ESSENTIAL PAPERS IN PSYCHOANALYSIS

Essential Papers on Borderline Disorders
  Michael H. Stone, M.D., Editor

Essential Papers on Object Relations
  Peter Buckley, M.D., Editor

Essential Papers on Narcissism
  Andrew P. Morrison, M.D., Editor

Essential Papers on Depression
  James C. Coyne, Editor

ESSENTIAL PAPERS ON NARCISSISM

Andrew P. Morrison, M.D.
Editor

 New York University Press
New York and London

Library of Congress Cataloging-in-Publication Data
Main entry under title:

Essential papers on narcissism.

(Essential papers in psychoanalysis)
Bibliography: p.
Includes index.
1. Narcissism—Addresses, essays, lectures.
I. Morrison, Andrew P., 1937–   . II. Series.
RC553.N36E77 1985   616.85′82   85-25845
ISBN 0-8147-5394-9 (alk. paper)
ISBN 0-8147-5395-7 (pbk.)

10 9 8 7 6

Clothbound editions of New York University Press books are
Smyth-sewn, and printed on permanent and durable acid-free paper.

Book design by Ken Venezio

Contents

Acknowledgments   vii

Introduction   1

Part I. Landmark Contributions   13

1. On Narcissism: An Introduction, *Sigmund Freud*   17

2. Pathologic Forms of Self-Esteem Regulation, *Annie Reich*   44

3. Forms and Transformations of Narcissism, *Heinz Kohut*   61

Part II. Overviews   89

4. Narcissism: The Term and the Concept, *Sydney E. Pulver*   91

5. Narcissism, *Arnold M. Cooper*   112

6. Self Relations, Object Relations, and Pathological Narcissism, *Marjorie Taggart White*   144

Part III. Differences in Theoretical Emphasis   165

A. Self and Identity   173

7. The Disorders of the Self and Their Treatment: An Outline, *Heinz Kohut and Ernest S. Wolf*   175

8. Toward a Functional Definition of Narcissism, *Robert D. Stolorow*   197

B. Object Relations   211

9. Factors in the Psychoanalytic Treatment of Narcissistic Personalities, *Otto F. Kernberg*   213

10. Further Contributions to the Treatment of Narcissistic Personalities, *Otto F. Kernberg*   245

11. A Narcissistic Defence Against Affects and the Illusion of Self-Sufficiency, *Arnold H. Modell*   293

12. The Theory of Narcissism: An Object-Relations
    Perspective, *Arnold Rothstein*   308

C. Affective States   321

13. Depression and Grandiosity as Related Forms
    of Narcissistic Disturbances, *Alice Miller*   323

14. Shame, Ideal Self, and Narcissism, *Andrew P. Morrison*   348

Part IV. Diagnostic and Therapeutic Applications   373

15. Some Narcissistic Personality Types, *Ben Bursten*   377

16. Narcissistic Personalities and Borderline Conditions:
    A Differential Diagnosis, *W.W. Meissner*   403

17. The Mirror and the Mask: On Narcissism and
    Psychoanalytic Growth, *Philip M. Bromberg*   438

    References   467

    Name Index   469

    Subject Index   473

Acknowledgments

We gratefully wish to acknowledge Basic Books, Inc., and Chatto & Windus for Sigmund Freud, "On Narcissism: An Introduction," from *The Standard Edition of the Complete Psychological Works of Sigmund Freud,* translated and edited by James Strachey.

We gratefully wish to acknowledge International Universities Press for permission to reprint Annie Reich, "Pathologic Forms of Self-Esteem Regulation," from *Psychoanalytic Study of the Child,* Vol. 15, pp. 205–32.

We gratefully wish to acknowledge International Universities Press for permission to reprint from *Journal of the American Psychoanalytic Association* the following: Heinz Kohut, "Forms and Transformations of Narcissism," Vol. 14: pp. 243–72; Sydney E. Pulver, "Narcissism: The Term and the Concept," Vol. 18: pp. 319–41; Otto F. Kernberg, "Factors in the Psychoanalytic Treatment of Narcissistic Personalities," Vol. 18: pp. 51–85; W. W. Meissner, "Narcissistic Personalities and Borderline Conditions: A Differential Diagnosis," Vol. 7: pp. 171–202.

We gratefully wish to acknowledge Basic Books, Inc., for permission to reprint Arnold M. Cooper, "Narcissism," from *American Handbook of Psychiatry,* edited by S. Arieti, Chapter 15, pp. 297–316.

We gratefully wish to acknowledge *International Journal of Psychoanalysis* for permission to reprint the following: Heinz Kohut and Ernest S. Wolf, "The Disorders of the Self and Their Treatment: An Outline," Vol. 59: pp. 413–25, 1978; Robert D. Stolorow, "Toward a Functional Definition of Narcissism," Vol. 56: pp. 179–85, 1975; Otto F. Kernberg, "Further Contributions to the Treatment of Narcissistic Personalities," Vol. 55: pp. 215–40, 1974; Arnold H. Modell, "A Narcissistic Defence Against Affects and the Illusion of Self-Sufficiency," Vol. 56: pp. 275–82, 1975; Alice Miller, "Depression and Grandiosity as Related Forms of Narcissistic Disturbances," Vol. 6: pp. 61–76, 1979; Ben Bursten, "Some Narcissistic Personality Types," Vol. 54: pp. 287–300, 1973.

We gratefully wish to acknowledge Human Sciences Press for permission to reprint from *The Psychoanalytic Review,* Arnold Rothstein, "The Theory of Narcissism: An Object-Relations Perspective," Vol. 66: pp. 35–47; and Marjorie Taggart White, "Self Relations, Object Relations, and Pathological Narcissism," Vol. 67: pp. 4–23.

We gratefully wish to acknowledge *Contemporary Psychoanalysis* for permission to reprint Andrew P. Morrison, "Shame, Ideal Self, and Narcissism, Vol. 19: pp. 295–318; Phillip M. Bromberg, "The Mirror and the Mask: On Narcissism and Psychoanalytic Growth," Vol. 19: pp. 359–87.

Introduction

The myth of Narcissus explores many of the themes to be elaborated in this volume. A handsome young man, Narcissus was much loved by the nymphs, including Echo, who was rejected by him. The Gods vowed to punish him for his callousness by causing him to fall in love with his own image as reflected in a mountain pool. However, the mirror image fragmented each time that Narcissus reached out to embrace it, causing him to pine away in melancholy, and ultimately to die. In his place, the nymphs found a flowering plant growing where once his body had been (see Cooper, Ch. 5; Rosenman, 1981). A *New Yorker* cartoon shows Echo standing behind the mythic hero, who is gazing wistfully into the water as she asks, "Is there someone else, Narcissus?"

Havelock Ellis introduced the term "narcissism" in 1898 to refer to a sexual perversion in which the person treats his own body as though it were a sexual object, but also to indicate a more generalized expression of self-admiration. Sadger and Rank also referred to narcissism as a normal stage of development on the way to object love. As we shall see, Freud (Ch. 1) elaborated the concept in 1914 in terms of primary and secondary states, the libidinal investment of the ego (including a heightened importance of the self over the object and a relative lack of importance of object relations), and the specific attributes of self-regard and the ego ideal. Following the ideas sketched at this time, however, Freud did not intend to expand his thoughts on narcissism significantly.

Wilhelm Reich (1949) described character formation as "essentially a narcissistic protection mechanism" against threats from the instincts and from the outside world. It was not until the elaborations of ego psychology, however, that renewed interest in, and study of narcissism would be evidenced by psychoanalytic theorists, following Hartmann's redefinition of narcissism as the libidinal investment of the self (1950). Considerations by Hartmann and Loewenstein (1962), Jacobson (1954), and others about the nature of the ego ideal and self and object representations rekindled this interest.

In the 1950s and 1960s, contributions to metapsychology examined primary and secondary narcissism, the role of the object representation in maintaining self-esteem, and narcissistic "entitlement" and the ego ideal. The subsequent impact of object relations theory then informed the investigation of narcissism, particularly with the contributions of Kernberg (Chs. 9 and 10) and others to be described later in this chapter. At the same time, the observations of Kohut (Chs. 3 and 7) were redefining narcissism, independent of object representations, as a normal developmental need for self-cohesion through availability of self-object functions optimally provided by empathically-attuned parents. Thus, the emphasis of study shifted from libidinal and drive manifestations to object representations, or to selfobject functions in establishing and maintaining self-cohesion.

Finally, as part of the call for diagnostic precision in the 1980s, much greater emphasis has been placed on the precise definition of narcissism in terms of symptoms, character pathology, and differential diagnosis. For example, in the description of narcissism in DSM-III (1980), the Diagnostic Criteria for Narcissistic Personality Disorder include a grandiose sense of self-importance; preoccupation with fantasies of unlimited success, power, brilliance, beauty, or ideal love; exhibitionism; cool indifference or rage, inferiority, shame, and emptiness; entitlement, exploitativeness, overidealization, or devaluation; and lack of empathy. Even as a reflection of the most current thinking in descriptive psychiatry, it is clear that these criteria rely heavily on the contributions and observations of psychoanalytic study. Yet, the "product" seems more pathological, more clinically pessimistic than the psychoanalytic view of narcissism.

The DSM-III criteria raise important questions. Is narcissism a diagnosis which relates essentially to character pathology? Does it reflect ego weakness, a paucity of self-esteem? Is it defined by an uncontrollable outpouring of unmodified, drive-derived aggression? Or does narcissism represent a defect of the self—an arrest in development of self-cohesion or stability of the self-representation? Does it relate to the ego's attempt to avoid investment in objects, or does it involve, instead, a vulnerability to rejection by overly invested objects? These are but some of the questions which will be addressed in the papers of this volume.

In this introductory essay, I will first make some clinical observations which seem to me central to narcissistic conditions. I will then borrow formulations from some of the papers *not* included in the volume, which will provide a framework from which to view the problem of narcissism.

In the book's part introductions, the reader will find critical summaries of the papers included in this book.

I

I have often heard statements similar to the following from patients suffering from a narcissistic disorder or in the throes of an acute state of narcissistic vulnerability: "If I am not the *only* person important (to me, in the transference, or to another, outside the therapeutic interaction) I feel like I am nothing." This need for absolute uniqueness, to be the sole object of importance to someone else, symbolizes the essence of narcissistic yearning. At such moments, the patient is cast back to a state of primitive, perhaps primary, narcissism, where there can be no one other than the self, in a state of merger with the representation or function of the idealized, all-powerful "other." We shall see later that this yearning is viewed by some as a moment of hunger for a predifferentiated, symbiotic state; others emphasize the voracious, demanding ego ideal; and still others focus on the state of the self in prestructural, age-appropriate need for a responsive selfobject. Nonetheless, I suggest that this moment of fantasied uniqueness is a clinically common occurrence in treatment, and does not necessarily reflect severe characterological pathology. However, it somehow captures the essence of what we regard as narcissism.

This yearning to be unique has several important implications. First of all, from an ego (or self) perspective, it suggests that the self is all-important, and the presence of any other, rivalrous individual is intolerable to a sense of well-being or self-esteem. Secondly, it implies an ego ideal of unyielding specialness, which is both objectively unrealistic, and unattainable. Superego manifestations are harsh and self-punitive. The need to share the stage with others may lead to an outpouring of aggression or retaliatory rage. The capacity to acknowledge the existence of another—to recognize or identify with an external object or its representation—is, at least temporarily, banished. Self-cohesion is undermined, and fragmentation—as indicated by the sense of nothingness—seems imminent.

What are the *affective* implications of this yearning for uniqueness? We have noted that it may lead to an outpouring of untamed aggression, or of reactive rage against the offending object. Internally, however, I suggest that such an experience leads to a sense of utter despair, profound depression, and reflects the paradoxical extremes of grandiose entitlement, on the one hand, and vulnerability to mortification, on the other. Underlying both of these states are, I believe, the common affects of shame and humiliation. Such shame may reflect both the recognition of overwhelming grandiosity, as well as feelings of utter unworthiness and insignificance. These points are elaborated in Chapter 14, but for now I would emphasize that shame (and its related affects of humiliation, embarrassment, despair, and mortification) are those feelings *central* to the experience of narcissism (much as guilt is central to neurotic conflict).

shame

To illustrate this point, let me quote from one of the patients who articulated her need to be the only person of importance to me. Again, this statement has been repeated by several other patients at moments of exquisite narcissistic vulnerability. "Humiliation is the most painful feeling that I can imagine." (This was said most recently by a woman in analysis who had progressed beyond some borderline manifestations to a fairly stable neurotic character and who was describing her feelings of dependency and smallness in the analytic situation.) I suggest that this painful experience of humiliation reflects narcissistic yearnings for specialness and uniqueness outlined above, and it is a response to fears of contempt from the "idealized other" over unremitting grandiosity and over these yearnings which can not be gratified.

I suggest that these qualities—yearnings for *uniqueness* with regard to an idealized object, and *shame* and *humiliation* over such yearnings and the vulnerability which they engender (with the everpresent danger of their nonfulfillment, or a response of contempt from the all-powerful object)—define an essential element of the narcissistic experience. This may reflect what Bursten (1977) calls the narcissistic course, or may, rather, indicate a temporary instability in the sense of self. Far from reflecting a negation of the importance of an object, they indicate how important the response of the (idealized) object is to the sense of wellbeing in states of narcissism. I offer these qualities as a guideline to the narcissistic experiences of our patients, and suggest that they be kept in mind as the essays in this volume are studied.

I shall now turn to a more systematic overview from which to examine the various theoretical and clinical perspectives on narcissism elaborated in this book.

II

In an interesting overview on narcissism, Teicholz (1978) considers some of the themes noted above with regard to views of the self, its relationship to external and internalized objects, object representations and functions, and the ego ideal and self-esteem. She summarizes some conceptualizations about these issues as follows:

1. A change in what is conceived of as the object or target of the libido in narcissism from the "ego" to the "self.". . .
2. The elaboration of the concept "self"
   a. as part of the structure ego, understood to mean the conscious, preconscious, and unconscious representations of the total person. . . .
   b. the elaboration of the process by which self- and object representations become differentiated and internalized as stable, enduring structures. . . .
   c. an elaboration of the role of identification in the structuring of the self-representations and other functions of the ego. . . .
   d. the distinction between self as structure, and self as experience, and an elaboration of the relation between structure and experience. . . .
3. Increasing emphasis on a distinction between internalized object relations as opposed to relations between the self and the objects in the external world:
   a. recognition of a certain quality of object relation in which the object is not perceived as a separate entity, but as part of the self and is used to correct a gap or defect in structural development. In such relationships, the object is needed to serve a function that is normally internalized and therefore carried out intrapsychically in the healthy personality. . . .
   b. a rejection of Freud's concept of an inverse ratio between self-directed libido and object-directed libido, and an alternative proposal that investment of libido in self and objects (internalized and external) is mutually enhancing rather than mutually exclusive. . . .
4. A clarification of the interrelationships in development and functioning between the hypothesized structures of the psyche: id, ego, and superego:
   a. the elaboration of the role of the ego ideal in personality functioning. . . .
   b. the elaboration of the concept self-esteem and an attempt to clarify the role of each structural entity in its regulation. . . .

Writing from an ego-psychological perspective, Teicholz concludes that narcissistic problems may be formulated in terms of dynamic conflicts which cause or result from them, in terms of structural defects and core inadequacies of psychic functioning; or of adaptive and defensive efforts which attempt to deal with the causative functional failures and resulting dysphoric affect. Moore (1975) also reviews narcissism from a historical perspective, concluding that "it has retained the implication of a positive, libidinal feeling towards the self," with cathexis of self and object representations with drive energies. He argues for the retention of the complexity and richness of narcissism as a concept, considering it seminal for Freud, providing an organizing matrix in his construction of psychoanalytic theory.

The question of self and object representations in narcissism has concerned many writers. Eisnitz (1974) defines "narcissistic object choice . . . wherein the major cathexis is directed to the self representation, and attachment object choice as that wherein the major cathexis is directed to the object representation." From this perspective, object choice is central, and narcissistic and attachment cathexes intertwine in normal and pathological development. There are no separate developmental lines for narcissism and object love (an issue which will be seen to play an important part in Kohut's work). A *narcissistic conflict* is seen "whenever the stability of the self-representation is threatened." From this perspective, narcissistic pathology reflects "restriction or impairment of ego functions, notably maintenance of adequate object relations, disturbances in identity, or the regulation of self-esteem." Hanley and Masson (1976) also argue that "narcissistic libidinal organizations and object libidinal organizations are dynamically interdependent," but these authors clearly place adequate object relations at the center of psychological health, stating that "narcissism serves a defensive, compensatory function in relation to the conflicts in object relations which are generated by these fixations." Kinston (1982) also indicates the interdependence of what he refers to as self-narcissism (with positive attitudes towards the self, in contrast with negatively valued self-images), and object narcissism (in which separateness is denied and the object is devalued or destroyed).

The relation of narcissism to choices of object-representation is emphasized by other authors. Reich (1953) relates the persistence of a grandiose, primitive ego ideal in women, who are suffering narcissistic injury from feelings of gender inferiority, to its externalization and fusion with a love object, leading to a form of narcissistic object choice which may feature idealization or masochism. Working from a Kleinian vantage point, Rosenfeld (1964) views narcissistic object relations as representing incorporation of an omnipotently experienced part object (e.g., the breast), with denial of any separate identity or boundary between self and object. This lack of separateness prevents object longing, rage, and envy; the object is devalued and may serve as a projected repository for all unwanted feelings. Other authors represented in this volume will be seen to focus on the *denial* of the importance of object relationships to the narcissistic patient (e.g., Modell), or on the self-regulating *function* of the object, minimizing its configurational qualities (e.g., Kohut).

Consistent with Reich's view of the primitive ego ideal as the source of narcissistic identification in some patients, Murray (1964) views the ego ideal as potentially capable of transformation and growth from narcissism to "higher" levels of function and abstraction. Thus, for Murray, the mature ego ideal functions antithetically to narcissism, opposing the "narcissistic entitlements" of the pregenital period and leading to more satisfactory object relations. Implicitly, then, for him narcissism represents arrogance and entitlement, which must be actively confronted and interpreted in psychoanalytic treatment.

Other writers have been concerned with the nature of the self in narcissism, some viewing it as *structure,* others as *experience.* The self as structure reflects a perspective in which the self's formal qualities, attributes, and representations are delineated, as an object for libidinal investment, or in terms of various self components. For instance, Joffe and Sandler (1967) refer to an *ideal state* as an affective state of well-being, the corollary of Freud's primary narcissism (Ch. 1); the *ideal self* denotes that particular shape of the self-representation at any given moment which embodies the fantasied ideal state, thus representing a formal, structured representation of the self. To these authors, psychological well-being is reflected in a substantial correspondence between representations of the actual state of and ideal shape of the self. Narcissistic disturbances reflect "a discrepancy between the mental representation of the actual self of the moment and an ideal shape of the self," the structural counterpart of painful affect. Thus, the affective experiences of narcissism—low self-esteem, feelings of failure and inferiority, shame and guilt—reflect failures in approximating the shape of the ideal self (see also Morrison, Ch. 14).

Van Der Waals (1965) examines narcissism in terms of unrealistic aspirations dictated by an excessively demanding ideal self and self-representation and concludes that healthy narcissism reflects an accurate representation of reality in establishing positive self-regard. Duruz (1981) also examines healthy narcissism, defining it "as the self-cohesiveness experienced by the ego, as it recognizes both the unifying and dividing aspects of its ideals."

Other authors approach the self, not as a structure, but in terms of subjective experience. For instance, Duruz (above) also discusses pathological narcissism in terms of two extremes: "either (1) an experience of self-unity, supported by an unlimited feeling of omnipotence, without apparent internal tension; or (2) an experience of a lack of self-unity, which leads to an identity crisis, where the individual no longer succeeds in saying 'I.' " Schwaber (1981) reflects the contributions of Kohut (e.g., Chs. 3, 7) in emphasizing that the self-experience, which she equates with the pathway of narcissism, has its own intrinsic developmental and maturational landmarks. In this important essay on narcissism and the listening perspective, Schwaber explicitly uses the term "self" as an "experiential construct which has a stability and continuity in time—*not* as a mental structure" (italics mine). Kohut himself never succinctly defined the self but alluded to an independent center of initiative; "the strengthened self becomes the organizing center of the skills and talents of the personality and thus improves the exercise of these functions; the successful exercise of skills and talents, moreover, in turn increases the cohesion, and thus the vigor, of the self" (Kohut, 1971). In his review of Kohut's contributions to the treatment of narcissistic disorders, Ornstein (1974) reminds us that "these patients have attained a cohesive self, which has remained more or less stable, though precariously balanced, and which shows a propensity for temporary fragmentation in response to narcissistic injury." These individuals can be identified as having narcissistic pathology only through a trial of analysis or psychoanalytic psychotherapy, during which one or more of the stable narcissistic transferences will become established. These experiential approaches to the self will be amply elaborated throughout this volume.

Some authors have examined narcissism from the vantage point of ego or self functions, such as identity and self-esteem regulation. Lichtenstein (1964) suggests that the various meanings of seeing oneself in a mirror are central to the concept of narcissism, which inevitably introduce problems of primary identity, identity confusion, and loss of identity as they relate to ego development. By emphasizing the relationship of "mirroring" to narcissism, Lichtenstein anticipates the perspective of Kohut. He equates "primary identity" with the construct of the self, viewing "narcissistic omnipotence as a result [of] identity maintenance through mirroring in the object." This view of identity formation inevitably calls to mind Kohut's emphasis on the selfobject function in establishing self-cohesion. Similarly, Val (1982) examines the need for the selfobject function to regulate self-esteem in regressive or arrested narcissism, but he argues that not all disturbances in self-esteem regulation reflect narcissistic pathology. Thus, it becomes clinically important to distinguish between problems in self-esteem regulation based on narcissistic (archaic selfobject) or structural (conflict) issues. This becomes an important point as we examine those discussions of narcissism which put self-esteem regulation at their center.

Some writers stress the defensive nature of narcissism in camouflaging underlying sexual and Oedipal problems. For instance, McDougall (1982) states, "Certain individuals, in their attempt to combat primitive castration fears of a narcissistic order, will seek to create a continuing series of narcissistic object relations with the hope of repairing the damaged self-image, and of stemming the rising tide of panic whenever threatened with separations and other such anxiogenic situations." McDougall points to a link between narcissistic structures and primitive fantasies of the primal scene, and emphasizes that narcissistic manifestations frequently represent barriers to painful object libidinal investments. Similarly, Rothstein (1979) examines narcissistic personality disorders from the perspective of underlying, but hidden, Oedipal conflicts.

Settlage (1977) presents a Mahlerian perspective of separation-individuation from which to view narcissistic and borderline problems, emphasizing the importance of the rapprochement subphase in establishing mastery, basic trust, a core sense of self, and in relinquishing omnipotence in favor of competence—developmental issues so central to narcissistic and borderline pathology. According to Settlage, problems arising during rapprochement, following successful self-object differentiation, "could account . . . for the later clinically observable deficit in self-esteem and sense of self, and the longing for but fear of intimacy in object relations." These qualities delineate narcissistic difficulties through maternal failures in response to the toddler's initial attempts at assertiveness and independence. In describing clinical approaches to the treatment of narcissism, Settledge emphasizes the patient's need for *control* over the analyst to promote internal self-regulation and avoidance of traumatic intrusiveness by the object. The analyst's constancy and helpful, empathic participation promote internalization of self-regulation and mastery over impulses and affects. Settledge suggests that the analytic process is *both* therapeutic and developmental in terms of "undoing psychopathology" and promoting development of new structure through a relationship which differs from that originally experienced during rapprochement. Gedo (1977) also considers therapeutic implications with regard to narcissism, examining manifestations in the transference of grandiosity (i.e., "vanity, exhibitionism, and arrogant ingratitude"). He suggests that the theoretical perspectives of Kernberg (narcissism as pathological, reflecting defense against infantile aggression), Mahler (narcissism as defensive against subjective feelings of helplessness and mortification), and Kohut (narcissism as a phase-appropriate expression of ambitions which elicited unempathic responses, leading to mortification) may each be appropriate to the developmental experiences of different patients. Thus, Gedo argues against "assumptions about normative criteria of early development with regard to grandiose ideation," emphasizing the importance of specific genetic reconstruction for each particular patient. Traumatic parental insensitivity, indentification with parental grandiosity, and constitutional aggressiveness may each play a part in the "primitive entitlement" of particular patients, underscoring the need for careful assessment of specific transference manifestations.

In this introductory essay, I have attempted to offer perspectives on narcissism from some of the many excellent presentations which could not be included in this volume. In the part introductions within the body of the work, I will attempt to integrate some of these themes and raise further questions through summaries of the papers that follow. I began this introduction with observations about narcissism from some of my own patients, reflecting their need/wish to be the *only* person of importance to me, the shame and mortification from recognition of this need, and from the realization that it would not likely be fulfilled. From our study so far, these needs seem to relate to self-esteem, archaic ego ideal manifestations, grandiosity, and vulnerability to empathic slights. Let us now proceed to the direct study of these essential papers on narcissism.

PART I

LANDMARK CONTRIBUTIONS

The first part of this volume includes three chapters considered "Landmark Contributions" because of their centrality to our thoughts about narcissism. Naturally, the first chapter is that of Freud, who, in 1914, set forth the guidelines and issues about narcissism which would be elaborated in many subsequent papers, including several which follow in this book. I shall not discuss in detail the themes set forth by Freud, since this is done effectively by other authors. Moore (1975) notes that there is a continuity in Freud's view about narcissism implying "a positive, libidinal feeling towards the self." Freud describes a *primary narcissism* in terms of an initial libidinal investment of psychic energy in the (predifferentiated) ego—a state of symbiotic bliss, which inevitably becomes altered with separation/individuation, as libidinal cathexis shifts from the ego to objects. Implicit in this view is the grounding of narcissism in the drives, and in libido distribution, as well as Freud's conclusion—widely contested by other authors—that with investment in external love objects, the ego's narcissistic supply is inevitably reduced. *Secondary narcissism* refers to a condition in which libido is withdrawn from external objects and turned anew onto the ego, or cathected to objects internalized within the ego. Finally, Freud elaborates the concept of the ego ideal, which he conceives as possessor of the lost perfection of primary narcissism. Thus, the ego ideal serves as a guide for the ego's aspirations and ultimately as the content of the self's perfection. Any deviation from this ideal determines the superego's punishments. In this paper, Freud also speaks of self-regard (the self-esteem which is seen as central to many authors' views of narcissism), relating it to primary narcissism, meeting the demands of the ego ideal, and to the reflected glory of love from the cathected object.

Freud's paper is rich and challenging, which, while rooted in his evolving theory of drives and psychic energy, nonetheless offers a way station which might well have led him in many new directions, especially with regard to elaboration of the ego ideal and self-esteem. In fact, he did not substantially move beyond his "Introduction," published in 1914. He chose, instead, to investigate the manifestations of psychic energy and the division of the mental apparatus into its three domains of ego, superego, and id. Not until Hartmann (1950) shifted Freud's libidinal cathexis from the ego to the self did further study of narcissism, and the influences of the ego ideal, self-esteem, and self- and object-representations, proceed.

I am curious about this decision of Freud's to leave the pursuit of narcissism to future generations of analysts (see also Moore [1975]). While there is not room to explore this question here, I suggest that it is fundamental as we consider the later contributions to the study of narcissism. It seems to me, however, that a partial answer may lie in the pressures that Freud felt in the political climate of the psychoanalytic movement at the time and in his determination to protect the "gold" of analysis from the "alloys" which he felt threatened it by some of the defectors from the psychoanalytic movement. As Jung abandoned infantile sexuality and Adler moved towards an ego-dominated, "social" psychology, might Freud have felt that the further study of narcissism would take him too far afield from elaboration of infantile sexuality and other drive manifestations, from the Oedipus Complex and the structures of the mental apparatus, towards the evanescent experience of self-regard, and the socially influenced ego ideal? I shall not here move further with this question, except to mention that the path taken by Freud meant a delay in the further study of narcissism until recent times. With it there was a delay in the investigation of the affect of shame in contrast with guilt, which flowed easily from his subsequent writings.

Annie Reich (Ch. 2) built on the contributions of Hartmann, Jacobson, and other ego psychologists to expand the conceptualization of narcissism from a state related to the (unanalyzable) psychoses to that of a normal aspect of neurotic conditions, especially with regard to the regulation of self-esteem. Thus, Reich picks up on one theme introduced by Freud, emphasizing, however, the capacity to "evaluate our potentialities and accept our limitations"—a capacity of the mature ego. By contrast, the pathological narcissist is seen to maintain "compensatory narcissistic self-inflation" in order to support a megalomanic concept of self—ideals aimed at protecting the self from threats to bodily intactness. Reich here emphasizes reality testing as a goal, implying that its absence in narcissistic conditions reflects an ego *defect,* resulting from an overly demanding ego ideal. She also indicates that one by-product of this concern for the integrity of the self is the temporary withdrawal of the libido from objects to the endangered self, underscoring the presence of "narcissistic injuries" during development which are manifest as "uncontrollable feelings of helplessness, anxiety, and rage." Thus, narcissists oscillate from feelings of grandiosity to those of worthlessness and dejection, reflecting wide shifts in self-esteem. With regard to objects, attempts to maintain self-esteem encompass feelings of magical identification, merger, and idealization, which are threatened by outbursts of envious rage and aggression leading to a cycle of object contempt, contempt for the self, and shame.

Reich, then, emphasizes the affective component of narcissism (i.e., self-esteem) to indicate its oscillations in narcissistic pathology. To the question of whether narcissism is defined by grandiosity or by vulnerability, she answers, "Both," implying, however, that vulnerability in self-esteem is fundamental, with narcissistic grandiosity being compensatory (i.e., defensive). She also introduces the importance of the object as a potential stabilizer of self-esteem through magical identification and merger with its idealized qualities, and through fluctuation of idealization and contempt towards self and other. These views will be seen to represent an ego-psychological precursor to the contributions of Kohut (Chs. 3, 7) and his followers.

Kohut's seminal work on narcissism (Ch. 3) represents a major departure from views of previous authors in that he questions the assumption that narcissism is fundamentally pathological. He does this by relegating the world of object relations to social psychology and by establishing the importance of the *function* of the object (through introjection of the idealized parental imago in forming the ego ideal), in contrast with the object's *representational* qualities. Thus, Kohut argues that narcissism may lead, not only to object love, but also to more mature forms of narcissism, which he elaborates in terms of humor, creativity, empathy, and wisdom. This exposition, still conceptualized by Kohut within the framework of drives and intrapsychic conflict, nonetheless represents the demarcation of two separate lines of development for narcissism. One is aimed towards object love and the other towards higher forms of narcissism. Earlier in the essay, he differentiates between the *ego ideal* (seen in terms of drive control through introjection of the idealized qualities of the object) and the *narcissistic self* (intertwined with drives and their tensions, and representing the self's ambitions, the exhibitionistic wish to be looked at and admired). The therapeutic implications of this division suggest that a premature closing off of the aspirations of the narcissistic self (through attempts at taming the drives) leads to repression and therapeutic inaccessibility. Thus, exhibitionism and grandiosity need to be kept open and brought into the therapeutic encounter, rather than being confronted and opposed. This view represents a radical change from previous approaches to narcissism.

Why did Kohut develop this conceptualization? I suggest that he felt constricted by the tenets of ego psychology, which he had absorbed and which had dominated psychoanalysis after World War II, particularly with regard to the presumed primacy of object love as a developmental endpoint. His essay clearly indicates rejection of object relations as the final arbiter of psychic health, both by equating object relations theory with social psychology, and by offering a developmental line independent of object love for mature narcissism. He states, "The object is important only insofar as it is invited to participate in the child's narcissistic pleasure and thus to confirm it." When the object inevitably fails to confirm the infant's grandiosity, the self experiences shame.

It is in this essay that Kohut speaks most extensively about shame, both in terms of the *object's* failure and rejection of the self (above), but also as a reflection of the ego's inability to provide expression for the narcissistic self's exhibitionistic demands. Thus, for Kohut it is the "ambitious, success-driven person," with poorly integrated grandiosity and exhibitionism, who is most likely to respond to any failures with shame.

1. On Narcissism: An Introduction

Sigmund Freud

I

The term narcissism is derived from clinical description and was chosen by Paul Näcke[1] in 1899 to denote the attitude of a person who treats his own body in the same way in which the body of a sexual object is ordinarily treated—who looks at it, that is to say, strokes it and fondles it till he obtains complete satisfaction through these activities. Developed to this degree, narcissism has the significance of a perversion that has absorbed the whole of the subject's sexual life, and it will consequently exhibit the characteristics which we expect to meet with in the study of all perversions.

Psycho-analytic observers were subsequently struck by the fact that individual features of the narcissistic attitude are found in many people who suffer from other disorders—for instance, as Sadger has pointed out, in homosexuals—and finally it seemed probable that an allocation of the libido such as deserved to be described as narcissism might be present far more extensively, and that it might claim a place in the regular course of human sexual development.[2] Difficulties in psychoanalytic work upon neurotics led to the same supposition, for it seemed as though this kind of narcissistic attitude in them constituted one of

[1] [In a footnote added by Freud in 1920 to his *Three Essays* (1905d, *Standard Ed.*, **7**, 218 *n.*) he said that he was wrong in stating in the present paper that the term 'narcissism' was introduced by Näcke and that he should have attributed it to Havelock Ellis. Ellis himself, however, subsequently (1928) wrote a short paper in which he corrected Freud's correction and argued that the priority should in fact be divided between himself and Näcke, explaining that the term 'narcissus-like' had been used by him in 1898 as a description of a psychological attitude, and that Näcke in 1899 had introduced the term '*Narcismus*' to describe a sexual perversion. The German word used by Freud is '*Narzissmus*'. In his paper on Schreber (1911c), near the beginning of Section III, he defends this form of the word on the ground of euphony against the possibly more correct '*Narzissismus*'.]

[2] Otto Rank (1911c).

the limits to their susceptibility to influence. Narcissism in this sense would not be a perversion, but the libidinal complement to the egoism of the instinct of self-preservation, a measure of which may justifiably be attributed to every living creature.

A pressing motive for occupying ourselves with the conception of a primary and normal narcissism arose when the attempt was made to subsume what we know of dementia praecox (Kraepelin) or schizophrenia (Bleuler) under the hypothesis of the libido theory. Patients of this kind, whom I have proposed to term paraphrenics,[3] display two fundamental characteristics: megalomania and diversion of their interest from the external world—from people and things. In consequence of the latter change, they become inaccessible to the influence of psycho-analysis and cannot be cured by our efforts. But the paraphrenic's turning away from the external world needs to be more precisely characterized. A patient suffering from hysteria or obsessional neurosis has also, as far as his illness extends, given up his relation to reality. But analysis shows that he has by no means broken off his erotic relations to people and things. He still retains them in phantasy; i.e. he has, on the one hand, substituted for real objects imaginary ones from his memory, or has mixed the latter with the former; and on the other hand, he has renounced the initiation of motor activities for the attainment of his aims in connection with those objects. Only to this condition of the libido may we legitimately apply the term 'introversion' of the libido which is used by Jung indiscriminately.[4] It is otherwise with the paraphrenic. He seems really to have withdrawn his libido from people and things in the external world, without replacing them by others in phantasy. When he *does* so replace them, the process seems to be a secondary one and to be part of an attempt at recovery, designed to lead the libido back to objects.[5]

The question arises: What happens to the libido which has been withdrawn from external objects in schizophrenia? The megalomania characteristic of these states points the way. This megalomania has no

[3] [For a discussion of Freud's use of this term, see a long Editor's footnote near the end of Section III of the Schreber analysis (1911c).]

[4] [Cf. a footnote in 'The Dynamics of Transference' (1912b).]

[5] In connection with this see my discussion of the 'end of the world' in [Section III of] the analysis of Senatspräsident Schreber [1911c]; also Abraham, 1908. [See also *Standard Ed.*, **14**, 86.]

doubt come into being at the expense of object-libido. The libido that has been withdrawn from the external world has been directed to the ego and thus gives rise to an attitude which may be called narcissism. But the megalomania itself is no new creation; on the contrary, it is, as we know, a magnification and plainer manifestation of a condition which had already existed previously. This leads us to look upon the narcissism which arises through the drawing in of object-cathexes as a secondary one, superimposed upon a primary narcissism that is obscured by a number of different influences.

Let me insist that I am not proposing here to explain or penetrate further into the problem of schizophrenia, but that I am merely putting together what has already been said elsewhere,[6] in order to justify the introduction of the concept of narcissism.

This extension of the libido theory—in my opinion, a legitimate one— receives reinforcement from a third quarter, namely, from our observations and views on the mental life of children and primitive peoples. In the latter we find characteristics which, if they occurred singly, might be put down to megalomania: an over-estimation of the power of their wishes and mental acts, the 'omnipotence of thoughts', a belief in the thaumaturgic force of words, and a technique for dealing with the external world—'magic'—which appears to be a logical application of these grandiose premises.[7] In the children of to-day, whose development is much more obscure to us, we expect to find an exactly analogous attitude towards the external world.[8] Thus we form the idea of there being an original libidinal cathexis of the ego, from which some is later given off to objects, but which fundamentally persists and is related to the object-cathexes much as the body of an amoeba is related to the pseudopodia which it puts out.[9] In our researches, taking, as they did, neurotic symptoms for their starting-point, this part of the allocation of libido necessarily remained hidden from us at the outset. All that we

[6] [See in particular, the works referred to in the last footnote. In *Standard Ed.*, **14**, 86, Freud in fact penetrates further into the problem.]

[7] Cf. the passages in my *Totem and Taboo* (1912–13) which deal with this subject. [These are chiefly in the third essay, *Standard Ed.*, **13**, 83 ff.]

[8] Cf. Ferenczi (1913a).

[9] [Freud used this and similar analogies more than once again, e.g. in Lecture XXVI of his *Introductory Lectures* (1916–17), and in his short paper on 'A Difficulty in the Path of Psycho-Analysis' (1917a), *Standard Ed.*, **17**, 139. He later revised some of the views expressed here. See the end of the Editor's Note, *Standard Ed.*, **14**, 71.]

noticed were the emanations of this libido—the object-cathexes, which can be sent out and drawn back again. We see also, broadly speaking, an antithesis between ego-libido and object-libido.[10] The more of the one is employed, the more the other becomes depleted. The highest phase of development of which object-libido is capable is seen in the state of being in love, when the subject seems to give up his own personality in favour of an object-cathexis; while we have the opposite condition in the paranoic's phantasy (or self-perception) of the 'end of the world'[11] Finally, as regards the differentiation of psychical energies, we are led to the conclusion that to begin with, during the state of narcissism, they exist together and that our analysis is too coarse to distinguish between them; not until there is object-cathexis is it possible to discriminate a sexual energy—the libido—from an energy of the ego-instincts.[12]

Before going any further I must touch on two questions which lead us to the heart of the difficulties of our subject. In the first place, what is the relation of the narcissism of which we are now speaking to auto-erotism, which we have described as an early state of the libido?[13] Secondly, if we grant the ego a primary cathexis of libido, why is there any necessity for further distinguishing a sexual libido from a non-sexual energy of the ego-instincts? Would not the postulation of a single kind of psychical energy save us all the difficulties of differentiating an energy of the ego-instincts from the ego-libido, and ego-libido from object-libido?[14]

As regards the first question, I may point out that we are bound to suppose that a unity comparable to the ego cannot exist in the individual from the start; the ego has to be developed. The auto-erotic instincts, however, are there from the very first; so there must be something added to auto-erotism—a new psychical action—in order to bring about narcissism.

[10] [This distinction is drawn here by Freud for the first time.]

[11] [See footnote 3, Standard Ed., 14, 74.] There are two mechanisms of this 'end of the world' idea: in the one case, the whole libidinal cathexis flows off to the loved object; in the other, it all flows back into the ego.

[12] [Some account of the development of Freud's views on the instincts will be found in the Editor's Note to 'Instincts and their Vicissitudes', Standard Ed., 14, 113 ff.]

[13] [See the second of Freud's Three Essays (1905d), Standard Ed., 7, 181–3.]

[14] [Cf. a remark on this passage in the Editor's Note to 'Instincts and their Vicissitudes', Standard Ed., 14, 115.]

To be asked to give a definite answer to the second question must occasion perceptible uneasiness in every psycho-analyst. One dislikes the thought of abandoning observation for barren theoretical controversy, but nevertheless one must not shirk an attempt at clarification. It is true that notions such as that of an ego-libido, an energy of the ego-instincts, and so on, are neither particularly easy to grasp, nor sufficiently rich in content; a speculative theory of the relations in question would begin by seeking to obtain a sharply defined concept as its basis. But I am of opinion that that is just the difference between a speculative theory and a science erected on empirical interpretation. The latter will not envy speculation its privilege of having a smooth, logically unassailable foundation, but will gladly content itself with nebulous, scarcely imaginable basic concepts, which it hopes to apprehend more clearly in the course of its development, or which it is even prepared to replace by others. For these ideas are not the foundation of science, upon which everything rests: that foundation is observation alone. They are not the bottom but the top of the whole structure, and they can be replaced and discarded without damaging it. The same thing is happening in our day in the science of physics, the basic notions of which as regards matter, centres of force, attraction, etc., are scarcely less debatable than the corresponding notions in psycho-analysis.[15]

The value of the concepts 'ego-libido' and 'object-libido' lies in the fact that they are derived from the study of the intimate characteristics of neurotic and psychotic processes. A differentiation of libido into a kind which is proper to the ego and one which is attached to objects is an unavoidable corollary to an original hypothesis which distinguished between sexual instincts and ego-instincts. At any rate, analysis of the pure transference neuroses (hysteria and obsessional neurosis) compelled me to make this distinction and I only know that all attempts to account for these phenomena by other means have been completely unsuccessful.

In the total absence of any theory of the instincts which would help us to find our bearings, we may be permitted, or rather, it is incumbent upon us, to start off by working out some hypothesis to its logical conclusion, until it either breaks down or is confirmed. There are var-

[15] [This line of thought was expanded by Freud in the opening passage of his paper on 'Instincts and their Vicissitudes' (1915c), *Standard Ed.*, **14**, 117.]

ious points in favour of the hypothesis of there having been from the first a separation between sexual instincts and others, ego-instincts, besides the serviceability of such a hypothesis in the analysis of the transference neuroses. I admit that this latter consideration alone would not be unambiguous, for it might be a question of an indifferent psychical energy which only becomes libido through the act of cathecting an object. But, in the first place, the distinction made in this concept corresponds to the common, popular distinction between hunger and love. In the second place, there are biological considerations in its favour. The individual does actually carry on a twofold existence: one to serve his own purposes and the other as a link in a chain, which he serves against his will, or at least involuntarily. The individual himself regards sexuality as one of his own ends; whereas from another point of view he is an appendage to his germ-plasm, at whose disposal he puts his energies in return for a bonus of pleasure. He is the mortal vehicle of a (possibly) immortal substance—like the inheritor of an entailed property, who is only the temporary holder of an estate which survives him. The separation of the sexual instincts from the ego-instincts would simply reflect this twofold function of the individual.[16] Thirdly, we must recollect that all our provisional ideas in psychology will presumably some day be based on an organic substructure. This makes it probable that it is special substances and chemical processes which perform the operations of sexuality and provide for the extension of individual life into that of the species.[17] We are taking this probability into account in replacing the special chemical substances by special psychical forces.

I try in general to keep psychology clear from everything that is different in nature from it, even biological lines of thought. For that very reason I should like at this point expressly to admit that the hypothesis of separate ego-instincts and sexual instincts (that is to say, the libido theory) rests scarcely at all upon a psychological basis, but derives its principal support from biology. But I shall be consistent enough [with my general rule] to drop this hypothesis if psycho-analytic work should itself produce some other, more serviceable hypothesis about the instincts. So far, this has not

[16] [The psychological bearing of Weismann's germ-plasm theory was discussed by Freud at much greater length in Chapter VI of *Beyond the Pleasure Principle* (1920g), *Standard Ed.*, **18**, 45 ff.]

[17] [See footnote 2, *Standard Ed.*, **14**, 125.]

happened. It may turn out that, most basically and on the longest view, sexual energy—libido—is only the product of a differentiation in the energy at work generally in the mind. But such an assertion has no relevance. It relates to matters which are so remote from the problems of our observation, and of which we have so little cognizance, that it is as idle to dispute it as to affirm it; this primal identity may well have as little to do with our analytic interests as the primal kinship of all the races of mankind has to do with the proof of kinship required in order to establish a legal right of inheritance. All these speculations take us nowhere. Since we cannot wait for another science to present us with the final conclusions on the theory of the instincts, it is far more to the purpose that we should try to see what light may be thrown upon this basic problem of biology by a synthesis of the *psychological* phenomena. (Let us face the possibility of error; but do not let us be deterred from pursuing the logical implications of the hypothesis we first adopted[18] of an antithesis between ego-instincts and sexual instincts (a hypothesis to which we were forcibly led by analysis of the transference neuroses), and from seeing whether it turns out to be without contradictions and fruitful, and whether it can be applied to other disorders as well, such as schizophrenia.

It would, of course, be a different matter if it were proved that the libido theory has already come to grief in the attempt to explain the latter disease. This has been asserted by C. G. Jung (1912) and it is on that account that I have been obliged to enter upon this last discussion, which I would gladly have been spared. I should have preferred to follow to its end the course embarked upon in the analysis of the Schreber case without any discussion of its premises. But Jung's assertion is, to say the least of it, premature. The grounds he gives for it are scanty. In the first place, he appeals to an admission of my own that I myself have been obliged, owing to the difficulties of the Schreber analysis, to extend the concept of libido (that is, to give up its sexual content) and to identify libido with psychical interest in general. Ferenczi (1913b), in an exhaustive criticism of Jung's work, has already said all that is necessary in correction of this erroneous interpretation. I can only corroborate his criticism and repeat that I have never made any such retractation of the libido theory. Another argument of Jung's,

---

[18] [*'Ersterwählte'* ('first selected') in the editions before 1924. The later editions read *'ersterwähnte'* ('first mentioned'), which seems to make less good sense and may be a misprint.]

namely, that we cannot suppose that the withdrawal of the libido is in itself enough to bring about the loss of the normal function of reality,[19] is no argument but a dictum. It 'begs the question',[20] and saves discussion; for whether and how this is possible was precisely the point that should have been under investigation. In his next major work, Jung (1913 [339–40]) just misses the solution I had long since indicated: 'At the same time', he writes, 'there is this to be further taken into consideration (a point to which, incidentally, Freud refers in his work on the Schreber case [1911c])—that the introversion of the *libido sexualis* leads to a cathexis of the "ego", and that it may possibly be this that produces the result of a loss of reality. It is indeed a tempting possibility to explain the psychology of the loss of reality in this fashion'. But Jung does not enter much further into a discussion of this possibility. A few lines[21] later he dismisses it with the remark that this determinant 'would result in the psychology of an ascetic anchorite, not in a dementia praecox'. How little this inapt analogy can help us to decide the question may be learnt from the consideration that an anchorite of this kind, who 'tries to eradicate every trace of sexual interest' (but only in the popular sense of the word 'sexual'), does not even necessarily display any pathogenic allocation of the libido. He may have diverted his sexual interest from human beings entirely, and yet may have sublimated it into a heightened interest in the divine, in nature, or in the animal kingdom, without his libido having undergone an introversion on to his phantasies or a return to his ego. This analogy would seem to rule out in advance the possibility of differentiating between interest emanating from erotic sources and from others. Let us remember, further, that the researches of the Swiss school, however valuable, have elucidated only two features in the picture of dementia praecox—the presence in it of complexes known to us both in healthy and neurotic subjects, and the similarity of the phantasies that occur in it to popular myths—but that they have not been able to throw any further light on the mechanism of the disease. We may repudiate Jung's assertion, then, that the libido theory has come to grief in the attempt to explain dementia praecox, and that it is therefore disposed of for the other neuroses as well.

[19] [The phrase is from Janet (1909): '*La fonction du réel*'. See the opening sentences of Freud, 1911b.]
[20] [In English in the original.]
[21] [All the German editions read '*Seiten*' ('pages'), a misprint for *Zeilen*'.]

II

Certain special difficulties seem to me to lie in the way of a direct study of narcissism. Our chief means of access to it will probably remain the analysis of the paraphrenias. Just as the transference neuroses have enabled us to trace the libidinal instinctual impulses, so dementia praecox and paranoia will give us an insight into the psychology of the ego. Once more, in order to arrive at an understanding of what seems so simple in normal phenomena, we shall have to turn to the field of pathology with its distortions and exaggerations. At the same time, other means of approach remain open to us, by which we may obtain a better knowledge of narcissism. These I shall now discuss in the following order: the study of organic disease, of hypochondria and of the erotic life of the sexes.

In estimating the influence of organic disease upon the distribution of libido, I follow a suggestion made to me orally by Sándor Ferenczi. It is universally known, and we take it as a matter of course, that a person who is tormented by organic pain and discomfort gives up his interest in the things of the external world, in so far as they do not concern his suffering. Closer observation teaches us that he also withdraws *libidinal* interest from his love-objects: so long as he suffers, he ceases to love. The commonplace nature of this fact is no reason why we should be deterred from translating it into terms of the libido theory. We should then say: the sick man withdraws his libidinal cathexes back upon his own ego, and sends them out again when he recovers. 'Concentrated is his soul', says Wilhelm Busch of the poet suffering from toothache, 'in his molar's narrow hole.'[22] Here libido and ego-interest share the same fate and are once more indistinguishable from each other. The familiar egoism of the sick person covers both. We find it so natural because we are certain that in the same situation we should behave in just the same way. The way in which a lover's feelings, however strong, are banished by bodily ailments, and suddenly replaced by complete indifference, is a theme which has been exploited by comic writers to an appropriate extent.

[22] [Einzig in der engen Höhle
Des Backenzahnes weilt die Seele.
Balduin Bählamm, Chapter VIII.]

The condition of sleep, too, resembles illness in implying a narcissistic withdrawal of the positions of the libido on to the subject's own self, or, more precisely, on to the single wish to sleep. The egoism of dreams fits very well into this context. [*Standard Ed.*, **14**, 223.] In both states we have, if nothing else, examples of changes in the distribution of libido that are consequent upon a change in the ego.

Hypochondria, like organic disease, manifests itself in distressing and painful bodily sensations, and it has the same effect as organic disease on the distribution of libido. The hypochondriac withdraws both interest and libido—the latter specially markedly—from the objects of the external world and concentrates both of them upon the organ that is engaging his attention. A difference between hypochondria and organic disease now becomes evident: in the latter, the distressing sensations are based upon demonstrable [organic] changes; in the former, this is not so. But it would be entirely in keeping with our general conception of the processes of neurosis if we decided to say that hypochondria must be right: organic changes must be supposed to be present in it, too.

But what could these changes be? We will let ourselves be guided at this point by our experience, which shows that bodily sensations of an unpleasurable nature, comparable to those of hypochondria, occur in the other neuroses as well. I have said before that I am inclined to class hypochondria with neurasthenia and anxiety-neurosis as a third 'actual' neurosis.[23] It would probably not be going too far to suppose that in the case of the other neuroses a small amount of hypochondria was regularly formed at the same time as well. We have the best example of this, I think, in anxiety neurosis with its superstructure of hysteria. Now the familiar prototype of an organ that is painfully tender, that is in some way changed and that is yet not diseased in the ordinary sense, is the genital organ in its states of excitation. In that condition it becomes congested with blood, swollen and humected, and is the seat of a

---

[23] [This seems to have been first hinted at in a footnote near the end of Section II of the Schreber case (1911c). It was again briefly, though more explicitly, mentioned by Freud in his closing remarks on masturbation at a discussion in the Vienna Psycho-Analytical Society (1912f). He returned to the subject later towards the end of Lecture XXIV of the *Introductory Lectures* (1916–17). At a much earlier period, Freud had already approached the question of the relation between hypochondria and the other 'actual' neuroses. See Section I (2) of his first paper on anxiety neuroses (1895b).]

multiplicity of sensations. Let us now, taking any part of the body, describe its activity of sending sexually exciting stimuli to the mind as its 'erotogenicity', and let us further reflect that the considerations on which our theory of sexuality was based have long accustomed us to the notion that certain other parts of the body—the 'erotogenic' zones—may act as substitutes for the genitals and behave analogously to them.[24] We have then only one more step to take. We can decide to regard erotogenicity as a general characteristic of all organs and may then speak of an increase or decrease of it in a particular part of the body. For every such change in the erotogenicity of the organs there might then be a parallel change of libidinal cathexis in the ego. Such factors would constitute what we believe to underlie hypochondria and what may have the same effect upon the distribution of libido as is produced by a material illness of the organs.

We see that, if we follow up this line of thought, we come up against the problem not only of hypochondria, but of the other 'actual' neuroses—neurasthenia and anxiety neurosis. Let us therefore stop at this point. It is not within the scope of a purely psychological inquiry to penetrate so far behind the frontiers of physiological research. I will merely mention that from this point of view we may suspect that the relation of hypochondria to paraphrenia is similar to that of the other 'actual' neuroses to hysteria and obsessional neurosis: we may suspect, that is, that it is dependent on ego-libido just as the others are on object-libido, and that hypochondriacal anxiety is the counterpart, as coming from ego-libido, to neurotic anxiety. Further, since we are already familiar with the idea that the mechanism of falling ill and of the formation of symptoms in the transference neuroses—the path from introversion to regression—is to be linked to a damming-up of object-libido,[25] we may come to closer quarters with the idea of a damming-up of ego-libido as well and may bring this idea into relation with the phenomena of hypochondria and paraphrenia.

At this point, our curiosity will of course raise the question why this damming-up of libido in the ego should have to be experienced as unpleasurable. I shall content myself with the answer that unpleasure is always the expression of a higher degree of tension, and that therefore

---

[24] [Cf. *Three Essays* (1905d), *Standard Ed.*, **7**, 183 f.]
[25] Cf. [the opening pages of] 'Types of Onset of Neurosis' (1912c).

what is happening is that a quantity in the field of material events is being transformed here as elsewhere into the psychical quality of unpleasure. Nevertheless it may be that what is decisive for the generation of unpleasure is not the absolute magnitude of the material event, but rather some particular function of that absolute magnitude.[26] Here we may even venture to touch on the question of what makes it necessary at all for our mental life to pass beyond the limits of narcissism and to attach the libido to objects.[27] The answer which would follow from our line of thought would once more be that this necessity arises when the cathexis of the ego with libido exceeds a certain amount. A strong egoism is a protection against falling ill, but in the last resort we must begin to love in order not to fall ill, and we are bound to fall ill if, in consequence of frustration, we are unable to love. This follows somewhat on the lines of Heine's picture of the psychogenesis of the Creation:

Krankheit ist wohl der letzte Grund
Des ganzen Schöpferdrangs gewesen;
Erschaffend konnte ich genesen,
Erschaffend wurde ich gesund.[28]

We have recognized our mental apparatus as being first and foremost a device designed for mastering excitations which would otherwise be felt as distressing or would have pathogenic effects. Working them over in the mind helps remarkably towards an internal draining away of excitations which are incapable of direct discharge outwards, or for which such a discharge is for the moment undesirable. In the first instance, however, it is a matter of indifference whether this internal process of working-over is carried out upon real or imaginary objects. The difference does not appear till later—if the turning of the libido on to unreal objects (introversion) has led to it being dammed up. In paraphrenics, megalomania allows of a similar internal working-over of

[26] [This whole question is discussed much more fully in 'Instincts and their Vicissitudes' (1915c), Standard Ed., **14**, 119 ff. For the use of the term 'quantity' in the last sentence, see Part I, Section 1, of Freud's 'Project' (1950a), written in 1895.]

[27] [A much more elaborate discussion of this problem too will be found in 'Instincts and their Vicissitudes' (1915c), Standard Ed., **14**, 134 ff.]

[28] [God is imagined as saying: 'Illness was no doubt the final cause of the whole urge to create. By creating, I could recover; by creating, I became healthy.' Neue Gedichte, 'Schöpfungslieder VII'.]

libido which has returned to the ego; perhaps it is only when the megalomania fails that the damming-up of libido in the ego becomes pathogenic and starts the process of recovery which gives us the impression of being a disease.)

I shall try here to penetrate a little further into the mechanism of paraphrenia and shall bring together those views which already seem to me to deserve consideration. The difference between paraphrenic affections and the transference neuroses appears to me to lie in the circumstance that, in the former, the libido that is liberated by frustration does not remain attached to objects in phantasy, but withdraws on to the ego. Megalomania would accordingly correspond to the psychical mastering of this latter amount of libido, and would thus be the counterpart of the introversion on to phantasies that is found in the transference neuroses; a failure of this psychical function gives rise to the hypochondria of paraphrenia and this is homologous to the anxiety of the transference neuroses. We know that this anxiety can be resolved by further psychical working-over, i.e. by conversion, reaction-formation or the construction of protections (phobias). The corresponding process in paraphrenics is an attempt at restoration, to which the striking manifestations of the disease are due. Since paraphrenia frequently, if not usually, brings about only a *partial* detachment of the libido from objects, we can distinguish three groups of phenomena in the clinical picture: (1) those representing what remains of a normal state or of neurosis (residual phenomena); (2) those representing the morbid process (detachment of libido from its objects and, further, megalomania, hypochondria, affective disturbance and every kind of regression); (3) those representing restoration, in which the libido is once more attached to objects, after the manner of a hysteria (in dementia praecox or paraphrenia proper), or of an obsessional neurosis (in paranoia). This fresh libidinal cathexis differs from the primary one in that it starts from another level and under other conditions.[29] The difference between the transference neuroses brought about in the case of this fresh kind of libidinal cathexis and the corresponding formations where the ego is normal should be able to afford us the deepest insight into the structure of our mental apparatus.

[29] [See some further remarks on this at the end of the paper on 'The Unconscious' *Standard Ed.*, **14**, 203–204.]

A third way in which we may approach the study of narcissism is by observing the erotic life of human beings, with its many kinds of differentiation in man and woman. Just as object-libido at first concealed ego-libido from our observation, so too in connection with the object-choice of infants (and of growing children) what we first noticed was that they derived their sexual objects from their experiences of satisfaction. The first autoerotic sexual satisfactions are experienced in connection with vital functions which serve the purpose of self-preservation. The sexual instincts are at the outset attached to the satisfaction of the ego-instincts; only later do they become independent of these, and even then we have an indication of that original attachment in the fact that the persons who are concerned with a child's feeding, care, and protection become his earliest sexual objects: that is to say, in the first instance his mother or a substitute for her. Side by side, however, with this type and source of object-choice, which may be called the 'anaclitic' or 'attachment' type,[30] psycho-analytic research has revealed a second type, which we were not prepared for finding. We have discovered, especially clearly in people whose libidinal development has suffered some disturbance, such as perverts and homosexuals, that in their later choice of love-objects they have taken as a model not their mother but their own selves. They are plainly seeking *themselves* as a love-object, and are exhibiting a type of object-choice which must be termed 'narcissistic'. In this observation we have the strongest of the reasons which have led us to adopt the hypothesis of narcissism.

(We have, however, not concluded that human beings are divided into two sharply differentiated groups, according as their object-choice con-

---

[30] ['*Anlehnungstypus.*' Literally, 'leaning-on type'. The term has been rendered in English as the 'anaclitic type' by analogy with the grammatical term 'enclitic', used of particles which cannot be the first word in a sentence, but must be appended to, or must lean up against, a more important one, e.g. the Latin '*enim*' or the Greek 'δέ'. This seems to be the first published appearance of the actual term '*Anlehnungstypus*'. The idea that a child arrives at its first sexual object on the basis of its nutritional instinct is to be found in the first edition of the *Three Essays* (1905*d*), *Standard Ed.*, **7**, 222; but the two or three explicit mentions in that work of the 'anaclitic type' were not added to it until the 1915 edition. The concept was very clearly foreshadowed near the beginning of the second of Freud's papers on the psychology of love (1912*d*), *Standard Ed.*, **11**, 180–1. The term '*angelehnte*' ('attached') is used in a similar sense near the beginning of Section III of the Schreber case history (1911*c*), but the underlying hypothesis is not stated there.—It should be noted that the 'attachment' (or '*Anlehnung*') indicated by the term is that of the sexual instincts to the ego-instincts, not of the child to its mother.]

forms to the anaclitic or to the narcissistic type; we assume rather that both kinds of object-choice are open to each individual, though he may show a preference for one or the other. We say that a human being has originally two sexual objects—himself and the woman who nurses him—and in doing so we are postulating a primary narcissism in everyone, which may in some cases manifest itself in a dominating fashion in his object-choice.)

A comparison of the male and female sexes then shows that there are fundamental differences between them in respect of their type of object-choice, although these differences are of course not universal. (Complete object-love of the attachment type is, properly speaking, characteristic of the male. It displays the marked sexual overvaluation which is doubtless derived from the child's original narcissism and thus corresponds to a transference of that narcissism to the sexual object. This sexual overvaluation is the origin of the peculiar state of being in love, a state suggestive of a neurotic compulsion, which is thus traceable to an impoverishment of the ego as regards libido in favour of the love-object.[31]) A different course is followed in the type of female most frequently met with, which is probably the purest and truest one. With the onset of puberty the maturing of the female sexual organs, which up till then have been in a condition of latency, seems to bring about an intensification of the original narcissism, and this is unfavourable to the development of a true object-choice with its accompanying sexual overvaluation. Women, especially if they grow up with good looks, develop a certain self-contentment which compensates them for the social restrictions that are imposed upon them in their choice of object. Strictly speaking, it is only themselves that such women love with an intensity comparable to that of the man's love for them. Nor does their need lie in the direction of loving, but of being loved; and the man who fulfils this condition is the one who finds favour with them. The importance of this type of woman for the erotic life of mankind is to be rated very high. Such women have the greatest fascination for men, not only for aesthetic reasons, since as a rule they are the most beautiful, but also because of a combination of interesting psychological factors. (For it seems very evident that another person's narcissism has a great attraction for those who have renounced part of their own narcissism and are in

---

[31] [Freud returned to this in a discussion of being in love in Chapter VIII of his *Group Psychology* (1921c), *Standard Ed.*, **18**, 112 f.]

search of object-love.) The charm of a child lies to a great extent in his narcissism, his self-contentment and inaccessibility, just as does the charm of certain animals which seem not to concern themselves about us, such as cats and the large beasts of prey. Indeed, even great criminals and humorists, as they are represented in literature, compel our interest by the narcissistic consistency with which they manage to keep away from their ego anything that would diminish it. It is as if we envied them for maintaining a blissful state of mind—an unassailable libidinal position which we ourselves have since abandoned. The great charm of narcissistic women has, however, its reverse side; a large part of the lover's dissatisfaction, of his doubts of the woman's love, of his complaints of her enigmatic nature, has its root in this incongruity between the types of object-choice.

Perhaps it is not out of place here to give an assurance that this description of the feminine form of erotic life is not due to any tendentious desire on my part to depreciate women. Apart from the fact that tendentiousness is quite alien to me, I know that these different lines of development correspond to the differentiation of functions in a highly complicated biological whole; further, I am ready to admit that there are quite a number of women who love according to the masculine type and who also develop the sexual overvaluation proper to that type.

Even for narcissistic women, whose attitude towards men remains cool, there is a road which leads to complete object-love. In the child which they bear, a part of their own body confronts them like an extraneous object, to which, starting out from their narcissism, they can then give complete object-love. There are other women, again, who do not have to wait for a child in order to take the step in development from (secondary) narcissism to object-love. Before puberty they feel masculine and develop some way along masculine lines; after this trend has been cut short on their reaching female maturity, they still retain the capacity of longing for a masculine ideal—an ideal which is in fact a survival of the boyish nature that they themselves once possessed.[32]

What I have so far said by way of indication may be concluded by a short summary of the paths leading to the choice of an object.

[32] [Freud developed his views on female sexuality in a number of later papers: on a case of female homosexuality (1920a), on the effects of the physiological distinctions between the sexes (1925j), on the sexuality of women (1931b) and in Lecture XXIII of his *New Introductory Lectures* (1933a).]

A person may love:—

(1) According to the narcissistic type:
    (a) what he himself is (i.e. himself),
    (b) what he himself was,
    (c) what he himself would like to be,
    (d) someone who was once part of himself.
(2) According to the anaclitic (attachment) type:
    (a) the woman who feeds him,
    (b) the man who protects him,

and the succession of substitutes who take their place. The inclusion of case (c) of the first type cannot be justified till a later stage of this discussion. [*Standard Ed.*, **14,** 101.]

The significance of narcissistic object-choice for homosexuality in men must be considered in another connection.[33]

The primary narcissism of children which we have assumed and which forms one of the postulates of our theories of the libido, is less easy to grasp by direct observation than to confirm by inference from elsewhere. If we look at the attitude of affectionate parents towards their children, we have to recognize that it is a revival and reproduction of their own narcissism, which they have long since abandoned. The trustworthy pointer constituted by overvaluation, which we have already recognized as a narcissistic stigma in the case of object-choice, dominates, as we all know, their emotional attitude. Thus they are under a compulsion to ascribe every perfection to the child—which sober observation would find no occasion to do—and to conceal and forget all his shortcomings. (Incidentally, the denial of sexuality in children is connected with this.) Moreover, they are inclined to suspend in the child's favour the operation of all the cultural acquisitions which their own narcissism has been forced to respect, and to renew on his behalf the claims to privileges which were long ago given up by themselves. The child shall have a better time than his parents; he shall not be subject to the necessities which they have recognized as paramount in life. Illness, death, renunciation of enjoyment, restrictions on his own will, shall not touch him; the laws of nature and of society shall be abrogated in his favour; he shall once more really be the centre and

---

[33] [Freud had already raised this point in Section III of his study on Leonardo (1910*c*), *Standard Ed.,* **11,** 98 ff.]

core of creation—'His Majesty the Baby',[34] as we once fancied our-selves. The child shall fulfil those wishful dreams of the parents which they never carried out—the boy shall become a great man and a hero in his father's place, and the girl shall marry a prince as a tardy com-pensation for her mother. At the most touchy point in the narcissistic system, the immortality of the ego, which is so hard pressed by reality, security is achieved by taking refuge in the child. Parental love, which is so moving and at bottom so childish, is nothing but the parents' narcissism born again, which, transformed into object-love, unmistak-ably reveals its former nature.

III

The disturbances to which a child's original narcissism is exposed, the reactions with which he seeks to protect himself from them and the paths into which he is forced in doing so—these are themes which I propose to leave on one side, as an important field of work which still awaits exploration. The most significant portion of it, however, can be singled out in the shape of the 'castration complex' (in boys, anxiety about the penis—in girls, envy for the penis) and treated in connection with the effect of early deterrence from sexual activity. Psycho-analytic research ordinarily enables us to trace the vicissitudes undergone by the libidinal instincts when these, isolated from the ego-instincts, are placed in opposition to them; but in the particular field of the castration complex, it allows us to infer the existence of an epoch and a psychical situation in which the two groups of instincts, still operating in unison and inseparably mingled, make their appearance as narcissistic inter-ests. It is from this context that Adler [1910] has derived his concept of the 'masculine protest', which he has elevated almost to the position of the sole motive force in the formation of character and neurosis alike and which he bases not on a narcissistic, and therefore still a libidinal, trend, but on a social valuation. Psycho-analytic research has from the very beginning recognized the existence and importance of the 'mas-

[34] [In English in the original. Perhaps a reference to a well-known Royal Academy picture of the Edwardian age, which bore that title and showed two London policemen holding up the crowded traffic to allow a nursery-maid to wheel a perambulator across the street.—'His Majesty the Ego' appears in Freud's earlier paper on *Creative Writers and Day-Dreaming* (1908e).]

culine protest', but it has regarded it, in opposition to Adler, as narcissistic in nature and derived from the castration complex. The 'masculine
protest' is concerned in the formation of character, into the genesis of
which it enters along with many other factors, but it is completely
unsuited for explaining the problems of the neuroses, with regard to
which Adler takes account of nothing but the manner in which they
serve the ego-instincts. I find it quite impossible to place the genesis of
neurosis upon the narrow basis of the castration complex, however
powerfully it may come to the fore in men among their resistances to
the cure of a neurosis. Incidentally, I know of cases of neurosis in which
the 'masculine protest', or, as we regard it, the castration complex,
plays no pathogenic part, and even fails to appear at all.[35]

Observation of normal adults shows that their former megalomania
has been damped down and that the psychical characteristics from
which we inferred their infantile narcissism have been effaced. What
has become of their ego-libido? Are we to suppose that the whole
amount of it has passed into object-cathexes? Such a possibility is
plainly contrary to the whole trend of our argument; but we may find a
hint at another answer to the question in the psychology of repression.

We have learned that libidinal instinctual impulses undergo the vicis-
situde of pathogenic repression if they come into conflict with the
subject's cultural and ethical ideas. By this we never mean that the
individual in question has a merely intellectual knowledge of the existence of such ideas; we always mean that he recognizes them as a
standard for himself and submits to the claims they make on him.
Repression, we have said, proceeds from the ego; we might say with
greater precision that it proceeds from the self-respect of the ego. The
same impressions, experiences, impulses and desires that one man
indulges or at least works over consciously will be rejected with the

[35] [In a letter dated September 30, 1926, replying to a question from Dr. Edoardo
Weiss (who has kindly brought it to our attention), Freud wrote: 'Your question, in
connection with my assertion in my paper on Narcissism, as to whether there are
neuroses in which the castration complex plays no part, puts me in an embarrassing
position. I no longer recollect what it was I had in mind at the time. To-day, it is true,
I could not name any neurosis in which this complex is not to be met with, and in any
case I should not have written the sentence to-day. But we know so little of the whole
subject that I should prefer not to give a final decision either way.'—A further criticism
of Adler's views on the 'masculine protest' will be found in the 'History of the Psycho-
Analytic Movement', *Standard Ed., 14*, 54 f.]

utmost indignation by another, or even stifled before they enter consciousness.[36] The difference between the two, which contains the conditioning factor of repression, can easily be expressed in terms which enable it to be explained by the libido theory. We can say that the one man has set up an *ideal* in himself by which he measures his actual ego, while the other has formed no such ideal. For the ego the formation of an ideal would be the conditioning factor of repression.[37]

This ideal ego is now the target of the self-love which was enjoyed in childhood by the actual ego. The subject's narcissism makes its appearance displaced on to this new ideal ego, which, like the infantile ego, finds itself possessed of every perfection that is of value. As always where the libido is concerned, man has here again shown himself incapable of giving up a satisfaction he had once enjoyed. He is not willing to forgo the narcissistic perfection of his childhood; and when, as he grows up, he is disturbed by the admonitions of others and by the awakening of his own critical judgement, so that he can no longer retain that perfection, he seeks to recover it in the new form *of an ego ideal.* What he projects before him as his ideal is the substitute for the lost narcissism of his childhood in which he was his own ideal.[38]

We are naturally led to examine the relation between this forming of an ideal and sublimation. Sublimation is a process that concerns object-libido and consists in the instinct's directing itself towards an aim other than, and remote from, that of sexual satisfaction; in this process the accent falls upon deflection from sexuality. Idealization is a process that concerns the *object;* by it that object, without any alteration in its nature, is aggrandized and exalted in the subject's mind. Idealization is possible in the sphere of ego-libido as well as in that of object-libido. For example, the sexual overvaluation of an object is an idealizaton of it. In so far as sublimation describes something that has to do with the instinct and idealization something to do with the object, the two concepts are to be distinguished from each other.[39]

---

[36] [Cf. some remarks in the paper on repression (1915*d*), *Standard Ed.,* **14,** 150.]

[37] [A comment on this sentence will be found in a footnote to Chapter XI of *Group Psychology* (1921*c*), *Standard Ed.,* **18,** 131 *n.*]

[38] [In the editions previous to 1924 this read '. . . is only the substitute . . .']

[39] [Freud recurs to the topic of idealization in Chapter VIII of his *Group Psychology* (1921*c*), *Standard Ed.,* **18,** 112 f.]

The formation of an ego ideal is often confused with the sublimation of instinct, to the detriment of our understanding of the facts. A man who has exchanged his narcissism for homage to a high ego ideal has not necessarily on that account succeeded in sublimating his libidinal instincts. It is true that the ego ideal demands such sublimation, but it cannot enforce it; sublimation remains a special process which may be prompted by the ideal but the execution of which is entirely independent of any such prompting. It is precisely in neurotics that we find the highest differences of potential between the development of their ego ideal and the amount of sublimation of their primitive libidinal instincts; and in general it is far harder to convince an idealist of the inexpedient location of his libido than a plain man whose pretentions have remained more moderate. Further, the formation of an ego ideal and sublimation are quite differently related to the causation of neurosis. As we have learnt, the formation of an ideal heightens the demands of the ego and is the most powerful factor favouring repression; sublimation is a way out, a way by which those demands can be met *without* involving repression.[40]

It would not surprise us if we were to find a special psychical agency which performs the task of seeing that narcissistic satisfaction from the ego ideal is ensured and which, with this end in view, constantly watches the actual ego and measures it by that ideal.[41] If such an agency does exist, we cannot possibly come upon it as a *discovery*—we can only *recognize* it; for we may reflect that what we call our 'conscience' has the required characteristics. Recognition of this agency enables us to understand the so-called 'delusions of being noticed' or more correctly, of being *watched,* which are such striking symptoms in the paranoid diseases and which may also occur as an isolated form of illness, or intercalated in a transference neurosis. Patients of this sort complain that all their thoughts are known and their actions watched and supervised; they are informed of the functioning of this agency by voices which characteristically speak to them in the third person ('Now she's thinking of that again', 'now he going out'). This complaint is justified; it describes the truth. A power of this kind,

[40] [The possible connection between sublimation and the transformation of sexual object-libido into narcissistic libido is discussed by Freud towards the beginning of Chapter III of *The Ego and the Id* (1923*b*).]

[41] [It was from a combination of this agency and the ego ideal that Freud was later to evolve the super-ego. Cf. Chapter XI of *Group Psychology* (1921*c*) and Chapter II of *The Ego and the Id* (1923*b*).]

watching, discovering and criticizing all out intentions, does really exist. Indeed, it exists in every one of us in normal life.

Delusions of being watched present this power in a regressive form, thus revealing its genesis and the reason why the patient is in revolt against it. For what prompted the subject to form an ego ideal, on whose behalf his conscience acts as watchman, arose from the critical influence of his parents (conveyed to him by the medium of the voice), to whom were added, as time went on, those who trained and taught him and the innumerable and indefinable host of all the other people in his environment— his fellow-men—and public opinion.

In this way large amounts of libido of an essentially homosexual kind are drawn into the formation of the narcissistic ego ideal and find outlet and satisfaction in maintaining it. The institution of conscience was at bottom an embodiment, first of parental criticism, and subsequently of that of society—a process which is repeated in what takes place when a tendency towards repression develops out of a prohibition or obstacle that came in the first instance from without. The voices, as well as the undefined multitude, are brought into the foreground again by the disease, and so the evolution of conscience is reproduced regressively. But the revolt against this 'censoring agency' arises out of the subject's desire (in accordance with the fundamental character of his illness) to liberate himself from all those influences, beginning with the parental one, and out of his withdrawal of homosexual libido from them. His conscience then confronts him in a regressive form as a hostile influence from without.

The complaints made by paranoics also show that at bottom the self-criticism of conscience coincides with the self-observation on which it is based. Thus the activity of the mind which has taken over the function of conscience has also placed itself at the service of internal research, which furnishes philosophy with the material for its intellectual operations. This may have some bearing on the characteristic tendency of paranoics to construct speculative systems.[42]

It will certainly be of importance to us if evidence of the activity of this critically observing agency—which becomes heightened into conscience and philosophic introspection—can be found in other fields as well. I will

---

[42] I should like to add to this, merely by way of suggestion, that the developing and strengthening of this observing agency might contain within it the subsequent genesis of (subjective) memory and the time-factor, the latter of which has no application to unconscious processes.

mention here what Herbert Silberer has called the 'functional phenomenon', one of the few indisputably valuable additions to the theory of
dreams. Silberer, as we know, has shown that in states between sleeping
and waking we can directly observe the translation of thoughts into visual
images, but that in these circumstances we frequently have a representation, not of a thought-content, but of the actual state (willingness, fatigue,
etc.) of the person who is struggling against sleep. Similarly, he has shown
that the conclusions of some dreams or some divisions in their content
merely signify the dreamer's own perception of his sleeping and waking.
Silberer has thus demonstrated the part played by observation—in the
sense of the paranoic's delusions of being watched—in the formation of
dreams. This part is not a constant one. Probably the reason why I
overlooked it is because it does not play any great part in my own dreams;
in persons who are gifted philosophically and accustomed to introspection
it may become very evident.[43]

We may here recall that we have found that the formation of dreams
takes place under the dominance of a censorship which compels distortion
of the dream-thoughts. We did not, however, picture this censorship as a
special power, but chose the term to designate one side of the repressive
trends that govern the ego, namely the side which is turned towards the
dream-thoughts. If we enter further into the structure of the ego, we may
recognize in the ego ideal and in the dynamic utterances of conscience the
dream-censor[44] as well. If this censor is to some extent on the alert even
during sleep, we can understand how it is that its suggested activity of self-
observation and self-criticism—with such thoughts as, 'now he is too
sleepy to think', 'now he is waking up'—makes a contribution to the
content of the dream.[45]

---

[43] [See Silberer (1909 and 1911). In 1914—the year in which he wrote the present
paper—Freud added a much longer discussion of this phenomenon to *The Interpretation
of Dreams* (*Standard Ed.*, 5, 503–6).]

[44] [Here and at the beginning of the next sentence, as well as *Standard Ed.*, 14, 100,
Freud makes use of the personal form, '*Zensor*', instead of his almost universal '*Zensur*'
('censorship'). Cf. a footnote to the passage in *The Interpretation of Dreams*, referred
to in the last footnote (*Standard Ed.*, 5, 505). The distinction between the two words is
clearly brought out in a sentence near the end of Lecture XXVI of the *Introductory
Lectures* (1916–17): 'We know the self-observing agency as the ego-censor, the conscience; it is this that exercises the dream-censorship during the night.']

[45] I cannot here determine whether the differentiation of the censoring agency from
the rest of the ego is capable of forming the basis of the philosophic distinction between
consciousness and self-consciousness.

At this point we may attempt some discussion of the self-regarding attitude in normal people and in neurotics.

In the first place self-regard appears to us to be an expression of the size of the ego; what the various elements are which go to determine that size is irrelevant. Everything a person possesses or achieves, every remnant of the primitive feeling of omnipotence which his experience has confirmed, helps to increase his self-regard.

Applying our distinction between sexual and ego-instincts, we must recognize that self-regard has a specially intimate dependence on narcissistic libido. Here we are supported by two fundamental facts: that in paraphrenics self-regard is increased, while in the transference neuroses it is diminished; and that in love-relations not being loved lowers the self-regarding feelings, while being loved raises them. As we have indicated, the aim and the satisfaction in a narcissistic object-choice is to be loved.[46]

Further, it is easy to observe that libidinal object-cathexis does not raise self-regard. The effect of dependence upon the loved object is to lower that feeling: a person in love is humble. A person who loves has, so to speak, forfeited a part of his narcissism, and it can only be replaced by his being loved. In all these respects self-regard seems to remain related to the narcissistic element in love.

The realization of impotence, of one's own inability to love, in consequence of mental or physical disorder, has an exceedingly lowering effect upon self-regard. Here, in my judgement, we must look for one of the sources of the feelings of inferiority which are experienced by patients suffering from the transference neuroses and which they are so ready to report. The main source of these feelings is, however, the impoverishment of the ego, due to the extraordinarily large libidinal cathexes which have been withdrawn from it—due, that is to say, to the injury sustained by the ego through sexual trends which are no longer subject to control.

Adler [1907] is right in maintaining that when a person with an active mental life recognizes an inferiority in one of his organs, it acts as a spur and calls out a higher level of performance in him through overcompensation. But it would be altogether an exaggeration if, following Adler's example, we sought to attribute every successful achievement to this factor of an original inferiority of an organ. Not all artists are handicapped with

---

[46] [This subject is enlarged on by Freud in Chapter VIII of his *Group Psychology* (1921c), *Standard Ed.*, **18**, 113 f.]

bad eyesight, nor were all orators originally stammerers. And there are plenty of instances of excellent achievements springing from *superior* organic endowment. In the aetiology of neuroses organic inferiority and imperfect development play an insignificant part—much the same as that played by currently active perceptual material in the formation of dreams. Neuroses make use of such inferiorities as a pretext, just as they do of every other suitable factor. We may be tempted to believe a neurotic woman patient when she tells us that it was inevitable she should fall ill, since she is ugly, deformed or lacking in charm, so that no one could love her; but the very next neurotic will teach us better—for she persists in her neurosis and in her aversion to sexuality, although she seems more desirable, and is more desired, than the average woman. The majority of hysterical women are among the attractive and even beautiful representatives of their sex, while, on the other hand, the frequency of ugliness, organic defects and infirmities in the lower classes of society does not increase the incidence of neurotic illness among them.

The relations of self-regard to erotism—that is, to libidinal object-cathexes—may be expressed concisely in the following way. Two cases must be distinguished, according to whether the erotic cathexes are ego-syntonic, or, on the contrary, have suffered repression. In the former case (where the use made of the libido is ego-syntonic), love is assessed like any other activity of the ego. Loving in itself, in so far as it involves longing and deprivation, lowers self-regard; whereas being loved, having one's love returned, and possessing the loved object, raises it once more. When libido is repressed, the erotic cathexis is felt as a severe depletion of the ego, the satisfaction of love is impossible, and the re-enrichment of the ego can be effected only by a withdrawal of libido from its objects. The return of the object-libido to the ego and its transformation into narcissism represents,[47] as it were, a happy love once more; and, on the other hand, it is also true that a real happy love corresponds to the primal condition in which object-libido and ego-libido cannot be distinguished.

The importance and extensiveness of the topic must be my justification for adding a few more remarks which are somewhat loosely strung together.

The development of the ego consists in a departure from primary narcis-

---

[47] ['*Darstellt.*' In the first edition only: '*herstellt,*' 'establishes'.]

sism and gives rise to a vigorous attempt to recover that state. This departure is brought about by means of the displacement of libido on to an ego ideal imposed from without; and satisfaction is brought about from fulfilling this ideal.

At the same time the ego has sent out the libidinal object-cathexes. It becomes impoverished in favour of these cathexes, just as it does in favour of the ego ideal, and it enriches itself once more from its satisfactions in respect of the object, just as it does by fulfilling its ideal.

One part of self-regard is primary—the residue of infantile narcissism; another part arises out of the omnipotence which is corroborated by experience (the fulfilment of the ego ideal), whilst a third part proceeds from the satisfaction of object-libido.

The ego ideal has imposed severe conditions upon the satisfaction of libido through objects; for it causes some of them to be rejected by means of its censor,[48] as being incompatible. Where no such ideal has been formed, the sexual trend in question makes its appearance unchanged in the personality in the form of a perversion. To be their own ideal once more, in regard to sexual no less than other trends, as they were in childhood—this is what people strive to attain as their happiness.

Being in love consists in a flowing-over of ego-libido on to the object. It has the power to remove repressions and re-instate perversions. It exalts the sexual object into a sexual ideal. Since, with the object type (or attachment type), being in love occurs in virtue of the fulfilment of infantile conditions for loving, we may say that whatever fulfils that condition is idealized.

The sexual ideal may enter into an interesting auxiliary relation to the ego ideal. It may be used for substitutive satisfaction where narcissistic satisfaction encounters real hindrances. In that case a person will love in conformity with the narcissistic type of object-choice, will love what he once was and no longer is, or else what possesses the excellences which he never had at all (cf. *(c) Standard Ed.*, **14,** 90). The formula parallel to the one there stated runs thus: what possesses the excellence which the ego lacks for making it an ideal, is loved. This expedient is of special importance for the neurotic, who, on account of his excessive object-cathexes, is impoverished in his ego and is incapable of fulfilling his ego ideal. He then seeks a way back to narcissism from his prodigal expenditure of libido

[48] [See footnote 44, p. 39.]

upon objects, by choosing a sexual ideal after the narcissistic type which possesses the excellences to which he cannot attain. This is the cure by love, which he generally prefers to cure by analysis. Indeed, he cannot believe in any other mechanism of cure; he usually brings expectations of this sort with him to the treatment and directs them towards the person of the physician. The patient's incapacity for love, resulting from his extensive repressions, naturally stands in the way of a therapeutic plan of this kind. An unintended result is often met with when, by means of the treatment, he has been partially freed from his repressions: he withdraws from further treatment in order to choose a love-object, leaving his cure to be continued by a life with someone he loves. We might be satisfied with this result, if it did not bring with it all dangers of a crippling dependence upon his helper in need.

The ego ideal opens up an important avenue for the understanding of group psychology. In addition to its individual side, this ideal has a social side; it is also the common ideal of a family, a class or a nation. It binds not only a person's narcissistic libido, but also a considerable amount of his homosexual libido,[49] which is in this way turned back into the ego. The want of satisfaction which arises from the non-fulfilment of this ideal liberates homosexual libido, and this is transformed into a sense of guilt (social anxiety). Originally this sense of guilt was a fear of punishment by the parents, or, more correctly, the fear of losing their love; later the parents are replaced by an indefinite number of fellow-men. The frequent causation of paranoia by an injury to the ego, by a frustration of satisfaction within the sphere of the ego ideal, is thus made more intelligible, as is the convergence of ideal-formation and sublimation in the ego ideal, as well as the involution of sublimations and the possible transformation of ideals in paraphrenic disorders.

[49] [The importance of homosexuality in the structure of groups had been hinted at in *Totem and Taboo* (1912–13), *Standard Ed.*, **13**, 144, and was again referred to in *Group Psychology* (1921c), *Standard Ed.*, **18**, 124 *n*. and 141.]

2. Pathologic Forms of Self-Esteem Regulation

Annie Reich

"Self-esteem," in common usage, is defined by Webster as a high opinion of oneself, respect for oneself. This positive evaluation of the self obviously is a precondition for one's well-being.

There are many ways in which human beings attempt to keep up a positive evaluation of themselves. The methods they use may vary according to numerous factors, such as age, character and capacities of the ego, individual nature of conflicts, and so on. A comprehensive study of these various ways would exceed the frame of a lecture. My discussion will limit itself to certain abnormal modes of self-esteem regulation which are characteristically found in some types of "narcissistic disturbances."

Obviously, disturbances of self-esteem are a frequent symptom in schizophrenic as well as in manic-depressive states. However, I shall not deal with the psychoses but intend to concentrate on "narcissistic neurosis."

I am well aware that Freud used the term "narcissistic neurosis" to designate exclusively psychotic illness, delimiting it from transference neurosis. But it seems to me that narcissistic pathology cannot be viewed as restricted to psychosis. I would like to use this term in a much wider sense. In the course of the last decades, we have become less inclined to regard clinical entities as pertaining exclusively to certain phases of development. We know overlapping of phases to be ubiquitous. There is usually a partial regression to earlier ego and libidinal states mixed with later, more highly developed structures. Even a marked narcissistic orientation need not be completely so; i.e., it need not be characterized by a withdrawal of the entire cathexis from objects. Indeed, we now even question the usefulness of a too narrowly circumscribed nosology. We are much concerned with so-called borderline conditions, and we tend to look upon the boundary between psychosis and neurosis as somewhat fluid.

Narcissism denotes a libidinal cathexis of the self, in contrast to object cathexis. Without repeating the well-known facts about the development from primary to secondary narcissism, I merely wish to stress that narcissism per se is a normal phenomenon. It becomes pathologic only under certain conditions: (1) in states of quantitative imbalance; e.g., when the balance between object cathexis and self-cathexis has become disturbed, and objects are cathected insufficiently or not at all; (2) in infantile forms of narcissism, which are frequently—but not always—present in the states of quantitative imbalance. Infantile narcissism consists in cathexis of the self at a time of incomplete ego differentiation and insufficient delimitation of self and object world. The absence of the ability, at this stage, to distinguish wish from reality manifests itself in the use of magic to achieve need satisfaction and mastery of reality; thus, the infantile narcissism has a megalomanic character.

Narcissistic pathology becomes especially noticeable in the methods used for self-esteem regulation.

Fenichel (1945), following the ideas of Ferenczi (1913), regards self-esteem as the expression of nearness to or distance from the infantile feeling of omnipotence. With advancing ego development, the values against which the self is measured change and become more realistic; equally, the methods that are used to keep self-esteem on a stable positive level. The longing for omnipotence, obviously, stems from fixation at a still undifferentiated ego level. By using it as a criterion, Fenichel thus framed a static definition leaving no room for the maturation of values. I prefer the more flexible one given by Edith Jacobson in her fundamental paper on "The Self and the Object World" (1954b), which has helped me to clarify many aspects of narcissistic disturbances. Her definition seems to cover the complexities of the problem more adequately. She considers self-esteem to be the expression of discrepancy or harmony between self-representation and the wishful concept of the self.

Or, to put it differently: in the course of growing up, we must learn to evaluate our potentialities and accept our limitations. Continued hope for the impossible represents an infantile wish, revealing a basic lack of ability to face inner and outer reality. Self-esteem thus depends on the nature of the inner image against which we measure our own self, as well as on the ways and means at our disposal to live up to it. That this inner image is influenced by many factors, expecially by the particular form of the superego, is obvious. Living up sufficiently to the demands of one's superego is a mature form of self-esteem regulation.

What we loosely describe as "narcissists" are people whose libido is mainly concentrated on themselves at the expense of object love. I shall not speak here of those who without visible conflict entertain an exceedingly high opinion of themselves. Another type of narcissists frequently has exaggerated, unrealistic—i.e., infantile—inner yard-sticks. The methods they use to deal with the resulting inner tension depend on the general state of their ego and often are infantile ones. This is the specific pathology I wish to discuss, concentrating at this time on the forms it takes in men. As a starting point, I may bring a few clinical data to illustrate some characteristic patterns of such pathologic self-esteem regulation.

Daniel K. was a very accomplished writer who wrote one book after another, with marked success. But he did not feel gratified by this. Nothing he did was as grandiose as he wanted it to be. He would feel reassured, for a time, when he looked at his book shelf and counted: "Here are seven books I wrote, six volumes I edited; there are twenty-three articles I brought out in other people's publications; I am quoted so and so many times:—*There are about two and a half feet of Mr. K. on the shelf.*" The phallic meaning of this little game was obvious. He had to reassure himself that his phallus was not only there, but of extraordinary size.

Daniel's life consisted to a large extent in behavior of this kind; he was constantly preoccupied with attempts to feel great and important. He was active in innumerable civic and cultural enterprises and had attained a leading position in his community. But neither this nor his prolific literary production nor his erotic successes sufficed to make him happy. He was a man of considerable talent, well informed, and rich in ideas. But frequently his writing was careless and superficial, not up to the level of his capacities, because he was driven to produce too fast. He could not *wait* for results, could not stand tension and unpleasure, although he *knew* better. He had an inner standard of quality for his work as well as the gift for it, but was unable to muster enough self-discipline to realize his potentialities. He had to have the immediate gratification of success. This need was so overwhelmingly strong that he had little control over it. He also was touchy, quick to take offense at the slightest provocation. He continually anticipated attack and danger, reacting with anger and fantasies of revenge when he felt frustrated in his need for constant admiration.

Obviously, Daniel was overconcentrated on himself; his object relationships were weak and apt to be relinquished under pressure. His main aim was to increase his self-esteem and to ward off the underlying danger of passivity by incessant masculine activity.

The narcissistic goal against which he measured himself was most clearly expressed by his fantasies in puberty: he would see himself successively as the Mayor of New York City, the President of the United States, and as the president of the world, until he had to stop with the painful question: "And then what?" Later, he wanted to be the outstanding genius of his time. Of course, no success in reality could measure up to such limitless inner demands, and his state of dissatisfaction was all the more intensified because he had to sacrifice more mature superego demands in reaching out for his illusory aims.

This bottomless need for grandiosity is clearly a compensatory striving. He has to be president of the world, he has to have a symbolic phallus two and a half feet long, because he is under the impact of unbearable castration fears.

Compensatory narcissistic self-inflation is among the most conspicuous forms of pathologic self-esteem regulation. Frequently, the attempt at compensation proves unsuccessful; instead of producing a feeling of "narcissistic bliss," it results in severe symptoms.

Thus Daniel continually felt not only slighted, unloved, unappreciated by others, but also awkward, embarrassed, and "self-conscious." Moreover, he harbored severe anxieties regarding his state of health. He was forever anticipating early death from cancer or heart attack, etc., and anxiously watched himself for signs of disease. "Self-consciousness" and hypochondriacal anxiety both are typical symptoms in persons with narcissistic pathology. They represent, so to speak, the reverse side of the narcissistic self-inflation. I shall have more to say about this later.

Two factors which are characteristic of the pathology in compensatory narcissistic self-inflation were implied in this material: (1) there is a large amount of unneutralized aggression which contributes to the hypochondriacal anxieties; (2) there is a superego disturbance that causes an overdependence on approval from outside, thus contributing to the symptom of "self-consciousness."

It should be stressed that in spite of his low tolerance of tension and unpleasure, Daniel's narcissistic orientation was not combined with a general regression to infantile narcissism. The pathology, in his case, rested predominantly on the megalomanic content of the ideals he had set up for himself. He tried to reach his goal of self-aggrandizement through achievement and did not indulge in regressive confusion between reality and fantasy .

However, owing to the regressive character of the narcissistic orientation, one often finds that the infantile-megalomanic ideal is accompanied by a barely disguised sexualization of originally non-sexual activities. Frequently the ambitious narcissistic fantasy is expressed in the form of sexualized and concrete images, thus revealing features of ego infantilism, deficient sublimation, and primitive thinking. In severer cases of this type the ego disturbance dominates the clinical picture and is not confined to an isolated area, as it was in the example given here.

Let us now examine the origin of the narcissistic imbalance which determines these compensatory efforts. The need for narcissistic inflation arises from a striving to overcome threats to one's bodily intactness. Obviously, such a threat is ubiquitous in all danger situations; but under favorable circumstances, defenses are mobilized that permit a permanent conflict solution. Anxiety is overcome via a modification or relinquishment of instinctual aims, while object cathexis can be retained. The development of reliable, solid defenses presupposes a considerable degree of ego integration. The ego must have the strength, while circumventing violent anxiety attacks and using small amounts of anxiety as a danger signal, to mobilize defenses and to influence the drives in the desired way. But if a traumatic situation occurs too early and is too overwhelming, at a time when the ego is still in a rather primitive state, the ego will not succeed in binding the anxiety. The impact of such early traumata thus can seriously interfere not only with the formation of defenses, but also with the integration and general development of the ego. States of panic in themselves represent grave disturbances in the balance of cathexis. That is to say, during intense anxiety there often occurs a *passing* withdrawal of psychic interest from objects to the self. Under the conditions of too frequently repeated early traumatizations, the narcissistic withdrawal of libido from the objects to the endangered self tends to remain permanent

Such early traumatization at a time of ego immaturity creates a predispositon to react in an infantile way to later danger situations. The imagined danger is taken for reality: it is not something that might occur in the future and might still be avoided, but something that has already occurred. In the case of my patient, for instance, the overwhelming castration anxiety stemmed from repeated early observations of primal scenes experienced as violence and total destruction, which had led to a feminine identification; i.e., to a latent homosexual orientation. The personality of the mother, a severe hypocondriac who constantly indulged in dramatic performances of being on the brink of castastrophic death, made a later re-evaluation of danger impossible. Femininity remained equated with complete annihilation. It represented not a threat in the future, but an accomplished fact. Hence the persistent orientation aiming at repair of the damage.

This infantile equation of danger with a castastrophe that has already occurred seems to be characteristic of such early disturbances. The only possible defense, therefore, consists in methods which were available to the infantile ego, particularly in *magical denial*: "It is not so. I am not helpless, bleeding, destroyed. On the contrary, I am bigger and better than anyone else. I am the greatest, the most grandiose, " Thus, to a large extent, the psychic interest must center on a compensatory narcissistic fantasy whose grandiose character affirms the denial.

Fantasies, to be sure, always have to do with easy ways of wish fulfillment. But they obviously differ vastly in kind, and they range from the most primitive to highly differentiated forms. Being rooted in magical denial and characterized by primitive features of an early ego state, the compensatory narcissistic fantasies often are poorly integrated into realistic, adult thinking.

The exclusive production of fantasies that aim at one's own aggrandizement reveals a serious disturbance of the narcissistic balance, particularly when these fantasies persist after puberty. For example, I remember a patient whose masturbation fantasies were consistently and exclusively concerned with self-adoration: "I am the greatest general in the world; I am the greatest all-round athlete; I am winning all Olympic ski races," etc. Grandiose fantasies of this type are not just a pleasant pastime whose wishful and unreal character is fully recognized, and which can be "turned off" at will. They have become an intrinsic part of the personality. Indeed, they have become life's main purpose, and the self is being measured against them.

I shall show later that such fantasies are based on primitive identifications with idealized infantile objects and thus represent primitive ego ideals.

The degree of pathology resulting from the persistence of these archaic ego ideals depends upon the structure of the ego. Ability to function adequately in reality, availability of sublimations, etc., determine whether any attempts can be made to transpose the fantasy at least partially into reality. Sometimes it may be tuned down to a pitch that is realizable in some degree, sufficiently to keep the self-esteem on a stable high level.

In the predominantly narcissistic personality, however, the withdrawal of interest from reality and object world frequently entails regressive trends. As a result, the wishful fantasy becomes or remains overcathected and the distinction between wish and reality will become blurred. Thus the fantasy is not only a yardstick, but is also experienced as magically fulfilled. The degree of pathology in a given case will depend on the degree of indulgence in such magic gratification and neglect of reality testing.

What is of interest for our special problem is the fact that such regressive abandonment of reality testing with respect to self-appreciation occurs frequently as an isolated lacuna in an otherwise well-coordinated personality. In other words, self-evaluation may remain infantile in certain restricted areas. For instance, the high sense of gratification which arose when the child was able to master certain difficulties may persist throughout later life, even though "objectively" such activity no longer represents any particular achievement. Rather minor activities and productions can thus be experienced as extremely important, sometimes, as though a hidden narcissistic fantasy had been realized. The resulting feeling of increased self-esteem, of exaggerated self-assurance, creates an impression of unwarranted conceit, since others cannot share the archaic value judgments which underlie it.

When an adult still finds magnificence, let us say, in being able to ride by himself in a train, he manifests an infantilism of inner standards. Usually the survival of such infantile values, too, is the end result of compensatory needs; but the intensity of inner conflict is less pronounced in these persons than in those with exaggerated standards. It is likely that their fixations took place on a somewhat higher level of development.

It would of course be artificial to delimit the compensatory narcissistic fantasy too sharply from the superego as the embodiment of "mature" values transmitted by education. Although the superego is the more complicated structure, both may exist simultaneously. They may overlap or may be fused and mixed with one another.

The differences between the two structures are self-evident. Narcissistic fantasies often stand in sharp contrast to superego demands, since they contain many elements of an unsublimated, instinct-fulfilling character. The primitive values comprised in them are expressions of body narcissism.

Overstrong body narcissism is rooted in traumatic experiences, pregenital as well as early genital, which had shattered primitive feelings of pleasure and unquestioned security. These traumata had thus destroyed the infantile feeling of power to subject the disobedient object world, including the own body, to the wishes of the infantile ego. Uncontrollable feelings of helplessness, anxiety, and rage ensued. These represent what we call "narcissistic injuries" that necessitate continuous reparative measures. The result is a turning away from love objects to an enormous overvaluation of the body or particular organs: of their intactness, size, strength, beauty, grandiosity. Most glaring here is the overvaluation of the phallus, in contrast to the concept of the female organs as being destroyed, bleeding, dirty, etc.

It should be stressed that castration threats, with ensuing overvaluation of the phallus, represent only the most conspicuous and the most tangible narcissistic traumata. However, any need for repair or restitution may be condensed into fantasies about phallic intactness and greatness. Castration thus is equated with object loss, emptiness, hunger, bowel loss and dirtiness, while phallic intactness also expresses the undoing of pregenital losses and injuries. Most important in this context is the equation of the whole body with a phallus, whose oral background was pointed out by Lewin (1933).

The megalomanic character of the body-phallus equation has to do with fantasies about incorporation of early objects (or of their organs) seen in an idealized way. Thus, to use Jacobson's formulation, fusion has taken place between self- and object images. The grandiosity originally attributed to the object belongs now to the self. Archaic object relationships of this kind, with fluid boundaries between self- and object image, represent the matrix of increased body narcissism.

The body-phallus equation usually reflects a narcissistic erotization of the whole body. This fantasy often has an out-and-out perverse quality and may lead to dire consequences.

To give an example: I once treated a professional actor, a handsome fellow, who was in a continual state of self-infatuation. That he really experienced his whole body as a penis was revealed by the fact that he liked to masturbate facing a mirror, with the fantasy that his neck was as thick as his head. This patient's constant preoccupation with his own body had disastrous effects. He became plagued by continuous, severe hypochondriacal anxieties. He was afraid of innumerable fatal diseases, worried that his nose would be disfigured by a chronic eczema, etc.

My other patient, Daniel K., showed the same pattern of self-adoration in a slight disguise when he admired his almost yard-long row of books. This transparent displacement from the body-phallus to his brain children did not avail him; he suffered from the same intolerable hypochondriacal fears as the actor.

Frequently, attempts are made to modify the sexual body narcissism and to transform it into something nonsexual and nonobjectionable; these attempts sometimes are on a rather primitive level. Certain tokens of masculinity are used in place of the real thing. I have repeatedly observed this in patients who attached a strong masculine connotation to particular garments or to the pipes they smoked, to the cars they drove, etc. This displacement represents a not very successful attempt at desexualization. The thinking remains symbolic, unrealistic, and incommunicable. (I never could establish, for instance, why one suit was regarded as more masculine than the other.)

Successful modification of body narcissism depends primarily upon the ego's capacity for sublimation and, as we shall see, deaggressivization.

Unsublimated, erotized, manic self-inflation easily shifts to a feeling of utter dejection, of worthlessness, and to hypochondriacal anxieties. *"Narcissists" of this type thus suffer regularly from repetitive, violent oscillations of self-esteem.*

It is as though the warded-off feeling of catastrophic annihilation, which had started off the whole process originally, were breaking through the elegant façade again each time. The brief rapture of elated self-infatuation is followed by a rude awakening. Usually the tiniest disappointment, the slightest physical indisposition, the most trifling experience of failure can throw the patient into extreme despair. He does not suffer from a cold: he has lung cancer. He did not meet with a minor setback because a contract fell through: his whole career is ruined; and so on. Thus, the grandiose body-phallus fantasy—for instance, "standing out high above everybody else, like an obelisk"—turns *suddenly* into one of total castration, often with a pregenital coloring: "I am falling apart at the seams," or "I am just a bagful of excrement," "I am full of poison that is going to kill me," etc. It is as though the original castration fear had extended from the penis to the whole body.

This infantile value system knows only absolute perfection and complete destruction; it belongs to the early time in life when only black and white existed, good and bad, pleasure and pain, but nothing in between. There are no shadings, no degrees, there are only extremes. Reality is judged exclusively from the standpoint of the pleasure principle; to evaluate it objectively is still impossible. Nor does a realistic evaluation of the self exist as yet. Like tolerance for others, tolerance for oneself is a late achievement.

The amount of aggression, both in the positive and in the negative phase, is conspicuous. The state of self-inflation is intensely competitive as a rule. My patient Daniel's grandiosity, for instance, could be measured in feet and inches, just as others measure theirs in dollars and cents. Such a concretization and oversimplification of values facilitates competition with others: "I am bigger than you—I am better—I am the best." The primitive correlation of value to size is of course a rather common phenomenon; this type of crude comparison easily lends itself to be used for purposes of aggressive competition. The very process of self-admiration involves contempt for others. Undisguised phallic-exhibitionistic impulses of this type generally are combined with unmitigated, primate aggression: the patient "blinds" others with his magnificence; he "rubs in" his successes, as though he were forcing his enormous penis on his audience.

But with the collapse of his phallic grandiosity, this vehement aggression instantly turns back upon his castrated self. Instead of admiring and loving himself the patient now hates himself. A drive diffusion has occurred, which the ego in its state of regression is unable to master. This explains, I believe, the intensity of the hypochondriacal anxieties regularly present in narcissistic disturbances.

In a number of these cases I have found the fantasy that only one grandiose phallus exists in the whole world. When the patient is in possession of it or is identified with it, everyone else is deprived of it and thus totally destroyed. In the negative phase, the tables are turned: the grandiose phallus belongs to somebody else—perhaps to its rightful, original owner—who, full of contempt, now destroys the patient. Either way, the acquisition of this glorified organ is accomplished through violent aggression.

This fantasy about the single glorified penis shows quite clearly that this and similar primitive forms of self-esteem regulation are based on a persistence of primitive types of object relationship; i.e., a fixation on infantile levels of libidinal and ego development.

At that early stage, the ability to perceive reality objectively is but *in statu nascendi.* Instinctual needs are so overwhelming that the sexual characteristics of the object flow together with the object as a person. Drives prevail toward oral—or anal—incorporation of the admired and envied objects; in this way, a feeling of *being* the object is temporarily achieved. But with growing ego differentiation, the child becomes increasingly aware of his own smallness as well as his separateness from objects. Hence the still completely sexualized and glorified object is set up as a primitive ego ideal, as something he longs to be. Under unfavorable conditions, however, the boundaries between this ideal and the self-image become blurred again, time after time.

Reverting to magical identification, the patient who has regressed to this infantile level may feel as though he *were* the magnificent phallus-father, as though he *were* his own ego ideal. Repair is achieved once more via magic fusion. But after a short time, as we have seen, this wishful identification turns into the opposite; it is doomed to break down, as the uncontrollably mounting aggression destroys the glorified object.

To relieve the ensuing intolerable feeling of annihilation, the aggression must be counteracted by a renewed elevation of the object; hence the grandiose phallus is restored to it and the entire process starts all over again. This state of affairs is reflected in the instability of moods, rapid oscillations of self-esteem, perpetual shifts from positive to negative feelings about the self, from megalomanic elation to hypochondriacal anxiety.

Let me illustrate this with a case characterized by a particular instability of self-esteem and body image. The origin of the primitive, still completely sexualized ego ideal in severe infantile traumatization can be clearly demonstrated here.

Robert L., a successful lawyer, suffers from repetitive mood swings. For a while he feels strong, victorious, much more creative and intelligent than his peers. He is proud of his slim figure; his whole body, to him, has definitely phallic characteristics. The analyst and everyone else during this period is seen as inferior, old, weak, defective. He feels that he is arousing envy in the analyst. He wishes to dazzle with his brilliance, to overpower by his masculinity. By exhibiting his own greatness he aggressively annihilates all others.

The slightest disappointment, however, or even the mere passage of time, transforms this state of phallic grandiosity into the opposite. Now he is afraid of the consequences of his aggressive wishes. He feels unsuccessful, hopeless, threatened by illness; he is affected by peculiar body sensations, as though he had a hangover. The analyst and other objects appear changed; they have gained in stature. The analyst looks younger, stronger; she is brilliant, wonderful. Now he wishes to be "adopted" and helped by her. She should give to him of her wisdom and her riches which will help to restore him. During such periods, he cannot evaluate objects at all critically or realistically. He hangs on every word of the analyst as a revelation, and it is as though her mere physical presence could do wonders for him. Now he idealizes the object, clings to it, wishes to become one with it. By this fusion he can participate again in the greatness of the glorified object.

Here we see not only the rapid change from phallic grandiosity to hypochondriacal anxieties and depression, but also a rapid change in the appearance and value of the object. Again, there are only extremes: the object either is glorious or it is nothing. Besides, the object is not experienced fully as a person. Like the patient's own body, it is treated only as a phallus, as a wonderful and life-giving breast, or as a gaping dirty wound.

This severe disturbance of object relationship was caused by a series of early traumatic events. When he was little more than six months old, Robert's obsessional mother started toilet training by means of regularly given enemas. For years to come, this interfered with his development of the sense of being a person separate from his mother: it was she who had power over his body. At the same time he experienced himself as an open bag full of excrement: things were put into him and came out of him. He could have no control over his body content. An operation early in his third year confirmed the feeling that the intactness of his body was constantly threatened. Then around the same time, his parents' marriage broke up. With the loss of his father he lost all security of permanent object relationships, particularly as the mother soon became involved with a series of lovers of whom Robert was intensely jealous.

Somewhat later, the little boy learned to retain his stools. He would sit for hours by himself, playing aggressive fantasy games in which he would kill and destroy tin soldiers, at the same time pushing and withholding a fecal column in his rectum. This gave him a feeling of mastery and of being completely solid and intact within his body, as though he had a powerful, aggressive anal phallus inside himself. In identification with his father, who was considered an aggressive monster by the mother, he became now "Freiherr von Richthofen," the German war pilot, seen as a murderous giant able to destroy the whole world. But this aggressive, anal-sadistic game led to a state of constipation which he could not overcome any more. It led to feelings of being sick and full of poison, to a new series of enemas, so that his sense of helpless annihilation broke through again.

These pregenital traumatic experiences were condensed with the child's envious admiration of his father's large penis and the simultaneous, terrifying awareness that the mother lacked this organ.

All this necessitated magical restitution. As we have seen, infantile states of elation persisted into adulthood in a slightly disguised form. They prevail for short periods, to be abruptly displaced by the sense of being worthless and destroyed. The peculiar "hangover" feeling, which assails the patient at the same time, can now be understood. By the destructive incorporation of everything that had caused his envy before, he destroyed the very power he acquired. He feels poisoned from within: he has incorporated something bad.

To repeat, the attempt at repair through primitive identification becomes intolerable due to the intensely aggressive feelings that may emerge at any moment. By destroying the object, the patient likewise destroys himself. Seeking to restitute himself, he again must endow the objects around him with ego-ideal qualities; and so the cycle is endlessly repeated.

This material throws into sharp relief that if the archaic character of the ego ideal has persisted, it invariably results in a complete failure of such attempts at self-esteem stabilization. Indeed, it is the primitive, crudely sexual quality of the ego ideals, conditioned by a fixation on the primitive levels where traumatization had occurred, that represents the quintessence of this pathology.

In the course of a more normal development, identifications with other than openly sexual aspects of the objects acquire importance. Hence the identifications lose their magical character. They bring about real changes in the structure of the ego, or they become more sublimated ideals to be incorporated in the superego. Primitive ego ideals may survive, nevertheless, while maturation of the personality progresses. In the "simpler" forms of self-esteem pathology I described before, their persistence expressed itself predominantly in a narcissistic orientation of the inner standards. The condition was not complicated by a reprojection of ego ideals onto the object world.

However, it should be stressed that a reprojection of ego ideals onto external objects need not by itself imply a greater degree of pathology. Ego ideals of a more sublimated nature may be so reprojected, and restitutive merging with real love objects may become a method of self-esteem stabilization. In my paper on "Narcissistic Object Choice in Women" (1953), I showed how the attempt to undo narcissistic injuries via identification with the partner's greatness may effect a rather stable solution if it is undertaken by a mature ego.

I should like now to come back briefly to another symptom which frequently occurs, as I mentioned before, in persons of the narcissistic structure here descibed, namely "self-consciousness." This excellent term, as far as I know, exists only in the English language. Webster defines it as follows: "prone to regard oneself as the object of observation of others. Embarrassed or stagy on account of failure to forget oneself in society." *Self-consciousness* thus describes an accentuated state of awareness of the own self and also indicates the assumption that the same exaggerated amount of attention is paid to one's person by others.

The remarks which follow are somewhat tentative. The symptom of self-conciousness is not restricted solely to the compensatory narcissistic personality. Structure and dynamics may be different under different conditions.

To be the object of admiring attention is frequently sought for as a means to undo feelings of insufficiency. But the imagined fulfillment of this wish can be experienced as extremely unpleasant. The attention desired from others is contained in and replaced by the ego's concentration upon the own self. The ego thus plays a double role: it is the observer and simultaneously the object of observation. What is relevant in pathologic cases of this kind is that cathexis has been shifted to the self not only from objects, but also from normally neutralized ego activities, to a degree which is intolerable.

Here the hypercathexis of the self is accompanied by a disturbance of sublimation, i.e., by a (voyeuristic-exhibitionistic) sexualization of ego activities. This reflects itself in the fact that any activity—any thought or feeling—exists not for its own sake, but exclusively for the purpose of narcissistic exhibition. It is as though the person would say: "Look, I am walking, speaking, thinking. Look, I have such beautiful feelings, deep interests, important thoughts." Normally such activities are invested not only with neutralized energy, but also with aim-inhibited "love" for some particular field, subject, etc. This type of "thing-love" or interest is precluded by the accentuated self-concentration we describe as "self-consciousness." The ensuing narcissistic imbalance generates disturbances of the sense of reality, ranging from feelings of emptiness or ungenuineness to severe depersonalization.

In addition, we must take into account the aggressive components of the narcissistic exhibitionistic strivings. Self-conscious people seek to undo feelings of inadequacy by forcing everyone's attention and admiration upon themselves, but they fail in this defensive attempt. They feel that attention is indeed focused on them in a *negative* way: as though others, instead of being dazzled, were discerning the warded-off "inferiority" behind the false front. The exhibitionistic drive contains contempt for those whose admiration is needed. Due to the re-emergence of inferiority feelings and to the concentration of cathexis on the self, the direction of the aggression changes; hence the contempt for others turns into self-contempt, which is experienced as shameful exposure.

The painfully increased self-awareness of the self-conscious persons thus results from a shifting back onto the self of resexualized and reaggressivized cathexis which can no longer be bound in a stable way by attachment to objects or ego activities.

Not rarely, the symptom of self-consciousness becomes further complicated by a deficiency of the self-evaluating functions. It is as though such persons were unable to form any independent moral judgment about themselves, but needed "public opinion" as a yardstick. Their superego is not fully internalized or, frequently, has become reprojected onto external objects. Here the impairment of ego functions, which is so often seen in narcissistically oriented persons, includes also a superego defect.

When the self-concious person imagines himself being judged by an outside observer, who stands for an externalized superego, he makes an unsuccessful attempt to get rid of inner conflicts, of unacceptable strivings, by means of projection. This contributes to the feelings of unreality and estrangement. It is as if he were saying: "I am not the one who wants to exhibit himself aggressively, but other people aggressively observe and judge me." Self-consciousness thus is a first step in the direction of a paranoid pattern, and this feature is in keeping with the disturbance of object cathexis which I described before.

It is obvious that the oscillations of self-esteem in compensatory narcissism bear similarities to cyclothymic states, but there are considerable differences. These mood swings are of shorter duration than the true cyclothymic ones. Notwithstanding the severity of the disturbance, large areas of the personality usually remain intact and are not involved in the pathologic process. Most noticeable is the difference of the role played by the superego. The sadistic intolerance of the superego, so predominant in the depressive phase of cyclothymia, is absent in the cases here described. The phase of lowered self-esteem is characterized preponderantly by anxiety and feelings of annihilation, not by guilt feelings. Thus, it is not the dissolution of an overstrict superego that brings about the positive phase, but a compensatory narcissistic fantasy of restitution via fusion with an archaic ego ideal. And while object loss causes regression to narcissistic identification in melancholia, these patients react with permanent vacillations between libidinous and aggressive hypercathexis of the self to an infantile traumatic situation necessitating endless attempts at repair.

BIBLIOGRAPHY

Bibring, E. (1953), The Mechanism of Depression. In: *Affective Disorders,* ed. P. Greenacre. New York: International Universities Press.

Deutsch, H. (1927), Über Zufriedenheit, Glück und Ekstase. *Int. Ztschr. Psa., XIII.*

——(1942), Some Forms of Emotional Disturbance and Their Relationship to Schizophrenia. *Psa. Quart.,* XI.

Fenichel, O. (1937), Early Stages of Ego Development. *The Collected Papers of Otto Fenichel,* II. New York: Norton, 1954.

——(1939), Trophy and Triumph. *The Collected Papers of Otto Fenichel,* II. New York: Norton, 1954.

——(1945), *The Psychoanalytic Theory of Neurosis.* New York: Norton.

Ferenczi, S. (1913), Stages in the Development of the Sense of Reality. *Sex in Psychoanalysis.* New York: Basic Books, 1950.

Freud, A. (1936), *The Ego and the Mechanisms of Defence.* New York: International Universities Press, 1946.

Freud, S. (1914), On Narcissism: An Introduction. *Standard Edition,* XIV. London: Hogarth Press, 1957.

——(1917), Mourning and Melancholia. *Standard Edition,* XIV. London: Hogarth Press, 1957.

——(1921), Group Psychology and the Analysis of the Ego. *Standard Edition,* XVIII. London: Hogarth Press, 1955.

——(1923),The Ego and the Id. *Standard Edition,* XVIII. London: Hogarth Press, 1955.

——(1926), Inhibitions, Symptoms and Anxiety. *Standard Edition,* XX. London: Hogarth Press, 1959.

Greenacre. P. (1947), Vision, Headache and the Halo. *Psa. Quart.,* XVI.

——(1952), *Trauma, Growth and Personality.* New York: Norton.

Hart, H. H. (1947), Narcissistic Equilibrium. *Int. J. Psa.,* XXVIII.

Hartmann, H. (1939), *Ego Psychology and the Problem of Adaptation.* New York: International Universities Press, 1958.

——(1950), Comments on the Psychoanalytic Theory of the Ego. *Psychoanal. Study Child,* V.

——(1953), Contribution to the Metapsychology of Schizophrenia. *Psychoanal. Study Child,* VIII.

——(1960), *Psychoanalysis and Moral Values.* New York: International Universities Press.

——Kris, E., & Loewenstein, R.M. (1949), Notes on the Theory of Aggression. *Psychoanal. Study Child,* III/IV.

Jacobson, E. (1953), Contribution to the Metapsychology of Cyclothymic Depression. In: *Affective Disorders,* ed. P. Greenacre. New York: International Universities Press.

——(1954a), Contribution to the Metapsychology of Psychotic Identifications. *J. Am. Psa. Assn.,* II.

——(1954b), The Self and the Object World: Vicissitudes of Their Infantile Cathexes and Their Influences on Ideational and Affective Development. *Psychoanal. Study Child,* IX.

Jones, E. (1913), The God-Complex. *Essays in Applied Psycho-Analysis,* II. London: Hogarth Press, 1951

Lewin, B. D. (1933), The Body as Phallus. *Psa. Quart.,* II.

——(1950), *The Psychoanalysis of Elation.* New York: Norton.

Reich, A. (1953), Narcissistic Object Choice in Women. *J. Am. Psa. Assn.,* I.

——(1954), Early Identifications as Archaic Elements in the Superego. *J. Am. Psa. Assn.,* II.

3. Forms and Transformations of Narcissism

Heinz Kohut

I

Although in theoretical discussions it will usually not be disputed that narcissism, the libidinal investment of the self,[1] is per se neither pathological nor obnoxious, there exists an understandable tendency to look at it with a negatively toned evaluation as soon as the field of theory is left. Where such a prejudice exists it is undoubtedly based on a comparison between narcissism and object love, and is justified by the assertion that it is the more primitive and the less adaptive of the two forms of libido distribution. I believe, however, that these views do not stem primarily from an objective assessment either of the developmental position or of the adaptive value of narcissism, but that they are due to the improper intrusion of the altruistic value system of Western civilization. Whatever the reasons for them, these value judgments exert a narrowing effect on clinical practice. They tend to lead to a wish from the side of the therapist to replace the patient's narcissistic position with object love, while the often more appropriate goal of a transformed narcissism (i.e., of a redistribution of the patient's narcissistic libido, and of the integration of the primitive psychological structures into the mature personality) is neglected. On the theoretical side, too, the contribution of narcissism to health, adaptation, and achievement has not been treated extensively.[2] This predilection, however, is justifiable on heuristic grounds since the examination of the relatively silent states of

---

[1] For the delimitation of narcissism as "strictly defined, libidinal cathexis of the self" and its differentiation from other libido distributions (such as those employed by ego functions or in "self-interest") see Hartmann (e.g., 32, esp. p. 185; and 33, esp. p. 433).

[2] Federn's statements in line with this approach were conjoined to form a chapter of the volume *Ego Psychology and the Psychoses* (9). Here, too, however, as is true with so many other of Federn's fascinating insights into ego psychology, the formulations remain too close to phenomenology, i.e., to the introspected experience, and are thus hard to integrate with the established body of psychoanalytic theory (cf. 31, p. 84).

narcissism in equilibrium is clearly less fruitful than the scrutiny of narcissism in states of disturbance. The disturbances of narcissistic balance to which we refer as "narcissistic injury" appear to offer a particularly promising access to the problems of narcissism, not only because of the frequency with which they occur in a broad spectrum of normal and abnormal psychological states but also because they are usually easily recognized by the painful affect of embarrassment or shame which accompanies them and by their ideational elaboration which is known as inferiority feeling or hurt pride.

In Freud's work two complementary directions can be discerned which analysts have tended to follow in their endeavor to fit the occurrence of some instances of narcissistic disequilibrium into a pre-established psychoanalytic context. On the one hand, Freud drew attention to certain functions of the ego which relate to the id, especially to the exhibitionistic aspects of the pregenital drives; i.e., he pointed to potential shame as a motive for defense (the ego's *Schamgefühl,* its sense of shame) and to the occurrence of shame with failures of the defense (14, pp. 169, 171, 178; 16, p. 242ff.; 26, pp. 99n., 106n,; furthermore, 17, p. 177f.; 18, p. 171; and 19, p. 108). On the other hand, Freud asserted that a part of the child's narcissism is transferred upon his superego, and thus narcissistic tensions occur in the ego as it strives to live up to the ego ideal. The superego, Freud said, is "the vehicle of the ego ideal by which the ego measures itself, which it emulates, and whose demands for ever greater perfection it strives to fulfil" (27, p. 64f.).

I cannot in the present context discuss the numerous contributions in the psychoanalytic and related literature which have followed Freud's lead concerning the two directions of the development of narcissism. Although in certain areas I arrived at conclusions which go beyond the outlines indicated by Freud, the general pattern of my own thought has also been determined by them.

Despite the fact that, in the present study, I shall frequently be referring to well-known phenomena on the psychological surface which can easily be translated into behavioral terms, the concepts employed here are not those of social psychology. The general definition of narcissism as the investment of the self might still be compatible with a transactional approach; but the self in the psychoanalytic sense is variable and by no means coextensive with the limits of the personality as assessed by an observer of the social field. In certain psychological states the self may expand far beyond the borders of the individual, or it may shrink and become identical with a single one of his actions or aims (cf. 43, p. 226f.). The antithesis to narcissism is not the object relation but object love. An individual's profusion of object relations, in the sense of the observer of the social field, may conceal his narcissistic experience of the object world; and a person's seeming isolation and loneliness may be the setting for a wealth of current object investments.

The concept of primary narcissism is a good case in point. Although it is extrapolated from empirical observations, it refers not to the social field but to the psychological state of the infant. It comprehends the assertion that the baby originally experiences the mother and her ministrations not as a you and its actions but within a view of the world in which the I-you differentiation has not yet been established. Thus the expected control over the mother and her ministrations is closer to the concept which a grownup has of himself and of the control which he expects over his own body and mind than to the grownup's experience of others and of his control over them.[3]

Primary narcissism, however, is not in the focus of the ensuing developmental considerations. Although there remains throughout life an important direct residue of the original position—a basic narcissistic tonus which suffuses all aspects of the personality—I shall turn our attention to two other forms into which it becomes differentiated: the *narcissistic self* and the *idealized parent imago*.

The balance of primary narcissism is disturbed by maturational pressures and painful psychic tensions which occur because the mother's ministrations are of necessity imperfect and traumatic delays cannot be prevented. The baby's psychic organization, however, attempts to deal with the disturbances by the building up of new systems of perfection. To one of them Freud (21, p. 136) referred as the "purified pleasure ego,"[4] a stage in development in which everything pleasant, good, and

[3] Bing, McLaughlin, and Marburg (3, p. 24) consider primary narcissism as a condition "in which the libido diffusely and in an undifferentiated way is invested in various parts of the organism." Their definition thus places primary narcissism as existing prior to the time when a psychological approach begins to be appropriate.

[4] The purified pleasure ego may be considered as a prestage of the structure which is referred to as *narcissistic self* in the present essay.

perfect is considered as part of a rudimentary self, while everything unpleasant, bad, and imperfect is considered as "outside." Or, in contrast to this at first attempted solution, the baby attempts to maintain the original perfection and omnipotence by imbuing the rudimentary you, the adult, with absolute perfection and power.[5]

The cathexis of the psychic representation of the *idealized parent imago* is neither adequately subsumed under the heading of narcissism nor of object love. Idealization may of course be properly described as an aspect of narcissism, i.e., of the (still undifferentiated) original bliss, power, perfection, and goodness which is projected on the parent figure during a phase when these qualities become gradually separated into perfection pertaining to pleasure, or power, or knowledge, or beauty, or morality. The intimate relationship between idealization and narcissism is attested to by the fact that homosexual libido is always predominantly involved even when the object is of the opposite sex. The ease, furthermore, with which the representation of the idealized object may at various stages of its development be taken back into the nexus of the self through identification is an additional piece of evidence for its narcissistic character, as Freud (23, p. 250), following Rank (46, p. 416), mentioned when he said that a "narcissistic type of object-choice" may lay the groundwork for the later pathogenic introjection of the depressed. Yet to subsume the idealized object imago under the heading of narcissism is telling only half the story. The narcissistic cathexis of the idealized object is not only amalgamated with features of true object love, the libido of the narcissistic cathexis itself has undergone a transformation, i.e., the appearance of idealizing libido may be regarded as a maturational step *sui generis* in the development of narcissistic libido and differentiated from the development of object love with its own transitional phases.

Although the idealization of the parent imago is a direct continuation of the child's original narcissism, the cognitive image of the idealized parent changes with the maturation of the child's cognitive equipment. During an important transitional period when gratification and frustration are gradually recognized as coming from an external source, the object alternatingly emerges from and resubmerges into the self. When separated from the self,

[5] For a discussion of the concept formed by the immature psyche of the all-powerful object and the child's relationship to it, see Ferenczi (10) and Jones (37). See also Sandler et al., who in this context speak of an "ideal object" (48, p. 156f.).

however, the child's experience of the object is total at each point of development, and the seemingly objective classification into "part" and "whole" objects rests on the adult observer's value judgment.

Form and content of the psychic representation of the idealized parent thus vary with the maturational stage of the child's cognitive apparatus; they are also influenced by environmental factors that affect the choice of internalizations and their intensity.

The idealized parent imago is partly invested with object-libidinal cathexes; and the idealized qualities are loved as a source of gratifications to which the child clings tenaciously. If the psyche is deprived, however, of a source of instinctual gratification, it will not resign itself to the loss but will change the object imago into an introject, i.e., into a structure of the psychic apparatus which takes over functions previously performed by the object. Internalization (although part of the autonomous equipment of the psyche and occurring spontaneously) is, therefore, enhanced by object loss. In the present metapsychological context, however, object loss should be conceived broadly, ranging from the death of a parent, or his absence, or his withdrawal of affection due to physical or mental disease, to the child's unavoidable disappointment in circumscribed aspects of the parental imago, or a parent's prohibitions of unmodified instinctual demands.

I would not contradict anyone who feels that the term object loss should not be employed for the frustrations imposed by education or other demands of reality. In the context of the preconditions for the internalization of drive-regulating functions, however, the differences are only quantitative. The kindly rejection of a child's unmodified instinctual demand, even if enunciated in the form of a positive value, is still a frustration which connotes the impossibility of maintaining a specific object cathexis; it may, therefore, result in internalization, and the accretion of drive-regulating psychic structure. The unique position of the superego among the drive-regulating psychic structures is correlated to the fact that the child has to achieve a phase-specific decathexis of his infantile object representations at the very time when the cathexis had reached the peak of its intensity.

If we apply these considerations to our specific topic, we may say that during the preoedipal period there normally occurs a gradual loss of the idealized parent imago and a concomitant accretion of the drive-regulating matrix of the ego, while the massive loss during the oedipal period contributes to the formation of the superego. Every shortcoming detected in the idealized parent leads to a corresponding internal preservation of the externally lost quality of the object.[6] A child's lie remains undetected; and thus one aspect of the omniscient idealized object is lost; but omniscience is introjected as a minute aspect of the drive-controlling matrix and as a significant aspect of the all-seeing eye, the omniscience of the superego. It is due to the phase-specific massive introjection of the idealized qualities of the object that, as Freud states, the superego must be regarded as the "vehicle of the ego ideal." Or, expressed in another way: the ego ideal is that aspect of the superego which corresponds to the phase-specific, massive introjection of the idealized qualities of the object. The fact that the idealized parent was the carrier of the originally narcissistic perfection and omnipotence accounts now for the omnipotence, omniscience, and perfection of the superego, and it is due to these circumstances that the values and standards of the superego are experienced as absolute. The fact, however, that the original narcissism has passed through a cherished object before its reinternalization, and that the narcissistic investment itself had been raised to the new developmental level of idealization, accounts for the unique emotional importance of our standards, values, and ideals in so far as they are part of the superego. Psychologically such a value cannot be defined in terms of its content or form. A funny story ceases to be amusing when its content is told without regard to the specific psychological structure of jokes. Similarly, the unique position held by those of our values and ideals which belong to the realm of the superego is determined neither by their (variable) content (which may consist of demands for unselfish, altruistic behavior or of demands for prowess and success) nor by their (variable) form (i.e., whether they are prohibitions or positive values, even including demands for specific modes of drive discharge), but by their genesis and psychic location. It is not its form or content but the

[6] A whole broad spectrum of possibilities is condensed here. Not only parental illness or death but also the parents' reactions to an illness of a young child may prematurely and traumatically shatter the idealized object imago and thus lead to phase-inappropriate, inadequate, massive internalizations which prevent the establishment of an idealized superego and lead later to vacillation between the search for external omnipotent powers with which the person wants to merge, or to a defensive reinforcement of a grandiose self concept.

Not only premature discovery of parental weakness, however, can lead to trauma in this area; a narcissistic parent's inability to permit the child the gradual discovery of his shortcomings leads to an equally traumatic result. The ultimate confrontation with the parent's weakness cannot be avoided and, when it occurs, the resulting introjection is massive and pathological.

unique quality of arousing our love and admiration while imposing the task of drive control which characterizes the ego ideal.

Our next task is the consideration of the *narcissistic self*. Its narcissistic cathexis, in contrast to that which is employed in the instinctual investment of the idealized parent imago and of the ego ideal, is retained within the nexus of the self and does not make that specific partial step toward object love which results in idealization. The ego ideal is predominantly related to drive control, while the narcissistic self is closely interwoven with the drives and their inexorable tensions. At the risk of sounding anthropomorphic, yet in reality only condensing a host of clinical impressions and genetic reconstructions, I am tempted to say that the ego experiences the influence of the ego ideal as coming from above and that of the narcissistic self as coming from below. Or I might illustrate my point by the use of imagery which pertains to the preconscious derivatives of the two structures and say that man is *led* by his ideals but *pushed* by his ambitions. And in contrast to the idealized parent imago which is gazed at in awe, admired, looked up to, and like which one wants to become, the narcissistic self wants to be looked at and admired.

The establishment of the narcissistic self must be evaluated both as a maturationally predetermined step and as a developmental achievement, and the grandiose fantasy which is its functional correlate is phase-appropriate and adaptive just as is the overestimation of the power and perfection of the idealized object. Premature interference with the narcissistic self leads to later narcissistic vulnerability because the grandiose fantasy becomes repressed and inaccessible to modifying influences.

The narcissistic self and the ego ideal may also be distinguished by the relationship of the surface layers of the two structures to consciousness. Perception and consciousness are the psychological analogue of the sensory organs which scan the surroundings. The fact that the ego ideal has object qualities facilitates, therefore, its availability to consciousness.[7] Even the surface aspects of the narcissistic self, however, are introspectively hard to perceive since this structure has no object qualities. In a letter to Freud (June 29, 1912) Binswanger mentioned that he "had been struck by his [Freud's] enormous will to power . . . to dominate. . . ."

---

[7] These considerations do not apply, of course, when aspects of the ego ideal have become concealed in consequence of endopsychic conflict. Corresponding to the special status of the ego ideal as an internal object, this concealment occupies a position which lies between repression and denial.

Freud replied (July 4, 1912): "I do not trust myself to contradict you in regard to the will to power but I am not aware of it. I have long surmised that not only the repressed content of the psyche, but also the . . . core of our ego [*"das Eigentliche unseres Ichs,"* i.e., the essential part of our ego] is unconscious. . . . I infer this from the fact that consciousness is . . . a sensory organ directed toward the outside world, so that it is always attached to a part of the ego which is itself unperceived" (4, p. 57f.).

As I mentioned before, the preconscious correlates of the narcissistic self and of the ego ideal are experienced by us as our ambitions and ideals. They are at times hard to distinguish, not only because ambitions are often disguised as ideals but also because there are indeed lucky moments in our lives, or lucky periods in the lives of the very fortunate, in which ambitions and ideals coincide. Adolescent types not infrequently disguise their ideals as ambitions and, finally, certain contents of the ego ideal (demands for achievement) may mislead the observer. If the metapsychological differences, however, are kept in mind, the phenomenological distinction is greatly facilitated.

Our ideals are our internal leaders; we love them and are longing to reach them. Ideals are capable of absorbing a great deal of transformed narcissistic libido and thus of diminishing narcissistic tensions and narcissistic vulnerability. If the ego's instinctual investment of the superego remains insufficiently desexualized (or becomes resexualized), moral masochism is the result, a condition in which the ego may wallow in a state of humiliation when it fails to live up to its ideals. In general, however, the ego does not specifically experience a feeling of being narcissistically wounded when it cannot reach the ideals; rather it experiences an emotion akin to longing.

Our ambitions, too, although derived from a system of infantile grandiose fantasies may become optimally restrained, merge with the structure of the ego's goals, and achieve autonomy. Yet here too, a characteristic, genetically determined psychological flavor can be discerned. We are driven by our ambitions, we do not love them. And if we cannot realize them, narcissistic-exhibitionistic tensions remain undischarged, become dammed up, and the emotion of disappointment which the ego experiences always contains an admixture of shame. If the grandiosity of the narcissistic self, however, has been insufficiently modified because traumatic onslaughts on the child's self esteem have driven the grandiose fantasies into repression, then the adult ego will tend to vacillate between an irrational overestimation of the self and feelings of inferiority and will react with narcissistic mortification (6) to the thwarting of its ambitions.

Before we can pursue our examination of the relationship between the narcissistic self and the ego, however, we must turn our attention to two subsidiary topics: exhibitionism and the grandiose fantasy.

Let me begin with the description of a mother's interaction with her infant boy from the chapter called "Baby Worship" from Trollope's novel *Barchester Towers* (51). "Diddle, diddle . . . , dum . . . ; hasn't he got lovely legs?" said the rapturous mother. ". . . He's a . . . little . . . darling, so he is; and he has the nicest little pink legs in all the world, so he has. . . . Well, . . . did you ever see? . . . My naughty . . . Johnny. He's pulled down all Mamma's hair . . . the naughtiest little man. . . . The child screamed with delight. . . ." The foregoing much abbreviated description of a very commonplace scene illustrates well the external surroundings correlated to two important aspects of the child's psychological equipment: his exhibitionistic propensities and his fantasies of grandeur. Exhibitionism, in a broad sense, can be regarded as a principal narcissistic dimension of all drives, as the expression of a narcissistic emphasis on the aim of the drive (upon the self as the performer) rather than on its object. The object is important only in so far as it is invited to participate in the child's narcissistic pleasure and thus to confirm it. Before psychological separateness has been established, the baby experiences the mother's pleasure in his whole body self, as part of his own psychological equipment. After psychological separation has taken place the child needs the gleam in the mother's eye in order to maintain the narcissistic libidinal suffusion which now concerns, in their sequence, the leading functions and activities of the various maturational phases. We speak thus of anal, of urethral, and of phallic exhibitionism, noting that in the girl the exhibitionism of the urethral-phallic phase is soon replaced by exhibitionism concerning her total appearance and by an interrelated exhibitionistic emphasis on morality and drive control.

The exhibitionism of the child must gradually become desexualized and subordinated to his goal-directed activities, a task which is achieved best through gradual frustrations accompanied by loving support, while the various overt and covert attitudes of rejection and overindulgence (and especially their amalgamations and rapid, unpredictable alternations) are the emotional soil for a wide range of disturbances. Although the unwholesome results vary greatly, ranging from severe hypochondria to mild forms of embarrassment, metapsychologically speaking they are all states of heightened narcissistic-exhibitionistic tension with incomplete and aberrant modes of discharge. In all these conditions the ego attempts to enlist the object's participation in the exhibitionism of the narcissistic self, but after the object's rejection the free discharge of exhibitionistic libido fails; instead of a pleasant suffusion of the body surface there is the heat of unpleasant blushing; instead of a pleasurable confirmation of the value, beauty, and lovableness of the self, there is painful shame.

Now I shall turn to an examination of the position which is held by the grandiose fantasy in the structure of the personality and of the function which it fulfills. While the exhibitionistic-narcissistic urges may be considered as the predominant drive aspect of the narcissistic self, the grandiose fantasy is its ideational content. Whether it contributes to health or disease, to the success of the individual or to his downfall, depends on the degree of its deinstinctualization and the extent of its integration into the realistic purposes of the ego. Take, for instance, Freud's statement that "a man who has been the indisputable favorite of his mother keeps for life the feeling of a conqueror, that confidence of success that often induces real success" (24, p. 26 [as transl. by E. Jones, 38, p. 5]). Here Freud obviously speaks about the results of adaptively valuable narcissistic fantasies which provide lasting support to the personality. It is evident that in these instances the early narcissistic fantasies of power and greatness had not been opposed by sudden premature experiences of traumatic disappointment but had been gradually integrated into the ego's reality-oriented organization.

We can now attempt to summarize the ultimate influence which is exerted by the two major derivatives of the original narcissism upon the mature psychological organization. Under favorable circumstances the neutralized forces emanating from the narcissistic self (the narcissistic needs of the personality and its ambitions) become gradually integrated into the web of our ego as a healthy enjoyment of our own activities and successes and as an adaptively useful sense of disappointment tinged with anger and shame over our failures and shortcomings. And, similarly, the ego ideal (the internalized image of perfection which we admire and to which we are looking up) may come to form a continuum with the ego, as a focus for our ego-syntonic values, as a healthy sense of direction and beacon for our activities and pursuits, and as an adaptively useful object of longing disappointment, when we cannot reach it. A firmly cathected, strongly idealized superego absorbs considerable amounts of narcissistic energy, a fact which lessens the personality's propensity toward narcissistic imbalance. Shame, on the other hand, arises when the ego is unable to provide a proper discharge for the exhibitionistic demands of the narcissistic self. Indeed, in almost all clinically significant instances of shame propensity, the personality is characterized by a defective idealization of the superego and by a concentration of the narcissistic libido upon the narcissistic self; and it is therefore the ambitious, success-driven person with a poorly integrated grandiose self concept and intense exhibitionistic-narcissistic tensions who is most prone to experience shame.[8] If the pressures from the narcissistic self are intense and the ego is unable to control them, the personality will respond with shame to failures of any kind, whether its ambitions concern moral perfection or external success (or, which is frequently the case, alternatingly the one or the other, since the personality possesses neither a firm structure of goals nor of ideals).

Under optimal circumstances, therefore, the ego ideal and the goal structure of the ego are the personality's best protection against narcissistic vulnerability and shame propensity. In the maintenance of the homeostatic narcissistic equilibrium of the personality, however, the interplay of the narcissistic self, the ego, and the superego may be depicted in the following way. The narcissistic self supplies small amounts of narcissistic-exhibitionistic libido which are transformed into subliminal signals of narcissistic imbalance (subliminal shame signals) as the ego tries to reach its goals, to emulate external examples and to obey external demands, or to live up to the standards and, especially, to the ideals of the superego (i.e., to the "ego ideal . . . whose demands for ever greater perfection it strives to fulfil" [27]). Or, stated in a whimsical fashion: the narcissistic self attempts to exhibit its perfection to the ego or, indirectly through the mediation of the ego, to the external world or the superego and finds itself wanting; the resulting minute faulty discharge of libido, however, alerts the ego about a potential experience of painful shame.

In contrast to the metapsychological explanation of the emotion of shame presented here, Saul (49, pp. 92–94), basing himself on Alexander (1), and in harmony with the approach of cultural anthropology (2), com-

---

[8] E. Jacobson (36, p. 203f.), in harmony with A. Reich (47), speaks cogently of the fact that such patients often blame their high ideals for their "agonizing experiences of anxiety, shame, and inferiority" but that in reality they suffer from conflicts relating to "aggrandized, wishful self images" and "narcissistic-exhibitionistic strivings."

pared guilt and shame as parallel phenomena; he suggested a differentiation between these two emotions by specifying that, unlike guilt, shame arises when people are unable to live up to their ideals. The question of the appropriateness of such structural distinctions (cf. especially Piers and Singer's comprehensive statement of this position [44]) is not germane to the present study and will not be pursued here. It was recently discussed by Hartmann and Loewenstein (34, p. 67) who maintain that it is inadvisable "to overemphasize the separateness of the ego ideal from the other parts of the superego," a theoretical procedure on which "the structural opposition of guilt and shame hinges."[9]

Sandler, Holder, and Meers (48, p. 156f.), on the other hand, retain the ego ideal within the context of the superego. Basing themselves on contributions by Jacobson (35) and A. Reich (47), however, they postulate the existence of an "ideal self" (as differentiated from the ego ideal), state that the child attempts to "avoid disappointment and frustration by living up to his ideal self," and conclude that shame arises when the individual fails "to live up to ideal standards which he accepts, whereas guilt is experienced when his ideal self differs from that which he feels to be dictated by his introjects."

The interplay between the narcissistic self, the ego, and the superego determines the characteristic flavor of the personality and is thus, more than other building blocks or attributes of the personality, instinctively regarded as the touchstone of a person's individuality or identity.[10] In many outstanding personalities this inner balance appears to be dominated more by a well-integrated narcissistic self (which channels the drives) than by the ego ideal (which guides and controls them). Churchill, for example, repeated again and again, in an ever-enlarging arena, the feat of extricating

---

[9] See also Kohut and Seitz (39, p. 135) who stress the importance of retaining the conception of the essential "functional and genetic cohesion" of the internal moral forces which reside in the superego, despite the heuristic advantages and the convenience of a differentiation according to the phenomenology of their psychological effects.

[10] It is difficult to find an appropriate place in psychoanalyis for the concept of "identity" (8) since, amphibologically, it is equally applicable in social and individual psychology. Under these circumstances an empirical approach to an area vaguely outlined by the impressionistic use of the term seems justified and, indeed, has occasionally (see, for example, Kramer [40]) led to illuminating findings, especially in the realm of psychopathology.

himself from a situation from which there seemed to be no escape by ordinary means. (His famous escape during the Boer war is one example.) I would not be surprised if deep in his personality there was hidden the conviction that he could fly and thus get away when ordinary locomotion was barred. In the autobiographical volume *My Early Life* (5, p. 43f.) he describes the following events. During a vacation in the country he played a game in which he was being chased by a cousin and a younger brother. As he was crossing a bridge which led over a ravine he found himself entrapped by his pursuers who had divided their forces. ". . . capture seemed certain" he wrote, but "in a flash there came across me a great project." He looked at the young fir trees below and decided to leap onto one of them. He computed, he meditated. "In a second, I had plunged," he continues, "throwing out my arms to embrace the summit of the fir tree." It was three days before he regained consciousness and more than three months before he crawled out of bed. Yet although it is obvious that on this occasion the driving unconscious grandiose fantasy was not yet fully integrated, the struggle of the reasoning ego to perform the behest of the narcissistic self in a realistic way was already joined. Luckily, for him and for the forces of civilization, when he reached the peak of his responsibilities the inner balance had shifted.

II

Up to this point I have surveyed the origin, development, and functions of two major forms of narcissism and their integration into the personality. Although the mutual influences between the narcissistic self, the ego, and the ego ideal were not ignored, our attention was focused predominantly on the narcissistic structures themselves and not on the ego's capacity to harness the narcissistic energies and to transform the narcissistic constellations into more highly differentiated, new psychological configurations. There exist, however, a number of acquisitions of the ego which, although genetically and dynamically related to the narcissistic drives and energized by them, are far removed from the preformed narcissistic structures of the personality, and which therefore must be evaluated not only as transformations of narcissism but even more as attainments of the ego and as attitudes and achievements of the personality.[11] Let me first enumerate those whose relationship to narcissism I shall discuss. They are: (i) man's creativity; (ii) his ability to be empathic; (iii) his capacity to contemplate his own impermanence; (iv) his sense of humor; and (v) his wisdom.

First we will briefly examine the relationship of narcissism to creativity. Like all complex human activities, artistic and scientific creativity serves many purposes, and it involves the whole personality, and thus a wide range of psychological structures and drives. It is therefore to be expected that the narcissism of the creative individual participates in his creative activity, for example, as a spur, driving him toward fame and acclaim. If there existed no further connection between narcissism and creativity, however, than the interplay between ambition and superior executive equipment, there would be no justification for discussing creativity specifically among the transformations of narcissism. It is my contention, however, that while artists and scientists may indeed be acclaim-hungry, narcissistically vulnerable individuals, and while their ambitions may be helpful in prompting them toward the appropriate communication of their work, the creative activity itself deserves to be considered among the transformations of narcissism.

The ambitions of a creative individual play an important role in his relationship to the public, i.e., to an audience of potential admirers; the transformation of narcissism, however, is a feature of the creator's relationship to his work. In creative work narcissistic energies are employed which have been changed into a form to which I referred earlier as idealizing libido, i.e., the elaboration of that specific point on the developmental road from narcissism toward object love at which an object (in the sense of social psychology) is cathected with narcissistic libido and thus included in the context of the self.

The analogy to the mother's love for the unborn fetus and for the newborn baby is inviting, and undoubtedly the single-minded devotion

---

[11] In his paper on poise Rangell (45) demonstrated the genetic and dynamic interrelatedness of specific drives with a whole integrative attitude of the ego. Poise, to state it in my words, rests on the desexualization of the crudely exhibitionistic cathexis of the narcissistic self and on the permeation of the neutralized libido into the whole physical and mental personality. Although poise may be nearer to the exhibitionistic drives than the various achievements of the ego to be discussed here, it too cannot be fully explained by reference to the drives which supply its fuel but must be considered as a new, broad configuration within the realm of the ego itself.

to the child who is taken into her expanded self, and her empathic responsiveness to him are similar to the creative person's involvement with his work. Nevertheless, I believe that the creative person's relationship to his work has less in common with the expanded narcissism of motherhood than with the still unrestricted narcissism of early childhood. Phenomenologically, too, the personality of many unusually creative individuals is more childlike than maternal. Even the experiments of some of the great in science impress the observer with their almost childlike freshness and simplicity. The behavior of Enrico Fermi, for example, while witnessing the first atomic explosion is described by his wife in the following way. He tore a piece of paper into small bits and, as soon as the blast had been set off, dropped them, one by one, watching the impact of the shock wave rise and subside (11, p. 239).

The creative individual, whether in art or science, is less psychologically separated from his surroundings than the noncreative one; the "I-you" barrier is not as clearly defined. The intensity of the creative person's awareness of the relevant aspects of his surroundings is akin to the detailed self perceptions of the schizoid and the childlike: it is nearer to a child's relationship to his excretions or to some schizophrenics' experiences of their body,[12] than to a healthy mother's feeling for her newborn child.

The indistinctness of "internal" and "external" is familiar to all of us in our relationship to the surrounding air which, as we take it in and expel it, is experienced by us as part of our selves, while we hardly perceive it as long as it forms a part of our external surroundings. Similarly, the creative individual is keenly aware of those aspects of his surroundings which are of significance to his work and he invests them with narcissistic-idealizing libido. Like the air which we breathe, they are most clearly experienced at the moment of union with the self. The traditional metaphor which is expressed by the term "inspiration" (it refers both to the taking in of air and to the fertilizing influence of an external stimulation upon the internal creative powers) and the prototypical description of creativity ("and the Lord God formed man of the dust of the ground, and breathed into his nostrils the breath of life; and

[12] I treated once a gifted schizoid young woman who at one point gave me an artistically detached, beautiful description of the areolar area of one of her nipples, with an almost microscopic knowledge about the details and a concentrated absorption as if it were the most fascinating landscape.

man became a living soul'' [Genesis 2:7]) support the assertion that there exists a close psychological proximity, on the one hand, between respiratory and creative inspiration and, on the other hand, between the coming to life of dust and the creative transformation of a narcissistically experienced material into a work of art.

Greenacre who recently discussed the nature of creative inspiration (30, p. 11f.) and who mentions the child's interest in the air as a mysterious unseen force which becomes a symbol for his dreams and thoughts, and for his dawning conscience, maintains that the future creative artist already possesses in infancy not only great sensitivity to sensory stimuli coming from the primary object, the mother, but also to those from peripheral objects which resemble the primary one. She uses the terms "collective alternates" and "love affair with the world" in describing the artist's attitude to his surroundings, and declares that it should not be considered as an expression of his narcissism but that "it partakes of an object relationship, though a collective one . . . (29, p. 67f.).

K. R. Eissler, too, refers to the problem of the artist's relationship to reality when he speaks of "automorphic techniques" (7, p. 544), i.e., artistic activities which take place in a borderland of autoplastic and alloplastic attitudes toward reality. A work of art, he explains, is autoplastic in so far as, like a dream or symptom, it serves the solution of an inner conflict and the fulfillment of a wish; it is simultaneously alloplastic, however, since it modifies reality by the creation of something original and new.

Greenacre and Eissler approach the problem of creativity from directions which are different from the one taken here, and arrive therefore at different conclusions. I believe, nonetheless, that their findings are consistent with the proposition that the artist invests his work with a specific form of narcissistic libido. Thus Greenacre's observation of the intensity of the future artist's early perception of the world, and of the persistence of this sensitivity during maturity, is in harmony with the contention that a leading part of the psychological equipment of creative people has been shaped through the extensive elaboration of a transitional point in libido development: idealization. In the average individual this form of the narcissistic libido survives only as the idealizing component of the state of being in love, and a surplus of idealizing libido which is not absorbed through the amalgamation with the object cathexis may account for the brief spurt of artistic activity which is not uncommon during this state. The well-established fact, furthermore, that creative people tend to alternate during periods of productivity between phases when they think extremely highly of their work and phases when they are convinced that it has no value, is a sure indication that the work is cathected with a form of narcissistic libido. The spreading of the libidinal investment upon "collective alternates" and ultimately upon "the world," which Greenacre describes, appears to me as an indication of a narcissistic experience of the world (an expanded self which includes the world) rather than as the manifestation of a "love affair" within an unqualified context of object love. The fact, too, that, as Eissler shows convincingly, the work of art is simultaneously the materialization of autoplastic and alloplastic psychic processes and that, in certain respects, the artist's attitude to his work is similar to that of the fetishist toward the fetish, lends support to the idea that, for the creator, the work is a transitional object and that it is invested with transitional narcissistic libido. The fetishist's attachment to the fetish has the intensity of an addiction, a fact which is a manifestation not of object love but of a fixation on an early object that is experienced as part of the self. Creative artists, and scientists, may be attached to their work with the intensity of an addiction, and they try to control and shape it with forces and for purposes which belong to a narcissistically experienced world. They are attempting to re-create a perfection which formerly was directly an attribute of their own; during the act of creation, however, they do not relate to their work in the give-and-take mutuality which characterizes object love.

I am now turning to empathy as the second of the faculties of the ego which, though far removed from the drives and largely autonomous, are here considered in the context of the transformation of narcissism.[13]

Empathy is the mode by which one gathers psychological data about other people and, when they say what they think or feel, imagines their inner experience even though it is not open to direct observation.

[13] Although, even concerning the other subject matters discussed in this study, I am, within the present limits, often not able to adduce sufficient empirical support for my assertions, the following considerations about empathy are more speculative in essence and, for their verification, are probably in need of a psychoanalytically oriented experimental approach.

Through empathy we aim at discerning, in one single act of certain recognition, complex psychological configurations which we could either define only through the laborious presentation of a host of details or which it may even be beyond our ability to define.[14]

Empathy is an essential constituent of psychological observation and is, therefore, of special importance for the psychoanalyst who, as an empirical scientist, must first perceive the complex psychological configurations which are the raw data of human experience before he can attempt to explain them. The scientific use of empathy, however, is a specific achievement of the autonomous ego since, during the act of empathy, it must deliberately suspend its predominant mode of operation which is geared to the perception of nonpsychological data in the surroundings.

The groundwork for our ability to obtain access to another person's mind is laid by the fact that in our earliest mental organization the feelings, actions, and behavior of the mother had been included in our self. This *primary empathy* with the mother prepares us for the recognition that, to a large extent, the basic inner experiences of people remain similar to our own. Our first perception of the manifestations of another person's feelings, wishes, and thoughts occurred within the framework of a narcissistic conception of the world; the capacity for empathy belongs, therefore, to the innate equipment of the human psyche and remains to some extent associated with the primary process.

Nonempathic forms of cognition, however, which are attuned to objects which are essentially dissimilar to the self become increasingly superimposed over the original empathic mode of reality perception and tend to impede its free operation. The persistence of empathic forms of observation outside of psychology is, indeed, archaic and leads to a faulty, prerational, animistic conception of reality. Nonempathic modes of observation, on the other hand, are not attuned to the experiences of other people

---

[14] The capacity to recognize complex psychological states through empathy has its analogy in the capacity to identify a face in a single act of apperception. Here, too, we do, in general, not add up details or go through complex theories of comparative judgment, and here, too, we are generally unable to define our certain recognition by adducing details. The similarity between the perceptual immediacy of the recognition of a face and the empathic grasp of another person's psychological state may not be only an incidental one; it may well be derived from the significant genetic fact that the small child's perceptual merging with the mother's face constitutes simultaneously its most important access to the mother's identity and to her emotional state (cf. 50, p. 103ff.).

and, if they are employed in the psychological field, lead to a mechanistic and lifeless conception of psychological reality.

Nonempathic forms of cognition are dominant in the adult. Empathy must thus often be achieved speedily before nonempathic modes of observation are interposed. The approximate correctness of first impressions in the assessment of people, by contrast with subsequent evaluations, is well known and is exploited by skillful men of affairs. Empathy seems here to be able to evade interference and to complete a rapid scrutiny before other modes of observation can assert their ascendancy. The exhaustive empathic comprehension, however, which is the aim of the analyst requires the ability to use the empathic capacity for prolonged periods. His customary observational attitude ("evenly suspended attention"; avoidance of note taking; curtailment of realistic interactions; concentration on the purpose of achieving understanding rather than on the wish to cure and to help) aims at excluding psychological processes attuned to the nonpsychological perception of objects and to encourage empathic comprehension through the perception of experiential identities.

Foremost among the obstacles which interfere with the use of empathy (especially for prolonged periods) are those which stem from conflicts about relating to another person in a narcissistic mode. Since training in empathy is an important aspect of psychoanalytic education, the loosening of narcissistic positions constitutes a specific task of the training analysis, and the candidate's increasing ability to employ the transformed narcissistic cathexes in empathic observation is a sign that this goal is being reached.

Could it be that among the obstacles to the use of empathy is also the resistance against the acknowledgment of unconscious knowledge about others? Could it be that to the "I have always known it" of the analysand when an unconscious content is uncovered (20, p. 148) may correspond an "I have always recognized it" in the analyst when he and the patient arrive at a valid reconstruction, or when the patient supplies a relevant memory?

Freud pondered the question whether thought transference does occur (27, pp. 54–56) and referred to such biological and social phenomena as the means by which "the common purpose comes about in the great insect communities" and the possibility of the persistence of an "original, archaic method of communication between individuals" which "in the course of phylogenetic evolution . . . has been replaced by the better method of giving information with the help of signals," yet which may still "put itself into effect under certain conditions—for instance, in passionately excited mobs'' (p. 55). To these statements one could add only that an intentional curbing of the usual cognitive processes of the ego (such as is brought about in the analytic situation) may free the access to empathic communication as does the involuntary trancelike condition which occurs in those who become submerged in an excited mob[15] and that the prototype of empathic understanding must be sought not only in the prehistory of the race but also in the early life of the individual. Under favorable circumstances, however, the faculty of perceiving the psychological manifestations of the mother, achieved through the extension of narcissistic cathexes, becomes the starting point for a series of developmental steps which lead ultimately to a state in which the ego can choose between the use of empathic and nonempathic modes of observation, depending on realistic requirements and on the nature of the surroundings that it scrutinizes.

Man's capacity to acknowledge the finiteness of his existence, and to act in accordance with this painful discovery, may well be his greatest psychological achievement, despite the fact that it can often be demonstrated that a manifest acceptance of transience may go hand in hand with covert denials.

The acceptance of transience is accomplished by the ego, which performs the emotional work that precedes, accompanies, and follows separations. Without these efforts a valid conception of time, of limits, and of the impermanence of object cathexes could not be achieved. Freud discussed the emotional task which is imposed on the psyche by the impermanence of objects, be they beloved people or cherished values (22, p. 303), and gave expression to the conviction that their impermanence did not detract from their worth. On the contrary, he said, their very impermanence makes us love and admire them even more: "Transience value is scarcity value in time."

Freud's attitude is based on the relinquishment of emotional infantilism, an abandonment even of a trace of the narcissistic insistence on the omnipotence of the wish; it expresses the acceptance of realistic values. More difficult still, however, than the acknowledgment of the imperman-

---

[15] For a striking description of the ego's perviousness to the dominant mental tendencies of an aroused multitude, and an illuminating discussion of the propensity of the individual who is trapped in an agitated group to shed ego autonomy and to respond regressively in narcissistic-identificatory compliance, see A. Mitscherlich (42, esp. p. 202f.).

ence of object cathexes is the unqualified intellectual and emotional acceptance of the fact that we ourselves are impermanent, that the self which is cathected with narcissistic libido is finite in time. I believe that this rare feat rests not simply on a victory of autonomous reason and supreme objectivity over the claims of narcissism but on the creation of a higher form of narcissism. The great who have achieved the outlook on life to which the Romans referred as living *sub specie aeternitatis* do not display resignation and hopelessness but a quiet pride which is often coupled with mild disdain of the rabble which, without being able to delight in the variety of experiences which life has to offer, is yet afraid of death and trembles at its approach. Goethe (28) gave beautiful expression of his contempt for those who cannot accept death as an intrinsic part of life in the following stanza:

Und so lang du das nicht hast,
Dieses: Stirb and werde!
Bist du nur ein trüber Gast
Auf der dunklen Erde.[16]

Only through an acceptance of death, Goethe says here, can man reap all that is in life; without it, however, life is dim and insignificant. I do not believe that an attitude such as the one expressed by Goethe is to be understood as a beautiful denial of the fear of death. There is no undertone of anxiety in it and no excitement. Conspicuous in it, however, is a nonisolated, creative superiority which judges and admonishes with quiet assurance. I have little doubt that those who are able to achieve this ultimate attitude toward life do so on the strength of a new, expanded, transformed narcissism: a cosmic narcissism which has transcended the bounds of the individual.

Just as the child's *primary empathy* with the mother is the precursor of the adult's ability to be empathic, so his *primary identity* with her must be considered as the precursor of an expansion of the self, late in life, when the finiteness of individual existence is acknowledged. The original psychological universe, i.e., the primordial experience of the mother, is "remembered" by many people in the form of the occasionally occurring

---

[16] Adapted from a translation by Ludwig Lewisohn (41):
And till thine this deep behest:
Die to win thy being!
Art thou but a dreary guest
Upon earth unseeing.

vague reverberations which are known by the term "oceanic feeling" (26, pp. 64–73). The achievement—as the certainty of eventual death is fully realized—of a shift of the narcissistic cathexes, from the self to a concept of participation in a supraindividual and timeless existence, must also be regarded as genetically predetermined by the child's primary identity with the mother. In contrast to the oceanic feeling, however, which is experienced passively (and usually fleetingly), the genuine shift of the cathexes toward a cosmic narcissism is the enduring, creative result of the steadfast activities of an autonomous ego, and only very few are able to attain it.

It seems a long way from the acceptance of transience and the quasi-religious solemnity of a cosmic narcissism to another uniquely human acquisition: the capacity for humor. And yet, the two phenomena have much in common. It is not by accident that Freud introduces his essay on humor (25, p. 161) with a man's ability to overcome the fear of his impending death by putting himself, through humor, upon a higher plane. "When . . . a criminal who was being led out to the gallows on a Monday remarked: 'Well, the week's beginning nicely'," Freud says that "the humorous process . . . affords him . . . satisfaction." And Freud states that "humour has something liberating about it"; that it "has something of grandeur"; and that it is a "triumph of narcissism" and "the victorious assertion of . . . invulnerability" (p. 162). Metapsychologically, however, Freud explains that humor—this "triumph of narcissism"—is achieved by a person's withdrawing "the psychical accent from his ego" and "transposing it on to his super-ego" (p. 164).

Humor and cosmic narcissism are thus both transformations of narcissism which aid man in achieving ultimate mastery over the demands of the narcissistic self, i.e., to tolerate the recognition of his finiteness in principle and even of his impending end.

There is no doubt that the claim that the ego has mastered its fear of death is often not authentic. If a person is unable to be serious and employs humor excessively, or if he is unwilling to face the pains and labors of everyday living and moves along continuously with his head in the clouds, we will become suspicious of both the clown and the saint, and we will most likely be right in surmising that neither the humor nor the otherworldliness are genuine. Yet, if a man is capable of responding with humor to the recognition of those unalterable realities which oppose the assertions of the narcissistic self, and if he can truly attain that quiet, superior stance which enables him to contemplate his own end philosophically, we will assume that a transformation of his narcissism has indeed taken place (a withdrawal of the psychical accent from the "ego," as Freud put it) and will respect the person who has achieved it.

A disregard for the interests of the self, even to the point of allowing its death, may also come about during states of supreme object cathexis. Such instances (for example, as a consequence of an upsurge of extreme, personified patriotic fervor) take place in a frenzied mental condition, and the ego is paralyzed, as if in a trance. Humor and cosmic narcissism, on the other hand, which permit us to face death without having to resort to denial, are metapsychologically based not on a decathexis of the self through a frantic hypercathexis of objects but on a decathexis of the narcissistic self through a rearrangement and transformation of the narcissistic libido; and, in contrast to states of extreme object cathexis, the span of the ego is here not narrowed but the ego remains active and deliberate.

A genuine decathexis of the self can only be achieved slowly by an intact, well-functioning ego; and it is accompanied by sadness as the cathexis is transferred from the cherished self upon the supraindividual ideals and upon the world with which one identifies. The profoundest forms of humor and cosmic narcissism therefore do not present a picture of grandiosity and elation but that of a quiet inner triumph with an admixture of undenied melancholy,

We have now reached our final subject matter, the human attitude which we call wisdom. In the progression from information through knowledge to wisdom, the first two can still be defined almost exclusively within the sphere of cognition itself. The term information refers to the gleaning of isolated data about the world; knowledge to the comprehension of a cohesive set of such data held together by a matrix of abstractions. Wisdom, however, goes beyond the cognitive sphere, although, of course, it includes it.

Wisdom is achieved largely through man's ability to overcome his unmodified narcissism and it rests on his acceptance of the limitations of his physical, intellectual, and emotional powers. It may be defined as an amalgamation of the higher processes of cognition with the psychological attitude which accompanies the renouncement of these narcissistic demands. Neither the possession of ideals, nor the capacity for humor, nor the acceptance of transience alone characterizes wisdom. All three have to be linked together to form a new psychological constellation which goes beyond the several emotional and cognitive attributes of which it is made up. Wisdom may thus be defined as a stable attitude of the personality toward life and the world, an attitude which is formed through the integration of the cognitive function with humor, acceptance of transience, and a firmly cathected system of values.

In the course of life the acquisition of knowledge clearly must be preceded by the gathering of information. Even from the point of view of its cognitive component, therefore, wisdom can hardly be an attribute of youth since experience and work must first have led to the acquisition of broadly based knowledge. Ideals are most strongly cathected in youth; humor is usually at its height during maturity; and an acceptance of transience may be achieved during the advanced years. Thus we can see again that the attainment of wisdom is usually reserved for the later phases of life.

The essence of this proud achievement is therefore a maximal relinquishment of narcissistic delusions, including the acceptance of the inevitability of death, without an abandonment of cognitive and emotional involvements. The ultimate act of cognition, i.e., the acknowledgment of the limits and of the finiteness of the self, is not the result of an isolated intellectual process but is the victorious outcome of the lifework of the total personality in acquiring broadly based knowledge and in transforming archaic modes of narcissism into ideals, humor, and a sense of supraindividual participation in the world.

Sarcasm occurs in consequence of the lack of idealized values and attempts to minimize the emotional significance of narcissistic limitations through the hypercathexis of a pleasure-seeking, omnipotent self. The most important precondition for the feat of humor under adverse circumstances, however, and for the ability to contemplate one's impending end, is the formation and maintenance of a set of cherished values, i.e., metapsychologically, a strong idealization of the superego. Wisdom is, in addition, characterized not only by the maintenance of the libidinal cathexes of the old ideals but by their creative expansion. And in contrast to an attitude of utter seriousness and unrelieved solemnity vis-à-vis the approaching end of life, the truly wise are able in the end to transform the humor of their years of maturity into a sense of proportion, a touch of irony toward the achievements of individual existence, including even their own wisdom. The ego's ultimate mastery over the narcissistic self, the final control of the rider over the horse, may after all have been decisively assisted by the fact that the horse, too, has grown old. And, lastly, we may recognize that what has been accomplished is not so much control but the acceptance of the ultimate insight that, as concerns the supreme powers of nature, we are all "Sunday riders."[17]

In concluding this presentation let me now give a brief résumé of the principal themes which I laid before you. I wanted to emphasize that there are various forms of narcissism which must be considered not only as forerunners of object love but also as independent psychological constellations, whose development and functions deserve separate examination and evaluation. In addition, I tried to demonstrate the ways by which a number of complex and autonomous achievements of the mature personality were derived from transformations of narcissism, i.e., created by the ego's capacity to tame narcissistic cathexes and to employ them for its highest aims.

I would finally like to say that I have become increasingly convinced of the value of these conceptualizations for psychoanalytic therapy. They are useful in the formulation of broad aspects of the psychopathology of the frequently encountered narcissistic personality types among our patients; they help us understand the psychological changes which tend to be induced in them; and, last but not least, they assist us in the evaluation of the therapeutic goal. In many instances, the reshaping of the narcissistic structures and their integration into the personality—the strengthening of ideals, and the achievement, even to a modest degree, of such wholesome transformations of narcissism as humor, creativity, empathy, and wisdom—must be rated as a more genuine and valid result of therapy than the patient's precarious compliance with demands for a change of his narcissism into object love.

BIBLIOGRAPHY

1. Alexander, F. Remarks about the relation of inferiority feelings to guilt feelings. *Int. J. Psychoanal.,* 19:41–49, 1938.
2. Benedict, R. *The Chrysanthemum and the Sword.* Boston: Houghton Mifflin, 1946.

[17] The German word *"Sonntagsreiter"* in the well-known joke mentioned by Freud (12, p. 275; and 15, p. 237) has been rendered as "Sunday horseman" in the English translations (13, p. 258; and 16, p. 231).

3. Bing, J. F., McLaughlin, F., & Marburg, R. The metapsychology of narcissism. *The Psychoanalytic Study of the Child*, 14:9–28. New York: International Universities Press, 1959.
4. Binswanger, L. *Erinnerungen an Sigmund Freud*. Bern: Francke Verlag, 1956.
5. Churchill, W. *My Early Life*. New York: Macmillian, 1942.
6. Eidelberg, L. *An Outline of a Comparative Pathology of the Neuroses*. New York: International Universities Press, 1954.
7. Eissler, K. R. *Goethe: A Psychoanalytic Study*. Detroit: Wayne State University Press, 1962.
8. Erikson, E. H. The problem of ego identity. *J. Am. Psa. Assn.*, 4:56–121, 1956.
9. Federn, P. On the distinction between healthy and pathological narcissism (1929, 1934, 1935). *Ego Psychology and the Psychoses*, ed. E. Weiss. New York: Basic Books. 1952, pp. 323–364.
10. Ferenczi, S. Stages in the development of the sense of reality (1913). *Contributions to Psychoanalysis*. New York: Robert Brunner, 1950, pp. 213–239.
11. Fermi, L. *Atoms in the Family*. Chicago: University of Chicago Press, 1954.
12. Freud, S. *Aus den Anfängen der Psychoanalyse* (1887–1902). London: Imago Publ. Co., 1950.
13. Freud, S. *The Origins of Psychoanalysis* (1887–1902). New York: Basic Books, 1954.
14. Freud, S. Further remarks on the neuro-psychoses of defence (1896). *Standard Edition*, 3:159–185. London: Hogarth Press, 1962.
15. Freud, S. Die Traumdeutung (1900). *Gesammelte Werke*, 2 & 3. London: Imago Publ. Co., 1942.
16. Freud, S. The interpretation of dreams (1900). *Standard Edition*, 4 & 5. London: Hogarth Press, 1953.
17. Freud, S. Three essays on the theory of sexuality (1905). *Standard Edition*, 7:125–245. London: Hogarth Press, 1953.
18. Freud, S. Character and anal erotism (1908). *Standard Edition*, 9:167–175. London: Hogarth Press, 1959.
19. Freud, S. Analysis of a phobia in a five-year-old boy (1909). *Standard Edition*, 10:3–149. London: Hogarth Press, 1955.
20. Freud, S. Remembering, repeating and working-through (1914). *Standard Edition*, 12:145–156. London: Hogarth Press, 1958.
21. Freud, S. Instincts and their vicissitudes (1915). *Standard Edition*, 14:109–140. London: Hogarth Press, 1957.
22. Freud, S. On transience (1916). *Standard Edition*, 14:303–307. London: Hogarth Press, 1957.
23. Freud, S. Mourning and melancholia (1917). *Standard Edition*, 14:237–258. London: Hogarth Press, 1957.
24. Freud, S. Eine Kindheitserinnerung aus "Dichtung und Wahrheit" (1917). *Gesammelte Werke*, 12:13–26. London: Imago Publ. Co., 1947.
25. Freud, S. Humour (1927). *Standard Edition*, 21:159–166. London : Hogarth Press, 1961.
26. Freud, S. Civilization and its discontents (1930). *Standard Edition*, 21:59–145. London: Hogarth Press, 1961.
27. Freud, S. New introductory lectures on psycho-analysis (1933). *Standard Edition*, 22:1–182. London: Hogarth Press, 1964.
28. Goethe, J. W. Selige Sehnsucht. In: West-östlicher Divan. *Goethes Werke. Vollständige Ausgabe letzter Hand*, Vol. 5. Stuttgart & Tübingen: Cotta, 1928, p. 26.

29. Greenacre, P. The childhood of the artist. *The Psychoanalytic Study of the Child,* 12:47–72. New York: International Universities Press, 1957.
30. Greenacre, P. A study of the nature of inspiration. *J. Am. Psa. Assn.,* 12:6–31, 1964.
31. Hartmann, H. Comments on the psychoanalytic theory of the ego. *The Psychoanalytic Study of the Child,* 5:74–96. New York: International Universities Press, 1950.
32. Hartmann, H. Contribution to the metapsychology of schizophrenia. *The Psychoanalytic Study of the Child,* 8:177–198. New York: International Universities Press, 1953.
33. Hartmann, H. The development of the ego concept in Freud's work. *Int. J. Psychoanal.,* 37:425–437, 1956.
34. Hartmann, H. & Loewenstein, R. M. Notes on the superego. *The Psychoanalytic Study of the Child,* 17:42–81. New York: International Universities Press, 1962.
35. Jacobson, E. The self and the object world. *The Psychoanalytic Study of the Child,* 9:75–127. New York: International Universities Press, 1954.
36. Jacobson, E. *The Self and the Object World.* New York: International Universities Press, 1964.
37. Jones, E. The God complex (1913). *Essays in Applied Psycho-Analysis,* 2:244–265. London: Hogarth Press, 1951.
38. Jones, E. *The Life and Work of Sigmund Freud,* Vol. 1. New York: Basic Books, 1953.
39. Kohut, H. & Seitz, P. F. D. Concepts and theories of psychoanalysis. In: *Concepts of Personality,* ed. J. M. Wepman & R. Heine. Chicago: Aldine, 1963, pp. 113–141.
40. Kramer, P. On discovering one's identity. *The Psychoanalytic Study of the Child,* 10:47–74. New York: International Universities Press, 1955.
41. Lewisohn, L. *The Permanent Horizon.* New York & London: Harper, 2nd ed., 1934, p. 110.
42. Mitscherlich, A. Meditationen zu einer Lebenslehre der modernen Massen. *Merkur,* 11:201–213, 335–350, 1957.
43. Piaget, J. *The Construction of Reality in the Child* (1937). New York: Basic Books, 1954.
44. Piers, G. & Singer, M. *Shame and Guilt.* Springfield, Ill.: Charles C Thomas, 1953.
45. Rangell, L. The psychology of poise. *Int. J. Psychoanal.,* 35:313–332, 1954.
46. Rank, O. Ein Beitrag zum Narzissmus. *Jb. psychoanal. psychopath. Forsch.,* 3:401–426, 1911.
47. Reich, A. Pathologic forms of self-esteem regulation. *The Psychoanalytic Study of the Child,* 15:215–232. New York: International Universities Press, 1960.
48. Sandler, J., Holder, A., & Meers, D. The ego ideal and the ideal self. *The Psychoanalytic Study of the Child,* 18:139–158. New York: International Universities Press, 1963.
49. Saul, L. *Emotional Maturity.* Philadelphia: Lippincott, 1947.
50. Spitz, R. A. The smiling response: a contribution to the ontogenesis of social relations. *Genet. Psychol. Monogr.,* 34:57–125, 1946.
51. Trollope, A. Baby worship. In: *Barchester Towers* (1857). New York: Doubleday, 1945, Chapter 16, pp. 133–144.

OVERVIEWS

Part II offers three valuable overviews of narcissism. Sydney Pulver
(Ch. 4) traces the evolution of narcissism as a concept leading to Freud's
paper published in 1914, and demonstrates the confusing multiple meanings ascribed to it. Pulver's basic position is that the term "narcissism"
is used to describe too many varying levels of abstraction about the
self. He suggests further elaboration and clarification in terms of ego
psychology. Specifically, he delineates problems with a "drive" concept of narcissism, reviewing its use clinically to refer to sexual perversion; genetically as a developmental stage; as a mode of object
relations (in which the self may play a more important role than configurational aspects of the object, or in which there is a paucity of actual
object relationships); or as the affective state of self-esteem. This essay
succinctly underscores the contradictions and haziness which surround
the use of narcissism by many authors writing from a drive perspective.
It specifically suggests abandoning the conception of narcissism as a
libidinal cathexis of the self.

I suggest that Pulver's essay is a useful summary and critique of
narcissism as conceived by authors prior to 1970, and as such it calls
for elaboration represented in many of the papers written subsequently.
Cooper provides one such review (Ch. 5), written ten years later, which
is both broader in the historical range of theorists concerned with the
self that are examined (e.g., Sullivan, Horney, Rado, Winnicott, and
Erikson) and, at the same time, more exactly diagnostic (reviewing
in detail the diagnostic criteria for Narcissistic Personality Disorder
included in DSM III). Cooper also clearly contrasts the more recent
contributions of Kohut and Kernberg. He includes cultural considerations in approaching the increased prominence of patients suffering
from narcissistic disorders. I think that this essay will provide a useful
perspective in that it moves beyond a classical psychoanalytic frame-

work to realms of neo-Freudian theorists and to cultural and diagnostic considerations.

White (Ch. 6) offers a useful overview which utilizes the contributions of Margaret Mahler (see also Settlage, 1977). She first reviews the contributions of Freud and ego psychology and then summarizes Mahler's view of the development of object- and self-relations. According to White, individuation—which she equates with the beginning of self-relations during the latter part of the symbiotic phase—occurs in the context of the mother's "holding behavior," it reflects the development of secondary narcissism. She cites Mahler's descriptions during the rapprochement subphase to support the concept of self-relations as a reflection of self-esteem, and the strengthening of the self-representation, through adequate maternal acceptance and empathy. White then reviews the work of Hartmann, Kohut, and Kernberg in terms of object- and self-relations and concludes that self-constancy involves "increased tolerance of our shortcomings and a self-love or appreciation subsuming our disappointments in ourselves."

4. Narcissism: The Term and the Concept

Sydney E. Pulver

In the voluminous literature on narcissism, there are probably only two facts upon which everyone agrees: first, that the concept of narcissism is one of the most important contributions of psychoanalysis; second, that it is one of the most confusing. The difficulties with the concept were apparent from the beginning. Freud himself was dissatisfied with his original formulations. He wrote to Abraham: "The narcissism was a difficult labor and bears all the marks of a corresponding deformation." "That you accept what I wrote about narcissism touches me deeply and binds us even closer together. I have a very strong feeling of vexation at its inadequacy" (Jones, 1955, p. 304).

We do not know just why Freud was dissatisfied, but most current theoreticians feel that our present difficulties are "due mainly to the fact that this concept has not been explicitly redefined in terms of Freud's later structural psychology" (Hartmann, 1950, p. 83). As Kernberg (1968) concisely puts it, narcissism as a descriptive term has been both abused and overused, and a more specific redefinition is long overdue.

At first glance it is surprising that the metapsychology of such an important concept has not been more adequately described. The reason for this, however, becomes apparent on closer inspection: Freud's original theoretical conception of narcissism as the libidinal investment of the ego[1] was essentially an economic one, and proved to be so nonspecific that the term came to be applied to many different psychic phenomena. These phenomena are often related to each other only in

[1] Taking this statement literally (as was done by many early writers) forces us to call certain things narcissistic which obviously are not. For instance, since object representations are part of the ego, their cathexis would have to be called narcissistic. Hartmann (1950) led us out of this dilemma by pointing out that Freud at this time used the term ego and self interchangeably, and suggesting that in his original definition Freud was using the term "ego" to mean "self" (or more accurately, self representation). A more accurate rendition, then, would be "the libidinal cathexis of the self." This definition is now commonly accepted, and I shall use it.

vague and obscure ways, and each has its own metapsychology. To the extent that the phenomena called narcissistic are unrelated, the meta-psychology of the phenomena is different. I believe that we cannot formulate a metapsychology of narcissism as long as the term is applied (as it now is) to relatively unrelated phenomena. To illustrate this I hope in this paper:

(1) to trace the evolution of the applications of the term narcissism to various psychic phenomena;
(2) to discuss the limitations of the original conceptualization of narcissism as the libidinal investment of the self;
(3) to categorize the phenomena currently called "narcissistic" and describe their interrelationships; and
(4) to consider possible solutions to the problems raised by the present terminological looseness.

In so doing, I have found it important to keep in mind the distinction between the use of the word narcissism to mean the metapsychological concept and its use to refer to specific psychic phenomena, two very different levels of description. I have tried to make this distinction explicit by calling narcissism "the concept" when used in the former sense and "the term" when used in the latter.

THE EVOLUTION OF THE VARIOUS USAGES

Prior to its adoption by psychoanalysis, the term narcissism denoted a very specific and delimited clinical phenomenon, described nicely by Freud (1914) as a kind of sexual perversion: narcissism now denotes "the attitude of a person who treats his own body in the same way in which the body of a sexual object is ordinarily treated—who looks at it, that is to say, strokes it and fondles it till he obtains complete satisfaction through these activities" (p. 73). This perversion had been described previously in the psychiatric literature, but was first connected with the name of Narcissus by Havelock Ellis, who discussed in detail its roots in literature and mythology. In his description, which appeared in English in 1898 and was abstracted in German in 1899, he not only referred to the specific perversion mentioned above, but adumbrated the psychoanalytic extension of the term narcissism to behavior not overtly sexual: "that tendency which is sometimes found, more especially perhaps in women, for the sexual emotions to be absorbed, and often entirely lost, in self-admiration.''

The brilliance of the psychoanalytic concept was the recognition that narcissism the perversion was a specific dramatic illustration of something more general in human behavior; that the sensual love of one's self existed as an underlying motivation in certain behavior which was not overtly sensual. It is interesting to note that this same theme—the recognition of the sensual element in overtly nonsensual behavior—marked many of the discoveries of early psychoanalysis. The parallel to the perversions of sadism, masochism, and exhibitionism is obvious.

It seems that narcissism made its appearance as a psychoanalytic concept in 1908 in a paper by Sadger. The paper was referred to by Stekel at a meeting of the Vienna Psychoanalytic Society on May 27, 1908. I have unfortunately been unable to obtain a copy of it, and cannot say how the term was used.[2]

In 1910, narcissism was mentioned by both Freud and Sadger. A footnote to *Three Essays* contains Freud's first written reference to narcissism, a genetic one, describing it as a phase in the libidinal development of inverts. Narcissism here still referred to the specific perversion. His brief reference to narcissism in *Leonardo* several months later used the term in the same way. At about the same time Sadger (1910) in the paper mentioned above made the first extension of the term from a perversion to a stage of normal development: ''the path to sexuality is always by way of narcissism; in other words, love of one's self.''

The next step in the development of the concept came in 1911 with Rank's publication of the first psychoanalytic paper devoted specifically to narcissism. In this paper narcissism was still considered primarily as the sensual love of the self, but it was connected for the first time with psychic phenomena which are not overtly sensual: vanity and self-admiration. Rank recognized that taking the self as a libidinal object is

---

[2] A minor item of priority should be mentioned here. Taking their lead from Jones (1955, p. 271), the Editors of the *Standard Edition* (1957, p. 69, 100) imply that Freud's mention of narcissism at the November 10, 1909, meeting of the Vienna Psychoanalytic Society was the first psychoanalytic use of the term. However, at that meeting Freud was discussing a paper later published by Sadger in 1910, and he clearly gave Sadger credit for introducing the concept: ''Sadger's comment with regard to narcissism seems new and valuable'' (Nunberg and Federn, 1967, p. 312).

not the only determinant of self-admiration: "loving their own bodies is a great factor in normal feminine vanity" (p. 406). While this indicates that Rank felt that it is not the *only* factor, the rest of the paper implies that it is the only one that makes any difference. This is in keeping with the libidinal emphasis of the time. Incidentally, Rank also for the first time described the defensive nature of this self-love: "The patient felt that men are so bad and so incapable of love, so lacking in ability to comprehend the beauty and worth of a woman, that she might better return to her former narcissistic state and, independent of man, love her own person."

In 1911 Freud amplified the genetic aspects of narcissism, using the word this time in terms of the self as a libidinal object.

By 1911, then, the term narcissism had been used genetically to describe a developmental stage, and dynamically to explain certain attitudes such as vanity and self-admiration. The *concept* of narcissism as the libidinal investment of the self had been mentioned, but only briefly.

In 1913 Freud used the concept to explain another group of phenomena: certain primitive aspects of thinking and feeling such as animism, magic, and omnipotence of thought. After describing these phenomena, Freud states: "This attitude may plausibly be brought into relationship with narcissism and regarded as an essential component of it" (p. 89).

By the time "On Narcissism" was written the foundations of the concept had been laid down. In this classical paper Freud elaborated on his previous uses of the term and used the concept to explain three additional phenomena: a type of object choice, a mode of object relationship, and self-esteem.

The first, the choice of an object on the basis of identification with some aspect of the self, is one of the paper's outstanding contributions:

A person may love:—
(1) According to the narcissistic type:
    (*a*) what he himself is (i.e. himself),
    (*b*) what he himself was,
    (*c*) what he himself would like to be,
    (*d*) someone who was once part of himself.
(2) According to the anaclitic (attachment) type:
    (*a*) the woman who feeds him,
    (*b*) the man who protects him [p. 90].

Freud's application of the term to a mode of object relationship resulted from his recognition that schizophrenia, organic disease, hypochondriasis, and sleep were all characterized by an overt withdrawal from objects. He explained this withdrawal theoretically as a withdrawal of libidinal cathexis from objects accompanied by an increased libidinal cathexis of the self, *ergo* narcissism.

The application of the term to self-esteem was only a peripheral part of the paper, touched upon in Freud's description of the ego ideal. From it, however, has arisen one of the most important current meanings of the term narcissism, its use as a synonym for self-esteem.

Very early in the psychoanalytic literature, then, the term narcissism was being used in several different ways:

1. Clinically, to denote a sexual perversion characterized by the treatment of one's own body as a sexual object.
2. Genetically, to denote a stage of development considered to be characterized by that libidinal state.
3. In terms of object relationship, to denote two different phenomena:
   (a) A type of object choice in which the self in some way plays a more important part than the real aspects of the object.
   (b) A mode of relating to the environment characterized by a relative lack of object relations.
4. To denote various aspects of the complex ego state of self-esteem.

All of these were conceptualized theoretically as repesenting in one way or another that state of the libido in which the self is taken as an object.

PROBLEMS WITH THE DRIVE CONCEPT OF NARCISSISM

In recent years questions have been raised about both the general drive concept of narcissism and its value in explaining certain specific clinical phenomena called narcissistic. The first of these questions has to do with the validity of the underlying theory upon which the concept is based. As has been stated, "libidinal investment of the self" is an expression of drive theory with economic implications. Yet the economic approach in general and drive theory in particular have been seriously challenged. A good review of both these controversies can be found in Apfelbaum (1965) and Holt (1967); they are too lengthy to go into here. Suffice it to say that if these aspects of psychoanalytic theory are ultimately found wanting, then this concept of narcissism must be also.

A second question concerns not the validity of the concept, but its usefulness. Obviously, the value of a theoretical concept in psychoanalysis lies in its ability to explain specific clinical material. The idea of specificity is important. For example, to conceptualize any particular object as "a collection of molecules" may be quite valid, but it is not useful, since "a collection of molecules" covers such a wide variety of objects. Similarly, the non-specific nature of the terms "libido" and "self" has resulted in the application of the term narcissism to such a large number of different things as to render it almost meaningless.

Originally, this broadness of meaning was not apparent. At the time "On Narcissism" was published, psychoanalytic instinct theory was based on the libidinal and ego instinct duality. Freud thus distinguished between self-directedness arising from libidinal investment of the self and other self-directedness arising from the ego instincts and called egoism: "Narcissism in this sense would not be a perversion, but the libidinal complement to the egoism of the instinct of self-preservation" (p. 73f.). Since narcissism was applied to only one kind of self-directedness, its meaning was somewhat delimited. However, as the theory of ego instincts was abandoned, this distinction disappeared. *All* self-directedness was then described as narcissism, broadening the concept considerably. Furthermore, as both "self" and "libido" were elaborated upon, more broadening occurred. A widening range of the "self" was described, ranging from the specific self-representation of a part of the body to the very general concept of identity. Libidinal investment of any of these was called narcissism. In addition, various vicissitudes of the libido, such as fusion, neutralization, and desexualization, were described. Investment of any of these aspects of the self by any of these vicissitudes of the libido all qualified as narcissism. At present, then, such widely varying clinical phenomena as a hypochondriacal preoccupation with bowel function, an adolescent's overconcern with the choice of a career, and mankind's general interest in the preservation of life have all been called narcissistic. A theoretical construct which can be applied to so many things is not necessarily meaningless, but its explanatory value is certainly reduced.

In addition to these general difficulties with the drive concept of narcissism, problems arise in the application of the concept to specific clinical phenomena. To illustrate these problems I have divided the widely differing clinical phenomena called narcissistic into four categories, which are described below.

Narcissism as a Sexual Perversion

The existence of a sexual perversion which might reasonably be called narcissism is not difficult to demonstrate. Perversions consist of the domination of adult sexual life by a component of infantile sexuality. Sexual interest in one's body occurs during infantile sexual development. It is seen not infrequently clinically, as, for example, in a patient of mine whose only overt sexual behavior was masturbation in front of a mirror with conscious fantasies about the size of his penis. This might reasonably be considered a perversion specifically called narcissism. In practice, however, the broader uses of the word have predominated, and the use of narcissism to mean a sexual perversion has been all but abandoned.

Narcissism as a Developmental Stage

As mentioned above, the use of the term narcissism to denote a developmental stage is found in the earliest psychoanalytic writings on the subject. Freud's first reference to narcissism is a genetic one:

In all the cases we have examined we have established the fact that the future inverts, in the earliest years of their childhood, pass through a phase of very intense but short-lived fixation to a woman (usually their mother), and that, after leaving this behind, they identify themselves with a woman and take *themselves* as their sexual object. That is to say, they proceed from a narcissistic basis, and look for a young man who resembles themselves whom *they* may love as their mother loved *them* [1905, p. 145, n. added in 1910].

In elaborating on the developmental aspects in "On Narcissism," Freud conceptualized two types: primary and secondary narcissism. Primary narcissism was defined as the libidinal investment of the self occurring before the investment of external objects, and secondary narcissism as occurring after such investment and resulting from the withdrawal of cathexis from external objects and reinvestment in the self. Freud's earlier writings are somewhat confusing as to the exact sequence of these phases. As Kanzer (1964, p. 529) points out: "Freud's terms and concepts were in constant evolutionary flux, and the interrelationship between autoerotism and narcissism . . . contradicted other formulations made at earlier and later dates." However, the developmental sequence of primary narcissism, then object love, and finally secondary narcissism was reaffirmed in Freud's later writings on the subject: "All that we know about it [the libido] relates to the ego, in which at first the whole available quota of libido is stored up. We call this state absolute, primary *narcissism*. It lasts till the ego begins to cathect the ideas of objects with libido" (1940, p. 150). In current usage, the narcissistic stage of development is conceptualized as being a stage of primary narcissism.

Using the concept of narcissism to delineate a stage of development has led to several problems. The first of these is the difficulty in fixing the exact duration of the stage. Freud never discussed the specific timing of this stage, and it has been described by subsequent authors as occurring over a wide chronological period in the infant's life. Some, e.g., Greene (1958), consider it to be exclusively interuterine. Others, e.g., Jacobson, (1964), consider it as a physiological discharge of energy into the various organ systems, and place it in earliest infancy before any psychic structure has yet occurred. Still others place it as late as the beginning of the second year of life. This lack of agreement on timing arises from uncertainty about the meaning of the concept of narcissism in terms of object relations. In contrast with the interest of our early instinct psychology in the *sources* of the instincts (oral, anal, and phallic), recent ego psychology has focused upon the *objects* of the instincts and the ego's relationship to these objects. Our best source of information about early infantile development—the direct observation of infants—yields information primarily about these vicissitudes of object relationships, and to a much lesser degree about the infant's investment of his self. This, plus the difficulty in defining just what libidinal investment of the self means in the infant, had led to the wide variation in timing just described.

Let us for the moment arbitrarily assign to this stage the duration which is most frequently used: the first six to eight months of life. A second difficulty then becomes apparent. A very complex period of development is being named by a concept, narcissism, which has little relationship to the developmental complexities occurring at the time. These complexities have become increasingly clear as psychoanalytic investigators have gathered information from the direct observation of infants. For a detailed review of these direct observations and their theoretical implications, Gouin Décarie's book (1965) is outstanding. Briefly it appears that the time before the "true objectal" period has at least two components, which Gouin Décarie calls the "narcissistic period" and the "intermediate period." The narcissistic period itself has at least two steps. In the first, during the initial week or two of life, cathexis is totally undifferentiated. In the second, certain experiences, such as that of nursing, become cathected, and the libido is distributed "between a subject who is as yet unaware of himself and an object which he does not perceive as being in the environment" (p. 80). In the intermediate period, lasting into the sixth month, certain aspects of the object are cathected as "pre-objects" (Spitz, 1950), the best known of which is the smiling human face. These pre-objects are not yet personified, but are considered as things. A gestalt is reponded to (cathected), rather than a human being: "the 3-month-old does not visually recognize the human partner as such; all he recognizes is the gestalt forehead-eyes-nose. If this gestalt is altered only slightly (e.g., by hiding one eye), the alleged object is not recognized" (p. 103). Fluctuations appear to occur in the subjective location of this gestalt. At times it is felt as external and at times as part of the self. Lastly, the perception of a true external object does not spring into being, but gradually develops over a number of months as the ego and its apparatuses mature.

These details are described in order to point out the complexities of this period in terms of the cathexis of the self and objects. Calling all or any part of the period "narcissistic" is an oversimplification which tends to obscure both the details of libidinal development and the other important developmental processes occurring at this time. Glover pointed this out many years ago (1956, p. 345): "It is some years now since I indicated that such terms had to a certain extent outworn their usefulness, that, for example, in the case of a narcissistic phase, the developmental range of this sytem called for some contraction and for a more specific description of the object systems in vogue during early ego-centric stages."

Still a third problem in designating these early months as a "narcissistic stage" of development must be described. The designation has led to the application of the term narcissistic to many psychic phenomena occurring during this period which in fact have little or nothing to do with the vicissitudes of libidinal investment. Worse, calling these phenomena "narcissistic" has led to the feeling that they are adequately *explained* as being due to the libidinal investment of the self, and that no further explanation is necessary. Their other, often more important, defensive and adaptive determinants in both the infant and the regressed adult have been frequently ignored.

For an example of this let us consider a cognitive phenomenon: the belief in animism and magic. In *Totem and Taboo* Freud (1913) explained these as manifestations of the libidinal investment of the self in infancy, and their occurrence in primitives as an infantile libidinal fixation. Since then, many other factors in their development have been described. Yet it is not uncommon to hear omnipotence of thoughts explained solely as being due to the patient's narcissism.

Another illustration of the same problem is provided by affective states originating during this period, which have also been called narcissistic. Note the following two quotations from Fenichel (1945):

Certain narcissistic feelings of well-being are characterized by the fact that they are felt as a reunion with an omnipotent force in the external world, brought about either by incorporating parts of this world or by the fantasy of being incorporated by it ("secondary narcissism") [p. 40].

The salvations frequently are experienced in a passive receptive way, showing signs of the narcissistic *unio mystica* of the deepest oral reunion of the subject with the universe and the re-establishment of the original "oceanic feeling" [p. 425].

"Narcissistic" in these quotations refers to those experiences of early "perfect" union with mother. The feelings are called narcissistic because they originally arise in the first six months of development. Again, the problem is that calling these affects narcissistic has led to the assumption that they are *caused* by the libidinal investment of the self. However, even our present unsatisfactory theory of affects will not accept this assumption. Affects, while often related to drive discharge, have many other nondrive determinants (Kaywin, 1966).

As a last example of the obscurations arising from calling certain early phenomena narcissistic, let us look at the metapsychology of megalomania. In "On Narcissism" Freud explained this on the basis of narcissism, and to this day it is common to find explanations of megalomania solely as manifestations of narcissistic regressions or fixations. However, these explanations ignore at least two important points: (1) Megalomania occurring as a clinical symptom in adults serves important defensive purposes best thought of in terms of structural theory rather than as a libidinal regression.[3] (2) Even during the early infantile stage omnipotence is due as much to aspects of ego development as to shifts of libido. For example, the immaturity of the infant's perceptual apparatus and his consequent inability to distinguish between the outer world and himself are important ego aspects of feelings of omnipotence. For all of these reasons, calling the earliest period of development narcissistic overlooks the important ego determinants which are present and tends to lead to several errors in conceptualizing this important period.

Narcissism as a Mode of Relating to Objects

Another important use of the term narcissism occurs in the sphere of the ego's relationship to objects. Two broad aspects of this relationship have been described. The first, "true object relationship," is generally considered to mean the perception of and reaction to the object as a separate individual with his own needs, desires, and reactions. Any mode of relating to objects in which true object relationships are impaired or do not exist is called narcissistic. This meaning of the term is sufficiently widespread to be given the status of a formal definition by Brenner (1955): "In general the term [narcissism] is used to indicate at least three somewhat different, though related things when it is applied to an adult. These are: (1) a hypercathexis of the self, (2) a hypocathexis of the objects of the environment, and (3) a pathologically immature relationship to these objects" (p. 113). The latter two are in terms of object relations and will be discussed below.

The term narcissism was applied to Brenner's (1955) second category, "a hypocathexis of the objects of the environment," on the basis of the logic that an increase of libidinal investment of the self must be accompanied by a decrease of cathexis of others. The validity of such a quantitative idea will be considered later. At this point let us look at a further assumption: that cathexis of others is decreased (a statement of theory) when overt observable relationships with objects in the environment are minimal or absent (a statement of clinical observation). Using this logic, which was quite consistent with the theory of the time,

[3] For a convincing demonstration of this see Arlow and Brenner (1964). These authors also point out that the ego aspects of narcissism, although not specifically described, were not lost to Freud, even in this early stage of theoretical development.

Freud applied the term narcissism to certain clinical situations such as organic disease, sleep, hypochondriasis, and schizophrenia. Others followed this usage, as illustrated by Ostow's paper (1967) on "narcissistic tranquillity": "The most striking dynamic feature of this syndrome is the detachment from objects. It may vary from the complete detachment of the schizophrenic to the relative inaccessibility of the aloof 'normal.'" "Detachment from objects" here refers to the overt behavior of the patient, rather than to his underlying dynamics.

The difficulty in using the term narcissism to refer to a type of overt behavior is that we no longer consider overt withdrawal from objects to be necessarily accompanied by either increased libidinal cathexis of the self or decreased object cathexis. Freud pointed out very early (Nunberg and Federn, 1962) that the apparent lack of overt objects does not mean that objects are not psychically present. At a meeting of the Vienna Psychoanalytic Society on February 13, 1907, Freud remarked that whereas Havelock Ellis used the concept of autoerotism only when *one person* is involved, he (Freud) uses it when there is no object. For example, he would not consider those who masturbate with images autoerotic. Indeed, the withdrawal is most often a defensive maneuver to avoid an anxiety-producing relationship with objects which remain highly cathected. Even when the overt withdrawal from objects is not primarily a defense, objects may remain intrapsychically important. For example, the apparent lack of object cathexis in sleep has been questioned by several authors (Balint, 1960; Kanzer, 1955; Lewin, 1953) who point out the persistence of object cathexis in fantasy as evidenced by the sleeper's dreams.

It appears, then, that applying the term narcissism to the concept of "hypocathexis of objects in the environment" has led to two areas of confusion. First, as will be shown later, increased libidinal investment of the self is not necessarily accompanied by decreased cathexis of objects. Second, "hypocathexis of objects in the environment" has come to mean lack of overt realationships with objects, an equation which is not necessarily true.

Let us now look at Brenner's third category of narcissism, pathologically immature relations to objects. Exactly how this usage arose is not clear. Perhaps it arose from clinical experiences in which the pathologically immature relations were accompanied by increased self-cathexis. The early connotation of pathology connected with narcissism probably also played a role, as did the simple equation that, if mature object relations indicate a greater consideration of objects, then immature relations indicate a greater consideration of the self, thus a greater libidinal investment of the self, and thus narcissism. Whatever the origin, a little reflection will reveal that immature object relations may be characterized by a very intense cathexis of external objects, as, for example, in the clinging, dependent, orally incorporative patient to whom mother or her imago is so vital. As Jacobson (1964) points out, this cathexis is based on very primitive incorporative and projective identification with loss of separation between self and object representations. Nevertheless, a cathexis of specific external object representations does occur. Clinically, the primitive mechanisms used to relate to these objects is at least as important as the heightened self-interest which may occur, a fact which is obscured by calling the relationships narcissistic.

It is interesting to note that both of these categories may embrace phenomena containing widely differing clinical and dynamic positions. The first may refer to an overt withdrawal from objects with an underlying intense attachment, while the second may refer to an overt intense attachment with an underlying focus on the self. It appears, then, that while narcissism may be a convenient term for both absent and immature object relations, it does not describe the underlying dynamics very well.

Narcissism as Self-Esteem

Perhaps the greatest difficulties have arisen out of the use of the term narcissism as a more technical name for self-esteem. This usage has a very long history. Rank (1911) implies it in his description of his narcissistic patient's self-admiration, while Freud (1914) made it explicit when he said: "we must recognize that self-regard has a specially intimate dependence on narcissistic libido" (p. 98). Freud (1926) recognized very clearly the difficulties inherent in explaining affects in terms of drives, but he continued to use self-regard (an affective concept) and narcissistic libido (a drive concept) interchangeably. Freud's use of the term as a synonym for self-regard (self-esteem) was widely adopted, particularly in clinical works, and has grown to be one of the most important meanings of the term. Although this usage has become so common that it is often part of the analyst's everyday vocabulary,[4] it might be of use to illustrate the manner in which it occurs in the literature.

When Hartmann and Loewenstein (1962) say, "The ego ideal can be considered a rescue operation for narcissism" (p. 61), they are using the term narcissism to refer to the self-esteem of the omnipotent infant in the process of disillusionment. Eidelberg's (1959) concept of "narcissistic mortification" refers to any experience of the feeling of helplessness, an affective state in the self-esteem spectrum. When Murray (1964) describes a "hopeful, expectant young man with a highly adequate self-image, part of a fine group of which he is justly proud. His legitimate narcissistic feelings ride easily and lightly on his shoulders" (p. 482), the meaning of the term narcissism as self-esteem is overt. When Kohut (1966) talks of "the personality's best protection against narcissistic vulnerability and shame propensity" (p. 255), he is speaking in terms of the maintenance of self-esteem. These are a few random examples; they could be multiplied endlessly.

The major drawback in using the term narcissism to mean self-esteem is that a word which basically refers to a theoretical drive concept is identified with a phenomenon (self-esteem) of much greater complexity. I do not mean to imply that the authors quoted above are equating self-esteem with the libidinal investment of the self. Rather, they seem to be using the term narcissism as a synonym for self-esteem while ignoring its libidinal meaning. However, in various discussions of this paper it became clear to me that a significant number of analysts will, when pressed, argue that self-esteem *is* the libidinal investment of the self, and even go so far as to assert that that is *all* it is. I would like, therefore, to briefly define some compounds of the word "self" which I believe will illustrate the inadequacy of that assertion. In spite of some disagreement about the exact meaning of "self," many of its compounds impart a sense of common understanding. For our purposes it will be sufficiently accurate to say that *self representations* are "the endopsychic representations of the bodily and mental self in the system ego" (Jacobson, 1964, p. 19). These consist initially of memory traces of inner experiences, sensations, and thought processes, and later of in-

---

[4] "His narcissism was injured" to mean "it was a blow to his self-esteem," for example.

direct self perception, i.e., the perception of the self as an object. These may or may not be linked with affective states of pleasure or unpleasure. When the link with affect is definite, we speak of *self images,* and when the varying self images become organized into a more cohesive affective picture of the self, we speak of *self-esteem,* with "high self-esteem" implying a predominance of pleasurable affects and "low self-esteem" of unpleasurable ones. All of these ego states of affect-self-representation linkages may be either conscious, preconscious, or unconscious, have complex origins, and many defensive and adaptive functions.

With all of this in mind, it should be clear that the proposition that self-esteem is simply the libidinal investment of the self is woefully inadequate. It is an explanation of a complex ego state in drive terms, and very nonspecific drive terms at that. It not only precludes the consideration of the multiple factors determining self-esteem, but tries in an indirect way to explain affects by drives. As I mentioned before, this is not currently acceptable.

Another problem in the narcissism-self-esteem equation was described in an excellent paper by Joffe and Sandler (1967), who were concerned particularly about the quantitative implications which the use of the term narcissism introduces into considerations of self-esteem. Explaining self-esteem as the libidinal investment of the self introduces the economic concept that self-esteem decreases as libido is invested in others and increases as it is withdrawn from others and invested in the self. This was implied by Freud in the well-known amoeba analogy and developed more fully by others. This type of quantitative fluctuation, however, does not fit the clinical facts. Individuals with high self-esteem are precisely those most able to be more interested in others, while those with low self-esteem are most likely to concentrate upon themselves. The phenomenon of being "in love," which at first glance appears to support the economic picture ("you are wonderful; I am worthless") has on deeper inspection complex dynamics in which the exact state of libidinal cathexis is very difficult to describe.

Joffe and Sandler (1967) were moved by these difficulties to propose a major revision in the meaning of the concept of narcissism. Rather than proposing that self-esteem no longer be called narcissism, they accepted the identity of narcissism and self-esteem as determined by long usage, and proposed a redefinition of narcissism in nondrive terms. They conclude that "the states which are important in any consideration of narcissism are not only determined by the state of the drives nor can they be understood in terms of the hypothetical distribution of energic cathexes" (p. 63). They describe an "ideal state" of well-being, "the state which is fundamentally affective and which normally accompanies the harmonious and integrated functioning of all the biological and mental structures" (p. 63), and imply that narcissism should be applied to this ideal state and its linkages to the self representations, that is, to self-esteem. They define the central feature of narcissistic disorders as, "the existence of an overt or latent state of pain which has constantly to be dealt with by the ego; and the defensive and adaptive manoeuvres which are responses to it can assume pathological proportions" (p. 65). In brief, they recommend abandoning the conceptualization of narcissism as a state of the libidinal investment of the self, and adopting instead its conceptualization in terms of the ideal state. I shall weigh this proposal later.

A last problem inherent in equating narcissism and self-esteem became apparent as analysts recognized two basically different types of self-regard. The history of this is interesting. Freud, in his original equation of self-regard and narcissism, was referring specifically to secondary narcissism—the libidinal investment of the self which occurred after the investment of objects. In secondary narcissism, libido is withdrawn from objects presumably because of the displeasure aroused by the original investment. In ego terms, the withdrawal of interest is a defensive maneuver designed to protect the individual against anxiety and other painful affects connected with objects. Since this appears most strikingly clinically as a pathological defense, the term narcissism came to be applied to such defensive inflations of self-regard as feelings of superiority and megalomania. However, it soon became apparent that a good opinion of oneself—high self-esteem—could exist as a realistic, nondefensive feeling. Since this was also called narcissism, both of these aspects of self-esteem were conceived of as being due to the libidinal investment of the self, and could not be easily differentiated. In attempting to find a way out of this dilemma, the idea of "good" and "bad" narcissism was developed, "good" narcissism referring to the basic essentially nondefensive self-esteem and "bad" narcissism referring to defensive pride. Unfortunately, though the concept of "good" and "bad" narcissism may reflect our value judgments, it does not lend itself to a real understanding of patients. Thought of in structural terms, however, the two kinds of self-esteem become much clearer.

"Good" narcissism is high self-esteem based on predominantly pleasurable affect-self-representation linkages, while "bad" narcissism is a self-centeredness or an apparent high regard for oneself utilized as a defense against underlying unpleasurable linkages. The use of the term narcissism to designate all self-esteem leads to the omission of these structural determinants, and the picture is muddled.

It appears from all of this that the two uses of the term narcissism—to designate the concept of the libidinal investment of the self and self-esteem—are incompatible.

Discussion

One thing emerges clearly from the above. The orginal theoretical concept of narcissism as the libidinal investment of the self no longer sufficiently explains all of the phenomena currently called narcissistic. Rather, the unifying concept seems to be a focus on some aspect of the self on any one of a number of levels. The orginal theoretical concept of narcissism deals with the relationship of the libidinal drive to the self. The narcissistic stage of development is that stage in which the boundaries between the self and object have not yet been clearly defined. Narcissistic object choice is the choice of an object resembling the self. Narcissism as a withdrawal from objects describes a kind of overt behavior in which the self is focused on to the exclusion of others. Narcissism as an immature relationship to objects describes a way of relating in which the focus upon the self distorts the real aspects of objects, or in which self-object boundaries are weakened Narcissism as self-esteem describes the linking of positive affect with the self representation. The common factor in all of these is the relationship to the self as contrasted to objects. This is not a new conclusion. In fact, it might almost be considered "official," as evidenced by the definition of narcissism in the *Glossary* of the American Psychoanalytic Association (Moore and Fine, 1967): "NARCISSISM: a concentration of psychological interest upon the *self*" (p. 57).

Our problem with narcissism is that it has been used to describe so many different aspects of the self on so many different levels of abstraction. It is clear now why Hartmann's call for a redefinition of the concept in structural terms has never been answered. Narcissism means many different things, each one of which can be independently defined structurally. This profusion of usages has led to the considerable confusion in the psychoanalytic literature pointed out above.

In seeking solutions to the problem, let us first consider the possibility of limiting the application of the term narcissism to one of its most important current meanings and renaming the rest. This has been suggested recently, most notably by Joffe and Sandler (1967) in the paper mentioned above. Recognizing the problems with the economic definition of narcissism, these authors advocate restricting the use of the term to the area of self-esteem, doing away not just with an economic definition of narcissism but with the drive concept of narcissism altogether, at least as its central characteristic. Unfortunately, there are several meanings of narcissism which are not easily subsumed under either a drive or a self-esteem concept. What, for instance, would we call "narcissistic object choice" if the term narcissism were reserved for certain basic self-esteem disturbances? And what would we call the primitive type of mental functioning "where the weakness of the boundaries between self and object images gives rise to fantasies or experiences of fusion between these images" (p. 40), which Jacobson (1964) calls "narcissistic" and which is not clearly either drive or self-esteem related? The same problem arises whenever we attempt to select any one of the important applications of the term narcissism and eliminate the others, and this seems to rule out a limited application as a practical possibility.

The solution which I find most satisfying is the reconceptualization of narcissism as found in the *Glossary*. This requires that we recognize that Freud's original concept of narcissism was both highly productive and useful in its time, but is now incomplete and at times misleading. Like so much of our metapsychology, it must now be replaced by a more comprehensive concept. With this in mind we would rename certain phenomena currently called narcissistic: those in which the concentration of psychological interest upon the self is only a minimal factor. I would nominate as leading candidate for such revision the use of the term narcissism to describe a developmental stage and to describe immature object relationships. In view of the many nonself aspects of early developments, it would seem to be much more meaningful to consider maturation in terms of "lines of development" as described by Anna Freud (1965), with the early stages of libidinal development designated by some less ambiguous term than narcissistic (perhaps "pre-objectal"?). Similarly, in view of the nonspecific relationship of self-interest to immature object relations, it would seem best to describe them by some other adjective than narcissistic.

We are left, then, with the term narcissism referring to a very broad, nonspecific concept describing a number of phenomena all in some way referring to some aspect of the self. When not absolutely clear from the context we would define it.[5] When possible and not burdensome, we would attempt to use a more specific term. Most important, we would resist the temptation to think of narcissism as simply the libidinal investment of the self, and attempt to keep in mind the dynamic and structural aspects of the phenomena to which we are referring. Perhaps in this way we can retain the value of the concept and the conciseness of expression, yet avoid the ambiguity which is currently giving us difficulty.

SUMMARY

In common with many of the other human sciences, psychoanalysis is constantly trying to redefine its terms to gain greater specificity and clarity of meaning. This paper looks at one of our most important concepts, narcissism, and the various applications of the term in our literature.

The term narcissism was originally used to name a number of phenomena which appeared to be explainable by assuming that the individual had taken himself as a sexual object—that he loved himself or some part of himself. Gradually, the application of the term was extended to almost any concentration of psychological interest upon the self. Many different phenomena fell into that category, and narcissism was applied to all of them. Very early in the psychoanalytic literature the term was being used in several different ways:
1. Clinically, to denote a sexual perversion.
2. Genetically, to denote a stage of development.
3. In terms of object relationships, to denote two different phenomena:
  (a) a type of object choice,

---

[5] Kernberg, for instance, does this in the opening paragraphs of his paper entitled, "Factors in the Psychoanalytic Treatment of Narcissistic Personalities" (1968), in which he states: "there does exist a group of patients in whom the main problem appears to be the disturbance of their self-regard in connection with specific disturbances in their object relationships."

(b) a mode of relating to the environment.
4. To denote various aspects of the complex ego state of self-esteem.

The use of the term narcissism to describe so many different aspects of self-interests and so many different levels of abstraction has led to considerable confusion in the psychoanalytic literature. It is not uncommon to find two authors differing about narcissism on apparently theoretical grounds. On closer inspection, however, the difference is semantic rather than theoretical. Each of the authors is discussing different phenomena, both of which have been called narcissistic. A more serious result of this vagueness is that the concept has not received the elaboration in terms of ego psychology which has been given to many other psychoanalytic concepts, and which it richly deserves.

BIBLIOGRAPHY

Apfelbaum, B. (1965), Ego psychology, psychic energy, and the hazards of quantitative explanation in psycho-analytic theory. *Int. J. Psycho-Anal.,* 46:168–182.

Arlow, J. A. & Brenner, C. (1964), *Psychoanalytic Concepts and the Structural Theory.* New York: International Universities Press.

Balint, M. (1960), Primary narcissism and primary love. *Psychoanal. Quart.,* 29:6–43.

Brenner, C. (1955), *An Elementary Textbook of Psychoanalysis.* New York: International Universities Press.

Eidelberg, L. (1959), Humiliation in masochism. *J. Amer. Psychoanal. Assn.,* 7:274–282.

Ellis, H. (1927), The conception of narcissism. *Psychoanal. Rev.,* 14:129–153.

Fenichel, O. (1945), *The Psychoanalytic Theory of Neurosis.* New York: Norton.

Freud, A. (1965), *Normality and Pathology in Childhood.* New York: International Universities Press.

Freud, S. (1905), Three essays on the theory of sexuality. *Standard Edition,* 7:125–243. London: Hogarth Press, 1953.

——(1910), Leonardo da Vinci and a memory of his childhood. *Standard Edition,* 11:63–137. London: Hogarth Press, 1957.

——(1911), Psycho-analytic notes on an autobiograpical account of a case of paranoia (dementia paranoides). *Standard Edition,* 12:9–82. London: Hogarth Press, 1958.

——(1913), Totem and taboo. *Standard Edition,* 13:1–161. London: Hogarth Press, 1955.

——(1914), On narcissism. *Standard Edition,* 14:69–102. London: Hogarth Press, 1957.

——(1915), Instincts and their vicissitudes. *Standard Edition,* 14:111–140. London: Hogarth Press, 1957.

——(1926), Inhibitions, symptoms and anxiety. *Standard Edition,* 20:77–175. London: Hogarth Press, 1959.

——(1940), An outline of psycho-analysis. *Standard Edition,* 23:144–207. London: Hogarth Press, 1964.

Glover, E. (1956), The future development of psycho-analysis. *On the Early Development of Mind.* New York: International Universities Press, pp. 333–351.

Gouin Décarie, T. (1965), *Intelligence and Affectivity in Early Childhood.* New York: International Universities Press.

Greene, W. A. (1958), Early object relations, somatic, affective and personal: an inquiry into the physiology of the mother-child unit. *J. Nerv. Ment. Dis.,* 126:225–253.

Hartmann, H. (1950), Comments on the psychoanalytic theory of the ego. *The Psychoanalytic Study of the Child,* 5:74–96. New York: International Universities Press.

——& Loewenstein, R. M. (1962), Notes on the superego. *The Psychoanalytic Study of the Child,* 17:42–81. New York: International Universities Press.

Holt, R. R. (1967), On the insufficiency of drive as a motivational concept in the light of evidence from experimental psychology. Read at the American Psychoanalytic Association, New York. Abstr. in: *J. Amer. Psychoanal. Assn.,* 16:627–632, 1968.

Jacobson, E. (1964), *The Self and the Object World.* New York: international Universities Press.

Joffe, W. G. & Sandler, J. (1967), Some conceptual problems involved in the consideration of disorders of narcissism. *J. Child Psychother.,* 2(1):56–66.

Jones, E. (1955), *The Life and Work of Sigmund Freud,* Vol. 2. New York: Basic Books.

Kanzer, M. (1955), The communicative function of the dream. *Int. J. Psycho-Anal.,* 36:260–266.

——(1964), Freud's uses of the terms autoerotism and narcissism. *J. Amer. Psychoanal. Assn.,* 12:529–539.

Kaywin, L. (1966), Notes on the psychoanalytic theory of affect. *Psychoanal. Rev.,* 53:278–280.

Kernberg, O. (1968), Factors in the psychoanalytic treatment of narcissistic personalities. Read at the Annual Meeting of the American Psychoanalytic Association, Boston.

Kohut, H. (1966), Forms and transformations of narcissism. *J. Amer. Psychoanal. Assn.,* 14:243–272.

Lewin, B. D. (1953), Reconsideration of the dream screen. *Psychoanal. Quart.,* 22:174–199.

Moore, B. E. & Fine, D., Eds. (1967), *A Glossary of Psychoanalytic Terms and Concepts.* New York: American Psychoanalytic Association, p. 57.

Murray, J. M. (1964), Narcissism and the ego ideal. *J. Amer. Psychoanal. Assn.,* 12:477–511.

Nunberg, H. & Federn, E., Eds. (1962, 1967), *Minutes of the Vienna Psychoanalytic Society,* 1:118 & 2:312. New York: International Universities Press.

Ostow, M. (1967), The syndrome of narcissistic tranquillity. *Int. J. Psycho-Anal.,* 48:573–583.

Rank, O. (1911), Ein Beitrag zum Narzissmus. *Jb. psychoanal & psychopathol. Forsch.,* 3:401–426.

Sadger, J. (1908), Psychiatrisch-Neurologisches in psychoanalytischer Beleuchtung. *Zbl. Gesamtgeb. Med. & ihre Grenzbeg.,* No. 7/8.

——(1910), Ein Fall von multipler Perversion mit hysterischen Absenzen. *Jb. psychoanal. & psychopathol. Forsch.,* 2:59–133.

Spitz, R. A. (1950), Psychiatric therapy in infancy. *Ameri. J. Orthopsychiat.,* 20:1–6.

5. Narcissism

Arnold M. Cooper

INTRODUCTION

Few concepts in psychiatry have undergone as many changes in meaning as has narcissism. Perhaps the single consistent element in these changes is the reference to some aspect of concern with the self and its disturbances. The word was introduced into psychiatry by Havelock Ellis.

The myth of Narcissus, as described by Bullfinch, clearly foreshadows many of the psychological descriptions that would come to be associated with the name. Narcissus was a physically perfect young man, the object of desire among the nymphs, for whom he showed no interest. One nymph, Echo, loved him deeply and one day approached him and was rudely rejected. In her shame and grief she perished, fading away, leaving behind only her responsive voice. The gods, in deciding to grant the nymphs' wish for vengeance, contrived that Narcissus would also experience the feelings of an unreciprocated love. One day, looking into a clear mountain pool, Narcissus espied his own image and immediately fell in love, thinking he was looking at a beautiful water spirit. Unable to tear himself away from this mirror image, and unable to evoke any response from the reflection, which disappeared every time he attempted to embrace it, he gradually pined away and died. When the nymphs came to bury him, he too had disappeared, leaving in place a flower.

H. G. Nurnberg[27] has pointed out that many of the features of narcissism are present in the myth; arrogance, self-centeredness, grandiosity, lack of sympathy or empathy, uncertain body image, poorly differentiated self and object boundaries, absence of enduring object ties, and lack of psychological substance.

Attempts to understand the concept of narcissism, the role of the self, and the nature of self-esteem regulation have occupied psychoanalysts and dynamic psychiatrists for three-quarters of a century. More recently, however, the "self," as a supraordinate organizing conception, has taken a more central place in the thinking of many clinicians and theorists, effecting a high yield in knowledge and understanding. This intensified interest in narcissism and the self relates to a number of current and historical trends. Some of these, briefly described, are:

1. The thrust of analytic research for several decades has emphasized the importance of early, that is, preoedipal developmental events. Psychiatrists and psychoanalysts have become increasingly interested in issues of early dependency, self-definition, separation and individuation, identity formation, and the earliest stages of object-relations. The theoretical movements of object-relational, interpersonal, and self-psychological schools have been highly influential. The works of Jacobson, Mahler, Winnicott, Rado, Horney, Sullivan, Kohut, Kernberg, Erikson, and others have been important.*

2. There has been an increasing willingness to alter or abandon traditional metapsychological language in favor of concepts that are closer to clinical experience. For instance, such designations as "self" and "identity" are incompatible with Freud's original natural science model of psychoanalysis and cannot easily be squared with the older concepts of energic and structural points of view. The concept of the self refers to a model that is more historical, experiential, intentionalistic, and action-oriented. Roy Schafer,[33] in discussing these issues, suggested that a new conceptual model for psychoanalysis is in the process of being developed, and the work of Kohut,[18,19,20,21] Jacobson,[15] Mahler,[24] and others represents a transitional step in this development. In part, the current interest in narcissism expresses a need felt by some therapists for a psychodynamic frame of reference that accommodates the unity of human behavior in terms that are appropriate to our current psychological thinking.

3. Our present interest in the self is concordant with powerful, contemporary currents in philosophy and culture. The concerns of such cultural historians as Lionel Trilling and Quentin Anderson, of philosophers such as Sartre, Heidegger, or Wittgenstein, as well as the themes of many contemporary novels and movies, are directed toward the

*See references 6, 14, 15, 16, 17, 18, 19, 20, 21, 24, 30, 34, and 35.

problem of maintaining a sense of self in an alienating modern world. Psychiatry and psychoanalysis, both in theory and practice, have always been powerfully influenced by, as well as influencing, the cultural milieu in which they exist. Many social observers, from Spiro Agnew to Christopher Lasch, have expressed the view that contemporary western civilization is characterized by an intense focus on private ambitions, a loss of concern with the needs of others, and a demand for immediate gratification—in effect, producing the "gimme" or "me first" culture. This change from an earlier sense of community and concern for one's fellow human beings is attributed to the influences of a television-dominated consumer culture, the loss of moral values, the breakdown of the stable authority-centered family, the focus on youth and beauty, the difficulty of perceiving one's valued place in society, and the uncertainity of future goals in a world of nuclear threat and political chaos.

4. In the intervening years between the early part of the century and the present, psychotherapists and psychoanalysts have perceived a change in the population presenting for therapy. Glover,[13] referring to the 1930s, and Lazar,[23] referring to the early 1970s, have discussed the scarcity of the "classical" neurotic patient described in the early psychoanalytic literature, and both have mentioned the increasing numbers of patients with characterologic disorders of some severity, epecially the narcissistic character.

While it is generally believed that this population change is genuine and a consequence of the cultural changes previously mentioned, there are some who feel that the change is largely in the perception of those psychotherapists who are both more sophisticated about, and interested in, character and early development. According to this view, deeper levels of personality organization are today being routinely explored, therapeutic ambitions have increased, and diagnoses have changed more than the patients.

Whether it is because of the changing population or changing diagnostic interest, therapists have been increasingly willing to undertake intensive psychotherapy or psychoanalysis with patients who previously would have been considered unsuitable because of their difficulties in forming a transference. Exploratory work with these patients has yielded new knowledge concerning narcissistic aspects of the personality.

All of these factors have played a role in engaging our interest in narcissism, and they have resulted in a greatly enriched description of the developmental and functional aspects of the self.

5. More recently, it has been the work of Heinz Kohut[18] and the publication of his *Analysis of the Self* that has kindled interest in narcissism. Without attempting to review what preceded his effort, Kohut boldly set forth an independent theory of the nature of narcissism and the therapy of narcissistic disorders. His work and its later modifications engaged the imagination of analysts and therapists, both pro and con, and has focused current discussion on the topic. (Kohut, and Kernberg, a major critic of his point of view, will be discussed separately in this chapter, and will not be included in the historical review.)

Finally, it should be emphasized that there is, today, general agreement that any concept of narcissism should include normal, as well as pathological, developmental and descriptive aspects. Current discussion emphasizes that narcissism is a universal and healthy attribute of personality, which may be disordered under particular circumstances.

HISTORY

Freud

Otto Kernberg[16] has pointed out that

psychoanalytic theory has always included the concept of the self, that is, the individual's integrated conception of himself as an experiencing, thinking, valuing and acting (or interacting) entity. In fact, Freud's starting point in describing the "I" ("das ich," so fatefully translated as "the ego" in English) was that of the conscious person whose entire intrapsychic life was powerfully influenced by dynamic, unconscious forces.

While this is undoubtedly the case, it is also true as Pulver[29] has indicated that Freud had extraordinary difficulty in conceptualizing the self within the libido theory and that this difficulty was compounded as Freud developed his structural point of view alongside the instinctual one. Because of variant historical usage, and because of the different meanings derived from different frames of reference, the term "narcissism" continues to have multiple meanings. As other workers began to take up the themes of narcissism, the concept took on even more varied meanings, dependent upon the historical period of the author's frame of reference. Pulver[29] points out that early in the psychoanalytic literature narcissism was used in at least four different ways.

1. Clinically, to denote a sexual perversion characterized by the treatment of one's own body as a sexual object.
2. Genetically, to denote a stage of development considered to be characterized by the libidinal narcissistic state.
3. In terms of object relationship, to denote two different phenomena:
   a. A type of object choice in which the self in some ways plays a more important part than the real aspects of the object.
   b. A mode of relating to the environment characterized by a relative lack of object relations.
4. To denote various aspects of the complex ego state of self-esteem. [p. 323]

The term "narcissism" was borrowed by Freud from Havelock Ellis, who used the Greek name to describe a form of sexual perversion in which the individual takes himself as a sexual object. Freud[10] described this as "the attitude of a person who treats his own body in the same way in which the body of a sexual object is ordinarily treated—who looks at it, that is to say, strokes it and fondles it till he obtains complete satisfaction through these activities." The term was also used by Freud[7] to describe a form of homosexual object choice in which the individual takes himself as his sexual object: "they perceive from a narcissistic basis and look for a young man who resembles them and whom *they* may love as their mother loved *them*." In 1911, in his account of the Schreber case—a patient with paranoia—Freud[8] expanded his use of the term to refer to the normal stage of libidinal development occurring between earliest autoerotism and object-love—the period in which the individual first unifies his sexual instincts by lavishing them upon himself and his own body. At this stage the self is the libidinal object, and fixation at this time could result in later perversion.

In 1913 Freud[9] described the magical omnipotent qualities of primitive or infantile thought and feeling, and considered them to be a component of narcissism.

In his paper "On Narcissism," Freud[10] elaborated the idea of narcissism as the libidinal investment of the self and described the kinds of object choice and the relationship to objects characterized by narcissism. The narcissistic individual will tend to choose and love an object on the basis of:

(a) what he himself is (i.e. himself),
(b) what he himself was,
(c) what he himself would like to be,
(d) someone who was once part of himself. [p. 90]

He described "primary" narcissism as the original libidinal investment of self and its consequent grandiose inflation, combined with
feelings of being perfect and powerful. "Secondary" narcissism was
seen as the self-involvement following a frustration in object-relations,
and the withdrawal of libido back into the ego.

Freud attempted to understand certain symptoms of schizophrenia
in terms of the withdrawal of libido into the ego, with the special
characteristic that the residua of the object-attachments have been
removed from fantasy. The outward manifestations of this development
include the withdrawal from objects, megalomania, and hypochondriasis—all indications of pathological excessive libidinal self-
involvement.

Self-regard (self-esteem) was considered by Freud[10] to be directly
proportional to the "size of the ego." "Everything a person possesses
or achieves, every remnant of the primitive feeling of omnipotence
which his experience has confirmed, helps to increase his self-regard."
Using the libidinal economic point of view, he also came to the conclusion that self-regard is lowered by being in love (since the self is divested
of libido, which is sent outwards toward the object) and raised in
schizophrenia. Because clinical experience demonstrates that many
persons in love experience an elevation of self-esteem and most schizophrenics suffer from damaged self-esteem, later workers thought to
revise that theory.

Freud[10] also considered the "ego-ideal" and the idealizing tendencies
of the ego in the formation of psychic structure. Freud at this time was
concerned with the criticisms of Jung and Adler, who maintained that
the psychoanalytic emphasis on sexuality offered no explanation of
nonsexual libidinal or aggressive behaviors. His response was to expand
the concept of narcissism to describe a variety of normal and pathological states, and to postulate the ego-libido. But while Freud continued
to refine his ideas on narcissism, they remained essentially intact. Elaborations of these views contributed to an explanation of depression,[12]
to understanding characterologic defiance,[11] and were the starting point
for the development of ego-psychology, which dominated later psy-

choanalytic thinking, Reich,[32] for example, took the concept of narcissim as an essential base for his description of character: "Character is essentially a narcissistic protection mechanism . . . against dangers . . . of the threatening outer world and the instinctual impulse." Reich thus further expanded the idea of narcissism as a way of conceiving defense mechanisms.

In the development of psychoanalytic theory, then, the concept of narcissism became increasingly complex as the term was adapted to fit the changing frames of reference demanded by libido-economic, topographic, developmental, genetic, and structural points of view.

In psychoanalytic literature since the development of ego psychology, the term "narcissism" has often been used either as a synonym for self-esteem or as a general reference to "a concentration of psychological interest upon the self."[27] It has become increasingly apparent that the term is so burdened with the baggage of its past that it has perhaps outlived its usefulness. The descriptive or explanatory (genetic or dynamic) ideas behind the term are not uniformly agreed-upon, and often the word is used as if it explained a phenomenon. One consequence of this trend has been an increasing focus on the concept of the "self" in an attempt to provide clearer opportunities for clinical description and research.

THEORISTS OF THE SELF

While many psychodynamic theorists proposed ideas about the role of self in personality, only the work of those few whose contributions were pivotal, although not always accorded full recognition at the time, will be described.

Sullivan

Harry Stack Sullivan was among the first psychoanalysts to accord a central role to the concept of the self in a systematic view of behavior. Sullivan[34] spoke of "self-dynamism," describing dynamism as "the relatively enduring patterns of energy transformation which recurrently characterize the interpersonal relations—the functional interplay of person and personifications, personal signs, personal abstractions, and personal attributions—which make up the distinctively human sort of being."

Sullivan described three types of interpersonal experience in infancy that contribute to the formation of self-dynamism: (1) that of a reward, which leads to a personification of a "good me"; (2) that of the occurrence of anxiety, which leads to the creation of a "bad me"; and (3) that of overwhelming and sudden anxiety, which leads to the creation of the sense of "not me." "Good me" personification organizes experiences of need satisfaction and the mother's soothing ministrations. "Bad me" personification represents experiences of the infant in which increased feelings of injury or anxiety coincide with increased tenseness and forbidding behavior on the part of the mother. Both of these experiences are communicable by the infant with relatively early development of speech capacity. The concept of the personification of "not me" relates to dream and psychotic experience and is a result of intense anxiety and dread, which in turn, results in dissociative behavior. Corresponding to the "good me" and "bad me" are personifications of a good and bad mother. These personifications of self-esteem are attempts to minimize anxiety that inevitably arises in the course of the educative process between mother and infant.

Sullivan[34] goes on to say that

the origins of the self-system can be said to rest on the irrational character of culture or, more specfically, society. Were it not for the fact that a great many prescribed ways of doing things have to be lived up to, in order that one shall maintain workable, profitable, satisfactory relations with his fellows: or, whether prescriptions for the types of behavior in carrying on relations with one's fellows were perfectly rational—then, for all I know, there would not be evolved, in the course of becoming a person, anything like the sort of self-system that we always encounter. If the cultural prescriptions characterizing any particular society were better adapted to human life, the notions that have grown up about incorporating or introjecting a punitive, critical person would not have arisen. . . . But do not overlook the fact that the self-system comes into being because of, and can be said to have as its goal, the securing of necessary satisfaction without incurring much anxiety. [pp. 168–169]

For Sullivan, this self-system was the central dynamism of human organization, the source of resistance to change in therapy as well as the source of stability in healthy functioning. Understanding the defects in the self-dynamism provides the major therapeutic opportunity for altering the more severe pathological states.

Horney

Karen Horney[14] felt that clinical observation did not support the conclusions of libido theory, which propounded that normal self-esteem is a desexualized form of self-love, and that persons tending toward self-concern or overevaluation of the self must be expressing excessive self-love. Building on H. Nunberg's concept of the synthetic function of the ego, she decided that the nuclear conflict of neurosis was not one of instincts, but one of self-attitudes. She suggested that narcissism be confined to situations of unrealistic self-inflation.

It means that the person loves and admires himself for values for which there is no adequate foundation. Similarly, it means that he expects love and admiration from others for qualities that he does not possess, or does not possess to as large an extent as he supposes.

According to my definition, it is not narcissistic for a person to value a quality in himself which he actually possesses or to like to be valued by others. These two tendencies—appearing unduly significant to oneself and craving undue admiration from others—cannot be separated. Both are always present, though in different types one or the other may prevail.

According to Horney this type of self-aggrandizement is always the consequence of disturbed relationships in early childhood, especially the child's alienation from others provoked by "grievances and fears." The narcissistic individual is someone whose emotional ties to others are tenuous, who suffers a loss of the capacity to love. Horney describes the loss of "the real me" as occurring under conditions of parental coercion in which the child suffers impairment of self-sufficiency, self-reliance, and initiative. Self-inflation (narcissism) is one attempt to cope with these tendencies.[14]

He escapes the painful feeling of nothingness by molding himself in fancy into something outstanding—the more he is alienated, not only from others but also from himself, the more easily such notions acquire a psychic reality. His notions of himself become a substitute for his undermined self-esteem; they become his "real me." [pp. 92–93]

This type of self-inflation also represents an attempt to maintain some life-sustaining self-esteem under conditions of potential annihilation, as well as being a desperate effort to attain admiration as a substitute for the unavailability of love. Horney describes three pathological consequences of narcissistic self-inflation: (1) increasing unproductivity because work is not satisfying for its own sake; (2) excessive expectations as to what the world owes the individual without effort on his part; and (3) increasing impairment of human relations due to constant grievances and hostility. Persons with narcissistic pathology tend to create ever more fantastic inflated versions of the self, which, lacking reality, lead to increasingly painful humiliations, which, in a vicious circle, lead to greater distortion of the self. Horney, therefore, sharply distinguishes between self-esteem, which rests on the genuine capacities that an individual possesses (which may be high or low), and self-inflation, which is an attempt to disguise a lack of qualities by a false presentation of capacities that do not exist. "Self-esteem and self-inflation are mutually exclusive."[14] Self-esteem represents the healthy development of the appropriate monitoring of self-approved action. Narcissism, therefore, is not an expression of self-love, but of alienation from the self.

She concludes:

In rather simplified terms, a person clings to illusions about himself because, and as far as, he has lost himself. As a consequence the correlation between love of self and love for others is not valid in the sense that Freud intends it. Nevertheless, the dualism which Freud assumes in his second theory of instinct—the dualism between narcissism and love—if divested of theoretical implications contains an old and significant truth. This is, briefly, that any kind of egocentricity detracts from a real interest in others, that it impairs the capacity to love others. [p. 100][14]

Rado

Sandor Rado,[30] in "Hedonic Control, Action-Self, and the Depressive Spell," attempted a description of what he termed the "action-self." The action-self is intended to be the organizing principle of behavior, replacing Freud's libidinal concepts.

Let me now give a rounded summary of these features of the action-self. Of proprioceptive origin, the action-self is the pivotal integrative system of the whole organism. Guided by willed action, it separates the organism's awareness of itself from its awareness of the world about it, and completes this fundamental separation by building up the unitary entity of total organism in contrast to the total environment. It is upon these contrasting integrations that the selfhood of the organism depends, as well as its awareness of its unbroken historical continuity. In accord with these functions, the action-self plays a pivotal part in the integrative action of the awareness process. This part is enhanced by its automatized organization of conscience, which increases the fitness of the

organism for peaceful cooperation with the group. By its expansion and contraction, the action-self serves as the gauge of the emotional stature of the
organism, of the ups and downs of its successes and failures. In its hunger for
pride, it continuously edits for the organism the thought-picture of its present,
past and future. [p. 304][30]

Rado attempted a functional description of a system of self-organization that was intended to replace the instinctual frame of reference
of Freud.

Winnicott

Winnicott,[35] in a paper written in 1960, described a True Self as the
spontaneous, biological comfort and enthusiasm that arise in the course
of development.

The True Self comes from the aliveness of the body tissues and the working
body-functions, including the heart's actions and breathing. It is closely linked
with the idea of the Primary Process, and is, at the beginning, essentially not
reactive to external stimuli, but primary. There is little point in formulating a
True Self idea except for the purpose of trying to understand the False Self,
because it does no more than collect together the details for the experience of
aliveness. [p. 148][35]

He went on to describe the False Self as a consequence of the failure
of the not-good-enough mother to meet the omnipotent fantasy of the
infant during the earliest stage of object relationships

A True Self begins to have life through the strength given to the infant's weak
ego by the mother's implementation of the infant's omnipotent expressions.
The mother who is not-good-enough is not able to implement the infant's
omnipotence, and so she repeatedly fails to meet the infant gesture; instead she
substitutes her own gesture which is to be given sense by the compliance of the
infant. This compliance on the part of the infant is the earliest stage of the False
Self, and belongs to the mother's inability to sense her infant's needs. [p. 145][35]

In Winnicott's theory, varying degrees of False Self are constructed in
an attempt to keep intact some hidden aspects of one's True Self, while
presenting a false compliance to environmental demands. In severe
degrees the False Self sustains the individual against the sense of total
annihilation through the loss of the True Self. Anticipating Kohut,
Winnicott described the extraordinary clinical importance of recognizing the existence of a False Self, and the failure of all therapeutic

measures that address only the False Self while failing to understand the hidden True Self. The analyst, however, must recognize initially that he can speak only to the False Self about the True Self. As a True Self begins to emerge, the analyst must be prepared for a period of extreme dependence, often created by degrees of acting out within the analysis. A failure on the part of the analyst to recognize this need to assume the caretaker role will destroy the opportunities for further analysis of the True Self. And finally, analysts who are not prepared to meet the heavy needs of patients who become extraordinarily dependent should be careful not to include False Self patients in their caseloads, since they will not be successful in treating them.

In psycho-analytic work it is possible to see analyses going on indefinitely because they are done on the basis of work with the False Self. In one case, a man had had a considerable amount of analysis before coming to me. My work really started with him when I made it clear to him that I recognized his non-existence. He made the remark that over the years all the good work done with him had been futile because it had been done on the basis that he existed, whereas he had only existed falsely. When I said that I recognized his non-existence he felt that he had been communicated with for the first time. What he meant was that his True Self that had been hidden away from infancy had now been in communication with his analyst in the only way which was not dangerous. This is typical of the way in which this concept affects psycho-analytic work. [p. 151][35]

While Winnicott did not attempt any rigorous definition of what a self is, his work is clearly clinically relevant to, and a precursor of, current issues in narcissism. He emphasized the importance of the early failure of the "holding environment" and the need for regression of the self in the analysis. The False Self, separated from the roots that compose the matrix of psychic structure, leads to an impoverishment of the capacities for play, creativity, and love; these qualities can be achieved only through a reestablishment of the predominance of the True Self.

Erikson

Erik Erikson, wrestling with similar questions concerning the organization of unified self-perception, self-judgment, and motivation, used the term "identity" or "ego identity." He was careful never to define his meaning with great precision, believing that the definition should grow out of its developing clinical use rather than be determined in advance by theoretical considerations. He spoke of the ego identity as

the accrued experience of the ego's ability to integrate these identifications with the vicissitudes of the libido, with the aptitudes developed out of endowment, and with the opportunities offered in social roles. The sense of ego identity, then, is the accrued confidence that the inner sameness and continuity are matched by the sameness and continuity of one's meaning for others, as evidenced in the tangible promise of a "career." [p. 228][6]

Identity for Erikson meant developing a sense of one's basic personal and interpersonal characteristics, beginning in early infancy with the advent of "basic trust" and continuing through each of the eight stages of man. Adolescence is seen by Erikson to be an especially crucial period in the formation of identity since it brings together many disparate elements of ego identity—sexual, vocational, dependent. Maturation is seen as a succession of developmental crises in which the respective optimal outcomes culminate in the achievement of an ego sense of trust, autonomy, initiative, industry, intimacy, generativity, and integrity. It is clear that self-esteem is dependent on the degree of success or failure in achieving satisfying ego images at each developmental stage.

Erikson allotted special emphasis to the interaction of biological and cultural influences in the formation of ego identity. The biological matrix, essentially that of Freud's psychosexual schema, takes on its particular psychological characteristics only through the effects of specific identifications and cultural expectations, which aid or hinder the achievement of identity goals at each developmental stage.

While Erikson did not specifically address his work to the theory of narcissism, and seems to eschew all metapsychological implications, his studies bear directly on attempts to understand the formation of stable self and object representations out of bodily perceptions, parent-child interactions, and social influence, as well as on the mechanisms of the maintenance of self-esteem. Erikson has made one of the most detailed efforts to relate the vicissitudes of the individual identity, or self, to the opportunities and disadvantages that each culture provides. In addition, he offers specific analyses of several historical phenomena and some of their psychological consequences.[6]

NARCISSISM AND CULTURE

There is a large popular and technical literature[3,22] that maintains with varying degrees of documentation that the typical personality met with in western culture today has been deformed by consumerism and by the atmosphere of selfishness that is fostered by a child-centered society where the welfare of the child is singled out at the expense of the welfare of the family. Furthermore, the sense of anomie and hopelessness that pervades the culture at the same time that glitter and glamour are displayed on all sides has led to a general feeling of uselessness and rage, as well as a powerful urge to possess all pleasures now, ignoring future pleasures as not worth waiting for. The high divorce rate, the loss of religion, the inability to maintain an extended family, the abandonment of the home by women who join the work force, the lack of traditional pursuits, which are valued for their own sakes rather than for the material rewards they bring—all of this and more have been cited as causes for, and evidence of, the so-called narcissistic generation. From this perspective, individuals are more than ever self-centered, incapable of self-sacrifice for another person, without deeper moral, spiritual, or emotional values, and capable of experiencing only shallow transference relationships—all of which ultimately subjects them to the perils of alienation, boredom, and insecure relationships.

Christopher Lasch,[22] in *The Culture of Narcissism,* has presented an elaborate and eloquent description of the decay of western individualistic society, in which narcissism has reached a pernicious flowering, creating a mockery of older values. According to Lasch, his book "describes a way of life that is dying—the culture of competitive individualism, which in its decadence has carried the logic of individualism to the extreme of a war against all, the pursuit of happiness to the dead end of a narcissistic pre-occupation with the self." Lasch then goes on to describe a culture in which there has been a loss of both independence and any sense of competence.

Narcissism represents the psychological dimension of this dependence. Notwithstanding his occasional illusions of omnipotence, the narcissist depends on others to validate his self-esteem. He cannot live without an admiring audience. His apparent freedom from family ties and institutional constraints does not free him to stand alone or to glory in his individuality. On the contrary, it contributes to his insecurity, which he can overcome only by seeing his "grandiose self'' reflected in the attentions of others, or by attaching himself to those who radiate celebrity, power and charisma. For the narcissist, the world is a mirror, whereas the rugged individualist saw it as an empty wilderness to be shaped in his own design. . . .

Today Americans are overcome not by the sense of endless possibility but by the banality of the social order they have erected against it. Having internalized the social restraints by means of which they formerly sought to keep possibility within civilized limits, they feel themselves overwhelmed by an annihilating boredom, like animals whose instincts have withered in captivity. A reversion to savagery threatens them so little that they long precisely for a more vigorous instinctual existence. People nowadays complain of an inability to feel. They cultivate more vivid experiences, seek to beat sluggish flesh to life, attempt to revive jaded appetites. They condemn the superego and exalt the lost life of the senses. Twentieth-century peoples have erected so many psychological barriers against strong emotion, and have invested those defenses with so much of the energy derived from forbidden impulses, that they can no longer remember what it feels like to be inundated by desire. They tend, rather, to be consumed with rage, which derives from defenses against desire and gives rise in turn to new defenses against rage itself. Outwardly bland, submissive, and sociable, they seethe with an inner anger, for which a dense, overpopulated, bureaucratic society can devise few legitimate outlets.[22]

While this idea seems logical and attractive, and is the theme of many novels and movies, there is little evidence that such a change of character has in fact taken place in a society that is as multifaceted as ours. It is very difficult to assess change in something as subtle as individual character or even in group behavior. Increased divorce rate, earlier appearance of sexual activity, and decline of religion need not be aspects of the failure in our ability to love, to work, or to value life itself. There has always been the tendency to blame the youth of any era for its lack of old-fashioned virtues, and as one follows the history of pop culture one must be impressed by the rapidity with which cultural movements change; for example, in a very few years an age of conformity (the 1950s) gave way to an age of rebellion (the 1960s), which in turn became an age of narcissism (the 1970s). But if we assume that character is fairly stable and slow to change, then these outward manifestations of cultural change reveal less about character than about a society that is predicated on technological goals. Of course others might say that the rapidity of cultural change is itself the source and measure of the problem of character.

Another claim for character change comes from psychoanalysts who feel that the classical neurotic patient suffering from a conflictual transference neurosis of primarily oedipal nature is now rare and has been replaced by the patient with narcissistic and even borderline features. It is difficult to know how to evaluate this claim. In the contemporary world, advances in psychoanalytic theory quickly permeate the general culture, so that even a vice-president who would later be indicted for fraud managed to have an opinion about defects in early child-rearing practices and the deformations of narcissistic character.

NARCISSISTIC PERSONALITY DISORDER

Diagnosis

Because the term narcissism involves issues of self-esteem regulation and the self-representation, aspects of narcissism will appear in all psychological functioning, and disturbances of narcissism are apt to appear as a part of all psychopathology.[5] The syndrome Narcissistic Personality Disorder has been separately defined in the third edition of the *Diagnostic and Statistical Manual of Mental Disorders:*[1]

The essential feature is a Personality Disorder in which there are a grandiose sense of self-importance or uniqueness; preoccupation with fantasies of unlimited success; exhibitionistic need for constant attention and admiration; characteristic responses to threats to self-esteem; and characteristic disturbances in interpersonal relationships that alternate between the extremes of over-idealization and devaluation, and lack of empathy.

The exaggerated sense of self-importance may be manifested as extreme self-centeredness and self-absorbtion. Abilities and achievements tend to be unrealistically overestimated. Frequently the sense of self-importance alternates with feelings of special unworthiness. For example, a student who ordinarily expects an A and receives an A minus may at that moment express the view that he or she, more than any other student, is revealed to all as a failure.

Fantasies involving unrealistic goals may involve achieving unlimited ability, power, wealth, brilliance, beauty, or ideal love. Although these fantasies frequently substitute for realistic activity, when these goals are actually pursued, it is often with a "driven," pleasureless quality, and an ambition that cannot be satisfied.

Individuals with this disorder are constantly seeking admiration and attention, and are more concerned with appearances than with substance. For example, there might be more concern about being seen with the "right" people than having close friends.

Self-esteem is often fragile; the individual may be preoccupied with how well he or she is doing and how well he or she is regarded by others. In response to criticism, defeat, or disappointment, there is either a cool indifference or marked feelings of rage, inferiority, shame, humiliation, or emptiness.

Interpersonal relationships are invariably disturbed. A lack of empathy (inability to recognize and experience how others feel) is common. For example, annoyance and surprise may be expressed when a friend who is seriously ill has to cancel a date.

Entitlement, the expectation of special favors without assuming reciprocal responsibilities, is usually present. For example, surprise and anger are felt because others will not do what is wanted; more is expected from people than is reasonable.

Interpersonal exploitativeness, in which others are taken advantage of in order to indulge one's own desires or for self-aggrandizement, is common; and the personal integrity and rights of others are disregarded. For example, a writer might plagiarize the ideas of someone befriended for that purpose.

Relations with others lack sustained, positive regard. Close relationships tend to alternate between idealization and devaluation ("splitting"). For example, a man repeatedly becomes involved with women whom he alternately adores and despises.

Associated features. Frequently, many of the features of Histrionic, Borderline, and Antisocial Personality Disorders are present; in some cases more than one diagnosis may be warranted.

During periods of severe stress transient psychotic symptoms of insufficient severity or duration to warrant an additional diagnosis are sometimes seen.

Depressed mood is extremely common. Frequently there is painful self-consciousness, preoccupation with grooming and remaining youthful, and chronic, intense envy of others. Preoccupation with aches and pains and other physical symptoms may also be present. Personal deficits, defeats, or irresponsible behavior may be justified by rationalization, prevarication, or outright lying. Feelings may be faked in order to impress others.

Impairment. By definition, some impairment in interpersonal relations always exists. Occupational functioning may be unimpaired, or may be interfered with by depressed mood, interpersonal difficulties, or the pursuit of unrealistic goals.

Prevalence. This disorder appears to be more common recently than in the past, although this may only be due to greater professional interest in the category. [pp. 315–317][1]

The Diagnostic Criteria for Narcissistic Personality Disorders are as follows:

The following are characteristic of the individual's current and long-term functioning, are not limited to episodes of illness, and cause either significant impairment in social or occupational functioning or subjective distress:

A.   Grandiose sense of self-importance or uniqueness, e.g., exaggeration of achievements and talents, focus on the special nature of one's problems.

B.   Preoccupation with fantasies of unlimited success, power, brilliance, beauty, or ideal love.

C.   Exhibitionism: the person requires constant attention and admiration.

D.   Cool indifference or marked feelings of rage, inferiority, shame, humiliation, or emptiness in response to criticism, indifference of others, or defeat.

E.   At least two of the following characteristics of disturbances in interpersonal relationships:

(1)   entitlement: expectation of special favors without assuming reciprocal responsibilities, e.g., surprise and anger that people will not do what is wanted

(2)   interpersonal exploitativeness: taking advantage of others to indulge own desires or for self-aggrandizement; disregard for the personal integrity and rights of others

(3)   relationships that characteristically alternate between the extremes of overidealization and devaluation

(4)   lack of empathy: inability to recognize how others feel, e.g., unable to appreciate the distress of someone who is seriously ill. [pp. 315–317][1]

Not all psychoanalysts would agree with all aspects of this definition, since it perhaps places excessive stress on the overt grandiose and exhibitionistic qualities of the self. In fact, many persons appropriately diagnosed as possessing narcissistic personality disorders maintain grandiose fantasies at unconscious or preconscious levels, being aware primarily only of shyness, feelings of unworthiness, fears of competition, and fears of exhibiting themselves.

A detailed description of the narcissistic personality has also been given by Otto Kernberg.[17]

On the surface, these patients may not present seriously disturbed behavior; some of them may function socially very well, and they usually have much better impulse control than the infantile personality.

These patients present an unusual degree of self-reference in their interactions with other people, a great need to be loved and admired by others, and a curious apparent contradiction between a very inflated concept of themselves and an inordinate need for tribute from others. Their emotional life is shallow. They experience little empathy for the feelings of others, they obtain very little enjoyment from life other than from the tributes they receive from others or from their own grandiose fantasies, and they feel restless and bored when external glitter wears off and no new sources feed their self-regard. They envy others, tend to idealize some people from whom they expect narcissistic supplies and to depreciate and treat with contempt those from whom they do not expect anything (often their former idols). In general, their relationships with other people are clearly exploitative and sometimes parasitic. It is as if they feel they have the right to control and possess others and to exploit them without guilt feelings—and, behind a surface which very often is charming and engaging, one senses coldness and ruthlessness. Very often such patients are considered to be dependent because they need so much tribute and adoration from others, but on a deeper level they are completely unable really to depend on anybody because of their deep distrust and depreciation of others.

Analytic exploration very often demonstrates that their haughty, grandiose, and controlling behavior is a defense against paranoid traits related to the projection of oral rage, which is central in their psychopathology. On the surface these patients appear to present a remarkable lack of object relationships; on a deeper level, their interactions reflect very intense, primitive, internalized object relationships of a frightening kind and incapacity to depend on internalized good objects. The antisocial personality may be considered a subgroup of the narcissistic personality. Antisocial personality structures present the same general constellation of traits that I have just mentioned, in combination with additional severe superego pathology.

The main characteristics of these narcissistic personalities are grandiosity, extreme self-centeredness, and remarkable absence of interest and empathy for others in spite of the fact that they are so very eager to obtain admiration and approval from other people. These patients experience a remarkably intense envy of other people who simply seem to enjoy their lives. These patients not only lack emotional depth and fail to understand complex emotions in other people, but their own feelings lack differentiation, with quick flare-ups and subsequent dispersal of emotion. They are especially deficient in genuine feelings of sadness and mournful longing; their incapacity for experiencing depressive reactions is a basic feature of their personalities. When abandoned or disappointed by other people they may show what on the surface looks like depression, but which on further examination emerges as anger and resentment, loaded with revengeful wishes, rather than real sadness for the loss of a person whom they appreciated.

Some patients with narcissistic personalities present strong conscious feelings of insecurity and inferiority. At times, such feelings of inferiority and insecurity may alternate with feelings of greatness and omnipotent fantasies. At other times, and only after some period of analysis, do unconscious fantasies of omnipotence and narcissistic grandiosity come to the surface. The presence of extreme contradictions in their self concept is often the first clinical evidence of the severe pathology in the ego and superego of these patients, hidden underneath a surface of smooth and effective social functioning.[17]

The chief attributes described in Kernberg's viewpoint are the individual's lack of emotional ties to others, the lack of positive feelings about his own activities, and his inability to sustain relationships except as sources of admiration intended to bolster his own faltering self-esteem. Kernberg further suggests that beneath the surface the pathological narcissist suffers from deep feelings of destructive rage and envy toward those people upon whom he depends. He also intimates that the inner fragmentation of those narcissistic individuals with good surface functioning may result in unexpected psychotic episodes during analytic treatment. Primitive defense mechanisms of splitting, projective identification, and denial are prevalent.

Kohut,[18] describing similar patients, emphasized the lack of genuine enthusiasm and joy, the sense of deadness and boredom, and the frequency of perverse activities. It is also his view that a final decision concerning the diagnosis can be made only on the basis of transference established in the course of psychoanalysis. For Kohut,[20] the person suffering a narcissistic personality disorder is someone who has achieved a cohesive self-organization—that is, someone who is not borderline or psychotic but whose self-organization is liable to fragmentation under conditions of stress. Typically, in analysis, they form self-object transferences of the "mirror" or "idealizing" type, and these are the hallmarks of the disorder.

Finally, it should be apparent that disturbances of a psychic structure as central as the self must have consequences for all developmental stages, as well as for other psychic structures and for content and quality of intrapsychic conflict.

Differential Diagnosis

While there is continuing disagreement about the precise criteria for diagnosis, narcissistic personality disorders must, in general, be distinguished from the borderline personalities at the sicker end of the spectrum, and from the higher level (oedipal, classical, or transference) neuroses at the other end.

The borderline personality represents a more severe failure to achieve self-integration, and is characterized by greater impulsivity, varieties of sexual acting out, shifting, intense unstable relationships, frantic refusal to be alone, psychotic manifestations under stress, evidence of severe identity disturbance ("I don't know who I am"), marked and rapid lability of mood, and tendencies toward severe self-damaging behavior, including suicidal gestures.[1] While persons suffering narcissistic personality disorders may show some of these manifestations, their functioning remains characterized by a cohesive, if defective, self-organization, while the behaviors mentioned for the borderline patients are only rarely present. Self-object differentiation has been achieved and reality testing is basically intact. Relatively high levels of functioning are possible for the narcissistic personality, although there is always the tendency to "burn out" as boredom and emptiness replace the pursuit for admiration.

At the other pole, it may be impossible initially to distinguish the patient with a narcissistic personality disorder from patients with narcissistic characterological defenses against oedipal conflict, since some disturbances of the self are present in all psychopathology.[20] It is Kohut's view that only the ongoing therapeutic effort in analysis and the clarification of the nature of the transference can clearly make the distinction between these disorders. In analysis, the "classical" transference neurosis patient will develop a full tripartite oedipal fantasy relationship with the therapist, and the nuclear oedipal conflict will become apparent as narcissistic defenses are analyzed and undermined. In the narcissistic personality the oedipal palimpsest provides an "as if" sense of interpersonal involvement that quickly collapses if narcissistic defenses are analyzed and the patient is threatened with the loss of a coherent self. Kernberg[17] further emphasizes that despite surface similarities with a variety of neurotic disorders in which narcissistic defenses for self-esteem are prominent, the narcissistic personality disorder is distinguishable by the absence of genuine warmth and concern for others.

Etiology

Disturbances of narcissism arise during the early phases of infantile development in relation to beginning separation from the mother and the clear differentiation of oneself as a separate individual. It is postulated that under optimum circumstances the very young infant enjoys some vague sense of omnipotence, autarchy, and perfect union with mother and environment, since all needs are gratified relatively quickly upon their being experienced and with no special effort on the part of the infant. The experience of hunger is followed by feeding, and the experience of bodily discomfort is followed by the soothing ministrations of the mother. This experience of satisfactory unity with the caretaking environment, usually the mother, builds in the young psyche a sense of omnipotence, a fantasy of total bliss and power. With increasing psychological development, experience, and the additional complexity of needs, the infant becomes increasingly aware of his need for the mother's care and help, an awareness that reaches one peak at the rapprochement phase (the stage in which the infant, now a toddler, increasingly separated from mother and without mother's automatic aid in achieving his wishes, experiences great anxiety and frustration and ambivalently seeks both to establish autonomy and reestablish ties to mother). It is assumed that the responses at this stage are crucial for the shaping of future narcissistic characteristics. Those infants who are able to begin gradually to delegate their own sense of omnipotence to a parent for whom they have loving feelings, and to share that omnipotence while gaining a feeling of greater effectiveness, both individually and through sharing, are likely to develop a sturdy and joyful sense of self. Those infants who respond with increasing frustration and rage to the recognition of their own helplessness in satisfying their needs, or who find that the mother on whom they are dependent is an unreliable gratifier of their needs, are likely to develop rage tinged with inadequate feelings of themselves as beings incapable of providing for their own gratification.

In a brief summary then, the development of an adequate sense of self requires a mother-child "fit" that is sufficiently gratifying to both parties, so that the mother can provide the child with: (1) a "holding environment"[25] that allows a maximum of psychological comfort, including pleasures in body sensations; (2) the phase-specific wax and wane of grandiose omnipotent fantasies of perfection; (3) identifications with idealized parent images; (4) adequate experiences of loving approval of the child's body, play, and achievements; (5) control and tolerence of the child's "badness"; (6) phase-appropriate encouragement of increasing autonomy; and (7) the sense of being empathically responded to, that is, understood in some way. Clearly all of these needs are never entirely fulfilled, and the rage and frustration that routinely occur in the mother-infant interaction as a result of failures of need gratifications and subsequent disruptions of omnipotent fantasy are a part of the normal maturational process, as are the attempts to repair these feelings of injury. While it is likely that constitutional, possibly genetic, factors contribute to certain infants' difficulty in integrating the many processes that contribute to the coherent sense of self, studies on this topic are not available.

Disturbances of the self are part of all psychological disturbances, and their treatment must be part of the treatment of the major psychopathology that is present. The narcissistic personality disorders, however, require a treatment designed to repair the primary flaws in the self-organization and the related broad disturbances of functioning that are likely to be manifested in all aspects of the personality—in stability of object relations, loss of affective capacity, diminished integrity of psychic structure, unstable self-esteem, and so forth. While outcome studies are unavailable, there is general agreement that lasting treatment effects are likely to occur only with deep intensive psychotherapy or psychoanalysis, with or without modifications. In recent years two major views concerning the nature of psychotherapy for this disorder have been developed—Kohut's and Kernberg's. They are described in the next section.

THERAPY

Kohut

Heinz Kohut's comprehensive theory of the development of the self and treatment of disorders of the self has been a major influence in current thinking.[19,21] While Kohut's views have gone through a lengthy evolution, in their current form they define a bipolar self composed on the one hand of tendencies toward exhibitionism and ambition, and on the other hand toward idealization of parent and self. Both of these tendencies derive from early infantile precursors. Kohut posits these inferences concerning early development primarily from the nature of transferences that occur in psychoanalytic treatment. Those aspects of what are labeled the "mirror transference" reveal primitive needs for being noticed, admired, and approved in one's grandiose aspirations. When these needs are met in the course of infantile development the normal construction of an infantile grandiose self is effected, and this is a necessary basis for healthy later development. Aspects of the "idealizing transference" reveal that the infant endows the caretakers in the environment with idealized capacities for power and omniscience with which the infant can identify and from which he can borrow strengths. One pole of narcissism thus relates to the development of ambition, strivings, and achievements, while the other pole of narcissism relates to the development of values and goals. It is Kohut's view that these developmental aspects of the self precede the development of drive and that they are the sources of coherent drive expression. Failures in the cohesive development of the self lead to drive derivative "disintegration products," expressed as pathological sexual and aggressive behaviors.

The psychopathology of the narcissistic character disorder is, in Kohut's view, one of arrest of the development of adequate psychic structure—that is, it is a deficiency disease. These failures in the development of self structure are prior to, and the source of, the apparent drive-related and conflictual materials that have been traditionally interpreted as the nucleus of neurosis. According to Kohut, the exclusive focus of traditional psychoanalysis on the conflictual aspects of the problem prevents the appearance of the significant underlying etiologic deficit. Furthermore, the objective inspectional, inferential stance of the analyst contributes to a consistent attitude of muted responsiveness, which for many narcissistic characters in analysis imposes a repetition of the deprivation circumstance—that is, the lack of empathy for the patient's need for vividness, responsiveness, and so forth, which were the original source of the developmental failure. The analyst's unavoidable periodic empathic failures in the transference situation present the possibility that these original empathic failures will be analyzed in the generally empathic treatment situation rather than repeated blindly.

In this view, the first object relations of the developing child consist of partial recognitions of the actual other person as part of one's internal monitoring of the state of one's self, and are termed by Kohut "self-objects." They are objects not yet perceived as autonomous in their own right but are internalized as aspects of the self and its own needs. In the later development of healthy narcissism, when the self is sufficiently sturdy and capable of providing its own gratifications, it then acknowledges the existence of the object as autonomous and as a source of gratifications as well as an opportunity for generous giving. The development of pathological forms of narcissim is largely dependent upon the actual failures of the environment to provide appropriate empathic responses to the infant's needs. For healthy development to occur, the mother must be empathically responsive to the infant's need for admiration ("mirroring") and to the later need to idealize the parent. Empathic failures result in a developmental arrest with fixation remaining at primitive levels of grandiosity and idealization, which leads to defensive rage and distorted sexuality. The arrest of self-development and its drive-disintegration products interfere with joyous expression and prevent the development of creativity. It is Kohut's view that while aspects of narcissistic pathology can be treated by a variety of psychotherapies, only a properly conducted psychoanalysis offers the greatest opportunity for therapeutic success.

The therapeutic task, therefore, is to permit the reconstruction within the psychoanalytic situation of the original self-strivings of the patient. The feelings of empathic failure that will arise as the analytic work periodically falters, because of real empathic failures on the analyst's part, permit a reexamination of the parents' original empathic failures and an opportunity for renewed growth as the analyst senses a new object. According to Kohut, the early phase of psychoanalysis should be devoted to allowing the fullest emergence of mirror and/or idealizing transferences. This requires care on the part of the therapist to avoid a too early interpretation of defensive secondary behaviors, since this could prevent the emergence of more basic narcissistic strivings. The patient, for example, who early in the analysis expresses rage at the analyst's inadequate attention, requires an empathic understanding of what has occurred within the analytic situation (that is, what has led him to feel unattended to) rather than an interpretation concerning the nature of his habitually excessive demands for attention. If the patient is permitted to regress in the analytic situation to the stage of fixation of self, and if the therapist does not interfere with the renewed infantile needs for mirroring and idealization, then normal growth processes will resume and a more mature self can be achieved.

The emphasis on empathy is an important aspect of Kohut's work. He stresses the necessity for the therapist consistently to maintain the empathic rather than objective stance. It is the therapist's task to imagine himself "into the skin" of the patient and to understand what each situation in the transference feels like to that patient. This is more important than the attempt, with the use of theory, to understand objectively what the situation is like in some larger or more objective context.

Kohut and his followers have made the claim that the insights and technical consequences of this new theory of the self have improved their abilities to treat the full range of narcissistic disorders by the methods already indicated, as well as enabling them to bring these patients to a level where more classical psychotherapeutic-psychoanalytic interpretive techniques will be successful. Their effort is to present the patient with comprehensive reconstructive interpretations derived from an empathic mode of observation and communication as opposed to the allegedly classical part-interpretations derived from an inferential mode of observation and communication.[28]

Critics of Kohut have maintained that his work is poorly supported by data and that the clinical data produced is adequately explained by existing theories. The plea for empathy is regarded by his critics as a return to a philosophy of gratifying the patient's neurotic needs without analyzing them. His critics also claim that he provides a "corrective emotional experience" rather than an experience of deepened understanding about the conflictual nature of the difficulty.

Kernberg

Otto Kernberg has attempted to understand the dynamics of narcissism within the structural dynamic and object-relational points of view. The works of Mahler,[24] Jacobson,[15] Reich,[31] and the British School had contributed significantly to Kernberg's conception of the self as a vital aspect of the early ego developing as an original fused self/object internalization. It is Kernberg's view that all early infantile experiences contribute to the differentiation and integration of internalized self and object representations, which consist of mixtures of affective, cognitive, and drive components. Kernberg[17] states that in the narcissistic personality disorder, stable ego boundaries are established (that is, reality testing is intact), but a refusal of already differentiated internalized self and object representations occurs as a defense against anxieties arising out of interpersonal difficulties. He postulates the creation of ideal self and object images, actual self and object images, and denigrated self and object images. Whereas the normal individual maintains a structural tension of idealized self and object images (the superego), and actual self and object images (the ego), the narcissistic character pathologically fuses ideal self, ideal object, and actual self images in the attempt to destroy the actual object. As a result, there are not only distortions of the self, but structural distortions of the superego. According to Kernberg, the narcissistic character is, in effect, saying:

I do not need to fear that I will be rejected for not living up to the idea of myself which alone makes it possible for me to be loved by the ideal person I imagine would love me. That ideal person and my ideal image of that person and my real self are all one and better than the ideal person whom I wanted to love me, so that I do not need anybody else any more.[17]

As a result of this process, denigrated unacceptable images of the self are projected onto those external objects viewed as dangerous, depriving, and attacking. The predominant self-image is itself a denigrated, hungry, weak, enraged, fearful, hating self. Kernberg discusses the feelings of emptiness, the lack of genuine feeling for others, and the paranoid projected rage that characterize these persons. Kernberg is in partial agreement with Kohut when he says that "chronically cold parental figures with covert, but intense aggression are a very frequent feature of the background of these patients."[17] The entire defensive effort of these patients is to maintain self-admiration, to depreciate others, and to avoid dependency. Kernberg's view is that the analytic task is to enable the patient to become familiar with his primitive oral rage, his hatred of the image of the aggressive mother, and to realize that this rage is linked with unfulfilled yearnings for loving care from the mother. The failure to integrate into one representation the loving and frustrating aspects of the mother—as represented in the figure of the analyst—will occupy a major portion of the analytic work. The patient's capacity to yield his own yearning for perfection in favor of accepting the terror of intimacy and the reality of another person as genuine, though imperfect, is the goal of the treatment. If successful, a new world of internalized objects is created that admits for the first time the feelings of genuineness and creative pleasure that were previously absent. Curiosity and interest in other persons, especially in the analyst, may begin to manifest themselves. The recognition of the reality of the analyst as a benign and actual whole person independent from the patient is, of course, the ultimate indicator of the success of the treatment.

It is Kernberg's view that narcissistic personalities can be treated without deviation from classical methods, that one must be alert to the borderline features which are displayed in more severe cases, and that one must be on the lookout for opportunities for narcissistic gratification which often hinder the analytic task. Kernberg does not agree with Kohut as to the need for a special preinterpretation phase of treatment. It is Kernberg's view that in the narcissistic personality the processes of idealization of self and object are not arrested but are faultily developed. Because the grandiose self regularly incorporates primitive components of ideal self and object, superego formation is defective and the internalized world of object-relations deteriorates, resulting in the severe disturbances of interpersonal relationships of pathological narcissism.[17] The therapeutic task is to enable the patient to arrive at new arrangements of existing structures and to undo pathological types of idealization rather than effect the resumption of growth of archaic tendencies toward idealization. For Kernberg the idealization of the analyst, early in the analysis of the narcissistic personality, would be a defensive measure related to covering underlying feelings of rage and emptiness rather than a conflict-free phase required for the building up of an adequate self. The pathological idealization is contaminated by rage, unlike the original idealization of the infant. Interpretation therefore will be aimed at helping the patient clarify his rage and greed; it will not require a preparatory phase of uncontaminated idealization.

Kernberg differentiates three levels of functioning of narcissistic personalities. The first group maintains effective surface adaptation in important areas of their lives; the patients are troubled by limited neurotic symptoms and have little insight into the inroads that narcissism has made in their lives. These patients are probably not yet willing to tolerate the anxieties that might be aroused in psychoanalysis, and are probably best treated by short-term psychotherapy. It is likely that later life experiences will bring home to them the full damage done to their personalities and they may then be amenable to psychoanalysis.

The second group of patients with narcissistic pathology is the most common and presents with severe disturbances in object relations and complicating symptoms in many areas of functioning. The treatment of choice in these cases is psychoanalysis. A third group of patients presents with borderline features and is likely to benefit from supportive-expressive psychotherapy.

Other Views

A variant of these views has been put forth by Cooper,[4] emphasizing the intermeshing of narcissistic and masochistic pathology. In his view early frustrations of narcissistic strivings lead to reparative attempts to maintain omnipotent fantasies, despite the helpless rage experienced by the infant in the course of ordinary failures of maternal care. One of these defensive efforts involves the attempt to master feelings of rage, frustration, and helplessness by the intrapsychic shift from pride in providing one's self with satisfactions to pride in the fantasy of control over a "bad mother," one who is responsible for the frustrations. Self-esteem takes on a pathological quality when an individual begins to derive satisfaction from mastery of his own humiliations, for example, when the infant begins to experience some sense of control and satisfaction when experiencing deprivations. A significant distortion of pleasure motivations has taken place and a pattern of deriving pleasure out of displeasure has begun. This pattern provides the groundwork for the later clinical picture of what Bergler[2] referred to as the behavior of the "injustice-collector." This individual engages in the following triad: (1) provocation or misuse of reality in order to suffer an injury; (2) defensive aggression designed both to deny responsibility for the unconsciously sought-for defeat and, secondarily, to escalate the self-punishment; and (3) depression, self-pity, and feelings of being singled out for "bad luck."

Cooper suggests that these individuals are basically narcissistic-masochistic characters and that their analysis regularly reveals that narcissistic defenses of grandiosity and entitlement are used to ward off masochistic tendencies toward self-abasement and self-damage. Concurrently, masochistic tendencies are used to disguise the full extent of the damage to the grandiose self. Treatment must therefore address both sides of the equation. Interpretation of narcissistic defenses produces masochistic reactions of victimization and self-pity, while interpretation of masochistic behaviors produces feelings of narcissistic humiliation.

Countertransference

Anyone who has attempted the treatment of narcissistic character pathology has noted the exceptional difficulties that arise in trying to maintain an appropriately attentive, sympathetic, and empathic attitude. The therapist is more than likely to find himself bored, or angry, or unable to make sense of the material, or just generally uneasy with the feeling of lifelessness presented in the treatment. Examination of the therapeutic situation will usually reveal that the therapist is responding to one or several of the following:

1. The patient's failure to acknowlege the therapist's existence in emotional terms. The therapist's interventions are ignored or denigrated; there is no curiosity about him, no indications that any tie exists between the two parties.
2. The patient's unspoken, grandiose, magical demand for total attention and effort on the part of the therapist, without any sense of a reciprocal relationship. The patient's feeling of icy control and detachment can be disconcerting.
3. Denigration of all therapeutic gain or effort, and destruction of all meaning.
4. Emergence of the extent of the patient's feelings of emptiness and hollowness, communicated to the therapist.
5. The patient's primitive idealizations of the therapist, arousing narcissistic anxieties in the therapist.
6. The patient's cold grandiosity, which arouses a retaliatory anger in the therapist.

Understanding the meanings of these reactions and making suitable preparations for them can aid the therapist to tolerate these periods, to remain alert for the shifts in the emotional climate of the treatment, and to avoid excessive guilt or anger on his own part.

SUMMARY

Issues of narcissism and the self have occupied a central role in psychodynamic theory and practice from the time of Freud's earliest researches. In the past several decades, increasing investigations into the diagnosis and treatment of the narcissistic personality disorders have been implemented by: (1) newer knowledge of infant development and the stages of individuation and separation; (2) developments in psychoanalytic theory that place greater emphasis on the central role of internal self and the object representations and the maintenance of self-esteem; and (3) possible changes in the culture that may have produced more frequent and more severe forms of pathological narcissism. While the treatment of these patients is difficult and challenging, significant advances have been made and worthwhile therapeutic goals can often be achieved.

BIBLIOGRAPHY

1. American Psychiatric Association. *Diagnostic and Statistical Manual of Mental Disorders,* 3rd ed. (DSM-III). Washington, D. C.: American Psychiatric Association, 1980.

2. Bergler, E. *The Superego*. New York: Grune & Stratton, 1952.
3. Coles, R. "Our Self-Centered Children: Heirs of the 'Me' Decade," *U.S. News and World Report*, February 25,1980.
4. Cooper, A. "The Masochistic-Narcissistic Character," abstracted in *Bulletin of the Association for Psychoanalytic Medicine*, 17 (1978): 13–17.
5. Eisnitz, A. "Narcissistic Object Choice, Self Representation," *International Journal of Psychoanalysis*, 50 (1969): 15–25.
6. Erikson, E. *"Childhood and Society,* 2nd ed. New York: Norton, 1963.
7. Freud, S. "Leonardo Da Vinci and a Memory of His Childhood," in Strachey, J., ed., *The Standard Edition of the Complete Psychological Works of Sigmund Freud* (hereafter *The Standard Edition)*, vol. 2. London: Hogarth Press, 1962, pp. 63–137 (originally published in 1910).
8. ——. "Psycho-Analytic Notes on an Autobiographical Account of a Case of Paranoia (Dementia Paranoides)," in Strachey, J., ed., *The Standard Edition*, vol. 12. London: Hogarth Press, 1958, pp. 9–82 (originally published in 1911).
9. ——. "Totem and Taboo," in Strachey, J., ed., *The Standard Edition*, vol. 13. London: Hogarth Press, 1958, pp. 1–162 (originally published in 1913).
10. ——. "On Narcissism: An Introduction," in Strachey, J., ed., *The Standard Edition*, vol. 14. London: Hogarth Press, 1957, pp. 69–102 (originally published in 1914).
11. ——. "Instincts and Their Vicissitudes," in Strachey, J., ed., *The Standard Edition*, vol. 14 London: Hogarth Press, 1957, pp. 109–140 (originally published in 1915).
12. ——. "Mourning and Melancholia," in Strachey, J., ed., *The Standard Edition*, vol. 14. London: Hogarth Press, 1957, pp. 237–258 (originally published in 1917).
13. Glover, E. *The Technique of Psycho-Analysis*. New York: International Universities Press, 1955.
14. Horney, K. *New Ways in Psychoanalysis*. New York: Norton, 1939.
15. Jacobson, E. *The Self and the Object World*. New York: International Universities Press, 1964.
16. Kernberg, O. "Contemporary Controversies Regarding the Concept of the Self," unpublished paper.
17. ——. *Borderline Conditions and Pathological Narcissism*. New York: Jason Aronson, 1975.
18. Kohut, H. *The Analysis of the Self: A Systematic Approach to the Psychoanalytic Treatment of Narcissistic Personality Disorders*. New York: International Universities Press, 1971.
19. ——. *The Restoration of the Self*. New York: International Universities Press, 1977.
20. ——. *The Psychology of the Self: A Casebook*, Goldberg, A., et al., eds. New York: International Universities Press, 1978.
21. ——. *The Search for the Self: Selected Writings of Heinz Kohut: 1950–1978, 2 vol.*, in Ornstein, P. H. ed., New York: International Universities Press, 1978.
22. Lasch, C. *The Culture of Narcissism: American Life in an Age of Diminishing Expectations*. New York: Norton, 1978.
23. Lazar, N. "Nature and Significance of Changes in Patients in a Psychoanalytic Clinic," *The Psychoanalytic Quarterly*, 42 (1973): 579–600.
24. Mahler, M., Pine, F., and Bergman, A. *The Psychological Birth of the Human Infant: Symbiosis and Individuation*. New York: Basic Books, 1975.
25. Modell, A. *Object Love and Reality*. New York: International Universities Press, 1968.

26. Moore B. E., and Fine B. D., eds. *A Glossary of Psychoanalytic Terms and Concepts.* The American Psychoanalytic Association,1968.
27. Nunberg, H. G. "Narcissistic Personality Disorder: Diagnosis," *Weekly Psychiatry Update Series,* 3 (1979): Lesson 17.
28. Ornstein, P., and Ornstein, A. "Formulating Interpretations in Clinical Psychoanalysis." Presented at the International Psycho-Analytic Congress, July 1979.
29. Pulver, S. "Narcissism: The Term and the Concept," *Journal of the American Psychoanalytic Association,* 18:2 (1970): 319–341.
30. Rado, S. "Hedonic Control, Action Self, and the Depressive Spell," in *Psychoanalysis of Behavior: Collected Papers.* New York: Grune & Stratton, 1956, pp. 286–311.
31. Reich, A. "Pathologic Forms of Self-Esteem Regulation," in Eissler, R. S., et al., eds., *The Psychoanalytic Study of the Child,* vol. 15. New York: International Universities Press, 1960, pp. 215–232.
32. Reich, W. *Character-Analysis,* 3rd ed., Wolfe, T. P. trans. New York: Orgone Institute Press, 1949, p. 158.
33. Schafer, R. "Concepts of Self and Identity and the Experience of Separation-Individuation in Adolescence," *The Psychoanalytic Quarterly,* 42 (1973): 42–59.
34. Sullivan, H. S. *The Interpersonal Theory of Psychiatry,* Perry, H. S. and Gowel, M. L., eds. New York: Norton, 1953, p. 168–169.
35. Winnicott, D. W. *The Maturational Processes and the Facilitating Environment: Studies in the Theory of Emotional Development.* New York: International Universities Press, 1965.

6. Self Relations, Object Relations, and Pathological Narcissism

Marjorie Taggart White

This above all, to thine own self be true. And it must follow, as the night the day. Thou canst not then be false to any man.[10]

With this exhortation, Shakespeare, in *Hamlet,* had Polonius, the Lord Chamberlain of Denmark, send his son, Laertes, off to seek his destiny. Polonius, sometimes seen as a symbol of the doddering father, too glib with clichés, was subsequently killed by Hamlet as a "rat" sneaking behind the curtains.

Polonius' fate as a champion of the importance of the self is reminiscent of the much earlier Greek myth of Narcissus, a beautiful youth who was bewitched into falling in love with his own reflection in a fountain, thinking it was "the presiding nymph of the place."[1] Narcissus "gradually pined away for love of this unattainable spirit" and jumped into the fountain where he died. The ill-fated youth thus came to symbolize the plight of those addicted to self-love, which was believed to lead to self-destruction. The idea of narcissism has been colored by this somber myth ever since. So Shakespeare, in Renaissance revival of Greco-Roman values, embodied the ambivalence about the prizing of the self in the ill-fated father figure of Polonius.

Christianity continued to emphasize the Greco-Roman value of self-abnegation, with selfishness easily slipping into the polar opposite of a vice. Yet competitiveness, which certainly implies self-advancement, was simultaneously encouraged in Greece and then in pagan and Christian Rome; religious wars, for example, eventuated in the precarious cultural domination by power struggles among multinational corporate giants.

Few thoughtful people would deny that Western culture (spreading into the East too) is pervaded, if not dominated by, an awareness of the importance of achieving visibility, even of becoming a celebrity. Being seen and heard on national (or preferably international) television has become an accolade of achievement, however much the more sophisticated may disparage it. "Publish or perish" continues to be the success prescription for professionals in almost every field. It seems that the competitive, self-advancing procedures involved in achieving as much visibility as possible are acceptable so long as they succeed.

Yet what about the archaic value system of self-abnegation implied in the virtues of modesty and unselfishness that we have inherited through the centuries? From the psychoanalytic viewpoint, the abrogation of the self is viewed as masochistic, a pathological condition. But in the therapeutic situation, there still seems to be much concern with "helping" the patient not to be demanding or "manipulative." Patients who want some kind of attention from the therapist, such as extra time, lower fees, telephone calls in stressful moments (e.g., suicidal attempts), or even verbal responses of encouragement, may be regarded as trying to control the therapist in terms of the patient's needs. Such patients, understandably, are a burden to the therapist. One could call such patients selfish and assume that their problems in living with other people stem from their self-centered needs, which are generally called infantile dependency needs. This attitude toward what we now know are indisputably early development deprivations can be regarded as a value judgment on the therapist's part, stemming from our dubious cultural heritage of the desirability of unselfishness and our human need not to be bothered by such patients. This archaic value could enter into an assumption by the therapist, bolstered by therapeutic training, that the needs of the self for attention and appreciation are somehow deviant. Could this involve the therapist's own ideal self-image and therefore color his or her expectations of the patient, regardless of the developmental needs and cultural counterforces that may be involved?

I have drawn some lines here between self-needs, object relations, expectations of oneself, expectations of others, the impact of the environment, and whatever may be the normal developmental needs. This is a complex conflict, but the awareness of it has led to significant findings in both theory and technique in psychoanalytic developmental psychology.

Let us start again with the self and go back to Freud, who published his ground-breaking article, "On Narcissism: An Introduction," in 1914.[5] Freud was concerned here with persons who took their own bodies as their exclusive sex objects, like the mythical Narcissus, and who, like psychotics, withdrew their interest from other people and the world. Freud was describing, in a very basic way, what we today term "pathological narcissism." He regarded this condition as a perversion. He also found such patients did not improve with psychoanalysis, because their lack of libidinal cathexis for other people interfered with the development of the usual transference reactions to the analyst. Although the necessary concepts and techniques for effectively treating pathological narcissism did not emerge for about twenty-five years, nevertheless, in this article Freud paved the way for this development and for the evolution of what I will call the concept of self relations. He raised the possibility that a so-called narcissistic libido might "claim a place in the regular course of human development" and formulated the concept of primary narcissism as "a libidinal complement to the egoism of the instinct of self-preservation, a measure of which may justifiably be attributed to every living creature."[5] Here Freud suggested that self-love could be a driving force for self-preservation. He originally saw self-preservation as a nonsexual ego instinct that later became an ego function when Freud presented the structural theory of the id, ego, and superego in 1923.[6] Freud found that the yearning for omnipotence and the belief in the magical power of wishes, words, and thoughts in dealing with the world are evident in the psychic life of children and of primitive peoples, thus attesting to the presence of this primary self-love in normal development as well as in pathology.

Hartmann, the father of ego psychology, took a fresh look at Freud's views on narcissism in 1950 in his article, "Comments on the Psychoanalytic Theory of the Ego."[8] Hartmann found that Freud defined narcissism as the libidinal cathexis of the ego prior to the structural theory when Freud made the ego one system in the tripartite psychic apparatus, a system which is defined by its functions. Yet Freud occasionally defined narcissism as the "cathexis of one's own person, of the body or of the self." Hartmann felt that to clarify narcissism, the self, or one's own person is to be distinguished from the object while the ego as a psychic system is to be distinguished from other substructures of personality. Hartmann says:

the opposite of object cathexis is not ego cathexis, but cathexis of one's own person, that is self-cathexis . . . it therefore will be clarifying if we define narcissism as the libidinal cathexis not of the ego but of the self. (It might also be useful to apply the term self-representation as opposed to object-representation.) Often, in speaking of ego libido, what we do mean is not that this form of energy cathects the ego, but that it cathects one's own person rather than an object representation.[8]

In this seemingly simple change in terminology, Hartmann makes it possible to think of the self or self-representations as a content of the ego, just as object representations are also regarded as a content of the system ego. The implications of this change, not only for the problem of narcissism but also for the processes of internalization and identification, are profound.

Freud speaks of primary narcissism as the happy state where the baby feels itself to be "the centre and core of creation."[5] Margaret Mahler, over 25 years ago, began to conceptualize primary narcissism in two phases. The first phase was termed normal autism. She says that "within that twilight state of early life . . . the infant shows hardly any sign of perceiving anything beyond his own body. He seems to live in a world of inner stimuli."[17] The second stage is what Mahler has termed normal symbiosis and has so fruitfully observed and elaborated upon with respect to both psychotic and normal infants. In an early formulation, Mahler says:

The presymbiotic, normal-autistic phase of the mother-infant unity gives way to the symbiotic phase proper from about the age of three months on. During his wakeful hungry periods of the day the three-four-month-old baby seems to perceive, temporarily at least, and, in a Gestalt kind of perception, that small part of external reality which is represented by the mother's breast, face, and hands, the Gestalt of her ministrations as such. This occurs in the matrix of the oral gratification-frustration sequences of the normal nursing situation. This phase of dim awareness of the "need-satisfying object" marks the beginning of the *phase of symbiosis* in which the infant behaves and functions as though he and his mother were an omnipotent system (a dual unity) within one common boundary (a symbiotic membrane as it were).[17]

The symbiotic dual unity consists of a psychic fusion of whatever memory traces have been laid down since birth and, perhaps before, of the baby's experience of its own inner sensations and of stimuli from the external world, especially of contacts with mother. These memory traces of beginning self-representations and representations of mother, the first object, are psychically fused in the symbiotic state with a coloration of omnipotence. Mahler more recently noted:

The entire life cycle constitutes a more or less successful process of distancing from and introjection of the lost symbiotic mother, an eternal longing for the actual or fantasied "ideal state of self," with the latter standing for a symbiotic fusion with the "all good" symbiotic mother, who was at one time part of the self in a blissful state of well being.[21]

In psychoanalytic developmental psychology, the symbiotic phase marks the beginning of object relations, with the dawning awareness of mother's ministrations along with the dawning awareness of the self that is gratified. This sense of blissful unity with the loved one is what is sought in the consummation of sexual love. This omnipotent gratification of all needs, including complete autonomy, is what the so-called narcissistic personality seeks in unconscious fantasies of retaining this self-object state. And this is the merger of self- and object representations to which the ego regresses in the borderline conditions and in psychosis, with varying degrees of severity.

Freud also saw object relations arising out of primary narcissism, but he did not have Mahler's concept of the symbiotic phase. Freud held that the libidinal cathexis of the baby's omnipotently experienced self—primary narcissism—became too much for the baby to discharge and overflowed on to objects, beginning with mother. Let us not forget that Freud thought of primary narcissism as the libidinal (i.e., the sexual) complement of the ego instinct for self-preservation. In Freud's view, the libidinal cathexis of the self underlies object love, and libido can be drawn back again to the self when major frustrations with objects occur. According to Freud, this drawing back of love from others to oneself is secondary narcissism, which becomes pathological unless love can again be returned to others. We will hear a different view of secondary narcissism from Mahler.[23]

But first I would like to summarize Freud's ideas on the antithesis he found between ego-libido and object-libido, which reflects his economics of love. He says "The more the one is employed, the more the other becomes depleted. The highest phase of development of which object-libido is capable is seen in the state of being in love, when the subject seems to give up his own personality in favour of an object-cathexis."[5] Freud's idea of the difference between self-love and object love underlies one of the most controversial concepts of Kohut,[14] a leading contemporary theorist on narcissism. Kohut holds that there are two lines of development involved here, one arising from normal infantile narcissism, which can lead to higher forms of healthy narcissism. The other line goes from infantile narcissism to object love, as Freud foresaw. Kohut states that these two lines of development coexist in every individual, that they may produce different problems, and that, at least in pathological narcissism, they have to be treated separately.

Mahler, in 1955, introduced the concept of "the separation-individuation phase," following the symbiotic phase. She described it as "a kind of second birth experience . . . a hatching . . . as inevitable as is biological birth."[22] More recently, she and her co-workers have considered the two processes somewhat separately. Individuation is described as the developmental process, which "consists of those achievements marking the child's assumption of his own individual characteristics."[23] On the basis of extensive observations of normal mother-child interactions, Mahler et al. say:

. . . We were most impressed by the tenacity of the pressure that the thrust of the individuation process exerts from the differentiation subphase onward. This finding caused us to regard *individuation* as an innate given, which reveals itself with particular force in the beginning of life and which seems to continue during the entire life cycle (Mahler is quoting Erikson here) (1959).[4, 23]

Individuation is conceived of as a complementary process to separation; it is "the child's emergence from the symbiotic fusion with the mother," beginning at about four or five months. Separation and individuation are seen as "intertwined but not identical developmental processes" (p. 4). Mahler et al. say:

We refer to the psychological birth of the individual as the separation-individuation process: the establishment of a sense of separateness from, and relation to, a world of reality, particularly with regard to the experience of *one's own body* and to the principal representative of the world as the infant experiences it, the *primary love object*. Like any intrapsychic process, this one reverberates throughout the life cycle.[23]

Mahler et al. hypothesize that "normal separation-individuation is the first crucial prerequisite for the development and maintenance of the 'sense of identity' defined as referring to

the earliest awareness of a sense of being, of entity—a feeling that includes in part, we believe, a cathexis of the body with libidinal energy. It is not a sense of *who* I am but *that* I am; as such, this is the earliest step in the process of the unfolding of individuality."[23]

The development of the self, of an intact sense of identity, as Mahler et al. have detailed it, thus takes place in the context of object relations. The normal mother is seen as having a "catalyzing function" in "facilitating not only the separateness of the child but also the specific patterning of his individuating personality by complementarity, contrast, identification or disidentification (Mahler is quoting Greenson, 1968)."[7,] [23] It is this facilitating function of the mother (necessarily including her own problems and inadequacies) that interacts with the infant's constitutional endowment and potential growth so that both normal self- and object relations can become vital parts of the ego's structure. Thus, Mahler says:

The normal separation-individuation process, following upon a developmentally normal symbiotic period, involves the child's achievement of separate functioning in the presence of, and with the emotional availability of the mother (Mahler, 1963);[19] the child is continually confronted with minimal threats of object loss (which every step of the maturational process seems to entail). In contrast to situations of traumatic separation, however, this normal separation-individuation process takes place in the setting of a developmental readiness for, and pleasure in, independent functioning.[23]

This emphasis on pleasure in independent functioning with the assistance of the mother could be seen as a counterbalance to the more familiar emphasis on optimal frustration as a vital component in bringing about a sense of separateness and fostering the growth of ego functions such as frustration tolerance, capacity for delay, reality testing, and anticipation of the future. Although optimal frustration is certainly a necessary and inevitable process, given life's vicissitudes, it has sometimes seemed that the qualification *optimal* has been forgotten and the focus on frustration per se has become excessive, both in regard to child rearing and in some treatment approaches to neurosis and the more severe disturbances. It is particularly in this respect that the concept of object relations as a catalyzing force in bringing about ego development may have led to an over-emphasis on the ungratifying and lonely aspects of separation, whether from mother or from the therapist. I believe that an appropriate concern for self relations, as an alternate term for healthy narcissism, can temper the deprivational aspects of object relations with an equal emphasis on the gratifications of independent functioning and fulfilling self relations.

Mahler's concept of secondary narcissism seems most relevant here.

As I noted, Freud used this term to mean the withdrawal of libido from an object after excessive frustration and a turning back of the libido on the self. Mahler suggests that secondary narcissism begins in the latter part of the symbiotic stage, when the infant starts to emerge from the omnipotent dual unity of symbiotic primary narcissism. In secondary narcissism the dawning of object relations along with self relations seems to start. Mahler says:[23] "The infant takes his own body, as well as the mother, as the object of his secondary narcissism." She adds: "Only when the body becomes the object of the infant's secondary narcissism, via the mother's loving care, does the external object become eligible for identification."

The libidinization of the infant's body through the mother's care very much involves the mother's "holding behavior," which Mahler calls "the symbiotic organizer—the midwife of individuation, of psychological birth."[23] Many types of "holding behavior" were observed in Mahler's research. One mother did not cradle the baby while breast-feeding but kept her arms free. The baby did not smile for a long time, perhaps reflecting the mother's ambivalence about wanting to hold the baby's body close. Another mother did not breast-feed but seemed to enjoy holding her little son, smiling and talking to him, cradling him even as she diapered him. Mahler reports that the little boy seemed happy and developed a specific smiling response very early. The related tender holding behavior seemed more important than breast-feeding when the latter was done in a mechanical way. The baby's affective responses in terms of specific smiling or not smiling to the caring or uncaring quality of the mother's physical ministrations are one clue to the elusive process of the gradual building up of psychic self-representations separate from the representations of mother, Mahler believes. It can also be a clue as to how the baby's self-image will be cathected as an adult.

Kohut[14] and Marian Tolpin[26] suggest the concept of "transmuting internalization." This involves a process where the mother's capacity to reduce physical and psychological tensions in the infant, (e.g., in soothing the infant to sleep) are gradually taken over by the baby through a manageable, bit-by-bit withdrawal of the mother's ministrations. In this way psychic structure develops, enabling the baby to soothe itself more and more. One could say that the care-taking, soothing functions of Winnicott's "good enough mother" have been internalized as a part of the self-representations thus providing a foundation for sound self relations later on. We are all familiar with patients who neglect themselves and appear unable to care for themselves, often despite adequate functioning with respect to others. They seem not only to have identified with their uncaring mothers but, as Kohut suggests, they may lack the psychic structure requisite for self-caring.

Mahler found, in her observations of child-mother interactions, that in focusing on the baby's movements, she and her co-workers could sometimes see "in *statu nascendi* affectomotor self-libidinization, which may be a forerunner of integration of body-self feelings." Both *in vivo* and in films, there are episodes as follows:

the 5-to-8-month-old, surrounded by the admiring and libidinally mirroring friendly adults, seemed electrified and stimulated by this mirroring admiration. This was evident by his excited kicking and flailing with the extremities, and stretching with an exaltedly pleasurable affect. This obvious tactile kinesthetic stimulation of his body-self, we believe, may promote differentiation and integration of his body image.[23]

This would seem to be an impressive validation of Freud's belief that the ego is first and foremost a "body ego"[6] as well as Kohut's concept[14] of how a cohesive self becomes integrated, on a bodily basis, through "the gleam in the mother's eye." Kohut proposes that this gleam "mirrors the child's exhibitionistic display, and other forms of maternal participation in and response to the child's narcissistic-exhibitionistic enjoyment (and) confirms the child's self-esteem."[14]

Mahler et al. cite unpublished research findings by McDevitt on babies' reactions to their mirror images. Before six months, a baby put on a mattress before a mirror becomes excited and flails its arms just as the baby previously cited reacted to admiring, mirroring adults. Later, Mahler et al. note, at eight months, "his movements slow down and he appears to become thoughtful as he seems to relate his own body movements to the movement of the image in the mirror." At nine to ten months, the baby makes deliberate movements, observing its image, as if "experimenting with, sorting out and clarifying for himself the relationship between himself and 'the image.' " Mahler et al. suggest that "mirror reactions are most relevant for following the process of self-representations and differentiating these from object representations." All of these findings seem to show the basis in the early stages of what Freud[5] described as the later tendency toward the narcissistic object choice where a person takes as a love object either himself or what he himself is, was, or would like to be. Freud says:

We say that a human being has originally two sexual objects—himself and the woman who nurses him—and in doing so we are postulating a primary narcissism in everyone, which may in some cases manifest itself in a dominating fashion in his object-choice.

Kohut, in line with Freud, believes that the fascination with oneself, in terms of body image and psychic achievements, is a natural phase of early development that can become fixated and repressed as an unconscious "grandiose self." This fixation is believed to occur when the child is confronted with massive disapproval, rejection, and neglect instead of the interest and encouragement needed to develop stable, libidinally cathected self-representations that lead to the integration in his or her ego of reliable self-esteem. In treating narcissistic personalities, Kohut[14] sees the patient's developmental need for acceptance of his or her infantile, exhibitionistic, grandiose self expressed in the "mirror transference." This may take the form of an archaic merger with the analyst experienced as a part of the patient's emerging omnipotent self, much as the baby appears to experience the good symbiotic mother. A less archaic form of the mirror transference is described by Kohut as the "alter ego or twinship" type, where the patient "assumes that the analyst is either like him or similar to him." In the treatment of narcissistic personalities, dreams or fantasies expressing wishes for a twin relationship would seem to be a possible intrapsychic corroboration of Freud's hypothesis about the narcissistic object choice as well as of Mahler et al.'s findings about the way babies observe themselves in a mirror and react with libidinal excitement and involvement. What Kohut describes as the most mature form of the mirror transference is where the analyst is clearly experienced "as a separate person" but, as Hartmann, the father of ego psychology, would say, on a need-gratifying level.

Kohut reminds us that the mother who appropriately responds to the child's exhibitionistic, body-integrating needs at this stage confirms the child's self esteem and, through a gradual selectivity of response, "begins to channel it in realistic directions." Similarly, the analyst working with this type of mirror transference is warned against prematurely demonstrating the unrealistic nature of the patient's needs and expectations before the patient has had a chance to bring the unconscious grandiose self out of repression and accept it as a necessary part of his or her early development. Only in this way, Kohut suggests, can the narcissistic libido fixated to the repressed pathological structure be made available to the ego for a fuller development of stable self and object relationships and other ego functions. The traditional interpretation of such grandiose needs in a narcissistic personality (e.g., the need to command another's admiration as a defense against an underlying oedipal conflict) usually elicits narcissistic rage from the patient which may be expressed in cold withdrawal and silence. The patient feels criticized for expressing what to him or her is a real, albeit, infantile, narcissistic need for approval. The patient also feels abandoned by the analyst who is not attuned to his or her needs for mirroring, as presumably mother had not been either. The result of such unattuned interpretations is not eventual insight nor even the mobilization of the more usual defenses against anxiety, but a withdrawal from the narcissistic transference and a re-repression of the emerging grandiose self. Such manifestations of narcissistic rage as a response to inappropriate interpretations are often involved in the stalemates or failures that have arisen in the treatment of narcissistic personalities.

Kohut believes that narcissistic rage is a reaction to feelings of helplessness.[14,15] The helplessness is believed to arise, particularly in relation to the unconscious grandiose self structure, out of the need to control others, as, ideally, one would like to control one's own body and mind. Therefore any real or imagined obstacle to such total control touches off a drop in self-esteem that is experienced as catastrophic, just as any inadequacy or failure perceived in one's body or mind may arouse feelings of intense helplessness. We might think here of Hartmann's concept[8] of the adaptive function of a defense mechanism (i.e., that the individual adapts to his or her experienced environment either through changing himself or herself or seeking to change the environment). Narcissistic rage might be seen, then, as a primitive defense against acknowledging the limitations of oneself as a separate, imperfect being in a world of imperfect people. Kohut says:

The enemy . . . who calls forth the archaic rage of the narcissistically vulnerable is seen by him not as an autonomous source of impulsions, but as a *flaw in a narcissistically perceived reality.* He is a recalcitrant part of an expanded self over which he expects to exercise full control and whose mere independence or other-ness is an offense.[15]

Kohut suggests that certain self-mutilations and suicides may be seen as expressions of narcissistic rage turned against the imperfect and therefore shameful self. He suggests that in self-mutilation, a "breakup of the body-self has occurred and that the fragments of the body-self which cannot be retained within the total organization of the body-self become an unbearably painful burden and are therefore removed" (e.g., the rejected, therefore evil, penis). Suicides arising from narcissistic rage, Kohut proposes, are "based on the loss of the libidinal cathexis of the self." He says that characteristically "these suicides are preceded not by guilt feelings but by feelings of unbearable emptiness and deadness or by intense shame, i.e., by the signs of profound disturbance in the realm of the libidinal cathexis of the self."[15]

The intensity of the aggressive and libidinal drive manifestations in pathological narcissism remind us of Hartmann's[9] concept of neutralization, defined as "the probably continuous process by which instinctual energy is modified and placed in the service of the ego." Neutralization, therefore, involves drive-taming processes that include the infant's developing capacity to delay drive discharge and use some of the drive energy to expand ego functions (e.g., when the hungry infant, turning to memory traces of past gratification, summons mother by a cry, the child has made the cry purposeful). In this connection, Blanck and Blanck[3] say "Object relations are built by transferring energy—which was formerly invested only in the drives—to the ego, for negotiation with the environment." Hartmann's concept of neutralization increases understanding of the more disturbed pathologies, including psychosis, since ego functions are impoverished because of the lack of neutralized energy normally accruing from the tamed drives. We have the situation where a weak rider is trying to master a wild horse.

A major problem with the hypothesized process of neutralization has been to conceptualize how it occurs, how the tamed drive energies are made available to the ego. It has been assumed that the drives are tamed through good enough mothering so that libido comes to predominate over aggression. But the psychic processes by which the tamed drives energize ego functions have only been hinted at. I suggest that it is through the developing positive cathexis of the self-representations, with growing self-experience and maternal encouragement of the expanding exploration of the body self, the mother and the world, that the tamed drive energies are channeled into the potential ego functions waiting to be triggered. As I indicated earlier in this article, Mahler seems to suggest this possibility in her concept of secondary narcissism and its implications for the baby's body image and for identification with mother.[18] In this connection, in a later study she says:

It is the mother's love of the toddler and her acceptance of his ambivalence that enable the toddler to cathect his self representation with neutralized energy. Where there is a great actual or fantasied lack of acceptance by the mother, there is a deficit in self-esteem and a consequent narcissistic vulnerability, which is also dependent on other factors, such as the drive distribution, the relative stability of self and object representations, and the course of subsequent development.[20]

As I noted earlier Kohut and Tolpin also suggest that in the concept of transmuting internalization it is through the soothing functions of the mother that the child is able to internalize these functions and eventually calm itself. In either case, the psychic receiving point of mother's loving care would be the self-representations, the awareness of the self having need tensions relieved, leading to what Sandler and Joffe[24] call the feeling of "well-being" and the quickened interest in exploring the world through expanding ego functions. The therapeutic implications are thought provoking: that encouraging the development of positively cathected self relations leading to stable self-esteem may be the most reliable way to foster neutralization and ego growth. Loewald[16] also suggests how this process may occur.

The child, by internalizing aspects of the parent, also internalizes the parent's image of the child, an image which is mediated to the child in the thousand different ways of being handled, bodily and emotionally. . . . The child begins to experience himself as a centered unit by being centered upon.

In proposing that it is the *positive* cathexis of the self-representations through attuned mothering that triggers ego functions, rather than the *libidinal* cathexis *per se,* I am allowing for the inclusion of both drives, the aggressive as well as the libidinal. This is designed to take account of the fact that attuned mothering fosters the development of individuation as the child moves toward autonomy and the consequent intrapsychic separation of self and object representations, while activating the ego functions involved. This proposal devolves upon the ego-psychological concept that the aggressive drive is related to growth as well as destruction. As I indicated earlier in this article, Mahler has conceptualized the separation-individuation phase as "the psychological birth of the infant.[22,23] She has come to conceive of individuation as an "intertwined but not identical" process with respect to separation and, in a footnote (p. 9)[23] she says: "We know now that the drive is not toward separation per se, but the innate given is the drive toward individuation which cannot be achieved without autonomous separation."

The growth-fostering role of the aggressive drive has also been elaborated upon by Gertrude and Rubin Blanck[3] who say:

. . . While *neutralized libido* builds object relations, *neutralized aggression* powers the developmental thrust toward separation-individuation. This is dramatically evident when the eighteen-month-old infant, in identification with the aggressor, begins to say "no." We have described how opposition is to be welcomed and supported as it proceeds further into the neutralized mode. Each step in differing with the object aids differentiation. At the Twenty-seventh International Congress of Psycho-Analysis, the theme of which was *aggression,* R. Blanck said:
1. Even though it awaits validation from biology, it has been postulated that the aggressive drive serves the aim of identity formation by providing the impetus for separation individuation. This view extends our thinking about the aggressive drive into the area of study of its role in ego development. Thus, aggression may no longer be regarded as stimulating solely hostile, pain-inflicting wishes, but as having the more positive aim of serving ego development as well.

The aggressive and libidinal drives of the narcissistic personality seem clearly to be more in the instinctual than in the neutralized mode, which would account for the intense rage at frustration and the overpowering quality of libidinal attractions, often followed by swift disappointment. As I noted before, Kohut sees narcissism as following a different developmental line from object cathexis. He says: "Narcissism . . . is defined not by the target of the instinctual investment (i.e., whether it is the subject himself or other people) but by the nature or quality of the instinctual charge."[14] With narcissistic rage, we have seen that it involves the need for complete control over others, as one needs to control one's own body and mind. Narcissistic libido often takes the form of idealizing an omnipotent other, and this tendency is activated in what Kohut calls the idealizing transference. Here the analyst becomes the omnipotent, idealized parent imago in a self object relation in which the patient experiences himself or herself as part of the analyst's perceived perfection and thus seeks to reinstate the lost symbiotic paradise. Like the grandiose self in the mirror transference, the patient's longing to merge with an idealized parent is also repressed. Unlike Freud and, as we will see, unlike Kernberg, Kohut advocates that the patient's idealization of the analyst be allowed to flower and take its full course, thus permitting the gradual disillusionment in the idealized parent imago that the patient should have experienced in normal development. Instead, Kohut stresses, as Edith Jacobson[12] did earlier, that the abrupt disillusionment in the parents at the critical toddler stage when the child becomes more aware of its own helplessness, leads to premature idealization either of parent imagoes or of the self as a perfect substitute for the disappointing parents. Treatment, therefore, is designed to reactivate the pathological structures and neutralize them gradually so that stable self-esteem and more realistic goals of achievement may be integrated into the ego and superego. The analyst's role is seen as helping the patient to accept either his or her own need to idealize others or to idealize himself or herself as part of normal development, which was thwarted. Unlike Kernberg, Kohut does not focus on the underlying aggression in these disorders but lets it manifest itself and relates it to disappointment either in the idealized analyst or in the idealized self. Kohut believes that the hyper-sensitivity of these patients calls for great empathy and tact on the part of the analyst, and he warns of the countertransference pitfalls arising when the analyst feels that he or she is only a part object or an impersonal function rather than a separate human being for the patient. The analyst's goal is to help the patient achieve a higher form of narcissism (i.e., a sound libidinal cathexis of the self and stable self-esteem, which would include neutralization of the narcissistic rage) as well as a release of the sublimatory potential in satisfying creative activity. Kohut notes that improvement in object relations is often a secondary consequence of his treatment approach, but it is not his goal.

Kernberg is also a contemporary theorist who has revived interest in narcissism both as a pathology and as a developmental fact. Like Kohut, Kernberg stresses that narcissistic disorders can be effectively dealt with, using a modified psychoanalytic approach. Kernberg[13] describes the narcissistic personalities' main problem as "the disturbance of their self-regard in connection with specific disturbances in their object rela-tionships." These patients are seen as very envious of "other people who seem to have things they do not have or who simply seem to enjoy their lives." This envy, of course, extends to the analyst, and one of

Kernberg's main concerns in treating such patients is to make them aware of how they envy the analyst's attributes even while devaluing the treatment. The combination of envy and devaluation is regarded by Kernberg as a very tough defense against becoming dependent on the analyst and thus allowing the treatment to have any impact for constructive change. Fear of dependence in these patients, Kernberg believes, arises from severe oral deprivation in the first year of life and leads to overwhelming aggression, which he thinks may be constitutional as well as the product of environmental neglect.

The narcissistic personality handles this aggression with primitive defenses, including the splitting of self- and object representations into all good and all bad, which leads to a lack of integration, dissociation, and alternating ego states in the perception both of the self and of other people. Today the analyst is an angel, tomorrow he or she will be beneath contempt, with only a vague recognition on the patient's part of this sudden affective change and little awareness of the reasons for it. The smooth social façade of the narcissistic personality tends to conceal the splitting operations with an affective emptiness in relating to the analyst. Kernberg advocates an alertness in pointing out this defense to the patient and eventually making him or her aware of the deep underlying aggression and the fear of dependency.

The idealization of the analyst is also regarded as a defense against the underlying envy and devaluation of the analyst, which must be consistently pointed out. Another major defense is projective identification, in which the patient projects on the analyst either the image of the patient's own worthless, infantile self, or omnipotent self image. Kernberg says that "in their fantasies, these patients identify themselves with their own ideal self images in order to deny normal dependency on external objects. . . . At the same time, the remnants of the unacceptable self images are repressed and projected onto external objects which are devaluated." These defensive operations, Kernberg points out, interfere with the normal development of the ego ideal as a part of the superego. The confusion and condensation in the narcissistic personality prevents the development of an integrated superego and makes for an aggressive, primitive superego that is easily reprojected in a paranoid fashion. Narcissistic patients, Kernberg believes, tend to have a kind of pseudomorality designed to secure admiration and ward off criticism.

Kernberg, like Kohut, regards the nature of the transference as a most important criterion in the diagnosis of narcissistic personalities. Kernberg believes the transference is essentially at a preoedipal level where the analyst is related to as a need-gratifying object and not as a person in his or her own right. Kernberg's objective with the narcissistic personality is, in a sense, to help the patient become a full person, with more mature object relations, capable of feeling guilt, dependent needs, and empathy with others. Kernberg, therefore, finds the presence of guilt in the beginning phase of treatment as a good prognostic sign and its absence as a somber warning. The treatment of narcissistic personalities, from Kernberg's standpoint, is a taxing one, fraught with countertransference pitfalls and intense pressures when the patient begins to face his or her aggression and fear of dependence. At this point, the patient may become suicidal or leave treatment. Kernberg says: "the more a person wishes to overcome feelings of emptiness, difficulties in empathizing with others, and his internal coldness, the better the prognosis."

With respect to pathological narcissism, Stolorow[25] has suggested that Kernberg's approach accords with the more traditional concept of narcissism as a defense against object-related instinctual conflicts. Certainly, Kernberg has focused attention on certain primitive defenses in the narcissistic personality that make treatment especially difficult, and he regards the oral aggression and fear of dependency as the central target for treatment, with the achievement of mature object relations as the goal. Stolorow sees Kohut as presenting "perhaps the most detailed account of how narcissistic patterns function to maintain the self-representation."

My own position, as I stated at the outset, is a concern with the relatively neglected field of self-relations. In line with the approach to self- and object representations as dynamic contents of the ego, developed by Hartmann, Jacobson, Mahler, and Blanck and Blanck, we can recognize that self-relations are just as important an ego function as object relations. Jacobson is in accord with Freud's recognition of healthy narcissism as a form of positive self-regard. She states it succinctly with, I think, implications that we are only beginning to appreciate. She says: "Normal ego functioning presupposes a sufficient, evenly distributed, enduring, libidinous cathexis of both object- and self-representations."[11] This suggests, in terms of an evenly distributed libidinal cathexis between self- and object representations, that normally we should love ourselves as much as we love others.

Jacobson's concept of an evenly distributed (i.e., fifty-fifty split) of libidinal cathexis between one's self and other people represents a departure from Freud's economics of love, where he saw the state of being in love as a depletion of self-regard in favor of the loved one. She seems to be suggesting that a healthy narcissism is a necessary foundation for an enduring love relation. Jacobson also recognizes that a libidinal approach to another person requires not only a hypercathexis of the object, perhaps what Freud would regard as an overvaluation of the other person, but also "the spur of a concomitant, libidinous hypercathexis of the self-representations which will encourage and guarantee the success of the action." The "libidinous cathexis extends to the representations, on the one hand, of the body parts and organs to be employed for the action and, on the other hand, of the whole self as an entity; the rising cathexis of the latter manifests itself in general feelings of increased self-confidence preceding and stimulating first the cathexis of the executive organs and then the action." The idea of a hypercathexis of the self, of heightened self-confidence as an important and perhaps necessary aspect of successful object relations, emphasizes again the necessity for healthy narcissism as an indispensable component in mature object relations.

Mahler has provided us with significant developmental findings for a greater understanding of how mature self relations and a stable sense of identity can build up from early self-representations under the pressure of the innate thrust toward individuation through psychic separation from the mother. The separation-individuation phase is divided into four subphases. Mahler has shown how the baby, with the crucial encouragement of the mother, gradually moves out from the omnipotent, symbiotic dual unity toward differentiating its body from mother and alertly noticing the surrounding world in the differentiation subphase. In the practicing subphase, the infant crawls and then toddles out to explore the world with the elation of secondary narcissism while retaining the anchorage in mother by checking back occasionally to be reassured of her presence. In the third subphase of rapprochement, the infant's increasing self-need to communicate its adventures in the world to mother and the deepening longing to be with her foreshadow the oedipal conflict and the open-ended fourth subphase of the consolidation of individuality and the beginnings of emotional object constancy.

Hartmann defined object constancy as the constant cathexis of the mental representation of the object, starting with mother, despite the frustrations the object may present and with neutralized love subsuming neutralized aggression.[9] The achievement of object constancy is regarded as an indication of the full psychic separation of object representations and self-representations and the arrival at a mature level of object relations. Mahler has given us the term "self constancy" as a counterpart of object constancy. She says:

> The task to be achieved by development in the course of the normal separation-individuation process is the establishment of both a measure of object constancy and a measure of self constancy, an enduring individuality as it were. The latter achievement consists of the attainment of the two levels of the sense of identity: (1) the awareness of being a separate and individual entity, and (2) a beginning awareness of a gender-defined self-identity. . . .
>
> We must emphasize again that the development of the sense of self is the prototype of an eminently personal, internal experience that is difficult, if not impossible, to trace in observational studies, as well as in the reconstructive psychoanalytic situation. It reveals itself by its failures much more readily than by its normal variations.

Just as object constancy requires acceptance of the object's needs, despite the frustrations this may impose, so we might think of the necessity of self-constancy as involving increased tolerance of our shortcomings and a self-love or appreciation subsuming our disappointments in ourselves. It may be that the current interest in narcissism is heralding a wider recognition of the developmental need for healthy self relations and is looking toward a new era in therapeutic technique as well as in theory. Hartmann stressed the adaptive functions of the defensive system, and this led Gertrude Blanck (1966) to suggest that the adaptive approach could be used even in the analysis of neurotics in order to help the patient accept what is often experienced as a critical attack on his or her mode of living in the analysis of defenses. Similar concern for the preservation and enhancement of the positive cathexis of the self in treatment, as Kohut has stressed, may make for important changes in technique and more success, especially in treating depression where the libidinal cathexis of the self may be so close to extinction that the forces for life may falter dangerously. The concept of self relations also could conceivably lead us to an increased fostering of the growth of that remarkable psychic organization, the ego, not only for coping with life's vicissitudes but also for an expanding appreciation of human resources.

REFERENCES

1. Benet W. R. (Ed.). *The Reader's Encyclopedia*. New York: Crowell, 1948.
2. Blanck, G. Some Technical Implications of Ego Psychology. *International Journal of Psycho-Analysis,* Vol. 47, 1966, pp. 6–13.
3. Blanck, G. and R. Blanck. *Ego Psychology: Theory and Practice.* New York: Columbia University Press, 1974.
4. Erikson, E. H. Identity and the Life Cycle. *Psychological Issues,* Monograph No. 1. New York: International Universities Press, 1959.
5. Freud, S. On Narcissism: An Introduction (1914). *Standard Edition,* Vol. 14. London: Hogarth Press, 1957, pp. 73–102.
6. ——The Ego and the Id (1923). *Standard Edition,* Vol. 19. London: Hogarth Press, 1961, pp. 13–66.
7. Greenson, R. R. Dis-identification. *International Journal of Psycho-Analysis,* Vol. 49, 1968, pp. 370–374.
8. Hartmann, H. Comments on the Psychoanalytic Theory of the Ego (1950), *Essays on Ego Psychology.* New York: International Universities Press, 1964, pp. 113–41.
9. ——Contribution to the Metapsychology of Schizophrenia (1953). *Essays on Ego Psychology.* New York: International Universities Press, 1964, pp. 182–206.
10. Holzknecht, E. J., and N. E. McClure (Ed.). Hamlet. In *Selected Plays of Shakespear,* Vol. 1. New York: American Book Company, 1936, pp. 420–559.
11. Jacobson, E. The Self and the Object World. In *The Psychoanalytic Study of the Child,* Vol. 9. New York: International Universities Press, 1954, pp. 75–127.
12. ——*The Self and the Object World.* New York: International Universities Press, 1964.
13. Kernberg, O. *Borderline Conditions and Pathological Narcissism.* New York: Aronson, 1975.
14. Kohut, H. *The Analysis of the Self.* New York: International Universities Press, 1971.
15. ——Thoughts on Narcissism and Narcissistic Rage. In *The Psychoanalytic Study of the Child,* Vol. 27. New York: Quadrangle Press, 1972, pp. 360–398.
16. Loewald, H. W. On the Therapeutic Action of Psychoanalysis, *International Journal of Psycho-Analysis,* Vol. 41, 1960, pp. 16–33.
17. Mahler, M. S. Autism and Symbiosis: Two Extreme Disturbances of Identity (1958). In *The Selected Papers of Margaret S. Mahler,* Vol. One. New York: Aronson, 1979, pp. 169–181.
18. ——On Sadness and Grief in Infancy and Childhood: Loss and Restoration of the Symbiotic Love Object (1961). In *The Selected Papers of Margaret S. Mahler,* Vol. One. New York: Aronson, 1979, pp. 261–279.
19. ——Thoughts about Development and Individuation. In *The Psychoanalytic Study of the Child,* Vol. 18. New York: International Universities Press, 1963, pp. 307–324.
20. ——*On Human Symbiosis and the Vicissitudes of Individuation: Vol. 1, Infantile Psychosis.* New York: International Universities Press, 1968.
21. ——On the First Three Phases of the Separation-Individuation Process. In Sci-

entific Proceedings-Panel Reports, reported by Muriel C. Winestine. *Journal of the American Psychoanalytic Association,* Vol. 21, 1971, pp. 135–154.

22. Mahler, M. S. and B. J. Gosliner. On Symbiotic Child Psychosis: Genetic, Dynamic, and Restitutive Aspects (1955). In The *Selected Papers of Margaret S. Mahler,* Vol. One. New York: Aronson, 1979, pp. 109–129.

23. Mahler, M. S., F. Pine and A. Bergman. *The Psychological Birth of the Human Infant: Symbiosis and Individuation.* New York: Basic Books, 1975.

24. Sandler, J. and W. G. Joffe. Toward a Basic Psychoanalytic Model. *International Journal of Psycho-Analysis,* Vol. 50, 1969, pp. 79–90.

25. Stolorow, R. D. Toward a Functional Definition of Narcissism. *International Journal of Psycho-Analysis.* Vol. 56, 1975, pp. 179–185.

26. Tolpin, M. On the Beginnings of a Cohesive Self. In *The Psychoanalytic Study of the Child,* Vol. 26. New York: Quadrangle Press, 1972, pp. 316–352.

DIFFERENCES IN THEORETICAL EMPHASIS

Part III, "Differences in Theoretical Emphasis," is divided into three sections, the first of which examines the "self"—its structure and functional supports—as the major component of narcissism. In Ch. 7, Kohut and Wolf provide an up-to-date summary of the psychology of the self, and offer, from this perspective, a classification of narcissistic character pathology. They succinctly review the source of the emergence of a psychology of the self from the discovery of specific narcissistic (i.e., selfobject) transferences in treatment which reflect a weakened or defective self; then they differentiate secondary (i.e., reactive) from primary self-disturbances. Among the primary self-disturbances, which also include the psychoses and borderline conditions, the authors consider only the narcissistic behavior and personality disorders to be analyzable. They explain this finding as a reflection of relative self-resiliency in narcissistic disorders, with only temporary fragmentation or depletion, and with the capacity to form the selfobject transferences (e.g., mirror and idealizing) noted above. Following a discussion of the etiology of self-pathology in terms of sustained empathic failures by parents who themselves generate a pathogenic developmental environment, the authors present a categorization of the patholgy of the self, which is divided into personality and behavioral disorders. In this formulation, new and challenging terms are introduced (such a *fragmenting, overstimulated,* and *over-burdened* self; and *mirror-hungry, ideal-hungry, merger-hungry,* and *contact-shunning* personalities).

These nosological entities represent an attempt to place the various manifestations of disorders of the self into a descriptive, clinically recognizable context. Also, they are relied upon to make a clear diagnostic statement from a self-psychological perspective. A section follows on the treatment of the narcissistic personality and behavior disorders, in which the authors advocate facilitating the emergence of narcissistic pathology through evolution and modification of the selfobject transferences, with acceptance, by the therapist, and genetic interpretation leading to change through the process of "transmuting internalization."

The essay by Kohut and Wolf represents a concise statement of the "state of the art" in self-psychology in the late 1970s and, as such, is a useful update on Kohut's earlier thinking (see Ch. 3). Again, we see the nonjudgmental attitude towards narcissistic manifestations, and treatment based on the reemergence of unintegrated grandiosity and idealizing needs in the selfobject transferences. According to this position, cure is achieved through the gradual integration of these experiences into the self. The cure attains further cohesiveness and vigor from the available selfobject functions provided by the therapist. This self-psychological perspective will be seen to differ dramatically from that of Kernberg (Chs. 9 and 10), who sees the narcissistic manifestations (which, incidentally, do not significantly differ from those described by Kohut) as being fundamentally pathological in origin, and who advocates confrontation and interpretation of excessive aggression. Also, by the time of this essay, Kohut and Wolf had abandoned the conflict-drive model of psychic energy, another major difference from Kernberg.

Stolorow (Ch. 8) further elaborates the viewpoint that the *economic* concept of narcissism, based on drive theory, is outmoded, and should be replaced by a *functional* framework which examines narcissism's utility to the sense of well-being of the self. He reviews the emphasis placed on self-esteem regulation by Freud and Reich, as noted earlier in my introduction, and suggests that narcissistic phenomena function "to maintain the cohesion, stability, and positive affective coloring of the self representation." To support this position, he refers to Pulver's paper (Ch. 4) and reinterprets the four categories of narcissism delineated—i.e., narcissism as sexual perversion, a mode of relating to objects, a developmental stage, and as self-esteem—in terms of their function with regard to the self. Stolorow views narcissism, not as a pathological diagnostic entity (as does Kernberg), but rather as "a dimension of psychopathology which cuts across all the traditional nosological entities." As such, he is firmly in agreement with Kohut's suggestion of a separate developmental line for narcissism, and, implicitly, would disagree with the diagnostic-categorization approach (Ch.

7). Finally, he suggests that the view of narcissism "in service of survival of the sense of self" is useful in helping to deal with counter-transference problems inherent in the therapist's reduction to the role of a function.

Stolorow's paper represents a further step in the evolution of self-psychological thinking away from conflict-drive metapsychology towards an essentially accepting position regarding narcissistic phenomena, and as an amplification of the central goal to create a new self-structure in psychotherapy with narcissistic patients. In addition, Stolorow presages the movement of self-psychology in subsequent theoretical applications beyond exclusive attention to narcissism, towards healthier, more mature, individuals.

The second section of this part presents an object relations perspective on narcissism, and includes two important contributions by Otto Kernberg (Chs. 9 and 10). Kernberg defines patients with narcissistic personalities as having disturbances of their self-regard and disturbed object relationships and manifesting a high degree of self-reference in interaction with other people. According to Kernberg, projection of oral rage, represented as anger and resentment towards others, is central to their psychopathology. "In their fantasies, patients identify themselves with their own ideal self images in order to deny dependency on external objects." Their superego is primitive and aggressive, deriving from intensely oral-aggressive drive fixations. For these patients, there is fusion of ideal self, ideal object, and self images; Kernberg does not take a stand as to whether this pathology reflects constitutionally strong aggressive drive manifestations, or severe (parental) frustration. Denial of dependency is based on a fear of envying the needed "other." Therapeutic implications of this viewpoint mandate that devaluation, anger, envy, and noninvolvement with the therapist/analyst be vigorously confronted and interpreted, along with the underlying aggression and dependency needs.

Differences between Kernberg and Kohut can clearly be seen. First, Kernberg much more strongly emphasizes the pathological (vs. the self-affirming) nature of narcissism, as well as its relationship to distorted object relations. No separate narcissistic line of development here! Narcissistic personalities are struggling with challenges of object love and dependency far more than with the fragile nature of their self-representation. The central issue for these patients is their oral aggression (i.e., untamed drives) as played out in the object world, not self-cohesion per se. Rather than inviting expression of unintegrated narcissistic yearnings, these manifestations must be confronted, interpreted, and brought under control.

In Ch. 10, Kernberg continues to elaborate narcissistic personality characteristics, including these patients with other, primitive, borderline types. He adopts Kohut's emphasis on grandiosity, but views this as inherently pathological, not as a normal developmental stage. Narcissistic rage is seen as a particularly poor prognosticator for analytic investigation, not simply as an expectable response to narcissistic injury in the course of treatment. He expands on the view that narcissistic and object investments occur simultaneously and must be explored in interaction with each other, relating the internalization of object relations to libidinal and aggressive drive derivatives. Idealization, too, is pathological in these patients, representing projective identification of grandiosity onto the analyst, whom the patient strives to control. "Unacceptable elements of the real self are dissociated and/or repressed," leading to devaluation and contempt towards external objects. Kernberg suggests that Kohut bypasses rage and deprecation in the transference, implicitly gratifying the primitive narcissistic demands.

The differences between Kernberg and Kohut thus seem clear-cut, with very different therapeutic implications. Teicholz (1978), however, has noted some very provocative similarities. Kohut and Kernberg believe that grandiosity lies at the heart of narcissism; both advocate bringing that grandiosity into the treatment situation rather than causing it to be banished or repressed. They agree on the potential analyzability of narcissistic disorders, thus differing from the more traditional view emanating from Freud that narcissistic patients are unable to form transference bonds to the analyst. Each acknowledges that "a somehow defective self is involved in pathological narcissism, [and] that archaically grandiose self-images and archaically idealized parent images play a psychopathological role . . ." (Teicholz, 1978). Finally, apathy towards, and denigration of the "real person" of the analyst is acknowledged by each, leading to countertransference problems specific to the treatment of pathological narcissism. Ornstein's (1974) question as to whether the two are describing the same patients should be noted.

Modell (Ch. 11) further contributes to our thinking about the relationship of narcissism to object relations through his attention to affects and the narcissistic patient's defense against them as reflected in a disavowal of the need for personal relationships. These patients establish an early, precocious sense of self, leading to a denial of object need, or what Modell calls "an illusion of self-sufficiency." He suggests that this illusion may reflect the environmental trauma of "the mother's failure to accept the child's separateness and autonomy, resulting in a fear of the mother's intrusiveness." This fear is also a barrier to the formation of a therapeutic alliance with such patients, who resist the therapist's "intrusiveness" experienced through interpretations and other therapeutic interventions.

Thus, Modell focuses on the haughty and disdainful aloofness of many narcissistic patients, which, he feels, reflects their defense against genuine affects from a fear of object intrusiveness. This perspective differs from that of Kernberg, who emphasizes the need to confront and interpret such patients' primitive rage and aggression. Yet both underscore the importance of the object representation to the narcissistic patient, differing in this way from Kohut's perspective.

In Ch. 12, Rothstein offers another view on the relevance of object relations to narcissism. Like Modell, he emphasizes the narcissistic response to separation anxiety, seeing separation as a loss of connectedness to the mother which, according to Rothstein, leads to "incorporative identification with the maternal object." However, he considers this incorporation an attempt to undo the object loss, with an illusion that the mother continues to exist within the "self-as-agent." Thus, the narcissistic feeling of perfection is aimed at restoring the predifferentiated sense of the self, fused with mother, as one. When maternal care is more narcissistic (i.e., less than adequately empathic), separation anxiety is greater, and the need for narcissistic investment in the self's sense of perfection is greater.

Thus we see an emphasis on the nature of object relatedness in the schema of narcissism as viewed by both Rothstein and Modell. While both emphasize the pathologic maternal relationship in the genesis of narcissistic phenomena, their views about attachment to the object are opposite. To Modell, inappropriate maternal intrusiveness leads to precocious (i.e., premature) attempts at separation and establishment of an independent self, with a haughty illusion of independence from others. To Rothstein, inadequate mothering leads to a fear of separation and a turning inward towards the fantasy of fused self-mother perfection. In each case, pathological narcissism is a manifestation of inadequate, unsatisfactory object relationships.

The third section of Part III deals with affective states. Certainly the contributions of Kernberg and Modell (Chs. 9, 10, and 11) also deal with affective considerations in narcissism, but their emphasis is more explicitly with the narcissistic manifestations towards objects. Miller (Ch. 13) emphasizes the relationship of grandiosity to depression in narcissistic disturbances representing loss of, or alienation from the self. Such patients regularly have been the product of narcissistic mothers, demonstrating grandiosity which leave them "excessively dependent on admiration from the object," and with "self-respect . . . dependent on qualities, functions and achievements which can suddenly fail." Miller sees depression as the constant companion of narcissistic grandiosity, appearing frequently when grandiosity breaks down, at other times as a phase repeatedly alternating with grandiosity, sometimes externalized in the person of an intimate companion, and in other cases split off from the ever-present grandiosity. Such depression is experienced whenever grandiosity fails, reflecting the patient's inevitable experience of a "false self" and underlying emptiness and despair. When depression and mourning are reached, however, there is hope for the successful treatment of the underlying narcissistic disturbance.

Miller's emphasis on depression in narcissistic disturbances is related to my own view of shame as the central affect in such patients (Ch. 13). While other authors have noted the presence of shame and shame vulnerability in narcissism (e.g., Chs. 2, 3, 9, 10, 13, 15, 16), I suggest that other affects of this disorder—rage and depression—are secondary to underlying shame and humiliation. Shame is here defined as "the affective response to falling short of a goal, to failure, to defect, to depletion of ideals. Shame motivates the individual to cover up, to hide, to withdraw." Since shame leads to concealment, it has been less fully appreciated than guilt in psychoanalytic treatment. Kohut's amplifications in self-psychology have created a framework which allows for the meaningful understanding and treatment of shame. For narcissistic patients, repeated failures to realize grandiose ambitions, the emptiness reflecting unattainable ideals, the absence of self-acceptance, lead to unmitigated shame. As Miller notes, such failures and emptiness lead as well to depression, but my observation is that depression is generated by the all-pervasive shame. However, I agree with Miller that the effective treatment of narcissistic disorders must somehow "reach behind" the manifest grandiosity to the underlying painful affects (e.g., shame, depression), and to the failures and anxieties which generate them.

A. Self and Identity

7. The Disorders of the Self and Their Treatment: An Outline

Heinz Kohut and Ernest S. Wolf

It is the aim of this survey to provide a summary of the concepts and theories of the psychoanalytic psychology of the self and of the clinical (diagnostic and therapeutic) formulations that are correlated to them. Although we wanted to be comprehensive and to convey a sense of the complexity of our subject matter, we tried to keep our presentation as brief as possible. While this goal needs no excuse, it may require a cautionary comment. In view of the fact that we had to keep our definitions terse and our formulations brief, we could not often indulge in the luxury of introducing qualifying statements. This is as we think it should be within the framework of a summarizing outline. It must be emphasized, however, that the paucity of restricting and modifying clauses does not imply any conviction on our part that we are presenting a finished or definitive system of thought. On the contrary, this survey should be considered to be a progress report about the present state of a step in the evolution of psychoanalysis that is itself only in its very beginning.

Why then a summary at such an early point? The answer to this question is simple. It is the very unsettledness of the state of scientific knowledge during a new developmental move that makes it advisable to take stock by dispassionately spelling out, simply and straightforwardly, the clinical discoveries that have been made and the theoretical constructions that have been formed. This stock-taking must, however, not lead to a hardening of our convictions. It should rather assist us in separating the wheat from the chaff—enable us to recognize those areas in which our investigations have been successful and those where they have so far failed. But let us now go to the heart of the matter and describe how the new psychology of the self came into being.

1. THE EMERGENCE OF A PSYCHOLOGY OF THE SELF

During recent years the psychoanalytic investigation of certain frequently encountered patients led to the recognition of a definable syndrome which at first appeared to be related to the psychoneuroses and
neurotic character disorders. It was clear from the outset that these
patients are characterized by a specific vulnerability: their self-esteem
is unusually labile and, in particular, they are extremely sensitive to
failures, disappointments and slights. It was, however, not the scrutiny
of the symptomatology but the process of treatment that illuminated
the nature of the disturbance of these patients. The analysis of the
psychic conflicts of these patients did not result in either the expected
amelioration of suffering or the hoped-for cessation of undesirable behaviour; the discovery, however, that these patients reactivated certain
specific narcissistic needs in the psychoanalytic situation, i.e. that they
established 'narcissistic transferences', made effective psychoanalytic
treatment possible. The psychopathological syndrome from which these
patients suffer was designated as *narcissistic personality disorder*. The
narcissistic transferences which are pathognomonic for these syndromes were subdivided into two types: (1) the *mirror transference* in
which an insufficiently or faultily responded to childhood need for a
source of accepting-confirming 'mirroring' is revived in the treatment
situation, and (2) the *idealizing transference* in which a need for merger
with a source of 'idealized' strength and calmness is similarly revived.
As the understanding of the symptomatology, core psychopathology,
and treatment of the narcissistic personality disorders increased, in
particular via the investigation of the narcissistic transferences, it became clear that the essence of the disturbance from which these patients
suffered could not be adequately explained within the framework of
classical drive-and-defense psychology. In view of the fact that it is a
weakened or defective self that lies in the centre of the disorder, explanations that focused on conflicts concerning either the libidinal or the
aggressive impulses of these patients could illuminate neither psychopathology nor treatment process. Some progress was made by expanding the classical libido theory and by revising the classical theory of
aggression. Specifically, the weakness of the self was conceptualized
in terms of its underlibidinization—as a cathectic deficit, to speak in
the terms of Freudian metapsychology—and the intense aggressions

encountered in the narcissistic personality disorders were recognized as the responses of the vulnerable self to a variety of injuries. The decisive steps forward in the understanding of these disorders, however, were made through the introduction of the concept of the selfobject and via the increasing understanding of the self in depth-psychological terms. *Selfobjects* are objects which we experienced as part of our self; the expected control over them is, therefore, closer to the concept of the control which a grown-up expects to have over his own body and mind than to the concept of the control which he expects to have over others. There are two kinds of selfobjects: those who respond to and confirm the child's innate sense of vigour, greatness and perfection; and those to whom the child can look up and with whom he can merge as an image of calmness, infallibility and omnipotence. The first type is referred to as the mirroring selfobject, the second as the idealized parent imago. The *self,* the core of our personality, has various constituents which we acquire in the interplay with those persons in our earliest childhood environment whom we experienced as selfobjects. A firm self, resulting from the optimal interactions between the child and his selfobjects is made up of three major constituents: (1) one pole from which emanate the basic strivings for power and success; (2) another pole that harbours the basic idealized goals; and (3) an intermediate area of basic talents and skills that are activated by the tension-arc that establishes itself between ambitions and ideals.

Faulty interaction between the child and his selfobjects result in a damaged self—either a diffusely damaged self or a self that is seriously damaged in one or the other of its continuents. If a patient whose self has been damaged enters psychoanalytic treatment, he reactivates the specific needs that had remained unresponded to by the specific faulty interactions between the nascent self and the selfobjects of early life—a selfobject transference is established.

Depending on the quality of the interactions between the self and its selfobjects in childhood, the self will emerge either as a firm and healthy structure or as a more or less seriously damaged one. The adult self may thus exist in states of varying degrees of coherence, from cohesion to fragmentation; in states of varying degrees of vitality, from vigour to enfeeblement; in states of varying degrees of functional harmony, from order to chaos. Significant failure to achieve cohesion, vigour, or harmony, or a significant loss of these qualities after they had been tentatively established, may be said to constitute a state of self disorder. The psychoanalytic situation creates conditions in which the damaged self begins to strive to achieve or to re-establish a state of cohesion, vigour and inner harmony.

Once the self has crystallized in the interplay of inherited and environmental factors, it aims towards the realization of its own specific programme of action—a programme that is determined by the specific intrinsic pattern of its constituent ambitions, goals, skills and talents, and by the tensions that arise between these constituents. The patterns of ambitions, skills and goals; the tensions between them; the programme of action that they create; and the activities that strive towards the realization of this programme are all experienced as continuous in space and time—they are the self, an independent centre of initiative, an independent recipient of impressions.

2. THE SECONDARY AND THE PRIMARY DISTURBANCES OF THE SELF

The experiential and behavioural manifestations of the *secondary disturbances of the self* are the reactions of a structurally undamaged self to the vicissitudes of life. A strong self allows us to tolerate even wide swings of self-esteem in response to victory or defeat, success or failure. And various emotions—triumph, joy; despair, rage—accompany these changes in the state of the self. If our self is firmly established, we shall neither be afraid of the dejection that may follow a failure nor of the expansive fantasies that may follow a success—reactions that would endanger those with a more precariously established self.

Among the secondary disturbances belong also the reactions of the self to physical illness or to the incapacities of a structural neurosis, e.g. the dejection or the anger experienced when incurable muscular paralysis or chronic neurotic anxiety inhibit a person from pursuing his central self-enhancing goals. And even certain reactions of relatively undamaged layers of the self to the consequences of its own primary disturbances—such as dejection over the fact that a damaged self's vulnerability has led to social isolation—should be counted among the secondary disturbances of the self.

The *primary disturbances of the self* can be divided into several subgroups, depending on the extent, severity, nature and distribution of the distrubance. If serious damage to the self is either permanent or protracted, and if no defensive structures cover the defect, the experiential and behavioural manifestations are those that are traditionally referred to as *the psychoses*. The nuclear self may have remained noncohesive (schizophrenia) either because of an inherent biological tendency, or because its totality and continuity were not responded to with even minimally effective mirroring in early life, or because of the interplay between or convergence of biological and environmental factors. It may have obtained a degree of cohesion but because of the interaction of inherent organic factors and a serious lack of joyful responses to its existence and assertiveness, it will be massively depleted of self-esteem and vitality ('empty' depression). It may have been almost totally deprived during the crucial periods of its formation of the repeated wholesome experience of participating in the calmness of an idealized adult (i.e. of a merger with an idealized selfobject), with the result, again decisively influenced by inherent biological factors, that an uncurbed tendency toward the spreading of unrealistically heightened self-acceptance (mania) or self-rejection and self-blame ('guilt'-depression) remains as a serious central weak spot in its organization.

A second subgroup of primary disorders of the self are the *borderline states*. Here the break-up, the enfeeblement, or the functional chaos of the nuclear self are also permanent or protracted, but, in contrast to the psychoses, the experiential and behavioural manifestations of the central defect are covered by complex defences. Although it is in general not advisable for the therapist to tamper with these protective devices, it is sometimes possible to make the patient's use of them more flexible by reconstructing the genesis of both the central vulnerability and of the chronic characterological defence. It may, for example, be helpful to the patient to understand the sequence of events, repeated on innumerable occasions, when as a child his need to establish an autonomous self was thwarted by the intrusions of the parental selfobject. At the very point, in other words, when the nascent self of the child required the accepting mirroring of its independence, the selfobject, because of its own incompleteness and fragmentation fears, insisted on maintaining an archaic merger.[1]

[1] Dr. Nathaniel J. London has questioned the 'writing style' of our paper. He thinks our language often suggests an athropomorphization of the concept 'self', in the same way that 'ego' used to be anthropomorphized. To illustrate his position he rewrote the

A significantly more resilient self is found in the next subgroup, the *narcissistic behaviour disorders,* even though the symptoms which these individuals display—e.g. perverse, delinquent or addictive behaviour—may expose them to grave physical and social dangers. But the underlying disorder, the break-up, enfeeblement or serious distortion of the self, is only temporary in these cases, and with the support of increasing insight into the genetic roots and the dynamic purpose of their symptomatic behaviour, they may become able to relinquish it and to substitute for it more mature and realistic supports for their self-esteem.

Closely related to the narcissistic behaviour disorders are the *narcissistic personality disorders* where break-up, enfeeblement or serious distortion of the self are also only temporary but where the symptoms—e.g. hypochondria, depression, hypersensitivity to slights, lack of zest—concern not primarily the actions and interactions of the individual but rather his psychological state.

Of the patients who suffer from disorders of the self, only those with narcissistic behaviour and personality disorders are capable of tolerating the frustrations of the reactivated narcissistic needs of their vulnerable self to which the working-through process in analysis exposes them

---

two sentences in our essay that precede the number in the text which leads to this note. Here is his version.

'It may, for example be helpful to the patient to understand the sequence of events, repeated on innumerable occasions, when as a child his need to establish an autonomous self was thwarted by an intrusive mother. At the very point, in other words, when the child required an accepting mirroring of his independence for the formation of his nascent self, his mother, because of her own incompleteness and fragmentation fears, insistently tried to achieve an archaic merger. Instead of serving as the source of a usable selfobject to the child, the mother provided an unmanageable and tyrannical selfobject which, among other ill-effects for development, left the child with an insatiable yearning for something that would allow him to feel whole and complete—something that he could only begin to define for himself in the nonintrusive atmosphere of the treatment situation.'

We fully agree with the spririt of Dr. London's critique—it is similar to Schafer's (1973)—and believe that it should be implemented, even in predominantly clinical communications, whenever such conceptual exactness can be adhered to without introducing undue stylistic complexity. But not at all cost, as an expression of a variant of that specific purity-of-thought-and-language morality of which Karl Kraus (see Janik & Toulmin, 1973, esp. pp. 67–91) was the most famous protagonist in our century. Since Dr. London can so easily grasp our meaning and translate it into more exact scientific language, we trust that others, too, will realize that the reifications of our language are not a manifestation of conceptual confusion but in the service of evocativeness and conciseness.

without a protracted fragmentation or depletion of the self. In other words, of all the primary disorders of the self only narcissistic behaviour and personality disorders are analysable.

3. THE AETIOLOGY OF SELF-PATHOLOGY

In view of the fact that the disorders of the self are, by and large, the results of miscarriages in the normal development of the self, we shall first present an outline of the normal development of the self. It is difficult to pinpoint the age at which the baby or small child may be said to have acquired a self. To begin with, it seems safe to assume that, strictly speaking, the neonate is still without a self. The new-born infant arrives physiologically pre-adapted for a specific physical environment—the presence of oxygen, of food, of a certain range of temperature—outside of which he cannot survive. Similarly, psychological survival requires a specific psychological environment—the presence of responsive-empathic selfobjects. It is in the matrix of a particular selfobject environment that, via a specific process of psychological structure formation called *transmuting internalization,* the *nuclear self* of the child will crystallize. Without going into the details of this structure-building process, we can say (1) that it cannot occur without a previous stage in which the child's mirroring and idealizing needs had been sufficiently responded to; (2) that it takes place in consequence of the minor, non-traumatic failures in the responses of the mirroring and the idealized selfobjects; and (3) that these failures lead to the gradual replacement of the selfobjects and their functions by a self and its functions. And it must be added that while gross identifications with the selfobjects and their functions may temporarily and transitionally occur, the ultimate wholesome result, the autonomous self, is not a replica of the selfobject. The analogy of the intake of foreign protein in order to build up one's own protein is very serviceable here—even as regards the detail of the splitting up and rearrangement of the material that had been ingested.

If we keep in mind the processes by which the self is created, we realize that, however primitive by comparison with the self of the adult the nuclear self may be, it is already at its very inception a complex structure, arising at the end-point of a developmental process which may be said to have its virtual beginnings with the formation of specific hopes, dreams and expectations concerning the future child in the minds of the parents, especially the mother. When the baby is born, the encounter with the child's actual structural and functional biological equipment will, of course, influence the imagery about its future personality that had been formed by the parents. But the parental expectations will, from birth onward, exert a considerable influence on the baby's developing self. The self arises thus as the result of the interplay between the new-born's innate equipment and the selective responses of the selfobjects through which certain potentialities are encouraged in their development while others remain unencouraged or are even actively discouraged. Out of this selective process there emerges, probably during the second year of life, a nuclear self, which, as stated earlier, is currently conceptualized as a bipolar structure; archaic nuclear ambitions form one pole, archaic nuclear ideals the other. The tension arc between these two poles enhances the development of the child's nuclear skills and talents—rudimentary skills and talents that will gradually develop into those that the adult employs in the service of the productivity and creativity of his mature self.

The strength of these three major constituents of the self, the choice of their specific contents, the nature of their relationship—e.g. which one of them will ultimately predominate—and their progress towards maturity and potential fulfilment through creative actions, will be less influenced by those responses of the selfobjects that are shaped by their philosophy of child rearing than by those that express the state of their own nuclear self. In other words, it is not so much what the parents *do* that will influence the character of the child's self, but what the parents *are*. If the parents are at peace with their own needs to shine and to succeed insofar as these needs can be realistically gratified, if, in other words, the parents' self-confidence is secure, then the proud exhibitionism of the budding self of their child will be responded to acceptingly. However grave the blows may be to which the child's grandiosity is exposed by the realities of life, the proud smile of the parents will keep alive a bit of the original omnipotence, to be retained as the nucleus of the self-confidence and inner security about one's worth that sustain the healthy person throughout his life. And the same holds true with regard to our ideals. However great our disappointment as we discover the weaknesses and limitations of the idealized selfobjects of our early life, their self-confidence as they carried us when we were babies, their security when they allowed us to merge our anxious selves with their tranquillity—via their calm voices or via our closeness with their relaxed bodies as they held us—will be retained by us as the nucleus of the strength of our leading ideals and of the calmness we experience as we live our lives under the guidance of our inner goals.

It is only in the light of our appreciation of the crucial influence exerted on the development of the self by the personality of the self-objects of childhood, that we are able to trace the genetic roots of the disorders of the self. Psychoanalytic case histories tended to emphasize certain dramatic incidents, certain grossly traumatic events—from the child's witnessing the 'primal scene' to the loss of a parent in childhood. But we have come to incline to the opinion that such traumatic events may be no more than clues that point to the truly pathogenic factors, the unwholesome atmosphere to which the child was exposed during the years when his self was established. Taken by themselves, in other words, these events leave fewer serious disturbances in their wake than the chronic ambience created by the deep-rooted attitudes of the self-objects, since even the still vulnerable self, in the process of formation, can cope with serious traumata if it is embedded in a healthily supportive milieu. The essence of the healthy matrix for the growing self of the child is a mature, cohesive parental self that is in tune with the changing needs of the child. It can, with a glow of shared joy, mirror the child's grandiose display one minute, yet, perhaps a minute later, should the child become anxious and over-stimulated by its exhibitionism, it will curb the display by adopting a realistic attitude *vis-à-vis* the child's limitations. Such optimal frustrations of the child's need to be mirrored and to merge into an idealized selfobject, hand in hand with optimal gratifications, generate the appropriate growth-facilitating matrix for the self.

Some parents, however, are not adequately sensitive to the needs of the child but will instead respond to the needs of their own insecurely established self. Here are two characteristic illustrations of pathogenic selfobject failures. They concern typical events that emerge frequently during the analysis of patients with narcissistic personality disorders during the transference repetitions of those childhood experiences that interfered with the normal development of the self. We must add here that the episodes depicted in the following vignettes are indicative of a pathogenic childhood environment only if they form part of the selfobjects' *chronic* attitude. Put differently, they would not emerge at crucial junctures of a selfobject transference if they had occurred as the consequence of a parent's unavoidable *occasional* failure.

First illustration: A little girl comes home from school, eager to tell her mother about some great successes. But the mother, instead of listening with pride, deflects the conversation from the child to herself, begins to talk about her own successes which overshadow those of her little daughter.

Second illustration: A little boy is eager to idealize his father, he wants his father to tell him about his life, the battles he engaged in and won. But instead of joyfully acting in accordance with his son's need, the father is embarrassed by the request. He feels tired and bored and, leaving the house, finds a temporary source of vitality for his enfeebled self in the tavern, through drink and mutually supportive talk with friends.

4. PSYCHOPATHOLOGY AND SYMPTOMATOLOGY

In the following we will present some syndromes of self-pathology, arising in consequence of the developmental failures described in the preceding section. It is clear that in many if not in most instances the various forms of self-disturbance which we separate from each other in the following classification will not be clearly identifiable in specific patients. Mixtures of the experiences characteristic of different types will often be present and, even more frequently, one and the same patient will experience the one or the other of the pathological states of the self at different times, often even in close proximity. The following descriptions should, however, be clinically helpful because they point out frequently occurring clusters of experience.

The *understimulated self.* This is a chronic or recurrent condition of the self, the propensity to which arises in consequence of prolonged lack of stimulating responsiveness from the side of the selfobjects in childhood. Such personalities are lacking in vitality. They experience themselves as boring and apathetic, and they are experienced by others in the same way. Individuals whose nascent selves have been insufficiently responded to will use any available stimuli to create a pseudo-excitement in order to ward off the painful feeling of deadness that tends to overtake them. Children employ the resources appropriate to their developmental phase—such as head-banging among toddlers, compulsive masturbation in later childhood, daredevil activities in adolescence.

Adults have at their disposal an even wider armamentarium of self-stimulation—in particular, in the sexual sphere, addictive promiscuous activities and various perversions, and, in the non-sexual sphere, such activities as gambling, drug and alcohol-induced excitement, and a life style characterized by hypersociability. If the analyst is able to penetrate beneath the defensive façade presented by these activities, he will invariably find empty depression. Prototypical is the compulsive masturbation of lonely, 'un-mirrored' children. It is not healthy drive-pressure that leads to the endlessly repeated masturbation, but the attempt to substitute pleasurable sensations in *parts* of the body (erogenous zones) when the joy provided by the exhibition of the *total* self is unavailable.

The *fragmenting self.* This is a chronic or recurrent condition of the self, the propensity to which arises in consequence of the lack of integrating responses to the nascent self in its totality from the side of the selfobjects in childhood. Occasionally occurring fragmentation states of minor degree and short duration are ubiquitous. They occur in all of us when our self-esteem has been taxed for prolonged periods and when no replenishing sustenance has presented itself. We all may walk home after a day in which we suffered a series of self-esteem-shaking failures, feeling at sixes and sevens within ourselves. Our gait and posture will be less than graceful at such times, our movements will tend to be clumsy, and even our mental functions will show signs of discoordination. Our patients with narcissistic personality disorders will not only be more inclined to react with such fragmentation symptoms to even minor disappointments, but their symptoms will tend to be more severe. If a normally tastefully dressed patient arrives in our office in a dishevelled attire, if his tie is grossly mismatched, and the colour of his socks does not go with that of his shoes, we shall usually not go wrong if we begin to search our memory with the question whether we had been unempathic in the last session, whether we had failed to recognize a narcissistic need. Still more serious degrees of fragmentation will finally be encountered during the psychoanalytic treatment of the most severely disturbed patients with narcissistic personality disorders. Here a patient might respond to even minor rebuffs, whether from the side of the analyst or in his daily life, with a deep loss of the sense of the continuity of his self in time and of its cohesiveness in space—a psychic condition that produces profound anxiety. The feeling, in particular, that various body parts are beginning not to be held together anymore by a strong, healthy awareness of the totality of the body-self, leads to apprehensive brooding concerning the fragments of the body, often expressed by the patient in the form of hypochondriacal worry concerning his health. Unlike the chronic hypochondriacal preoccupations encountered in some psychoses, however, even the most severe and quasi-delusional analogous worries in the narcissistic personality disorders are the direct consequence of some specific, identifiable narcissistic injury, and they disappear, often with dramatic speed, as soon as a bridge of empathy with an understanding self-object has been built. A frequently occurring sequence of events during the analysis of patients who have established a mirror transference will demonstrate this point. When the mirror transference is in balance, the patient, sensing the analyst's empathic attention, feels whole and self-accepting. Subsequent to an erroneous interpretation, however—e.g. following a session in which the analyst had addressed himself to some *detail* of the patient's psychic life when, in fact (after some progress in treatment, for example, or after some external success), the patient had offered his *total* self for approval—the patient's feeling of wholeness which had been maintained via the transference disappears. It is re-established when the analyst restores the empathic tie to the selfobject by correctly interpreting the sequence of events that had led to its disruption.

The *overstimulated self*. The propensity towards recurrent states during which the self is overstimulated arises in consequence of unempathically excessive or phase-inappropriate responses from the side of the selfobjects of childhood, either *vis-à-vis* the activities of the grandiose-exhibitionistic pole of the child's nascent self or *vis-à-vis* the activities of the pole that harbours the guiding ideals, or both.

If it was the grandiose-exhibitionistic pole of a person's self that had been exposed to unempathic overstimulation in childhood, then no healthy glow of enjoyment can be obtained by him from external success. On the contrary, since these people are subject to being flooded by unrealistic, archaic greatness fantasies which produce painful tension and anxiety, they will try to avoid situations in which they could become the centre of attention. In some such individuals creativity may be unimpaired so long as no exhibition of the *body*-self is involved, directly or indirectly. In most of them, however, the creative-productive potential will be diminished because their intense ambitions which had remained tied to unmodified grandiose fantasies will frighten them. In view of the fact, furthermore, that the selfobjects' responses had focused prematurely and unrealistically on the fantasied performance or the fantasied products of the self but had failed to respond appropriately to the exhibitionism of the nascent nuclear self of the child as the initiator of the performance and as the shaper of products, the self will, throughout life, be experienced as separate from its own actions and weak in comparison with them. Such people will tend to shy away from giving themselves over to creative activities because their self is in danger of destruction by being siphoned into its own performance or into the product it is shaping.

If it is predominantly the pole that harbours the ideals that had been overstimulated—e.g. by the unempathically intense and prolonged display of a parental selfobject in need of admiration—then it will be the persisting, intense need for the merger with an external ideal that will threaten the equilibrium of the self. Since contact with the idealized selfobject is, therefore, experienced as a danger and must be avoided, the healthy capacity for enthusiasm will be lost—the enthusiasm for goals and ideals which people with a firm self can experience *vis-à-vis* the admired great who are their guide and example or with regard to the idealized goals that they pursue.

Closely related to the overstimulated self is the *overburdened self*. But while the overstimulated self is a self whose ambitions and ideals had been unempathically responded to in isolation, without sufficient regard for the self *in toto,* the overburdened self is a self that had not been provided with the opportunity to merge with the calmness of an omnipotent selfobject. The overburdened self, in other words, is a self that had suffered the trauma of unshared emotionality. The result of this specific empathic failure from the side of the selfobject is the absence of the self-soothing capacity that protects the normal individual from being traumatized by the spreading of his emotions, especially by the spreading of anxiety. A world that lacks such soothing selfobjects is an inimical, a dangerous world. No wonder, then, that a self that had been exposed in early life to states of 'overburdenedness' because of the lack of soothing selfobjects, will under certain circumstances experience its environment as hostile. During states of 'overburdenedness' in adult life—e.g. after the therapist had been unempathic, in particular by failing to give to his patient the right interpretation with regard to his emotional state, or by pouring too much insight into him all at once, oblivious to the fact that the absorption of the new understanding confronts the patient with an excessive task—a patient might dream that he lives in a poisoned atmosphere or that he is surrounded by swarms of dangerous hornets; and, in his wakeful awareness, he will tend to respond to otherwise hardly noticeable stimuli as if they were attacks on his sensibilities. He will, for example, complain of the noises in the therapist's office, of unpleasant odours, etc. These reactions of patients with narcissistic personality disorders, especially when they involve an overall attitude of irritability and suspiciousness, may at times strike us as alarmingly close to those we encounter in the psychoses, in particular of course in paranoia. Unlike the more or less systematized, chronic suspiciousness and counter-hostility of the paranoiac, however, these manifestations of the overburdened state of the self appear, like the analogous hypochondriacal preoccupations in states of self-fragmentation, always as the direct consequence of a specific narcissistic injury, as a consequence of the unempathic, overburdening response of a selfobject. They disappear speedily when an empathic bond with the selfobject has been re-established, i.e. in therapy, when a correct interpretation has been made.

5. BEHAVIOURAL PATTERNS AND THE INJURED SELF

It is with a good deal of reluctance that the psychoanalyst undertakes to present a typology of behaviour, even if he has been able to correlate his descriptions of frequently occurring clusters of specific surface manifestations with specific underlying dynamic constellations or with specific foci of genetic experience. The best efforts of the past—Freud's (1908, 1910, 1916, 1931); Abraham's (1921, 1924, 1925)—are no exception to the rule that the simplified correlation of specific patterns of manifest behaviour with universally present psychological conditions which of necessity forms part of any such typology will, in the long run, impede scientific progress. Why then, do we persist in the attempt to devise characterologies? The answer is that such classifications, even though we must be aware of the fact that they may eventually limit our thinking and stand in our way, can for a while be valuable guides in psychological territory in which we feel not yet at home. There is no question, for example, about the fact that an analyst who adheres strictly to the thought patterns so beautifully laid out by Abraham in 1921, will be hampered in his ability to understand some of his patients. Had Mr. W.'s 'obsessional' description of the contents of his trouser pocket (Kohut, 1977, pp. 164–9) been seen unquestioningly as a manifestation of his 'anal character', the crucial significance of his behaviour, in the service of the maintenance of his endangered self, would not have been understood and the crucial genetic data would not have come to light. But does that mean that it would have been better for analysis if Abraham had never given us his typology? Decidedly not. It was of the greatest help to generations of analysts and, so long as we are aware of the limitations of its applicability, continues to be of limited service even today.

But although we therefore feel that the setting up of typologies is justified, it behooves us to be explicit about the shortcomings inherent in any such attempt. We have no doubt, for example, about the fact that the concept of a 'mirror-hungry personality', to be sketched out shortly, will be helpful as an orientating device within the framework of the psychology of the self, just as Abraham's 'anal character' was helpful within the framework of drive-psychology. But we must immediately say that there are some mirror-hungry individuals whose personality structure is different from the one which, according to our dynamic interpretation, is correlated to their mirror-hungry behaviour—it is different because it was not formed as the result of the specific traumata in childhood which, according to our genetic reconstruction, are the responsible agents. Mr X.'s behaviour (Kohut, 1977, pp. 199–219) might well be characterized as that of a mirror-hungry personality. Yet his insistent claims for attention and praise, his arrogant superiority, were not manifestations of the specific personality structure—characterized by simple deficiencies due to insufficient mirroring attention in childhood—that we should expect to encounter on the basis of our description of '*the*' mirror-hungry person. His mirror-hungry behaviour was embedded in a much more complexly organized pathological personality. His behaviour was the manifestation of a sector of his personality that was isolated from his nuclear self by a 'vertical split'—a split that had come about not because of a *lack* of mirroring attention in childhood but because of a specific *fault* in his mother's responses to him. While, to state it more exactly, her approval of him had indeed been excessive, the focus of her mirroring had not been selected in accordance with *his* needs—namely, to develop an independent and vigorous self—but in accordance with *hers*—namely, to keep him dependent on her, indeed to retain him within her own personality organization, in order to brace up her own, precariously constituted self.

There are many cases, however, where our brief explanation of the 'mirror-hungry personality' is more nearly correct. Miss F., for example (Kohut, 1971, pp. 283–93), became indeed 'mirror-hungry'—i.e. self-righteously demanding exclusive attention and reassuring praise—because her phase-appropriate needs for mirroring had not been met by her self-absorbed mother. But even in these cases the patients' demandingness is not simply the present-day expression of normal, self-assertive needs of childhood that have persisted because they had not been appropriately responded to in the past. Because of the intensity of these needs, and, *par excellence,* because of these patients' conviction that they will not find an echo of understanding empathy, they arouse deep shame which, in turn, leads to their suppression, manifested by depressed and hopeless withdrawal—the latter behaviour sometimes, in particular in the narcissistic behaviour disorders, alternating with bursts of enragedly expressed but not effectively pursued demands that the wrong that had been done be set right.

Having in the foregoing given voice to some of the arguments that speak for and against psychoanalytic characterologies in general and to some of the pros and cons regarding a classification of behavioural syndromes in the area of the disturbed self in particular, we will now throw further caution to the winds and outline some frequently encountered narcissistic personality types.

Mirror-hungry personalities thirst for self-objects whose confirming and admiring responses will nourish their famished self. They are impelled to display themselves and to evoke the attention of others, trying to counteract, however fleetingly, their inner sense of worthlessness and lack of self-esteem. Some of them are able to establish relationships with reliably mirroring others that will sustain them for long periods. But most of them will not be nourished for long, even by genuinely accepting responses. Thus, despite their discomfort about their need to display themselves and despite their sometimes severe stage fright and shame they must go on trying to find new selfobjects whose attention and recognition they seek to induce.

Ideal-hungry personalities are forever in search of others whom they can admire for their prestige, power, beauty, intelligence, or moral stature. They can experience themselves as worthwhile only so long as they can relate to selfobjects to whom they can look up. Again, in some instances, such relationships last a long time and are genuinely sustaining to both individuals involved. In most cases, however, the inner void cannot forever be filled by these means. The ideal-hungry feels the persistence of the structural defect and, as a consequence of this awareness, he begins to look for—and, of course, he inevitably finds—some realistic defects in his God. The search for new idealizable selfobjects is then continued, always with the hope that the next great figure to whom the ideal-hungry attaches himself will not disappoint him.

Alter-ego-personalities need a relationship with a selfobject that by conforming to the self's appearance, opinions, and values confirms the existence, the reality of the self. At times the alter-ego-hungry personalities, too, may be able to form lasting friendships—relationships in which each of the partners experiences the feelings of the other as if they had been experienced by himself. 'If thou sorrow, he will weep; if thou wake, he cannot sleep; thus of every grief in heart he with thee doth bear a part' (Shakespeare, *The Passionate Pilgrim*). But again, in most instances, the inner void cannot be filled permanently by the twinship. The alter-ego-hungry discovers that the other is not himself and, as a consequence of this discovery, begins to feel estranged from him. It is thus characteristic for most of these relationships to be short-lived. Like the mirror- and ideal-hungry, the alter-ego-hungry is prone to look restlessly for one replacement after another.

The preceding three character types in the narcissistic realm are frequently encountered in everyday life and they should, in general, not be considered as forms of psychopathology but rather as variants of the normal human personality, with its assets and defects. Stated in more experience-distant terms, it is not primarily the intensity of the need that brings about the typical attitude and behaviour of these individuals but the specific direction into which they are propelled in their attempt to make up for a circumscribed weakness in their self. It is the location of the self-defect that produces the characteristic stance of these individuals, not the extent of the defect in the self. By contrast, the following two types are characterized less by the location of the defect and more by its extent. They must, in general, be considered as lying within the spectrum of pathological narcissism.

Merger-hungry personalities will impress us by their need to control their selfobjects in an enactment of the need for structure. Here, in contrast to the types sketched out before, it is the need for merger that dominates the picture, the specific type of merger, however—whether with a mirroring or an idealized selfobject or with an alter ego—is less important in determining the individual's behaviour. Because the self of these individuals is seriously defective or enfeebled, they need selfobjects in lieu of self-structure. Their manifest personality features and their behaviour are thus dominated by the fact that the fluidity of the boundaries between them and others interferes with their ability to discriminate their own thoughts, wishes and intentions from those of the selfobject. Because they experience the other as their own self, they feel intolerant of his independence: they are very sensitive to separations from him and they demand—indeed they expect without question—the selfobject's continuous presence.

Contact-shunning personalities are the reverse of the merger-hungry just described. Although for obvious reasons they attract the least notice, they may well be the most frequent of the narcissistic character types. These individuals avoid social contact and become isolated, not because they are disinterested in others, but, on the contrary, just because of their need for them is so intense. The intensity of their need not only leads to great sensitivity to rejection—a sensitivity of which they are painfully aware—but also, on deeper and unconscious levels, to the apprehension that the remnants of their nuclear self will be swallowed up and destroyed by the yearned-for all-encompassing union.

6. THE TREATMENT OF THE NARCISSISTIC BEHAVIOUR AND PERSONALITY DISORDERS

The essential therapeutic goal of depth-psychology is the extensive amelioration or cure of the central disturbance, not the suppression of symptoms by persuasion or education, however benevolently applied. Since the central pathology in the narcissistic behaviour and personality disorders is the defective or weakened condition of the self, the goal of therapy is the rehabilitation of this structure. True, to external inspection, the clusters of symptoms and personality features that characterize the narcissistic behaviour disorders on the one hand, and the narcissistic personality disorders, on the other hand, are completely different: the self-assertive claims of the first group appear to be too strong, those of the second not strong enough. But depth-psychological investigation demonstrates that the psychopathological basis of both disorders—the disease of the self—is, in essence, the same.

With regard to those patients with self-pathology, those with narcissistic behaviour disorders, who make overly loud narcissistic claims, and whose behaviour appears to be overly self-assertive, the therapist might be tempted to persuade them to relinquish their demands and to accept the limitations imposed by the realities of adult life. But doing this is like trying to persuade a patient who suffers from a structural neurosis to give up his phobia, his hysterical paralysis, his compulsive ritual. The overtly expressed excessive narcissistic demands of these patients and what appears to be their overtly displayed excessive self-assertiveness are a set of characterologically embedded symptoms—they are not the manifestations of an archaic narcissism that had not been tamed in early life and that must now be tamed belatedly. On the contrary, it is the essence of the disease of these patients that the access to their childhood narcissism is barred. The unfulfilled narcissistic needs of their childhood with which they must learn to get in touch, which they must learn to accept, which they must learn to express, lie deeply buried beneath their clamorous assertiveness, guarded by a wall of shame and vulnerability. If, on the basis of a therapeutic maturity- or reality-morality, the therapist concentrates on censuring the patient's manifest narcissism, he will drive the repressed narcissistic needs more deeply into repression—or he will increase the depth of the split in the personality that separates the sector of the psyche that contains the unresponded-to autonomous self from the noisily assertive one that lacks autonomy—and he will block the unfolding of the narcissistic transference. These considerations apply whether the patient's overt narcissistic demands are expressed via quietly persistent pressure, via attacks of scathing narcissistic rage, or via emotional means that lie between these two extremes. We all know people who annoy us by asking us again and again to repeat our favourable comments concerning some successful performance of theirs. And we all also know others who, throughout their life, go from one selfishly demanding rage attack to another, seemingly oblivious to the rights and feelings of those toward whom their demands are directed. If the analyst responds to these demands by exhortations concerning realism and emotional maturity or, worse still, if he blamefully interprets them as the expression of their insatiable oral drive that needs to be tamed or of a primary destructiveness that needs to be neutralized and bound by aggression-curbing psychic structures, then, as we said, the development of the narcissistic transference will be blocked. But if he can show to the patient who demands praise that, despite the availability of average external responses, he must continue to 'fish for compliments' because the hopeless need of the unmirrored child in him remains unassuaged, and if he can show to the raging patient the helplessness and hopelessness that lie behind his rages, can show him that, indeed his rage is the direct consequence of the fact that he cannot assert his demands effectively, then the old needs will slowly begin to make their appearance more openly as the patient becomes more empathic with himself. And when the repressions are thus ultimately relinquished—or when the split maintained via disavowal is bridged—and the narcissistic demands of childhood are beginning to make their first shy appearance, the danger is not that they will now run to extremes, but that they will again go into hiding at the first rebuff or at the first unempathic response. Experience teaches us, in other words, that the therapist's major effort must be concentrated on the task of keeping the old needs mobilized. If he succeeds in this, then they will gradually—and spontaneously—be transformed into normal self-assertiveness and normal devotion to ideals.

The foregoing conclusions hold also with regard to those individuals with self-pathology, those with narcissistic personality disturbances, who are overtly shy, unassertive and socially isolated, but whose conscious and preconscious fantasies—'The Secret Life of Walter Mitty'—are grandiose. If the therapist believes that the patient's timidity, shyness and social isolation are due to the persistence of archaic illusions, specifically that they are due to the persistence of his untamed childhood grandiosity as manifested in the form of his grandiose fantasies, then he will feel justified in the attempt, through the application of educational and moral pressure, to persuade the patient to relinquish these fantasies. But neither the patient's fantasies nor his social isolation are the cause of his illness. On the contrary, together they constitute a psychological unit which, as a protective device, attempts to maintain the patient's precariously established self by preventing its dangerous exposure to rebuff and ridicule. If the therapist is educational rather than analytic, if he restricts his approach to the attempt to persuade the patient to give up his fantasied grandiosity, then the distance between the patient's defective self, on the one hand, and the therapist as the hoped-for empathic responder to the patient's narcissistic needs, on the other hand, will increase and the spontaneously arising movement towards the first significant breach in the wall of sensitivity and suspicion, the establishment of a narcissistic transference, will be halted. If, however, the therapist can explain without censure the protective function of the grandiose fantasies and the social isolation and thus demonstrate that he is in tune with the patient's disintegration anxiety and shame concerning his precariously established self, then he will not interfere with the spontaneously arising transference mobilization of the old narcissistic needs. Despite disintegration fears and shame, the patient will then be enabled, cautiously at first, later increasingly more openly, to re-experience the need for the selfobject's joyful acceptance of his childhood grandiosity and for an omnipotent surrounding—healthy needs that had not been responded to in early life. And again, as in the case of the narcissistic behaviour disorders, the re-mobilized needs will gradually—and spontaneously—be transformed into normal self-assertiveness and normal devotion to ideals.

In the foregoing we demonstrated that the therapeutic principles which we enunciated and the therapeutic strategy correlated to them are based on the understanding of the central psychopathology of the analysable disorders of the self and that they have as their aim the amelioration and cure of this central psychopathology. Since the psychopathology of both major types of analysable disorders is identical, it follows that despite their divergent symptomatology—noisy demands and intense activity in the social field in the narcissistic behaviour disorders; shame and social isolation in the narcissistic personality disorders—the process of treatment also is identical in its essence. And the same, of course, holds for the nature of the wholesome result that is achieved by the treatment: it is the firming of the formerly enfeebled self, both in the pole that carries the patient's self-confidently held ambitions and in the pole that carries his idealized goals. It only needs to be added now that the patient's revitalized self-confidence and the revitalized enthusiasm for his goals will ultimately make it possible for him, whether he suffered from a narcissistic behaviour disorder or a narcissistic personality disorder, to take up again the pursuit of the action-poised programme arched in the energic field that established itself between his nuclear ambitions and ideals, will make it possible for him to lead a fulfilling, creative-productive life.

With the preceding remarks about some clinical lessons, derived from the application of the psychology of the self to the therapeutic situation, our survey of the psychology of the self has reached its end. Since it would serve no good purpose if we now made the attempt to summarize an essay which, in itself, is in its essence a summary of the results of previous investigations, we shall restrict our final statement to emphasizing once more that the brevity of our presentation does not imply any conviction on our part that we were offering the outline of a finished system of thought. We simply tried to describe briefly the current state of a new development in psychoanalysis—a development, it must be added, which not only has by no means come to its end but which, on the contrary, appears to have lost none of its initial momentum. The foregoing pages should, therefore, be considered as a survey of the current state of the psychoanalytic psychology of the self—a survey that should assist us in planning the further investigation of an as yet incompletely explored psychological field.

REFERENCES

Abraham, K. (1921). Contributions to the theory of the anal character. In *Selected Papers*. London: Hogarth Press, 1927.

Abraham, K. (1924). The influence of oral erotism on character-formation. In *Selected Papers*. London: Hogarth Press, 1927.

Abraham, K. (1925). Character-formation on the genital level of the libido. In *Selected Papers*. London: Hogarth Press, 1927.

Freud, S. (1908). Character and anal erotism. *S.E.* **9.**

Freud, S. (1910). A special type of choice of object made by men. *S.E.* **11.**

Freud, S. (1916). Some character-types met with in psychoanalytic work. *S.E.* **14.**

Freud, S. (1931). Libidinal types. *S.E.* **21.**

Janik, A. & Toulmin, S. (1973). *Wittgenstein's Vienna*. New York: Simon & Schuster.

Kohut, H. (1971). *The Analysis of the Self*. New York: Int. Univ. Press.

Kohut, H. (1972). Thoughts on narcissism and narcissistic rage. *Psychoanal. Study Child* **27.**

Kohut, H. (1977). *The Restoration of the Self*. New York: Int. Univ. Press.

Schafer, R. (1973). Concepts of self and identity and the experience of separation-individuation in adolescence. *Psychoanal. Q.* **42,** 42-59.

Wolf E. S. (1976). Ambience and abstinence. *Ann. Psychoanal.* **4.**

8. Toward a Functional Definition of Narcissism

Robert D. Stolorow

Traditional usage, within the economic model and psychoanalytic drive theory, defines narcissism as pertaining to the libidinal cathexis of the self. The difficulties inherent in this economic concept of narcissism have been cogently reviewed in a recent paper by Pulver (1970). Citing the work of Apfelbaum (1965) and Holt (reported by Dahl, 1968), Pulver notes that the economic model and drive theory in general have been subjected to serious criticisms. He further argues convincingly that the non-specific nature of the terms 'libido' and 'self' has introduced a good deal of conceptual confusion into our thinking about narcissism, so much so that the drive concept of narcissism is of little use in clinical practice. Pulver concludes that a 'serious result of this vagueness is that the concept [narcissism] has not received the elaboration in terms of ego psychology which . . . it richly deserves.' The present paper is in the spirit of such an elaboration.

Since the advent of the structural theory, a trend in modern psychoanalytic ego psychology has been to move away from a preoccupation with purely economic explanations, and to move towards *functional* explanations. Armed with modern ego-psychological concepts, we are somewhat less interested in explaining mental activity primarily in terms of a hypothetical flow of instinctual energies (a highly abstract level of theorizing which is far removed from empirical and phenomenological verification), and we are more interested in understanding the multiple functions which a given mental activity serves in the interplay of id, ego and superego forces within the personality (a level of theorizing which is much closer to actual clinical observations) (Waelder, 1930; Arlow & Brenner, 1964). In keeping with this trend, I am offering the following functional definition of narcissism, which I believe captures the state of our knowledge about the unique function served by those mental activities which clinicians have labelled as narcissistic:

Mental activity is narcissistic to the degree that its function is to maintain the structural cohesiveness, temporal stability and positive affective colouring of the self-representation.

In the paragraphs which follow, I shall first review the work of some authors who have made significant contributions to our understanding of narcissism in functional terms. I shall then attempt to demonstrate that a functional conception of narcissism can be very helpful in clearing up some of the ambiguities and contradictions which have arisen as a result of the traditional drive concept of narcissism.

CONTRIBUTIONS TO A FUNCTIONAL UNDERSTANDING OF NARCISSISM

Numerous authors (e.g. Arlow & Brenner, 1964; Freeman, 1964; Eisnitz, 1969) have pointed out that narcissistic activity may function as a defence, in order to ward off a multitude of object-related instinctual (incestuous, sadomasochistic) conflicts. An excellent example of this orientation is Kernberg's (1970) detailed interpretation of the 'splendid isolation' and cold, contemptuous attitudes of the narcissistic personality as representing a defensive retreat from dreaded object relationships characterized by intense dependency, oral envy and primitive oral sadism, and the resulting guilt and fears of retaliation. The correctness of such interpretations cannot be doubted in many cases. However, since virtually *any* mental activity can serve to defend against instinctual conflicts and dreaded object relationships, such interpretations do not appear to enhance our understanding of the *unique* function of activity which clinicians have labeled narcissistic. Hence, I shall restrict my brief review to explanations which I believe have contributed to our insight into the specific and unique function of narcissistic activity as proposed in the definition which I presented above.

A crucial bit of groundwork for a functional understanding of narcissism was Hartmann's (1950) conceptual distinction between the *ego* (a structural mental system), the *self* (the whole person of an individual, including his body and body parts as well as his psychic organization and its parts), and the *self-representation* (the unconscious, preconscious and conscious endopsychic representations of the bodily and mental self in the system ego). Taking off from Hartmann's distinction, Jacobson (1964) was able to point out that narcissism is not identical with the libidinal endowment of the system ego or of ego functions as Freud (1914) had originally postulated. Narcissism, according to Jacobson, refers to the libidinal cathexis of the self-representation, which is constituted in the course of ego development. While Jacobson's formulation remains rooted within the economic model, it is nevertheless very useful in delineating the arena in which narcissistic activity exercises its function; namely, the arena of the self-representation.

That Freud himself was hazily aware of the functional relationship between narcissistic activity and the maintenance of the self-representation is suggested by his remark (1914) that 'the self-regard has a very intimate connection with the narcissistic libido'. Freud noted that in narcissistic object choice the aim is to be loved and he stated further that to be loved raises the self-regard. The clear implication is that the function of narcissistic object choice is to regulate self-esteem (i.e. to maintain the positive affective colouring of the self-representation). However, Freud was unable to carry this implication further, apparently because he did not yet have a clear concept of the self-representation as distinct from the system ego.

To my knowledge it was Reich who first spelled out with crystal clarity the way in which certain patterns, traditionally labelled narcissistic, function to maintain the self-representation. In the earlier of two important papers (1953), she demonstrated how a woman may form a narcissistic object tie to an aggrandized phallic ideal in order to undo the trauma of her imagined castration and her resulting sense of defect and inferiority. Union with a phallic ideal was understood as a magic method of repairing the damaged self-representation and restoring injured self-esteem. In the later paper (1960), Reich showed how various other narcissistic patterns (e.g. grandiose self-inflation, body narcissism, and ceaseless cravings for admiring attention) may represent compensatory attempts to repair damage done to the self-representation by early traumatic experiences. Reich clearly interpreted clinically observed 'narcissistic disturbances' as abortive attempts to restore and stabilize self-esteem.

Numerous authors have buttressed and amplified Reich's groundbreaking formulations. Elkisch (1957) observed that certain of her patients would gaze at their images in the mirror in order to restore a lost sense of self-identity. Referring to the myth of Narcissus, Lichtenstein (1964) formulated that narcissism refers not to the love of oneself but to the love of one's mirror image, and argued that 'the mirror and the act of mirroring introduce problems of the emergence of a primary identity, of identity confusion, of loss of identity, and of identity maintenance as well'. Narcissistic object relationships are to be understood as regressive efforts at identity maintenance through mirroring in the object. Eisnitz (1969) formulated that narcissistic object choices serve to stabilize and supplement a weakened self-representation. Arlow & Brenner (1964), Murray (1964), Kernberg (1970), and Oremland & Windholz (1971) all noted that grandiose fantasies of magic omnipotence and unlimited entitlement may be attempts to repair various injuries to and degradations of the self-representation and to ward off the threat of its dissolution.

Perhaps the most detailed account of how narcissistic patterns function to maintain the self-representation has been presented by Kohut (1971). The nuclear pathology in narcissistic disturbances, according to Kohut, is an absence of or defect in internal structures that maintain self-cohesiveness and self-esteem. In narcissistic object relationships, the object functions as a substitute for the missing or defective self-esteem regulating endopsychic structures. The object performs basic functions in the realm of self-esteem regulation that the individual's own psyche is unable to provide. Archaic narcissistic configurations are mobilized (e.g. in which the individual requires continuous mirroring of his grandiose fantasies or merger with an aggrandized omnipotent object) in order to solidify a fragile and precarious sense of self-cohesion and self-esteem, and to ward off the ultimate threat of fragmentation and structural disintegration of the self-representation.

It is surprising that, despite the above *clinical* formulations which stress the structure-maintaining function of narcissistic activity, the authors listed seem unwilling to take the ultimate *metapsychological* step of freeing the concept of narcissism from an economic definition which it has outgrown, and redefining narcissism in functional terms. Kohut, for instance, in struggling to define a narcissistic object relationship metapsychologically, says, 'Narcissism . . . is defined not by the target of the instinctual investment (i.e. whether it is the subject himself or other people) but by the nature or quality of the instinctual charge. The small child . . . invests other people with narcissistic cathexes and thus experiences them narcissistically . . .'. In a narcissistic object relationship the object is invested with narcissistic cathexes. But what is a narcissistic cathexis? In struggling to reconcile his excellent clinical observations with an outmoded economic concept of narcissism, Kohut presents us with either a tautology or a notion that there is a *qualitative* difference between narcissistic energies and object-related energies—a highly speculative proposition. A way out of this conceptual mulberry bush, which would be totally consistent with Kohut's clinical formulations, would be to simply define a narcissistic object relationship as one whose function is to maintain the cohesiveness, stability and positive affective colouring of the self-representation. In the following paragraphs, I shall try to show that other conceptual difficulties can be cleared up by replacing the drive concept of narcissism with a functional definition.

CLARIFICATIONS ACHIEVED WITH A FUNCTIONAL DEFINITION OF NARCISSISM

After a review of the literature, Pulver (1970) concluded that the term narcissism has been used clinically to refer to (1) a sexual perversion, (2) a mode of relating to objects, (3) a developmental stage and (4) self-esteem. I shall now attempt to demonstrate that a functional definition lends clarification to our understanding of narcissism in each of these four usages. I shall also attempt to show that a functional definition clarifies the issue of healthy versus unhealthy narcissism and helps us to avoid certain countertransference pitfalls with narcissistic patients.

1. Narcissism as a sexual perversion.

Narcissism as a sexual perversion refers to the taking of one's own body, or more specifically the mirror image of one's own body, as a sexual object. In modern clinical thinking it is insufficient to interpret a sexual perversion solely in drive theory terms as a libidinal fixation (in this case, a libidinal fixation on the self as sexual object). It is also necessary to understand the function served by perverse activity within the personality. With regard to the narcissistic perversion, Elkisch (1957) and Lichtenstein (1964) have noted that patients become preoccupied with their mirror image in order to restore and stabilize a crumbling self-representation. A narcissistically disordered patient of my own would gaze lovingly at his mirror image (with or without masturbatory activity) as a reparative device following injurious experiences which threatened his self-representation with fragmentation. Reich (1960) and

Kohut (1971) have both observed that a wide variety of sexual perversions may function as sexualized attempts to ward off self-depletion and self-fragmentation, to revive the sense of having a cohesive self, and to restore self-esteem. Hence, it would seem that a functional conception of narcissism in terms of the maintenance of the self-representation contributes significantly to our understanding of the narcissistic perversion and perverse activity in general.

2. Narcissism as a mode of relating to objects.

Again following Pulver (1970), narcissism as a mode of relating to objects has been used to refer to (a) a mode of relating to the environment characterized by a relative lack of object relationships—i.e. withdrawal from overt observable relationships with objects in the environment, and (b) a type of object choice in which the self plays a more important part than the real aspects of the object.

With regard to (a), Pulver points out that the difficulty applying the drive concept of narcissism to overt withdrawal from objects, is that lack of overt object relationships does not mean that objects are not psychically present; i.e. despite defensive overt withdrawal, objects may remain intensely important intrapsychically. Kohut (1971) too stresses that a person's seeming isolation may cloak a wealth of object investments. The difficulty is cleared up by applying the functional definition of narcissism: withdrawal behaviour is narcissistic depending on its function, or the function of the accompanying fantasies. If the withdrawal behaviour and/or the fantasies into which the individual retreats function to buttress the cohesiveness, stability and positive affective colouring of a threatened self-representation, the withdrawal may be called narcissistic.

With regard to (b), Pulver (1970) notes, as have may others (Reich, 1953; Lichtenstein, 1964; Einstein, 1969; Kohut, 1971), that narcissistic object ties may be characterized by a very intense overt attachment to external objects. In other words, increased involvement with the self is not necessarily accompanied by a decreased cathexis of objects as implied in the drive concept of narcissism. Freud's (1914) economic hypothesis of a mutually excluding reciprocity between narcissistic libido and object libido does not appear to hold up clinically. As mentioned earlier, I believe that the contradictions spawned by the drive concept of narcissism are rather easily cleared up by a functional definition, according to which a narcissistic object choice is defined as one whose function is to maintain the cohesiveness, stability and positive affective colouring of the self-representation. It is clear that an intensely cathected object relationship can serve a primarily narcissistic function. The supposed antithesis between narcissism and object relationship is an artifact of an outmoded economic concept of narcissism.

3. Narcissism as a developmental stage.

Though Freud's conception of narcissism as a developmental stage frequently changed (Kanzer, 1964), in his later writings he reaffirmed his earlier theory of a stage of primary narcissism (Freud, 1914). According to this theory, primary narcissism refers to the earliest stage in the infant's libidinal economy, in which all of the libido invested in the self and object cathexes have not yet developed. According to Pulver's (1970) review, in current usage narcissism as a developmental stage is synonymous with primary narcissism. Pulver aptly criticizes this usage on the basis that the drive concept of (primary) narcissism as the libidinal cathexis of the self does not do justice to the developmental complexities, including the vicissitudes of object relationships, occurring during the period in question (first six to eight months of life).

Perhaps the most pointed critique of the theory of primary narcissism can be found in the writings of Balint (1960), who argues cogently that most of the observations on which Freud and others based the hypothesis of primary narcissism prove only the existence of secondary narcissism occurring subsequent to frustration by the environment. Balint suggests further that in deeply regressive states, such as those found in schizophrenia and in dreamless sleep (see Lewin, 1954), the fixation point is not primary narcissism, but a primitive form of relationship in which a probably undifferentiated environment is intensely cathected. In opposition to the theory of primary narcissism, Balint proposes that the neonate is born into a primary state of intense relatedness to his environment—a state of harmonious fusion with the environment termed 'primary love'. According to Balint, all narcissism is secondary to this primary love and is caused by a disturbance between the infant and environment leading to frustration. Other authors (e.g. Rosenfeld, 1964) have similarly claimed that the earliest period of infancy is characterized not by a primary state of self-absorption but rather by primitive object relationships.

The controversy about primary narcissism versus primary object relatedness appears to me to be another red herring created by the drive concept of narcissism. In the earliest infantile stage the self and object world are undifferentiated—the neonate cannot discriminate between his own sensations and the objects from which they are derived (Jacobson, 1964). Since self and object images are not yet differentiated, it makes no logical sense to think of this earliest neonatal stage in terms of *either* primary narcissism (self-cathexis) or primary love (object-cathexis). It seems more appropriate to the phenomenology of this stage to describe it as a state of undifferentiated symbiotic fusion. It is only with the beginning of self-object differentiation that the issue of primary narcissism versus primary object relatedness becomes at all meaningful. But even here the controversy is rendered insubstantial by a functional conception of narcissism. The newly differentiated self-representation of the infant is highly vulnerable and fragile, lacking in cohesiveness and stable boundaries. Hence, the infant's earliest object relationships *of necessity* serve a basically narcissistic function—i.e. serve to consolidate the infant's rudimentary self-representation. In other words, the earliest manifestations of the narcissistic function occur in relation to primary objects, and the earliest object relationships serve a basic narcissistic function. Primitive object relationship and primitive narcissism are two inseparable sides of the same coin. The controversy about which came first, an artifact of the economic conception of narcissism, fades away when narcissism is understood in functional terms. Within the framework of a functional definition, narcissism as a developmental line pertains to stages in the growth of structures that maintain the cohesiveness, stability, and positive affective colouring of the self-representation. Growth proceeds from primitive prestructural narcissistic object relationships towards higher forms of narcissism by way of a gradual accretion of internal structure which takes on the function of maintaining the self-representation (Jacobson, 1964; Kohut, 1971).

4. Narcissism as self-esteem.

Pulver's (1970) criticism of equating the drive concept of narcissism (libidinal cathexis of the self) with self-esteem (a complex ego state) is worth quoting at some length:

When the varying self images become organized into a more cohesive affective picture of the self, we speak of *self-esteem,* with 'high self-esteem' implying a predominance of pleasurable affects and 'low self-esteem' of unpleasurable ones. All of these ego states of affect-self-representation linkages may be either conscious, preconscious or unconscious, have complex origins, and many defensive and adaptive functions . . . With all of this in mind, it should be clear that the proposition that self-esteem is simply the libidinal investment of the self is woefully inadequate. It is an explanation of a complex ego state in drive terms, and very nonspecific drive terms at that. It not only precludes the consideration of the multiple factors determining self-esteem, but tries in an indirect way to explain affects by drives.

Pulver also cites the point made by Joffe & Sandler (1967) that explaining self-esteem as the libidinal investment of the self introduces the economic notion that self-esteem decreases as libido is invested in objects and increases as it is withdrawn from objects and invested in the self. Obviously, such a notion is not supported by clinical observations that object relationships can serve (with varying degrees of success) to enhance self-esteem, and that the loss of object ties can be catastrophic for the self-esteem.

These conceptual difficulties are eliminated and the relationship between narcissistic activity and self-esteem is clarified, if the drive concept of narcissism is replaced by the functional definition proposed here. Narcissism, as functionally defined, is not synonymous with self-esteem, which is conceived as a complex affective state multiply determined by many factors (not the least of which is the vicissitudes of aggression). Narcissism embodies those mental operations whose *function* is to regulate self-esteem (the affective colouring of the self-representation) and to maintain the cohesiveness and stability of the self-representation (the structural foundation upon which self-esteem rests). The relationship of narcissism to self-esteem is analogous to the relationship between a thermostat and room temperature. A thermostat is not equivalent to room temperature, nor is it the only determinant of room temperature. It as the function of a thermostat to regulate and stabilize room temperature in the face of a multitude of forces which threaten to raise or lower it. Similarly, self-esteem is vulnerable to the impact of a multitude of internal and external forces (see Jacobson, 1964). But when self-esteem is threatened, significantly lowered or destroyed, then narcissistic activities are called into play in an effort to protect, restore, repair and stabilize it. With regard to the point made by Joffe & Sandler (1967), narcissism functionally defined as being in the service of self-esteem regulation is not incompatible with intense object relationships, which indeed may be in the same service.

5. Healthy versus unhealthy narcissism.

As Pulver (1970) points out, the drive concept of narcissism makes it difficult to differentiate metapsychologically between pathological inflations of the self and a realistic good feeling about oneself, since with the drive concept both are conceived as being due to the libidinal cathexis of the self. Indeed, it seems to me that the drive concept leads to the erroneous view that narcissism is by definition unhealthy since it is at the expense of object cathexis. In contrast, a functional definition of narcissism (indeed, a functional definition of any activity) contains a built-in criterion for differentiating between healthy versus unhealthy narcissism; namely, the criterion of how successful or unsuccessful a given narcissistic activity is in exercising its function. The issue of whether a piece of narcissism is healthy or unhealthy reduces to the question of whether or not it succeeds in maintaining a cohesive, stable and positively coloured self-representation. For instance, beyond the developmental stage at which they are phase-appropriate, attempts to maintain the self-representation through a narcissistic object tie to an idealized external object often fail, since such relationships tend to go through highly conflictual vicissitudes, and the state of the self-representation will be highly vulnerable to the fate of the usually unstable relationship (Reich, 1953). On the other hand, self-esteem regulation by means of a depersonified, abstract, fully internalized and realistically tempered superego ideal system represents a highly successful exercise of the narcissistic function. As Jacobson (1964) points out, the development of such an autonomous central endopsychic regulatory system, independent of external objects, contributes greatly to the stability of the self-representation 'which cannot be as easily affected as before by experiences of rejection, frustration, failure and the like', and to the successful maintenance of 'a sufficiently high average level of self-esteem, with a limited margin for its vacillations, apt to withstand to some extent psychic or even physical injuries to the self'.

6. Countertransference.

It is my belief that the drive concept of narcissism (and even the very term 'narcissism', which derives from drive theory) can exacerbate the countertransference problems elicited by narcissistic patients. The drive concept of narcissism as self-love may lead us to develop overt or covert rejective and contemptuous attitudes toward our narcissistic patients in so far as it encourages us to view such patients as selfish, self-engrossed, self-indulgent infants. As a result, we would tend to identify these patients with rejected aspects of our own infantile selves or of our childhood objects. In contrast, I believe a functional conception of narcissism helps to alleviate the countertransference problems that arise with narcissistic patients, because it helps us to recognize that their narcissism is literally in the service of the psychic survival of the self. A functional orientation helps us to achieve empathy with such patients, as we become intrigued with understanding the function of their narcissistic operations and what has made them necessary. A functional definition helps us to sympathetically accept primitive narcissistic attitudes as comprehensible and indispensable in view of a patient's level of ego development, and to endure our humble and at times thankless role in the narcissistic transferences of being nothing more than the embodiment of a function which the patient's mental apparatus cannot yet perform itself (Kohut, 1971). And finally, an accurate functional understanding of narcissism helps us to avoid the (sometimes countertransference-motivated) pitfall of routinely interpreting narcissistic configurations as defences against object-instinctual investments (Oremland & Windholz, 1971).

SUMMARY

A critique of the traditional economic concept of narcissism as the libidinal investment of the self has been offered. A functional definition was proposed, according to which mental activity is narcissistic to the degree that its function is to maintain the cohesiveness, stability and positive affective colouring of the self-representation. Contributions to a functional understanding of narcissism were reviewed. It was argued that the proposed functional conception of narcissism lends clarification to our understanding of the narcissistic perversion, narcissistic object relationships, narcissism as a developmental line, the relationship of narcissistic activity to self-esteem, and the issue of healthy versus unhealthy narcissism. Lastly, the claim was made that a functional understanding of narcissism can help analysts avoid certain counter-transference pitfalls encountered with narcissistic patients.

REFERENCES

Apfelbaum, B. (1965). Ego psychology, psychic energy, and the hazards of quantitative explanation in psychoanalytic theory. *Int. J. Psycho-Anal.* **46**, 168–182.

Arlow, J. & Brenner, C. (1964). *Psychoanalytic Concepts and the Structural Theory.* New York: Int. Univ. Press.

Balint, M. (1960). Primary narcissism and primary love. *Psychoanal. Q.* **29**, 6–43.

Dahl, H. (*Reporter*) (1968). Panel on 'Psychoanalytic theory of the instinctual drives in relation to recent developments'. *J. Am. Psychoanal. Ass.* **16**, 627–632.

Eisnitz, A. (1969). Narcissistic object choice, self-representation. *Int. J. Psycho-Anal.* **50**, 15–25.

Elkisch, P. (1957). The psychological significance of the mirror. *J. Am. Psychoanal. Ass.* **5**, 235–244.

Freeman, T. (1964). Some aspects of pathological narcissism. *J. Am. Psychoanal. Ass.* **12**, 540–561.

Freud, S. (1914). On narcissism: an introduction. *S.E.* **14**.

Hartmann, H. (1950). Comments on the psychoanalytic theory of the ego. *Psychoanal. Study Child* **5**.

Jacobson, E. (1964). *The Self and the Object World.* New York: Int. Univ. Press.

Joffe, W. & Sandler, J. (1967). Some conceptual problems involved in the considera-tion of disorders of narcissism *J. Child Psychother.* **2**, 56–66.

Kanzer, M. (1964). Freud's uses of the terms 'autoerotism' and 'narcissism'. *J. Am. Psychoanal. Ass.* **12**, 529–539.

Kernberg, O. (1970). Factors in the psychoanalytic treatment of narcissistic person-alities. *J. Am. Psychoanal. Ass.* **18**, 51–85.

Kohut, H. (1971). *The Analysis of the Self.* New York: Int Univ. Press.

Lewin, B. (1954). Sleep, narcissistic neurosis and the analytic situation. *Psychoanal. Q.* **23**, 487–510.

Lichtenstein, H. (1964). The role of narcissism in the emergence and maintenance of a primary identity. *Int. J. Psycho-Anal.* **45**, 49–56.

Murray, J. (1964). Narcissism and the ego ideal. *J. Am. Psychoanal. Ass.* **12**, 477–511.

Oremland, J. & Windholz, E. (1971). Some specific transference, countertransference and supervisory problems in the analysis of a narcissistic personality. *Int. J. Psycho-Anal.* **52**, 267–275.

Pulver, S. (1970). Narcissism: the term and the concept. *J. Am Psychoanal. Ass.* **18**, 319–341.

Reich, A. (1953). Narcissistic object choice in women. *J. Am. Psychoanal. Ass.* **1**, 22–44.

Reich, A. (1960). Pathological forms of self-esteem regulation. *Psychoanal. Study Child* **15.**

Rosenfeld, H. (1964). On the psychopathology of narcissism: a clinical approach. *Int. J. Psycho-Anal.* **45,** 332–337.

Waelder, R. (1930). The principle of multiple function. *Psychoanal. Q.* **5,** (1936), 45–62.

B. Object Relations

9. Factors in the Psychoanalytic Treatment of Narcissistic Personalities

Otto F. Kernberg

In this paper I shall discuss the etiology, diagnosis, prognosis, and some factors in the treatment of patients with narcissistic personality structure. I do not expect to treat the subject exhaustively, but I hope to shed new light on certain areas. This paper deals mainly with the clinical problem of narcissism, and such metapsychological considerations as will be presented shortly have to do only with the etiology of pathological narcissism and not with the broader issue of the theory of narcissism in psychoanalysis.

I suggested in an earlier paper (8) that narcissistic as a descriptive term has been both abused and overused, but that there does exist a group of patients in whom the main problem appears to be the disturbance of their self-regard in connection with specific disturbances in their object relationships, and whom we might consider almost a pure culture of pathological development of narcissism. It is for these patients that I would reserve the term narcissistic personalities. On the surface, these patients may not present seriously disturbed behavior; some of them may function socially very well, and they usually have much better impulse control than the infantile personality.

These patients present an unusual degree of self-reference in their interactions with other people, a great need to be loved and admired by others, and a curious apparent contradiction between a very inflated concept of themselves and an inordinate need for tribute from others. Their emotional life is shallow. They experience little empathy for the feelings of others, they obtain very little enjoyment from life other than from the tributes they receive from others or from their own grandiose fantasies, and they feel restless and bored when external glitter wears off and no new sources feed their self-regard. They envy others, tend to idealize some people from whom they expect narcissistic supplies and to depreciate and treat with contempt those from whom they do not expect anything (often their former idols). In general, their relationships with other people are clearly exploitative and sometimes parasitic. It is as if they feel they have the right to control and possess others and to exploit them without guilt feelings—and, behind a surface which very often is charming and engaging, one senses coldness and ruthlessness. Very often such patients are considered to be dependent because they need so much tribute and adoration from others, but on a deeper level they are completely unable really to depend on anybody because of their deep distrust and depreciation of others.

Analytic exploration very often demonstrates that their haughty, grandiose, and controlling behavior is a defense against paranoid traits related to the projection of oral rage, which is central in their psychopathology. On the surface these patients appear to present a remarkable lack of object relationships; on a deeper level, their interactions reflect very intense, primitive, internalized object relationships of a frightening kind and an incapacity to depend on internalized good objects. The antisocial personality may be considered a subgroup of the narcissistic personality. Antisocial personality structures present the same general constellation of traits that I have just mentioned, in combination with additional severe superego pathology.

The main characteristics of these narcissistic personalities are grandiosity, extreme self-centeredness, and a remarkable absence of interest in and empathy for others in spite of the fact that they are so very eager to obtain admiration and approval from other people. These patients experience a remarkably intense envy of other people who seem to have things they do not have or who simply seem to enjoy their lives. These patients not only lack emotional depth and fail to understand complex emotions in other people, but their own feelings lack differentiation, with quick flare-ups and subsequent dispersal of emotion. They are especially deficient in genuine feelings of sadness and mournful longing; their incapacity for experiencing depressive reactions is a basic feature of their personalities. When abandoned or disappointed by other people they may show what on the surface looks like depression, but which on further examination emerges as anger and resentment, loaded with revengeful wishes, rather than real sadness for the loss of a person whom they appreciated.

Some patients with narcissistic personalities present strong conscious feelings of insecurity and inferiority. At times, such feelings of inferiority and insecurity may alternate with feelings of greatness and omnipotent fantasies (12). At other times, and only after some period of analysis, do unconscious fantasies of omnipotence and narcissistic grandiosity come to the surface. The presence of extreme contradictions in their self concept is often the first clinical evidence of the severe pathology in the ego and superego of these patients, hidden underneath a surface of smooth and effective social functioning.

The defensive organization of these patients is quite similar to that of the borderline personality organization in general. They present a predominance of primitive defensive mechanisms such as splitting, denial, projective identification, omnipotence, and primitive idealization. They also show the intense, primitive quality of oral-aggressive conflicts characteristic of borderline patients. What distinguishes many of the patients with narcissistic personalities from the usual borderline patient is their relatively good social functioning, their better impulse control, and what may be described as a "pseudosublimatory" potential, namely, the capacity for active, consistent work in some areas which permits them partially to fulfill their ambitions of greatness and of obtaining admiration from others. Highly intelligent patients with this personality structure may appear as quite creative in their fields: narcissistic personalities can often be found as leaders in industrial organizations or academic institutions; they may also be outstanding performers in some artistic domain. Careful observation, however, of their productivity over a long period of time will give evidence of superficiality and flightiness in their work, of a lack of depth which eventually reveals the emptiness behind the glitter. Quite frequently these are the "promising" geniuses who then surprise other people by the banality of their development. They also are able to exert self-control in anxiety-producing situations, which may at first appear as good anxiety tolerance; however, analytic exploration shows that their anxiety tolerance is obtained at the cost of increasing their narcissistic fantasies and of withdrawing into "splendid isolation." This tolerance of anxiety does not reflect an authentic capacity for coming to terms with a disturbing reality.

In short, the surface functioning of the narcissistic personality is much better than that of the average borderline patient; therefore, their capacity for regression—even to the level of psychotic functioning when undergoing psychoanalysis—may come as a real surprise to the analyst.

ETIOLOGICAL AND DYNAMIC FEATURES

An early effort to classify the narcissistic character as one form of libidinal type (5) did not become generally accepted, for reasons mentioned by Fenichel (3). Van der Waals (21) has clarified the issue of "pathological narcissism" by pointing out that severe narcissism does not reflect simply a fixation in early narcissistic stages of development and a simple lack of the normal course of development toward object love, but that it is characterized by the simultaneous development of pathological forms of self-love and of pathological forms of object love. According to van der Waals, normal narcissism develops simultaneously with normal object relationships, and pathological narcissism with pathological object relationships. He has also pointed out that progress in the understanding of pathological narcissism has been hampered by the fact that in psychoanalytic literature the clinical problems of narcissism are intermingled with the issue of narcissism as a metapsychological problem.

Jacobson (6) has clarified the relationship between psychotic regression on the one hand and defensive refusion of early self and object representations on the other. According to Jacobson, in the earliest stages of an individual's development, when self and object images are differentiated from each other and thus contribute to the development of reality testing and of ego boundaries, extremely severe frustrations in relationships with significant early objects may bring about a dangerous refusion of self and object images, a mechanism which allows the individual to escape the conflict between the need for the external object and the dread of it. Under these circumstances, a blurring of ego boundaries, the loss of reality testing, in short, psychotic regression, may occur. Such a development does not take place in the case of narcissistic personalities, whose ego boundaries are stable and whose reality testing is preserved. A. Reich (12) has suggested that in narcissistic personalities a regressive fusion takes place between a primitive ego ideal and the self.

I propose that a process of refusion of the internalized self and object images does occur in the narcissistic personality at a level of development at which ego boundaries have already become stable. At this point, there is a fusion of ideal self, ideal object, and actual self images as a defense against an intolerable reality in the interpersonal realm, with a concomitant devaluation and destruction of object images as well as of external objects. In their fantasies, these patients identify themselves with their own ideal self images in order to deny normal dependency on external objects and on the internalized representations of the external objects. It is as if they were saying, "I do not need to fear that I will be rejected for not living up to the ideal of myself which alone makes it possible for me to be loved by the ideal person I imagine would love me. That ideal person and my ideal image of that person and my real self are all one, and better than the ideal person whom I wanted to love me, so that I do not need anybody else any more." In other words, the normal tension between actual self on the one hand, and ideal self and ideal object on the other, is eliminated by the building up of an inflated self concept within which the actual self and the ideal self and ideal object are confused. At the same time, the remnants of the unacceptable self images are repressed and projected onto external objects, which are devaluated. This process is in marked contrast to the normal differentiation between ideal self images on the one hand and ideal object images on the other, both of which represent the internalized demands of objects as well as gratification from these objects if the demands are met. The normal superego integrates ideal self images and ideal object images; the tension between actual self images and such integrated ideal ones becomes tension between the ego and superego. In patients presenting pathological narcissism, however, the pathological fusion between ideal self, ideal object, and actual self images prevents such integration of the superego, because the process of idealization is highly unrealistic, preventing the condensation of such idealized images with actual parental demands and with the aggressively determined superego forerunners. Also, actual self images, a part of the ego structure, are now pathologically condensed with forerunners of the superego, and, therefore, they interfere with the normal differentiation of the superego and ego. Although some superego components are internalized, such as prohibitive parental demands, they preserve a distorted, primitive, aggressive quality because they are not integrated with the loving aspects of the superego which are normally drawn from the ideal self and object images and are missing in these patients (17). Because there is so little integration with other superego forerunners, the generally aggressive and primitive kind of superego is easily reprojected in the form of paranoid projections. I want to stress that the primitive and aggressive nature of their superego ultimately derives from the intense oral-aggressive quality of their fixations. Narcissistic patients characteristically adapt themselves to the moral demands of their environment because they are afraid of the attacks to which they would be subjected if they do not conform, and because this submission seems to be the price they have to pay for glory and admiration; however, one frequently finds that patients of this kind, who have never shown evidence of antisocial activity, think of themselves as "crooks" and as capable of antisocial behavior "if they could get away with it." Needless to say, they also experience other people as basically dishonest and unreliable, or only reliable because of external pressures. This concept of themselves and others, of course, becomes very important in the transference.

One result of the defensive fusion of ideal self, ideal object, and actual self images is the devaluation and destruction not only of external objects but also of internalized object images. Actually, this process never goes so far that there are no internal representations of external objects: it would probably be impossible to live under such conditions. To want to be admired and loved by others requires that others should appear at least somewhat "alive," internally as well as externally. The remnants of the internalized object representations acquire the characteristics of real, but rather lifeless, shadowy people. This experience of other people, especially those who are not idealized, as lifeless shadows or marionettes, is quite prevalent in the patients I am considering. Idealized people, on whom these patients seem to "depend," regularly turn out to be projections of their own aggrandized self concepts. Idealized representatives of the self, the "shadows" of others, and—as we shall see—dreaded enemies, are all that seem to exist in the inner world of these patients. A narcissistic patient experiences his relationships with other people as being purely exploitative, as if he were "squeezing a lemon and then dropping the remains." People may appear to him either to have some potential food inside, which the patient has to extract, or to be already emptied and therefore valueless. In addition, these shadowy external objects sometimes suddenly seem to be invested with high and dangerous powers, as the patient projects onto others the primitive characteristics of his own superego and of his own exploitative nature. His attitude toward others is either deprecatory—he has extracted all he needs and tosses them aside—or fearful—others may attack, exploit, and force him to submit to them. At the very bottom of this dichotomy lies a still deeper image of the relationship with external objects, precisely the one against which the patient has erected all these other pathological structures. It is the image of a hungry, enraged, empty self, full of impotent anger at being frustrated, and fearful of a world which seems as hateful and revengeful as the patient himself.

This, the deepest level of the self concept of narcissistic patients, can be preceived only late in the course of their psychoanalytic treatment, except in the case of narcissistic patients with overt borderline features who show it quite early. British psychoanalysts who have analyzed patients with this character structure have reported the central importance of such basic dread of attack and destruction. In less disorganized patients, that is, narcissistic personalities with relatively stronger egos, one eventually encounters in the transference paranoid developments, with feelings of emptiness, rage, and fear of being attacked. On an even less regressed level, the available remnants of such self images reveal a picture of a worthless, poverty-stricken, empty person who feels always left "outside," devoured by envy of those who have food, happiness, and fame. Often the surface remnant of this line of primitive self images is undistinguishable from the shadowy remnant of devaluated object images. This devaluated concept of the self can be seen especially in narcissistic patients who divide the world into famous, rich, and great people on the one hand, and the despicable, worthless, "mediocrity" on the other. Such patients are afraid of not belonging to the company of the great, rich, and powerful, and of belonging instead to the "mediocre," by which they mean worthless and despicable rather than "average" in the ordinary sense of the term. One patient, after years of analytic treatment, began to yearn to become "average," meaning he wanted to be able to enjoy being an ordinary person, without an overriding necessity to feel great and important in order to cancel feelings of worthlessness and devaluation.

What brings about the crucial pathological fusion of ideal self, ideal object, and actual self images? These patients present a pathologically augmented development of oral aggression and it is hard to evaluate to what extent this development represents a constitutionally determined strong aggressive drive, a constitutionally determined lack of anxiety tolerance in regard to aggressive impulses, or severe frustration in their first years of life.

Chronically cold parental figures with covert but intense aggression are a very frequent feature of the background of these patients. A composite picture of a number of cases that I have been able to examine or to treat shows consistently a parental figure, usually the mother or a mother surrogate, who functions well on the surface in a superficially well-organized home, but with a degree of callousness, indifference, and nonverbalized, spiteful aggression. When intense oral frustration, resentment, and aggression have developed in the child within such an environment, the first condition is laid for his need to defend against extreme envy and hatred. In addition, these patients present some quite specific features which distinguish them from other borderline patients. Their histories reveal that each patient possessed some inherent quality which could have objectively aroused the envy or admiration of others. For example, unusual physical attractiveness or some special talent became a refuge against the basic feelings of being unloved and of being the objects of revengeful hatred. Sometimes it was rather the cold hostile mother's narcissistic use of the child which made him "special," set him off on the road in a search for compensatory admiration and greatness, and fostered the characterological defense of spiteful devaluation of others. For example, two patients were used by their mothers as a kind of "object of art," being dressed up and exposed to public admiration in an almost grotesque way, so that fantasies of power and greatness linked with exhibitionistic trends became central in their compensatory efforts against oral rage and envy. These patients often occupy a pivotal point in their family structure, such as being the only child, or the only "brilliant" child, or the one who is supposed to fulfill the family aspirations; a good number of them have a history of having played the role of "genius" in their family during childhood.

I am not sure whether these observations explain the entire story. Once, however, the kind of mechanism mentioned—defensive fusion of ideal self, ideal object, and self images—comes into operation, it is extremely effective in perpetuating a vicious circle of self-admiration, depreciation of others, and elimination of all actual dependency. The greatest fear of these patients is to be dependent on anybody else, because to depend means to hate, envy, and expose themselves to the danger of being exploited, mistreated, and frustrated. In the course of treatment, their main defenses are erected against the possibility of depending on the analyst, and the development of a situation in which they do feel dependent immediately brings back the basic threatening situation of early childhood (14).

This kind of person's incapacity to depend on another person is a very crucial characteristic. These patients often admire some hero or outstanding individual and establish with such a person what on the surface looks like a dependent relationship, yet they really experience themselves as part of that outstanding person; it regularly emerges in treatment that the admired individual is merely an extension of themselves. If the person rejects them, they experience immediate hatred and fear, and react by devaluating the former idol. If their admired person disappears or is "dethroned," they immediately drop him. In short, there is no real involvement with the admired person and a simple narcissistic use is made of him. When narcissistic personalities are themselves in a position of objective importance—for example, heading a political institution or a social group—they love to surround themselves with admirers in whom they are interested as long as the admiration is new. Once they feel they have extracted all the admiration they need, they perceive their admirers as "shadows" once more and mercilessly exploit and mistreat them. At the same time, these patients are extremely offended when one of their "slaves" wants to free himself. In the analytic situation this relationship is constantly re-enacted. These patients at times idealize the analyst and are convinced that he is the greatest analyst on earth. At the same time, on a deeper level, they experience themselves as the only patient of the analyst; I have found the literal fantasy in several patients that, when they are not in session, their analyst disappears or dies or is no longer brilliant. Typically, over weekends and during vacations, these patients completely forget the analyst and do not permit themselves the mourning reactions that separations from the analyst induce in the usual psychoneurotic case. In short, the idealized analyst is only an extension of themselves, or they are extensions of the idealized analyst; it is the same situation in either case. There exists the danger of looking upon these patients as very dependent because of the satisfaction they obtain from such "closeness." It comes as a surprise to some therapists that patients who seemed happy to come to their sessions over many years with unending expressions of praise and admiration for their therapist are all of a sudden willing and able to drop the relationship for the slightest reason or frustration.

These patient's feelings of emptiness and boredom are intimately related to their stunted ego development, which in turn is connected with their inability to experience depression. Many authors have pointed out that the capacity for tolerating depression, linked to the capacity for mourning over a lost good object or a lost ideal image of oneself, is an important prerequisite for emotional development and especially for the broadening and deepening of feelings. In addition, the devaluation of objects and object images on the part of patients with pathological narcissism creates a constant emptiness in their social life and reinforces their internal experience of emptiness. They need to devaluate whatever they receive in order to prevent themselves from experiencing envy. This is the tragedy of these patients: that they need so much from others while being unable to acknowledge what they are receiving because it would stir up envy; in consequence, they always wind up empty. One patient fell in love with a woman whom he considered very beautiful, gifted, warm, in short, completely satisfying. He had a brief period of awareness of how much he hated her for being so perfect, just before she responded to him and decided to marry him. After their marriage he felt bored with her and became completely indifferent toward her. During his psychoanalysis he came to understand how he treated his analyst in a similar way: he depreciated everything he was receiving from his analyst in order to prevent his envy and hatred from coming to the surface. After that, the patient gradually developed strong suspiciousness and hatred toward his wife for having all that he felt he did not have, and he was also afraid that she would abandon him and leave him with even less. At the same time, however, he was able for the first time to become aware of and to be moved by her expressions of love and tenderness. His awareness of his aggressive disqualification of her and his analyst, and his increasing ability to tolerate his hatred without having to defend against it by destroying his awareness of other people made both his wife and his analyst "come alive" as real people with independent existences, and eventually permitted him to experience not only hatred but also love toward them.

DIFFERENTIAL DIAGNOSIS

The descriptive features of narcissistic personalities usually permit their differentiation from other forms of character pathology in which narcissistic character defenses are present. All character defenses have, among other functions, a narcissistic one: they protect self-esteem. In addition, there are patients with all kinds of character pathology who present marked character defenses especially erected to protect or enhance self-esteem. These latter cases have "narcissistic character defenses" in an essentially nonnarcissistic personality structure, which has to be differentiated, therefore, from the narcissistic personality in the narrow sense used in this paper. Thus, for example, the stubbornness or oppositionalism of obsessive personalities often has a strong narcissistic quality; however, there is much more stability and depth in the interpersonal relationships of obsessive personalities than in those of narcissistic personalities, in spite of the fact that both may appear superficially as quite "cold." Also, the value systems of narcissistic personalities are generally corruptible, in contrast to the rigid morality of the obsessive personality.

The differential diagnosis in distinction to hysterical character structure is also not too difficult. An exaggeration of narcissistic traits, especially those linked with exhibitionistic trends, is quite prevalent in hysterical personalities; however, the need to be admired, to be the center of attention of the hysterical personality—usually a narcissistic reaction formation against penis envy—goes together with a capacity for deep and lasting relationships with others. Women with narcissistic personalities may appear as quite "hysterical" on the surface, with their extreme coquettishness and exhibitionism, but the cold, shrewdly calculating quality of their seductiveness is in marked contrast to the much warmer, emotionally involved quality of hysterical pseudo-hypersexuality.

A. Reich (11), further analyzing narcissistic types of object choice made by women as presented in Freud's classical paper on narcissism (4), described two types of object choice in women which, broadly speaking, correspond to the differentiation between narcissistic defenses in hysterical women on the one hand and the narcissistic personality as described in this paper on the other. A. Reich's first type is the woman who develops extreme submissiveness toward men who represent her own, infantile, grandiose ego ideal; such a woman appears to wish to fuse with idealized men, overcoming in this way her experience of herself as a castrated being. These women are able to establish meaningful object relationships with men, and their fusion with and idealization of men are based on at least some realistic and discriminating evaluation of the objects. The second type of woman which A. Reich describes corresponds to the "as if" type of personality: such a woman establishes transitory pseudoinfatuations with men, infatuations which represent a more primitive, narcissistic fusion with easily devaluated and poorly differentiated objects. This latter form of object choice reflects, A. Reich says, a more severe degree of pathology and lack of differentiation of the ego ideal, which goes hand in hand with an insufficiently developed superego and with a "predominance of aggression against the objects on whom the ego ideal is built" (11).

From a diagnostic and prognostic viewpoint, it is very important for the analyst to observe what kind of new transference developments appear when narcissistic transference resistances are interpreted. A good diagnostic study involving structural considerations should make it possible to differentiate between narcissistic personalities and character structures and narcissistic features. The effects of consistent interpretation of narcissistic transference resistances should clarify the diagnosis in cases in which doubts about the character structure still remain. For example, an obsessive patient may start out in analysis with strong narcissistic defenses against oedipal fears or against sadomasochistic dispositions; a hysterical woman may develop initially strong narcissistic defenses against oedipal involvement and especially against penis envy. In all these cases the analysis of such narcissistic character defenses soon opens the road to the underlying transference dispositions, with intense and highly differentiated transference involvements, in contrast to the process in the case of patients with narcissistic personalities. In the latter, narcissistic defenses do not change into other transference paradigms, but remain stubbornly linked to primitive, oral-aggressive drive derivatives and related primitive defensive operations. Here the characteristics of the transference involvement oscillate between narcissistic grandiosity and aloofness on the one hand, and primitive, predominantly paranoid trends on the other. The patient's complete incapacity, maintained over many months and years of analytic work, to experience the analyst as an independent object is characteristic of narcissistic personalities, and is in sharp contrast to the transference involvements in other forms of character pathology where the transference may shift to reveal different, highly specific conflicts of varying psychosexual stages of development and with a highly differentiated awareness by the patient of the analyst as an independent object.

From a structural viewpoint, the main difference between narcissistic personalities and other forms of character pathology is the different nature and functioning of the ego ideal. Normally, idealized images of the parental figures and idealized self images are first condensed into the ego ideal (6), which then is further modified by the integration and incorporation of more realistically perceived parental demands, of the sadistic forerunners of the superego, and of the more advanced aspects of the prohibitive superego. Such a "toned down," less grandiose, and more attainable ego ideal permits one the normal narcissistic gratification of living up to the internalized ideal parental images, and this gratification in turn reinforces self-esteem, one's confidence in one's own goodness and one's trust in gratifying object relationships. In character pathology other than the narcissistic personality, the excessive development of narcissistic character defenses results from an exacerbation of the early infantile ego ideal as a defense against fear and guilt over multiple conflicts. Thus, for example, in the case of many female patients with hysterical personalities, the need to live up to internal fantasies of being beautiful and powerful may be a protection against feelings of inferiority which in turn stem from penis envy and castration anxiety. Again, in obsessive personalities, living up to primitive ideals of perfection and cleanliness may be a most effective protection against anal-sadistic guilt and conflicts. In all these cases, the exacerbation of or fixation at the infantile ego ideal is not accompanied by a primitive fusion of the self concept with such an ego ideal, nor by a concomitant devaluation of object representations and external objects. But in narcissistic personalities, such a primitive fusion of the self with the ego ideal, and concomitant processes of devaluation of external objects and object images, do take place in order to protect the self against primitive oral conflicts and frustration. These fixations at the level of normal infantile narcissism, which are pathological in any case, have to be differentiated from the more severe, particular distortion of all internalized object relations that take place in the narcissistic personality.

The following two cases illustrate the presence of narcissistic character defenses in nonnarcissistic personalities. The first, a female patient with hysterical personality structure, had a strong, although deeply repressed, conviction that underneath what she considered her ugly, distasteful body and genitals, there was the body and the genitals of a unique, extremely beautiful woman toward whom men would feel impelled to pay homage. At that deeper level, she fantasied herself as the most attractive woman on earth, a "mother-queen-goddess" who would achieve a perfect relationship with an ideal, great "father-husband-son." In the transference, she was willing to give her love to the analyst-father if he in return would comply with that perfect image which she had of herself by admiring her and never questioning her perfection and integrity. The patient experienced the analyst's interpretations as threatening to that image of herself, a severe attack on her self-esteem, and a shattering criticism which induced quite intense depression. When her haughty, derogatory attitude toward the analyst, a part of her narcissistic self-aggrandizement, was pointed out to her, she became angry and depressed, and at that point experienced the analyst as a narcissistic, self-involved, grandiose father image. Her reaction represented part of the way she had actually experienced her father in her childhood at the height of her oedipal development. Disappointed at what she perceived as the analyst-father's "attacks" on her, she then felt lost and rejected by this idealized father, and defeated in her fantasies by other, idealized women-mothers in the competition for the father. Thus, she developed a full-fledged oedipal transference. This transference emerged after the undoing of her narcissistic character defenses, which in turn had stemmed from penis envy. At no point did she completely devaluate the transference object, or oscillate between primitive, orally determined paranoid transference distortions on the one hand, and narcissistic withdrawal into a more primitive self-idealization on the other. Since these latter elements were lacking, we may conclude that her narcissistic transference resistances did not reflect a narcissistic personality structure.

The second illustration of a narcissistic character defense was provided by a male patient with an obsessive personality structure. He was quite derogatory toward the analyst, revealed in his own interpretations of his material, and saw the analyst mainly as a background figure whose function was to applaud and admire these interpretations and insights. When this attitude was systematically examined, however, and the patient was consistently confronted with this defensive pattern, a new, deeper, transference pattern evolved. In this new facet of the transference, the patient saw the analyst as a cold, indifferent, unloving mother image, and experienced feelings of sadness and loneliness, representing an early longing for his idealized mother. In this second illustration, too, when narcissistic character defenses broke down, other transference patterns emerged in which the patient maintained a differentiated object relationship, neither devaluating the object nor taking flight into an idealized self image. In summary, both of these cases developed new, differentiated transference relationships after the narcissistic character defenses had been dissolved, whereas the narcissistic patient cannot acknowledge the analyst as an independent object and continuously and stubbornly regards him as a simple extension of the patient's own self concept, although the regression within this same transference paradigm may fluctuate.

CONSIDERATIONS IN REGARD TO TECHNIQUE

Many experienced clinicians consider these narcissistic personalities as unlikely candidates for analysis, but at the same time as hopeless candidates for any method of treatment other than psychoanalysis. Against this extremely guarded prognosis, Stone (18) expresses a somewhat more optimistic viewpoint about the analyzability of these patients. E. Ticho (20), recognizing both the problems and the challenges of these cases, has proposed that narcissistic personalities constitute a "heroic indication for psychoanalysis." In my opinion, the fact that some of these patients not only improve with psychoanalytic treatment, but improve dramatically, shows that efforts to study the technical and prognostic features of these cases more thoroughly are well warranted.

Jones (7) published a paper on pathological narcissistic character traits as early as 1913. In 1919, Abraham (1) wrote the first paper on the transference resistances of these patients, in which he warned the therapist about the dangerous effects of narcissistic character defenses on the psychoanalytic process. He pointed to the necessity for consistent interpretation of these patients' tendencies to look down on the analyst and to use him as an audience for their own independent "analytic" work. Riviere (13), in her classic paper on the negative therapeutic reaction, describes patients who have to defeat the psychoanalytic process: they cannot tolerate the notion of improvement, because improvement would mean acknowledgment of help received from somebody else. She states that these patients cannot tolerate receiving something good from the analyst because of the intolerable guilt over their own basic aggression. Rosenfeld (14) has stressed how basic the intolerance of dependency is on the part of patients with narcissistic personality structure. Kohut (10) has illustrated how a patient with this personality structure could not tolerate the analyst's being a different, independent person. These papers all emphasize the severity of the transference resistances of narcissistic patients.

I should like to illustrate this problem of transference resistance with a case history. A patient with narcissistic character structure spent hour after hour over many months of treatment telling me how monotonous and boring analysis had become, that in his associations the same contents kept coming up again and again, and that treatment was definitely a hopeless enterprise. At the same time, he felt rather good in his life outside the analytic hours, with some relief from his feelings of insufficiency and insecurity, but he was unable to understand why this had happened. I pointed out to him that, implicit in his description of his psychoanalysis, was a description of me as the provider of useless and silly treatment. The patient denied this at first, stressing that it was only his problem, not mine, that analysis could not work. I then pointed out to him that, at the beginning of his treatment, he had considerably envied my other patients, who had already received so much more from me than he had, and that it was strange now that he should feel no envy at all of the other patients, especially in view of his statement that it was his problem only that he could not benefit from analysis. I also pointed out to him that his previous, strong envy of me had completely disappeared, for reasons which had remained obscure to him. At this point the patient became aware that he really thought that it was entirely my fault that his analysis was, according to him, a failure. He now felt surprised that he was so satisfied to continue his treatment while considering me so inefficient. I pointed out to him how much satisfaction it gave him for me to be a failure while he was a success in his life. I also pointed out that it was as if I had become the worthless self of him, while he had taken over the admired self of me. At that point he became very anxious and developed the fear that I hated him and that I would take revenge. Fantasies came up in which he thought that I was telling his superiors and the police about activities of which he was very much ashamed. I pointed out to him that his fear of attack from me was one reason which prevented him from really considering himself in analysis and that he reassured himself that he was not really a patient by asserting that nothing was going on in the sessions. At that point the patient experienced feelings of admiration toward me because I had not become confused and discouraged by his constant repetition that analysis was a failure. At the next moment, however, he thought that I was very clever, and that I knew how to use "typical analytic tricks" to keep "one up" over patients. He then thought that he himself would try to use a similar technique with people who might try to depreciate him. I then pointed out that as soon as he received a "good" interpretation, and found himself helped, he also felt guilty over his attacks on me, and then again envious of my "goodness." Therefore, he had to "steal" my interpretations for his own use with others, devaluating me in the process, in order to avoid acknowledging that I had anything good left as well as to avoid the obligation of feeling grateful. The patient became quite anxious for a moment and then went completely "blank." He came in the next session with a bland denial of the emotional relevance of what had developed in the session before, and once again the same cycle started all over, with repetitive declarations of his boredom and the ineffectiveness of analysis.

At times it is difficult to imagine how frequent and how repetitive such interactions are, extending as they do over two or three years of analysis; this resistance to treatment illustrates the intensity of the narcissistic patient's need to deny any dependent relationship. It is obvious that consistent examination of the negative transference is even more crucial in these patients than in others undergoing psychoanalysis. These narcissistic patients persistently seek to devaluate the analytic process, to deny the reality of their own emotional life, and to confirm the fantasy that the analyst is not a person independent from themselves. A recent motion picture by Ingmar Bergman, *Persona,* illustrates the breakdown of an immature but basically decent young woman, a nurse, charged with the care of a psychologically severely ill woman presenting what we would describe as a typical narcissistic personality. In the face of the cold, unscrupulous exploitation to which the young nurse is subjected, she gradually breaks down. She cannot face the fact that the other sick woman returns only hatred for love and is completely unable to acknowledge any loving or human feeling expressed toward her. The sick woman seems to be able to live only if and when she can destroy what is valuable in other persons, although in the process she ends up destroying herself as a human being. In a dramatic development, the nurse develops an intense hatred for the sick woman and mistreats her cruelly at one point. It is as if all the hatred within the sick woman had been transferred into the helping one, destroying the helping person from the inside.

This screen play reproduces in essence the transference-countertransference situations that develop in the treatment of severely narcissistic patients. All the patients' efforts seem to go into defeating the analyst, into making analysis a meaningless game, into systematically destroying whatever they experience as good and valuable in the analyst. After many months and years of being treated as an "appendix" of the patient (a process which may be subtle enough to remain unnoticed for a long time) the analyst may begin to feel really "worthless" in his work with such a case. All his comments and interventions seem to dissolve into meaninglessness, and whatever sympathetic feeling he had for the patient is systematically destroyed by the latter. Following an unsuccessful, long treatment, a defensive devaluation of the patient on the analyst's part may occur, reinforcing the patient's feeling that his analyst is becoming one of those dangerous objects from whom he had attempted to escape; or some minor frustration of the patient may grow into a general awareness on the patient's part that he is no longer in control of the analyst. Interruption of treatment may occur at this point; the patient escapes from a hated, frustrating transference object, which he eventually reduces to a "shadow" once more, and the analyst's countertransference may reflect a corresponding feeling of "emptiness," as if the patient had never existed.

There are several technical implications of the above considerations. First, the analyst must continuously focus on the particular quality of the transference in these cases and consistently counteract the patient's efforts toward omnipotent control and devaluation. Then the analyst also has to watch carefully for his long-term countertransference developments. He should bring the countertransference into the analytic process, not by revealing to the patient what his own reaction is, but by consistently recognizing in the countertransference the hidden intention of the patient's behavior. For example, when the patient systematically rejects all the analyst's interpretations over a long period of time, the analyst may recognize his own resultant feelings of impotence and point out to the patient that he is treating the analyst as if he wished to make him feel defeated and impotent. Or, when antisocial behavior in the patient makes the analyst, rather than the patient, worry about the consequences, the analyst must point out that the patient seems to try to let the analyst feel the concern over his behavior because the patient himself cannot tolerate such a feeling. Because these patients treat the analyst as extensions of themselves, or vice versa, the analyst's emotional experience reflects more closely than usual what the patient is struggling with internally, and thus the use of countertransference reactions is particularly revealing in treatment.

One technical problem which is especially difficult for the therapist to handle is the occurrence of sudden "switches" in the emotional attitude of the patient. Especially following moments of understanding or relief, the patient tends to drop an entire subject matter rather than to be obliged either to feel grateful to the analyst for his help, or to be motivated to deepen his understanding of that particular issue. The tendency to devaluate the analyst operates here, together with an effort to rob the analyst of his interpretation; one has to be very attentive to this sudden "disappearance" of what only minutes ago, or a session ago, appeared as an important problem.

One final word about technique. One should probably not treat many of these patients at the same time, because they put a great stress and many demands on the analyst. In addition, it may help to keep in mind that these patients require the longest psychoanalytic treatments in order to break through the pathological character structure activated in the transference.

In the past some clinicians felt that these patients did not develop a transference, and that they always kept a "narcissistic noninvolvement" toward the analyst which prevented analytic work. Actually, these patients develop a very intensive transference that I have described above; what appears as distance and uninvolvement on the surface is underneath an active process of devaluation, depreciation, and spoiling. The undoing of this transference resistance typically brings about intense paranoid developments, suspiciousness, hatred, and envy. Eventually, after many months and sometimes years of treatment, guilt and depression may appear in the patient; awareness of his aggression toward the analyst may develop into guilt over it, and more human concern for the analyst as a person in combination with a heightened tolerance of guilt and depression in general. This is a crucial moment in the treatment of these patients and represents an essential prognostic factor at the same time. Those patients who have at least some tolerance for guilt and depression when the treatment starts do better than those who cannot tolerate these feelings at all. This observation leads us into our next topic: the general issue of prognosis in the psychoanalysis of these patients.

PROGNOSTIC CONSIDERATIONS

The overall prognosis for narcissistic personalities is guarded. The rigidity and smoothness in functioning of this character structure are great obstacles to analytic progress. From the viewpoint of the patient's pathology, the advantage of a complete characterological "isolation" from any meaningful interpersonal relationship is hard to give up. These patients are able internally to withdraw from social life as effectively as the most severe schizoid character. And yet, they usually seem to be in the center of things, efficiently extracting "narcissistic supplies" while subtly protecting themselves from the painful experience of more meaningful emotional interactions.

I suggested in an earlier paper (9) that narcissistic personalities, in spite of the fact that their defensive organization is, broadly speaking, similar to that of the borderline personality, benefit very little from expressive, psychoanalytically oriented treatment approaches geared to that category of patients, and that psychoanalysis is the treatment of choice for narcissistic personalities. Some of these patients not only tolerate the analytic situation without excessive regression but are so extremely resistant to any effort to mobilize their rigid pathological character defenses in the transference that they remain untouched by analysis. In patients with narcissistic personalities and overt borderline characteristics (multiple symptomatology, severe nonspecific manifestations of ego weakness, regression to primary process thinking) psychoanalysis is contraindicated. These patients usually cannot tolerate the severe regression and reactivation of very early pathogenic conflicts in the transference, necessary to their analytic treatment, without psychotic decompensation. A supportive treatment approach seems best for this group. In regard to those narcissistic patients who seem capable of undergoing psychoanalysis, I have found the following prognostic considerations useful in individual cases.

Tolerance of Depression and Mourning

The prognosis improves with patients who preserve some capacity for depression or mourning, especially when their depressions contain elements of guilt feelings. For example, one narcissistic patient began his treatment by discussing his feelings of remorse over having gotten involved with a woman who had three small children and who was very much in love with him. The children also loved him and he suddenly found himself "surrounded" in an atmosphere of friendliness and love which prevented him from carrying out his usual behavior of "dropping out" after having "made" a woman. (The transference implications of these feelings were taken up only later in his treatment.) This patient was able to improve markedly over a period of several years of analysis.

Two incidents in the treatment of this patient illustrate his gradually increasing tolerance of guilt and depression. After the first year of treatment, and after the exploitative nature of his relationship to women had been explored, the patient impulsively married the same woman and interrupted treatment for several months; he later explained this action as caused by his fear of the analyst's interference with his decision to marry. The marriage represented at this point both a defense against deepening of his guilt feelings and an acting out of his guilt feelings. Two years later we examined an episode which had repeated itself quite frequently. The patient's work led him to other cities where he would briefly become involved with women and then completely forget them the moment he left town. After two years of analysis, he had to visit one town, and he decided not to visit a girl there with whom he had been involved for many years. She still thought that he might eventually marry her, seemed always happy with his visits, and conveyed the impression to the patient that she could not get involved with any other man as long as he was still in her life. In the analysis, we had examined the exploitative nature of his relationships with her and his need to defend against guilt feelings in regard to this girl. After arriving in his hotel at that city, the patient thought with intense pain of the disappointment that she would experience after he left her once more. He also felt an intense sexual excitement pressuring him into seeing her. For hours these two feelings struggled in him and he finally had a crying spell with feelings of sadness and sorrow for both the girl and himself. He felt that to see her would only stir up again false hopes in her, and would be bad for her and for the better part of himself. He also was aware that his sexual excitement represented a wish to gratify her sexually and, thus, to allay his guilt feelings toward her, and was also an attempt to escape from his awareness of the entire problem. He finally decided not to see her, experiencing then an increase in his feelings of love and gratitude toward the girl, together with feelings of sadness and mourning, experiencing her as a good, lost object, and feeling that it was now too late to start a new life with her. I must stress that I had at no point interfered with his wishes to see her; his not seeing her did not represent a submission to my will. After this episode the patient became much more tolerant of people who were incapable of action because of their strong feelings, people whom he had always depreciated in the past.

Secondary Gain of Analytic Treatment

Unfortunately, there are social and professional conditions which give a strong secondary gain to "learning" the method of analysis. The defensive operation of "robbing" the analyst of what he has to give in order to defend oneself against the envy of the analyst and against the need to acknowledge dependency upon him is strongly reinforced under such "learning" conditions. One minister, who had been sent to analysis because of promiscuous sexual behavior, was very happy with the prospect of analytic treatment, which would give him advantages in the professional field of education in which he was involved. This felt advantage presented an insoluble resistance; the gratification of "learning" analysis compensated most effectively for the underlying depreciation of the analyst and for the patient's inability to accept himself as a patient. Candidates for psychoanalytic institutes should not present a narcissistic personality structure (15), but some applicants with such characteristics do manage to be accepted for psychoanalytic training, especially since the intellectually gifted kind of narcissistic personality may have a very promising aura of originality and intellectual curiosity (19). Such candidates remain in analysis in spite of the emotional emptiness that develops in their analyses, and they may even manage to complete their training with no appreciable change in their narcissistic features. What happens is that the ultimate gratification of becoming a psychoanalyst is sufficient to compensate for the envy and hatred of the "giving" analyst, and the candidate's inability to depend on the analyst and to establish a full-fledged transference neurosis on the level of his basic oral-aggressive conflicts remains unnoticed. Eventually, most candidates with narcissistic personality structes stop doing analytic treatment, even if they have graduated from institutes, because their lack of interest in and involvement with patients makes psychoanalysis a boring procedure to them.

Transference Potential for Guilt versus Transference Potential for Paranoid Rage

Riviere (13) stressed that these patients are incapable of tolerating a dependent relationship with the analyst because of deeply buried but ever-present feelings of unconscious guilt. In contrast, Rosenfeld (14) mentions the underlying paranoid disposition, and the strong oral-sadistic transference, behind these patients' incapacity to tolerate dependency. There are narcissistic patients with each kind of underlying transference potential. Once the typical transference defenses of magic, narcissistic fusion with the analyst and devaluation of him as an independent person, together with the accompanying struggle against real dependency on the analyst, have been resolved, some patients develop intense paranoid reactions in the transference, while other patients seem able to experience at least some guilt and concern over what they are doing to the analyst. Even if their previous history has not given evidence of conscious guilt, this second type of patient (resembling the type described by Riviere) has a better prognosis than the type who experiences a pure paranoid reaction in the transference.

The Quality of the Sublimatory Potential

Patients who have been able to achieve some really creative development in a certain area of their life have a better prognosis than those who have no capacity in this regard. Sometimes it is difficult to evaluate this factor, but careful attention to the patient's interests and aspirations will provide this information. For example, one patient had vivid and chronic fantasies of accumulating a collection of antique art, and was very envious of people who possessed ceramics or other objects of this kind. He was, however, completely incapable of differentiating between anything of value and third-rate imitations, and unable or unwilling to inform himself meaningfully about issues of quality. In short, he only wanted to decorate his house the way the people who collected antiques and whom he envied decorated theirs. I must stress that collecting antiques was his main aspiration in regard to personal wealth and yet it was a superficial interest. Another patient was interested in existential philosophy, talked very much about it, and after months of treatment it turned out that he had read only a few books popularizing this particular philosophy. A third patient, although he had reached a high professional level requiring a great deal of reading and formal education, did not read anything other than what was required for his examinations, and, once graduated, was incapable of doing any further reading. In this last case, once the problem of envy of what other people knew and could contribute was analyzed, he was able to read and learn from what he was reading, at the same time being able to learn from his own analysis.

In all the cases just mentioned, the patients had a low sublimatory potential in spite of the fact that superficially they exhibited a special talent or interest. The next few cases present a higher sublimatory potential, and a better prognostic outlook. The patient mentioned above, who impulsively married in the beginning stage of his analysis, was a merchant, interested in history. His interest seemed genuine and was a source of real pleasure for him; he had achieved real depth in that area and yet devaluated his own achievements, because of the unconscious fear that if he were triumphant in anything other people's envy would destroy it. Another patient was an amateur musician, and during the early stages of analysis frequently stated that when he played the piano, the only thing that was good about him came to the surface. Music was like an ideal though mysterious companion; the patient felt that whenever he deeply enjoyed listening or playing, some vaguely experienced trust or confidence in goodness was being reconfirmed.

The Degree and Quality of Superego Integration

I have already mentioned that superego integration in narcissistic personalities is poor. Their superegos mainly contain derivatives of primitive, aggressive, distorted parental images without the normal integration of aggressive forerunners with ideal self and ideal object images, and without the later phase of superego depersonalization and abstraction. Some of these patients, however, do present a depersonalized and abstracted superego in some areas. For example, they may be honest in money matters, in keeping promises, and in emotionally uninvolved daily interactions with others. They may experience shame, if not guilt, when they break minor conventions surrounding interpersonal relationships. These patients have a better prognosis than those in which there is very little of such "minor morality" left. Patients who lie to the analyst over a long period of time, as well as to other people, or present other forms of antisocial behavior, have a bad prognosis. It almost goes without saying that the antisocial personality structure, which represents an extreme form of this lack of superego development, has the worst prognosis of all. There is nothing new in mentioning the absolutely hopeless prognosis for the analytic treatment of antisocial personalities, but I am stressing here the continuum between the narcissistic personality and the antisocial personality which I see as an extreme form of pathological narcissism with, among the features, a complete absence of an integrated superego. In contrast, those narcissistic personalities with obsessive features have a better prognosis. One has to be careful, though, in diagnosing obsessive characteristics in narcissistic patients, because they may convey a false impression of an obsessive person. This is especially true for narcissistic personalities who are highly intellectual and cultivated: the smooth and cold quality of their thinking processes and the absence of emotional reactions may be mistaken for obsessive traits. However, in the truly obsessive personality we find intense and deep emotional reactions at points of anxiety, and at points which represent displacements of their emotional conflicts. For example, obsessive personalities may feel strongly about social, cultural, and political issues, and they may develop a surprising understanding of emotional depth in others while being apparently so "cold" themselves. In contrast, narcissistic personalities show superficial emotions of a quick and transitory kind, against a background of emotional blandness and indifference.

Presence of Life Circumstances Granting Unusual Narcissistic Gratifications

One element in the patient's life circumstances that leads to a poor prognosis is the opportunity for the patient to act out his needs for power, social importance, and admiration. A power-oriented narcissistic patient may already have achieved such a position in his profession and social life that it may appear to him quite "normal" and, therefore, it is difficult to analyze this form of "chronic acting out." In the same way that the candidate of a psychoanalytic institute may use his analysis as a ladder to professional status, a patient may use a pre-existing outlet for the gratification of his pathological narcissistic needs outside the analytic relationship and thereby compensate for frustration suffered in analysis, resulting in a therapeutic stalemate.

Impulse Control and Anxiety Tolerance

Narcissistic patients often have relatively good impulse control in all but a few areas which represent a compromise formation permitting the gratification of pathological narcissistic needs. For example, one patient had very good impulse control except for periods of homosexual acting out, in which he would pick up an occasional partner in such an impulsive way that he endangered his social position and risked conflict with the law. This patient used a homosexual experience to escape from the rage that any frustration from his girl friend brought about. If she appeared critical of him, he would leave in his car, pick up a man in a public rest room, have him perform fellatio on him, and then drop that man with a feeling of disgust and return home relieved. It gradually emerged that in the homosexual interaction he had the fantasy that the man who was sucking his penis needed him terribly and that the patient was the owner of all the love and fulfillment that was available in the interaction. He could give this love to the other man, thus proving to himself that he was the wealthy one. Later, after dropping his partner abruptly and depreciating him, he identified himself with the hostile and derogatory mother whom he had envied and hated and with the girl friend who represented his mother. By the whole action, he also took revenge on his girl friend-mother by reassuring himself that he did not need her sexually. In this example, what appeared on the surface to be a lack of impulse control was a specific defensive organization which could be understood and resolved analytically. The prognosis is better for these patients than for those who exhibit poor or nonexistent impulse control, who lose themselves in acting out, such as so-called "chaotic" personalities, or those who combine some form of sexual deviation with an impulse neurosis—alcoholism, drug addiction, etc. Prognosis is also guarded for those patients in whom anxiety immediately brings about generalized acting out or intensification of other symptoms: in short, for those whose anxiety tolerance is very low.

Regression toward Primary Process Thinking

I suggested above that the combination of overt borderline character-istics and narcissistic personality structure usually contraindicates psy-choanalytic treatment. Some narcissistic patients may show little symp-tomatology, good impulse control, and not even too low an anxiety tolerance and, yet, primary process thinking is surprisingly near the surface. For example, one patient functioned quite well in his life, but he had developed over the years the pleasurable fantasy that there was something "Christlike" about him and he enjoyed speculating about the characteristics he shared with Christ. He correctly assessed these fantasies as unrealistic, but at the same time he felt they were very pleasurable. At the beginning of his treatment, the intensity of these fantasies increased to the point that he wondered whether perhaps he was not Christ after all; then he regressed acutely into a schizophrenic reaction, which probably would not have occurred at that point had he not been offered an expressive psychotherapy.

One other point in regard to the regressive potential of the patient; overt borderline features, especially a lack of impulse control, an in-ability to tolerate anxiety, and a tendency toward primary process thinking, contraindicate psychoanalysis in these cases even if they show the presence of guilt and a potential to experience depression, because in these cases the depression that develops during treatment may re-gress into a psychotic depression or serious suicidal attempts. Every narcissistic character who is to be successfully treated must undergo periods of severe depression and suicidal fantasies, and if he does not have sufficient ego strength to tolerate this development, his life is in serious danger. In those cases where the ego is weak, supportive psy-chotherapy is indicated. Among the patients studied in the Psychoth-erapy Research Project of The Menninger Foundation, those with se-vere narcissistic character structure combined with overt borderline functioning could be treated quite successfully with a purely supportive approach.

The Motivation for Treatment

The crucial test of the motivation of these patients comes only after a period of analysis. The usually acceptable motivations for treatment, such as the wish to get rid of symptoms, may prove quite spurious in patients with narcissistic personalities. They may really want to become "perfect," and may enter analysis with such expectations. The question of whether "perfection" will turn out to mean for them freedom from symptoms so that they can be superior to everybody else, or whether it will be exchanged for the wish to get rid of their crippled emotional lives is often difficult to answer at the initiation of treatment. In any case, the more a person wishes to overcome feelings of emptiness, difficulties in empathizing with others, and his internal coldness, the better the prognosis.

A CRUCIAL PERIOD IN THE TREATMENT

After the patient systematically works through the defensive organizations of pathological narcissism, his primitive oral conflicts regularly come to the surface. His intense hatred and fear of the image of a dangerous, aggressive mother are projected onto the analyst as well as onto all other significant beings in his life. At some point, the patient has to become aware that this fear of attack from the mother represents a projection of his own aggression, linked to the rage caused by his frustration by mother. He also has to become aware that his ideal concept of himself is a fantasy construction which protects him from such dreaded relationships with all other people, and that this ideal self concept also contains a hopeless yearning and love for an ideal mother who would come to his rescue. The deep aspiration and love for such an ideal mother and the hatred for the distorted, dangerous mother have to meet at some point, in the transference, and the patient has to become aware that the feared and hated analyst-mother is really one with the admired, longed-for analyst-mother.

At this point, an extremely difficult emotional situation comes about for the patient: he must acknowledge the realistically good aspects of the analyst (mother) which he has previously denied and devaluated and bring upon himself a shattering feeling of guilt because of his previous aggression toward the analyst. The patient may feel despair because he has mistreated the analyst and all the significant persons in his life, and he may feel that he has actually destroyed those whom he could have loved and who might have loved him. Now he may have intense suicidal thoughts and intentions, but if he has been selected for analysis because of his good ego strength, he may work through this conflict without premature reassurance from his analyst. As the narcissistic patient works through this crucial period in the analysis, he comes to acknowledge the analyst as an independent being to whom he can feel love and gratitude. Simultaneously, the patient will begin to acknowledge the independent existence of other significant persons in his life. For the first time he may show an authentic curiosity about, interest in, and satisfaction with what goes on in other human beings. It is as if people were coming alive in the patient's external world as well as in his internal world of objects and self experience, his "representational world" (16). This stage in the analysis contrasts strikingly with the previous emptiness of the fantasy and emotional life of the patient.

Normal regression in the service of the ego involves one special dimension, namely, the reactivation of past internal object relationships as a source of internal support in times of crisis, of loss of external support, or of loneliness. Normally, the emotional wealth derived from past happy relationships with others not only permits the empathic enjoyment of the present happiness of others, but also is a source of internal consolation when reality threatens to bring about loss of self-esteem. Narcissistic patients are not able to resort in this way to their own past. If they are treated successfully, they come to realize a deeper and more meaningful life, and begin to draw from sources of strength and creativity in their newly developing world of internalized object relationships.

The following case history illustrates this crucial period of treatment in one particular patient. At one time, this patient had become aware that he had always treated the analyst as a "mirror" of himself, and had built the analyst up as a kind of powerful slave, totally at the patient's service, something like the genie in the fairy tale of Aladdin's Lamp. He realized that, between the sessions, he had had the feeling that the analyst had disappeared into an only potential existence, as if the analyst were confined in a bottle that the patient could put away. At this point, for the first time after years of analysis, the patient exhibited curiosity about the life of the analyst and envy of the analyst's private life. He became aware of anger and regret at being separated from the analyst over the weekends, and also had feelings of gratitude because the analyst had been willing to "stick with him" in spite of his chronically derogatory behavior. This patient had always depreciated literature, especially poetry, and everything that did not deal with "strong, cold, useful facts."

Then one day he remembered a fairy tale that had impressed him in his early childhood but that he had completely forgotten since. It was the story of "The Nightingale" by Andersen (2) and the patient, an unimaginative person, spontaneously interpreted the story through associations and dreams over a period of several days. He understood that he himself was the Emperor of China in the story, because he was as deprecatory of everybody else as the Emperor. China itself, in that fairy tale, was like the fantasy world of the patient, because everybody was depreciating everybody else in it. The nightingale (the live, real one) was the only warm and loving creature in that world, but the Emperor was not able to love it. Although he enjoyed its song, he dropped it without remorse when the shiny, jewel-covered mechanical substitute was offered to him. The mechanical nightingale covered with jewels and gold represented the Emperor's (patient's) own mechanical lifeless self. When the Emperor became ill and longed for the nightingale's song in order to become well again, the mechanical bird broke down and was no longer available, because the Emperor himself, the patient felt, had destroyed everything surrounding him. One night, when the Emperor was about to die, all the good and bad deeds of his life came back to him and made him suffer. The patient understood this to be an expression of the Emperor's final awareness of the bad sides of himself, and of his despair at ever undoing all the wrongs he had done. The patient felt very moved by the idea that the real-life nightingale came back at last, to sing by the dying Emperor's window and thus saved his life. The patient said, with deep feeling, that he now understood why, as a child, he had been moved to tears by this story and he cried at that point. The survival of the real, good nightingale in the story reaffirmed the patient's faith in the existence of a good being who was still available and had not been killed, in spite of all the Emperor's— and the patient's—greed and destructiveness. The Emperor was saved because he had kept inside of himself such a good and forgiving object. The nightingale also represented the good analyst who had not been killed by the patient's destructiveness.

This example illustrates not only the patient's understanding of a crucial problem in himself, but also his generally deepening awareness of emotional life; for the first time, he could accept a previously depreciated form of literature. To see a patient come alive during treatment, and begin to feel for the first time real concern for and interest in others as well as in an internal life of his own, is a gratifying experience for the analyst. It compensates for the many months and years of emptiness and meaninglessness with which these patients try to drown the analytic situation.

The prognostic considerations examined in this paper illustrate the limitations and difficulties in the psychoanalytic treatment of patients with narcissistic personality structures. Even if we cannot successfully treat many of these patients, at least they permit us to better understand and resolve narcissistic defenses in patients with less intensive overall character pathology. I believe that careful selection of these cases may bring about more encouraging therapeutic results with those who initially are considered hopeless and are, therefore, not treated, or who are taken into analysis under the erroneous assumption that they fall into the category of the ordinary character neurosis and cause disappointment after many years of analytic work.

SUMMARY

A general hypothesis regarding the etiology of the narcissistic personality structure is proposed, involving the relationships between pathological narcissism and pathological object relationships. Technical problems in the psychoanalytic treatment of narcissistic personalities are examined—especially their typical transference resistances—and prognostic criteria are outlined.

BIBLIOGRAPHY

1. Abraham, K. A particular form of neurotic resistance against the psychoanalytic method (1919). *Selected Papers on Psycho-Analysis*. London: Hogarth Press, 1949, pp. 303–311.
2. Andersen, H. C. The nightingale. In: *Tales of Grimm and Andersen*. New York: Modern Library, 1952, pp.714–721.
3. Fenichel, O. Typology. *The Psychoanalytic Theory of Neurosis*. New York: Norton, 1945, pp. 525–527.
4. Freud, S. On narcissism: an introduction (1914). *Standard Edition*, 14:67–102. London: Hogarth Press, 1957.

5. Freud, S. Libidinal types (1931). *Standard Edition,* 21:215–220. London: Hogarth Press, 1961.
6. Jacobson, E. *The Self and the Object World.* New York: International Universities Press, 1964.
7. Jones, E. The God complex (1913). *Essays in Applied Psycho-Analysis,* 2:244–265. New York: International Universities Press, 1964.
8. Kernberg, O. Borderline personality organization. *J. Am. Psychoanal. Ass.,* 15:641–685, 1967.
9. Kernberg, O. The treatment of patients with borderline personality organization. *Int. J. Psycho-Anal.,* 49:600–619, 1960.
10. Kohut, H. Transference and countertransference in the analysis of narcissistic personalities. Presented at the 2nd Pan-American Congress of Psychoanalysis, Buenos Aires, Argentina, August, 1966.
11. Reich, A. Narcissistic object choice in women. *J. Am. Psychoanal. Ass.,* 1:22–44, 1953.
12. Reich, A. Pathologic forms of self-esteem regulation. *The Psychoanalytic Study of the Child,* 15:215–232. New York: International Universities Press, 1960.
13. Riviere, J. A contribution to the analysis of the negative therapeutic reaction. *Int. J. Psycho-Anal.,* 17:304–320, 1936.
14. Rosenfeld, H. On the psychopathology of narcissism: a clinical approach. *Int. J. Psycho-Anal.,* 45:332–337, 1964.
15. Sachs, H. Observations of a training analyst. *Psychoanal. Quart.,* 16:157–168, 1947.
16. Sandler, J. & Rosenblatt, B. The concept of the representational world. *The Psychoanalytic Study of the Child,* 17:128–145. New York: International Universities Press, 1962.
17. Schafer, R. The loving and beloved superego in Freud's structural theory. *The Psychoanalytic Study of the Child,* 15:163–188. New York: International Universities Press, 1960.
18. Stone, L. The widening scope of indications for psychoanalysis. *J. Am. Psychoanal. Ass.,* 2:567–594, 1954.
19. Tartakoff, H. H. The normal personality in our culture and the Nobel prize complex. In: *Psychoanalysis—A General Psychology,* ed. R. M. Loewenstein, L. M. Newman, M. Schur, & A. J. Solnit. New York: International Universities Press, 1966, pp. 222–252.
20. Ticho, E. Selection of patients for psychoanalysis or psychotherapy. Presented at the 20th Anniversary Meeting of the Menninger School of Psychiatry Alumni Association, Topeka, Kansas, May, 1966.
21. Van der Waals, H. G. Problems of narcissism. *Bull. Menninger Clin.,* 29:293–311, 1965.

10. Further Contributions to the Treatment of Narcissistic Personalities

Otto F. Kernberg

This paper continues my earlier studies of the diagnosis and psychoanalytic treatment of a specific constellation of character pathology, that of the narcissistic personality (Kernberg, 1967, 1970a, 1971a). In recent years, a consensus has been gradually developing regarding the definition of this pathological character structure and the indication of psychoanalysis as the treatment of choice (Jacobson, 1964; P. Kernberg, 1971; Kohut, 1966, 1968, 1971; Rosenfeld, 1964; Tartakoff, 1966; E. Ticho, 1970; van der Waals, 1965). However, despite the evolving agreement about the descriptive, clinical characteristics of this constellation, divergent views have developed regarding the underlying metapsychological assumptions and the optimal technical approach within a psychoanalytic modality of treatment. In particular, Kohut's approach to the psychoanalytic treatment of narcissistic personality disorders (1971) is very different from the approach I outlined in an earlier paper (Kernberg, 1970a), which is more closely related to the views of Abraham (1919), Jacobson (1964), Riviere (1936), Rosenfeld (1964), Tartakoff (1966) and van der Waals (1965). Therefore, in this paper I will focus particularly on those aspects of my approach to the understanding and treatment of narcissistic personalities which highlight agreements and disagreements with Kohut's approach.

CLINICAL CHARACTERISTICS OF THE NARCISSISTIC PERSONALITY AS A SPECIFIC TYPE OF CHARACTER PATHOLOGY

With respect to clinical characteristics, there is agreement between Kohut's view and that of the other authors whom I have mentioned as representing an alternative view and myself. I describe patients with narcissistic personalities as presenting excessive self-absorption usually coinciding with a superficially smooth and effective social adaptation, but with serious distortions in their internal relationships with other people. They present various combinations of intense ambitiousness, grandiose fantasies, feelings of inferiority, and overdependence on external admiration and acclaim. Along with feelings of boredom and emptiness, and continuous search for gratification of strivings for brilliance, wealth, power and beauty, there are serious deficiencies in their capacity to love and to be concerned about others. The lack of capacity for empathic understanding of others often comes as a surprise considering their superficially appropriate social adjustment. Chronic uncertainty and dissatisfaction about themselves, conscious or unconscious exploitiveness and ruthlessness towards others are also characteristics of these patients. Perhaps one difference in my description from that derived from Kohut's work is my stress on the pathological nature of their internalized object relations, regardless of the superficially adaptive behaviour of many of these patients. In addition, I stress the presence of chronic, intense envy, and defences against such envy, particularly devaluation, omnipotent control and narcissistic withdrawal, as major characteristics of their emotional life.

THE RELATIONSHIP OF NARCISSISTIC PERSONALITY TO BORDERLINE CONDITIONS AND THE PSYCHOSES

Regarding this point, important differences exist between my approach and that of Kohut. Kohut differentiates the narcissistic personality disorders from the psychoses and borderline states, but does not make a clear differentiation of 'borderline cases' from schizophrenic psychoses (1971), p. 18). In my view, however, the defensive organization of narcissistic personalities is both strikingly similar to and different in a specific way from borderline personality organization, which I will outline below. In contrast to Kohut's view, I see important structural differences between borderline personality organization and psychotic structures, and I would not rule out psychoanalysis as the treatment of choice for some borderline conditions.

The similarity of the defensive organization of narcissistic personalities to that of borderline conditions is reflected in the predominance of mechanisms of splitting or primitive dissociation as reflected in the presence of mutually dissociated or split-off ego states. Thus haughty grandiosity, shyness and feeling of inferiority may coexist without affecting each other. These splitting operations are maintained and reinforced by primitive forms of projection, particularly projective identification, primitive and pathological idealization, omnipotent control, narcissistic withdrawal and devaluation. From a dynamic viewpoint, pathological condensation of genital and pregenital needs under the overriding influence of pregenital (especially oral) aggression characterizes narcissistic personalities as well as borderline personality organization in general.

In this connexion, it is interesting that Kohut acknowledges the presence of 'conscious but split-off aspects of the grandiosity' (1971, p. 179) and describes in detail 'the side-by-side existence of disparate personality attitudes in depth' (p. 183), and the analyst's need to relate the central sector of the personality to the split-off sector. In practice, therefore, Kohut acknowledges a defensive organization which is related to splitting as a predominant mechanism, although he does not relate it to particular vicissitudes of the structural development of the ego.

The difference between narcissistic personality structure and borderline personality organization is that in the narcissistic personality there is an integrated, although highly pathological grandiose self, which, as I have suggested earlier (Kernberg, 1970a), reflects a pathological condensation of some aspects of the real self (the 'specialness' of the child reinforced by early experience), the ideal self (fantasies and self-images of power, wealth, omniscience and beauty which compensated the small child for the experience of severe oral frustration, rage and envy) and the ideal object (the fantasy of an ever-giving, ever-loving and accepting parent, in contrast to the child's experience in reality; a replacement of the devalued real parental object). I am adopting here the term 'grandiose self', suggested by Kohut, because I think it expresses better the clinical implications of what I referred to earlier as the pathological self-structure, or what Rosenfeld (1964) called the 'omnipotent mad' self. The integration of this pathological, grandiose self compensates for the lack of integration of the normal self-concept which is part of the underlying borderline personality organization: it explains the paradox of relatively good ego functioning and surface adaptation in the presence of a predominance of splitting mechanisms, a related constellation of primitive defences, and the lack of integration of object representations of these patients. This pathological, grandiose self is reflected in clinical characteristics which, as mentioned before, mostly coincides with the observations of all the authors mentioned. However, a basic disagreement exists between Kohut's views and mine regarding the origin of this grandiose self, and whether it reflects the fixation of an archaic 'normal' primitive self (Kohut's view), or whether it reflects a pathological structure, clearly different from normal infantile narcissism (my view).

Before examining this difference in views, a special group of patients needs to be mentioned, who, in my opinion, present the clearest illustration of the intimate relationship between borderline personality organization and the development of the pathological grandiose self. I am referring to those narcissistic personalities who, in spite of a clearly narcissistic personality structure, function on what I have called an overt borderline level, i.e. present the nonspecific manifestations of ego weakness characteristic of borderline personality organization, in addition to the generally similar defensive constellation mentioned. These narcissistic patients present severe lack of anxiety tolerance, generalized lack of impulse control, striking absence of sublimatory channelling, primary process thinking clearly noticeable on psychological tests, and proneness to the development of transference psychosis. In these patients, the pathological narcissistic structure does not provide sufficient integration for effective social functioning, and they usually present a contraindication for analysis (often even for the modified psychoanalytic procedure that I have recommended for most patients with borderline personality organization). These patients characteristically present the repetitive, chronic activation of intense rage reactions linked with ruthless demandingness and depreciatory attacks on the therapist, i.e. 'narcissistic rage'. One also finds such intense outbursts of rage in borderline patients, usually as part of alternating activation of 'all good' and 'all bad' internalized object relations in the transference. However, the relentless nature of this rage, the depreciatory quality which seems to contaminate the entire relationship with the therapist, evolves as a complete devaluation and deterioration of all the potentially good aspects of the relationship for extended periods of time so that the continuity of treatment is threatened.

The following case illustrates this development. A patient with a rather typical narcissistic personality, a single woman in her early twenties, came to a psychiatric hospital after gradual breakdown of school performance and social relations, and sexual promiscuity characterized by her tendency to drop any man whom she could not completely control. Both her parents were rather narcissistic and withdrawn, and presented some mild antisocial trends. An older sister was in treatment for antisocial tendencies. Her lack of significant involvement with others started in nursery school, was later smoothed over by the patient's joining mother's efforts to control and manipulate their social environment, and culminated in the chaos of the patient's social life, work, and sexual involvements. After two months of treatment, in which subtle derogation of the therapist and all treatment staff and ongoing manipulation and splitting of staff and predominant features, the therapist absented himself for a week. The patient then changed her controlled derogation into overt anger and rage, and in spite of the efforts of staff managed to convince her parents to take her out of treatment two months later. Throughout this time, the sessions were characterized by ongoing attacks and derogation of the therapist, in short, by narcissistic rage, which could not be treated by an expressive approach.

Narcissistic personalities whose defences against primitive object relationships related to conflicts around oral aggression have been substantially worked through in analysis may present such rage reaction in the transference at advanced stages of treatment. At times, the transformation of a previously bland, mostly indifferent, apparently well-controlled narcissistic personality into such an openly and chronically raging person may be quite striking. However, it usually can be worked through in more advanced stages of the treatment, and may represent an important move forward. In this connexion, careful analysis of the history of such patients often reveals temper tantrums and aggressive outbursts which occurred in the past when they were frustrated, particularly under conditions when they felt they should be securely in control of the situation, and later again in life, when they felt superior to or in control of those against whom their rage was directed.

The situation, therefore, is different in cases where narcissistic rage appears as part of the initial clinical constellation (in narcissistic personalities functioning on an overtly borderline level), as compared to cases where it develops as part of the resolution of pathological narcissism at later stages of the treatment. Early and open expression of narcissistic rage represents a serious risk for the treatment. This is particularly true in narcissistic personalities functioning on a borderline level who present antisocial features or a sexual deviation with strong sadistic components, such as open physical violence toward the objects of their sexual exploits. Also, adolescents with narcissistic personality structure and antisocial behaviour frequently show such rage reactions.

For narcissistic personalities functioning on an overt borderline level (particularly the prognostically more guarded cases of narcissistic rage mentioned before), a supportive psychotherapeutic approach may be the treatment of choice. Ideally, the treatment may shift into the general approach for borderline patients that I have recommended, namely, consistent interpretation (not only of the origin of the narcissistic rage, but of the secondary gains derived from its expression in the transference), and limit setting when such secondary gain cannot be avoided by interpretive means alone. When it is possible to structure the external life of the patient in such a way that acting out of narcissistic rage can be controlled and the treatment situation protected so that the analyst can maintain a relatively neutral stance, a systematic interpretation of the defensive functions of the expression of aggression toward the analyst may be possible, with ultimate resolution of the narcissistic rage. In addition to direct expression of primitive aggression, such rage reactions may have the defensive function of protecting the patient against primitive fears of the analyst, or against overwhelming guilt toward him, or against separation anxiety.

In patients with narcissistic personalities in which narcissistic rage develops during later stages of the treatment it is usually less difficult to analyse the origin and functions of rage in the transference. The patient's angry outbursts over minor frustrations, real or fantasied, from the analyst may be an important move forward from the previously subtle devaluations of the analyst so characteristic of narcissistic resistances. To angrily devalue the analyst in an effort to eliminate him as an important object who would otherwise be feared and envied, and on whom the patient so desperately needs to rely, is a characteristic function of the rage reaction. The analyst's internal security and his conviction in what he has to offer realistically to the patient are very important in reassuring the patient against his fantasies of the overwhelming nature of his own aggression.

In summary, then, the pathological grandiose self compensates for the generally 'ego weakening' effects of the primitive defensive organization, a common characteristic of narcissistic personalities and patients of a borderline personality organization, and explains the fact that narcissistic personalities may present an overt functioning which ranges from the borderline level to that of better integrated types of character pathology. The differential diagnosis of narcissistic personalities from other types of character pathology can usually be arrived at in a careful analysis of the clinical features; I have examined in earlier papers the differential diagnosis of narcissistic personalities with hysterical personalities, infantile pesonalities, and obsessive compulsive personalities (Kernberg, 1967, 1970a,b). In cases where doubts persist, or the diagnosis cannot be made before the initiation of treatment, the characteristic development of a narcissistic transference differentiates narcissistic personalities from the usual transference neurosis of other cases. On this point, I think, Kohut and I agree.

THE RELATIONSHIP OF NORMAL TO PATHOLOGICAL NARCISSISM

Developmental arrest or pathological development?

Kohut (1971) thinks that narcissistic personalities remain 'fixated on archaic grandiose self-configurations and/or on archaic, overestimated, narcissistically cathected objects' (p. 3) He clearly establishes (p. 9) a continuity of pathological and normal narcissism, in which the grandiose self represents an archaic form of what normally, and in the course of treatment, may become the normal self in a continuous process. His analysis focuses almost exclusively on the vicissitudes of development of libidinal cathexes, so that his analysis of pathological narcissism is essentially unrelated to any examination of the vicissitudes of aggression. Kohut (1971) states (p. xv): 'Specifically, this study concentrates almost exclusively on the role of the libidinal forces in the analysis of narcissistic personalities; the discussion of the role of aggression will be taken up separately.' In addition, Kohut examines narcissism so predominantly from the viewpoint of the quality of the instinctual charge, that he seems to imply the existence of two entirely different, narcissistic and object-oriented, libidinal instincts determined by intrinsic qualities rather than by the target (self or object) of the instinctual investment. In his words (p. 26): 'Narcissism, within my general outlook, is defined not by the target of the instinctual investment (i.e.

whether it is the subject himself or other people) but by the nature or quality of the instinctual charge.' He repeats the essence of this statement later (p. 39, footnote) and considers the development of object love largely independent from that of lower to higher forms of narcissism (pp. 220, 228, 297). Kohut conveys the impression that he analyses the vicissitudes of normal and pathological narcissism and of normal and pathological object relationships as mostly dependent upon the quality of libidinal cathexes rather than in terms of the vicissitudes of internalized object relations.

I disagree with these viewpoints, and like Jacobson (1964), Mahler (1968) and van der Waals (1965), I think that one cannot divorce the study of normal and pathological narcissism from the vicissitudes of both libidinal and aggressive drive derivatives, and from the development of structural derivatives of internalized object relations (Kernberg, 1971*b*, 1972). In what follows, I will provide clinical material as well as theoretical considerations in support of the following viewpoints:

(1) The specific narcissistic resistances of patients with narcissistic personalities reflect a pathological narcissism which is different from both the ordinary, adult narcissism and from fixation at or regression to normal infantile narcissism. The implication is that narcissistic resistances that develop in the course of interpretation of character defences in patients other than narcissistic personalities are of a different nature, require a different technique, and have a different prognostic implication than narcissistic resistances of patients presenting pathological narcissism.

(2) Pathological narcissism can only be understood in terms of the combined analysis of the vicissitudes of libidinal and aggressive drive derivatives. Pathological narcissism does not simply reflect libidinal investment in the self in contrast to libidinal investment in objects, but libidinal investment in a pathological self-structure. This pathological self has defensive functions against underlying libidinally invested and aggressively invested primitive self and object images which reflect intense, predominantly pregenital conflicts around both love and aggression.

(3) The structural characteristics of narcissistic personalities cannot be understood simply in terms of fixation at an early level of development, or lack of development of certain intrapsychic structures. They are a consequence of the development of pathological (in contrast to

normal) differentiation and integration of ego and superego structures, deriving from pathological (in contrast to normal) object relationships.

To summarize these three viewpoints into one overall statement: Narcissistic investment (i.e. investment in the self), and object investment (that is, investment in representation of others and in other human beings), occur simultaneously, and intimately influence each other, so that one cannot study the vicissitudes of narcissism without studying the vicissitudes of object relationships, in the same way one cannot study the vicissitudes of normal and pathological narcissism without relating the development of the respective internalized object relations to both libidinal and aggressive drive derivatives.

Differential qualities of infantile and pathological narcissism

What follows are some pertinent clinical observations. The differential diagnosis of narcissistic personalities with obsessive, depressive-masochistic, and hysterical personalities (i.e. of the relatively better functioning narcissistic patients with other types of character pathology) illustrates how narcissistic patients not only seem to love themselves excessively, but do so in a rather poor, often self-demeaning way, so that one concludes that these patients do not treat themselves better than the other people with whom they have relationships. Their conviction of being 'phony', their deep lack of confidence in anything basically good and worthwhile that could emerge from honest self-exploration, and their occasionally surprising neglect and disregard for their 'public image' in terms of honesty, decency and convictions about values, are poor ways of loving oneself.

The following features distinguish pathological narcissism from the normal narcissism of small children: (1) The grandiose fantasies of normal small children, their angry efforts to control mother and to keep themselves in the centre of everybody's attention, have by far a more realistic quality than is the case of narcissistic personalities. (2) The small child's overreaction to criticism, failure, and blame, as well as his need to be the centre of attention, admiration and love, coexist with simultaneous expression of genuine love and gratitude, and interest in his object at times when he is not frustrated, and above all, with the capacity to trust and depend upon significant objects. A two and a half year old child's capacity to maintain a libidinal investment in mother during temporary separations is in striking contrast to the narcissistic patients' inability to depend upon other people (including the analyst) beyond immediate need gratification. (3) Normal infantile narcissism is reflected in the child's demandingness related to real needs, while the demandingness of pathological narcissism is excessive, cannot ever be fulfilled, and regularly reveals itself to be secondary to a process of internal destruction of the supplies received. (4) The coldness and aloofness of patients with pathological narcissism at times when their capacity for social charm is not in operation, their tendency to disregard others except when temporarily idealizing them as potential sources of narcissistic supply, and the contempt and devaluation prevalent in most of their relationships are in striking contrast to the warm quality of the small child's self-centeredness. Pursuing this observation into the historical analysis of narcissistic patients, one finds from the age of two to three years a lack of normal warmth and engagement with others, and an easily activated, abnormal destructiveness and ruthlessness.

(5) The normal infantile narcissistic fantasies of power and wealth and beauty which stem from the pre-oedipal period do not imply an exclusive possession of all that is valuable and enviable in the world; the normal child does not need that everybody should admire him for being the exclusive owner of such treasures; but this is a characteristic fantasy of narcissistic personalities. In normal infantile narcissism, fantasies of narcissistic triumph or grandiosity are mingled with wishes that acquisition of these values will make the child lovable, acceptable by those whom he loves and by whom he wants to be loved.

The implication of all this is that pathological narcissism is strikingly different from normal narcissism.

Manifestations of pathological narcissism in the analytic situation

In the transference, one main function of the narcissistic resistances of narcissistic personalities is to deny the existence of the analyst as an independent, autonomous human being, without a simultaneous fusion in the transference such as can be observed with more regressed patients. It is as if the analyst were tolerated in a type of 'satellite existence'; over many months and years there are likely to be frequent role reversals in the transference relationship, without any basic change in the total transference constellation. The grandiose self permits the denial of dependency on the analyst. Regularly, however, when it has been possible to work through this defensive constellation, it turns out that this denial of dependency on the analyst does not represent an absence of internalized object relations or of the capacity to invest in objects, but a rigid defence against more primitive, pathological object relations centred around narcissistic rage and envy, fear and guilt because of this rage, and yet a desperate longing for a loving relationship that will not be destroyed by hatred. This defensive constellation is strikingly different from the activation of narcissistic defences in other types of character pathology.

In patients who do not have the narcissistic personality structure, resentment toward the analyst, disappointment reactions, feelings of shame and humiliation in the process of character analysis are temporary and less intense; and their reactions coexist with a clear capacity for dependence upon the analyst as indicated by separation anxiety or mourning reactions in the transference. In contrast, generalized devaluation and contempt of the analyst are prevalent in the case of narcissistic personalities, often rationalized as 'disappointments'. There is a persistent absence of separation anxiety or mourning reactions at weekends, vacation, or illness of the analyst, so that even at times of apparent idealization of the analyst the difference between such idealization and that which obtains in other transferences is striking.

Expression of anger and rage in the course of the predominantly negative transference related to the analysis of character defences in non-narcissistic patients will not bring about the massive devaluation of the analyst which is typical of narcissistic personalities. The alternation of childlike demands in times of anger with manifestations of love, gratitude, and guilt-activated idealization characteristic of non-narcissistic patients, gives an entirely different quality to the transference. Narcissistic personalities' curiosity about the analyst's life in areas other than those related to the immediate needs of the patient is often absent for many months or years. The presence of what on the surface seems 'normal' (although infantile) idealization simultaneous with almost complete obliviousness toward the analyst alerts us to the difference between normal and pathological idealization. The absence of the capacity to depend upon others on the part of narcissistic personalities, in contrast to the clinging dependency and persistent capacity for a broad spectrum of object relations in borderline patients, contributes fundamentally to the differential diagnosis of narcissistic personalities functioning on an overt borderline level from usual borderline patients. Other elements in this differential diagnosis are the specific characteristics of pathological idealization, the prevalence of omnipotent control and particularly of contempt and devaluation, and the narcissistic withdrawal in the case of narcissistic personalities. Again, the analytic situation provides abundant clinical evidence of a fundamental difference between normal infantile narcissism, fixation at infantile narcissism typical of patients with character pathology other than narcissistic personalities, and the pathological narcissism of narcissistic personalities.

Genetic considerations

This difference becomes even more striking when, in the course of psychoanalytic treatment, the genetic determinants of these patients' narcissistic resistances and related character defences are analysed. Such genetic analysis reveals that in contrast to fixation at infantile narcissistic stages of development directly related to frustrations and failures of the mothering figure and other significant childhood objects, narcissistic personalities repeat in the transference early processes of devaluation of significant external objects and of their intrapsychic representations as a secondary elaboration and defence against underlying conflicts around oral rage and envy. They need to destroy the sources of love and gratification in order to eliminate the source of envy and projected rage, while simultaneously withdrawing into the grandiose self which represents a primitive refusion of the idealized images of the parental figures and idealized images of the self, so that they escape from a vicious circle of anger, frustration and aggressive devaluation of the potential source of gratification at the cost of serious damage to internalized object relations. In short, devaluation processes rationalized as 'disappointment' reactions in the transference repeat pathological devaluation of parental images, while the defensive structure of the grandiose self actualizes the pathological condensation of components stemming from object relationships reflecting those conflicts.

I mentioned in an earlier paper (Kernberg, 1970a) that it is an open question to what extent inborn intensity of aggressive drive participates in this picture, and that the predominance of chronically cold, narcissistic and at the same time overprotective mother figures appears to be the main etiological element in the psychogenesis of this pathology. The inclusion of the child in the narcissistic world of mother during certain periods of his early development creates the predisposition for the 'specialness' of the child, around which the fantasies of the grandiose self become crystallized. The narcissistic character defences protect the patient not only against the intensity of his narcissistic rage, but also against his deep convictions of unworthiness, his frightening image of the world as being devoid of food and love, and his self-concept of the hungry wolf out to kill, eat and survive. All these fears are activated in the transference at the time when the patient begins to be able to depend upon the analyst. The patient now fears his destructive envy of the analyst, and he is uncertain whether his need for love will survive or be stronger than his aggressive onslaughts on the analyst. These developments determine an intensively ambivalent and frightening transference paradigm which needs to be worked through.

Types of idealization and the relationship of narcissistic idealization to the grandiose self

Regarding the nature of the defensive operations in pathological narcissism, I have already alluded to the fact that these patients' idealization of the analyst is markedly different from the primitive idealization of borderline patients, and from the idealization that occurs in other types of character pathology. Borderline conditions are characterized by what I have called 'primitive idealization', namely an unrealistic, 'all good' image of the analyst as a primitive good, powerful gratifying object, used as a protection against the 'contamination' of the analyst with paranoid projections of an 'all bad', sadistic, primitive object. In other words, this primitive level of idealization is related to the predominance of splitting mechanisms. In contrast, in the non-narcissistic types of character pathology and the symptomatic neuroses, the idealization of the analyst as a good, loving, forgiving parental image is related to the patient's ambivalence, his guilt and concern over the simultaneous presence of both intense love and hatred for the analyst. At this higher level of idealization, the analyst is seen as a parental figure who is all-understanding and tolerant and who loves the patient in spite of his 'badness'. This higher level of idealization is followed by the still more mature type of idealization which includes the projection on to the idealized objects of higher level superego functions dealing with abstract, depersonified value systems: in essence, a normal phenomenon which is characteristic particularly of adolescence and falling in love.

These different types of idealization can be seen as a continuum, from normal primitive to normal adult functioning. All of them, however, are in striking contrast to the idealization of the narcissistic personality, which reflects the projection on to the analyst of the patient's grandiose self. The narcissistic patient extends his own grandiosity to include the analyst, and thus, while apparently free associating in the presence of the analyst, really talks to himself expanded into a grandiose 'self-observing' figure to which the patient becomes, temporarily, an attachment or satellite. It needs to be stressed that insofar as the patient 'withdraws' that idealization at the end of the hour, and shows a complete absence of real dependency on the analyst, there is no real merger taking place, thus indicating the difference of this reaction from more primitive self–object fusion which characterizes what Jacobson (1954) calls psychotic identification and Mahler (1968) described as the symbiotic phase of development. Rather than a fusion of self and object image reflecting regression to a very early level of development at which ego boundaries have not yet stabilized, reality testing in a strict sense is maintained in the hours, and transference psychosis does not develop.

Also, insofar as the idealization of the analyst does not alternate with intense projection of a 'bad object' on to him (as in the usual borderline conditions), nor involve guilt and reparation (as in normal infantile types of idealization during transference neurosis), narcissistic idealization is a pathological process rather than a normal developmental stage. The genetic origins of this pathology must be located somewhere in between the stage of self–object differentiation (i.e. beyond the level of development characteristic of the psychoses) and the stage of normal integration of self-images into a normal self-structure and of object images into integrated object representations (i.e. the object-relations-derived structures underlying the usual forms of character pathology and symptomatic neuroses). Insofar as a pathological, grandiose self is projected on to the analyst and the patient's 'empathy' with that projected self remains, and he attempts to exert maximum control to have the analyst follow exactly what is required in order to maintain the projection and to avoid the emergence of the analyst as an independent, autonomous object, this entire defensive operation reflects what I have described operationally (reformulating Melanie Klein's use of this term) as 'projective identification' (1967), another characteristic mechanism of borderline conditions and narcissistic personalities. The practical consequences of the patient's continuing efforts to force the analyst to behave exactly as the patient needs to see him correspond quite closely to Kohut's descriptions of the mirror transference. What I want to stress again, however, is the specific, peculiar nature of the constellation of pathological narcissism in contrast to narcissistic developments in other types of pathology.

Kohut's thinking about narcissistic idealization is in contrast to the foregoing formulation. He sees narcissistic personalities as suffering from a lack of optimal internalization of the archaic, rudimentary self-object—the idealized parent imago (1971, pp. 37–47). He stresses that the small child's idealizations belong genetically and dynamically into a narcissistic context, a proposition which makes sense in the context of Kohut's stress that it is the quality of the libidinal cathexes and not the target of the instinctual investment which determines whether an internalization is basically narcissistic or object oriented. Because of traumatic loss of the idealized object, or a traumatic disappointment in it, optimal internalization does not take place, and, Kohut suggests:

The intensity of the search for and of dependency on these objects is due to the fact that they are striven for as a substitute for the missing segments of the psychic structure. They are not objects (in the psychological sense of the term) since they are not loved or admired for their attributes, and the actual features of their personalities, and their actions, are only dimly recognized. They are not longed for but are needed in order to replace the functions of a segment of the mental apparatus which had not been established in childhood (pp. 45–6).

In short, he suggests that the idealizing transference of narcissistic personalities corresponds to a fixation at an archaic level of normal development.

In my view, the idealizing transference reflects a pathological type of idealization, and corresponds to the massive activation of the grandiose self in the transference. Thus, what Kohut calls the mirror transference, and what he calls idealizing transference correspond in my thinking to the alternative activation of components belonging essentially to a condensed, pathological self. This self stems from the fusion of some aspects of the real self, the ideal self, and the ideal object. This condensation is pathological, and does not simply represent fixation at an early stage of development. Kohut himself, in referring to the idealized parent imago, refers to it as an archaic, rudimentary 'self–object', and describes 'typical regressive swings' during the analysis of narcissistic personality disorders (cf. 1971, diagram 2, p. 97, illustrating how shifts occur from idealizing transference to activation of grandiosity in the patient). I have found the alternative projection of the grandiose self on to one participant of the analytic relationship, while the other one represents the remnants of the real self incorporated as it were in a magical union with the idealized partner, a regular feature of narcissistic resistances.

In my view, the early idealization of the analyst in the transference does not constitute a paradigm essentially different from the projection of the grandiose self on to him, and frequently contains many elements of the characteristics of the grandiose self. In addition, in the early stages of the analysis, idealization of the analyst serves to re-create the patient's usual incorporative relationships with potential sources of gratification, the idealization of such sources representing the gratifying fantasies that other people, in this case the analyst, still have something valuable that the patient has not yet incorporated and that he needs to make his. The early idealization is also a defence against the danger of emergence of intense envy, and against the processes of devaluation of the analyst. Devaluation of the analyst may protect the patient against envy, but it also destroys his hope of receiving something new and good, and, on a deeper level, reconfirms his fear of not ever being able to establish a mutually loving and gratifying relationship.

Thus, in the early stages of analysis, narcissistic patients typically develop fantasies that their analyst is the best analyst that exists; they do not need to envy any other patients having another analyst; they are the only patients of the analyst, or at least the most interesting patient whom the analyst prefers over all others, etc. Gradually, the idealized features of the analyst, which at first reflect rather conventionally ideal attributes, shift into directions which reveal a particular nature of the patient's grandiose self. Throughout this entire process, switches occur during which the otherwise ideal analyst is supposedly lucky to have such an unusual patient, and the patient can be reassured of the analyst's exclusive interest because no other patient of any other analyst could match such a gratifying analytic experience, etc. This sudden shift from periods in which the analyst is seen as a perfect, God-like creature, into a complete devaluation of the analyst and self-idealization of the patient, only to revert later to the apparent idealization of the analyst while the patient experiences himself as part of the analyst, indicate the intimate connexions of the components of the overall condensed structure—the grandiose self—which characterizes narcissistic resistances. The analysis of all these components of this pathological structure reveals defensive functions against the emergence of direct oral rage and envy, against paranoid fears related to projection of sadistic trends on the analyst (representing a primitive, hated and sadistically perceived mother image), and against basic feelings of terrifying loneliness, hunger for love, and guilt over the aggression directed against the frustrating parental images.

One patient, a fellow professional in treatment with a colleague, felt in the early stages of his treatment that his psychoanalyst had a perfect technique of interpretation. From what he said he had heard and from his own observations about his analyst, he construed the picture of a very thorough, meticulous, somewhat cold and distant but perfectionistic technician, who would see to it that all of the patient's defences and conflicts would be resolved systematically in the right order. The patient gradually elaborated this vision of his analyst into that of a man who was absolutely certain of himself, incorruptible, rigid but completely stable and reliable, who would not let emotions get in his way, and would interrupt the patient with scientific precision only when and if needed. He felt very reassured by this image of perfection, and one might have thought that this transference constituted an idealization of the analyst as an external object. However, it gradually turned out that the patient had been reading the technical work of a leading psychoanalyst from another city, with the intention of shifting from the present analyst to the other one in case he discovered any shortcoming in his present analyst. In a subtle way, he attempted to force his analyst into conforming with his picture of the perfect analysing machine, with the qualities of coldness, distance, and olympian untouchability emerging as the main features. This patient presented characterological attitudes very similar to those of the analyst of his fantasies, and had a distant and unfeeling attitude about his own patients while attempting to copy the technique of this analyst. The patient was very proud of his careful, precise, intellectual approach; he also became extremely irritated when anybody invaded what he considered his personal space or time. He presented strong disappointment reactions when the analyst did not conform to the patient's self-image, or when the analyst would give indications of personality characteristics different from those known and particularly understood by the patient thus threatening him with the presence of an independent, autonomous person. This case illustrates the intimate connexion of the idealization of the analyst as representing part of the patient's grandiose self, and the related pathological nature of the idealization process.

Structural characteristics and origins of the grandiose self

What are the structural origins and functions of the pathologically condensed grandiose self? In my view, idealized object images which normally would be integrated into the ego ideal and as such, into the superego, are condensed instead with the self-concept. As a result, normal superego integration is lacking, ego–superego boundaries are blurred in certain areas, and unacceptable aspects of the real self are dissociated and/or repressed, in combination with widespread, devastating devaluation of external objects and their representations. Thus, the intrapsychic world of these patients is populated only by their own grandiose self, by devaluated, shadowy images of self and others, and by potential persecutors representing the non-integrated sadistic superego forerunners, as well as primitive, distorted object images on to whom intense oral sadism has been projected. It needs to be stressed again that these developments occur at a point when self and object images have been sufficiently differentiated from each other to assure stable ego boundaries, so that the pathological condensation occurs after the achievement of the developmental line which separates psychotic from non-psychotic structures. Thus created, the pathological grandiose self permits a certain integration of the ego providing a better overall social adaptation than achieved by borderline patients in general. The splitting of the self characteristic of borderline patients is thus compensated for, but at the price of a further deterioration of object relationships, the loss of the capacity to depend, and an ominous capacity for self-protection from emotional conflicts with others by withdrawing into the splendid, grandiose isolation which gives the specific seal to the narcissistic organization.

Another consequence of these developments is that, insofar as superego elements and ego elements are condensed into the grandiose self, certain superego elements will not be available for superego integration, particularly the normal components of the ego ideal. Under these circumstances, the sadistic forerunners of the superego predominate, and superego integration would represent a terrible danger for the ego of pressure from a sadistic, primitive superego. Also, as the normal integration of the ego ideal with other superego structures is missing, the forerunners of later value systems are also missing, and so is the precondition for the internalization of later superego components, mainly the more realistic parental images derived from oedipal conflicts which normally constitute a major cement of superego integration (Jacobson, 1964). Devaluation of the parents, rationalized as disappointment reactions, is also fostered by this defective development of advanced superego functions, and further interferes with the normal integration of value systems as part of total personality and the related development of sublimatory potentials.

The final, and most crucial consequence of the establishment of the grandiose self, is the rupture of the normal polarity of self and object images which have been part of the internalized units which fixate and reproduce satisfactory relations with others. The grandiose self permits the denial of dependency on others, protects the individual against narcissistic rage and envy, creates the precondition for ongoing depreciation and devaluation of others, and contributes to distort both the future narcissistic and object investments of the patient.

For all these reasons, pathological narcissism cannot be considered simply a fixation at the level of normal primitive narcissism. Normal narcissism stems from the libidinal investment in an originally undifferentiated self and object image from which later, libidinally invested self and object images will develop. These will eventually determine an integrated self, which incorporates libidinally determined and aggressively determined self-images under the predominance of the libidinally determined ones. This integrated self is surrounded by integrated object representations which in turn reflect the integration of earlier, libidinally invested and aggressively invested object images, the integration also occurring under the predominance of predominantly libidinal object images. In pathological narcissism this normal 'representational world' (Sandler & Rosenblatt, 1962) is replaced by a pathological constellation of internalized object relations.

Thus, in contrast to Kohut's view about the nature of the superego pathology in narcissistic personalitites, I think these cases do not simply reflect a lack of development of the idealized fore-runners of the super-ego (the components of the ego ideal), but the pathological condensation of such forerunners with ego components. Thus, normal ego and superego boundaries are blurred, and the development of primitive superego structures into an advanced, normal superego is interfered with. There is not merely a 'lack' of internalization of certain normal idealized superego forerunners, but an active distortion of them simultaneously with pathological devaluation of the eternal objects. In more general terms, there is not simply an 'absence' of certain structures, but a pathological development of earlier structures so that the later normal ones cannot develop.

PSYCHOANALYTIC TECHNIQUE AND NARCISSISTIC TRANSFERENCE

If I understand him correctly, Kohut's overall strategy of technique aims at permitting the establishment of a full narcissistic transference, especially the unfolding of the mirror transference reflecting the activation of the grandiose self. He implies that this transference development completes a normal process that has been arrested, namely that of the internalization of the ideal self-object into the superego and the related growth from primitive into mature narcissism. Kohut suggests that 'during those phases of the analysis of narcissistic character disturbance when an idealizing transference begins to germinate, there is only one correct analytic attitude: to accept the admiration' (1971, p. 264). The analyst, Kohut adds,

interprets the patient's resistances against the revelation of his grandiosity; and he demonstrates to the patient not only that his grandiosity and exhibitionism once played a phase-appropriate role but that they must now be allowed access to consciousness. For a long period of the analysis, however, it is almost always deleterious for the analyst to emphasize the irrationality of the patient's grandiose fantasies or to stress that it is realistically necessary that he curb his exhibitionistic demands. The realistic integration of the patient's infantile grandiosity and exhibitionism will in fact take place quietly and spontaneously (though very slowly) if the patient is able, with the aid of the analyst's empathic understanding for the mirror transference, to maintain the mobilization of the grandiose self and to expose his ego to its demands (1971, p. 272).

Kohut acknowledges, 'At first hearing I might seem to be stating that, in instances of this type, the analyst must indulge a transference wish of the analysand; specifically, that the patient had not received the necessary emotional echo or approval from the depressive mother, and that the analyst must now give it to her in order to provide a "corrective emotional experience" (p. 290). In objecting to this interpretation, Kohut states, 'Although for tactical reasons (e.g. in order to insure the cooperation of the segment of the patient's ego), the analyst might in such instances transitorily have to provide what one might call a reluctant compliance with the childhood wish, the true analytic aim is not indulgence but mastery based on insight, achieved in a setting of tolerable analytic abstinence' (p. 291).

In discussing the results of his approach, he states, 'The primary and essential results of the psychoanalytic treatment of narcissistic personalities lie within the narcissistic realm, and the changes achieved, constitute in the majority of cases, the most significant and therapeutically decisive results' (p. 298). He considers the increase and the expansion of the patient's capacity for object love as 'the most prominent nonspecific change' (p. 296), and says that 'the increasing availability of object-instinctual cathexes as the analysis proceeds usually does not indicate that a change of the mobilized narcissism into object love has taken place; it is rather due to a freeing of formerly repressed object libido; i.e. it is the result of therapeutic success in sectors of secondary psychopathology (transference neurosis) in a patient who is primarily suffering from a narcissistic personality disorder' (pp. 296–7).

In my view, Kohut's approach neglects the intimate relationships between narcissistic and object related conflicts, and the crucial nature of conflicts around aggression in the psychopathology of patients with narcissistic personality. While I certainly agree that it is important to permit a full development of the transference rather than prematurely interpreting it, and that the analyst needs to avoid—as in all analytic cases—any moralistic attitude regarding the inappropriate nature of the patient's grandiosity, Kohut's approach may unwillingly foster an interference with the full development of the negative transference aspects, maintain the patient's unconscious fear of his envy and rage, and thus hinder the working through of the pathological, grandiose self. Kohut implies that the mirror transferences which reflect the activation of the grandiose self must be tolerated to permit its full development, because otherwise the narcissistic grandiosity may be driven underground. It seems to me that systematic analysis of the positive and negative aspects of the patient's grandiosity from an essentially neutral position better achieves the goal of full activation of the narcissistic transference.

I agree with Kohut that the psychoanalytic treatment of narcissistic personalities centres on the activation of the grandiose self and the need for helping the patient achieve full awareness of it in a neutral analytic situation, but I think that focusing exclusively on narcissistic resistances from the viewpoint of libidinal conflicts with an almost total disregard of the vicissitudes of aggression in these cases interferes with a systematic interpretation of the defensive functions of the grandiose self. In my view, both the primitive idealization of and the omnipotent control over the analyst need to be interpreted systematically; the patient needs to become aware, obviously in a non-critical atmosphere, of his need to devalue and depreciate the analyst as an independent object, in order to protect himself from the reactivation of underlying oral rage and envy and the related fear of retaliation from the analyst. Fear of retaliation from the analyst (derived from projected sadistic reactions activated by real or fantasied frustrations from him), and fear of guilt (because of the patient's attack on the analyst as a primitive giving object) are prominent motives against which narcissistic resistances have been erected. They need to be explored and interpreted systematically before the transference shifts into the ordinary transference paradigms characteristic of transference neurosis. The patient's efforts to hold on to his grandiose self, and to avoid acknowledging the analyst as an independent, autonomous person, consistently reveal his defence against the intense envy, against the feared relationship with the hated and sadistically perceived mother image, and his dread of a sense of empty loneliness in a world devoid of personal meaning.

In the course of this work, what regularly emerges is that behind the consciously remembered or rediscovered 'disappointments' from the parents are the devaluations of the parental images and the real parental figures, carried out in the past in order to avoid the underlying conflict with them. The patients' disappointments in the analyst reveal not only fantasied—or real—frustrations in the transference: they also reveal dramatically the total devaluation of the transference object for the slightest reason, and thus, the intense, overwhelming nature of the aggression against the object. Direct rage because of frustrations is an infinitely more normal, although an exaggerated type of response. In addition, the implication of 'either you are as I want you, or you cease to exist' is also the acting out of unconscious need for omnipotent control of the object, and reflects defences against aggression. 'Disappointment reactions' in these cases reflect conflicts about aggression as well as libidinal strivings and, more immediately, a protection against general activation of oral-aggressive conflicts. The narcissistic transference, in other words, first activates past defences against deeper relationships with the parents, and only then the real past relationships with them. As is true in so many cases with borderline conditions, the parents did, indeed, disappoint the patient, but in ways and areas which the narcissistic patient usually did not suspect and which only become clear in the later part of the treatment. In short, disappointments in the analyst, unrealistic idealization of him which hides the patient's refusal to acknowledge him as an independent object, and the complex motives for narcissistic withdrawal, need to be carefully scrutinized for underlying contempt and devaluation. This is a striking difference from the technical requirements in the analysis of infantile narcissistic reactions in other types of character pathology.

A crucial technical issue with these patients is the focus on such remnants as the patient possesses of the capacity for love and object investment, and on his realistic appreciation of the analyst's efforts, in order to help the patient avoid misinterpreting the focus on the latent negative transference as the psychoanalyst's conviction that the patient is 'all bad'. In short, the analyst needs to focus both the positive and negative transference. In this connexion, Kohut quotes me as saying that ego distortions 'temporarily require a bit of educational pressure' (1971, p. 179), which is a misunderstanding of my views. The analyst certainly needs to avoid educational pressures or a moralistic stance, and I think that the best way to achieve this is by analysing the motives which determine narcissistic defences, including the activation of the grandiose self. One prominent reason why these patients cannot tolerate facing their feelings of hatred and envy is because they fear such feelings will destroy the analyst, destroy their hope for a good relationship with him, and crush their hope of being helped. At a deeper level, these patients fear that their aggression will not only destroy the potentially loving and giving object but also their own capacity to give and receive love. Narcissistic patients also attempt, in denying the reality of their emotional relationship with the psychoanalyst, to deny the danger of their destructiveness and to preserve the illusion of being able to 'start all over again'. This can be observed in some patients with sexually promiscuous narcissistic behaviour, in which one function of the promiscuity is to preserve the hope for a better relationship with new objects, and to protect the objects of the patients' sexual impulses from destruction. Often, neglecting to interpret the negative aspects of the transference may heighten the patient's fear over his own aggression and destructiveness, and intensify the need for activation of the narcissistic resistances. In short, the optimal technique for resolution of the narcissistic resistances is the systematic interpretation of both the positive and negative transference aspects rather than focusing exclusively on libidinal elements, or the misunderstanding that interpretation of latent negative resistances means exclusive focus on aggression.

It is important to keep in mind that, except in the most severe cases of narcissistic personality, there are certain normal ego functions which are maintained and certain realistic aspects of the self-concept which continue in existence, side-by-side with the grandiose self. These, of course, constitute the basis for the establishment of a therapeutic alliance, and the related capacity to really listen to the analyst and to identify with him in thinking psychologically about himself. These normal self-aspects can be diagnosed, preserved, and expanded by focusing upon the patient's tendency to split off or devaluate these very functions in himself. The realistic wish to maintain a good relationship with the analyst and to be helped by him is the starting point, one might say, of the recuperation of normal infantile and mature dependency and self-evaluation. Insofar as narcissistic resistances against full awareness of the underlying rage and contempt are also at the service of preserving the good relationship with the analyst, the interpretation of this double function of the narcissistic resistance may greatly help the patient face his split-off contempt and envy. In short, non-critical interpretation of the negative aspects of the transference may help reduce the patient's fear of his own destructiveness and doubts about his goodness.

However, there are cases in which the narcissistic resistances cannot be worked through, and the patient after lengthy periods of stalemate prefers to terminate the treatment, or the analyst feels that he cannot help the patient any further. Under these conditions, a shift into a more supportive approach of the kind which in my opinion is implied (although not intended) in Kohut's approach may be very helpful. This is particularly true for patients with relatively effective social adaptation, who consult because of a symptom which improves in the course of the analysis before working through of their basic narcissistic resistances; and for cases in which secondary gains, particularly important narcissistic gratifications linked to their pathological character structure, militate against the painful nature of analytic work. There are also patients with intense negative therapeutic reactions who can accept certain improvement only at the cost of simultaneously defeating the analyst in his purpose to bring about further change. In many cases of this kind, the treatment may have to shift at some point, into a supportive tolerance of the narcissistic constellation in combination with preparation for termination of the treatment.

There is, however, a dramatic difference between the changes brought about under these circumstances, and the changes brought about when pathological narcissism is systematically worked through. When the pathological narcissism cannot be worked through, and analysis shifts into a supportive approach, the patient's social functioning usually improves noticeably, and his capacity to understand better what goes on in other people and in his interactions with them improves the patient's relationships with others and himself. The patient's ambitions become more realistic, the ways to achieve them more in harmony with his overall life situation and goals, and there is usually an increase of the tolerance of the feelings of boredom and restlessness which are so typical of narcissistic personalities. However, there usually persists a lack of capacity for empathy in depth with others, and a lack of capacity for full development of love relations. Their attitude toward work often reveals the pursuit of some specialized interest or small area of personal investment—whether it is in business, professions, studies, hobbies or collections—where the patient obtains a sense of control and superiority while isolating himself from the broader area of which this particular interest is part.

Paradoxically, narcissistic personalities functioning rather poorly on an overt borderline level, who have undergone supportive psycho-therapy, may present a higher level of improvement than patients who originally functioned more effectively and were more intelligent, crea-tive and ambitious. The persistent feelings of emptiness, the 'burned out' quality of interests and ambitions that one observes in narcissistic personalities functioning on a borderline level leaves them more willing to settle for rather conventional, often over-conventional ways and styles, replacing their old ambitiousness and flamboyance with a grati-fication of having their life and immediate needs stable and under con-trol. In contrast, the highly gifted, brilliant narcissistic personalities who have undergone psychoanalytic treatment which did not resolve their narcissistic personality structure, tend to experience more dissat-isfaction with themselves and with life. They feel that while they can no longer hold on to their old grandiosity, they cannot accept the essentially 'mediocre' nature of ordinary life.

The observation of former psychoanalytic candidates (graduated or not) who have undergone psychoanalytic treatment in which the nar-cissistic resistances were not systematically analysed and resolved (usu-ally in connexion with lack of full exploration of the negative transfer-ence dispositions) provide a good illustration of these developments. A composite picture of traits one particularly finds among this group are: a gradual disappointment with intensive psychotherapeutic work with patients, a feeling of boredom when considering the perspective of intensive work with a patient over a period of months or years, and rationalizations of this loss of interest in clinical work in terms of theoretical criticisms of psychoanalytic theory or technique. Frequently these former candidates—or analysts—eagerly explore new treatment methods, particularly those which promise to bring about an immediate activation of emotional reactions or regression. They feel more com-fortable with methods which permit 'instant intimacy' of a non-differ-entiated nature rather than the lengthy, complex building-up of personal relationships in depth. Intelligent and gifted therapists with this char-acter constellation may have a great sensitivity for 'small and complex issues' in the treatment, but lose sight of the emotional constellation expressing what is going on between them and the patient. It is inter-esting to observe how in the post-analytic stage patients with narcissistic personality who have not undergone systematic working through of the narcissistic resistances continue to idealize their analyst for a time, and then gradually shift into a basic indifference. Their retrospective evaluation of analysis is that while it was a very helpful experience, they did not learn anything really new about themselves.

The following case illustrates the patient's pressure for premature termination of the treatment and a consequent shift into a supportive approach. This patient, a businessman in his early 40s with a typical narcissistic personality structure, came because of homosexuality. Over a period of four years of psychoanalysis he improved to the extent that his homosexual impulses and acting out disappeared, and his general adaptation to his family life and work improved markedly. He felt he had achieved the main goal for which he had entered treatment, and was satisfied with his present life in spite of the persisting sensation of boredom, difficulty in empathizing with other people, and an awareness of his limitations in caring for others. His chronic conflicts about envy had decreased, partly because his wishes for wealth and prestige had been gratified. After a lengthy period in which he met my interpretive efforts by insisting that he had achieved all he had expected from psychoanalysis, we finally agreed to consider termination. In the six months before the termination of the analysis, and after a date for termination had been set, his main fear was that I was angry and disappointed because of this decision, and, on a deeper level, he felt that termination represented his escape from a perfectionistic, never-satisfied analyst-mother. At this point, I focused on the patient's fear of rejection by me without persisting in my previous attempts to analyse the underlying conflicts (mainly his paranoid fear of attack and betrayal by me as a sadistic, withholding primitive mother). I did, however, point out to him his fear that I was seeing him as sadistically withholding further analytic work from me, and that he was attributing to me the kind of suspiciousness which he had previously experienced toward me. I also explored with him his fear that I would not accept him as a person in his own right if he did not live up to some kind of perfect standards, which reflected a projection on to me of his own, highly unrealistic aspirations for perfection that we had explored in the past. In the course of this process, the patient's experience of me as an idealized person who could accept him as he was in his own right provided an important source of support to him, helped him tone down his own narcissistic aspirations and achieve further improvement in his relationship with himself as well as with his family. This patient did not experience a full-blown mourning process during the last part of the analysis, nor, as I learned from follow-up information years after the termination of this analysis, did he experience such a period of mourning after the termination. Over the years, his general symptomatic improvement has persisted, and he had gradually accepted the limitation of his internal emotional life. In short, this case illustrates how the protection of narcissistic defences as part of the process of treatment termination may be helpful when full resolution of the pathological narcissism cannot be achieved.

However, whenever possible, one should attempt to resolve this serious psychopathology in order to achieve a fundamental change in the patient's internal relationship with himself and with others—a shift, in short, from pathological narcissism and object relationships to normal narcissism and object relationships.

The following vignettes illustrate various features of narcissistic transferences.

VIGNETTE 1

A male patient reacted to the information that I would not be able to see him for one of his appointments later that week with anger, and then, feeling distant and empty in the hour, withdrew into a monotonous recital of disconnected thoughts going through his mind. Exploration of his anger revealed that he felt shocked about the suddenness of the announcement, and about the fact that it did not fit into what he considered to be a predictable pattern (my letting him know weeks ahead when I would not be able to see him, or my secretary letting him know about some unexpected development, i.e. an illness on my part). This patient showed no reactions to weekend separations, and would resume his sessions after vacations as if his last hour had been yesterday. We had explored in some depth his angry reactions to minor frustrations on my part, and his tendency to forget me completely (and his fantasies that, actually, I ceased to exist in between hours) when he felt I had behaved in a stable, completely predictable manner (for example, my comments would confirm his own observations, and I would thus show neither more nor less knowledge about him that he had). During this session, his associations to his anger led into fantasies that one of my children must be ill, and that I was cancelling my appointments because

I wanted to be with the child. He then expressed fantasies that I had unusually bright or attractive children, and speculated about the ways in which I was spending my free time with my family. In the course of these associations, it became clear that he saw me as a potential source of love and concern for him, and as teasingly withholding that love and concern from him, giving it instead to my children, of whom he felt intensely jealous. At this point he became sad, and commented that it was understandable enough that I should prefer my children rather than a demanding, self-centred person such as he. His reaction then shifted abruptly to a feeling of annoyance with me and of having been trapped by me. At that point, he felt that I was demanding and selfish, asking him to come at hours which were convenient to me, and cancelling his hours without any regard to his needs. He felt it was a typical analyst's manipulation to have him think about his motivations when obviously something was wrong with me. His associations then focused on other aspects of my personality which seemed to confirm to him that I had a self-centred, manipulative character, and that I really did not care about him at all. He felt I had simply cancelled his hour in order not to have to change my schedule.

What I wish to stress is the suddenness of the shift in the emotional relationship of the patient with me: in contrast to the consistent, many hours of 'calm' narcissistic control, he presented a brief period of intense and changing emotional reaction. His reaction illustrates the utilization of the narcissistic defence against his feeling rejected by a hypocritical mother, and the feelings of guilt and unworthiness because of what he considered his excessive demandingness on her. His reaction also illustrates the projection of his demandingness and self-centeredness on her, and the secondary disappointment and devaluation of this maternal image in the transference, thus reestablishing the narcissistic balance.

There was abundant evidence in this case that his mother was, indeed, very self-centred, and had a chronic tendency to manipulate him through guilt feelings; but his feelings of abandonment and unworthiness were intolerable to him, because they were compounded by guilt over his anger toward his mother, and by the projection on to her of his own angry, revengeful feelings.

In this case, the feeling of sadness reflected a temporary awareness of his angry, demanding behaviour toward me, and toward his mother in the last resort. However, the sadness also involved his acknowledgement that, in spite of the frustration that he had just experienced from me, I was also the person who could give him love and concern. It was also sadness over his feeling that he could not respond in a loving way to me, that is, to his mother image. I pointed out to the patient that one of the reasons he felt it was so difficult to tolerate his anger and loneliness, and his longing for a good relationship with his analyst (mother) was his despair over his own badness, as if his aggressive fantasies and feelings would eliminate or destroy his right to expect a loving relationship, and his trust in his capacity to give. Again, systematic interpretation of both the positive and negative transference reactions defended against by pathological narcissistic resistances help to integrate love and hatred and, in the last resort, the contradictory self and object images which are split off as part of the primitive ego organization of these patients.

VIGNETTE 2

A college student in her early 20s was furious because I would be gone for a week, and expressed ragefully her disappointment in what she experienced as my callousness and negligence. She threatened to terminate the treatment, and made me responsible for anything that might happen to her during the time I was away. I interpreted to her the anger over my leaving her, and her projection of that anger on to me so that my going away acquired dangerous, sadistic qualities. I also pointed out to her that because she was so angry with me she was disqualifying me completely not only as a professional, but also, as it were, tearing apart my image inside of her, so that nothing was left but bleak emptiness and my leaving became much worse. In earlier hours, she had expressed the fantasies that I would go away on a professional trip to boastfully let others know about my success with patients, and she had imagined my trip as an ongoing series of feasts which would start out with my proclaiming my greatness and continue with huge, endless dinner parties in which I would greedily devour food ordinarily only available to a select few. These fantasies, expressed in the middle of intense rage, alternated with periods of disdainful calmness in which the patient would act completely indifferent and bored. I now reminded her of these fantasies, and suggested that one of the functions of her intense rage was to erase me as the source of unending envy for her. At this point, still angry but somehow more thoughtful, she exclaimed that what she was really envious of was that I could be satisfied with myself, that I would not crumble under the guilt feelings which she would try to evoke in me, and that I could tolerate feelings of guilt without losing my determination to do what I had decided to. This same patient, at another time when she was again considering termination of her treatment, said that although she knew she really did need to continue in treatment, the idea that she would rob me of the treatment success would go a long way to make life more pleasurable without continuing in treatment.

VIGNETTE 3

Another patient, after many months of what appeared on the surface to be detachment, gave continuous indication of his need to reassure himself against relentless envy. This was a young college professor who continuously compared the achievements of all other people with his own, and obtained endless gratification from the reassurance that he had achieved much more than anybody else at the same age. He would calculate the relationship between the level of income and the age of friends, the size of houses in relationship to the age of the owner, the number of professional honors and publications of other colleagues in comparison to what he had achieved at the same age, etc. Although he speculated intellectually that perhaps his complete indifference toward me might be related to the fear that he might develop the same reaction with me, and, feeling superior, might evoke my envy and hatred, it took many months until this became an emotional reality. At one point he was able to face the humiliating and painful awareness that to really feel he needed me caused him to envy me because of this very need. If I really had understanding to offer which he lacked, every confirmation of this would create a pang of envy.

VIGNETTE 4

Still another patient, an industrialist in his middle thirties, came to analysis with the expectation that he was to be 'brain washed' into a state of satisfaction with himself, and to be given a clear system of values and principles for guiding his daily life to replace his chronic sense of uncertainty and futility and his feelings of being 'phony'. He had become disillusioned with religion, in spite of strenuous efforts in . early years to find magic help through a religious commitment, and he was quite aware of his efforts to replace his search for religion with psychoanalysis. In the early stages of his analysis, he saw me as a rigid, dogmatic but deeply convinced high-priest of psychoanalysis, an ambivalent idealization which turned out to be a protective structure against his vision of me as a hypocrite, a man who went through empty rituals because it fitted his pocket—in short, a 'phony' as the patient saw himself. It became quite striking to him that there were only three ways in which he could perceive me: either I was a convinced, dogmatic, arbitrary 'brain washer' who could sadistically force him to submit to psychoanalytic dogma; or a cynical manipulator who could exploit him financially; or, even worse, an impotent fool who would believe in a phony method and theory such as psychoanalysis. It took many months for the patient to become aware that in these three alternatives he had excluded the possibility that I, as a psychoanalyst, might have something real and concrete to offer, and that my convictions might reflect my awareness of this fact. This patient insisted on acquiring the 'magical' tools of psychoanalysis for achieving happiness, instead of carrying out a realistic work in collaboration with the analyst, partly because he was fearful of his envious impulses.

At one point, he became aware that he used to rapidly scan my office at the beginning of the sessions to make sure everything was exactly as it had been before. It turned out that he was afraid that new objects, books or papers would appear on my desk indicating new acquisitions or tributes that I had received, and it was with a great sense of relief that the patient reassured himself that there was nothing new that would upset him. He also became aware that, at times when he did find new acquisitions in the office, the intrusive thoughts would come to mind that I was Jewish, that Jewish people were extremely grabby and voracious, and that new possessions of mine confirmed my belonging to an empty, hungry, exploitative race. The patient was very much afraid of exploring these fantasies about me, fearing that my self-esteem would crumble under these 'poisonous' attacks, and that therefore he would be unable to obtain help and relief in the analysis. Systematic interpretation of the fear over his own aggression, with implicit acknowledgement of the patient's wish to preserve me as an intact, potentially helpful person in the transference as part of his total reaction, permitted the gradual uncovering of the conflicts around contempt, greediness, and hatred against which narcissistic defences had been erected.

COUNTERTRANSFERENCE AND THERAPEUTIC MODIFICATION OF THE NARCISSISTIC RESISTANCES

Kohut suggests that unresolved narcissistic disturbances in the analyst may cause the analyst's uneasiness at being idealized, and bring about a subtle tendency to reject the patient's idealization (1971, p. 263). While I agree that unresolved narcissistic conflicts of the analyst may bring about pathological reactions in him to the patient's idealization, I also feel they may foster excessive acceptance as well as rejection of the patient's idealization. Unfortunately, at times analysts treating these patients accept uncritically some aspects of the patient's idealization. To accept the admiration seems to me an abandonment of a neutral position in the same way as does critical 'over-objectivity'. Narcissistic patients readily react to interpretations as if they were 'rejections' and if acceptance of the patient's admiration means to abandon a neutral interpretative stance, there exists a danger of the analyst being forced into a situation which the patient can easily interpret, sometimes with justification, as a seduction of the analyst. I have been impressed by how skilfully some narcissistic patients sense those aspects of their idealization of the analyst which fit into the analyst's own narcissistic 'weak spots'.

The 'analyst's uneasiness' regarding the idealization may stem from the peculiar quality of this idealization, namely the combination of the controlling elements in it, and its particular 'switch on–switch off' quality. In other words, the analyst may sense the negative as well as the positive transference implications.

In my experience, the main problem regarding the counter-transference reactions to narcissistic patients is related to the patient's consistent efforts to deny the existence of the psychoanalyst as an independent person. In this regard, I agree with Kohut's description of the reactions of the analyst to the primitive forms of the mirror transference. Kohut says that, while the analyst 'may feel oppressed by the patient's unqualified yet silent demands which, from the point of view of the target of the merger transference, are tantamount to total enslavement—the absence of object-instinctual cathexes often makes it difficult for him to remain reliably attentive during prolonged periods' (p. 275). But I disagree with the implication that the problem is one of the nature of the cathexes, for it seems to me that what is involved is the unconscious tendency to control the analyst, the unconscious mechanisms of deval-uation, and the activation of primitive types of projection related to the grandiose self.

A careful study of Kohut's case of Miss F. (1971, p. 283–95), illus-trating the analyst's reactions to mirror transferences, lends itself to an interpretation along the lines I have suggested in this paper. At one point, the patient was able to 'establish connexions between the rage which she experienced against me when I did not understand her de-mands and the feelings she had experienced in reaction to the narcis-sistic frustration which she had suffered as a child' (p. 293). Kohut states: 'I was finally able to tell her that her anger at me was based on narcissistic processes, specifically on a transference confusion with a depressed mother who had deflected the child's narcissistic needs on to herself. These interpretations were followed by the recall of clusters of analogous memories concerning her mother's entering a phase of depressive self-preoccupation during later years of the patient's life' (1971, p. 292). In the light of the overall information given about this case, I would raise the question to what extent, in making this interpre-tation, was the analyst implicitly blaming the patient's mother for having caused the patient's anger and protecting the patient from full exami-nation of the complex origins of her own rage? In more general terms, I see a danger of a seductive effect given by the combination of the analyst's unquestioning acceptance of the patient's idealization, and by the immediate referral back to the original object of the negative trans-ference without exploring fully the patient's participation in the devel-opment of pathological rage within the here and now of the transference.

I have suggested that the patient's subtle, unconscious efforts to deny meaning to the analytic relationship (which may induce in the analyst a chronic sense of frustration, helplessness, boredom, and lack of un-derstanding) are much more difficult for the analyst to tolerate than the unrealistic, primitive idealization, which by its very nature alerts the analyst to the narcissistic functions of this idealization. While it is true that analysts with unresolved conflicts regarding their own narcissism may react with anxiety and rejection, or with uncritical acceptance of the patient's idealization, the main danger is the internal rejection by the analyst of the patient because of the patient's chronic devaluation of the analyst. The analyst may feel, at times, as if the patient were convincing him that there is no such thing as an internal life, that psychological matters are incomprehensible and senseless, and that the patient as well as the total analytic situation has a strange, lifeless, mechanical quality. At other times, the analyst may have a sense of understanding but of complete paralysis, as if he no longer would be able to decide regarding what or when to intervene, or as if the emotional connexions among the different aspects of the material were unavailable. At times, there are strong temptations for the analyst to just sit back and let things go, hoping that he will find a way back to an intuitive understanding of the patient later on. If at this point, alerted by this development, the analyst is able to gather the objective evidence in the verbal and non-verbal manifestations of the patient which is related to treating the analyst as non-existent, immediate changes may occur in the transference making the analytic relationship come alive. The sense of deadening monotony in the analytic situation may derive from very specific aspects of the patient's associations and non-verbal behaviour which need to be diagnosed and interpreted.

In one session in the middle of his analysis, I pointed out to a narcissistic patient that I was puzzled by the fact that he seemed to talk about important memories of his past in such a monotonous, subdued tone that it was difficult for me to follow them, and that there seemed to be an obvious discrepancy between what he was saying and the way he was saying it. The patient first had a startled reaction, and after I finished talking, he said that he had not been able to listen attentively to what I was saying, but that he had all of a sudden become aware of my presence. In response to my suggestion to associate to this sudden shock, the patient became aware that he had felt very comfortable exploring his past, feeling that letting his thoughts go into all directions would throw them, as it were, into a big, expectant void—a kind of open, receptive world—which would order and automatically bring back into his mind all that he was expressing, with a clear understanding of what it meant and how it would increase the emotional wealth of his experience. The patient also felt annoyed about my intrusion, and he had the fantasy that I might feel frustrated and incompetent because he could do his analytical work alone. Later in the session, he said, smilingly, that perhaps he had not been able to pay attention to what I had said, because if I really had something to add which would make a change, this would be a very rude disruption of his feeling that he could do it all alone.

Gradually, in the course of working through of narcissistic resistances, the analyst will experience shifts in the sensation of paralyzing stalemate, such as acute awareness of fleeting emotional states of loneliness, or fears of loss of meaning or of love, or of fears of threatening attacks or of rejection by others, feelings within the analyst which reflect the dissociated, repressed and/or projected self and object images which are coming alive in the transference. These regressive 'flashes' of emotional experience, or a gradual shift in the analyst's emotional reaction to the patient's efforts to deny emotional meaning to the hours, is a useful index of the working through of narcissistic resistances. At times, a sudden feeling of becoming 'widely awake' to aspects of the material which earlier made no emotional sense, will indicate the shift in the transference–counter-transference equilibrium. Insofar as a patient will gladly accept any kind of intellectual explanation which he can 'learn' and absorb in his 'self-analysis', he will accept the analyst's interpretations; however, the analyst's reflection on such momentary states of mood perceived by him on the basis of what has been conveyed by the patient, or of the analyst's emotional perception of the patient's self-images or object-images activated in the hours will often be arduously resisted by the patient and require much emotional alertness on the analyst's part. It is as if at this stage the analyst would become the depository of the patient's more differentiated self and object images linked with the emotional experiences of abandonment, loneliness, frustration, hopelessness against which the patient was defending himself. It is as if the analyst were now experiencing that part of the normal infantile self of the patient which he had been unable to tolerate and had to dissociate or repress and replace by his pathological grandiose self.

At this stage of development in his analysis, a narcissistic patient drove past a sidewalk on to which a dead cat had been thrown, obviously run over by another car. There was something peculiar in his description of the dead cat, in the way he conveyed the sense of abandonment and total misery expressed in the frozen attitude of the dead animal, but before I had time to explore this matter further, other issues seemed to erase its emotional significance. A few days later, the patient mentioned a hungry cat that had been picked up by his children, and he talked about the desperate way this cat would devour food, always ready to escape from possible blows or attack. When I asked him to associate about this, the patient thought of powerful cats roaming the streets at night and chasing away all rivals while searching for food in garbage cans, with an obvious shift from the hungry, frightened, lonely kitten to the powerful, aggressive, 'callous' cat. The subject-matter came up again in a brief fantasy of a dark, rainy night and a lonely kitten having difficulty in finding shelter.

What is hard to convey in this brief vignette is the mutual isolation of these rather specific descriptions of a certain state of mind which the patient found very difficult to tolerate in himself. What predominated by far, during that stage, was the patient's haughty self-affirmation, his feeling of powerful superiority as a member of a social group which had inborn stamina and deep roots in the country, in contrast to people he despised, such as foreigners, particularly traumatized refugees. The transference was predominantly narcissistic-grandiose, and we ex-plored consistently his tendency to disregard or forget my comments, to treat me as non-existent, and to analyse himself on his own. It was now, however, that my own experience shifted from that of meaning-less, random listening to material with lack of emotional depth, to the strange experience of occasional moments of strong empathy with the isolated, fleetingly activated descriptions of this image of the hungry little cat, and for the dead cat thrown on to the sidewalk. Only then was I able to grasp the connexion between the image of the lonely kitten and the traumatized refugee. It was as if the patient was activating whatever deep sources existed in my own past implying a conviction of loneliness and agonizing incapacity to express the need for love and shelter. Again, these were only fleeting experiences in the hours with this patient, and at first it was hard for me to connect these experiences with the material.

However, these experiences and fantasies, and memories of relevant dreams of my own past, would only come up in the hours with this patient, and I gradually discovered their connexion with the peculiar cat fantasy material that regularly preceded them. I finally was able to interpret to the patient that he was projecting on to me an image of himself, of his early childhood in which he felt deeply unloved. I reconstructed with him the physical and familiar environment in the context of which he had these experiences on the basis of the different aspects of the 'cat material' as well as the general knowledge that we had developed to that point. Retrospectively, the connexion of the cat fantasy material with his past was pretty obvious, but I wish to stress how difficult it was to capture this material directly from isolated associations in a stage of the analysis in which the patient was engaged in a defensive deterioration of all meaningful communication, and in which the activation of projected, dissociated remnants of the real infantile self occurred in split-off bits in the countertransference over periods of many sessions.

Acting out of the countertransference reactions motivated by the patient's ongoing efforts of omnipotent control of the analyst may take the form of 're-educative' efforts on the analyst's part, such as pointing out to the patient how he is 'undermining' the analytic process, 'paying lip service to free association,' etc. The analyst may be tempted, at such times, to become moralistic, or to concern himself excessively with the long-range prognosis of the case, in contrast to evaluating his difficulty in empathizing with the immediate transference development. Psychoanalysts with important unresolved narcissistic conflicts may, during periods of lengthy devaluation on the part of the patient, react by suddenly rejecting narcissistic patients whom they previously considered extremely interesting and 'rewarding' (particularly at times when the projection of the grandiose self on to the analyst would feed into the analyst's own narcissistic needs).

The most general point I wish to stress again is that, underlying the narcissistic resistances there exist significant, primitive internalized object relations which are activated in the transference, and may be diagnosed gradually as the narcissistic resistances are worked through. This clinical observation constitutes, it seems to me, a most important documentation of the theoretical assumption that narcissism and object relationships always go hand-in-hand, a point articulately stressed by van der Waals (1965).

What follows is the summary of the sequence of transference paradigms representing approximately two years of an advanced stage in the psychoanalytic treatment of a narcissistic personality. The patient was a successful architect in his late 30s, a senior partner of a large architectural firm. This patient's transference remained at a level of a typical narcissistic transference paradigm for over three years. During that time, an early phase of idealization of the analyst, reflecting mainly a reaction formation against pervasive devaluating tendencies, was followed by what might best be called an oscillating situation with alternative activation of the pathological grandiose self and the projection of such a grandiose self on to the analyst. The gradual working through of this paradigm activated intense primitive envy and competitiveness based upon oral envy (rather than oedipal strivings), and eventually, a more direct expression of ambivalence with shifts from oral demandingness and anger to longing for a dependency on a loving, protective father-mother image, and strong guilt feelings for his attacks on the analyst. This transference shifted, in turn, toward a more stable dependency on a loving, protective, father image in the transference, and the patient, after over three years of psychoanalysis, for the first time became really dependent upon the analyst with the development of neurotic mourning reactions to separations from the analyst, and the emergence of material from various levels of childhood conflicts. This stage was followed by a reactivation of emotional withdrawal, and a general emotional emptiness in the hours, which on the surface appeared as a repetition of the earlier stage of narcissistic resistances. However, there was a difference in the patient's reaction, which now had the quality of a suspicious, disgruntled withholding of material, together with what appeared as an unconscious attempt to put the analyst to sleep, or at least to maintain him in a chronic frustration created by monotonous repetitions. The patient, during this time, frequently referred to his mother's sadistic, withholding tendencies, and eventually became aware of his identification with such a mother image, while projecting his own, frustrated, infantile self on to the analyst.

This identification with the aggressor was different from the earlier narcissistic withdrawal in the transference, and the interpretation of this transference pattern brought about an immediate shift, with further deepening of the dependent relationship toward the analyst. The patient now saw him as a protective, loving father toward whom he could turn for the gratification of his dependent childhood needs; and he now felt he could 'abandon himself' to the analytic situation. He was struck by this new experience for him, which influenced the relationship with his wife and children, and made him understand the dependent needs of them as well as deepen his own involvement with his family. Now, for the first time, the patient became aware of how his entire attitude toward the analyst had been influenced by his basic conviction that no real relationship would ever occur between him and the psychoanalyst. For example, for a long time he harboured fantasies that a friendly although distant relationship with his psychoanalyst would occur after the termination of the analysis, and that he and the analyst had a secret understanding that in reality the analytic relationship had nothing to do with the descriptions of intense emotional conflicts supposedly occurring during the treatment.

The patient also became aware of the existence of an internal world which was not under his conscious control, and of the excitement and fear in facing this world in the analytic situation.[1] A year later the full development of oedipal conflicts emerged in the transference, and the analysis acquired features of the usual resistances and manifestations of these conflicts.

In general, at times of heightened resistances, earlier, previously abandoned narcissistic resistances may become reactivated, similarly to what occurs with past, abandoned character defence during stages of shift into new lines of resistance. However, the context in which such reactivation of narcissistic defences occur, and the differentiated quality of the internalized object relations connected with these resistances, confirm the important structural changes that have taken place in the patient.

PROGNOSIS OF NARCISSISM, TREATED AND UNTREATED

I have referred to prognostic factors in the psychoanalytic treatment of narcissistic personalities in earlier papers (Kernberg, 1970a, 1971a), and will limit myself here to briefly enumerating these factors, modifying and adding to my earlier considerations.

Secondary gain of illness, such as life circumstances granting unusual narcissistic gratification to a patient with a socially effective narcissistic personality structure, may be a major obstacle in the resolution of narcissistic resistances. This is also the case when there is secondary

[1] It needs to be stressed that it took over three years of analysis of the narcissistic resistances to bring about a transference situation which with less severe types of character pathology occurs during the early stages of the treatment.

gain from analytic treatment itself, such as in the case of candidates with narcissistic personality in psychoanalytic training. The question may be raised whether unusual life gratifications in early adulthood of gifted patients generally militate against treatment in some cases of narcissistic personalities, and whether psychoanalysis during middle and later adulthood might not have better prognosis in some of them.

Another major prognostic factor is the extent to which negative therapeutic reactions develop, typically linked with particularly severe, repressed or dissociated conflicts around envy. This is a type of negative therapeutic reaction not derived from superego factors and more severe than that seen in depressive-masochistic patients with a sadistic although integrated superego. Cases with relatively good quality of superego functioning (reflected in the capacity for real investment in values transcending narcissistic interests) have a good prognostic implication, in contrast to cases in which there are subtle types of manipulative and antisocial behaviour, even in the absence of major antisocial features (which would make the prognosis very bad indeed). In simple terms, honesty in their daily life is a favourable prognostic indicator for the analysis of narcissistic personalities. Insofar as a good development of sublimatory channels is intimately linked to the capacity for investment in value systems transcending narcissistic needs, the sublimatory potential of the patient is important too.

In contrast to the outstanding importance of the prognostic factors mentioned so far, tolerance of depression and mourning, and a predominance of transference potential for guilt versus a potential for paranoid rage, are of somewhat less overriding importance. Of even less prognostic importance are the non-specific manifestations of ego weakness, such as lack of impulse control and of anxiety tolerance, and even the potential for regression to primary process thinking if and when the patient does not function on an overt borderline level. This brings us to the general limitation of a strictly psychoanalytic approach for certain patients with narcissistic personality, namely, the disorganizing effect that psychoanalysis may have for narcissistic patients functioning on an overt borderline level. For such people, I consider this approach generally contraindicated.

A particularly difficult prognostic estimate is involved in the case of potential candidates for psychoanalytic training with narcissistic personality structure. Obviously, the problem only comes up in those relatively well-adjusted narcissistic personalities whose social and professional functioning is satisfactory, who present high intelligence and particular talents, and at times appear unusually promising. In reviewing a number of cases in which, retrospectively, it appeared that mistakes had been made both in accepting and rejecting some candidates, the two major prognostic factors that stand out as prognostically significant are the quality of object relationships and the integrity and depth of the value systems and superego functioning. It needs to be stressed again that I use the concept 'quality of object relations' to refer more to the quality of internalized object relations, i.e. the depth of the patient's internal relationships with others, rather than to the extent to which he is involved in social interactions. This clarification may be particularly relevant in discussing Kohut's work, because he tends to use the term 'object relation' in its behavioural sense rather than in the sense referred to in this paper. For instance, he states: 'The antithesis to narcissism is not the object relation but object love. An individual's profusion of object relations, in the sense of the observer of the social field, may conceal his narcissistic experience of the object world; and a person's seeming isolation and loneliness may be the setting for a wealth of current object investments' (1971, p. 228). Again (p. 283): 'The patient established object relations not primarily because she was attracted to people but rather as an attempt to escape from the painful narcissistic tensions.' In my view, narcissism (investment in the self), and object relations (investment in significant objects and their representations), go hand-in-hand, and their depth depends not only upon the vicissitudes of the libidinal investment, but, as stressed throughout this paper, on the aggressive investment as well. For practical purposes, object relations in depth involve the capacity both to love well, and to hate well, and particularly to tolerate varying combinations of loving and hateful feelings, and their toned down mingling in the relationship with the same object and with the self. Normal object relations as well as normal narcissism include an integrative conception in depth of others and oneself. All this is in striking contrast to the frequent blandness and uninvolvement, the lack of commitment to others as well as to any convictions about himself that one sees in narcissistic patients. Paradoxically, such lack of emotional depth and commitment may permit a better social functioning, for example, in certain political and bureaucratic organizations in which lack of commitments means survival and access to the top.

Applying all this to the particular case of prospective psychoanalytic candidates, systematic attempts to evaluate the realness, the aliveness of other people as they come through in the descriptions of the candidate, and the depth of the candidate as he describes himself, are important indicators of the quality of object relations, in addition to more observable aspects of stability, depth, and richness of the relationships with others and himself. The extent to which there is authentic human warmth and depth may be more difficult to evaluate but is even more important than the extent to which there is a commitment to ethical, intellectual, cultural or aesthetic values, the other major prognostic indicator in the special cases under examination. Sometimes the very good outcome in cases of psychoanalytic candidates who at first seemed highly questionable warrants to consider carefully all the elements of individual cases; and with the improvement in our therapeutic techniques there should be an increase in successful outcomes in the future.

While Kohut does not, as far as I can tell, refer specifically to prognostic differences with his approach for narcissistic personalities functioning on various levels of ego and superego integration, he conveys a generally optimistic outlook. Regarding the outcome with this approach he states: 'The most prominent nonspecific change is the increase and the expansion of the patient's capacity for object love; the specific changes take place in the realm of narcissism itself' (p. 296). Kohut describes, as the result of his treatment approach, the internalization of the idealized parent imago (the archaic aspects of the imago) into the general structure of the ego and into the superego (the late pre-oedipal and oedipal aspects of the imago), leading to an improved functioning of the superego (1971, p. 288–9). Regarding the grandiose self, he states: 'The infantile grandiosity becomes gradually built into the ambitions and purposes of the personality and lends not only vigour to a person's mature strivings but also a sustaining positive feeling of the right to success' (p. 299). In my view, and on the basis of Kohut's published writings, his approach leads to a higher level functioning and better adaptation of the grandiose self, in the context of the patient's shift from more primitive to more adaptive levels of mirror transferences, without a basic resolution of what I consider the pathological structure of the grandiose self. This may well be the reason why, in Kohut's findings, there is no direct, specific relationship between the changes in the patient's narcissism and the patient's object relations. It seems to me that the effects of his approach, if not his intentions and technique, have re-educative elements in them which foster a more adaptive use of the patient's grandiosity. A major question, that necessarily must remain open at this point, is what are the long-range effects of such an approach, or, for that matter, of both Kohut's approach and the alternative one I have outlined? A major test of the effectiveness of the treatment of narcissistic personalities is the adaptation of these patients to the stress and crises which the later stages of life unavoidably will bring about. We will need careful follow-up over long periods of time in order to separate the short-range consequences of treatment from the long-term consequences on their personality, intrapsychic as well as social functioning. This brings me to the last issue of this paper, namely, the prognosis of untreated narcissism.

I strongly agree with Kohut's conviction that narcissistic personality disorders should be treated by psychoanalysis whenever possible. Even in cases which are functioning quite successfully except for some relatively minor symptoms, and where the combination of intelligence, talents, luck and success provide sufficient gratifications to compensate for the underlying emptiness and boredom, one should keep in mind the devastating effects that unresolved pathological narcissism often has during the second half of life. In my view, if psychoanalytic treatment can be carried out and is successful, improvement in these cases means a resolution of their pathological narcissism, the development of normal infantile and adult narcissism in the context of normal object relationships in depth, and what often amounts to a dramatic enrichment of life. In contrast, pathological narcissism has ominous long-range prognostic implications, even in cases of relatively young patients with excellent surface adaptation and very little awareness of illness or suffering on the patient's part. If we consider that throughout an ordinary life span most narcissistic gratifications occur in adolescence and early adulthood, and that even though narcissistic triumphs and gratifications are achieved throughout adulthood, the individual must eventually face the basic conflicts around ageing, chronic illness, physical and mental limitations, and above all, separations, loss, and loneliness—then we must conclude that the eventual confrontation of the grandiose self with the frail, limited and transitory nature of human life is unavoidable.

It is dramatic how intense the denial of this long-range reality can be in narcissistic personalities, who under the influence of the pathological, grandiose self are unconsciously (and sometimes consciously) convinced of their eternal youth, beauty, power, wealth and the unending availability of supplies of confirmation, admiration and security. For them, to accept the breakdown of the illusion of grandiosity means to accept the dangerous, lingering awareness of the depreciated self—the hungry, empty, lonely primitive self surrounded by a world of dangerous, sadistically frustrating and revengeful objects. Perhaps the most frightening experience that narcissistic personalities need to ward off and eventually may have to face is that of a surrounding world empty of love and human contact, a world of dehumanized objects within which animate as well as inanimate objects have lost their previous, magically satisfying qualities.

One patient, a nationally known politician, had developed a serious physical illness which brought about the loss of his professional functions. He became depressed and developed deep feelings of defeat and humiliation accompanied by fantasies in which his political opponents were gloating with satisfaction over his defeat. His depression diminished. He went into retirement, but gradually devaluated the areas of political science in which he had been an expert. This was a narcissistic depreciation of that in which he was no longer triumphant, which brought about a general loss of interest in professional, cultural and intellectual matters. His primary areas of professional and intellectual interests no longer seemed exciting and reminded him again and again of his failure. He was resentful of his dependency upon his wife and children, whom he had previously disregarded while dedicating all his energies to his professional life. His fears of being depreciated by his family motivated him toward ever increasing demands for reassurance and respect. Envious of the professional success of his children, and unable to obtain gratification of this success by means of empathic identification with them, he experienced an increasing sense of estrangement which finally evolved into the recurrence of a now severe, chronic depression, with a predominance of impotent rage over mourning processes as such.

The frightening sensation of futility and emptiness, the panic over the disintegration of the personal meaning of one's immediate environment that has been so dramatically evoked in the plays of Samuel Beckett, or in Eugene Ionesco's *The Chairs* and *Exit the King,* illustrate, it seems to me, the devastating effect of the conflicts of old age on persons with narcissistic personality. The normal reaction to loss, abandonment and failure is the reactivation of internalized sources of love and self-esteem intimately linked with internalized object relations, and reflects the protective function of what has been called 'good internal objects'. Regression in the service of the ego often takes the form of regression to such reactivated internalized object relations of a protective kind, a regression which in turn reactivates, strengthens and broadens the patient's capacity for meaningful relations with others and with humanity and value systems at large. The capacity to work through mourning processes, to be in love, to feel empathy and deep gratification in identifying with loved people and values, a sense of transcendence with nature, of continuation within the historical process, and of oneness with a social or cultural group, are all intimately linked to the normal activation of internalized object relationships at the time of loss, failure and loneliness.

This is in striking contrast to the vicious circle triggered off by narcissistic loss in the case of narcissistic personalities, where defensive devaluation, primitive envy and panic because of the reactivated sense of impoverishment further complicate narcissistic loss and failure. This becomes particularly evident in the narcissistic patient's inability to come to terms with old age, to accept the fact that a younger generation now possesses many of the previously cherished gratifications of beauty, wealth, power and, particularly, creativity. To be able to enjoy life in a process involving a growing identification with other people's happiness and achievements is tragically beyond the capacity of narcissistic personalities. Therefore treatment geared to radically changing pathological narcissism may show its ultimate benefits over the entire life span left to the patient.

The clinical study of narcissistic personalities illustrates that the relationships of the individual with himself and with his surrounding human and inanimate world depends upon the development of normal or pathological internalized object relations. The loss of the world of loving and loved internal objects brings about the loss of meaning of the self and of the world. Psychotic depression represents, in many ways, the terrifying stage of awareness of the loss of love and meaning against which narcissistic personalities need to defend themselves, and schizoid emotional dispersal or a paranoid—not necessarily psychotic—reorganization of the world represents an alternative protection for these patients against the bleakness of depression, but at the cost of bringing about further dehumanization and emptiness. Therefore, and in spite of the limited number of patients whom we are able to help and the very extensive analyses required in these cases, it seems worthwhile to invest much effort in the treatment of what so often on the surface, looks deceivingly as if we were dealing with an almost 'normal' person.

REFERENCES

Abraham, K. (1919). A particular form of neurotic resistance against the psychoanalytic method. *Selected Papers*. London: Hogarth Press, 1927.

Jacobson, E. (1954). Contribution to the metapsychology of psychotic identifications. *J. Am. psychoanal. Ass.* **2**, 239–262.

Jacobson, E. (1964). *The Self and the Object World.* New York: Int. Univ. Press.

Kernberg, O. (1967). Borderline personality organization *J. Am. psychoanal. Ass.* **15**, 641–685.

Kernberg, O. (1970a). Factors in the psychoanalytic treatment of narcissistic personalities. *J. Am. psychoanal. Ass.* **18**, 51–85.

Kernberg, O. (1970b). A psychoanalytic classification of character pathology. *J. Am. psychoanal. Ass.* **18**, 800–822.

Kernberg, O. (1971a). Prognostic considerations regarding borderline personality organization. *J. Am. psychoanal. Ass.* **19**, 595–635.

Kernberg, O. (1971b). New developments in psychoanalytic object-relations theory. (Paper read to the American Psychoanalytic Association.)

Kernberg, O. (1972). Early ego integration and object relations. *Ann. N.Y. Acad. Sci.* **193**, 233–247.

Kernberg, P. (1971). The course of the analysis of a narcissistic personality with hysterical and compulsive features. *J. Am. psychoanal. Ass.* **19**, 451–471.

Kohut, H. (1966). Forms and transformations of narcissism. *J. Am. psychoanal. Ass.* **14**, 243–272.

Kohut, H. (1968). The psychoanalytic treatment of narcissistic personality disorders. *Psychoanal. Study Child* **23**.

Kohut, H. (1971). *The Analysis of the Self.* New York: Int. Univ. Press.

Mahler, M. S. (1968). *On Human Symbiosis and the Vicissitudes of Individuation,* vol. 1: *Infantile Psychosis.* New York: Int. Univ. Press.

Riviere, J. (1936). A contribution to the analysis of the negative therapeutic reaction. *Int. J. Psycho-Anal.* **17**, 304–320.

Rosenfeld, H. (1964). On the psychopathology of narcissism: a clinical approach. *Int. J. Psycho-Anal.* **45**, 332–337.

Sandler, J. & Rosenblatt, B. (1962). The concept of the representational world. *Psychoanal. Study Child* **17.**

Tartakoff, H. H. (1966). The normal personality in our culture and the Nobel Prize complex. In R. M. Loewenstein *et al.* (eds.), *Psychoanalysis: A General Psychology.* New York: Int. Univ. Press.

Ticho, E. (1970). Differences between psychoanalysis and psychotherapy. *Bull. Menninger Clin.* **34,** 128–138.

Van der Waals, H. G. (1965). Problems of narcissism. *Bull. Menninger Clin.* **29,** 293–311.

11. A Narcissistic Defence Against Affects and the Illusion of Self-Sufficiency

Arnold H. Modell

We are familiar with the observation that the defences of the ego are variegated, but if one particular defence predominates it contributes to the structure of a specific character type (thus the predominance of repression is associated with hysteria, and isolation and intellectualization with the obsessive compulsive personality). A specific narcissistic defence against affects that we shall describe here may be looked upon in a similar fashion: it determines the ego structure of a variety of personality types. When it predominates it contributes to the formation of the personality structure that we associate with the narcissistic character disorder. To define a character type by means of a principal ego defence is in a sense an operational definition, for it is an observation made predominantly by means of the psychoanalytic process itself, and this implies that the defences in question not only characterize the mode of resistance to psychoanalysis but are also linked to the qualities of developing transference so that the nature of the transference itself can form the basis for nosology. I have suggested that borderline states can be defined by their characteristic transference (Modell, 1968), and Kohut (1971) has similarly defined the narcissistic character disorder by the absence of a transference neurosis and the development of a characteristic 'idealizing and mirror' transference. So our discussion of a characteristic ego defence is necessarily associated with a discussion of the effect of ego structure upon the developing transference, and this will be dealt with in a later section.

The analyst first becomes aware of this particular narcissistic defence when he observes that there is a massive affect block in the opening phase of psychoanalysis. If other characteristics of an obsessive compulsive personality are present, this defence may be confused with that of isolation. Although there are subtle phenomenological differences that serve to contrast isolation and this narcissistic affect block, the clearest difference derives from the fact that the narcissistic defence is motivated by a fear of closeness to the object of the analyst. Isolation is a more purely intrapsychic defence, as Anna Freud (1936) has described, resulting from the fear of being overwhelmed by the intensity of affects. As I said, there are also phenomenological differences— when there is this narcissistic defence against affects one perceives after a while that there are not two people in the consulting room—the patient acts as if the analyst is not there and is talking to himself or behaves as if *he* is not there. The patient is 'turned off' emotionally— he does not communicate feelings, for to do so would strengthen the object tie to the analyst.

The analyst's countertransference can usually be relied upon to differentiate the subtle differences in the phenomenology between the defence of isolation and the narcissistic defence against affects. In both there is an affect block but in the obsessive compulsive defence there is still a perception on the analyst's part that the patient is relating to him. When the analyst is continuously in the presence of another person who does not seem to be interested in him, or indeed acts as if he was not there, he may experience this as an affront to his own narcissism and may accordingly become bored and sleepy (Kohut, 1971). Therefore our boredom and sleepiness should alert us to the possibility that this is in response to the patient's narcissistic defence against affects. Though the analyst's withdrawal may be defensive, I do not believe that it is necessarily neurotic—it is a very human response to the patient's state of non-relatedness.

When this defence against affects is present, one can invariably observe that it is supported by a fantasy of grandiose self-sufficiency. This illusion of self-sufficiency is maintained in the face of a profoundly dependent relationship with the analyst and the analytic process; their state of non-relatedness is paradoxically associated with that of intense involvement. Grandiose and omnipotent fantasies permit these patients to maintain the illusion that they need nothing from others, that they can provide the source of their own emotional sustenance. Affects in this sense signify object seeking and object hunger, so that their absence supports the illusion that they seek nothing from the person of the analyst.

These people have an accurate endopsychic perception of their relationship to objects. They describe themselves as encased in a 'plastic bubble' or feel that they are really not 'in the world'[1]—they are in a cocoon: a cocoon provides sustenance for its occupant and protects it from the dangers of the environment; it is like a fortress which nothing leaves and nothing enters. A cocoon, no matter how well insulated, needs to be attached to something, and these people who may deny their dependent needs usually crave admiration.

SOME STRUCTURAL CONSIDERATIONS

Freud (1924, 1940) observed that when the ego is in conflict with the environment it attempts to resolve the conflict by means of denying a piece of reality. It does so at the expense of modification of its own structure. Freud employed the metaphor of a split in the ego—a failure of the ego's synthetic functions. The mechanism of denial is thus in contrast to the mechanism of repression where the ego itself remains intact.[2]

As we have said earlier, a defensive alteration of the ego's structure is necessarily linked to the phenomenon of transference: the 'classical' neurotic—one who is capable of developing a transference neurosis— is one whose ego development is relatively unimpaired. In the 'classical' neurotic there is relatively good differentiation of psychic structures— conflicts are primarily internalized and not primarily between the individual and the environment. Further, in the 'classical' neurosis we assume a capacity to form a therapeutic alliance. Correspondingly, where there is ego impairment, this impairment will be reflected in a limitation of the ego's ability to form a therapeutic alliance, as is the case in the narcissistic character disorder.

The narcissistic defence against affects that we have been describing is similar to that of denial as it does involve a disturbance of the ego's relation to the environment with profound consequences to the ego's structures.[3] It differs, however, from denial in that it is a defence

---

[1] Volkan (1973) described a patient who felt encased in an iron ball and used his fantasies as a transitional object.

[2] Kohut (1971) has described this distinction between repression and denial using the terms horizontal and vertical split, where the vertical split corresponds to Freud's description of denial.

[3] In an earlier discussion of denial I have tried to connect the mechanisms of denial to a failure to accept the separateness of objects (Modell, 1961).

primarily against affects and not, as in denial, the perception of a particular piece of reality. But perhaps this narcissistic defence must be supported by a denial of reality—it may all be of one piece. Furthermore, this narcissistic defence against affects is similar to denial in that it can exist in a transitory form which is relatively benign or in a more permanent characterological form which is not benign. It is this characterological formation that we shall consider further.

PRECOCIOUS AUTONOMY

We have observed that in our patients with narcissistic character disorders, there is probably a disturbance in the process of the development of the autonomy of the self *vis-à-vis* the child's relationship to its mother. Although the specifics of the environmental trauma will vary, we have observed that the trauma results in the need to defend the sense of the separateness of the self against the intrusiveness of the mother.[4] This is a confirmation of what Khan (1971) has described: 'The ego of the child has prematurely and precociously brought the traumata of early childhood under its omnipotence and created an intrapsychic structure in the nature of an infantile neurosis which is false self organization.'

We have the impression that environmental trauma at the time when the child is developing a sense of self leads to the establishment of a precocious and vulnerable sense of autonomy. The environmental trauma may take the form of a disillusionment with the mother based on an accurate perception of the mother's faulty judgement.[5] For example, one patient who was in fact intellectually precocious perceived at the age of two or three that his mother was mad, although the extent of her madness was hidden and this fact was not acknowledged by her family or by her neighbours. The child, however, observed that his mother's judgement was off and that he could not rely on her. Another

[4] Kohut (1971) recognizes the central importance of the fear of intrusiveness but does not see the process as object related. He states: ' . . . the central anxiety encountered in the analysis of narcissistic personality disorders is not castration anxiety but the fear of dedifferentiating intrusion of the narcissistic structures and their energies into the ego' (p. 152).

[5] Rycroft (1955) has suggested that idealization is a response to actual object loss linked to the disappointment with a frustrating object. Kohut (1971) stresses the trauma that ensues from the mother's lack of empathy (p.46).

patient perceived his mother at the same age to be flighty, childish and fatuous. The human child, as is true of all primates, is dependent upon the mother to protect it from the dangers of the environment so that the perception of the mother's unreliability must have profound consequences. We suggest that it leads in some patients to the formation of a precocious separation from the mother which is supported by fantasies of omnipotence. The perception that the mother's judgement is off may also be accompanied by the need to defend oneself from the mother's excessive intrusiveness. For example, one patient's mother consistently undressed in front of him as if he were not a separate person and it did not really matter. In yet another patient, a woman, the mother did not respect the separateness and autonomy of the patient's body— she successfully toilet trained my patient by inserting rectal suppositories from the age of six months and thereafter whenever it was thought to be needed.

Although the specific form of the environmental trauma may vary, we suggest that there is a common denominator in that these environmental traumata induce the formation of a precocious and premature sense of self—which retains its fragility and must be supported by omnipotent and grandiose fantasies.

THE STRUCTURAL DIFFERENCE BETWEEN THE BORDERLINE AND NARCISSISTIC CHARACTER

Our description of a precocious structural formation resulting from environmental trauma forces us to clarify further the differences between this description and that of borderline states. For the borderline character is believed to be, at least in some measure, the result of environmental trauma that Winnicott has described as a failure of 'good enough' mothering. We must further remind ourselves that this narcissistic defence against affects that we associate with narcissistic character disorder may also exist as a defence in the borderline patient. We are reminded here of a very useful metaphor employed by Robert Knight (1954) and originally attributed to Freud, where the defensive structures of a given personality are likened to the troops of an army. An army's defences may be strung out in an uneven fashion: troops may appear to be defending a forward position but the main body of forces may be well to the rear. The point of this metaphor is that ego arrests and regressions that form part of character are highly uneven, that defences are variegated in that our nosological distinctions are a description of where the main body of troops is (see Gedo & Goldberg, 1973, for a detailed discussion of this issue).

Thus the precocious internalization of the self that we believe characterizes the narcissistic character disorder may be a facet of the personality organization of a borderline patient, but that is not where his major forces reside. In contrast to the patient with the narcissistic character disorder, the borderline patient evidences an intense object hunger. He is seeking objects and affects are communicated and, correspondingly, the countertransference affects are intense in the analyst. The borderline patient does not attempt to maintain an illusion of self-sufficiency—instead he invests the person of the analyst with the qualities of a transitional object placed between himself and a dangerous environment, so that his safety in the world depends on the presence of the therapist (Modell, 1968). Accordingly, the therapist experiences the patient's conflict with the environment directly, and he becomes the target of the patient's rage at reality. This is in marked contrast to the affect block experienced in the opening phases of analysis with a narcissistic character disorder. Affects are therefore the leading edge of this differential diagnosis (see also Modell, 1973). The intensity of affects in the borderline state and the non-relatedness of the narcissistic character disorder reflect differences in ego structure and it is this issue that we shall examine further.

A structural differentiation can be illustrated by reference to Gitelson's (1962) distinction of the 'open' and 'closed' system, as observed in the opening phase of psychoanalysis. Gitelson quotes Anna Freud as follows: 'The infant and child do not present us with a "closed system", and therefore it is necessary to pay more regard to the environment and less to the biological reasonableness and synthetic functions of the ego. The aim with children is to lift them to a secondary level of development through the use of the analyst as a new object.' Gitelson observes that 'we may say that this "secondary level of development" is an intrapsychic structure which in the end is, effectively, a "closed system" leading to relatively greater autonomy *vis-à-vis* the environment.'

The structural difference between the narcissistic character disorder and the borderline state is a consequence of the fact that the former has achieved some degree of secondary level development and presents us with a closed system, while the borderline patient remains in this more regressive open system. We believe, with Winnicott, that the borderline state may result from a failure of the maternal environment in the first and second years of life, i.e. a relative failure in 'good enough' mothering (Winnicott, 1960). This relative failure of an object relationship results in a miscarriage of the normal process of identification, a failure to take something in which is specifically a failure to identify with the pre-oedipal mother. As a result, a relative autonomy from the human environment has not been achieved and consequently there is persistent object hunger with the illusion that an object stands between the person and the dangers of the environment. This is analogous to a young child who makes executant use of its mother before identification has been achieved.

We suspect that the environmental trauma which may predispose to the development of narcissistic character disorder is less severe as compared to that which leads to a borderline state. A disturbance in the mother-child relationship may be more subtle. As we have described before, the mother may be reliable in the sense that she is there, but her judgement may be faulty and she may not respect the child's separateness and autonomy. We have suggested that this type of trauma may be such as to induce a precocious but fragile development of the sense of self. In contrast to the borderline patient something *is* taken in. This precocious autonomy is based on what might be described as a primary identification with the pre-oedipal mother. It is as if the child states: 'I cannot trust my own mother; therefore I will become a better mother to myself.' This internalization, however, does not lead to a sublimation of instinctual demands nor has true autonomy been achieved. The affect block that accompanies this structural deformation defends against the closeness of an object tie. There is a fear that this fragile sense of self will disintegrate if the object is permitted to intrude. And further, true autonomy from the object has not been achieved as infantile dependency persists. Thus we have the paradox of a state of non-relatedness, yet there is a sense of an enormous involvement in the analyst and the analytic process.

The affect block signifies a profound disturbance in the relationship of the self to the external world. It reflects a state of illusionary self-sufficiency. The sharing and communication of affects is object seeking.

By means of the illusion of self-sufficiency the individual is removed from the fear of closeness to objects, for he denies any instinctual demand made upon the object.

NARCISSISTIC CHARACTER AND THE FALSE SELF

One advantage of the structural approach is that it may help to unify seemingly disparate clinical observations. For I believe that the false self described by Winnicott and the narcissistic disorder outlined by Kohut refer to similar if not identical clinical types. I would add also that the earlier description of the 'as if' personality by Helene Deutsch (1942) bears a close familial resemblance. In comparing these various clinical syndromes we believe that it may be clarifying to start with a consideration of a specific defence which is linked to a disturbance in the sense of self and which may exist as an admixture with other character defences, notably the obsessive compulsive's defence of isolation (Khan, 1971). I am suggesting that our description of this defence against affects may be covering the same clinical ground as Winnicott's description of the false self (Myerson has also addressed himself to this issue). Winnicott, however, intended his false self description to be that of a syndrome rather than of a specific defence of the ego. Winnicott's description of the false self is primarily a description of a disturbance of affects (Winnicott, 1960). Winnicott understood that the experiencing and sharing of feelings helps to organize an early sense of self; and alternatively, that one can keep oneself hidden by one's failure to share genuine feeling. Where there is a false self, what is shared and displayed is essentially false because it is based on compliance. In psychoanalysis one learns to use one's countertransference perceptions to separate true and false affects (Modell, 1973). One learns, e.g. that anger may be feigned, that the patient's tears do not move us, that transference feelings may not be genuine but intended as a manipulation. We know, from Winnicott's description and from our own observations, that these people are not only unable to communicate genuine feeling to others but are cut off from an internal experience of their own affects. a similar lack of genuine emotional experience was observed by Helene Deutsch who described how patients show 'a completely passive attitude to the environment with a highly plastic readiness to pick up signals from the outer world and to mould oneself and one's behaviour accordingly' (p.

265). Further we know that in the presence of such compliance there is massive unconscious defiance. There is the implicit attitude that 'if you are fooled into accepting the feeling I display as the truth, you are contemptible.' And the analyst's failure to be fooled is reassuring.

Kohut, in contrast to Winnicott, does not place his clinical observations in an object relation context. I believe it is these theoretical differences that may have obscured the fact that the false self syndrome and the narcissistic personality disorder may designate identical clinical phenomena. Whether we consider the 'false self' to be a syndrome or to be a defence may be related to a quantitative structural issue. The well differentiated structures of the classical neurotic capable of a transference neurosis is in a sense idealized. For all of us carry with us vestiges of ego arrests. The narcissistic defence that we have been describing may be observed in a transitory form in otherwise mature personalities, and in the analysis of a classical neurotic who is capable of a transference neurosis it is not uncommon to observe at times affect blocking based upon fantasies of self-sufficiency. Similarly, I have noted that vestiges of the transitional object relationship may also exist in a mature love relationship where there is acceptance of the separateness of the object. If the quality of the transference can be used as the basis of our nosology this would imply a quantitative factor—that the structural deformation must be substantial. It is the introduction of this quantitative factor that allows us to think of the structural deformation accompanying the narcissistic defence against affects as occupying either a partial sector of the personality, i.e. as a defence, or as constituting a character syndrome.

THE THERAPEUTIC ALLIANCE IN NARCISSISTIC CHARACTER DISORDERS

I have suggested that theoretical differences may have obscured the recognition that similar clinical phenomena were being observed, i.e. that Winnicott's false self syndrome and Kohut's description of narcissistic character disorder may describe identical clinical phenomena. However, when we consider the question of the therapeutic alliance in narcissistic character disorders—a concept related to problems of psychoanalytic technique as well as an hypothesis concerning how psychoanalysis obtains its results—we move into an area of greater controversy. Although we may be able to agree on the description of the clinical phenomena, there is little agreement regarding the inferences that can be drawn from these observations, i.e. the question of the analysability of narcissistic character disorders.

Where there is a precociously developed and fragile sense of self defended by fantasies of omnipotence and self-sufficiency, a therapeutic alliance is not possible. Zetzel (1956, 1958) has linked the capacity to form a therapeutic alliance to the ego's capacity to form mature object relations. It is assumed that in order to form a good therapeutic alliance there must be a sufficiently mature sector of the patient's personality for him to perceive the analyst as a separate person and to separate the transference neurosis from his perception of the analyst as a unique and separate individual. This concept is based on the earlier observations of Sterba (1934) and Bibring (1937) of the split in the ego that enables the relatively mature portion of the patient's ego to identify with the analyst as a 'real' person and to share with the analyst the common goals of the therapeutic aims of psychoanalysis. This capacity to form a therapeutic alliance has been equated by some to be synonymous with analysability (see also Greenson, 1965).

To state it simply: the capacity to form a therapeutic alliance assumes some capacity to accept the separateness and the reality of the analyst (the reality of the analyst refers to his qualities both as an analyst and as a person). As we have described earlier, at least in the opening phase of psychoanalysis with narcissistic character disorders, there is the illusion that there is only one person in the consulting room—either the analyst is not there or the patient is not there. What substitutes for a therapeutic alliance is a magical belief that to be in the presence of the idealized analyst will effect a change—they will acquire the idealized characteristics not by means of an active identification but by means of a magical process. As one patient described it, choosing the right analyst is like joining the proper club—one derives a sense of identity by means of contiguity.

We know that alongside the idealization of the analyst is the very opposite—an intense derogation. What the analyst says is negated and dismissed, as if his words were worthless. I have described the narcissistic defence as a cocoon which nothing leaves and nothing enters. The analyst experiences the frustration that his clarifications and interpretations have not been heard: nothing seems to be getting through.

With a relative absence of a therapeutic alliance, we cannot count on the patient's ability to identify with the observing ego of the analyst. Indeed an identification is warded off defensively for fear of being intruded upon, of being unduly influenced or being taken over. I believe Winnicott (1969) has this problem in mind when he describes: 'For instance, it is only in recent years that I have become able to wait and wait for the natural evolutional transference arising out of the patient's growing trust in the psychoanalytic technique and setting, and to avoid breaking up this natural process by making interpretations' (page 86). Interpretations are perceived by the patient as a threat to his autonomy. Envy of the analyst's knowledge is also a factor in rejecting his interpretations. It is not, however, the predominant issue as is the case in patients with a pronounced negative therapeutic reaction (Modell, 1965). There the analyst's interpretations are taken in but they lead to a worsening of the patient's condition.

After several years of analytic labour, an embryonic therapeutic alliance may develop with these patients, but they may never establish an analytic setting where the analyst's communications are received with suspended independent judgment to be worked over, to be either accepted or rejected.

There is indeed a question as to whether the therapeutic progress which may occur in spite of the absence of the therapeutic alliance is the result of the analyst's interpretations or may be the result of processes that are preverbal. Anna Freud has expressed her scepticism concerning the therapeutic results of an analysis that relies predominantly on preverbal processes. She states (1969),

What strikes the observer first is the change in the type of psychic *material* with which the analysis is dealing. Instead of exploring the disharmonies between the various agencies within the structured personality, the analyst is concerned with the events which lead from the chaotic, undifferentiated state towards the initial building up of a psychic structure. This means going beyond the area of intrapsychic conflict, which has always been the legitimate target for psychoanalysis, and into the darker area of an interaction between innate endowment and environmental influence. The implied aim is to undo or to counteract the impact of the very forces on which the rudiments of personality are based (p. 38).

The first issue, which Anna Freud raised by implication, is the comparison of the results obtained from a psychoanalysis of a patient capable of forming a transference neurosis and a therapeutic alliance to the result of the psychoanalysis of a narcissistic character disorder. There is also a separate issue: what is it in the psychoanalytic process itself that facilitates growth and maturation and promotes the differentiation of psychic structure in the narcissistic character? My own observations lead me to believe that there is a possibility of significant growth in the psychoanalysis of narcissistic character disorders but that the narcissistic character may not achieve a full resolution of his neurosis as can sometimes be achieved with the analysis of a transference neurosis. We suspect that the healing forces may be of a different order in patients with structural deformation; the healing may be facilitated by the analytic setting itself serving as a holding environment (in Winnicott's sense). There is gratification implicit in the constancy and reliability of the analyst's judgment as well as the analyst's capacity to perceive the patient's unique identity. The analyst, unlike the patient, is able to maintain the patient's identity to focus over time. This is the mirroring function that Spitz (1965) observed in the mother's response to the child's smile. This is the capacity to perceive the patient as a 'thou' (in Buber's terms). Lest I be misunderstood, I am not suggesting the introduction of special parameters of activity in Ferenczi's sense. But I am suggesting, as others have, that there is gratification in the object tie to the analyst without the need for the analyst to demonstrate his affection or friendliness.[6]

The healing process in the analytic setting may move silently so that the analyst may experience the feeling during this phase that nothing seems to be happening. I would suggest that during this period the patient may be experiencing a silent structural growth that may correspond to the idealizing transference described by Kohut. It is a phase prior to the development of the therapeutic alliance.

This idealizing phase gives way to a more negative transference relationship and this negativity itself may support the patient's growing sense of individuation (Winnicott, 1969). When there is growing perception of the analyst as a separate person, there may be concurrently a vestigal capacity to form a therapeutic alliance and fragments of the transference neurosis may begin to appear.

[6] I have suggested in another paper that this process may have instinctual backing from the instincts that observe object ties in contrast to the more directly sexual instinct seeking immediate discharge (Modell, 1974).

Although we acknowledge that the psychoanalysis of narcissistic character disorders can lead to significant therapeutic gains, such analyses may prove to be interminable if the gains do not also result in the establishment of a transference neurosis and therapeutic alliance.

SUMMARY

A narcissistic defence against affects, unlike isolation, is a defence against an object relationship. Object relations are strengthened by the sharing of genuine affects so that the failure to share feelings or the presentation of false feelings creates distance between the self and other objects. The defence is similar to that of denial in that it entails a modification of the ego's own structure. We have suggested that this modification consists of a precocious but fragile establishment of a sense of self.

The defence may occupy a sector of the personality or reflect a more massive structural arrest. When there is this structural arrest, we believe that this narcissistic defence forms the basis for the narcissistic character disorder described by Kohut and the false self of Winnicott.

This precocious sense of self leading to an illusion of self-sufficiency may also be found in other disorders, including the borderline patient, but the borderline patient, in contrast, suffers from a failure of internalization which leads to object hunger in contrast to the denial of object need of the narcissistic disorder. We suspect that the environmental trauma that may contribute to the narcissistic disorder is less severe as compared to the borderline states and may consist of the mother's failure to accept the child's separateness and autonomy, resulting in a fear of the mother's intrusiveness.

The fear of the maternal object's intrusiveness contributes to the relative inability to form a therapeutic alliance in the psychoanalysis of narcissistic character disorders. The analyst's interpretations are experienced as dangerous, not necessarily because of their content but due to the fear of the analyst's intrusive influence. Our understanding of the means of effecting therapeutic change must be modified in patients with narcissistic character disorders for, in contrast to the 'classical' neurotic, analytic progress is not obtained by means of interpreting the transference neurosis in the context of a working or therapeutic alliance. Although we acknowledge that the psychoanalysis of narcissistic disorders can lead to significant therapeutic gains, such analyses may prove to be interminable if the gains do not also result in the establishment of a transference neurosis and therapeutic alliance.

REFERENCES

Bibring, E. (1937). [Contribution to the] Symposium on the theory of the therapeutic results of psychoanalysis. *Int. J. Psycho-Anal.* **18,** 170–189.

Deutsch, H. (1942). Some forms of emotional disturbance and their relationship to schizophrenia. In *Neuroses and Character Types.* New York: Int. Univ. Press, 1965.

Freud, A. (1936). *The Ego and the Mechanisms of Defence.* New York: Int. Univ. Press, rev. ed. 1967.

Freud, A. (1969). *Difficulties in the Path of Psychoanalysis.* New York: Int. Univ. Press.

Freud, S. (1924). The loss of reality in neurosis and psychosis. *S.E.* **19.**

Freud, S. (1940). Splitting of the ego in the process of defence. *S.E.* **23.**

Gedo, J. & Goldberg, A. (1973). *Models of the Mind.* Chicago: Univ. of Chicago Press.

Gitelson, M. (1962). The first phase of psychoanalysis. [Contribution to a symposium on 'the curative factors in psychoanalysis'.] *Int. J. Psycho-Anal.* **43,** 194–205.

Greenson, R. R. (1965). The working alliance and the transference neurosis. *Psychoanal. Q.* **34,** 155–181.

Khan, M. M. R. (1971). Infantile neuroses as a false-self organization. *Psychoanal. Q.* **40,** 245–263.

Knight, R. (1954). Borderline states. In *Psychoanalytic Psychiatry and Psychology.* New York: Int. Univ. Press.

Kohut, H.(1971). *The Analysis of the Self.* New York: Int. Univ. Press.

Modell, A. H. (1961). Denial and the sense of separateness. *J. Am. psychoanal. Ass.* **9,** 533–547.

Modell, A. H. (1965). On having the right to a life: an aspect of the superego's development, *Int. J. Psycho-Anal.* **46,** 323–331.

Modell, A. H. (1968). *Object Love and Reality.* New York: Int. Univ. Press.

Modell, A. H. (1973). Affects and psychoanalytic knowledge. The *Annual of Psychoanalysis,* vol. 1. New York: Quadrangle Books.

Modell, A. H. (1975). The ego and the id—fifty years later. *Int. J. Psycho-Anal.* **56,** 57–68.

Myerson, P. G. (1975). The false self condition. (Unpublished manuscript.)

Rycroft, C. (1955). Two notes on idealization, illusion and disillusion as normal and abnormal psychological processes. *Int. J. Psycho-Anal.* **36,** 81–87.

Spitz, R. (1965). *The First Year of Life.* New York: Int. Univ. Press.

Sterba, R. (1934). The fate of the ego in analytic therapy. *Int. J. Psycho-Anal.* **15,** 117–126.

Volkan, V. D. (1973). Transitional fantasies in the analysis of a narcissistic personality. *J. Am. psychoanal. Ass.* **21,** 351–376.

Winnicott, D. W. (1960). The theory of the parent-infant relationship. In *The Maturational Processes and the Facilitating Environment.* New York: Int. Univ. Press, 1965.

Winnicott, D. W. (1969). The use of an object and relating through identifications. In *Playing and Reality*. New York: Basic Books, 1971.

Zetzel, E. (1956). The concept of transference. In *The Capacity for Emotional Growth*. New York: Int. Univ. Press, 1970.

Zetzel, E. (1958). Therapeutic alliance in the analysis of hysteria. In *The Capacity for Emotional Growth*. New York: Int. Univ. Press, 1970.

12. The Theory of Narcissism: An Object-Relations Perspective

Arnold Rothstein

A premise of this paper is that secondary narcissistic investment is a defensive response of the ego to the signal of separation anxiety stimulated by the perception of a state of separateness. Separation anxiety is an implicit potential in all character neuroses. Therefore, narcissistic investment and separation anxiety are a ubiquitous component of the human condition.

Mahler[13] has described the normal processes of primary separation-individuation. Although these are normal developmental processes, they stimulate defensive responses of the toddler's immature ego. In *Beyond the Pleasure Principle* Freud[4] explored the defensive nature of these processes in an attempt to explain the repetition compulsion. An ego confronted with the frightening perception of its separateness experiences separation anxiety. This anxiety and concomitant perceptions of helplessness and vulnerability motivate the ego to engage in activity that symbolically represents the ability of the toddler subject to control the maternal object. Freud describes a child:

At the age of one and a half he could say only a few words. . . . He was, however, on good terms with his parents and their one servant girl and tributes were paid to his being "a good boy." He did not disturb his parents at night, he conscientiously obeyed orders not to touch certain things . . . and above all he never cried when his mother left him. At the same time he was very attached to his mother. . . . This good little boy had the disturbing habit of taking any small objects he could get hold of and throwing them away from him into the corner, under the bed and so on, so that hunting for his toys and picking them up was quite a business. As he did this he gave vent to a long drawn out "o-o-o-o" accompanied with an expression of interest and satisfaction. . . . The child had a wooden reel with a piece of string tied around it. . . . What he did was to hold the reel by the string and throw it over the edge of his curtained cot, so that it disappeared. . . . He then pulled the reel out of the cot again. . . . and hailed its appearance with a joyful "da" (there). This then was the complete game. Disappearance and return.[4a]

Freud presents a child with a close, warm tie to his mother. Behaviorally the child does not seem to be having trouble with separation, yet his ego is involved in activities that are designed to give the illusion of a capacity to control the object and its disappearance, i.e., to prevent separation. He joyfully repeats his successful functioning ad infinitum. This joyful feeling derives from the defensive illusion created by the symbolic meaning of the activity. His separation anxiety diminishes because the activity creates the illusion that the ego has the capacity to control the object, thereby implying the self will survive. This is one type of narcissistic investment of ego activities designed to protect against separation.

Mahler[14] has exquisitely described subphases of the separation-individuation process. During the "practicing subphase" the infant stands erect and feels infused with omnipotent power. At this stage a definitive self-representation has not been established. An experience of vulnerability, such as a fall, fills the toddler with diffuse anxiety. He runs in panic to snuggle physically and gain sustenance from contact with his mother. Furer has termed this "refueling." It seems to represent a reuniting of self with maternal object. It probably emphasizes a primal human wish to stay connected and a part of the maternal object. When that object is felt to be part of the self, security seems assured. A maternal smile can offer a similar sense of security. A few months later, by the middle of the second year of life, the toddler subject has a more clearly defined sense of self. This perception is frightening because the ego perceives its relative helplessness and vulnerability. Without the mother's presence the subject cannot survive.

Thus, separateness implies an object loss because the self no longer perceives itself as connected to the gratifying maternal object. Prior to the more constant perception of separateness, the gratifying aspects of the maternal object could be felt to be a part of the self. Now the object is lost to the self. Yet in *The Ego and the Id* Freud[5] felt that people are probably unable to accept object loss and that object loss stimulates defensive processes. He said that when "a person has to give up a sexual object there quite often ensues an alteration of his ego which can only be described as a setting up of the object inside the ego" and "It may be that this identification is the sole condition under which the id can give up its object."[5a]

The core premise of this paper is that secondary narcissistic investment is motivated by feelings of separation anxiety implicit in the perception of a separate sense of self. The perception of separateness stimulates separation anxiety and the experience of object loss. This anxiety stimulates an incorporative identification with the maternal object. This representation is integrated within the "self-as-agent."*

It is as if the object loss has been undone. There is the illusion that the mother exists and is present within the "self-as-agent." The ego has memories of activities that elicited a maternal smile and resulting elated feelings of union. If the "self-as-agent or object" can perform in a manner that elicits the internalized representation of a maternal smile, there is the illusion that the mother is present and part of the self, leaving the toddler with a feeling of safety. The ego experiences the representational awareness of itself as an agent or an object. This experience and the proposed relationship of the self smiling at itself undoes the feeling of object loss implicit in the separation-individuation experience. The "self-as-agent or object" performing to elicit a smile from the "self-as-agent" is the prototypical secondary narcissistic representational relationship as it exists within a differentiated self. If the self were able to verbalize its feelings, it would say "*I* love *me*." Because, in part, I equals mother, it means, "Mother smiles at me, loves me, nurtures and protects me."

This state of the self smiling at itself is analogous to Kohut's "narcissistic self."[9a] The representational presence of the mother internalized as an identification within the "self-as-agent" and the internalized means of eliciting a representational maternal smile assuages the terror that results from the perception of vulnerability implicit in separateness. There is now an illusory means of avoiding the impact of integrating one's ultimate separateness. Narcissistic investment preserves the illusion of the omnipotent mother smiling at and united with the self.

---

*Schafer[16] has developed concepts I find most valuable for organizing the subjective or feeling aspects of the self. He states: "In subjective experience the person aware of his engagement with internal objects or introjects feels himself to be engaged with something other than himself; yet he will acknowledge that the object is within him and thus within his subjective self. . . . To deal with this ambiguity, it appears necessary to differentiate at least three kinds of subjective self: the self-as-agent (the 'I'), the self-as-object (the 'me'), and the self-as-place (for which no pronoun is specific)."[16a] He indicates that the "self-as-place" is often "conceived in bodily terms, that is, inhabited by a psychological self (agent, object)." Introjects are experienced as part of the "self-as-place." Identifications are part of the "self-as-agent or object."

Reality and its inevitable frustrations intrude on this neat, internalized illusion system. The limitations of the self and the object are inevitable. These limitations are mortifying injuries to one's omnipotent sense of self. They are perceived as symbolic separations and stimulate separation anxiety which results in additional defensive responses.

We have been exploring the normal development of narcissistic investment. I will attempt to explore the normal vicissitudes of postindividuated narcissistic investment and some of the factors that may lead to pathological distortions.

For postindividuated development to proceed, a number of factors are necessary. First, the toddler's biological ego endowment must be adequate for maturational sequences to continue. Second, as Mahler has emphasized, "Optimal maternal availability is required."[13a] Implicit also, as development proceeds, is adequate paternal availability and familial harmony. Parents are the limit-setters. They impose many of the injuries experienced by the narcissistic self. If these are imposed with a quality of love, empathy, and understanding, the toddler begrudgingly, gradually, and partially relinquishes his omnipotent strivings and accepts limits. As Freud has pointed out, man

is not willing to forgo the narcissistic perfection of his childhood . . . he seeks to recover it in the new form of an ego ideal. What he projects before him as his ideal is the substitute for the lost narcissism of his childhood in which he was his own ideal.[2a]

The original narcissistic perfection is the primary narcissistic experience of the preindividuated era. Kohut's representational form of the narcissistic self is comprised of the previously described relationship between the "self-as-agent," which includes a smiling maternal representation and its response to performances of the "self-as-agent or object." As perceptions of reality violate representations of the "narcissistic self," the toddler seeks additional solutions to preserve the illusion of the possibility of narcissistic perfection. It is as if the toddler said, "If I could be like the omnipotently perceived parental object [Kohut's second representational form, the idealized parental imago[9a]], I might recapture the lost feeling of union with Mother." These representational forms, the "narcissistic self" and the "idealized parental imago," are important components of the ego ideal. As Freud[2] has emphasized this is the substitute for the original narcissistic perfection.

As I have been attempting to emphasize, this feeling of perfection recalls preindividuated memory traces of the gratifying maternal object as part of the self. To defend against this loss, the postindividuated ego attempts to preserve the illusion of these feelings within the secondary narcissistic representational forms: the "narcissistic self" and the "idealized parental imago."

As differentiation proceeds, the ego is more and more impressed with the perception of its limitations. The best it can do is gain narcissistic satisfaction by attempting to live up to the standards of its ego ideal. The single most important factor for the successful formation of a healthy relationship between the self and its ideal is loving, empathic, and respectable parents who are relatively happy with themselves and their lives. When the superego judges that the "self-as-agent or object" has performed up to the standards of its ideal, the subject feels a sense of well-being. The same sense of well-being derives from the activation of the representation of a maternal smile. This smile is integrated in different ways. There is an object representation that is part of the ego ideal. This representation derives from the postindividuated era. It is felt to be separate from the self and smiling at it. At a more primal level there is the representation of a maternal smile within the "self-as-agent." The performance of those ego functions that result in a sense of well-being are narcissistically invested because they give the subject the feeling that he can elicit a maternal smile and hence the illusion of the ability to control his mother's presence. At times these feelings are closer to elation than well-being. The elated feeling recaptures more than a sense of a separate smiling maternal presence. It recaptures the feeling of unity with the maternal object.

Aspects of these same ego functions are often characterized as secondarily autonomous and sublimated. At this point I will attempt to explore the possibility that these object representational hypotheses concerning secondary narcissism may be helpful in clarifying the issue of sublimation. Freud states in *On Narcissism,* following his introduction of the concept of the ego ideal, "We are naturally led to examine the relation between this forming of an ideal and sublimation."[2a] He defines sublimation as "a process that concerns object libido and consists in the instinct directing itself towards an aim other than, and remote from, that of sexual satisfaction."[2a] He states that "the ego ideal demands such sublimation but it cannot enforce it."[2b] This leads us to the interesting question of what it is about the ego ideal that influences the ego's capacity for sublimation. Freud identifies the fact that "in neurotics we find the highest differences of potential between the development of their ego ideal and the amount of sublimation of their primitive libidinal instincts."[2] Annie Reich elaborates upon this relationship with reference to male narcissistic character pathology: "It is the primitive crudely sexual quality of the ego ideals that represents the quintessence of this pathology."[15a] and "Successful modification of body narcissism depends primarily upon the ego's capacity for sublimation and, as we shall see, de-aggressivization."[15b] In *The Ego and the Id* Freud elaborates the idea that secondary narcissism may be the universal route to sublimation. He states, "the transformation of object-libido into narcissistic libido which thus takes place obviously implies an abandonment of sexual aims, a desexualization—a kind of sublimation, therefore. Indeed, the question arises, and deserves careful consideration, whether all sublimation does not take place through the mediation of the ego, which begins by changing sexual object libido into narcissistic libido and then, perhaps, goes on to give it another aim."[5b] In an elaborating footnote on the same page, he reminds us that secondary narcissism is due to "the libido which flows into the ego owing to the identifications described above."

The question still remains: why do different egos have differing capacities for sublimation? Because the ego is built, in part, of identifications, perhaps there is an important relationship between the ego's identifications and its capacity for sublimation. Hartmann in his discussion of sublimation (neutralization) reminds us that "Hart (1948) has particularly emphasized that renunciation which comes from love is more likely to promote neutralization than one which comes from fear."[6a]

What does the ideal of "renunciation which comes from love" mean? An ideal maternal love is one in which joy is derived primarily from nurturing the child for its own sake. We refer to this as object-related love. The child is treated predominantly as a separate object rather than as a narcissistically invested extension of the maternal self-representation. The parents' primary concern is with the child's needs rather than with their own. This requires parents who are relatively happy with their lives and moderately accepting of their limitations. The antithesis is narcissistic love in which the child is treated predominantly as a narcissistic object who is of value only insofar as he aggrandizes the parents' self-representation. Realistically, healthy parental love is composed of a balance of the two with the empathic object-related investment maintaining a primacy over the narcissistic investment. A mother with a healthy capacity to love nurtures her child so that the process of internalization of the maternal smile within the "self-as-agent" leads to an optimally integrated identification. Healthy maternal love affects the quality of the primary building blocks of the original narcissistic representational forms. A healthy narcissistic self-representation is one in which the "self-as-agent" is comprised, in part, of memory traces of being loved consistently and empathically. This experience has allowed the "self-as-agent" to develop an internalized expectation of being loved primarily for himself rather than for his performance. It is as if there is a kind of synchrony between the representation of a primal maternal smile structured with the "I" and the other aspects of the "I" and "me." It is as if self wants to reciprocate for the mother within the "I." Renunciation is easier and even pleasurable. If we could articulate the feelings of "self-as-agent," they would be expressed, "Because she gave to me of herself I want to give to her of myself." In such a situation energy is more easily available for nonconflictual reality-related activities that would please the mother. The subject can renounce his own direct pleasure wishes because he has been given to and wants to reciprocate.

A number of factors influence the quality of the development of narcissistic investments. I have been stressing the quality of maternal love. Individuals with healthier narcissistic investments seem to have experienced a more related parental involvement which facilitated a process of more integrated internalizations.

A disturbance in the development of narcissistic investments correlates with disturbances within the mother-child relationship. Many authors (Easser,[1] Jacobson,[7] Kernberg,[8] Kohut,[9,10,11,12] A. Reich,[15] and implicitly Mahler[13]) have emphasized pre-Oedipal disturbances in the mother-child relationship in the genesis of narcissistic pathology. These are best summarized under the rubric of disturbances of "optimal maternal availability."[13a] A number of problems of maternal relatedness are subsumed under the rubric of maternal availability. Mothers may be unempathic, cold, hostile, anxious, or overinvolved and excessively gratifying. Other mothers are inconsistent and alternate between one or another of these attitudes. What seems similar in all these situations is that their relationship to their children is not motivated predominantly by a wish to nurture in a phase-appropriate manner. Rather, it seems driven predominantly by more self-oriented motivations. The toddler exposed to such a disturbed quality of maternal relatedness does not feel loved for himself. Rather he feels a possibility of love only when he performs adequately in a manner that will elicit a maternal smile. As a consequence, as he separates he feels his separateness with greater profundity. He is painfully alone. He feels no confidence emanating from a smiling representation within the "self-as-agent." Instead he has a greater awareness that the "self-as-agent and object" will obtain a representational smile only in response to specific performances. This smile is not well integrated within the "self-as-agent." Rather it is tenuously integrated within the "self-as-place." At moments when the "self-as-agent" performs well, there is harmony between the "I" and the introject within the "self-as-place." This depends on good perform- ances that are fueled by separation anxiety. These relatively unrelated mothers are more intolerant of and angry at their toddlers when they fail. Hence, there is greater potential for more intense separation anx- iety in these children. They have to integrate their phase-appropriate separateness, their perception that their mother smiles only in response to specific performances and, often, expressions of rage at them for existing. They experience her rage as destructive. Her destructiveness is embellished by the toddler's projection of his oral cannibalistic urges.

These toddlers feel less loved and are more anxious and angry. This results in a narcissistic self preoccupied with a more intense urge to control the object. The integration of the maternal smile within the "I" has been interfered with. When extremes of deprivation have been experienced, the subject may not even feel a sense of "I." When he has experienced less extreme deprivation, the subject feels that the "I" (the "self-as-agent") is defective and unlovable. Milder disorders of maternal relatedness leave the subject feeling lovable but only in re- sponse to specific performances. In the latter instances the integration of the maternal smile is more tenuous. The subject has an internalized feeling, "I will not be loved for myself but only in response to specific performances." Performance and renunciation are motivated by the fear that could be expressed, "If I don't perform I will be alone and unloved." Freud's example of an apparently normal child attempting to symbolically control separation underlines the ubiquitous nature of these issues.[4] In more disturbed children the need for control and mastery is more intense. When the toddler is unable to perform, dedifferentiation occurs with the self. The tenuously internalized smile within the "self-as-place" is undone. By virtue of the rage the subject feels toward the maternal representation and in consequence of fear of the introject's rejection and retaliation, the introject imbued with primary-process qualities is felt to be frightening. This frightening internalization may be further defended against by mechanisms of splitting and externalization. This splitting leaves the toddler and his budding sense of self more vulnerable to separation anxiety. To defend himself against this imminent separation anxiety, the subject judges he must develop those narcissistically invested functions of the "self-as-agent" which can elicit a smile from the maternal representation within the "self-as-place."

In summary, the toddler whose mother is less empathic (or stated another way, whose investment in him is more narcissistic) will experience more intense separation anxiety. This is the result of three factors. First, there is a disturbance of integration of the maternal representation within the "self-as-agent." Second, he fears he will not be able to perform for the introject within the "self-as-place." Finally, he fears his rage will destroy the object.

The more intense the separation anxiety, the more defensive is the secondary narcissistic investment in the self-representation. The resulting illusion of perfection assuages his fear of being alone. Without this illusion he feels he will die. These feelings contribute to the dramatic use of metaphors of death so frequently expressed by patients with significant defensive narcissistic investments in their self representation.

As the toddler enters the individuated epoch, his disordered narcissistic development leaves him with a potential to feel narcissistic gratification when he can control the frustrating object. Limit-setting accompanied by expressions of parental anger, particularly of a corporal nature, potentiate disorders of narcissistic development. I will attempt to explore some of the potential disturbances as they occur and correlate them with anal and Oedipal experiences. The quality of the child's separation-individuation experience and particularly the quality of mothering he has provides the foundation that influences his experience of later conflict-laden events.

Freud was keenly aware of this. In *On Transformations of Instinct as Exemplified in Anal Eroticism* he demonstrates an understanding of the renunciation of narcissistic pleasures in return for parental love:

> For its feces are the infant's first gift, a part of the body which he will give up only on persuasion by someone he loves, to whom indeed he will make a spontaneous gift of it as a token of affection; . . . Defecation affords the first occasion on which the child must decide between a narcissistic and an object-loving attitude. He either parts obediently with his feces, "sacrifices" them to his love, or else retains them for purposes of autoerotic satisfaction and later as a means of asserting his own will. If he makes the latter choice we are in the presence of defiance (obstinacy) which, accordingly, springs from a narcissistic clinging to anal eroticism.[3a]

Defiance represents the wish to experience a victory over the unloving frustrater. Implicit in the narcissistic victory is a combination of anger and elation. The child maintains the feeling that he does not have to submit; he can preserve his original omnipotence and its illusion of union with an all-gratifying mother. Many later power struggles bear the stamp of this defiant struggle of an angry "self-as-agent" against a relatively "unavailable" frustrater. Ego functions, which are employed in power struggles with frustraters, become part of the self-representation and are narcissistically invested because they recapture the illusion of maintaining control of the maternal smile. This is defensive, because implicitly the subject is acting as if he could force the parent to be like the gratifying parent he remembers from an earlier era. Earlier moments of satisfaction structured within the narcissistic self influence his narcissistic denial of reality. In this sense it defensively perpetuates the struggle to make the parents more loving and available and avoids finally integrating the impossibility of the wish. It defends against the loss and depression that would result from definitively integrating the reality of who his parents were.

The Oedipal situation represents a monumental experience of limits. The quality of previous frustrations will certainly influence its resolution. Previous difficulties interfere with the integration of the narcissistic injuries implicit in the Oedipal defeat.

Invariably castration anxiety is one of the important factors that encourages the child to relinquish or repress his Oedipal wishes. When castration anxiety is intense, there is a tendency to regress to defensive activity of a narcissistic nature. Numerous factors may account for increased castration anxiety. Freud stated, "The ego ideal is therefore the heir of the Oedipus Complex."[5c] As has been noted, the formation of a well-integrated ego ideal depends on loving and admirable parents. If a boy has a loving father he can admire and respect, he will identify with him, accept Oedipal limits, and experience castration anxiety that is less intense. Parents who do not fulfill these requirements contribute to ego-ideal disorders of the type described by A. Reich.[15] This leaves the child more vulnerable to intense castration anxiety. The representation of a loving and respected father is not internalized within the ego ideal. Rather, a tenuously internalized representation of an angry, jealous, potentially retaliating castrator exists within the "self-as-place." Any situation that represents an Oedipal wish stimulates the vivification of this castrating presence within the "self-as-place." This perception stimulates castration anxiety. Situations that represent the gratification of an Oedipal wish stimulate more intense castration anxiety. The child feels that his wish and its symbolic success will result in his annihilation. In the absence of a well-integrated ego ideal and superego, and under the impact of fear from more primitive representations, the child may seek safety within the illusions of greatness implicit in narcissistic defenses. It is as if the subject feels he can be safe from the castrator only if he can be great. Because his mother's smile is infused in the greatness of the narcissistic defenses, it is as if the child were seeking a representational recapitulation of the "refueling" safety he felt in his mother's arms. In this case he seeks the representational illusion of a protecting mother from a castrating father. If his narcissistic defenses work, he feels protected. When they function effectively, his castration anxiety diminishes because of two representational illusions: (1) the child feels more powerful than the castrating father, and (2) he feels protected by an omnipotent mother.

When these defenses fail, castration anxiety is intense. Its intensity is reinforced by the pre-Oedipal fixation upon which these narcissistic defenses are constructed. There is the loss of the illusion of the presence of a smiling, protecting mother. That loss may be associated with the activation of the representation of a dissatisfied, biting mother. This biting imagery reinforces the representation of a castrating Oedipal father resulting in the intense castration anxiety so nicely described by A. Reich.[15]

In summary, in this paper the theory of narcissism has been explored from an object-relations perspective, with the premise that secondary narcissistic investment in the self-representation is motivated by the feelings of separation anxiety implicit in the perception of a separate sense of self. The influence of the quality of mothering on the resulting narcissistic investments has been examined. A relationship between these investments and the ego's capacity for sublimation has been explored. Finally, possible vicissitudes of postindividuated narcissistic investments have been delineated.

REFERENCES

1. Easser, B. R. Affect, the Self and Psychoanalytic Technique. Paper presented at the Sandor Rado Memorial Lecture, New York City, 1973.
2. Freud, S. On Narcissism (1914). *Standard Edition.* Vol.14. London: Hogarth Press, 1957, pp. 69–102: (a) 94; (b) 95.
3. ——.On Transformations of Instinct as Exemplified in Anal Eroticism (1917). *Standard Edition,* Vol. 17. London: Hogarth Press, 1955, pp. 125–133: (a) 130.
4. ——.Beyond the Pleasure Principle (1920). *Standard Edition,* Vol. 18. London: Hogarth Press, 1955, pp. 7–64: (a) 14-15.
5. ——.The Ego and the Id (1923) *Standard Edition,* Vol. 19. London: Hogarth Press, 1961, pp. 13–66: (a) 29; (b) 30; (c) 36.
6. Hartmann, H. Notes on the Theory of Sublimation. *The Psychoanalytic Study of the Child,* Vol. 10. New York: International Universities Press, 1955, pp. 9–29: (a) 26.
7. Jacobson, E. The Self and the Object World. *The Psychoanalytic Study of the Child,* Vol. 9. New York: International Universities Press, 1954, pp. 75–126.
8. Kernberg, O. Factors in the Psychoanalytic Treatment of Narcissistic Personalities. *Journal of the American Psychoanalytic Association,* Vol. 18, 1966, pp. 51–85.
9. Kohut, H. Forms and Transformations of Narcissism. *Journal of the American Psychoanalytic Association,* Vol. 14, 1966, pp. 243–272: (a) 246.
10. ——.The Psychoanalytic Treatment of Narcissistic Personality Disorders. *Psychoanalytic Study of the Child,* Vol. 23. New York: International Universities Press, 1968, pp. 86–113.
11. ——. *The Analysis of the Self.* New York: International Universities Press, 1971.
12. ——.Thoughts on Narcissism and Narcissistic Rage. *The Psychoanalytic Study of the Child,* Vol. 27. New York: International Universities Press, 1972, pp. 360–400.
13. Mahler, M. A Study of the Separation-Individuation Process and Its Possible Application to Borderline Phenomena in the Psychoanalytic Situation. *The Psychoanalytic Study of the Child,* Vol.26. New York: International Universities Press, 1971, pp. 386–402: (a) 410.

14. ———.On the First Three Subphases of the Separation-Individuation Process. *International Journal of Psycho-Analysis,* Vol. 53, 1972, pp. 333–338.
15. Reich, A. Pathologic Forms of Self-Esteem Regulation. *The Psychoanalytic Study of the Child,* Vol. 15. New York: International Universities Press, 1960. pp. 215–231 (a) 228; (b) 224.
16. Schafer, R. *Aspects of Internalization.* New York: International Universities Press, 1968: (a) 80.

C. Affective States

13. Depression and Grandiosity as Related Forms of Narcissistic Disturbances

Alice Miller

INTRODUCTION

I would like to present some ideas which have occurred to me over the years in the course of my analytic work. This work has included analyses, supervision and many interviews with people who have been looking for an analyst, and whom I have seen for one or two sessions. In these short encounters, the tragedy of each individual destiny can often be seen with moving clarity and intensity. What is described as depression, and experienced as emptiness, futility, fear of impoverishment and loneliness, is frequently recognizable as the tragedy of loss of the self, or alienation from the self, which is seen regularly in our generation and society. Thanks to years of reconstructive work with my analysands, I think I have come nearer to the child origins of this alienation from the self.

The observations of early mother–child interaction recorded by M. Mahler, R. Spitz, and J. Robertson, confirmed my suppositions. On reading Winnicott I felt on familiar ground and encouraged to continue along this path. Lastly, H. Kohut's studies on narcissism, especially his concept of *narcissistic cathexis,* helped me to conceptualize the relationships I had discovered.

In what follows I shall dispense with the meta-psychological language of structure theory and try to develop the connections I want to show on the basis of the mother–child relationship. Obviously a large part of the events here described take place intra-psychically, but an object relationship precedes every internalization and its language seems to me to be emotionally truer, and, for many analysts, more understandable.

A. THE VICISSITUDES OF NARCISSISTIC NEEDS

According to H. Kohut (1971), an object is narcissistically cathected when we experience it not as the centre of its own activity but as a part of ourselves. If the object does not behave in the way in which we expect or wish, we may at times be immeasurably disappointed or offended, almost as if an arm ceased to obey us, or a function that we take for granted (such as memory) lets us down. This sudden loss of control can also lead to intense narcissistic rage.

This sort of attitude is met far more frequently in adults than one might imagine, however much we live to regard it as pathological, unrealistic or egocentric. At the beginning of life, however, it is the only attitude possible. Not only during the phase of primary narcissism (the symbiotic phase) but also after the gradual separation between self- and object-representations, does the mother normally remain a narcissistically cathected object, a function of the developing individual.

Every child has a legitimate narcissistic need to be noticed, understood, taken seriously, and respected by its mother. In the first weeks and months of life it has to have the mother at its disposal, must be able to use her and to be mirrored by her. This is beautifully illustrated in one of Winnicott's images: the mother gazes at the baby in her arms, and the baby gazes at its mother's face and finds itself therein . . . provided that the mother is really looking at the unique, small, helpless being and not projecting her own introjects on to the child, nor her own expectations, fears and plans for the child. In that case, the child would not find itself in its mother's face but rather the mother's own predicaments. It would remain without a mirror, and for the rest of its life would be seeking this mirror in vain.

i. Healthy narcissism

If a child is lucky enough to grow up with a mirroring mother, who allows herself to be cathected narcissistically, who is at the child's disposal, that is, who allows herself to be 'made use of' as a function of the child's narcissistic development, as M. Mahler (1968) says, then a healthy self-feeling can gradually develop in the growing child. Ideally this should be a mother who can also provide the necessary emotional climate and understanding of the child's needs. But even a mother who is not especially warm-hearted can make this development possible, if she only refrains from preventing it. This enables the child to acquire from other people what its mother lacks. Various investigations have shown the incredible ability which a healthy child displays in making use of the smallest affective 'nourishment' (stimulation) to be found in its surroundings.

I regard as a healthy self-feeling, the unquestioned *certainty* that the feelings and wishes which one experiences are a *part of one's self*. This certainty is not something based upon reflection, but is there like one's own pulse, which one does not notice as long as it functions normally.

This automatic, natural contact with his own emotions and wishes gives an individual strength and *self esteem*. He may live out his feelings, be sad, despairing or in need of help, without fear of making the introjected mother insecure. He can allow himself to be afraid when he is threatened, or angry when his wishes are not fulfilled. He knows not only what he does not want, but also what he does, and is able to express this, irrespective of whether he will be loved or hated for it.

I will now enumerate some characteristics of a successful narcissistic development but would like to make it clear that here, as also later on, I am describing constructions of phenomena which are only approximated in reality. Instead of 'healthy narcissism,' it would be possible also to speak of inner freedom and vitality.

1. *Aggressive impulses* could be neutralized because they did not upset the confidence and self esteem of the mother.
2. *Strivings towards autonomy* were not experienced as an attack.
3. The child was allowed to experience and express *'ordinary'* impulses (such as jealousy, rage, defiance) because his mother did not require him to be 'special,' for instance to represent her own ethical attitudes.
4. There was no need to please anybody (under optimal conditions) and the child could develop and *exhibit* whatever was active in him during each developmental phase.
5. He could use his parents because they were independent of him.
6. These preconditions enabled him to *separate self- and object-representations* successfully.
7. Being able to display ambivalent feelings, the child could learn to regard both his self and the object as *'both good and bad,'* and did not need to split off the 'good' from the 'bad' object.
8. *Object love* was made possible because the parents also loved the child as a separate object.
9. Provided there were phase-appropriate and non-traumatic frustrations, the child was able to *integrate* his narcissistic needs and did not have to resort to repression or splitting.
10. This integration made their transformation possible, as well as the development of a drive regulating matrix, based on the child's own *trial and error experiences*.

ii. Narcissistic disturbance

What happens if the mother not only is unable to take over the narcissistic functions for the child, but also, as very often happens, is herself in need of narcissistic supplies? Quite unconsciously and counter to her own good intentions, the mother then tries to assuage her own narcissistic needs through her child, i.e. *she cathects him narcissistically*. This does not rule out strong affection. On the contrary, the mother often loves her child as her self-object passionately, but not in the way he needs to be loved. Among other things, therefore, the continuity and constancy that would be so important, are missing from this love, but above all, also the framework within which the child could experience *his* feelings and *his* emotions. Instead, he develops something which the mother needs, and which certainly saves his life (the mother's love) at the time, but nevertheless may prevent him, throughout his life, from being himself. The literature speaks, in this connection, of the 'false self' (D. Winnicott, 1971) or of the 'as if' mechanism (M. Mahler, 1968).

In such cases the natural narcissistic needs appropriate to the child's age, as described above, cannot be integrated into the developing personality, but are split off, partially repressed, and retain their archaic form which makes their later integration still more difficult.

M. Mahler (1968) writes: 'It is the specific unconscious need of the mother that activates, out of the infant's infinite potentialities, those in particular that create for each mother "the child" who reflects her own unique and individual needs.' In other words, the mother communicates a 'mirrored frame-work' in infinitely varied ways to which the infant's primitive self accommodates itself. If her primary occupation with her child, i.e. her mirroring function during the period of early childhood, is *unpredictable, insecure, anxiety-ridden* or *hostile,* or if her confidence in herself as a mother is shaken, then the child has to face the period of individuation without a reliable frame-work for *emotional* checking back to his symbiotic partner. The result is a disturbance in his primitive 'self-feeling.'

With two exceptions, the mothers of all my patients had a narcissistic disturbance, were extremely insecure and often suffered from depression. The child, an only one or often the first-born, was the narcissistically cathected object. What these mothers had once failed to find in their own mothers, they were able to find in their children; someone at their disposal who can be used as an echo, who can be controlled, is completely centred on them, will never desert them, and offers full attention and admiration. If the child's demands become too great (as once did those of her own mother) she is no longer so defenceless, does not allow herself to be tyrannized; she can *bring the child up* in such a way that it neither cries nor disturbs her. At last she can make sure that she receives consideration and respect.

This can be illustrated best with an example. A patient who herself had four children, brought only scanty memories of her own mother. At the beginning of treatment she described her as an affectionate, warm-hearted woman who spoke to her 'openly about her own troubles' at an early age, who was very concerned for her own children and sacrificed herself for her family. She must have had the ability to empathize with other people, for she was often asked for advice by others within the sect to which the family belonged. The patient reported that her mother had always been especially proud of her daughter. She was now old and invalided, and the patient was very concerned about her health. She often dreamed that something had happened to her mother and woke with great anxiety.

During the further course of the analysis, this picture of her mother changed as a consequence of the emotions which arose in the transference. Above all, when the period of toilet training entered the analysis, she experienced her mother in me as domineering, demanding, controlling, manipulating, bad, cold, stupid, petty, obsessional, touchy, easily offended, over-wrought, false and hard to please. Even if this picture included the projection of her long-dammed-up anger, many childhood memories did in fact include these characteristics.

It was only in the course of the analysis, during which she re-enacted a great deal from her childhood, that this patient could discover what her mother was really like, through observing her own relationship to her children. Towards the end, she felt that when her mother had felt insecure in relation to her, she had in fact often been cold and treated her badly. Her anxious concern for the child had been a reaction formation to ward off her aggression and envy. Since the mother had often been humiliated as a child she needed to be valued by her daughter. Gradually, the two pictures of the loving mother and of the wicked witch were united into that of a single human being whose weakness, insecurity and over-sensitivity made it necessary for her to have her child at her disposal. The mother, who apparently functioned as well, was herself basically still a child in her relationship to her own child. The daughter, on the other hand, took over the understanding and caring role until, with her own children, she discovered the demanding child within herself who seemed compelled to press others into her service.

Not all children of narcissistically deprived mothers have to suffer from such a disturbance. The siblings can usually obtain a certain freedom when one child has already accepted this role. Children who have a nurse or another stranger caring for them from the beginning are usually freer to develop in their own way because they are less often the object of narcissistic cathexis.

In his novel *The Lily in the Valley,* Honoré de Balzac described his childhood. His mother preferred his brother, gave Honoré first into the care of a nurse and then sent him away to school. He suffered greatly and all his life he courted his mother in the guise of different women. But perhaps he was fortunate that *this mother* did not use him as a glorification of herself. The very hopelessness of his wooing gave him the possibility of developing *his own* emotional wealth and the ability to develop freely his exceptional capacity for suffering. Perhaps the same is true of Vincent van Gogh, whose mother, throughout her life, mourned and idealized the *first* Vincent who had died very young (H. Nagera, 1967).

The narcissistically cathected child has the possibility to develop his intellectual capacities undisturbed but not the world of his emotions, and this has far-reaching consequences for his well-being. The intellect assumes a supportive function of incalculable value in strengthening the defence mechanisms, but behind it the narcissistic disturbance can deepen.

In fact, various mixed forms and nuances of narcissistic disturbances can be found. For the sake of clarity I shall try to describe two extreme forms of which I consider one to be the reverse of the other: grandiosity and depression. Behind manifest grandiosity, depression is constantly lurking, and hiding behind a depressive mood there are often unconscious (or conscious but split off) fantasies of grandiosity. In fact, grandiosity is the defence against depression and depression is the defence against the real pain over the loss of the self.

1. Grandiosity. The person who is 'grandiose' is admired everywhere and needs this admiration, indeed cannot live without it. He *must* perform brilliantly everything he undertakes, which he is surely capable of doing (otherwise he just does not attempt it). *He* admires himself as well—on account of his qualities: his beauty, cleverness, talents; and on account of his success and achievements. Woe betide if one of them fails him, for then the castastrophe of a severe depression is imminent. It is usually considered normal that sick or aged people who have suffered a great loss, or, for example, women at the time of the menopause, should become depressive. There are, however, other personalities who can tolerate the loss of beauty, health, youth, or loved ones, and although they mourn them they do so without depression. In contrast, there are those with great gifts, often precisely the most gifted, who suffer from severe depression. One is free from depression when self-esteem is based on the authenticity of one's own feelings and not on the possession of certain qualities.

The collapse of self-esteem in a 'grandiose' person shows clearly how it had been hanging in the air, *'hanging from a balloon'* (dream of a female patient). The balloon flew very high in a good wind but then suddenly got a hole and then lay like a ragged fragment on the ground. Something that is genuine and which could have given strength later on, had never been developed.

The partners (including sexual partners) of a 'grandiose' person are also narcissistically cathected. The others are there to admire him and he himself is constantly occupied, body and soul, with gaining this admiration. This is how his torturing dependence shows itself. The childhood trauma is repeated, he is always the child whom his mother admires, but at the same time he senses that so long as it is his qualities which are being admired, he is not loved for the person he really is at any given time. Dangerously close to pride in the child, shame is concealed, lest it should fail to fulfil the expectations.

In a field study from Chestnut Lodge in 1954, the family backgrounds of 12 patients with manic-depressive psychosis were examined. The results strongly confirm the conclusions I have reached, by other means, about the aetiology of depression, and, as I believe, of narcissistic disturbances as a whole.

'All the patients came from families who were socially isolated and felt themselves to be too little respected in their neighbourhood. They therefore made special efforts to increase their prestige with their neighbours through conformity and outstanding achievements. The child who later became ill had been assigned a special role in this effort. He was supposed to guarantee the family honour, and was loved only in proportion to the degree to which he was able to fulfil the demands of his family ideal by *means of his special abilities, talents, his beauty, etc,* (my italics). If he failed in this he was punished by being cold-shouldered or thrown out of the family group, and by the knowledge that he had brought great shame on his people' (M. Eicke-Spengler, 1977, p. 1104). I have found a similar isolation in the families of my patients but I saw this as the result, rather than the cause, of the parents' narcissistic disturbance.

It is thus impossible for the grandiose person to cut the tragic link between admiration and love. In his compulsion to repeat he seeks insatiably for admiration, of which he never gets enough because admiration is not the same thing as love. It is only a substitute gratification of the primary needs for respect, understanding and being taken seriously, which have remained unconscious.

When Kernberg (1974) spoke of the remarkably strong envy shown by narcissistically disturbed patients in a discussion group at the Paris Congress in 1973, he remarked, almost as an aside: 'These people are envious of everything, even of other people's object relations.' Do we not have to assume that it is precisely there that the unconscious roots of their excessive envy are to be found? A patient once said she had the feeling that she had always been walking on stilts. Is somebody who always has to walk on stilts not bound to be constantly envious of those who can walk on their own legs, even if they seem to him to be smaller and more 'ordinary' than he is himself? And is he not bound to carry dammed-up rage within himself, against those who have made him afraid to walk without stilts? In this way, envy of other things can appear, the result of the defence mechanism of displacement. Basically he is envious of healthy people because they do not have to make a constant effort to earn admiration, and because they do not have to do something in order to impress, one way or the other, but are free to be 'average'.

Manifest grandiosity, especially in the erotic sphere, is often described as 'phallic narcissism'. The women with the structure and pathogenesis described here usually attained their 'special position' in the sexual sphere during the oedipal phase or even earlier (in cases where the mother was emotionally replaced by the father). They had been specially predestined to this by their development during the pre-oedipal period as narcissistic show-pieces of the mother. If seductive behaviour on the father's side is added, then the woman is forced, by the compulsion to repeat, to go on looking for a special position in her relationships to men. She also has to repress the painful rivalry of the oedipal triangle in order to maintain the fantasy of her favoured position with her father. The inability to develop genuine object love is also narcissistically mortifying, since being a *complete* woman, i.e. being capable of loving, is part of her ambition. Paradoxically, she owes this to her introjected and subsequently transformed mother as well.

Things may be simpler with the so-called 'phallic man'. He is his mother's *special* son and in the seduction situation, her preferred sexual object.[1] The 'phallic man' is forced to be a really splendid fellow if he wants to feel like a man at all. However, as soon as he has to be something specific and is not allowed to be what he really is, he loses, understandably, his sense of self. He then tries all the more to blow up his self-esteem which again leads to narcissistic weakening and so on *ad infinitum*. Fellini's *'Casanova'* portrayed this person and his anguish most impressively.

The grandiose person is never really free, (1) because he is excessively dependent on admiration from the object, and (2) because his self-respect is dependent on qualities, functions and achievements which can suddenly fail.

2. *Depression as the Reverse of Grandiosity.* In the group of patients known to me, depression was coupled with grandiosity in many ways.

(a) Depression sometimes appeared when the grandiosity broke down as a result of sickness, disablement or ageing. The source of external narcissistic supplies, for example, gradually dried up in the case of an unmarried woman as she grew older. She no longer received, from men, constant confirmation of her attractiveness which had had a directly supportive function as a substitute for the missing mirroring by her mother.

Superficially, her despair about getting old seemed to be due to the

[1] Cf on the aetiology of perversion, Chasseguet-Smirgel (1973): denial of the generation gap and overcoming the narcissistic insult in boys who feel themselves to be superior to their fathers.

absence of sexual contacts but, at a deeper level, early pre-oedipal fears of being abandoned (stemming from the symbiotic phase) were being aroused, and this woman had no new conquests with which to counteract them. All her substitute mirrors were broken, and she again stood helpless and confused like the small girl once did before her mother's face in which she had not found herself but her mother's confusion.

The so-called 'phallic narcissistic men' can experience their ageing in a similar way even if a new love affair may seem to create the illusion of their youth for a time and in this way introduce brief manic phases into the early stages of the depression caused by their ageing.

(b) This combination of alternating phases of grandiosity and depression can be seen in many other people. They are the two sides of the medal which could be described as the 'false self', a medal which was actually once given for achievements.

An actor, for example, on the evening of his success, can play before an enthusiastic audience and experience feelings of heavenly greatness and almightiness. Nevertheless, his sense of emptiness and of futility, even of shame and anger, can return the next morning if his happiness the previous night was due not only to his creative activity in playing and expressing the part, but also, and above all, was rooted in the substitute satisfaction of old needs for echoing, mirroring and being seen and understood. If his success the previous night only serves as the denial of childhood frustrations, then, like every substitute, it can only bring momentary satiation. In fact, proper satiation is no longer possible since the time for that is irrevocably past. The former child no longer exists, nor do the former parents. The present parents—if they are still alive—are now old and dependent, have no power over their son any more, are delighted with his success and with his infrequent visits. In the present, the son enjoys *success and recognition* but these things cannot offer him more than they are, they cannot fill the old gap. Again, as long as this is denied with the help of illusion, that is, in the intoxication of success, the old wound cannot heal. Depression comes close to it, but only mourning what was missed, *missed at the crucial time,* can lead to real healing[2]

[2] A remark of Igor Stravinsky's can be cited as an example of successful mourning: 'I am convinced that it was my misfortune that my father was spiritually very distant from me and that even my mother had no love for me. When my oldest brother died unexpectedly (without my mother transferring her feelings from him on to me and my

(c) Continuous outstanding achievements may sometimes enable an individual to maintain the illusion of constant attention and availability of his self-object (whose absence, in his early childhood, had made him deny his own emotional reactions). Such a person is usually able to ward off threatening depression with increased brilliance, thereby deceiving both himself and those around him. However, he quite often chooses a marriage partner who either already has strong depressive traits or at least within their marriage unconsciously takes over and enacts the depressive components of the grandiose partner. This means that *the depression is outside*. The grandiose one can look after his 'poor' partner, protect him like a child, feel himself to be strong and indispensable, and thus gain another supporting pillar for the building of his own personality which actually has no secure foundations and is dependent on the supporting pillars of success, achievement, 'strength' and, above all, of denying his own childhood world of feeling.

(d) Lastly, depression can be experienced as a constant and overt dejection which appears to be unrelated to grandiosity. However, the repressed or split-off fantasies of grandiosity of the depressive are easily discovered, for example in his moral masochism. He has especially severe standards which apply only to himself. In other people he accepts without question thoughts and actions which, in himself, he would consider mean or bad when measured against his high ego ideal. Others are allowed to be 'ordinary', but he himself may not.

Although the outward picture of depression is diametrically opposite to that of grandiosity and has a quality which expresses the tragedy of the loss of self to a great extent, both have the same roots in the narcissistic disturbance. Both are indications of an *inner prison*, because the grandiose and the depressive individuals are *compelled* to fulfil the introjected mother's expectations: whereas the grandiose person is her successful child, the depressive sees himself as a failure.

father, also, remaining as reserved as ever) I resolved that one day I would show them. Now this day has come and gone. No-one remembers this day but me, who was its only witness.' This is in marked contrast to the statement by Samuel Beckett: 'One could say that I had a happy childhood, although I showed little talent for being happy. My parents did all that can be done to make a child happy, but I often felt very lonely.' (Both quotations are from an article by H. Mueller-Braunschweig, 1974.) Here the childhood drama has been fully introjected, and idealization of the parents was maintained with the help of denial, but the boundless isolation of his childhood found expression in Beckett's plays.

They have several points in common:

1. A 'false self' which has led to the loss of the potential 'true self'.
2. A fragility of self-esteem which is based on the possibility of realising the 'false self' because of a lack of confidence in one's own feelings and wishes.
3. Perfectionism, a very high ego ideal.
4. Denial of the rejected feelings (the missing of a shadow in Narcissus' reflected image).
5. A preponderance of narcissistic cathexes of objects.
6. An enormous fear of loss of love and therefore a great readiness to conform.
7. Envy of the healthy.
8. Strong aggression which is split off and therefore not neutralized.
9. Over-sensitivity.
10. A readiness to feel shame and guilt.
11. Restlessness.

Thus depression can be understood as a sign of the loss of self and consists of a denial of one's own emotional reactions and feelings. This denial begins in the service of an absolutely essential adaptation during childhood, to avoid losing the object's love. Subsequently, it continues under the influence of the introjects. That is the reason why depression indicates a very early disturbance. There had been a deficit, right in the beginning at infancy, in certain affective areas which would have been necessary for stable self-confidence. From the reconstructions available through analyses, I have gained the impression that there are children who have not been free to experience the very earliest feelings such as discontent, anger, rage, pain, even hunger and, of course, enjoyment of their own bodies.

Discontentment and anger had aroused uncertainty in the mother over her maternal role; pain made her anxious. The enjoyment of their bodies sometimes produced envy, sometimes shame about 'what other people would think' or else it disturbed the mother's reaction formations (A. Miller, 1971). Thus, under certain circumstances, a child may learn very early what it is not allowed to feel, lest it runs the risk of losing its mother's love.

A patient in her fourth year of analysis came to a session several weeks after the birth of her third child and told me how free and alive she felt with this baby, compared with the two previous ones. With them she had constantly felt that excessive demands were made on her, that she was a prisoner and that the child took advantage of and 'exploited' her so that she rebelled against his justified demands and, at the same time, felt that this was very bad of her; as in depression she was separated from her true self. She thought this might have been rebellion against her mother's demands for now she experiences nothing of this sort. The love for which she had then struggled now came of its own accord. She could enjoy her unity with this child and with herself. Then she spoke of her mother in the following words:

'I was the jewel in my mother's crown. She often said: "Maja can be relied upon, she will cope." And I did cope, I brought up the smaller children for her so that she could get on with her professional career. She became more and more famous, but I never saw her happy. How often I longed for her in the evenings. The little ones cried and I comforted them but I myself never cried. Who would have wanted a crying child? I could only win my mother's love if I was competent, understanding and controlled, if I never questioned her actions nor showed her how much I missed her; that would have limited her freedom which she needed so much. That would have turned her against me. At that time, nobody ever would have thought that this quiet, competent, useful Maja could be so lonely and have suffered so much. What could I do but be proud of my mother and help her?

The deeper the hole in my mother's heart was, the bigger the jewels in her crown needed to be. My poor mother needed these jewels because, at base, all her activity served only to suppress something in herself, perhaps a longing, I don't know. . . . Perhaps *she* would have discovered it if she had been fortunate to be a mother in more than a biological sense. It is not her fault. She tried so hard. But she had not been given the gift.

And how all of this repeated itself with Peter! How many empty hours my child had to spend with the maids so that I could get my diploma, which only took me further away from him and from myself. How often I deserted him without seeing what I was doing to him, because I had never been able to experience my own sense of being deserted? Only now do I begin to realize what motherhood without crown or jewels or a halo can be like.'

A German magazine for women (which tries to speak openly of truths that have been tabooed) published a reader's letter in which the tragic story of her experience of motherhood was told without camouflage. It is in the nature of the problem that she could not really experience either her own tragedy or that of her child, since her own emotionally inaccessible childhood was the real beginning of the story. Her report ends with the following passage: 'And then the breast-feeding! The baby was put to the breast all wrong and soon my nipples were all bitten. God, how that hurt. Just two hours and then it was back: another one . . . the same . . . while it was sucking there, I was crying and swearing above it. It was so terrible that soon I couldn't eat any more and had a temperature of 40. Then I was allowed to wean it and suddenly felt better. It was a long time before I noticed any maternal feelings. I wouldn't have minded if the baby had died. And everybody expected me to be happy. In despair I telephoned a friend who said that I'd get fond of it in time through being busy with it and having it around all the time. But that did not happen either. I only *began to be fond* of it when I could go back to work and only saw it when I came home, as a *distraction and toy,* so to speak. But quite honestly, a little dog would have been just as good. Now that he is gradually getting bigger and I see that *I can train him and that he is devoted to me and trusts me,* I am beginning to develop *tender feelings* for him and am glad that he is there. [My italics.]

I have written all this because I think it is good thing that someone should, at last, say that there is no such thing as mother love—not to speak of a maternal instinct' ('Emma', Jul 1977).

B. THE MYTH OF NARCISSUS

The myth of Narcissus actually shows the tragedy of the narcissistic disturbance. Reflected in the water, Narcissus falls in love with his own beautiful face, which his mother was surely proud of. The nymph Echo also answers the young man's calls because she is in love with his beauty, like the mothers of our patients. Echo's answering calls deceive Narcissus. His reflection deceives him as well since it only shows his perfect, wonderful side and not the other side. His back view, for example, and his shadow remain hidden from him; they do not belong to and are cut off from his beloved reflection.

This stage of rapture can be compared with grandiosity, just as the next (the consuming longing for himself) can be likened to depression. Narcissus wanted to be *nothing but the beautiful youth.* He denied his true self, wanted to be at one with the beautiful picture. This leads to a giving up of himself, to death or, in Ovid's version, to being changed into a flower. This death is the logical consequence of the fixation to the false self. It is not only the 'beautiful', 'good' and pleasant feelings that make us really *alive,* deepen our existence and give us crucial insights but often precisely the unacceptable and unadapted ones which we would prefer to escape from: impotence, shame, envy, jealousy, confusion and mourning. These feelings can be experienced in the analyst's room and grow beyond their archaic form there. In this way this room is also a mirror of the analysand's inner world which is much richer than the 'beautiful countenance'!

Narcissus was *in love with* his idealized picture, but neither the grandiose nor the depressive 'Narcissus' can *really love* himself. His passion for his false self not only makes object love impossible but also love towards the one person who is fully entrusted to his care—namely, himself.

C. DEPRESSIVE PHASES DURING ANALYSIS

A grandiose person only looks for an analyst if depressive episodes come to his aid. As long as the grandiose defence is effective, this form of narcissistic disturbance exerts no pressure through visible suffering, except when other members of the family (spouse or children) have to seek psychotherapeutic help for depression or psychosomatic disorders. In our analytic work, we encounter grandiosity coupled with depression. On the other hand, we see depression in almost all our patients, either in the form of a manifest illness or in distinct phases of depressive moods. These phases can have different functions.

i. Signal function

Every analyst is familiar with sessions where the patient arrives complaining of depression and later leaves the consulting room in tears but much relieved and free from depression. Perhaps he has been able to experience a long-dammed-up rage against his mother, or to express his mistrust of the analyst's superiority, or, to feel for the first time, his sadness over the many lost years of his life during which he did not really live, or his anger over the impending holidays and separation. It is irrelevant which of these feelings are involved; the important thing is that they could be experienced. The depression had signalled their proximity but also their denial. The analytic session enabled the feelings to break through and then the depression disappeared. Such a mood can be an indication that parts of the self which had been rejected (feelings, fantasies, wishes, fears) have become stronger without finding discharge in grandiosity.

ii. Self-denial

There are some patients who, after coming close to the core of their selves in a session and feeling content and understood, organize a party or something else equally unimportant to them at that moment, where they feel empty and inadequate again. After a few days they complain of *self-alienation* and *emptiness,* again of having lost the way to themselves. Here the patient has actively, though unconsciously, provoked a situation which shows the repetition of what used to happen to him as a child: when he could really sense himself in play, feeling creative in Winnicott's sense, he would be asked to do something 'more sensible', to achieve something, and his world, which was just beginning to unfold, would be *overthrown.* These patients, even as children, probably reacted to this by withdrawing their feelings and by becoming depressed.

iii. The accumulation of strong, hidden feelings

Patients who are no longer depressive sometimes have depressive phases which may last several weeks before *strong emotions* from their childhood break through. It is as though the depression had held back the affect. When it can be experienced, insight and associations related to the primary objects follow, often accompanied by significant dreams. The patient feels fully alive again until a new depressive phase signals something new. This may be expressed in the following fashion: 'I don't feel myself any more. How can it happen that I should lose myself again? I have no connection with what is within me. It is all hopeless. . . . It will never be any better. Everything is pointless. I am longing for my former sense of being alive.' An aggressive outbreak may follow, with reproaches against the analyst, and only after this outbreak does a new link become clear and new vitality is felt.

iv. The struggle with the introjects

During an analysis there are also times of depressive moods after the patient has started to resist the demands of his introjects, e.g. for demands for achievement, but has not yet fully freed himself from them. Then he lands again in the cul-de-sac of *pointlessly excessive demands* which he is making on himself and only becomes aware of this when a depressive mood arises. This finds expression in the following way, for instance: 'Yesterday I was so happy, my work went easily, I was able to do more work for the exam than I had planned for the whole week. Then I thought I must take advantage of this good mood and do another chapter in the evening. I worked all evening but without any enthusiasm and next day I couldn't do any more. I felt such an idiot, nothing stayed in my head. I didn't want to see anyone either, it felt like the depressions I used to have. Then I "turned the pages back" and found where it had begun. I had spoiled my pleasure as soon as I made myself do more and more. And why? Then I remembered how my mother used to say: "You have done that beautifully, now you could just do this as well. . . . " I got angry and left the books alone. I suddenly trusted myself to know when I was ready to work again. And, of course, I did too. But the depression went sooner—at the point where I noticed that I had bowled myself over again.'

D. THE INNER PRISON AND ANALYTIC WORK

Probably everybody knows from his own experience about depressive moods which can, of course, also express or hide themselves in psychosomatic suffering. If one pays attention it is easy to see that they regularly appear and check spontaneity when an impulse or undesirable feeling is suppressed. If an adult, for example, cannot experience mourning when he loses somebody dear to him but tries to distract himself from his sadness, or if he suppresses and hides from himself his indignation over an idealized friend's behaviour from fear of losing his friendship, he must reckon with the probability of depression (unless his grandiose defence is constantly at his disposal). When he begins to pay attention to these connections in his analysis he can benefit from his depression and use it to learn the truth about himself.

A child does not yet have this possibility. He cannot yet see through his mechanism of self-deception and, on the other hand, he is far more threatened than an adult by the intensity of his feelings if he does not have a holding, empathic environment. Winnicott compared the infant's world of feeling with that of a psychotic and there is something convincing about this comparison. What they have in common, in addition to the lack of structuring, is the extreme intensity of feeling which is otherwise to be found only in puberty. But the recollection of the pains of puberty, of not being able to understand or to place our own impulses is usually more accessible than the first narcissistic traumata which are often hidden behind the picture of an idyllic childhood or even behind an almost complete amnesia. This is perhaps one reason why adults less often look back nostalgically to the time of their puberty than to that of their childhood. The mixture of longing, expectation and fear of disappointment which, for most people, accompanies the festivities they have known from their childhood, can perhaps be explained by their search for the intensity of feeling they knew in childhood which they cannot regain.

It is precisely because a child's feelings are so strong that they cannot be repressed without serious consequences. The stronger a prisoner is, the thicker the prison walls have to be, which impede or completely prevent later emotional growth.

Once a patient has experienced a few times in the course of his analysis, that the breakthrough of intense early-childhood feelings (characterized by the specific quality of non-comprehension) can relieve a long period of depression, this experience will bring about a gradual change in his way of approaching 'undesired' feelings, above all those of pain. He discovers that he is no longer compelled to follow the former pattern of disappointment, suppression of pain and depression, since he now has another possibility of dealing with disappointment, namely, that of experiencing the pain. In this way he at least gains access to his earlier experiences, i.e. to the parts of himself and of his fate that were previously hidden from him.

A patient, in the closing phase of his analysis, expressed it thus: 'It was not the beautiful or pleasant feelings which give me new insight but the ones against which I had fought most strongly: feelings which made me experience myself as shabby, petty, mean, helpless, humiliated, demanding, resentful or confused. And above all sad and lonely. However, it was precisely from these experiences, which I had avoided for so long, that I gained the certainty of understanding, stemming from the core of my being, something which I could not have learnt from any book!'

This patient was describing the process of *creative insight* in psycho-analysis. Interpretations play an important part in this process. They can accompany it, support ('hold') and encourage, but they can also disturb, hamper and delay, or even prevent it or reduce it to mere intellectual insight. A patient with narcissistic problems is all too ready to give up his own pleasure in discovery and self-expression and ac-commodate himself to his analyst's concepts—from fear of losing the latter's affection, understanding and empathy for which he has been waiting all his life. Because of his early experiences with his mother, he cannot believe that this need not necessarily be so. If he gives way to this fear and adapts himself, the analysis slides over into the sphere of the 'false self' and the truth remains hidden and undeveloped. It is therefore extremely important that the analyst does not cathect the patient narcissistically, that is, his own needs should not impel him to formulate connections which the patient himself is *discovering with the help of his own feelings*. Otherwise he is in danger of behaving like a friend who brings some good food to a prisoner in his cell, at the precise moment when he has the opportunity of escaping, perhaps to spend his first night without shelter and hungry, but nevertheless in freedom. Since this step into unknown territory requires a great deal of courage in the first instance, it can happen that the prisoner, comforting himself with his food and shelter, misses his chance and stays in prison.

Recognizing the fragility of a creative process obviously does not mean that the analyst must adopt a mostly silent and hurtful attitude but merely that he must exercise care in this respect. Provided that the analyst respects the analysand's need to discover things for himself, it is possible, for example, that his compulsion to repeat can be of good service to his creative self-discovery, especially if its indirect commu-nications are understood. This will come about through producing a variety of new situations through which an old, unremembered situation can, for the first time, be consciously experienced in its fullest tragedy and then finally be mourned. It is part of the dialectic of the mourning process that such experiences both encourage and are dependent on self-discovery (A. Miller, 1979).

Grandiosity is the counterpart of depression *within the narcissistic disturbance.* The patient can therefore be freed from his depression for a while if the psycho-therapist knows how to let him share in his own grandiosity, that is, when he can enable the patient to feel big and strong as a part of the idealized therapist. The narcissistic disturbance then appears in a different guise for a while even though it still exists. Achieving *freedom from both forms* of narcissistic disturbance in analysis is hardly possible without deeply-felt mourning. This ability to mourn, i.e. to give up the illusion of his 'happy' childhood, can restore vitality and creativity to the depressive, and (if he comes to analysis at all) free the grandiose person from the exertions of and dependence on his Sisyphean task. If a person is able, during this long process, to experience that he was never 'loved' as a child for what he was but for his achievements, success and good qualities, and that he sacrificed his childhood for this 'love', this will shake him very deeply, but one day he will feel the desire to end this courtship. He will discover in himself a need to live according to his 'true self' and no longer be forced to earn love, a love which, at root, still leaves him empty-handed since it is given to the 'false self' which he has begun to relinquish.

The true opposite of depression is not gaiety or absence of pain, but vitality, i.e. the freedom to experience feelings which are spontaneous. It is part of the kaleidoscope of life that these feelings are not only cheerful, 'beautiful' and 'good' but that they can display the whole scale of human experience, including envy, jealousy, rage, disgust, greed, despair, and mourning. But this freedom cannot be achieved if childhood roots are cut off. Access to the 'true self' is thus only possible, for a person with narcissistic problems, when he no longer has to be afraid of the intense 'psychotic' emotional world of his childhood. Once he has experienced it during the analytic process, it is no longer strange and threatening and need no longer be hidden behind the prison walls of illusion.

A good deal of advice for dealing with depressive patients (e.g. turning his aggression from the inner to the outer world) has a clearly manipulative character. S. Levin, for example, suggested that one should demonstrate to the patient that 'his hopelessness is not rational' or make him aware of his 'oversensitivity' (R. Fischer, 1976). In my opinion, such a procedure will only strengthen the 'false self' and emotional conformity, i.e. bascially reinforce the depression too. If we don't want to do that then we must take *all* his feelings seriously. It is precisely his over-sensitivity, shame and self-reproach (how often a depressive patient knows that he reacts over-sensitively and how much does he reproach himself for it) which form a *continuous thread throughout his analysis* even before we understand what they really relate to. The more unrealistic such feelings are and the less they fit present reality, the more clearly they show that they are concerned with unremembered situations from the past which are still to be discovered. If, however, the feeling concerned is not experienced but reasoned away, the discovery cannot take place and depression will be triumphant.

After a long depressive phase, accompanied by suicidal thoughts, a 40-year-old patient was at last able to experience her violent, very early, ambivalence in the transference. This was not immediately followed by visible relief but by a period full of mourning and tears. At the end of this period she said: 'The world has not changed, there is so much evil and meanness all around me, and I see it even more clearly than before. Nevertheless, for the first time I find life really worth living. Perhaps this is because, for the first time, I have the feeling that I am really *living my own life*. And that is an exciting adventure. On the other hand, I can understand my suicidal ideas better now, especially those I had in my youth—it seemed pointless to carry on because in a way I had always been living a life that wasn't mine, that I didn't want and that I was ready to throw away.'

E. A SOCIAL ASPECT OF DEPRESSION

One might ask whether adaptation must necessarily lead to depression. Is it not possible, and are there no examples of emotionally conforming individuals living quite happily? There are such examples, and above all there were more in the past, for depression is a disease of our time. Within a culture which was shielded from other value systems, such as that of orthodox Jewry in the ghetto, or negro families in the southern states a hundred years ago, an adapted individual was not autonomous and did not have his own individual sense of identity (in our sense) which could have given support, but he did feel supported by the group. The sense of being a 'devout Jew' or a 'loyal slave' gave him a measure of security in this world. Of course, there were some exceptions, people for whom that was not sufficient and who were strong enough to break away. Today it is hardly possible for any group to remain as isolated from others who have different values. This means it is necessary for the individual to find his support in himself if he is not to become the victim of various interests and ideologies. This strength within himself, i.e. through access to his own real needs and feelings and the possibility of expressing them, thus becomes crucially important for him on the one hand, and on the other is made enormously more difficult through living in contact with various different value systems, These factors can probably explain the rapid increase of depression in our time and also the fascination with groups.

Within the partially adapted child there are latent powers which resist this adaptation. As the child grows, particularly in puberty, these powers attach themselves to new values, which are often opposed to those of the parents, and thus they create new ideals which they try to put into practice. Since this attempt is nevertheless not rooted in awareness of his own true needs and feelings, the adolescent accepts and *conforms to the new ideals* in a similar way to that which he previously adopted in relation to his parents. He again gives up and denies his true self in order to be accepted and loved by the heirs of the primary objects (whether in his ego-ideal or in the group). But all that is of little avail against depression. This person is not really himself, nor does he know or love himself: he does everything to make a narcissistically cathected object love him, in the way he once, as a child, so urgently needed it. But whatever could not be experienced at the right time in the past, can never be attained later on.

There are innumerable examples of this and I would like to include two of them:

1. A young woman wants to free herself from her patriarchal family in which her mother was completely subjected by the father. She marries a submissive man and seems to behave quite differently from her mother. Her husband allows her to bring her lovers into the house. She does not permit herself any feelings of jealousy or tenderness and wants to have relations with a number of men without any emotional ties, so that she can feel as autonomous as a man. Her need to be 'progressive' goes so far that she allows her partners to abuse and humilate her as they wish, and suppresses all her feelings of mortification and anger in the belief that this makes her modern and free from prejudice. In this way she carries over both her childhood obedience and her mother's

submissiveness into these relationships. At times she suffers from severe depression.

2. A patient from an African family grew up alone with his mother after his father had died whilst he was still a very small boy. His mother insists on certain conventions and does not allow the child to be aware of his narcissistic and libidinal needs in any way, let alone express them. On the other hand, she regularly massages his penis until puberty, ostensibly on medical advice. As an adult her son leaves his mother and her world and marries an attractive European with a quite different background. Is it due to chance or to his unerring instinct that this woman not only torments and humiliates him but also undermines his confidence to an extreme degree, he being quite unable to stand up to her or leave her? This sado-masochistic marriage, like the other example, represents an attempt to break away from the parents' social system with the help of another one. The patient was certainly able to free himself from the mother of his adolescence but he remained emotionally tied to the oedipal and pre-oedipal mother whose role was taken over by his wife as long as he was not able to experience the feelings from that period. In his analysis he encountered his original ambivalence. It was terribly painful for him to realize the extent to which he had needed his mother as a child and at the same time had felt abused in his helplessness; how much he had loved her, hated her and been entirely at her mercy. The patient experienced these feelings after four years of analysis, with the result that he no longer needed his wife's perversions and could separate from her. At the same time he was able to see her far more realistically, including her positive sides.

F. POINTS OF CONTACT WITH SOME THEORIES OF DEPRESSION

When we conceptualize depression as the giving-up of one's real self in the service of maintaining object love, we can find within this view the main elements of the most important theories of depression:

1. Freud's factor of *impoverishment* of the ego is, of course, centrally contained in this concept, allowing for the fact that, at the time of writing 'Mourning and Melancholia' (1917), he used the term 'ego' in the sense in which we now use the term 'self'.
2. What Abraham (1912) described as *turning aggression against the self* is equally closely related to the idea of loss of the self which I tried to describe.

The 'destruction' of feelings, needs and fantasies which are unwelcome to the primary object is an aggressive act against the self. The feelings which are 'killed' by the depressive may vary according to the child's specific situation—they are not merely linked to aggressive impulses.

3. Sandler and Joffe (1965) (cf. also Joffe & Sandler, 1965) define depression as a possible *reaction to psychic pain* caused by the discrepancy between the actual and the ideal self-representation. Congruity of these representations leads to a feeling of well-being. In the language of object relations that would mean: the ideal self-representation is the heir of the primary objects whose approval and love ensure a sense of well-being, just as the discrepancy brings the danger of loss of love. If this pain could be risked and experienced there would be no depression, but for that a 'holding' environment would have been necessary.

4. Finally, according to E. Jacobson (1971), the conditions for a depressive development arise when loss of the ideal object is denied. Loss here does not only mean real separation from the self-object, or disappointment which is traumatic if it is not phase-appropriate, but also the unavailability of the self-object.

The narcissistically disturbed patient did not have a self-object at his disposal during the symbiotic phase, nor a 'usable' object in Winnicott's sense (1971), i.e. one which would have survived its own destruction. Both the depressive and the grandiose person *deny this reality completely* by living as though the availability of the self-object could still be salvaged: the grandiose person, through the illusion of achievement and the depressive through his constant fear of losing the self-object. Neither of them can accept the truth that this loss or this unavailability has *already happened* in the past, and that *no effort* whatsoever *can ever change this fact.*

SUMMARY

Whereas 'healthy narcissism' can be characterized as the full access to the true self, the narcissistic disturbance can be uderstood as a fixation on a 'false' or incomplete self. This fixation can be seen as the intra-psychic heir to the narcissistic cathexis of the child by his parents. In order to maintain the object's love, these children developed only those capacities which they felt their parents needed and admired. The un-acceptable feelings had to be hidden from the environment and from themselves in order to avoid rejection or shame. This selective function is then taken over by the introjects. If anger, envy, despair and other undesirable feelings cannot be avoided completely, they have to be split off and cannot be integrated which leads to a marked impoverishment of the personality. This loss of important parts of the self can be denied by grandiosity or can find expression through depression. The grandiosity, once based on the hope of reaching the real object, is later continued in an intense struggle with the introjects. Yet, if there is an awakening of a greater sense of reality, the defensive function of grandiosity breaks down in a depression. And now there is a greater awareness of the real state of affairs. Nevertheless, the depressed person feels like an empty house, still defending against pain.

Clinical vignettes illustrate how the newly-freed ability to mourn and to face pain leads to the dissipation of the depression and allows the patient to feel genuine intensity of the life processes.

REFERENCES

Abraham, K. (1912). Ansätze zur psychoanalytischen Erforschung und Behandlung des manisch-depressiven Irreseins und verwandter Zustände. In *Psychoanalytische Studien*, Bd. II. Frankfurt: J. Fischer, 1971.

Chasseguet-Smirgel, J. (1973). L'ideal du moi, XXIIIe Congres des Psychanalystes de Langues romanes. R.F.P. 5 Juin, 1973.

Eicke-Spengler, M. (1977). Zur Entwicklung der psychoanalytischen Theorie der Depression. *Psyche* **31**, 1079–1125.

Fischer, R. (1976). Die klassiche und die ichpsychologische Theorie der Depression. *Psyche* **30**, 924–946.

Freud, S. (1917). Mourning and melancholia. *S.E.* **14**.

Jacobson, E. (1971). *Depression*. New York: Int. Univ. Press.

Joffe, W. & Sandler, J. (1965). Notes on pain, depression and individuation. *Psychoanal. Study Child* **20**.

Kernberg, O. (1974). Further contributions to the treatment of narcissistic personalities. *Int. J. Psycho-Anal.* **55**, 215–240.

Kohut, H. (1971). *The Analysis of the Self*. New York: Int. Univ. Press.

Mahler, M. (1968). *On Human Symbiosis and the Vicissitudes of Individuation*. New York: Int. Univ. Press.

Miller, A. (1971). Zur Behandlungstechnik bei sogenannten narzisstischen Neurosen. *Psyche* **25**, 641–668.

Miller, A. (1979). The drama of the gifted child and the psychoanalysts narcissistic disturbance. *Int. J. Psycho-Anal.* **60**, 47–58.

Mueller-Braunschweig, H. (1974). Psychopathologie und Kreativität. *Psyche* **28**, 600–634.

Nagera, H. (1967). *Vincent van Gogh*. London: Allen and Unwin.

Sandler, J. & Joffe, W. (1965). Notes on childhood depression. *Int. J. Psycho-Anal.* **46**, 88–96.

Winnicott, D. W. (1971). *Playing and Reality*.London: Tavistock Publns.

14. Shame, Ideal Self, and Narci₅

Andrew P. Morrison

Much of the literature on shame begins with t!
affect has been ingored, little appreciated, or
choanalytic writings. This observation has I
made, in some intriguing and useful accounts,
of work on this important subject has accrued,
to the differentiation of shame from guilt. Ma
assumed that guilt is the "weightier" subject, ₹
a phenomenon of the ego's response to social d
little significance compared to guilt's internal (
waged between the agencies id, ego, and supe

With some other authors (Lewis, 1971; Ly
Wurmser, 1981) I shall assume throughout th⁷
affect of equal importance, theoretically and
guilt. I shall also include within the designatic
phenomena of humiliation, mortification, remorse, apathy, embarass-
ment, and lowered self-esteem. While there is good reason to attempt
differentiation of these phenomena from shame and from one another,
I believe that, for the purposes of this examination, they are closely
enough related emotions to be subsumed under "shame" as a signifying
affect. Shame has been relegated to second-order importance in classic
psychoanalytic literature, I believe, because it relates directly to a
construct which until recent writings has not been easily integrated into
the mainstream of Freudian concepts—that of the *self*. Thus, much of
the significant work on shame has emerged from writers working within
Sullivanian (and other neo-Freudian) perspectives. As we shall see, the
classical construct of the ego ideal, a poorly differentiated element of
the system superego, has been previously invoked in discussions of
shame. That loving function of the superego has traditionally been less
accessible than its punitive function, regularly associated with guilt.

With the work of Kohut, the construct of the self has been elaborated
and elevated to a place in psychoanalytic conceptualization which

should allow for a more systematic and helpful examination of the phenomenon of shame. In this paper I shall attempt to re-examine shame in the context of Kohut's contributions. First, I shall review the concept of shame (and its relation to guilt), including some thoughts on why shame has been insufficiently considered in the classical literature. I shall then turn to the construct of the *ideal self* and its relationship to shame. Finally, I shall attempt to utilize conceptualizations from Kohut's recent writings to indicate that shame is an affect central to the application of his theory, representing in fact a seminal dilemma for the narcissistic personality.

THE PSYCHOLOGY OF SHAME

Freud's development of structural theory (1914, 1923) led to the evolution of the constructs superego and ego-ideal, and with them the potential for an understanding of shame. However, his emphasis and interests lay in other directions, and, under the sway of libido and conflict theory, he focused on the development of guilt in relation to Oedipal strivings and superego retaliation. He added little to the understanding of shame (Hazard, 1969), suggesting only that it reflected danger from exposure to others through genital visibility and vulnerability when man assumed the upright position (1930); and also the sense of genital deficiency in women (1933), with shame emerging primarily as a feminine characteristic. With Thrane (1980), I note the relationship of this conceptualization to Adler's "organ inferiority" and "inferiority complex", suggesting that Freud may have avoided the affect of shame in part because of its proximity to Adler's contributions. Also, Freud alluded to shame as a reaction to forbidden libidinal wishes and sexual exhibitionism, never clearly differentiating it from the guilt resulting from overstepping the sexual taboo.

A major psychoanalytic statement on shame and guilt was that of Piers and Singer (1953). Piers defined guilt as the painful internal tension whenever an emotionally charged barrier of the superego is transgressed, as by id impulses to aggression and sexuality. The resultant danger from such transgression is dismemberment and annihilation (i.e., castration). Shame, on the other hand, results from a tension between the ego and that ill-defined substructure of the superego—the ego ideal. According to Piers, shame is manifest when a goal of the ego ideal is not attained, and therefore is the result of failure. As the threat from guilt is castration, so the threat from shame is abandonment and rejection. Piers describes the ego ideal as containing narcissistic omnipotence, the sum of positive identifications and social roles, and an awareness of the ego's potentialities and goals. He also describes a guilt-shame cycle, in which an id impulse is inhibited (guilt), leading to passivity (shame), and subsequent overcompensation and impulse expression, which in turn leads again to guilt, and inhibition of the impulse. The guilt-shame cycle is Piers' attempt to integrate the two affects, and to overcome the reductionistic tendency in his differentiation between them. Finally, according to Piers, shame is a reflection of body functions and comparison of self to others, with resultant feelings of inferiority. Such comparisons lead to the shame phenomena of blushing, and of hiding (i.e., the defective body part). Shame, then, leads to hiding and compensatory activity to camouflage a defect.

Thus, with his emphasis on failure and the ego ideal, Piers' conceptualization of shame leads inevitably to the concept of "self", an entity more global and less circumscribed than the structures id, ego, and superego. Also, Piers introduces the concept of narcissism in relationship to shame, which I will develop later in this paper. Lewis (1971), in her study of the phenomenology of shame and guilt, further develops the concept of self. She demonstrates that Freud came late to the 'self', failing to clearly differentiate it from ego and ego ideal. Such a clarification in Freudian theory had to await Hartmann (1950) and Jacobson (1954). However, the self concept is central to Lewis' understanding of shame. According to her, "The self is, first of all, the experiential registration of the person's activities as his own" (Lewis, p. 30). Shame, according to Lewis, is about the whole self, and its failure to live up to an ideal; as such, it is a "narcissistic" reaction. A typical defense against shame is hiding, or running away. Hostility against self is experienced in a passive mode, and therefore leaves the shame-prone individual subject to depression. Guilt, on the other hand, refers to a transgression, an action, and therefore has a more specific cognitive or behavioral antecedent than shame, referring less globally to the subjective sense of self. Lewis states, "Shame of failure is for an involuntary event. It results from incapacity. Guilt for transgression is, by implication, guilt for a voluntary act or choice. The proximal stimulus to shame is thus deficiency of the self; while the proximal stimulus of guilt is some action (omission) by the self, which by implication is able. Shame thus feels involuntary; guilt feels as if it were more voluntary" (Lewis, p. 86).

Lewis, an experimental researcher as well as psychotherapist, studies the interesting relationship between field dependence and independence to shame. Field dependence is a perceptual style in which individuals have difficulty perceiving an object as separate from its "embedding context" (background). Thus, field-dependent persons tend to be more "other-directed" and influenced by the opinions of others than are field-independent persons. Through detailed analyses of transcripts of field-dependent and independent patients, Lewis demonstrates that field-dependent individuals are more prone to the affect of shame; tend to be women; and are more likely to experience depression. Field-independent patients, on the other hand, tend more to experience guilt, to isolate affect, and to be men. It would be interesting to repeat Lewis' studies in the context of the women's movement, and resultant variations in women's self-esteem.[1]

The referent of shame, then, is the self, which is experienced as defective, inadequate, and having failed in its quest to attain a goal. These goals of the self relate to ideals internalized through identification with the "good" (or idealized) parent, and as such reflect that portion of the superego contained within the ego ideal. However, in considering the construct of self, a second concept comes under scrutiny which is critical in our consideration of shame—the concept of identity. Erikson (1950) develops "identity" as part of his pioneer work on developmental stages, where he speaks of the stage of Autonomy vs. Shame and Doubt. Identity relates to conscious and unconscious strivings for continuity, and synthesis of personality, maintenance of congruence with the ideals and identity of one's chosen social group, and a conscious awareness of who one is. Lynd (1958) indicates that Erikson "includes in the meaning of identity the self as subject and object, as observer and observed-meanings that are sometimes kept separate in an effort to make exclusive distinctions between the concepts self and ego" (p. 204). According to Lynd, shame and doubt relate to the development of self-esteem, and thus imply a consciousness of the whole self. In

[1] A thoughtful paper by Sederer and Seidenberg (1976) speaks to the shame-proneness of women, and their pressure to meet the separate and conflicting goals of expressing womanhood through procreation and the home, and attaining aspirations in the male-dominated work world.

addition, it is associated with "unconfronted aimless anxiety" (p. 207), which drives the individual into irrational flight, covering or hiding of the exposed vulnerability, or into denial of that defect or vulnerability. Shame, then, reflects feelings about a defect of the self, a lowering of self-esteem, falling short of the values of the ego ideal, a flaw in one's identity representation.

The external danger from the experience of shame is abandonment or rejection (Piers, 1953; Levin, 1967), in contrast with punishment and castration in relationship to guilt (Piers, 1953). Levin further indicates that anxiety about the potential for shame leads to a specific affect which he describes as shame anxiety. Since shame is experienced in relationship to a "perceiving other," it may lead to recoil and withdrawal from significant objects (Levin, 1967). One disagreement in the literature on shame is the question of how closely tied it is to a social context. Lowenfeld (1976) suggests, for instance, that shame is a social phenomenon, and as such plays an important role in upholding the structure of society. Thrane (p. 332) indicates that shaming, as in the early anal stage of development, is a central first step in the socialization process. On the other hand, others argue that shame reflects feelings about failure to live up to one's deepest ideals and morals. Since the "ego ideal" refers to internalization of idealized objects and values, shame can also be viewed as reflecting prior development of a moral system, and thus relates to the individual's deepest held values and personal identity which "fall short" of his self-expectations (Thrane, p. 338). How closely tied one's sense of identity and self-esteem are to a social context may well be a reflection of the nature of an individual's field dependence or independence, as described by Lewis.

Another important relationship is that between shame and narcissism. It is not a coincidence that Freud first evolved the ego ideal construct in his paper On Narcissism (1914), where he states, "It would not surprise us if we were to find a special psychical agency which performs the task of seeing that narcissistic satisfaction from the ego ideal is ensured and which, with this end in view, constantly watches the actual ego and measures it by that ideal." Since shame is experienced in relationship to the self, libidinal energy associated with the shame experience is closely tied to narcissism and its vicissitudes.

Lewis (p. 37) observes that shame "is thus a narcissistic reaction, evoked by a lapse from the ego-ideal." Lowenfeld (1976) notes that "shame, so weakened in reaction to moral standards, is still experienced when a person's narcissism is involved." Finally, Jacobson (1964) pointed out that shame is related to the vicissitudes of narcissistic libido, whereas guilt relates more closely to the vicissitudes of object-libido. I shall consider the relationship of shame to narcissistic injury later in this paper, but at this point it suffices to point out that, where a defect or failure of the self is perceived, the resultant shame carries with it a decrease in narcissistic self-esteem.

The "Low Profile" of Shame in Psychoanalytic Writings

Lewis (p. 100) believes that the relative paucity of attention to shame in psycho-analytic literature may reflect the late, and relatively sparse, attention paid the concept of self in comparison to the ego. Freud's discussions of the superego focused almost exclusively on guilt and its relationship to castration anxiety and the Oedipus complex, with relative inattention to positive identifications and the ego ideal (Thrane, p. 322). Thrane suggests that Freud may well have been influenced in this emphasis by western culture's preoccupation with, and Christianity's emphasis on, guilt. Erikson suggests that, in western civilization, shame is early and easily absorbed by guilt.

A second explanation of shame's "low profile" is that guilt has been generally considered to be a more worthy, deep, and structurally-based emotion than shame. From Erikson's paradigm, the crisis of shame-autonomy precedes that of guilt-initiative. Implicit in Erikson's conceptualization is the view that shame reflects a passive orientation, while guilt, involving as it does the transgression of a boundary, reflects an active one. Freud's attention to aggressive and libidinal wishes, and the consequent retaliatory response of the superego (castration anxiety and Oedipal resolution), linked guilt much more explicitly to conflict psychology. Since psychoanalysis has evolved so clearly as the study of intrapsychic conflict, and guilt results from the conflict between unbridled libidinal and aggressive wishes and the fear of superego punishment, guilt has become a major leitmotif in pschoanalytic study.

Shame, on the other hand, does not so clearly reflect internal (intersystemic) conflict, resulting, as I have argued, from failure to attain a superego goal or ideal (i.e., a goal of the self). Successful attainment of a goal generates pride, or enhanced self-esteem.[2] I have suggested that

_____

[2] However, the notion that shame results from failure by no means excludes the

these goals and ideals are frequently internalized, just as libidinal or aggressive impulses are internal. However, the frequent linkage of shame to external expectations by many psychoanalytic writers has caused it to seem more superficial and socially embedded, less a product of internal forces, than is guilt. For these reasons classical psychoanalysis has contributed less to the psychology of shame (see Levin, 1967, 1971; Wurmser, 1981, for exceptions) than have some other authors.

In addition, because of the individual propensity to hide and withdraw in the face of shameful feelings, they have been less easy to identify and analyze than have been guilt feelings. Quoting Tarachow, Levin (1967) states that "guilt feelings bring material into the interview, shame keeps it out." Thrane suggests that guilt seeks confession, and for that reason guilty thoughts or actions are frequently brought into analysis or psychotherapy, as the patient seeks forgiveness from the therapist. Shame feelings are more painful and repugnant, leading to the intimate danger of exposure. At risk in the exposure of shameful feelings to the analyst is rejection and abandonment (Levin, 1967); the hope in sharing shame feelings is to attain acceptance and understanding. In the Western, Judeo-Christian and male-dominated ethos of psychoanalytic therapy, forgiveness may seem more easily attainable than acceptance. As Schecter (1979) remarks aphoristically, "there is no problem so great as the shame of it."

The Ideal Self and Shame

In this section, I shall reconsider the constructs ego ideal and superego, and their relationship to the ideal self, suggesting that the ideal self is a more useful concept than ego ideal in assisting our understanding of shame. As already indicated, Freud did not significantly clarify the ego ideal construct, or its relationship to the other functions of the superego. Subsequent work by Hartmann (1950) and Jacobson (1954) more sharply delineated the concepts of self and ego. Jacobson (1964) also considered

presence of conflict in its genesis. Consider, for instance, the conflict inherent in prioritizing the goals of the self. Also, failure to attain the perfectionistic goals of a grandiose self may reflect internal prohibitions against unbridled ambitions. The guilt-shame cycle of Piers is relevant here to demonstrate interaction between the two affects. However, the conflict attending shame is intrasystemic, whereas the conflict of guilt is ubiquitous, more globally intersystemic.

the ego ideal, viewing it as a "'pilot' and 'guide' for the ego." Other writers (e.g., Hartmann and Loewenstein, 1962; Reich, 1954, 1960) have attempted to elaborate the ego ideal and to differentiate it from super-ego, sometimes embedding the former as one function of the latter. In general, the ego ideal has been viewed as the set of goals, values, and esteemed objects towards which the ego strives. The superego, on the other hand, represents the conscience, and as such stands as judge, persecutor of the ego. When viewed as part of the superego, the ego ideal represents internalization of valued objects' goals and ideals through the mechanism of *introjection*. Sandler et al. review the development of the ego ideal in Freud's writings, pointing to conflicts which suggest that this construct first refers to the individual's ideal for himself (efforts to regain infantile narcissism), then to the "conscience," (superego), and finally to the introjected parental ideals. It becomes what Schafer (1960) calls the loving and beloved superego, or what Schecter (1979) refers to as the "comforting modality of the superego" in contrast to the "persecuting" functions of the (judgmental) superego so clearly delineated by Freud.

Sandler et al. identified the ideal self as a self-representation which reflects "desired shape of the self—the self-as-I-want-to-be." As suggested above, there may be conflicts of choice between various shapes of the ideal self at any given moment. The authors also suggest that failure to attain the given goals of the ideal self may lead to lowered self-esteem and shame.

In two recent papers, Schecter (1974, 1979) has grappled with the concepts of ego ideal and ideal self, and their relationship to shame. Speaking of an ideal, Schecter describes "the ultimate perfect shape—or structure—of the wish on the one hand, and of the cultural imperative on the other. As the self and object-person become organized in experience and in our mental representations, they soon come to be comparatively monitored as to what the self and other ought to be like in their most perfect form" (1974, p. 104). About the ideal self, Schecter suggests that it "may come to have dimensions of activity (vs. passivity), intense stimulation (vs. an impoverishment of stimulation), playful, masterful body and mental activities, loving forms of relatedness—and more—all of which become organized as ideal states, images or concepts yet to be achieved" (1974, p. 111). In his second paper, Schecter advances as a major goal of psychoanalysis a modification of the superego structure through "1) a mellowing and taming of the harshness of the persecuting superego combined with more realistic standards; and 2) a growth and development of the loving superego in the direction of a greater strength and protectiveness, especially in relation to the persecuting superego." Schecter suggests that this superego modification is attained in analysis through assistance in forgiving the self or other "to give up his chronic resentment, his reproachfulness and harsh irrational claims against himself or the other, as emotional debtor or creditor; in short to forgive." Modell (1976) also suggests similar therapeutic actions in modifying the strictures of the harsh superego.[3]

How does this discussion help us in our effort to differentiate the ego ideal from the ideal self? While they are closely related, the ego ideal represents, I suggest, the classification of goals, ideals, and valued object representations which the patient internalized as a check-list against which to compare himself. The ideal self, on the other hand, is the more subjective, less specific and cognitive, sense of self, towards which the individual aspires with regard to ideals and standards.[4] Schecter (1979, p. 368) uses the metaphor of "the North Star which guides and orients us though we cannot expect to actually reach it." The North Star analogy represents, I suggest, the ego ideal, while the subjective sense of how closely one approximates that beacon's direction represents the ideal self. I will use the ideal self representation as a goal, with failure to attain it reflecting the subjective sense of self-defect and shortcoming so central to the experience of shame.

Contributions of Heinz Kohut

From any initial perspective in the assessment of Kohut's contributions, his emphasis on the central role of the self must be viewed as the essential ingredient (Kohut, 1971, 1977). I shall deal briefly with Kohut's own definition of self—briefly, because Kohut himself does not spend

---

[3] Following my earlier differentiation between the palliative goals in reparation of guilt and shame, I suggest that the loving superego seeks more appropriately to accept rather than to forgive the self for falling short of its ideals, and that psychoanalytic therapy can help to strengthen the loving superego through modifying, making more flexible and less rigid, the goals and aspirations of the ego ideal.

[4] Schafer (1967) emphasizes that ideal self refers to a self-representation which is "an image or concept of oneself as one would be if one had satisfied a specific ideal."

much time on attempting a definition. In discussing the endstage of analysis—the termination phase Kohut comes closest to a definition of the self as "a center of productive initiative—the exhilarating experience that I am producing the work, that I have produced it" (1977, p. 18). Thus, the self as a center of initiative is a subjective representation, linked as it is by Kohut to the "exhilarating experience" of action.[5] However, throughout this work he goes no further in attempting to define the self, and at the end he states, "My investigation contains hundreds of pages dealing with the psychology of the self—yet it never assigns an inflexible meaning to the term self, it never explains how the essence of the self should be defined" (1977, p. 310). He offers a definition in a narrow sense, as a "specific structure in the mental apparatus," or a broader one, as "the center of the individual's psychological universe." It is in the latter sense, as the center of the subjective, experience-near attributes of individual identity, that I shall use the term.[6]

In his 1966 paper, Kohut discusses shame in relationship to the ego ideal. At this stage in the development of his views on narcissism, he still works within the framework of structural and drive psychology. He sees the ego ideal as "related to drive control," while the narcissistic self is the source of ambition, the wish "to be looked at and admired" (1966, p. 435–6). Later he states, "Shame, on the other hand, arises when the ego is unable to provide a proper discharge for the exhibitionistic demands of the narcissistic self" (p. 441). The shame-prone individual is ambitious and success-driven, responding to all failures (in the pursuit of moral perfection or external success) with shame.

In 1972, Kohut mentions the relationship of shame to exhibitionistic libido and defective body parts; suicide and disturbance in libidinal cathexis of the self; defect in the omnipotent grandiose self; and the response of insatiable rage to narcissistic injuries. He comes closest to the themes elaborated in this paper by stating, "The most intense experiences of shame and the most violent forms of narcissistic rage

---

[5]The reader will note the similarity of Kohut's definition of "self" to that of Lewis cited above.

[6]Again, it is striking that Kohut follows his statement about the ambiguity of the self concept by indicating that "I admit the fact (i.e., that the self is not knowable in its essence) without contrition or shame." This is the closest that Kohut himself comes in the 1977 work to linking self with shame.

arise in those individuals for whom a sense of absolute control in an archaic environment is indispensable because the maintenance of self-esteem—and indeed of the self—depends on the unconditional availability of the approving-mirroring functions of an admiring selfobject or on the ever-present opportunity for a merger with an idealized one.''

However, Kohut does not further elaborate the place of shame in the constellation of self-psychology, an elaboration which is attempted in the present paper. In subsequent sections, I shall consider the relationship of shame to the following constructs of Kohut: the Bipolar Self (grandiosity and the idealized parent imago); defensive and compensatory structures; mirroring and idealized selfobjects; the self in relation to ambitions and goals and ideals; Guilty vs. Tragic Man; and the self in the transference. I shall not attempt to evaluate the theoretical soundness of self psychology, or to establish whether in fact it represents a substantive difference from or break with classical theory. Others have recently attempted this (e.g., Friedman, 1980; Rothstein, 1980). Rather, I shall review the relationship of shame to self psychology, as an example of the application of Kohut's work to an important clinical phenomenon. Part of an assessment of the usefulness of any theoretical framework must include its capacity to clarify or amplify our understanding of such phenomena.

The *Bipolar Self* is a construct central to Kohut's theoretical system, encompassing as it does much of what has preceded in the evolution of self psychology. The Bipolar Self refers to Kohut's assertion that "the child has two chances as it moves toward the consolidation of the self"—two chances, that is, in the establishment of a healthy, cohesive self; severe self pathology occurs only when both of these opportunities fail to provide adequate experiences. Kohut continues (1977, p. 185), "The two chances relate, in gross approximation, to the establishment of the child's cohesive grandiose-exhibitionistic self (via his relation to the empathically responding merging-mirroring-approving selfobject), on the one hand, and to the establishment of the child's cohesive idealized parent-imago (via his relation to the empathically responding selfobject parent who permits and indeed enjoys the child's idealization of him and merger with him), on the other." In essence, then, the two chances for development of self-cohesion arise either early, usually with the mother, relating to adequate and empathic mirroring in response to the exhibitionistic self; and later (ages 3–6), usually with the father, reflecting empathic acceptance of the child's "voyeuristic" idealization and wish for merger. Put differently, Kohut suggests (1977, p. 190) that between the two poles of the self, a tension arc exists, an "action-promoting condition" between a person's ambitions (relating to adequate mirroring by the early selfobject), and his goals and ideals (developed later in relationship to the empathic, idealized selfobject). Success in traversing at least one of these encounters with the empathic selfobject is a prerequisite for the development of a cohesive, non-fragmented nuclear self. Implicit in the model of the Bipolar Self is the concept of a "second chance" at self-development; if the mirroring selfobject fails, some of the damage may be compensated for by the empathic idealized selfobject later on.

What constitutes pathology of the nuclear self in terms of exhibition-istic and idealizing needs in relation to the selfobject and how does it arise developmentally? According to Kohut (1977, pp. 3–4), there are defects in the early development of psychological structure of the self, and secondary structures related to the primary defect—the defensive and compensatory structures. A defensive structure functions to cover over the self's primary defect, whereas the compensatory structure strives to compensate for the defect. Thus, the compensatory structure attempts to make up for a weakness in one pole of the self (usually, in the area of exhibitionism and ambitions) by increasing self-esteem through the pursuit of ideals. Pseudovitality in a narcissistic patient may be defensive against (i.e., attempt to hide) "low self-esteem and depression—a deep sense of uncared-for worthlessness and rejection, an incessant hunger for response, a yearning for reassurance" (1977, p. 5).[7]

Kohut goes on to relate the primary structural defect in the nuclear self to the genetic failure of the mother as selfobject in mirroring the child's healthy exhibitionism; defects in the self's compensatory struc-tures frequently reflect failure of the father as selfobject in responding to the child's idealizations (1977, p. 7). Again, we see the first pole in self-formation (ambitions-exhibitionism, the nuclear self) occurring early, the second pole (ideals-voyeurism, the compensatory structures)

---

[7]This description by Kohut of a narcissistic personality disorder fits well, I suggest, the psychodynamics of manic-depressive illness. I believe that shame is a central affect for the manic-depressive, which the manic flight attempts to hide through fan-tasied merger with the ideal self.

occurring later in development. The process of psychoanalytic treatment becomes, then, either reparation of the self's nuclear defect through repeated transmuting internalizations (within the analytic context, through transference to the mostly-empathic analyst as a responsive selfobject); or through modification of the compensatory structures, by establishing more flexible and realistic ambitions, goals, and ideals. Central to my discussion of shame is modification of grandiose ambitions and/or the ideal of perfection which may occur through identification with the accepting empathic selfobject/analyst.

Kohut's psychology also explicates the steps necessary for the development of a firm nuclear self through merger with the empathic selfobject; "empathic merger with the selfobject's mature psychic organization and participation in the selfobject's experience of an affect signal instead of affect spread; . . . (and) need-satisfying actions performed by the selfobject" (1977, p. 87). In other words, the selfobject (parent) must meet the needs of the infant/child by affirming (mirroring) the child's healthy exhibitionism and/or by allowing for merger/identification with his own mature, empathic self. According to Kohut, defects which represent self pathology reflect inadequacies in the structure of the parent's self, which deprive the child of phase-appropriate adequate merger (through inadequate mirroring or idealization). Reparation through psychoanalysis occurs when the analyst provides a context of empathic mirroring, and allows for optimal idealization. Adequate nuclear self structure can be built anew, or adequate compensatory structure created, through exploration and interpretation of the perceived empathic micro-failures by the analyst, allowing for the transmuting internalizations and structure-building necessary to strengthen the patient's self.

One final point in self psychology is relevant to my subsequent discussion—Kohut's suggestion of the two major forms of self pathology. The most severe form of self-pathology is disintegration and fragmentation of the self (see 1977, pp. 76-77, 120–121); the second is emptiness, enfeeblement, and depletion of the self. Although Kohut is ambiguous on this point, I suggest that disintegration of the self reflects pathology from earlier major empathic failures of the selfobject—inadequate mirroring of the exhibitionistic self and its ambitions. Depletion of the self tends to reflect later problems with the compensatory structures, and deficiency in the responsiveness of the idealized selfobject to the voyeuristic goals and ideals of the self. Such a distinction (i.e., between mirroring/affirming and idealized selfobject functions) cannot be made too arbitrarily, in that less severe frustration of exhibitionistic needs and ambitions can stimulate development of compensatory structures (e.g., formation of ideals) rather than causing primary defects of the nuclear self (see below).

This formulation assumes that there is a severity gradient in disorders of the self, with disintegration/fragmentation representing the most severe, primitive degree of pathology. Kohut has equated the depleted self with "empty depression" (1977, p. 243); he states (1977, pp. 241–2), "And . . . there are others, who despite the absence of neurotic conflict, are not protected against succumbing to the feeling of the meaninglessness of their existence, including . . . the agony of the hopelessness and lethargy of pervasive empty depression . . ." That depletion (empty depression) reflects, I suggest, not the primary defect of a fragmented, disintegrated self, but failures in the compensatory structures, in the absence of goals and ideals. In his discussion of the case of Mr. M., Kohut supports this assumption of a relation between the "genetically later" failure of compensatory structures and "the father's selfobject function as an idealized image" (1977, p. 7). The absence of ambitions, goals and ideals as a result of failure in selfobject responsiveness, and subsequent failure in compensatory structures, is the primary source of self-depletion.

How does this brief review of Kohut's recent contributions help us in our understanding of the psychology of shame? I suggest that shame is an emotion experienced in relation to self-critical judgments, to failures and defects of the ideal self, and as such is specifically relevant to self psychology and to a thorough understanding of the narcissistic character. I hope that this paper will further delineate the importance of shame within the system of self psychology.

Shame and the Psychology of the Self

In Kohut's 1977 book, there is only one indexed reference to shame (that relating to narcissistic rage). However, throughout the book there are descriptions of the self and of self pathology which relate to the experience of shame (and related phenomena of humiliation, despair, mortification, lowered self-esteem and lethargy). For instance (italics mine), "The unresponded-to self has not been able to transform its archaic grandiosity and its archaic wish to merge with an omnipotent selfobject into *reliable self-esteem,* realistic ambitions, attainable goals" (1977, pp. 81–2);

A psychology of the self will be most important and most relevant whenever we scrutinize those states in which experiences of *disturbed self-acceptance* and/or of the fragmentation of the self occupy the center of the psychological stage (as is the case par excellence with the narcissistic personality disorders) (1977, p. 94); . . . and the success or failure of our libidinal and aggressive pursuits may result in changes of *self-esteem,* which manifested as the triumph of victory (heightened self-esteem) or as the *dejection of defeat (lowered self-esteem)* may in turn become important secondary forces on the psychic stage (1977, p. 97); Still, because the repressed content is not the same in the two classes of disorders—incestuous drive-wishes vs. fear of punishment (castration anxiety) in the one; the needs of a *defective* self vs. the avoidance of the mortification of being re-exposed to the narcissistic injuries of childhood in the other. . . . (1977, p. 137); the experiences that relate to the crucially important task of building and maintaining a cohesive nuclear self (with the correlated joy of achieving this goal and the correlated *nameless mortification* . . . . of not achieving it) and, secondarily, to the experiences that relate to the crucially important striving of the nuclear self, once it is laid down, to express its basic patterns (with the correlated triumph and *dejection* at having succeeded or failed in this end) (1977, p. 224);

and finally,

. . . . the struggle of the patient who suffers from a narcissistic personality disorder to reassemble himself, the despair—the *guiltless despair,* I stress, of those who in late middle age discover that the basic patterns of their self as laid down in their nuclear ambitions and ideals have not been realized. . . . This is the time of utmost hopelessness for some, of utter lethargy, of that depression without guilt and self-directed aggression, which overtakes those who feel that they have failed and cannot remedy the failure in the time and with the energies still at their disposal. The suicides of this period are not the expression of a punitive superego, but a remedial act—the wish to wipe out the *unbearable sense of mortification and nameless shame* imposed by the ultimate *recognition of a failure* of all-encompassing magnitude (1977, pp. 238, 241).

I submit that these quotes from Kohut utilize the language of shame as described earlier: 'self-esteem'', "disturbed self-acceptance'', "dejection of defeat'', "defective self'', "mortification of being exposed'', "guiltless despair'', "hopelessness'', "lethargy'' and finally, "nameless shame imposed by the ultimate recognition of a failure of all-encompassing magnitude." Although only in the last quote does Kohut directly identify shame as the emotional experience of the narcissistic personality disorder, I suggest that it is the language of shame which permeates his work.

How does Kohut believe that psychoanalysis can overcome the shame experience of the fragmented or depleted self?

> This working-through process begins in most instances with the mobilization of archaic needs for mirroring and for merger; as working through is maintained, it gradually transforms the patient's ideas of archaic greatness and his wishes for merger with the omnipotent objects into healthy self-esteem and wholesome devotion to ideals" (1977, p. 150).

Thus, the analyst mobilizes the patient's primitive (previously unresponded-to) needs for mirroring, merger, and idealization through the process of "protracted emphatic emersion" (1977, p. 302) and, through transmuting internalizations provided by interpretations of the microempathic failures of the analyst, solidifies and nurtures the patient's self, heals and modifies his ambitions, goals and ideals to conform to his talents and abilities. In the language of this paper, the patient cures and reduces his shame through attainment of a cohesive, plentiful self which allows for self-acceptance, and so attains believable acceptance by the selfobject/analyst.

Several questions remain in our study of shame and its relationship to self-pathology. First of all, is the experience of shame the same for the patient with disintegration anxiety (the more primitive narcissistic personality disorder) and the one with depletion anxiety (the less severely impaired narcissistic character)? I suggest that a certain level of attainment of self cohesion is necessary in order to experience shame. Kohut states (1977, p. 191),

> I suggest that we first sub-divide the disturbances of the self into two groups of vastly different significance; the primary and the secondary (or reactive) disturbances. The latter constitute the acute and chronic reactions of a consolidated, firmly established self to the vicissitudes of the experiences of life, whether in childhood, adolescence, maturity, or senescence. The entire gamut of emotions reflecting the states of the self in victory and defeat belongs here, including the self's secondary reactions (rage, despondency, hope) to the restrictions imposed on it by the symptoms and inhibitions of the psychoneuroses and of the primary disorders of the self.

I believe that shame deserves a prominent place in the list of the self's secondary reactions. However, the experience of shame requires a certain degree of self-cohesion to register nonresponsiveness of a self-object, failure in attainment of a goal, disappointment with regards to ideals, or even to bodily functions. A self that is disintegrating or fragmenting does not have the energy or luxury to register shame, but rather is overwhelmed with panic and boundary diffusion.

As a "secondary reaction" of the self, I believe that shame is a prominent response to the failure of a compensatory self structure. The reader will recall that Kohut defined "compensatory structure" as attempting to compensate for a defect in the self (in contrast to a defensive structure, which attempts to cover over the primary self defect). One characteristic example of compensatory structure offered by Kohut is the enhancement of self-esteem through the pursuit of ideals. From my earlier discussion of shame, failure in attaining an ideal goal is a major precipitant to shame, with the concomitant threat of rejection or abandonment by the "significant object." This threat of abandonment or rejection may also reflect an earlier experience of failed responsiveness (e.g., affirmation or mirroring) by the parental selfobject to the self's healthy exhibitionistic attempts. Such defeat of healthy exhibitionistic strivings may lead to compensatory creation of ideals, aimed at reversing the perceived disinterest and apathy of the parental selfobject. In this way, defensive strivings may be transformed into compensatory structure in healthier narcissistic patients. However, recurrent failure in attaining responsiveness from the selfobject to the idealized quest for merger will lead to a sense of emptiness, depletion and despair. In this sense, shame becomes a response to failure in attaining the goal of the ego-ideal, or in the language of this paper, a response to a defect in the ideal self.

Kohut speaks of self pathology in terms of disintegration and depletion anxiety. Although he does not say so, I suggest that depletion anxiety is the product of less severe self pathology, the result of a failure of the "more or less" cohesive self, and thus a failure of a compensatory structure to attain an ideal, including the ideal of gaining for the striving self the admiration/mirroring of a responsive selfobject. Shame, then, can be understood as one reaction to failure in the self's quest to gain responsiveness/affirmation by the selfobject, or to generate ideals. It reflects the subjective experience of the defeated self depleted of energy, falling short of attaining ambitions and ideals. Within Kohut's framework, we have arrived at the complement in self-esteem, the hallmark of shame in the previous writings cited above.

If the reader accepts my suggestion that shame reflects self depletion—failure to attain ambitions and ideals—we must address the relationship between shame and depression. I have already considered Kohut's statement of the "guiltless despair" resulting from the self's failure to realize its ambitions and ideals. He indicates the relationship of self depletion to the depression of middle life over failure to attain the goals of the nuclear self. Bibring (1953) also relates depression to decrease in self-esteem.[8] The reader will recall that Lewis, in her discussion of shame and field-dependency, related shame to depression in the field-dependent patient (Lewis, p. 55).

Thus, Kohut's (and Bibring's) explanation of depression is complementary to that of classical conflict-drive theory, suggesting an alternate view within the theoretical framework of self-psychology—that there is a close relationship between shame and depression (through depletion of the nuclear self, failure of the ideal self); and that, for some patients (e.g., those suffering from narcissistic personality disorders) the relationship of depression to failure in attaining ambitions and ideals may be most compelling.

When considered in the context of self psychology, must the experience of shame be relegated only to those patients suffering from the (relatively serious) personality disorder of narcissism? Certainly, we know that all individuals, including the relative healthy (possessors of a firmly cohesive "nuclear self"), suffer at times from the affect of shame (especially, as Lewis has described, those who are relatively field-dependent). I suggest that shame in healthy people can also be understood in terms of micro-failures of the (relatively differentiated) ideal self. Put another way, the ideal self is a construct relevant to the neuroses as well as to more primitive psychopathology. At issue here

---

[8] Bibring's discussion of depression is very closely related to Kohut's notion of depletion of the self, and the failure to attain ambitions and ideals. While he does not explicitly discuss shame, Bibring approximates the conceptualizations of this paper when he states, ". . . the depressions sets in whenever the fear of being inferior or defective seems to come true, whenever and in whatever way the person comes to feel that all the effort was in vain, that he is definitely doomed to be a 'failure' " (p. 25). Again, he states "In depression, the ego is shocked into passivity not because there is a conflict regarding the goals, but because of its incapacity to live up to the undisputed narcissistic aspirations" (p. 30).

is the intensity and magnitude of failure, not the existence of failure in affirmation of ambitions and development of attainable ideals. When viewed from the perspective of self in the "broader" sense, we can understand that failures in attaining aspirations of the ideal self need not necessarily reflect severe psychopathology.

Guilty Man vs. Tragic Man

Kohut has recently designated the individual suffering from pathology of structural conflict as Guilty Man, contrasting with major self pathology as Tragic Man. "I identify these (two directions of man's functioning) by speaking of *Guilty Man* if the aims are directed toward the activity of his drives and of *Tragic Man* if the aims are towards the fulfillment of the self" (1977, p. 132). He amplifies that, because of enviromental pressures and inner conflict, Guilty Man is often unable to achieve his goals. So too, Tragic Man frequently fails to attain the goals of his nuclear self in terms of self-expression and creativity. About Guilty Man, Kohut asserts that "the end result remains that of classical analysis: a conception of man as endowed with either a well-functioning or a malfunctioning psychic apparatus—of man spurred on by his drives and shackled by castration anxiety and guilt" (1977, p. 233). However, to understand Tragic Man, the constructs of self psychology are needed:

Nuclear ambitions and ideals are the poles of the self; between them stretches the tension arc that forms the center of the pursuits of Tragic Man. . . . The psychology of the self is needed to explain the pathology of the fragmented self (from schizophrenia to narcissistic personality disorder) and of the depleted self (empty depression, i.e., the world of unmirrored ambitions, the world devoid of ideals)—in short, the psychic disturbances and struggles of Tragic Man (1977, p. 243).

If guilt is the dominant experience of man suffering from the structural disorders, are we not justified in considering shame (and the previously mentioned related phenomena) as the major affect of Tragic Man, particularly of the depleted self, suffering as it does, in Kohut's terms, the empty, guiltless depression of the self with unmirrored ambitions, and devoid of ideals? I have suggested that patients suffering from fragmentation and disintegration of the self (i.e., schizophrenics, borderlines, and severe narcissistic personality disorders) are too overwhelmed, devoid of a registering and firm self, to readily experience shame. Their experience is more appropriately the nameless terror and panic of psychosis. However, I have argued that the gradient of failures of the less primitive narcissistic disorders in attaining ambitions, objects, and ideals (relating to the experience of depression and depletion of the self) generates in such patients the affect of shame—shame at the failure to realize ambitions, to gain response from others, at the absence of ideals. While shame and guilt coexist for these patients (through the guilt-shame cycle of Piers), *shame* remains a distinguishing affective experience for them, the heathier representatives of Kohut's Tragic Man.

Shame and Narcissism

In the epilogue to his 1977 work, Kohut makes the interesting suggestion that problems of the self (i.e., narcissistic problems) are increasing in current western society, while problems of inner structural conflicts are decreasing. Some observers have argued that there is not an absolute increase in narcissistic disorders, but rather that these disorders are being more frequently and correctly identified. Whatever the statistical truth on this question will prove to be, it is certainly true that psychoanalysis is accepting more frequently for its specialized treatment patients who suffer disordered narcissism (patients whom Kohut designated as suffering from pathology of the nuclear self). He suggests that this shift in the increase of narcissistic problems reflects understimulation of children by the emotional life of their parents in contemporary society, while previously they were more frequently overstimulated. Overstimulation due to parental over-closeness led to the structural disturbances of neuroses, and reflected parental acting out of their own neurotic conflict (1977, p. 273). On the other hand, "understimulation due to parental remoteness that is a pathogenic factor in disorders of the self is a manifestation of a disorder of the self in the parent" (1977, p. 274). Again, ". . . . the child's essential loneliness, i.e. . . . neither the child's pridefully offered exhibitionism nor enthusiastically expressed idealizing needs had been phase-appropriately responded to and that the child, therefore, becomes depressed and lonesome. Such a child's self is psychologically undernourished and its cohesion is weak" (1977, p. 275).

Thus, in Kohut's view, parental self pathology (i.e., narcissistic disorder) generates self pathology in the child, through insufficient mirroring and inadequate response by the selfobject to idealization. The child, then, evolves without adequate response to his ambitions and ideals, and frequently develops with impoverishment, depletion of his nuclear self. While an argument can be offered in favor of over-stimulation as a source of certain narcissistic pathology, this paraphrasing of Kohut describes, I suggest, the more frequent pattern and dilemma of the narcissistic character treated currently in analysis. Such patients present with a grandiosity which defensively covers an emptiness of self, an absence of attainable ambitions, sustaining ideals, or meaningful affirming personal relations, making them resistant to traditional psychoanalytic treatment.

Further, I suggest that shame is one of the dominant, excruciatingly painful experiences of such patients. Encumbered with grandiose fantasies which have been unmodified through empathic, realistic responses by a sustaining selfobject, these patients face repeated failures to achieve their (unrealistic) ambitions. They feel empty and worthless, because their world is so devoid of sustaining objects and ideals. As we have seen earlier, their shame is experienced in relation to repeated failure to realize their exhibitionistic, grandiose ambitions: to the emptiness (depletion) of their self with regard to ideals; and failure too in their attempt to establish close, meaningful interpersonal relationships. The shame over this emptiness and repeated failure is accompanied by depression, but too often it is only the depression which is treated, and not the concomitant shame which leads to it. In essence, these are individuals who cannot attain even a modicum of self-acceptance, who cannot believe that anyone else could possibly accept them, for all their emptiness and failure at their own self-appointed, grandiose life tasks. This lack of acceptance by self and others is, I suggest, a central narcissistic dilemma; relates to the deeply felt shame of the narcissistic patient; and should be a target in treatment of the narcissistic personality.

Psychoanalytic Treatment of Shame

A long discourse on the psychoanalysis of shame is also beyond the scope of this paper, and must await further elucidation. Let me return to Kohut, however, to offer an explanation of the psychoanalytic process. "In my view, then, the essence of psychoanalysis lies in the

scientific observer's protracted empathic emersion into the observed"
i.e., the inner life of man, "for purpose of data-gathering and observation" (1977, p. 302). Since empathy is so central a construct to Kohut's
psychology, let us review his definition of that capacity; "our ability to
know via vicarious introspection—my definition of empathy. . . . —
what the inner life of man is, what we ourselves and what others think
and feel" (1977, p. 306).

As the finale to this consideration of shame and its relationship to
failures and depletion of the self, I wish to suggest, along with Levin
(1971, p. 361), that the careful analysis of shame should be one of the
major goals of the analytic process. Protracted empathic emersion into
the feeling state of any patient (but particularly into the world of the
narcissistic patient) will unveil deep and painful shame feelings. These
are often difficult to detect, for many defenses are directed at covering
over shame experiences, and the defects, failures, and emptiness which
engender them. However, their discovery, examination, working
through the patient, and the ultimate realization that the analyst and
patient alike can accept them, represent a major curative factor in each
and every successful analysis. In achieving this goal, the analyst should
be helped and guided by his own recognition, through the vicarious
introspection of empathy, of his own failures to achieve goals, to realize
ambitions and ideals, of his own defects—in short, the analyst must be
willing to face and acknowledge his own shame, and the pain which
accompanies it.

Many have argued that the tenets of self psychology can be well
integrated into the theoretical framework of classical psychoanalytic
theory. However, with regard to the affective experience of shame, it
seemed that structural theory could not completely encompass and
explain its importance, particularly in the narcissistic patient's psychopathology. Unlike guilt, which can be understood in terms of the conflicting vectors of traditional metapsychology, shame can best be appreciated as a reflection, not of conflicting drives, but of passive failure,
defect, or depletion. Heuristically, then, I have chosen to view shame
within the context of self psychology and the ideal self.

Shame is the affective response to falling short of a goal, to failure,
to defect, to depletion of ideals. Shame motivates the individual to
cover up, to hide, to withdraw. As guilt motivates the patient to confess,
shame motivates him to conceal—for this reason, shame has been less

richly evaluated in psychoanalytic literature, and less frequently dealt with in psychoanalytic therapy. For guilt, the antidote is forgiveness; shame tends to seek the healing response of acceptance—of the self despite its weaknesses, defects, and failures. A lack of self-acceptance underscores the distress of the depleted, empty depressed narcissistic patient—which Kohut calls the patient's "guiltless despair"—and the selfobject/analyst must strive to facilitate self-acceptance through his own protracted empathic emersion into the patient's psychological depths.

Our inquiry has unearthed areas which require further study. A definitive historical review of the self-concept has been long overdue. The relationship of shame to manic-depressive illness, guiltless depleted depression reflecting lowered self-esteem, and the depression of women in current western society require further examination. Elaboration of shame with regard to the related phenomena of humiliation, mortification, remorse, apathy, embarrassment, and lowered self-esteem is a necessary task. And finally, a technical exploration of the psychoanalysis of shame has yet to be undertaken in the context of Kohut's contributions. I hope that this exploration will stimulate further work on these important issues.

REFERENCES

Bibring, E. (1953). The Mechanism of Depression. In Greenacre, P., *Affective Disorders*. New York: International Universities Press.

Erikson, E. H. (1950). *Childhood and Society*. New York: Norton.

Freud, S. (1914). On narcissism: an introduction. *S.E.* **14.**

Freud, S. (1923). The ego and the id. *S.E.* **21.**

Freud, S. (1930). Civilization and its discontents. *S.E.* **21.**

Freud, S. (1933). New introductory lectures on psycho-analysis. *S.E.* **22.**

Friedman, L. (1980). Kohut: A book review essay. *Psychoanalytic Quarterly* **XLIX,** 393–422.

Hartmann, H. (1950). Comments on the psychoanalytic theory of the ego. *Psychoanalytic Study Child,* **V,** 74–96.

Hartmann, H. and Loewenstein, R. (1962). Notes on the superego. *Psychoanalytic Study Child,* **XVII,** 42–81.

Hazard, P. (1969). Freud's teaching on shame. *Naval Theologique et Philosophique,* **25:** 234–267.

Jacobson, E. (1954). The self and the object world: vicissitudes of their infantile cathexis and their influences on ideational and affective development. *Psychoanalytic Study Child.* **IX,** 75–127.

Jacobson, E. (1964). *The Self and the Object World.* New York: International Universities Press.

Kohut, H. (1966). Forms and transformations of narcissism. *Journal of the American Psychoanalytic Association,* **14,** 243–272.

Kohut, H. (1971). *The Analysis of the Self.* New York: International Universities Press.

Kohut, H. (1972). Thoughts on narcissism and narcissistic rage. *Psychoanalytic Study of the Child,* **XXVII,** 360–399.

Kohut, H. (1977). *The Restoration of the Self.* New York: International Universities Press.

Levin, S. (1967). Some metapsychological considerations on the differentiation between shame and guilt. *International Journal of Psycho-Analysis,* **48,** 267–276.

Levin, S. (1971). The psychoanalysis of shame. *International Journal of Psycho-Analysis,* **52,** 355–362.

Lewis, H. B. (1971). *Shame and Guilt in Neurosis.* New York: International Universities Press.

Lowenfeld, H. (1976), Notes on shamelessness. *Psychoanalytic Quarterly,* **45,** 62–72,

Lynd, H. M. (1958). *On Shame and the Search for Identity.* New York: Harcourt Brace and World.

Modell, A. (1976). The holding environment and therapeutic action. *Journal of the American Psychoanalytic Association,* **24,** 285–307.

Piers, G. and Singer, M. (1953). *Shame and Guilt.* New York: W. W. Norton.

Reich, A. (1954). Early identifications as archaic elements in the superego. *Journal of the American Psychoanalytic Association,* **II,** 218–238.

Reich, A. (1960). Pathologic forms of self-esteem regulation. *Psychoanalytic Study of the Child,* **XV,** 215–232.

Rothstein, A. (1980). Toward a critique of the psychology of the self. *Psychoanalytic Quarterly,* **XLIX,** 423–455.

Sandler, J., Holder, A., and Meers, D. (1963). The ego ideal and the ideal self. *Psychoanalytic Study of the Child,* **XVIII,** 139–158.

Scarf, M. (1980). *Unfinished Business.* Garden City: Doubleday.

Schafer, R. (1960). The loving and beloved superego in Freud's structural theory. *Psychoanalytic Study of the Child,* **XV,** 163–188.

Schafer, R. (1967). Ideals, the ego ideal, and the ideal self. In Holt, R. *Motives and Thought: Psychoanalytic Essays in Honor of David Rapaport. Psychological Issues,* **5,** 131–174.

Schafer, R. (1976). *A New Language for Psychoanalysis.* New Haven: Yale University Press.

Schecter, D. (1974). The ideal self and other. *Contemporary Psychoanalysis,* **10,** 103–115.

Schecter, D. (1979). The loving and persecuting superego. *Contemporary Psychoanalysis,* **15,** 361–379.

Sederer, L. and Seidenberg, R. (1976). Heiress to an empty throne: ego-ideal problems of contemporary women. *Contemporary Psychoanalysis,* **12,** 240–251.

Thrane, G. (1980). Shame and the construction of the self. *Annual of Psychoanalysis,* **VII,** 321–341.

Weissman, M. (1980). The epidemiology of depression in women. Presented at the 133rd Annual Meeting of the American Psychiatric Association, San Francisco.

Wurmser, L. (1981). *The Mask of Shame.* Baltimore: Johns Hopkins University Press.

PART IV

Diagnostic and Therapeutic Applications

Part IV presents diagnostic and therapeutic applications. Two papers reflect diagnostic applications. Bursten (Ch. 15) offers a characterological categorization of different narcissistic personality types, having first divided character diagnosis into complementary, narcissistic, and borderline types. "Narcissistic characters" are broadly defined in terms of their quest to achieve "the bliss and contentment characteristic of the primary narcissistic state" through reunion of the self with an all-powerful, nourishing object. Thus, Bursten's view is similar to the object-relations perspective offered by Rothstein (Ch. 12), but is further distinguished by personality subtypes, from the most primitive to the most mature. The *craving personality* is clinging and demanding of support by others, lacking energy to function without satisfaction of these needs; the *paranoid personality* is hypersensitive, suspicious, jealous, self-important, and blames others; the *manipulative personality* attempts to influence others to do things his way, and tends to feel satisfied if he "puts something over" on the other; the *phallic narcissistic personality* tends to show off, exhibit clothes, manliness, or sexuality, and to radiate arrogance. These subtypes are then compared in terms of "the mode of narcissistic repair, the degree of selfobject differentiation, and the value system."

Bursten indicates that the narcissistic mechanism of repair in each type relates to ridding the self of shame (see Ch. 15). Bursten aims at integrating libidinal, object-relations, and affectual components into a character typology which attempts at developmental and diagnostic clarity. Meissner (Ch. 16) looks at many of the same issues, again within a diagnostic framework, but this time with an emphasis on differences between narcissistic and borderline personalities. Meissner makes use of Bursten's classification, emphasizing the phallic narcissist's underlying sense of inferiority and shame through identification with a weak father, with compensation through arrogance, and expectation of acclaim from the analyst for his own therapeutic efforts. Manipulative patients utilize contempt in their exploitation of others in an attempt to externalize their shame. They, then, are highly dependent on their victim, and strongly resemble the antisocial personality. In general, Meissner views the patients' object relationships as the main locus of their narcissistic pathology (see Chs. 9-12), as in the craving personality's demand to be given to by the significant object. Meissner then elaborates the transferences formed by, and the quality of self cohesion in, narcissistic personalities from a perspective consistent with Kohut. He evolves a helpful differentiation between narcissistic and borderline personalities in terms of the organization of introjects, reflecting "the quality of a developmental experience, particularly in the crucial rapprochement phase."

These related diagnostic frameworks might usefully be compared with the nosology of Kohut and Wolf (Ch. 7), whose paper was included under the section "Self" because of its elaboration of self-psychology, but which could as well have been considered under diagnostic applications. For example, is the "mirror-hungry personality" similar to the "craving personality" of Meissner and Bursten? Does the "overstimulated self" have elements of the "manipulative and phallic-narcissistic personalities" in terms of use of objects? Such comparisons bring to the fore the relationship of object relations and representations in classical theory to the function of the selfobject in self psychology. The relationships and differences between object representations and self-object functions are at the core of the question of separate or unified developmental lines of narcissism, as articulated by Kohut and negated by many of his critics.

In the final paper, therapeutic applications are specifically considered. Bromberg (Ch. 17) writes, rather optimistically, from an interpersonal (i.e., Sullivanian) perspective, suggesting that the analytic (or therapeutic) setting must meet the patient's shifting need for affirmation in order to lead to personal growth. With Modell (Ch. 11) he sees detachment and unrelatedness as the essence of narcissistic pathology, reflecting an attempt to maintain structural stability of the self by denying dependency on the other. Rigid interpretation of transference resistance is experienced as attack by such patients, and Bromberg emphasizes the analyst's contribution to a facilitating climate of affirmation *and* anxiety which invites openness to the therapeutic encounter. He sees therapy moving, within an interpersonal context, from acceptance and affirmation exclusively, towards more interpretation and confrontation as the relationship begins to unfold. Thus, Bromberg emphasizes the interpersonal setting of analysis and therapy, and, unlike Kohut, views the evolution of a meaningful interactive relationship between patient and therapist as central to the success of treatment. This position differs also from that of Kernberg and other object representation rather than its interactive qualities.

15. Some Narcissistic Personality Types

Ben Bursten

I

Human beings appear in such a rich assortment of personalities that attempts to classify them into types are difficult and must be to some degree arbitrary. Our classifications are based on our observations, but what we observe, what we attend to and how we see it depend on our theoretical assumptions and our particular interests. This was true of the ancient humoral classification of temperament based on blood, phlegm, and yellow and black bile; it is equally true of modern approaches, such as Fromm's (1947) receptive, exploitative, hoarding, marketing and productive types, and Riesman's (1950) tradition-directed, inner-directed, and other-directed types.

If, indeed, our categories depend in great measure on the orientation from which we start, why is it so important that we categorize? At least two reasons come to mind; some ordering is necessary for us to cope with, or even to retain, the vast variety of personality data, and classification enables us to relate one set of observations to another and to apply to a new situation the knowledge gained from a former one.

In psychoanalytic thought, too, evolution of our theoretical concepts has led to changes in our categorization. The early characterology emphasized the stages of libidinal development as a basis for classification. Freud (1908, 1913) and Abraham (1921, 1924a, 1925), for example, stressed the instinctual underpinnings of character structure. In his 1913 paper, Freud acknowledged the incompleteness of a theory resting on only the stages of development of the libido; however, the corresponding phases of ego development were yet to be charted, for example by Erikson (1950).

As our understanding of the ego evolved, particularly with the formulation of the structural theory (Freud, 1923), other bases for classifying character arose. Fenichel (1945, pp. 470 ff.), for example, described sublimative and reactive character types, and he separated the latter into pathological behaviour towards the id, which leaned heavily on the stages of libidinal development, pathological behaviour towards the superego and pathological behaviour towards external objects. That this is essentially an ego classification can be recognized when we recall that these three targets of pathological behaviour constitute the 'dependent relationships of the ego' described by Freud in 'The Ego and the Id'. And as early as 1916, Freud had described some character types representing not libidinal fixation points (the relationship to the id), but in large measure the relationship to what was later to be called the superego.

In 1931, although Freud utilized structural concepts in his characterology, his biological orientation impelled him to maintain that 'if we confine our effort to setting up purely psychological types, the libidinal situation will have a first claim to serve as a basis for our classification'. Accordingly, he described narcissistic, obsessional and erotic types as well as mixtures of these three types. More recently, however, character classification based on stages of instinctual development does not seem to be fashionable. While Hartmann (1952), in discussing ego formation, proposed an *enlargement* of our scope from only considerations of instinctual development to include considerations of aggression and 'the partly independent elements in the ego', nowadays we seem to hear more about the latter considerations and less about the former. indeed, some analysts seem to have all but repudiated the importance of instinct theory as out of date. Guntrip (1969, p. 124) maintains that 'a dynamic psychology of the ''person'' is not an instinct-theory but an ego-theory, in which instincts are not entities *per se* but functions of the ego . . . Instinct-theory *per se* becomes more and more useless in clinical work, and ego-theory more and more relevant'. And Kernberg (1970a), in his valuable contribution to characterology, rejects a classification based on the stages of libidinal development. The libidinal components he employs are conceived of as 'levels' of instinctual development: genital, pregenital, and a pathological condensation of genital and pregenital with a preponderance of pregenital aggression.

In part, this underplaying of instinctual theory is due to some very solid advances in ego psychology. However, I cannot escape the concern raised by Stein (1969), who points out that, even among analysts, repression of instinctual life may affect our observations and our study of character differences. And I believe that, in contrast to ego theory, instinct theory is most vulnerable to such repression.

The issue may be further clarified by referring to the distinction between the aim and the object of an instinct (Freud, 1905, 1915). The aim of an instinct is satisfaction and its expression has reference to various bodily zones. The object, not originally connected to the instinct, 'becomes assigned to it only in consequence of being particularly fitted to make satisfaction possible' (Freud, 1915, p. 122). Hoffer (1952) has warned us about the importance of keeping this distinction in mind. In terms of the present discussion, I am suggesting that instinctual development, as characterized by its aim, is of basic importance in the understanding of variations in character. I do not imply that objects, ego organization, superego considerations, etc., all of which have their instinctual aspects, are of lesser importance; they are of great significance, but not to the exclusion of aims.

II

We may approach the subject of narcissistic personality types through Freud's (1914) two categories of object choice—narcissistic and anaclitic. The term 'narcissistic object choice' is generally well accepted; it refers to an object who represents what the person is, was in whole or in part, or would like to be. Oremland & Windholz (1971) discuss the narcissist as one whose relationships are characterized by a sense of identity with himself. As Pulver (1970) indicates, there is no implication that the narcissist does not relate to others; rather it is the type of relationship—one characterized by seeing himself in the other person—that is important.

The term 'anaclitic' is, as Eisnitz (1969) points out, out of date, in that it refers to an earlier concept of instincts. What then shall we call the other type of object choice? Eisnitz suggests Freud's synonym, 'attachment'. I hesitate to adopt this term; it suffers from the same theoretical difficulty as 'anaclitic'. Further, it is ambiguous—what could be more attached than an object seen as a part of or extension of oneself? Other sets of terms, such as 'narcissistic v. object love' or 'narcissistic personality v. transference neuroses' are also ambiguous. As we have seen, narcissists do love objects, although the objects represent the narcissists themselves. And in psychoanalysis, narcissists do form a transference along the particular lines of their type of object relationships, although identification might be a better term than transference. Thus I choose the term 'complementary relationship' to denote the other type of object choice. This term implies a fitting in with the person's needs and yet a sense of separateness from the other person which the narcissistic relationship lacks.

Now the separation of persons with complementary object relationships (complementary personalities) from narcissistic personalities is based on object choice, not instinctual aim. When Freud (1914, p. 88) differentiated these two types of relatedness, he disclaimed that he was proposing a character typology: 'We have not, however, concluded that human beings are divided into two sharply differentiated groups, according as their object choice conforms to the anaclitic or the narcissistic type; we assume rather that both types of object choice are open to each individual, though he may show a preference for one or the other.' However, later in the same paper he mentioned certain kinds of people, such as criminals and humorists who 'compel our interest by the narcissistic consistency with which they manage to keep away from their ego anything that would diminish it' (p.89). When a narcissistic preference reaches such a consistency that it dominates the ego's repertoire of defences and adaptations, it may fairly be called a character type. And subsequent writings (Freud, 1931; Kernberg, 1970b; Kohut, 1971) have distinguished a type of person called a 'narcissistic personality'.

Narcissistic personalities are distinguishable not only from complementary personalities, but also from people with borderline personalities. And here again, the chief element in the distinction is not the instinctual aims but consideration of the objects—or more properly, the internalized object representations. The borderline personality has a less cohesive self; he is easily subject to fragmentation. Likewise, the boundary between himself and others is less clear. The narcissistic personality may have transient episodes of fragmentation, but he more readily recovers his sense of self (Kohut, 1971, pp.1 ff.).

Thus the broad group of narcissistic personalities may be distinguished, with reasonable if imperfect clarity, from complementary personalities on the one hand and borderline personalities on the other. Kernberg (1970a), Frosch (1970) and Kohut (1971) among others have elaborated on the distinguishing characteristics; I shall touch only very briefly on them here.

In contrast to borderline personality, the narcissistic personality has a firmer sense of self, feels (and is) in less danger of fragmenting and has a better sense of reality testing. As Kohut (pp. 11 f.) has pointed out, narcissistic concerns, such as grandiosity and the need for omnipotent others are prominent in borderline personalities, but the 'narcissistic structures . . . are hollow . . . brittle and fragile'. While the narcissistic personalities have a firmer, more cohesive and stable ego organization than borderline personalities, they are not so able to separate themselves from others as are complementary personalities. This is seen, of course, in the narcissistic object choice—a reflexion or extension of the narcissist, himself, with little ability to respect the object as a person in his own right. The cohesiveness of the ego is firmer in the complementary personalities; repression rather than splitting is a fundamental defence mechanism, and complementary personalities are not subject to the fleeting, psychotic-like regressions which are experienced by narcissistic personalities. Complementary personalities are guided more by guilt; narcissistic personalities, more by shame. We may view narcissistic personalities, then, as more or less intermediate between borderline personalities and complementary personalities, and, as we shall see when we examine the gamut of narcissistic personalities, they tend to merge with these other groups at the ends of the range.

We may look at one other distinguishing aspect—that which Frosch (1970) calls 'the nature of the conflict and danger' and I shall call the task of the character structure. The primary task of the complementary personality is to resolve Oedipus complex—to combat the castration fear and overcome the guilt. The main task of the narcissistic personality is to achieve the bliss and contentment characteristic of the primary narcissistic state, and this implies the reunion of the self which must be very grand with an object which must be nourishing and powerful (Rado, 1928; Lewin, 1950; A. Reich, 1960). Self-esteem, the approval of others and the confirmation of one's sense of worth by the ability to use others are as I have described elsewhere (Bursten, 1973, pp. 100 ff.), derivatives of the earliest narcissistic state. The primary task of the borderline personality is to prevent disintegration and dissolution. It may be seen to be related to the task of the narcissistic personality, for dissolution and psychic death is, in a sense, a return to the primary undifferentiated state. However, the narcissistic personality is governed by a need to satisfy the later derivatives of this primary state (Kohut, 1966); the borderline personality must struggle to prevent a regression towards the primary state itself.

I should point out here what may be a difference in emphasis between my formulation and that of Kohut (1971, pp. 15 ff., 152 f.). He speaks of the 'central vulnerability' of narcissistic personalities as the danger of fragmentation or disintegration when the narcissistic relationship is ruptured. Nonetheless, narcissistics have a resilience which borderline personalities lack and they tend to 'snap back' and repair their narcissism. Thus I think of their fragmentation as a consequence of the failure of the central task—the reunion. Whereas the threat of fragmentation is central (in the sense of exerting a prominent influence upon the character traits) in the borderline patient, I emphasize the threat of the rupture of the narcissistic relationship as central to the narcissistic personality.

These three broad personality groupings, then, are distinguishable primarily by criteria other than the instinctual aims to which I referred in the first section of this paper. Nonetheless, instinctual aims are important also. Complementary personalities have a primary task related to the oedipal phase of development. Borderline and narcissistic personalities have tasks expressive of orality. The role of the instincts in the differentiation of borderline from narcissistic personalities is more obscure, possibly because this differentiation occurs in a period when ego and id are so intertwined that it is difficult for us to separate the instinctual components from the more easily understandable ego components.

I shall not linger further over the differentiation of these three groups. Early in life a course seems to be set for the establishment of personality type according to one of these three categories. Let us turn now to the group of narcissistic personalities to examine the particular character types within this group.

III

In the course of my work at a U.S. Veterans Hospital I have had the opporunity to observe a large number of narcissistic personalities. I have seen them in the context of the social situation of a psychiatric ward, in the context of direct interviews with them, and through the eyes of psychiatric residents under my supervision. I have been fortunate to have been able to supplement these 'direct' observations with material from my psychoanalytic work with each of the narcissistic personality types I shall describe shortly with the exception of the paranoid personality. I draw my material from a predominantly male population; nevertheless, I believe that the formulations to be presented here are generally applicable to women as well as to men.

From these observations, I have come to classify four types of narcissistic personalities—the craving, the paranoid, the manipulative and the phallic narcissistic personalities. These are not necessarily new classifications, although some of them do not exactly coincide with classifications of the current psychiatric nomenclature. These personality types can often be distinguished on clinical grounds and I shall describe some of their more obvious features at this point.

The craving personality includes many people who have been called 'dependent' or 'passive aggressive'. Indeed, their interpersonal relationships are characterized by the need to have others support them. They are clinging, demanding, often pouting and whining. They act as though they constantly expect to be disappointed, and because of their extraordinary neediness, disappointment comes frequently. When not given to, they often seem to lack the energy to function, except for the function of increasing their demands in obvious or subtle ways. In social situations, some of these people seem quite charming and lively; however, one can often discern a certain desperation behind their charm, and their liveliness has a driven quality. Others are less socially inclined; they may cling to one person, or to a very small group of people. The essential features of their personalities can often be seen in their marriages. Even in those cases where they seem to function adequately at their jobs, they collapse at home unless their wives give them a great deal of attention.

I do not feel that 'dependent' or 'passive aggressive' really grasps the essential feature of this personality. Like Rosenfeld (1964) and Kernberg (1967), I doubt whether these people can be dependent. It is precisely because they cannot depend on anyone that they are so clinging. But I have still another reason for rejecting these terms. Among many of our psychiatric colleagues, there seems to be an inordinate fear of patients' dependency needs or attempts to be passive. Activity (of a socially approved type, of course) and independence are highly valued. These psychiatrists view the therapeutic situation as a struggle in which the therapist must constantly try to force the patient to be independent. 'Dependency' and 'passive-aggressiveness' play into this struggle.

A better term was suggested to me by one of my patients. I was talking about his constant state of neediness and he corrected me. 'Neediness,' he said, 'it isn't just neediness. It's craving. I'm like a little bird with a wide-open beak.'

The clinical features of the paranoid personality are well described in the *Diagnostic and Statistical Manual of Mental Disorders* (American Psychiatric Association, 1968):

This behavioural pattern is characterized by hypersensitivity, rigidity, unwarranted suspicion, jealousy, envy, excessive self-importance, and a tendency to blame others and ascribe evil motives to them.

These people are not psychotic. They should be differentiated from those patients with paranoid states (Cameron, 1959), who are delusional. Much of the literature on paranoid conditions refers to paranoid schizophrenia on the one hand and paranoid states on the other. These psychotic conditions occur when there is a failure of the more usual copying mechanisms; in the paranoid personality there is no such failure. In fact, many paranoid personalities lead active and productive lives—especially in vocations where scepticism, suspiciousness and criticism are important components. Often these people are litigious. They are generally argumentative. Their anger runs the gamut from querulousness and scepticism to jealous rages.

The manipulative personality has been previously described by me (Bursten 1972, 1973, pp. 153 ff.). This personality type includes some, but not all, persons generally known as 'anti-social personalities' or 'sociopaths'. I find the current designations inadequate because they rely on a combination of psychological and sociological criteria. Too often the diagnosis is made on the basis of a record of repeated offences and conflicts with the law. The clinical features of the manipulative personality centre around manipulativeness, whether in the context of socially approved activities as in the case of some businessmen and administrators, or otherwise as in the case of confidence men.

I define manipulation in a restricted way (Bursten, 1973, pp. 8 ff.). It is an intrapsychic phenomenon and thus is independent of whether the manipulation succeeds. The manipulator perceives that another person's goal conflicts with his own, he intends to influence the other person and employs deception in the influencing process, and he has the satisfying feeling of having put something over on the other person when the manipulation works. These components of manipulation are readily available to consciousness; the manipulator knows what he is doing. This criterion excludes a great many behaviours which other psychiatrists term 'manipulative'. The mere fact that a person's actions influence another to treat him in a certain way does not constitute manipulation. Indeed, wherever one person is expressive and another empathic, influence is likely to occur. It is the conscious existence of these four components—conflict of goals, intention to influence deception, and the feeling of putting something over—which comprise manipulation.

In addition to his central feature of manipulativeness, the manipulative personality is characterized by a propensity for lying (deception), little apparent guilt transient and superficial relationships, and considerable contempt for other people. Some of these people are aggressively antisocial. Because they repeatedly get into trouble it has been felt that they do not learn from experience. Cleckley (1959) wrote: 'The psychopath often makes little or no use of what he attains as a result of deeds that eventually bring him to disaster.' In order to understand the manipulative personality, we must focus not on the obvious rewards of his manipulations, but on the inner compulsion to manipulate.

The phallic narcissistic personality has been described by W. Reich (1933, pp. 200 ff.), although he includes a wider variety of personalities in this category than I do. These are the 'men's men'. Often they are called 'passive-aggressive'. They parade their masculinity, often along athletic or aggressive lines. In common with some manipulative personalities, they tend to be both exhibitionist and reckless. While the exhibitionism of the manipulative personality tends more to call attention to his 'good behaviour' and reputation, the phallic narcissist tends more to show himself off and to exhibit his body, clothes, and manliness. The manipulative person is more reckless in his schemes, deceptions and manipulations; the phallic narcissist tends more towards feats of reckless daring, such as driving automobiles at excessive speeds, in order to prove his power. Many phallic narcissistic men seem to have a dual attitude to women. On the one hand, they talk about them in the contemptuous terms of locker-room language. On the other hand, they are the defenders of motherhood and the sanctity of women.

This personality type is not limited to men, although, because of the nature of my work, I have seen many more men than women. Phallic narcissistic women are often confused with hysterical women because of their narcissistic exhibitionism. Like their male counterparts, they tend to be very conscious of their clothes, cars, etc. They are usually much colder and haughtier than hysterics. Arrogance, above all, is a feature of phallic narcissism.

The relationships of these personality types to each other have particularly attracted my interest. I shall discuss these relationships along three dimensions—the mode of narcissistic repair, the degree of self-object differentation, and the value system.

It is the dimension of the mode of narcissistic repair which brings considerations of instinctual aims to the forefront. To understand this, we must return to the chief task of the narcissistic personality as outlined above. The primary narcissism of the undifferentiated state sets the tone for this task. As the infant develops and his mental apparatus begins to differentiate, the basic pattern takes on instinctual and ego aspects. Lewin's (1950) oral triad describes the instinctual component; the ego components are self-esteem and the affects—anxiety and depression when the instinctual aims are thwarted and self-esteem falls, and bliss, contentment and elation when the instinctual aims are gratified and self-esteem is maintained or restored (Bibring, 1953; Rapaport, 1959). Rado's (1928) formulation of the reunion of the self with the nourishing breast is a crucial part of this pattern having both instinctual aspects (oral gratification) and ego aspects (reunion and fusion of self and object representations). Complete fusion, of course, expresses the state of primary narcissism; secondary narcissism is built on reunion. The ability to obtain oral gratification is the basis for self-esteem and the grandiose self; the notion of powerful and nourishing breast with which to unite is the basis for the omnipotent object, or idealized parent imago. The development of these two aspects of narcissism has been set forth in detail by Kohut (1966, 1971). As the child grows older, the nature of the reunion takes on different colorations. The basic narcissistic pattern, however, is laid down in early infancy. It is not simply a fixation on the oral level. From the instinctual side, the vicissitudes of early orality are very important; the frustrations and disappointments due to inadequate and unempathic mothering (Jacobson, 1946; Kohut, 1971, pp. 63 ff.) set the stage for susceptibility to narcissistic wounds. The ego aspects of this drama—reunion, self-esteem, and the affects— set the stage for the narcissism itself, and the subsequent measures which will be employed to sustain and restore it.

For the person with a narcissistic personality, then, the essential task is that of maintaining and restoring the self-esteem which accompanies the reunion of a grandiose self representation with an omnipotent object representation. The manner in which these four personality types go about this task is what I call the mode of narcissistic repair—'repair' because their narcissism is so vulnerable that keeping it in repair is a lifetime project. And, if one listens very carefully to the complaints offered by all of these types, they have a common underlying theme of having been disappointed and betrayed by someone who was not powerful enough or ready enough to give when they needed it.

The mode of narcissistic repair employed by the craving personality is so beautifully illustrated by my patient's comment. When in danger, he opens his beak ever wider. Here we can see very clearly the instinctual component of the character trait. The craving personality must be fed. He is devastated if supplies and nourishment are not forthcoming, and with the expression of his predominantly oral orientation, he sucks harder, and sometimes he bites and grasps. He does this not only for the instinctual satisfaction of being fed. His libido is also pressed into the service of narcissistic repair. While he is unfed, his self-esteem suffers; where is his specialness and where are the nourishing objects? Reunion is effected mainly by crying out, 'I'm hungry!, I'm starving!'

Let us look now at the role of aggression in the narcissistic repair. All narcissistic personality types are capable of flying into cold rages; they have this capability in common and it may represent a regression to a diffuse infantile rage in the face of severe feelings of narcissistic injury. However, the role of aggression is seen to be different among the various types when the wound is not so great as to call for the rage; when the aggressive discharge is modulated it becomes admixed with the libidinal elements of the narcissistic repair. Such admixture has been described by A. Freud (1949). In the case of the craving personality, we see pouting and sulking. Adatto (1957) has described the oral nature of pouting. It is essentially an inactive form of angry appeal for supplies. No work is done on the object or the world in order to bring about satisfaction. Some psychiatrists, following the transactional method of analysis, refer to this behaviour as extremely manipulative; however, several patients have made it clear to me that they do not see themselves playing an active part in the process (Bursten, 1973, pp. 58 ff.). One woman had a prolonged sulking attitude toward her mother. When the mother gave her a casserole dish as a present, she was delighted until her husband revealed that he had told the mother that she had needed a casserole dish. This spoiled the whole gift—it had to come spontaneously in response to her needs; it lost its value if she (or her husband) played an active role in getting it. This is the difference which Freud (1911b) distinguished in this manner:

[The infant] betrays its unpleasure where there is an increase of [internal] stimulus and an absence of satisfaction, by motor discharge of screaming and beating about with its arms and legs and then it experiences the satisfaction it has hallucinated. [That is, mother, realizing the baby is hungry, feeds it.] Later, as an older child, it learns to employ these manifestations of discharge intentionally.

Pouting and sulking, while more modulated, have much of the aspect of expressions of discomfort rather than intentional demanding.

The same process was shown by another craving patient. He had moved in with his girl friend and he fully expected that she would work, and that their combined income would be supplemented by her parents—regardless of the fact that they disapproved of their daughter's living with this man. He just could not understand why money was not forthcoming. On an intellectual level, he could see the problem, but it was clear that it had no real meaning to him. As time went on and no money arrived, he pouted and ran out of energy. Increasingly, he expected his girl-friend to anticipate his demands in some empathic way. For example, he would lie on his bed hoping the girl would perform fellatio. Seeing his unhappiness, she would ask what she could do for him. This made him furious. He felt she should know without his having to tell her.

The needs and demands of the craving personality can drain the object dry. This clinging attitude has been described by A. Freud (1949) as a fusion of erotic and aggressive tendencies on the anal level. 'Whoever has dealt with toddlers knows the peculiarly clinging, possessive, tormenting, exhausting kind of love which they have for their mothers, an

exacting relationship which drives many young mothers to despair.'
While this behaviour must, of course, wait until the infant is more
mobile, there is much here to suggest oral grasping and greed. I suggest
that these are orally tinged behaviours rather than anal ones. They suck
their mothers dry, and they hold on to the external object rather than
retain or expel an internal one. As one patient put it, 'I've gone through
two women now who have said, "I've taken, taken, taken, and I've
given nothing".' And while he could understand their complaints intellectually, he really could not grasp why he was so unlucky that he
couldn't find a 'loving' woman.

One further clinical vignette, this time from a joint interview with a
hospitalized patient and his wife, will illustrate the aggressive and receptive aspects of the sulking. This patient was describing his temper—
he got so angry sometimes, particularly when his authority as a father
was challenged, that he wouldn't speak to any of the family for several
days. He and his wife were groping for the right word to express the
anger. I said, 'It sounds like you're sulking.' Both of them seized the
word; that was exactly it. The wife went on to say that she was the one
who had to stop the sulk—by apologizing, by offering him sex, or by
being especially nice to him.

The sulking and complaining of the craving personality takes on a
much more hostile tone in the paranoid personality whose mode of
narcissistic repair is expressed through argumentativeness, jealousy
and critical suspiciousness. As I mentioned earlier, these people are
not psychotic, nor is this personality type necessarily the forerunner of
paranoid psychotic conditions.

Like all narcissistic personalities, they feel a sense of disappointment
and betrayal by those whom they felt had the power to give to them
when they were in need. With paranoid personalities, one does not have
to listen very hard to hear the complaint of betrayal. It is apparent in
their jealousy and suspiciousness. Much of the critical attitude of this
type of person says, 'Why does he get things and I don't? And he
doesn't even deserve it.' Although Jacobson (1971, p. 315) says that
none of her paranoid patients 'ever complained about having felt "betrayed" by his parents', I have seen several such patients, some of
whom were so bitter that they refused to have anything to do with their
parents.

We can hardly talk about the mechanisms used by paranoid personalities without at least a brief discussion of the content underlying the argumentativeness, etc. In the first place, content and form (mechanism) are interwined; secondly, Freud's (1911a) classic formulation in the Schreber case of the content of the mechanisms in paranoia cannot be overlooked. In this formulation, the projections served as a defence against homosexual impulses. As White (1961) observed, although Freud spoke of the paranoia as a fixation on the narcissistic level of libidinal development, his was essentially a negative oedipal formulation. Knight (1940) and Bak (1946) emphasized the anal aspects of paranoia especially in regard to its sadomasochistic features. White, in my view quite correctly, pointed out the oral underpinnings of the conflict in terms of fusion with the mother. And, if we examine the case material presented by Knight and Bak we can easily see the reunion fantasies which underlie the homosexual urges. Bak presented his patient's dream, just prior to his paranoid episode, where he 'resolved the differences with his father and at the final reconciliation, they wept'. This led to feelings of great power. Knight described his patient's feeling that he had a brilliant mind (grandiose self); he and Knight would sit together at seminars and exchange knowing nods (reunion with powerful object). The homosexual aspect of the suspiciousness and anger both in paranoid psychoses and paranoid personalities derives in great part from the need to reunite with a powerful and nourishing figure. In the paranoid psychotic, such a reunion would be a fusion which risks the dangerous loss of ego structure. In the paranoid personality, such a reunion should fortify the narcissism as it does in the craving personality.[1] His complaints and jealousy portray his need to be the special selected one. Why, then, does he struggle against this reunion by suspicion, criticism, and arguing? These manoeuvres only drive people away. And how do such manoeuvres serve to repair and maintain his narcissism?

Whether it be a reunion with the representation of the father with its homosexual implications or a reunion with a representative of the mother with implications of weakness and/or incest (and usually it is both), the narcissistic personality struggles against it because of shame.

---

[1] This distinction is, of course, overdrawn for purposes of illustration. Some of the dynamics of the paranoid personality's struggle against reunion are also seen in the case of the paranoid psychotic.

Fantasies of humiliation, embarrassment, and mortification are common. Shame is the enemy of the grandiose self and it makes the narcissist feel unacceptable to the omnipotent object. Thus, the task of the narcissistic repair mechanism is to be rid of the shame.

The narcissistic repair mechanism of the paranoid personality, then, is involved in getting rid of his shame—or more nearly correctly, his shameful self concept. Waelder (1951) provides us with an important key to understanding this mechanism: paranoia rests on denial. The patient is making a statement, albeit in the negative. He is saying, 'I do not love him or her' and 'I am not shameful'. The simple statement does not suffice; externalization and projection are necessary. Thus the statement 'I am not shameful' becomes 'he or she is shameful'. The instinctual aspects of this mechanism are eliminative. Jacobson (1946) has shown that the forerunner of this mode is disgust, spitting and vomiting. That which has been taken in is thrown out again and devalued. As anal erotism gains primacy, the expulsion of faeces serves as the vehicle for getting rid of the worthless material. And, as Jacobson (1957) points out, denial is a relatively primitive mechanism, developed when thinking tended to be very concrete. Thus spitting and defecation could well serve as the basis for the expulsion of a shameful introject (Abraham, 1924b; Rosenfeld, 1964) and the denial and projection of a shameful self-concept.

Now the paranoid psychotic can sufficiently distort reality to cement his conviction; the paranoid personality must continually work at this mode of supporting his narcissism. Thus he is critical, argumentative, suspicious, and he constantly looks for signs of shameful conduct in others, both as a public repudiation of his own inner feelings (Waelder, 1951) and as external affirmation and support of his projections.

Jacobson (1971, pp. 302 ff.) has described another feature of paranoid patients which dovetails with this formulation: they often betray their former allies by playing other people off against them. My own observations of several paranoid personalities confirm her findings. The patient, ashamed of his subordinate and sometimes masochistic or passive homosexual position with one ally, will form a new alliance by helping the new friend hurt, and sometimes ruin, the old. This clearly shows the use of the paranoid criticism as a means of effecting a union (or in narcissistic terms, a reunion) with the anticipated source of power. It is a way of saying, 'Don't classify me with the bad guys—I'm one of the good guys like you.' It is also eliminative as the patient has literally got rid of the 'bad guy'—the projected image of his shameful self.

With one paranoid personality, the eliminative mode was very graphic. Time after time, he could make new friends, only to become quickly 'disillusioned'. He would then devalue his 'friend' and complain about him to others in the most faecal terms. On one occasion, he defecated into a box, wrapped it and sent it to a man with whom he had had a falling out.

Another narcissistic patient who was not predominantly a paranoid personality had been in analysis with me for several years. He had been quite unable to express any strong affect or acknowledge that there was anything more than a kind of intellectual collaboration between us.

The patient had a strong identification with his mother who was crippled. From her wheelchair, she had wielded enormous influence, however, and, in the manner of many mothers of narcissists, she exploited her son. He was her legs; he pushed her chair, opened doors for her, and ran her errands. Although he realized his resentment of this role, any move toward independence caused him enormous anxiety; he was certain his mother could not survive if he were severed from her.

As he began to become more acutely aware of this theme, and more particularly, as he became aware of its reactivation in the transference, he found it harder and harder to ignore me. When the next opportunity for self-assertion presented itself, he could no longer employ his usual passivity. Instead he became paranoid, not in a psychotic way but in the manner of a paranoid personality. This period was ushered in by his report of a fantasy of being on a podium where he was supposed to give a speech. Instead of words, he threw little pellets of faeces at the audience and laughed at them. 'Wait!' he said, becoming my intellectual collaborator again, 'that's defensive. I feel humiliated so I humiliate them.'

In the ensuing weeks he was argumentative and critical and he saw exploitative motives in everyone. Toward the end of this period, he pondered whether he could ever respect me. At first he said he could not because it was too risky to have feelings towards me; I might exploit and betray him. Then he revised his reason. 'I can't drop my contempt for you,' he said. 'If I do, I'll feel humiliated with my little penis. I'll just be a shitty little boy.' The danger of loving me made him feel weak, homosexual and shitty—truly a cripple. It was this shit which he expelled by projecting (throwing) it on to others. They were the devalued ones—and at the same time exploitative (a reprojection of the introject of his crippled mother).

It is not diffficult to see the aggression fused with the eliminative mode of narcissistic repair used by the paranoid personality. Both Knight (1940) and Bak (1946) have described the anal-sadistic aspects of the paranoid mechanisms; they need no further comment here.

Now you will recall Jacobson's (1971, pp. 302 ff.) reference to the fact that paranoid patients often betray their former allies by setting up a situation where others will harm them. These 'schemes' come very close to manipulations, and in a conceptual way, can be seen as a bridge between paranoid and manipulative personalities. Contempt and devaluation, so prominent in the paranoid personality, is also a central feature of the manipulative personality, although it is perhaps more subtle. The mode of narcissistic repair of the manipulative personality is 'putting something over' on the other person. I have described this mechanism in detail elsewhere (Bursten, 1973, pp. 97 ff.). I shall sketch it briefly here. Putting something over involves contempt and a feeling of exhilaration when the deception succeeds in making the manipulation work. The instinctual component of the contempt is that described for the paranoid personality. It is a purging of a shameful, worthless self-image and its projection on to the victim. The exhilaration is the elation of the reunion fantasy when the 'cleansed' self is now glorified and powerful. As a manipulative analysand put it, his parents expected him to put up a good appearance—which he interpreted as being clean and not obviously aggressive. He was plagued, however, with inner feelings of worthlessness. One day he felt particularly dirty. 'The problem, I guess, is how to get rid of all that shit without letting on,' he said. 'That's what I do, I play tricks on them and they never really know they got shit on.' And a few days later, when he was feeling exceptionally successful he recalled with great exhilaration a childhood fantasy of lying in bed waiting for the sky to open up and God to take him. He shouted, 'I'm the *one,* the brains, the best.'

Thus the manipulative personality, while employing the eliminative mode of the paranoid personality, keeps up appearances by attenuating his aggression and applying it to being clever and tricky. He also enters more actively into competition with his victim. While the paranoid inclines toward destruction, the manipulator leans toward proving his superiority (and acceptability for reunion) by defeating the other person. Thus, in the manipulative personality, we see not only the eliminative mode, but also some phallic themes.

These phallic themes occupy centre stage, of course, in the phallic narcissist. His sense of shame often comes from an identification with a father whom he felt was weak. One of my patients 'saw through' his father's self-assurance; it was really his mother who wielded the power in the family. He was very moved and upset one day when he happened to see a former radio announcer who had been a boyhood idol of his. The announcer looked old, dissipated, and beaten down while his wife still had youth and verve. This scene was called to mind again and again in the analysis. The shame of being weak is repaired by arrogance, self-glorification, aggressive competitiveness and pseudo-masculinity. The body, representing the phallus, is adorned with clothes and sometimes with insignia. Phallic narcissistic personalities, even more than manipulative personalities, are risk-takers, often engaging in foolish acts of 'bravery.' A. Reich's (1960) formulation describes the narcissistic repair mechanism. Constantly in fear of the shame of castration, these men deny the shame and unconsciously fantasy they have the greatest phallus possible. (Here, I insert a step: the disappointing father representation is also denied.) As his megalomanic self-image is reunited with the fantasied giant phallus of the father, nothing can stop him. He is powerful and is protected by a powerful, benevolent fate. Greenacre (1945) speaks to the same point when she points out how these risk-takers feel they will be miraculously saved.

When we turn to the area of selfobject differentiation we begin to clarify a remark I made earlier. You will recall that I stated that early in life a course seems to be set for one of the three broad personality types. With regard to the narcissistic group, this course has its instinctual roots in early orality, although, as we have seen, it is modified by contributions from later libidinal stages as well. From the ego side, the processes of separation and individuation described by Mahler (1967) play a major role. Mothers of narcissistic patients, in varying degrees, have difficulty in letting their children separate. Their own narcissism so influences the child's object relations throughout his infancy that the libidinal stages take on the coloration of narcissistic object relationships. Lichtenstein (1964) describes the situation thus: the infant's primary identity is set down in the earliest attempts to emerge from the symbiosis. The mother serves as a mirror showing the infant what he is supposed to be. This same mother will bring her influence to bear throughout his infancy and the later transformations of his sense of identity will become variations on the theme of the primary identity.

Thus we may postulate that all narcissistic personalities share common features in the relationships of their separation-individuation process. However, there must also have been some differences among them which are reflected in the four personality types. Perhaps we might say that narcissism is the primary identity while the four types are variations on the theme.

It is my impression that the craving personality most often exhibits manifest features of symbiosis. The clinging and desperate seeking show the need for actual physical proximity. Some of these patients show 'as if' types of relationships. Others crumble and are literally lost (with no self) if left alone. One of my patients could not function when her husband went to sleep. She demanded he stay up (not necessarily actually to help her) until her work was finished.

I believe that paranoid personalities represent features of negativism seen when the infant has begun actively to disengage from the mother–child symbiosis (Mahler & Gosliner, 1955). The effect of the paranoid behaviour is to wall the patient off from someone toward whom he is drawn. This disengagement process can be seen in Jacobson's (1971, pp. 302 ff.) descriptions of how paranoid patients become disenchanted with their former allies and betray them.

The manipulative personality is more secure in his separation; he does not have to try so hard. Thus, he has more energy available for doing work in the world, and concomitantly, his appreciation of reality is firmer. A good manipulator can size up a situation and move people around in such a manner that his own wishes are gratified. The process of individuation and firmness of self can be seen in the area of suggestibility and influence (Bursten, 1972, pp. 81 ff.). The craving personality tends to be more suggestible; having no firm sense of self, when he empathizes with others, he cannot relinquish the trial identification (Fliess, 1942) and he becomes the other person. The successful manipulator has a firmer sense of self; he can relinquish the trial identification involved in sizing up a situation and use the knowledge gained from it to influence others.

Phallic narcissists seem even more firm in their sense of self. While still maintaining a predominantly narcissistic orientation, as W. Reich (1933, p. 201) noted, 'they often show strong attachments to people and things outside.' There is a greater admixture of complementarity in the phallic narcissist than in the other narcissistic personality types, and this reflects their greater degree of individuation. The need to be admired as a competitor reflects the reunion motif and the earlier symbiosis where the infant can exist only in conjunction with a mother; however, whereas the craving personality needs this relationship almost continuously and on a direct basis, the phallic narcissist has more successfully internalized his sources of approval. While he still needs external sources of flattery, he can also flatter himself. In both personality types we can see evidence of mirroring as described by Elkisch (1957). However, the quality of the mirroring in the craving personality is much closer to the direct mirroring of the infant. The phallic narcissist can often carry his mirror around with him. He is also freer to work, to perform, to compete and then to check with his mirror, because his sense of self is not so urgently dependent on the mirror.

Let us now briefly consider the four personality types from the point of view of the value system. In our discussion of the mode of narcissistic repair we encountered the shame and humiliation of being weak. Bibring (1953) indicated that the basic problem of self-esteem in the infant is the shock of helplessness in the face of needs which are frustrated. All subsequent conditions of helplessness or diminution of his sense of power will injure his self-esteem.

I have only fragmentary data relevant to how this paradigm is translated into the different conditions causing shame among the four personality types. What will be shameful and how it will be counteracted depends in great measure on the values the patient has internalized from his family, for it is they who set up his ego-ideal and it is the internalized images of them with which he must reunite.

I believe that the mothers of craving personalities value their sons as babies. Therefore these sons can be openly weak, passive and demanding. The mother of one such patient preserved her intimate attachment to her son by developing a special language for them to use. Another mother applauded her child only when he was 'cute.' In both of these patients, the image of the 'weak' father was quite conscious and identification with him provided a way of winning mother's love. Where a younger sibling enters the picture, the child may soon learn to inhibit his aggressive and assertive rivalry in favour of becoming the 'good' (i.e. weak) little boy.

One of my craving patients, who had an intense identification with his mother, said, 'My mother doesn't concern herself with work. She's intuitive, not practical. With her, things will just happen. My father is practical—it's a whole world I can't understand. I can't write or publish, I just expect to be famous. I never learned how to work.'

In the cases of the other three narcissistic personality types, the situation is somewhat different; weakness becomes a threat to the reunion and causes a loss in self-esteem. In some of these patients, it has been very clear that the mother saw the son as her phallus and that the patient's struggle between strength and weakness reflected the mother's conflict over having a phallus-son on the one hand while not being able to tolerate the notion that a man's penis really counted for anything on the other. These patients are caught between being strong and manly in order to be useful to (acceptable to) mother and yet not really strong and manly because basically they must be 'mama's boys'.

Jacobson's (1971, pp. 302 ff.) paranoid patients grew up in families where there was overt cruelty and fights between the patients. She emphasizes the sadomasochistic family atmosphere and marital infidelity which sets the stage for the development of the child's own sadism. While I have seen this atmosphere in the families of some paranoid personalities, it has not been overt or obvious in all. However, even where it is not obvious, this atmosphere (and consequently these values) may come across in subtle ways. In one such family the weak father adored his phallic wife; he was her tool. She was an active clubwoman and he would write her speeches for her while staying in the background. The patient's mother was over-concerned with her favourite son's control of his impulses with the result that he developed a harsh superego. It was only later in life that the subtle paranoid atmosphere broke through the surface. By that time, the son had a typical paranoid personality. His mother became actively psychotic in her advanced years; she was suspicious to the point of delusion, accused her probably innocent husband of infidelity, had a most cruel temper, and became a hoarder of useless newspapers.

The family of the manipulative personality plays out its conflicts on the stage of public image (Greenacre, 1945). Johnson & Szurek (1952) have described the double messages given to children in these families: the manifest message is 'Be good and obey society's rules', while the latent message is 'Have fun so we parents can enjoy it vicariously'. The child is thus freed to engage in hidden mischief as long as his public image is clear. This sets the stage for deceptions. As I have explained elsewhere (Bursten, 1973, pp. 162 ff.), the manipulative personality is reasonably well aware that he is a liar, but it does not matter; in his family the public image counted more than the truth. With this latitude, he does not have to treat himself so harshly as the paranoid personality, and he is less destructive.

The family of the phallic narcissist has usually put a high premium on 'masculinity'. The theme may be 'Be a man like your father' or 'Be a man like I wish your father were'. If the encouragement to manliness were genuine, the child might not be narcissistic at all. However, mother cannot let go—the child has to be *her* man, her phallus, and as I mentioned earlier, she undercuts his manhood because she cannot tolerate a real or independent man. And this mother–son relationship, like all such relationships of narcissistic mothers with their children, is built upon earlier years of inadequate mothering, so that the child's sense of his self and his confidence in others has already been severely compromised.

These few remarks do not do justice to the complexities of the value systems of these personality types. What they are meant to convey is the fact that the family settings, prompted by the needs of the parents, dovetail with the levels at which the issues of shame and the restoration of pride are enacted, and that they become internalized to provide a value system which coordinates with the othe factors determining just which type of narcissistic personality as individual will have.

IV

In clinical psychiatric practice, especially in a large hospitalized population, it is often easy to identify patients who predominantly display the features of one or another of these personality types. As with all our diagnostic categories, however, I have not seen a pure case of one type or another. Most often, although it is possible to classify a patient as primarily a particular type of personality, we see features of an 'adjacent' type as well. Thus some manipulative personalities have a tendency to be competitively phallic, some craving personalities complain to the point of jealousy and querulousness, etc. Other patients, although exhibiting primarily one type of personality, show a remarkable fluidity in their use of features of all the types. In addition, all of these narcissistic personality types exhibit some features of the craving personality from time to time; they can become very demanding and clinging. Often this behaviour is seen when they are physically sick or drunk. Perhaps the craving personality is closest to the primary identity and the subsequent identity transformations melt away under stress.

As we examine the aspects of the four personality types I have described, we see a progression from the craving personality with its emphasis on features of early infantile life through the paranoid and manipulative personalities, to the phallic narcissistic personality which manifests features of later development. These four categories probably do not exhaust the types of narcissistic personalities, but they do serve as guideposts along this progression. It is in the sense of this progression that I have spoken above about 'adjacent' types. And, as I mentioned in Part II of this paper, at the lower end, this progression blends into the borderline personality, while at the upper end, the phallic narcissist approaches the complementary personality types.

Kohut has distinguished two forms of narcissism; the grandiose self and the idealized parent image (here called the 'omnipotent object'). At first glance, the clinical pictures presented by these personality types suggest that craving personalities are largely expressing omnipotent object fantasies, while phallic narcissists largely express the grandiose self, and the other two types lie somewhere in between. However, analysis reveals the enormous grandiosity of the craver and the fantasies of omnipotence which the phallic narcissist gives to his objects. Both forms of narcissism are active in all four personality types. While the roles they play in the differentiation of the types are not clear to me, I do have some preliminary thoughts. In the earlier personality types, such as the craver, the omnipotent object has been less adequately internalized; this would go along with his greater structural vulnerability, for, as Kohut (1971, pp. 49 ff.) has indicated, structure building is dependent on this internalization. Thus he shows on the surface a greater need for an external source of supplies, mirroring, etc. The later-stage personality types, such as phallic narcissists, have firmer structure, as I have indicated in Part III. There is evidence of greater internalization of the archaic omnipotent object and its transformation into goals and ideals which generally have to do with appearances. The archaic grandiose self of the later personality types is also transformed so as to be more useful to the ego, for example, as in ambition. As Kohut explains (1971, p. 187), 'the structures built up in response to the claims of the grandiose self appear in general to deal less with the curbing of narcissistic demands but with the channeling and modification of their expression.' Thus we can see the grandiose self showing through the ambition and competitiveness of the phallic narcissist, but the reliance on the omnipotent object is hidden in the internalized structures. In the paranoid personality, with less firm structuralization, we can see the omnipotent object in the complaints about 'their' influence, albeit malevolent, and the frequent search for new alliances. The manipulative personality shows less of this; his contempt is attenuated and his sense of self-glorification is aided by his initiative.

V

I shall recapitulate some of the relationships developed in this paper. I have distinguished three broad personality groupings. The borderline group has as its central task the prevention of fragmentation and disintegration. The narcissistic group has reunion as the central task. The central task of the complementary group is the resolution of the Oedipus complex. The three groups are on a continuum which is derived from the development of selfobject differentiation and the firmness of the sense of self.

Within the narcissistic group, I have distinguished four personality types—the craving, the paranoid, the manipulative and the phallic narcissistic personalities. These types represent a progression both in terms of the instinctual stages predominantly represented in the execution of the narcissistic central task (reunion) and in the degree of separation and individuation. The values held by each of these types represent parental values which have dovetailed with the particular stage of libidinal emphasis and degree of separation and individuation. I have discussed some of the theoretical implications of this progression.

REFERENCES

Abraham, K. (1921). Contributions to the theory of the anal character. In *Selected Papers on Psycho-Analysis*. London: Hogarth Press, 1927.

Abraham, K. (1924*a*). The influence of oral erotism on character formation. *Ibid.*

Abraham, K. (1924*b*). A short study of the development of the libido viewed in the light of mental disorders. *Ibid.*

Abraham, K. (1925). Character-formation on the genital level of libido development. *Ibid.*

Adatto, C. P. (1957). On pouting. *J. Am. psychoanal. Ass.* **5,** 245–249.

American Psychiatric Association (1968). *Diagnostic and Statistical Manual of Mental Disorders*. Washington, D.C.: American Psychiatric Association.

Bak, R. C. (1946). Masochism in paranoia. *Psychoanal. Q.* **15,** 285–301.

Bibring, E. (1953). The mechanism of depression. In P. Greenacre (ed.), *Affective Disorders*. New York: Int. Univ. Press.

Bursten, B. (1972). The manipulative personality. *Archs gen. Psychiat.* **26,** 318–321.

Bursten, B. (1973). *The Manipulator: A Psychoanalytic View*. New Haven: Yale Univ. Press.

Cameron, N. (1959). Paranoid conditions and paranoia. In. S. Arieti (ed.), *American Handbook of Psychiatry,* vol. 1. New York: Basic Books.

Cleckley, H. (1959). Psychopathic states. *Ibid.*

Eisnitz, A. J. (1969). Narcissistic object choice, self representation. *Int. J. Psycho-Anal.* **50,** 15–25.

Elkisch, P. (1957). The psychological significance of the mirror. *J. Am. psychoanal. Ass.* **5,** 235–244.

Erikson, E. H. (1950). *Childhood and Society*. New York: Norton.

Fenichel, O. (1945). *The Psychoanalytic Theory of Neurosis*. New York: Norton.

Fliess, R. (1942). The metapsychology of the analyst, *Psychoanal. Q.* **11,** 211–227.

Freud, A. (1949). Aggression in relation to emotional development: normal and pathological. *Psychoanal. Study Child* **3–4.**

Freud, S. (1905). Three essays on the theory of sexuality. *S.E.* **7.**

Freud, S. (1908). Character and anal erotism. *S.E.* **9.**

Freud, S. (1911*a*). Psycho-analytic notes on an autobiographical account of a case of paranoia. *S.E.* **12.**

Freud, S. (1911*b*). Formulations on the two principles of mental functioning. *S.E.* **12.**

Freud, S (1913). The disposition to obsessional neurosis. *S.E.* **12.**

Freud, S. (1914). On narcissism: an introduction. *S.E.* **14.**

Freud, S. (1915). Instincts and their vicissitudes. *S.E.* **14.**

Freud, S. (1916). Some character-types met with in psycho-analytic work. *S.E.* **14.**

Freud, S. (1923). The ego and the id. *S.E.* **19.**

Freud, S. (1931). Libidinal types. *S.E.* **21.**

Fromm, E. (1947). *Man For Himself.* New York: Rinehart.

Frosch, J. (1970). Psychoanalytic considerations of the psychotic character. *J. Am. psychoanal. Ass.* **18,** 24–50.

Greenacre, P. (1945). Conscience in the psychopath. *Am. J. Orthopsychiat.* **15,** 495–509.

Guntrip, H. (1969). *Schizoid Phenomena, Object Relations and the Self.* New York: Int. Univ. Press.

Hartmann, H. (1952). The mutual influences in the development of ego and id. *Psychoanal. Study Child* **7.**

Hoffer, W. (1952). The mutual influences in the development of ego and id: earliest stages. *Psychoanal. Study Child* **7.**

Jacobson, E. (1946). The effect of disappointment on ego and superego formation in normal and depressive development. *Psychoanal. Rev.* **33,** 129–147.

Jacobson, E. (1957). Denial and repression. *J. Am. psychoanal. Ass.* **5,** 61–92.

Jacobson, E. (1971). *Depression.* New York: Int. Univ. Press.

Johnson, A. M. & Szurek, S. A. (1952). The genesis of antisocial acting out in children and adults. *Psychoanal. Q.* **21,** 323–343.

Kernberg, O. F. (1967). Borderline personality organization, *J. Am. psychoanal. Ass.* **15,** 641–685.

Kernberg, O. F. (1970a). A psychoanalytic classification of character pathology. *J. Am. psychoanal. Ass.* **18,** 800–822.

Kernberg, O. F. (1970b). Factors in the psychoanalytic treatment of narcissistic personalities. *J. Am. psychoanal. Ass.* **18,** 51–85.

Knight, R. P. (1940). The relationship of latent homosexuality to the mechanism of paranoid delusions. *Bull. Menninger Clin.* **4,** 149–159.

Kohut, H. (1966). Forms and transformations of narcissism. *J. Am. psychoanal. Ass.* **14,** 243–272.

Kohut, H. (1971). *The Analysis of the Self.* New York: Int. Univ. Press.

Lewin, B. D. (1950). *The Psychoanalysis of Elation.* New York: Norton.

Lichtenstein, H. (1964). The role of narcissism in the emergence and maintenance of a primary identity. *Int. J. Psycho-Anal.* **45,** 49–56.

Mahler, M. S. (1967). On human symbiosis and the vicissitudes of individuation. *J. Am. psychoanal. Ass.* **15,** 740–763.

Mahler, M. S. & Gosliner, B. J. (1955). On symbiotic child psychosis, *Psychoanal. Study Child* **10.**

Oremland, J. D. & Windholz, E. (1971). Some specific transference, countertransference and supervisory problems in the analysis of a narcissistic personality. *Int. J. Psycho-Anal.* **52,** 267–275.

Pulver, S. (1970). Narcissism: the term and the concept. *J. Am. psychoanal. Ass.* **18,** 319–341.

Rado, S. (1928). The problem of melancholia. *Int. J. Psycho-Anal.* **9,** 420–438.

Rapaport, D. (1959). Edward Bibring's theory of depression. In *Collected Papers.* New York: Basic Books, 1967.

Reich, A. (1960). Pathological forms of self-esteem regulation, *Psychoanal. Study Child* **15.**

Reich, W. (1933). *Character-Analysis.* New York: Noonday Press.

Riesman, D. (1950). *The Lonely Crowd.* New Haven: Yale Univ. Press.

Rosenfeld, H. (1964). On the psychopathology of narcissism: a clinical approach. *Int. J. Psycho-Anal.* **45,** 332–337.

Stein, M. H. (1969). The problem of character theory. *J. Am. psychoanal. Ass.* **17,** 675–701.

Waelder, R. (1951). The structure of paranoid ideas: a critical survey of various theories. *Int. J. Psycho-Anal.* **32,** 167–177.

White, R. (1961). The mother-conflict in Schreber's psychosis. *Int. J. Psycho-Anal.* **42,** 55–73.

16. Narcissistic Personalities and Borderline Conditions: A Differential Diagnosis

W. W. Meissner

INTRODUCTION

One of the basic sources of confusion and difficulty in attempts to understand the lower-order forms of character pathology has been the lack of clarity in discriminating between forms of borderline disorder and the so-called narcissistic personalities. The primary contenders for recognition in this area are the notion of borderline personality provided by Kernberg (1967, 1968, 1971, 1975, 1976) and Kohut's (1971, 1972) approach to the narcissistic personality disorders.[1]

The Kernberg description of borderline personality organization arose out of a context in which the borderline conditions were a poorly defined and poorly conceptualized spectrum of disorders which were neither clearly psychotic nor classically neurotic. The major contribution of Kernberg's analysis is that he was able to define this intermediate range of pathology and establish certain specific and definable characteristics. The emphasis in his approach was to delimit the boundaries of the borderline range and to distinguish it from the psychoses at the lower level of pathological organization and from the more clearly

---

[1] Implicit in this comparison is the supposition that the respective ideas of Kernberg and Kohut can be related within a single framework. I have indicated elsewhere (Meissner, 1978c) my view of the theoretical divergence between them. However, the emphasis in the present study falls on a complex diagnostic discrimination to which both authors address themselves. Here the extent to which theoretical premises overlap or diverge remains secondary to the core diagnostic issue which is fundamentally descriptive or phenomenological.

But I trust the reader will not allow himself to be misled by this footnote. The *status quaestionis* here is not the differentiation of Kohut's account of narcissistic personality from Kernberg's account of borderline personality. The *status quaestionis* is the diagnostic differentiation between narcissistic personalities and the borderline conditions. It is based on no prior commitment to either account. Consequently, in the present study the assessment of both narcissistic personalities and borderline conditions may come to differ from both prior accounts.

established neuroses at the higher level. Consequently, his description of the borderline conditions tends to lump them into a common category which, in effect, groups together a number of pathological conditions that fill in the space between the higher forms of neurosis and neurotic character on the one hand and psychotic conditions on the other.

Obviously, a problem arises from the fact that the narcissistic personalities fall somewhere within this spectrum: between the neurotic character disorders, such as the hysterical or obsessive-compulsive characters, and the borderline conditions. On the one hand an attempt has been made to extend the analysis of borderline personality structure to include the narcissistic personalities. Kernberg, for example, sees narcissistic personalities in terms of underlying borderline features (1967), tends to emphasize the similarities of defensive organization, including the use of primitive defenses of splitting, denial, omnipotence, and idealization (1970), and in general emphasizes the common denominators, particularly in terms of narcissistic character traits and narcissistic deficits, in both types of personality organization (1971).

On the other hand, Kohut (1971) describes the narcissistic personality disorders essentially as cohesive self organizations manifesting specific archaic narcissistic configurations.[2] He leaves open the question of vulnerability to regression, so that the actual delineation from border-

---

[2] A further clarifying point is in order in this regard. The argument could be (and has been) made that Kernberg's approach to the borderline is based on descriptive object-relations data whereas Kohut's approach to narcissistic problems is based on subjective experience or personal meaning. Any attempt at comparison would run afoul of this essential difference—you can't add apples and oranges. Fair enough! But I would not be ready to endorse this supposition. I do not think that the respective approaches can be so easily dichotomized. The theoretical divergences are plain enough, but even the differential emphases do not disguise or obliterate the common elements. Kohut's emphasis on inner subjective experience of self does not prevent his parallel emphasis of the experience of-and-with objects and the nature of narcissistic object relations. Kernberg, on the other hand, speaks a language of object relations, but his concern is not so much with the relationships with objects as with the organization and experiencing of self and object representations (Meissner, 1978c). The attempt to dichotomize the respective approaches on these grounds may have certain ad hoc advantages, but it remains to a degree artificial and does not do justice to the complexity of thought of either approach.

It should also be noted that attempts to drive a wedge between objective observational aspects of psychoanalysis and its subjective, meaning-signifying aspects have not met with general acceptance. Because the psychoanalytic enterprise is fundamentally more complex than reductive attempts of any kind allow, such dichotomizations sacrifice something for whatever gain in clarity they offer.

line conditions is somewhat obscured, even though he asserts their differentiation from borderline states. He writes:

The central psychopathology of the narcissistic personality disturbances, on the other hand, concerns primarily the self and the archaic narcissistic objects. These narcissistic configurations are related to the causative nexus of psychopathology in the narcissistic realm in the following two ways: (1) they may be insufficiently cathected and are thus liable to temporary fragmentation; and (2) even if they are sufficiently cathected or hypercathected and thus retain their cohesiveness, they are not integrated with the rest of the personality, and the mature self and other aspects of the mature personality are deprived of a sufficient or reliable supply of narcissistic investments [p. 19].

Consequently, the relative descriptions of borderline and narcissistic personalities overlap considerably both in the narcissistic characteristics and in the tendency to regression, particularly to transient and partial regressions. Kernberg also remarks on the regressive potential of narcissistic personalities (1970, 1974) and makes no attempt to distinguish between them on this basis. One way to summarize this problem is to say that Kernberg writes as though the diagnostic spectrum stretching between the psychoses and the neuroses were filled by nothing but forms of borderline personality. At the same time, Kohut writes as though the same diagnostic vacuum were filled by nothing but forms of narcissistic personality.

Kohut does attempt to differentiate these conditions on the basis of the relative cohesion of nuclear narcissistic structure. As he sees it, the narcissistic personalities are characterized by an insecure cohesiveness of the nuclear self and selfobjects and by only fleeting fragmentation. He contrasts this with borderline conditions in which the symptomatology hides the fragmentation of nuclear narcissistic structures or in which the breakup of such structures remains an ever-present potential which can be prevented by avoiding the regression-inducing narcissistic injuries—as in schizoid personalities. These intermediate conditions are again distinguished from the frank psychoses in which the narcissistic structures are permanently fragmented and in which the symptoms openly reflect their decompensation. The discrimination between the fleeting fragmentation of the narcissistic personality and the hidden or potential breakdown of nuclear narcissistic structures in the borderline (including schizoid) conditions is difficult to grasp, if not tenuous in conceptualization.

The upshot of the ambiguities in these approaches is that there is considerable diagnostic confusion and difficulty in making appropriate discriminations between these various forms of psychopathology. In fact, Ornstein (1974b) has argued that Kohut's classification of the narcissistic personality disorders has now come to encompass those conditions previously considered to be borderline or psychotic characters, and may even include some of those previously diagnosed as neurotic characters or psychoneuroses.

This differential emphasis in approach to narcissistic personality disorders has given rise to differences in therapeutic approach as well. Building on his concept of archaic narcissistic configurations such as the grandiose self as part of a normal developmental progression, Kohut emphasizes the need for empathic responsiveness and acceptance of the patient's grandiosity and needs to idealize the analyst. Kernberg, however, sees these archaic narcissistic formations as forms of developmental arrest or of pathological development. Consequently, rather than stressing empathic acceptance, Kernberg insists on the interpretation of narcissistic structures as defensive elaborations against both more primitive and more mature object relationships. His emphasis is on the defensive aspects of the narcissistic configuration and on the need to work through narcissistic issues in terms of the related aggressive and libidinal concerns (Ornstein, 1974a).

Ornstein's suggestion that the argument may founder on the fact that it is concerned with essentially different patient populations is a cogent one and further points to the possibility that part of the difficulty arises from ambiguities in diagnosis. My attempt in the present paper is to elucidate further this problem in differential diagnosis. The strategy will be to try to define the essentials of the narcissistic personality organization and then to clarify the differentiating aspects of the borderline conditions. At the end of the paper we may then be able to take up certain structural and developmental differentiations which may help to clarify the diagnostic discrimination.

ASPECTS OF NARCISSISTIC PERSONALITY ORGANIZATION

Certainly it is clear that all forms of personality organization have narcissistic elements which influence the form of the pathology. However, we are discussing here forms of character pathology in which the narcissistic disorder forms the central core of the patient's pathology. The wide spectrum of narcissistic pathology is not equivalent to the more restrictive diagnosis of narcissistic personality. An essential note on which that diagnosis rests is the capacity for forming stable and at least potentially analyzable narcissistic transferences.[3] We need also to remind ourselves that these narcissistic disorders will cover a pathological spectrum which will include those personalities whose level of functioning is quite good as well as those in which functioning may be relatively impaired.

In trying to order the narcissistic personality types Bursten (1973) has suggested that the highest level of narcissistic personality organization is found in the phallic narcissistic personality. The exhibitionism, pride in prowess, show-offishness, and the often counterphobic competitiveness and risk-taking in the service of narcissistic exhibitionism are quite familiar. Such individuals tend to be self centered, and to have an exorbitant need for approval and admiration from others—particularly admiration. Their relationship with others often has a quality of arrogance or contempt which is defensive in tone and tends to mask underlying and often repressed feelings of inadequacy or inferiority.

This inner sense of inferiority often stems from a sense of shame derived from an underlying identification with a weak father figure

---

[3] It has been argued that Kohut's focusing on transference phenomena as essential to the diagnosis of narcissistic personalities stands in opposition to descriptive diagnostic categories, such as those used in general psychiatry. This objection presupposes that Kohut uses no phenomenological elements in defining his categories. However, we do not observe anything in psychoanalysis that is not phenomenal. Even our judgments of transference are based on phenomenological observations of transference manifestations (behaviors or verbal reports of inner states) from which the construct "transference" can be derived. Further, psychoanalytic observations of transference phenomena do not stand in opposition to descriptive observations, any more than psychoanalysis stands in opposition to general psychiatry. Psychoanalysis merely adds a different dimension to psychiatric observations that has to do with the fantasy-related, affective, transferential, and object-relations aspects of psychological functioning. The position taken in the present study is that psychoanalytic and psychiatric observations are complementary. Consequently, any attempt at diagnosis or diagnostic differentiation, based either on behavioral description or on transference and object-relations phenomena, must remain partial and incomplete. This position does not override the possibility that different diagnostic schemata may be evolved by psychiatrists or psychoanalysts in terms of different needs, emphases, objectives, and purposes of their respective approaches. It does mean that such schemata remain incomplete and demand further elaboration.

which is compensated by the arrogant, assertive, aggressively competitive, often hyper-masculine and self-glorifying façade. In other words,
the unconscious shame from the fear of castration is continually denied
by phallic assertiveness. This may even be accompanied by a sense of
omnipotence and a feeling of invulnerability which allows such individuals, feeling that some miraculous fate of good luck will carry them
through, to continually take risks. Narcissistic personality types tend
to have a firmly established and cohesive sense of self which shows
little tendency to regression or fragmentation.

Seemingly strong inner resources enable them to maintain their independence and express little need for others beyond the sort of admiration and acknowledgment we have described. The intense attachment to self-objects that may be found in other forms of narcissistic
pathology is not usually apparent in these patients or is concealed
behind a façade of hyperadequacy. The extent of their real dependency
becomes apparent only when the love or support of such objects is lost.
These personalities may have elements of grandiosity and omnipotence
which reflect the persistence of the grandiose self in Kohut's terms, and
objects may be idealized which then serve as models for imitation or
identification. The vulnerabilities of such personalities are generally
well concealed by counterphobic and counterdependency mechanisms.

Nonetheless, they remain susceptible to the ravages of time and
diminishing capacity and potency. The diminished capacity to perform
with advancing age, whether sexually, physically, or intellectually, can
constitute a narcissistic trauma with rather severe pathological results.
The outcome is usually a depression.

Such individuals do not generally show a dramatic regressive crisis,
but under conditions of severe stress the regression may be severe and
at times irreparable. One wonders whether the cases of war neurosis in
which individuals seemed to suffer from little or no fear or anxiety about
danger prior to the traumatic event, but who seemed incapable of
reconstituting in the usual way to pretraumatic levels of functioning,
were in fact phallic narcissistic characters. In such cases the assault on
the individual's self image created by the traumatic event would have
so damaged the individual's self image and self esteem that they proved
relatively incapable of reconstitution.[4] Their self image had been based

---

[4] A striking literary portrayal of just this form of narcissistic pathology is provided
in the character of Marrow, the "hero" of John Hersey's *The War Lover* (1959).

on a view of themselves as fearless and as capable of withstanding any amount of stress or danger. The experience of severe anxiety would have destroyed that image and would have created an impediment to its reconstitution or effective treatment (Zetzel and Meissner, 1973).

A more subtle variant of this form of narcissistic pathology was described by Tartakoff (1966) nearly a dozen years ago in her study of the apparently well-adjusted, sociologically "healthy" personality. Her subjects were often academically or professionally successful individuals who were able and ambitious, often had achieved significant professional respect and recognition, but who found themselves dissatisfied with their current life situation. Difficulties arose in connection with competitive feelings or in competitive situations, or in their inability to gratify the needs of others in intimate human relations with family, close friends, etc. Some of these individuals could recognize reactive depressions, or anxiety attacks under stress, or a variety of psychosomatic symptoms. Others were essentially asymptomatic, recognized no underlying motivation for treatment, but sought analysis essentially as a way of broadening their professional training. They shared the conviction that their exceptional abilities, talents, or virtues would win them success if they worked properly at it. Achieving these goals or life expectations had become essential to their psychic harmony. For the most part they experienced little difficulty in life since their abilities and endowments usually allowed them to gain some measure of narcissistic gratification and recognition from the environment, or at least to maintain the hope of fulfilling their narcissistic expectations—a facet of their experience that could receive considerable cultural and social reinforcement from prevailing attitudes in our society. It is when the reinforcements began to fail or the expectations began not to be met that narcissistic imbalance and symptomatic manifestations arose.

In analysis, success in therapy was seen as a means to this end. Active mastery of the analytic situation and the conflicts it mobilized was a first line of defense for these patients. They treated the analysis as an adaptive task which carried the unspoken assumption that they would gain acceptance or acclaim from the analyst as a reward for their efforts. Their behavior was defensive, often competitive with the analyst, with an implicit expectation of gaining a special relation with him. It was often expressed in the fantasy of being a special patient, especially interesting or especially difficult, preferred to other patients, even loved—exclusively—by the analyst.

When the adaptive function of the patient's attempts to master the analytic situation is seen and understood as a repetition of previously successful endeavors, a second line of preoedipal transference emerges in the idealization of the analyst. This externalization of the ego ideal comes closer to Kohut's (1971) notion of the idealizing parental imago. Conformity to the analyst's expectations holds the promise that the patient will be rewarded by success in the analysis and will thereby be endowed with the qualities of omnipotence and omniscience he attributes to the analyst. Such fantasies may continue to be unspoken and may become a secret source of resistance. Insofar as the analyst fails to meet these narcissistic expectations, the patient's disillusionment and narcissistic rage may become intense. In describing these patients, Tartakoff (1966) refers to the "Nobel Prize complex" which embraces two predominant fantasies: (1) an active grandiose fantasy of being powerful and omnipotent, and (2) a more passive fantasy of being special, singled out for special recognition by reason of exceptional talents, abilities, virtues, etc.

At a somewhat more pathological level, the narcissistic need expresses itself not simply in terms of the drive to gain recognition and admiration, but in the entitlement to use, manipulate, or exploit others for the purposes of self enhancement or aggrandizement. Bursten (1973) described such personalities as "manipulative." His description of them comes close to the description of psychopathic or antisocial personalities, and it is undeniable that the pathology may frequently be more or less flagrantly similar. However, the antisocial or psychopathic quality of such personalities cuts across the discrimination we are attempting to make between narcissistic and borderline personalities.

Nonetheless, the contempt for others, the implicit notion that they have potential value only in terms of their exploitability or manipulability in the service of self enhancement, the high value often placed on putting something over on others or getting away with something, even though that may involve deceptive or even dishonest practices, all carry the narcissistic stamp of this sort of personality and reflect the persistence of residues of the grandiose self. The exploitative form of narcissistic repair covers an underlying narcissistic vulnerability to exploitation or manipulation by others. Yet the self is constantly turning the tables, as it were. The inherent sense of shame, vulnerability, and worthlessness attached to this narcissistically vulnerable self image is equivalently projected onto the victim of the subject's exploitation, so that the denial and reassurance that one's self is not really entrapped in this impoverished self image is gained through the projection and subsequent exploitation of the victim. It should be noted that in these circumstances the victim is of vital importance to the subject as a means of maintaining his narcissistic equilibrium—in no sense valued or idealized, but rather held in a devalued posture or even regarded with contempt. This contrasts with the normal narcissism described above, in which there is little pressure to seek favor or support from objects, or *a fortiori* to manipulate or exploit them. Rather, a feeling of exceptional endowment and precocity has led to an expectation of success and admiration, thus lessening the need to gain or extort such narcissistic feedback from others. Dependence on others is focused on the related narcissistic gratification, which leads to impairment in the capacity for meaningful love relationships.

The sense of self in more exploitative patients is relatively well established and subject to little regression, as long as the resources for continuing narcissistic repair are available. These patients maintain a sense of separateness in their relations with others and have considerable difficulty in developing meaningful or mutually gratifying relationships, since the premise of any meaningful relationship rests on the underlying narcissism which requires that the other be put in the service of the self. When the means of narcissistic repair fail or become unavailable, such patients generally fall prey to depression. Depending on the severity of the pathology, the depression can be quite severe and even suicidal. Something similar can be seen even more dramatically in the effects of inpatient confinement and restricted mobility on criminal psychopaths (Vaillant, 1975). When such patients are confined and control is established over their behavior so that flight is impossible and they are relatively immobilized, the underlying depression becomes much more clinically apparent. Such psychopathic personalities are more primitive than exploitative narcissistic personalities, and fall within the borderline spectrum.

At more pathological levels, however, the narcissism becomes even more needy, clinging, and demanding. The need to be given to, supported, and taken care of, which reflects a sense of peremptory and uncompromising entitlement, is heightened, and may be so profound as to take on a symbiotic quality which results in intensely dependent and needy involvements. Frequently such involvements have a highly ambivalent, hostile-dependent quality since the object is never quite capable of satisfying the patient's narcissistic demand and expectation. Consequently, these patients are constantly exposed to the threat of disappointment and frustration, feeling deprived and often desperate. In such states they can become sullen and pouting, even whining and complaining, in their attempts to wheedle the necessary response from the important other.

Like all narcissistic personalities these individuals have as well a capacity for charm and the ability to entertain, flatter, and influence others. But the quality of this activity is quite different from that of the phallic narcissist for whom the objective is gaining admiration, or from that of the more exploitative narcissistic personality who is compelled to put the other in the service of his own narcissistic objectives. In these more severely disturbed narcissistic patients, the objectives are much more directed toward drawing others into the position of giving, supporting, taking care of, or otherwise filling up the intense neediness and deprived emptiness that characterize their narcissistic vulnerability. Consequently, the quality of behavior in such individuals is intensely oral and has been aptly characterized by Bursten (1973) as "craving."

At all levels of narcissistic pathology there are degrees of both narcissistic vulnerability and grandiosity. It should be noted that these qualities are inherently linked and are never found in isolation. Frequently one dimension or the other may be found as a more explicit or conscious manifestation of the narcissistic aspects of a given personality, but even in such cases the correlative aspect of the narcissistic pathology can also be found on further clinical investigation. Thus, the phallic or exploitative narcissistic character who displays his vanity and grandiosity in a variety of more or less public ways can be found to carry a concealed core of narcissistic vulnerability and feelings of inferiority, shame, weakness, and susceptibility. Similarly, the clinging, dependent, needy, and demanding type—the more primitive narcissistic character—will be found on closer evaluation and more extensive investigation to be concealing a core of grandiosity that underlies the infantile expectations and extreme sense of entitlement which makes them feel that they have a right to demand concern, care, and attention from others often to the point of considerable self sacrifice and disadvantage or detriment to the other. This same grandiosity may also be manifested by the sulking, pouting, whining, and demanding quality of the efforts to gain narcissistic supplies.

There is often an implicit supposition that others owe it to the subject to make up for the deprivation and deficits that he feels he has suffered. The obligation falls upon others, therefore, to undo the wrongs that have been done to the subject, thus relieving the subject himself of the responsibility for dealing with his own difficulties. This goes along with a general tendency to lay the responsibility for the individual's difficulties at the door of others—frequently parents or other caretakers, but not infrequently other family members, friends, employers, coworkers, etc. In its more extreme forms this tendency may take a paranoid expression. As we have noted elsewhere (Meissner, 1977), the narcissistic pathology forms a substantial part of the core of paranoia.

Actually Kernberg's (1967) early desciption of narcissistic characters is quite apt and may be useful at this point. He writes:

These patients present an unusual degree of self-reference in their interactions with other people, a great need to be loved and admired by others, and a curious apparent contradiction between a very inflated concept of themselves and an inordinate need for tribute from others. Their emotional life is shallow. They experience little empathy for the feelings of others, they obtain very little enjoyment from life other than from the tributes they receive from others or from their own grandiose fantasies, and they feel restless and bored when external glitter wears off and no new sources feed their self-regard. They envy others, tend to idealize some people from whom they expect narcissistic supplies, and to depreciate and treat with contempt those from whom they do not expect anything (often their former idols). In general, their relationships with other people are clearly exploitative and sometimes parasitic. It is as if they feel they have the right to control and possess others and to exploit them without guilt feelings—and behind a surface which very often is charming and engaging, one senses coldness and ruthlessness. Very often such patients are considered to be "dependent" because they need so much tribute and adoration from others, but on a deeper level they are completely unable to really depend on anybody because of their deep distrust and depreciation of others [p. 655].

It is easy to see that it is but a short step from this description to the borderline characteristics that Kernberg has described so well. In fact, he does take this step, consistent with the inclusive methodology that he uses in defining the borderline syndrome.

The primary and most discriminating locus of narcissistic pathology is in the patient's object relationships. Here the need to be loved and the investment in and use of objects as a means of redressing and maintaining narcissistic equilibrium are the predominant aspects. Over a quarter of a century ago, Reich (1953) described some varieties of narcissistic object choice in women which she ascribed to a repressive resolution of the oedipal-castration trauma by regression to a pregenital level of narcissistic passivity and demandingness. In these women the feelings of shame and inferiority were resolved by a narcissistic object choice which was seen as undoing the trauma of castration and re-establishing the narcissistic balance.

She described two predominant patterns: one in which a dependent and subservient attachment was established with one man who became the admired and indispensable idealized object, and another character-ized by brief, intense infatuations, in which there was an admiring idealization accompanied by a transient imitative mirroring of the man's characteristics. These idealizing infatuations would quickly burn out and turn to devaluing rejection, which then would lead to a re-creation of the cycle with another object. Reich compared this type of object choice with Deutsch's (1942) "as-if" personality. To this latter type of narcissistic object involvement can be added the more or less exploit-ative use of objects for sexual and narcissistic gratification which con-stitute deeper and more troublesome narcissistic threats when they seem to signal the prospect of more long-lasting involvement and com-mitment. In this case the prospect of giving or sharing in an enduring relationship is seen as a narcissistic loss rather than a gain.

These early characterizations are quite consistent with the more recent formulations provided by Kohut (1971). Kohut has emphasized, as the predominant characteristic of narcissistic personalities, the for-mation of cohesive narcissistic configurations around which the per-sonality organization takes shape. These configurations on the objective side involve the idealized parent imago, and on the subjective side the grandiose self. These relatively stable configurations are cathected with narcissistic libido, either idealizing or grandiose-exhibitionistic, and manifest themselves in various forms of object relations and in analytic transferences.

The therapeutic activation of the omnipotent and idealized object leads to the formation of an idealizing transference in which residues of the lost infantile experience of narcissistic perfection are restored by assigning it to a transitional selfobject, the idealized parent imago. Thus, all power and strength are attributed to this idealized object, so that the subject feels empty and powerless when separated from it. Consequently, he must bend every effort to maintain contact and union with this object. Thus, the continuing contact and union with an idealized selfobject seems to characterize one of Reich's (1953) forms quite adequately. The second form, however, is unable to sustain a consistent object attachment and vacillates quickly between narcissistic configurations, between infatuation and contempt, idealization and devaluation. This instability and the defects of object constancy give rise to an "as-if" quality and suggest that such narcissistic attachments are essentially borderline.

Such idealizing transferences can reactivate archaic narcissistic states which stem from one of several levels of development and which may include primitive mergings of the self with an idealized maternal imago or may reflect later developmental traumata that produce specific narcissistic fixations. Such traumata or narcissistic disappointments may create impediments in the development of the child's idealization, or may contaminate or undo idealizations of objects which are insecurely established. In either case, because of failure of internalizations, insufficient idealization of the superego and secondary structural deficits may result from fixations on the narcissistic aspects of preoedipal and oedipal objects. Kohut (1971) notes:

Persons who have suffered such traumas are (as adolescents and adults) forever attempting to achieve a union with the idealized object since, in view of their specific structural defect (the insufficient idealization of their superego), their narcissistic equilibrium is safeguarded only through the interest, the responses, and the approval of present-day (i.e. currently active) replicas of the traumatically lost self-object [p. 55].

These varieties of pathogenic narcissistic fixation give rise to differentiable transferences. Certain varieties of idealizing transference reflect the disturbances of later stages of the development of the idealized parent imago, particularly at the time of introjection of the idealized object in the formation of the ego ideal. More archaic forms of narcissistic idealization may reflect themselves in the expression of global mystical or even religious concerns associated with awe-inspiring qualities that do not seem to emanate from a clearly delimited, single admired figure. Although such primitive idealizing elements tend to be more diffuse and vague, particularly when merged with elements of the grandiose self, the special bond and the idealizing attachment to the analyst are never in doubt. In such cases the restored narcissistic equilibrium, along with feelings of esthetic and moral perfection, is experienced as a sense of omnipotence and omniscience. These feelings are maintained as long as the patient believes he is united and sustained by the idealized analyst. Moreover, the symptomatology due to the narcissistic imbalance—particularly the diffused depression, disturbed work capacity, irritability, feelings of shame or inferiority, hypochondriacal preoccupations, etc.—becomes diminished. The establishment of union with the idealized object also minimizes the threat of further narcissistic regression, perhaps to even more archaic precursors of the idealized parent imago (Kohut, 1971). The narcissistic dynamics in the Wolf Man's case seem to have followed such a pattern (Meissner, 1977).

In some individuals the narcissistic fixation leads to the development of the grandiose self. The reactivation in analysis of the grandiose self provides the basis for the formation of mirror transferences, of which Kohut (1971) has described three forms:

> The cohesive therapeutic reactivation of the grandiose self in analysis occurs in three forms; these relate to specific stages of development of this psychological structure to which pathognomonic therapeutic regression has led: (1) the archaic *merger through the extension of the grandiose self;* (2) a less archaic form which will be called *alter-ego transference* or *twinship;* and (3) a still less archaic form which will be referred to as *mirror transference* in the narrower sense [p. 114].

In the most primitive merger form of mirror transference, the analyst is experienced only as an extension of the subject's grandiose self, and consequently he becomes the repository of its grandiosity and exhibitionism. Kohut uses such terms as merger or symbiosis to describe this extension, but reminds us that what is at issue here is not merger with an idealized object, but rather a regressive diffusion of the borders of the self to embrace the analyst who is then experienced as united to the grandiose self. The analogy to the adult experience of cathexis of one's own body or mind reflects the kind of unquestioned control or dominance that the grandiose self expects to exert over the invested object. With such patients the analyst may find himself forced to resist the oppressive tyranny with which the patient seeks to control him (Kohut, 1971). The quality of this merging and extension of the grandiose self seems to eliminate the object as such and to make it simply a reflection of the self. Consequently, merging of this nature must be regarded as severely regressive and comes closer to the modalities of incorporation which I have described elsewhere (Meissner, 1971, 1979a). To this extent it may be regarded as psychotic in character, or at least regressively borderline.

At a somewhat less primitive level of organization, the activation of the grandiose self leads to the experiencing of the narcissistic object as similar to, and to that extent a reflection of, the grandiose self. In this variant, the object as such is preserved but is modified by the subject's perception of it to suit his narcissistic needs. This form of transference is referred to as alter-ego or twinship transference. Clinically, dreams or fantasies referring to such as alter-ego or twinship relationship with the analyst may be explicit. As Kohut (1971) notes:

The pathognomonic therapeutic regression is characterized by the fact that the patient assumes that the analyst is either like him or similar to him, or that the analyst's psychological makeup is like, or is similar to that of the patient [p. 115].

In this type of transference, then, the reality of the analyst is preserved, but it is modified after the fashion of a transitional object by a projection of some aspects of the patient's grandiose self onto the analyst.

In the most mature and most developed form of the mirror transference the analyst is experienced as a separate person, but nonetheless one who becomes important to the patient and is accepted by him only to the degree that he is responsive to the narcissistic needs of the reactivated grandiose self. Kohut appeals here to the model of the gleam in the mother's eye which responds to and mirrors the child's exhibitionism. In this way the mother participates in and reinforces the child's narcissistic pleasure in himself. Thus, in this strictest sense of the mirror transference, the analyst's function becomes one of admiring and reflecting the grandiosity and exhibitionism of the patient. This need on the part of the patient may also take a more subtle form in which the patient seeks such admiration and confirmation from the analyst, but constantly acts in a way that reflects the fear of not getting it. Consequently, the patient becomes extremely resistant out of a continuing fear that the revelation of less than ideal impulses, fantasies, or wishes may deprive him of the analyst's admiring eye. For such patients, the grandiose self is not so much confirmed as maintained intact behind a highly defensive façade. In such cases the analyst runs the risk of becoming a threat to the vulnerability of the grandiose self and may even be seen in persecutory or paranoid forms of transferential distortion.

The Kohut argument carries an assumption that where the "archaic" narcissistic configurations or their transferential expressions are identifiable, one is dealing by definition with narcissistic personality disorders as such. This may be one source of diagnostic confusion since both narcissistic configurations can be found expressed in varying degrees and modalities not only in the lower levels of pathological organization, even the psychotic, but also at higher levels of organization, in relatively well-organized more or less neurotic personalities. According to this assumption wherever the idealized imago or grandiose self is identifiable, one is dealing with a narcissistic personality. It seems more reasonable, from the perspective taken in the present study, to view the formulations Kohut has provided as fundamental forms of pathological narcissistic organization that can be found expressed at many different levels of pathology and character structure. Consequently, one can view the narcissistic personality as having one or the other or both of these configurations as a predominant part of the personality structure, but the diagnostic formulation does not rest simply on the identification of these configurations. It must include other factors as well.

One of the primary aspects of narcissistic personality organization and a significant dimension of it₃ diagnosis is the element of self cohesion. Kohut has emphasized that these patients have developmentally attained the stage of cohesive self organization and that for this reason they are capable of establishing stable narcissistic transferences. Moreover, Ornstein (1974b) has emphasized that the establishment and maintenance of a cohesive self is a *sine qua non* for psychoanalysis and lays the ground for the formation of narcissistic transferences. Bursten (1978) marks this relatively greater degree of self cohesion as a central characteristic of the narcissistic personality organization. He writes:

People with narcissistic personality types have a firmer sense of self. Generally, they confirm their sense of self more easily. Kohut (1971) indicates that they have a more cohesive self and are less vulnerable to fragmentation. However, the confirmers utilized in the maintenance of this cohesive sense of self give them their typical narcissistic stamp; they are self-oriented. Self-esteem and the use of omnipotent others to bolster themselves are characteristic [p. 18].

Not only has Kohut (1971) emphasized this cohesiveness of the structure and functioning of the self in such narcissistic personalities, but he sees these factors as significant in discriminating them from primitive borderline or psychotic forms of organization. He comments:

Disturbing as their psychopathology may be, it is important to realize that these patients have specific assets which differentiate them from the psychoses and borderline states. Unlike the patients who suffer from these latter disorders, patients with narcissistic personality disturbances have in essence attained a cohesive self and have constructed cohesive idealized archaic objects. And, unlike the conditions which prevail in the psychoses and borderline states, these patients are not seriously threatened by the possibility of an irreversible disintegration of the archaic self or of the narcissistically cathected archaic objects. In consequence of the attainment of these cohesive and stable psychic configurations, these patients are able to establish specific, stable narcissistic transferences, which allow the therapeutic reactivation of the archaic structures without the danger of their fragmentation through further regression: they are thus analyzable [p. 4].

DISCRIMINATIVE ASPECTS OF THE BORDERLINE CONDITIONS

I would like to turn to those aspects of the borderline conditions that may serve as potential points of differentiation from the narcissistic personality disorders as delineated above. It is important to note in attempting to make a more careful delineation of these syndromes that the extant descriptions of the borderline conditions, dominated of course by Kernberg's (1967) delineation of the borderline personality organization, embrace a fairly wide spectrum of pathological conditions and forms of characterological deficit. Certain aspects of the description of borderline disorders apply to some borderline patients and not to others, whereas other aspects of the description apply to specific subgroups.

One would have to conclude that the borderline conditions constitute a heterogeneous group of diagnostic entities within which further diagnostic specification and refinement are required in order to make sense out of the total clinical picture (Meissner, 1979b). The diagnostic reach of such borderline conditions stretches all the way from the schizophrenia-like conditions described as "pseudoneurotic schizophrenia" (Hoch and Cattell, 1959; Hoch and Polatin, 1949; Hoch et al., 1962) to the forms of borderline personality which seem to present a relatively well-organized and well-functioning neurotic façade, and which begin to be manifested only under conditions of regressive inducement, such as the analytic situation. There is a radical clinical distinction between patients whose borderline features are activated only under conditions of regressive inducement, and then only gradually and in relatively minor degree, and those patients who come to clinical attention under conditions of acute regressive crisis usually requiring hospitalization. The quality of transient regressive psychotic-like states and the marked borderline propensity for acting out, often in self-destructive ways, are characteristic of the lower-order borderline pathologies, such as the psychotic characters and the pseudoneurotic schizophrenias. A fairly large proportion of borderline patients, however, have much better organized and better functioning personality structure and may show little or none of the regressive qualities which have become classically attributed to borderline personality structure. If they show any indications of such propensities, it is often in very subtle or minor degrees, or in periods of transient regressive stress.

In attempting to draw a distinction between the narcissistic personalities and the borderline conditions, Kohut (1971, 1972) has emphasized the relatively greater propensity for regression and regressive disorganization in borderline as compared to narcissistic personalities. That discriminating point retains its validity in reference to forms of borderline personality in which such regressive potential is a marked feature, but it is of considerably less utility in distinguishing between, let us say, the analyzable borderline and the analyzable narcissistic personality.

Other points of discrimination relative to regression may have some validity. Adler (1975) has noted that borderline patients are more likely to regress from a variant of narcissistic transference to a hungry, demanding, clinging stage when the narcissistic longings or needs are not met. Additional hints may be taken from the quality of anxiety in such regressive states; it must be remembered that severe or structural regressions are much less likely to be seen in narcissistic than in borderline patients. The narcissistic emphasis falls much more heavily on the maintenance of narcissistic equilibrium, and the typical narcissistic signal affects of shame and depression reveal the loss of such equilibrium. Anxiety is much less likely to appear though it is much more available to the borderline, and in borderlines frequently has a dramatic life-or-death quality connected with issues of separation or even survival anxiety (Corwin, 1974). When such severe separation or survival anxiety related to the fear of inner fragmentation or dissolution of the self is found in patients whose transferences have a markedly narcissistic quality, they must be regarded diagnostically as falling within the borderline range.

The quality of regressive borderline involvement with objects, that is, the more or less chronically regressed quality of object relationships in lower-order borderlines and the quality of object relationships in higher-order borderlines in transient regressive states, has been described often and well (Kernberg, 1967; Masterson, 1972; Blum, 1972; Adler, 1974; Corwin, 1974). In the therapeutic context Kernberg (1974) has particularly emphasized the expressions of ego weakness, the proneness to transference psychosis, and the repetitive and chronic activation of intense rage reactions with a quality of ruthless demandingness or depreciating attacks on the therapist of borderline patients. These reflect the alternate activation in Kernberg's terms of all-good or all-bad internalized object relations in the transference, the increase of pathogenic splitting reflected in mutually dissociative ego states (such as haughty grandiosity coexisting with feelings of inferiority), the forms of pathological idealization and omnipotent control alternating with narcissistic withdrawal and devaluation. Along with the pathological influence of pregenital and oral aggression, these elements seemed to be quite characteristic of such regressive borderline states.

Kernberg distinguishes these personalities as forms of narcissistic personality which function on a borderline level; the category of narcissistic personality, therefore, is used by him inclusively, as opposed to Kohut's exclusive usage which opposes narcissistic personalities to borderline and psychotic categories. Kernberg (1974), however, also recognizes that the presence of a coherent narcissistic configuration characterizes the narcissistic personality in opposition to the borderline. Such a configuration can give rise to differences in patterns of primitive idealization. The pattern of intense attachment with forms of primitive idealization, found most frequently in women with infantile or borderline personalities who cling desperately and unrealistically to idealized men, may form nonetheless a more enduring pattern than the transitory involvements of narcissistic personalities. The primitive idealization in such borderline patients of the all-good object acts as a defense against the projection of aggression onto the all-bad object and, in Kernberg's view, may even have positive implications as a first step in the direction of establishing a love relationship different from the intolerably ambivalent love-hate relationship to the primary objects. In such patients, when the splitting is modified, the relationship with the love object may be able to begin to tolerate and resolve their primitive pregenital conflicts against which the idealization provides a defense (Kernberg, 1974).

On the other hand, the regressive activation of the grandiose self may serve as the basis for a narcissistic withdrawal and isolation which give rise to a schizoid picture. The role of such schizoid withdrawal as a defense against affects and particularly as a defense against affective involvement with the analyst and the narcissistic quality of the illusion of self sufficiency that accompanies it have been clearly delineated by Modell (1973, 1975).

Although the organization of defenses and the patterns of functioning in such patients can be recognized as specifically narcissistic, we are suggesting here that this recognition may not be an adequate basis for diagnostic discrimination. Rather than simply extending the narcissistic categories to more primitive levels, it may be more useful in the long run to regard these more primitive forms as variants of the borderline syndrome, regarding the variants of schizoid psychopathology as one subsection of borderline pathology (Meissner, 1978a). As Kohut (1971) notes:

The first modification of the dynamic consequences on a specific weakness in the basic narcissistic configurations of the personality concerns a particular mode of defense against the dangerous regressive potential that is associated with the central defect, a defense which usually results in what is referred to as the *schizoid personality*. This defensive organization (which should be included among the borderline states) is characteristically encountered in personalities whose basic pathological propensity is toward the development of psychosis; it is, however, not encountered in patients with analyzable narcissistic personality disturbances. The schizoid defensive organization is the result of a person's (pre)conscious awareness not only of his narcissistic vulnerability, but also, and specifically, of the danger that a narcissistic injury could initiate an uncontrollable regression which would pull him irreveresibly beyond the stage of the nuclear, cohesive, narcissistic configurations [p. 12].

Horner (1976) has noted the oscillatory patterns of object relations in borderline patients. She notes, for example, the double approach-avoidance conflict involving, on the one hand, object loss as the consequence of continuing separation and individuation and, on the other hand, the danger of the loss of self connected with regressive attempts at restitution of the union with the symbiotic object through merger. Driven by separation anxiety and depression on the one hand, and the fear of loss of self on the other, the borderline patient is seen as chronically oscillating between two object-relational positions without being able to gain any stabilization at either. Similarly, Horner sees the borderline patient as alternating between the position of the narcissistic personality, in which the object is seen as existing for or to meet the demands of the self, and the schizoid position, in which the individual flees from any sense of attachment or dependence on the object.

The description of such oscillatory patterns is reminiscent of Kernberg's emphasis on splitting and the maintenance of alternating or often coexistent yet contradictory ego states. Although such patterns are frequently identifiable in the more labile and more primitively organized borderlines, at the lower range of the borderline conditions, they are not at all characteristic of higher-order borderline personality configurations, except under conditions of transient regressive disorganization. Nor do they present a predominant or even identifiable aspect of the day-by-day functioning of such personalities.

The alternation of omnipotence and devaluation frequently seen in such borderline states is a case in point (Kernberg, 1968). Such highly narcissistic extremes serve as a defense against threatening needs and narcissistic vulnerabilities connected with the involvement with others. As Kernberg (1968) notes:

Such "self-idealization" usually implies magical fantasies of omnipotence, the conviction that he, the patient, will eventually receive all the gratification that he is entitled to, and that he cannot be touched by frustration, illness, death, or the passage of time. A corollary of this fantasy is the devaluation of other people, the patient's conviction of his superiority over them, including the therapist. The projection of that magical omnipotence onto the therapist, and the patient's feeling magically united with or submissive to that omnipotent therapist, are other forms which this defensive operation can take [p. 615].

It is quite correct clinically that the more one finds the pattern of such alternation or oscillation present in a patient, the more likely it is that the underlying personality organization is borderline. In the more primitively organized borderline, this may become quite readily apparent insofar as the contradictory ego states and their corresponding transferential paradigms may be quickly mobilized and projected onto the analyst. In the more highly organized borderline patients, however, such oscillatory patterns are by no means immediately evident and may only begin to express themselves after quite long periods of analytic experience and after some significant effects of the analytic regression have taken place. It is only then that the underlying borderline features become apparent, whereas initially such patients may present as looking very neurotic or at times even normal. At that unregressed level of functioning one of these polar positions is usually more or less stabilized while the other is repressed. In contrast, in the narcissistic personality, one is much more likely to find a consistent and coherent, although narcissistically impregnated and vulnerable, configuration, around which the patient's personality is organized and functions.

These differences in the capability for and quality of object relations express themselves in the transference. Within the therapy the borderline patient constantly tends to distort the relationship with the therapist by projections which can undermine an often tenuous therapeutic alliance. These projective distortions may thrust upon the therapist magical expectations of omniscience and omnipotence, while at the same time they subject him to devaluations and counterattacks which reflect the patient's own inner fears of vulnerability and impotence (Adler, 1970). The assigning of omnipotence to the therapist is accompanied by an assumption of impotence, need, and dependence in the patient. His only course is to submit in compliant acceptance, thereby inducing the therapist (he hopes) to use his omnipotence on his behalf. Such patients tend to set unrealistic and grandiose goals so that change or progress in the therapy cannot approach the fantasy and therefore gives little satisfaction.

In the more severely disturbed borderlines there can be rapid oscillation of projections and introjections which affect the organization of self and object representations, creating a fragmentary and shifting configuration of elements of both the self and the perception of objects. Consequently, the perception of other people becomes grossly inconsistent and variable, showing a lack of awareness of contradictions from state to state, a rapid fluctuation between contradictory states, and a volatility of behavior which seems to parallel the perceptual fluctuations. Consequently, the capacity to perceive others as separate, to relate to them realistically in terms of a variety of traits and qualities, gives way to a relationship based on the projection of parts of the self which must then be controlled by possessing or destroying the object.

Such projective turmoil is found only in the more primitive forms of borderline pathology or in borderline regressive states. By and large, in the general run of borderline patients, one does not see this sort of chaotic and fragmentary projective distortion. Nonetheless, significant relationships tend to be discolored by projective expectations and interpretations. Such projective distortions may take place in reasonably healthy or neurotic individuals just as easily, but they present more of a problem for the borderline, since they tend to dominate his perception of the object more pervasively and are less available to correction by other qualifying or contradictory pieces of evidence.

These characteristic and often shifting projective transference distortions are quite different in character from the transference paradigms associated with the narcissistic personality. Narcissistic personalities tend to present relatively stable narcissistic transference paradigms, in which the analyst is related to as one or other form of selfobject. Although the constitution of such selfobjects requires a projective aspect (Meissner, 1978b), its quality is quite different since it is put in the service of maintaining narcissistic equilibrium. Certainly it does not show the shifting and fragmentary pattern frequently seen in the borderline patient.

As Ross (1976) has observed, borderline pathology has more directly to do with failures in the cohesiveness of the self than with specifiable ego defects. Certainly some distinction is necessary here, since ego defects related to specific developmental impediments can be found in the lower-order borderline conditions, but less so in those of a higher order. In this latter realm of borderline pathology, ego functions and their correlative structures seem relatively well integrated, whereas the impairments have more to do with the integration and cohesiveness of the self (Meissner, 1978c). Consequently, attempts to describe borderline pathology in terms of pervasive ego defects have run afoul of this basic differentiation.

Thus, a common impairment in the borderline conditions is the inherent fragility and vulnerability of nuclear narcissistic structures which result in impaired cohesiveness of the self. The potential disruption of such nuclear structures is a continual threat which must be countered by a variety of defensive and avoidance measures, Kernberg has observed with regard to his "lower level" of character pathology that these individuals have a poor integration of self representations so that caricatures of both the good and the bad aspects of important objects come to dominate the inner world without any effective integration. These residues of object relations, the introjects (Meissner, 1979a), serve as the basis for the integration of the self.

In the borderline, the self is thus composed of a chaotic amalgamation of shameful, threatened, impotent, and yet at the same time exalted and omnipotent images. Such a patient may leap from one isolated or more or less coherent self image to the next without any intervening connections to maintain the continuity of self experience. Attempts to help him to gain a measure of synthesis are resisted, and he unconsciously relies on the fantasied magical power of the analyst to provide what is missing and to transform him into a more integrated whole person. As Frances et al. (1977) have noted:

> The borderline patient has integrative deficits in self-constancy which are manifested by persistent fragmentation and splits in his self-structure, occurring in time both cross-sectionally and longitudinally. As a result, his present self-experience is not securely placed within a context of past and future selves. Instead, his ongoing experience of himself contains continual potential newness, unfamiliarity and dissonance—more than the usual discontinuity in the self over time [p. 328].

An important discrimination in terms of the capacity to maintain self cohesiveness must be made between narcissistic personalities and the borderline conditions. In general, narcissistic personalities have been able to establish a relatively cohesive sense of self which is firmer, more consistent, and more stable than that of the borderline. Whereas the narcissistic concerns of grandiosity and the need for an omnipotent other are prominent in the pathology of narcissistic characters, the narcissistic structures remain somewhat vulnerable to transient regression as a consequence of disruption of essential self-supporting relationships. But the danger of fragmentation or disintegration is relatively minor and is buffered by the relatively good resilience of such character structures and the maintenance of well-integrated ego capacities and functioning.

The borderline, however, has a generally less cohesive self which is more readily subject to regression and fragmentation and in which the boundaries between self and object are less securely established. As Bursten (1973) has noted, the threat of inner fragmentation is relatively more central in borderline conditions, whereas the threat of disruption of a narcissistic relationship plays a more central role in the narcissistic personalities. He (1978) notes further that the borderline personality types have to deal with a central difficulty of maintaining a firm sense of self. The self integration is unstable and is at constant risk of dissolution. The narcissistic self is firmer and less at risk, less in danger of fragmentation, but nonetheless needs continual confirmation. The characteristic devices of narcissistic personalities, including narcissistic object choices and the archaic narcissistic configurations described by Kohut, may be seen in this perspective as ways of confirming a threatened or unstable sense of self. Another way of putting it is that the borderline issues are concerned with self cohesion more than self esteem; the narcissistic issues are concerned with self esteem more than self cohesion. In both diagnostic areas, both aspects remain problematic, but the emphasis is different.

The vulnerability of the borderline sense of self and its fragile cohesiveness give rise to attempts to regain or stabilize the self. At times this may be accomplished by fanatical dedication or infatuation with causes, religious movements, or other sources of dedication which allow the borderline to gain some sense of definition of self and a corresponding sense of identity. However, these commitments tend to remain inconstant and often are subject to sudden shifts of conviction in quite different directions. Such involvement in extrinsic causes tends not be characteristic of narcissistic personalities.

STRUCTURAL DIFFERENTIATIONS

I would like to attempt a structural differentiation which might bring some greater clarity to the diagnostic differentiation and to some extent help to explain it. A differentiation can be made in terms of the introjective organization which characterizes these respective forms of psychopathology.

The introjects represent those basic internalizations which form the core elements around which the individual's sense of self is constructed (Meissner, 1971, 1979a). They reflect the defensive and developmental vicissitudes that arise in the experience of object relations, particularly but not exclusively in those relationships that pertain to the primary objects. The organization of the introjects takes place along two primary dimensions, the narcissistic and the aggressive. Consequently, the intrapsychic organization of these introjective configurations can take place along primarily narcissistic lines or along aggressive lines, or in terms of some combination of both.

Each of these dimensions tends to be organized in terms of a polar distribution, which tends to be extreme or absolute in proportion to the degree of psychopathology. Thus, in the narcissistic dimension the introjective configuration can take on the aspect of superiority and grandiosity in one direction, but can also take on the aspect of inferiority and shame-filled insignificance and worthlessness in the other. Similarly, along the aggressive dimension, the introjective configuration expresses itself in terms of polar attributes of hateful, evil, and powerful destructiveness on the one hand, and impotent, helpless, weak vulnerability on the other. I have applied the terms ''aggressor-introject'' and ''victim-introject'' to express these polar coordinates of the aggressive dimension in the organization of pathogenic introjects. By the same token the polar distribution in the narcissistic dimension can be described in terms of the ''superior-introject'' and the correlative ''inferior-introject.''

It should be noted that these polar coordinates are always present together and express correlated and reciprocally linked aspects of the patient's psychopathology. For example, where one finds evidence of the victim-introject, as it might find expression in the patient's sense of vulnerability, helplessness, weakness, or impotence, we can be sure that careful exploration will also turn up evidence of the aggressor-introject—a side of the patient which feels itself to be powerful, destructive, and perhaps even evil and dangerous. Correspondingly, the narcissistic organization of the introjects also has this same reciprocal dimension between the superior and the inferior introject. Where we find the evidence of narcissistic impoverishment and a sense of shameful insignificance and worthlessness, we may be sure that lurking in the background of the patient's unconscious mind is a corresponding configuration which sees itself as special, privileged, and entitled to admiration and special consideration. Behind the sense of shame lurks an exhibitionistic wish, just as behind a sense of inferiority and worthlessness lurks the residues of the grandiose self that Kohut (1971) has described so aptly. Correspondingly, when the patient's narcissistic self aggrandizement and self inflation are a more apparent part of the clinical picture, it can be presumed that the inferior-introject is playing itself out in less apparent and often unconscious ways.

In better organized personalities, the pathological aspects of the organization of the patient's self have a tendency to cluster around one of these introjective configurations with the corresponding repression of the others. Thus, in the depressive neurotic, the components of the inferior-introject reflecting the patient's inherent narcissistic vulnerability and sense of inferiority and worthlessness are easily identifiable, but it is usually only after long and aften arduous therapeutic work that the more hidden and repressed elements of the patient's narcissism become evident, particularly in terms of his inherent sense of narcissistic entitlement and residual grandiosity.

In the somewhat more primitive forms of personality organization we are discussing here, the various aspects of the introjective organization are much more dominant. Not only does the introjective configuration dominate the patient's sense of self, but it is relatively more likely that the various polar aspects of the introjective configuration will come to play a more prominent part in the patient's pathology and often are much more intrusive on his self awareness or much more expressive in various aspects of his pathology than in better organized personalities. This can be seen quite strikingly in forms of borderline pathology in which the various aspects of the introjective configuration are never far from consciousness and are often intrusive, either in the form of determinations of the patient's own sense of self, or in the form of projective distortions of significant objects. Thus, we have become quite familiar with the characteristic picture of the somewhat regressed borderline patient who plays out the role of helpless and impotent victim, while at the same time he projects the elements of aggressive destructiveness and powerful persecutory threat onto the therapist. Both these aspects of the patient's pathology reflect the organization of the introjects in terms of the aggressive polarities implied in the victim- and aggressor-introjects.

Not only is the ready attribution of one polar dimension to the self and the other projectively to the object a characteristic of borderline functioning, but these introjective characterizations can also alternate within the subject himself. Thus, it is not all unusual for the borderline to feel himself the helpless and impotently vulnerable victim at one point and to shift into the opposite introjective posture, that of powerfully destructive agent of hostility, at another. Thus, the victim-introject or the aggressor-introject may come to dominate the patient's sense of himself, and in the less stable and labile forms of regressive expression he may alternate between them, often quite rapidly and dramatically.

It may be possible to try to understand the differences in the organization of the pathological aspects of the narcissistic personalities in contrast to that of the borderline personalities in terms of the organization of these respective introjects. From this point of view, it seems reasonable to say that the narcissistic personality has organized itself around the narcissistically impregnated introjects and that the narcissistic apsects of these internal structures dominate the organization and functioning of the personality. The major preoccupations of the narcissistic personality, therefore, are directed toward the maintenance of the sense of self which requires the corresponding preservation of and narcissistic integrity of these introjective configurations.

Since the predominant introjective configuration is organized around issues of narcissism it has its own inherent characteristics of vulnerablity which have to do with maintenance of narcissistic supplies and supports. Even so, to the extent that the individual is able to maintain these necessary supplies and supports, he is able to maintain a relatively high degree of self integration and cohesiveness. In the moderate degrees of narcissistic impairment and in circumstances in which the individual's ability to gain the necessary narcissistic input is adequate, he runs little risk of severe psychological impairment and is correspondingly reasonably well protected against the threats of regressive disorganization or impairment in self cohesiveness or even of any sense of loss of self or diffusion of identity.

The picture is quite different in the borderline patient. Here the introjective configuration does not center specifically or solely around issues of narcissism, but around a more pathogenic and combined complex of issues having to do with both narcissism and aggression. Whereas the narcissistic personality must deal primarily with the vicissitudes the superior and inferior introjects and with the corresponding narcissistic vulnerabilites, the borderline patient must deal not only with these narcissistic configurations but with the added burden of the aggressor- and victim-introjective configurations as well. Thus, whereas the pathology of the narcissistic personality is more or less confined to the narcissistic sector of the personality, as it affects the integration and functioning of the patient's self, the more prominent intrusion of issues having to do with vicissitudes of aggression make the picture considerably more complex for the borderline personality, and the disruptive influence of unresolved aggressive elements, often stemming from relatively primitive and even oral aggressive-sadistic levels, contributes an additional burden and an additional set of vulnerabilities.

The issues of victimization and victimizing in the borderline personalities play a prominent role not only in their pathology but in their therapy as well (Nadelson, 1976). Thus, the maintenance of a sense of self and a sense of inner organization is made more difficult for the borderline since he must deal not only with the narcissistic issues and the narcissistic vulnerabilities that characterize the narcissistic personality, but with the vicissitudes imposed by unresolved and relatively primitive aggressive components. In terms of their motifs of victimization and threatening destructiveness, therefore, these aggressive components play themselves out in much more dramatic and apparent ways in the psychotherapy of the borderline patient than in that of the narcissistic. The difficulties with aggression in narcissistic patients remain relatively secondary and usually arise in the form of a narcissistic rage which is secondary to narcissistic insult or is a vehicle for redressing narcissistic wrongs.

The vicissitudes of aggression in the borderline patient, however, play a much more primary role and contribute significantly to his inability to establish and maintain a coherent sense of self around any of the available introjective configurations. Consequently, the borderline patient has greater difficulty in establishing or maintaining a sense of object constancy, is only capable of maintaining a sense of inner cohesiveness in relatively partial and unstable ways, and is considerably more vulnerable to regressive pressures and stresses. Although these vicissitudes may be seen most dramatically and clearly in the lower order of borderline pathology and in regressive borderline states, these same parameters play themselves out in more modulated and often more subtle ways through the whole range of borderline pathology. Thus, even in the higher-order and better functioning borderline patient who might be suitable for analysis, the personality may be relatively consistently organized around an integrated self concept which allows for a considerable degree of autonomous functioning. However, under the stress induced by an analytic regression or by a severe narcissistic insult or disappointment, that relatively vulnerable cohesiveness may begin to deteriorate so that the component introjective configurations come to dominate the functioning of the personality and begin to express themselves in a variety of pathological forms.

The same structural and dynamic differentiations suggest that developmentally the borderline patient has not been able to integrate partial good/bad, giving/denying, satisfying/frustrating images of both self and objects. The hostile and loving parts of parental imagos have failed to achieve satisfactory integration due to unresolved aggressive components derived from hostile or ambivalent relations with the significant caretaking objects. The unresolved aggression derives in some sense from drive sources but remains unresolved because of aggressively contaminated internalizations (introjections) from external objects. The result is a form of impaired synthesis of introjective components (splitting) and the tendency to projection of hostility. The organization of object representations fails to achieve a reliable constancy, and self cohesion remains precarious and vulnerable to regressive strain. These developments, as has been suggested by Mahler (1972) and Mahler et al. (1975), probably take place in the rapprochement phase of separation-individuation and reflect deviant resolutions of the "rapprochement crisis."

The narcissistic personality has been shaped by different developmental experiences. The passage through separation and individuation has not been contaminated to the same degree by aggressive derivatives. The narcissistic child does not meet the same degree of parental rejection, disapproval, hostility, or destructiveness. The relationship with both parents is not caught up in an excess of ambivalence, so that the resolution and integration of aggression is a less pressing developmental issue. Rather, the problems for the narcissistic child lie more specifically in the narcissistic sector. The problem in separation and individuation concerns the loss, potential or actual, of the narcissistic communion or narcissistic availability of the parent as separation and the establishing of autonomy assert themselves. The narcissistic personality is left with a greater sense of individuation and correlative self cohesion, but with a pervasive sense of narcissistic need and a sense of narcissistic vulnerability from the potential or actual loss of narcissistically invested objects.

In a recent discussion of developmental aspects of both narcissistic and borderline pathologies, Settlage (1977) offers the following comment:

The distinction between narcissistic and borderline disorders in terms of differences in their specific determinants and psychopathologies has not yet been adequately drawn. As one possibilty, these differences may prove to be due to a difference in the timing of traumatic experience in the developmental sequence. The generally held clinical impression that borderline disorders are more severe than narcissistic disorders may be accounted for by a developmentally earlier, and therefore more devastating, trauma in the borderline disorder. A second possibility is that the difference between these two conditions will be explained by the degree of traumatic impact and the extremity of defensive response. And thirdly, the difference may come to be understood in terms of the area of personality involved in developmental arrest and pathologic formation, for example, involvement of the sense of self and identity as these can be distinguished from ego capacities and functions per se [pp. 810–811].

All these possibilities remain possible. We have not yet come to terms with the heterogeneity of borderline conditions and the fact that diagnostic differentiations (Meissner, 1978a) may shed important discriminating light on their theoretical diversity (Meissner, 1978c). I have suggested in the present study that the nature and level of structural deficit vary from higher-order borderline conditions to lower-order. Difficulties in self integration and functioning in the former give way to both self and ego deficits in the latter, and these reflect specific developmental impairments.

However, if both narcissistic and borderline conditions reflect vicissitudes of the rapprochement period and crisis (Settlage, 1977), the differences between these conditions—let us say specifically between narcissistic personalities and higher-order borderline conditions—may lie in the quality of that experience and its resolution. The continuity of libidinal availability of the mother may play a crucial role. Mothers who experience difficulty in accepting and fostering the child's assertive thrust into emerging autonomy, with its often resistant and protecting noncompliance, can react defensively by emotional withdrawal or by excessive anger and attempts to control the child's impulse to individuate.

We might wonder to what extent these variant patterns of response play a role in altering the titer of narcissistic threat resulting in the closure of personality organization around introjective residues of an infantile grandiose self, or of heightened ambivalence and aggressive conflict resulting in the internalization of aggressive conflicts which prejudice the consolidation of introjective self components and jeopardize the integration of object representations in the achievement of libidinal object constancy.

SUMMARY

I have attempted a diagnostic differentiation, based on descriptive clinical and structural considerations, between narcissistic personality disorders and the borderline conditions. I have argued that the narcissistic personality disorders constitute a group of higher-order character pathologies characterized by stable narcissistic transferences (described by Kohut, 1971) and possessing evidences of achieved self cohesion, stable characterological traits, minimal regressive tendency, and a stability of functioning. Narcissistic needs and the seeking of narcissistic stability through the gaining of narcissistic supplies and supports from narcissistically invested objects predominate.

More primitive forms of narcissistic pathology with severer degrees of impairments in self cohesion and heightened regressive tendencies should not be regarded as forms of narcissistic personality, but fall more appropriately within the borderline category. The fact that these more primitive forms of narcissistic pathology also manifest archaic narcissistic formations, typically the grandiose self and the idealized parental imago, should not argue to the diagnosis of narcissistic personality disorder, but should simply reflect more primitive forms of narcissistic pathology existing in other developmentally earlier and more severe forms of psychopathology. The borderline conditions, on the other hand, form a spectrum of forms of psychopathology extending from higher-order borderline conditions (primitive hysteric, borderline personality) in which the more typical borderline features emerge only after significant regression, whether induced analytically or precipitated by stress, to more primitive forms of borderline organization characterized by tendencies to regression, emotional lability, instability, tendencies to act out, more subtle forms of thought disorder, and other indexes of more primitive personality functioning and organization.

The diagnostic discrimination between narcissistic personalities as such and the higher-order borderline conditions, especially those manifesting narcissistic impairments, is difficult, and in specific cases it may be impossible, with room for some diagnostic overlap. Nonetheless, subtle indicators may be identifiable which facilitate a differentiation even at this level. Yet it is suggested that the narcissistic and borderline disorders may differ less in the timing of traumatic experience in the developmental sequence or in the degree of traumatic impact and defense, or even in the area of personality involved in developmental arrest, than in the quality of developmental experience, particularly in the crucial rapprochement phase. These other aspects of developmental fixation and failure or arrest may shed greater light on the differentiation between the narcissistic and higher-order borderline conditions and the more primitive lower-order borderline conditions.

REFERENCES

Adler, G. (1970), Valuing and devaluing in the psychotherapeutic process. *Arch. Gen. Psychiat.*, 22: 454–461.

——(1974), Regression in psychotherapy: Disruptive or therapeutic? *Internat. J. Psycho-Anal. Psychother.*, 3:252–264.

——(1975), The usefulness of the "borderline" concept in psychotherapy. In: *Borderline States in Psychiatry*, ed. J. E. Mack. New York: Grune and Stratton, pp. 29–40.

Blum, H. P. (1972), Psychoanalytic understanding and psychotherapy of borderline regression. *Internat. J. Psycho-Anal. Psychother.*, 1(1):46–60.

Bursten, B. (1973), Some narcissistic personality types. *Internat. J. Psycho-Anal.*, 54:287–300.

——(1978), A diagnostic framework. *Internat. Rev. Psycho-Anal.*, 5:15–31.

Corwin, H. A. (1974), The narcissistic alliance and the progressive transference neurosis in serious regressive states. *Internat. J. Psychoanal. Psychother.*, 3:299–316.

Deutsch, H. (1942), Some forms of emotional disturbance and their relation to schizophrenia. In: *Neurosis and Character Types*. New York: International Universities Press, 1965, pp. 262–286.

Frances, A., Sacks, M., & Aronoff, M. S. (1977), Depersonalization: A self-relations perspective. *Internat. J. Psycho-Anal.*, 58:325–331.

Hersey, J. (1959), *The War Lover*. New York: Knopf.

Hoch, P. H. & Polatin, P. (1949), Pseudoneurotic forms of schizophrenia. *Psychoanal. Quart.*, 23:248–276.

—— & Cattell, J. P. (1959), The diagnosis of pseudoneurotic schizophrenia. *Psychoanal. Quart.*, 33:17–43.

—— ——Strahl, M. O., & Pennes, H. (1962), The course and outcome of pseudoneurotic schizophrenia. *Amer. J. Psychiat.*,119:106–115.

Horner, A. J. (1976), Oscillatory patterns of object relations and the borderline patient. *Internat. R. Psycho-Anal.*, 3:479–482.

Kernberg, O. F. (1967), Borderline personality organization. *J. Amer. Psychoanal. Assn.*, 15:641–685.

——(1968), The treatment of patients with borderline personality organization. *Internat. J. Psycho-Anal.*, 49:600–619.

——(1970), Factors in the psychoanalytic treatment of narcissistic personalities. *J. Amer. Psychoanal. Assn.*, 18:51–85.

——(1971), Prognostic considerations regarding borderline personality organization. *J. Amer. Psychoanal. Assn.*, 19:595–635.

——(1974), Contrasting viewpoints regarding the nature and psychoanalytic treatment of narcissistic personalities: A preliminary communication. *J. Amer. Psychoanal. Assn.*, 22:255–267.

——(1975), *Borderline Conditions and Pathological Narcissism*. New York: Jason Aronson.

——(1976), Technical considerations in the treatment of borderline personality organization. *J. Amer. Psychoanal. Assn.*, 24:795–829.

Kohut, H. (1971), *The Analysis of the Self*. New York: International Universities Press.

——(1972), Thoughts on narcissism and narcissistic rage. *The Psychoanalytic Study of the Child*, 27:360–400. New York: Quadrangle Books.

Mahler, M. S. (1972), Rapprochement subphase of the separation-individuation process. *Psychoanal. Quart.*, 41:487–506.

——Pine, F., & Bergman, A. (1975), *The Psychological Birth of the Human Infant: Symbiosis and Individuation*. New York: Basic Books.

Masterson, J. F. (1972), *Treatment of the Borderline Adolescent: A Developmental Approach*. New York: Wiley.

Meissner, W. W. (1971), Notes on identification. 2: Clarification of related concepts. *Psychoanal. Quart.*, 40:277–302.

——(1977), The Wolf Man and the paranoid process. *Ann. Psychoanal.*, 5:23–74. New York: International Universities Press.

——(1978a), Notes on the potential differentiation of borderline conditions. *Internat. J. Psycho-Anal. Psychother.*, forthcoming.

——(1978b), *The Paranoid Process*. New York: Jason Aronson.

——(1978c), Theoretical assumptions of concepts of the borderline personality. *J. Amer. Psychoanal. Assn.*, 26:559–598.

——(1979a), Internalization and object-relations. *J. Amer. Psychoanal. Assn.*, 27:345–360.

——(1979b), Notes on the levels of differentiation within borderline conditions. *Psychoanal. Rev.*, forthcoming.

Modell, A. H. (1973), Affects and psychoanalytic knowledge. *Ann. Psychoanal.*, 1:117–124. New York: International Universities Press.

——(1975), A narcissistic defense against affects and the illusion of self-sufficiency. *Internat. J. Psycho-Anal.*, 56:275–282.

Nadelson, T. (1976), Victim, victimizer: Interaction in the psychotherapy of borderline patients. *Internat. J. Psycho-Anal. Psychother.*, 5:115–129.

Ornstein, P. H. (1974a), Discussion of the paper of Otto F. Kernberg, "Further contributions to the treatment of narcissistic personalities." *Internat. J. Psycho-Anal.*, 55:241–247.

——(1974b), On narcissism: Beyond the inroduction. *Ann. Psychoanal.*, 2:127–149. New York: International Universities Press.

Reich, A. (1953), Narcissistic object choice in women. *J. Amer. Psychoanal. Assn.*, 1:22–44.

Ross, M. (1976), The borderline diathesis. *Internat. Rev. Psycho-Anal.*, 3: 305–321.

Settlage, C. F. (1977), The psychoanalytic understanding of narcissistic and borderline personality disorders: Advances in developmental theory. *J. Amer. Psychoanal. Assn.*, 25:805–833.

Tartakoff, H. H. (1966), The normal personality in our culture and the Nobel Prize complex. In: *Psychoanalysis—A General Psychology*. ed. R. M. Loewenstein, L. M. Newman, M. Schur, & A. J. Solnit. New York: International Universities Press, pp. 222–252.

Vaillant, G. E. (1975), Sociopathy as a human process: A viewpoint. *Archiv. Gen. Psychiat.*, 32:178–183.

Zetzel, E. R. & Meissner, W. W. (1973), *Basic Concepts of Psychoanalytic Psychiatry*. New York: Basic Books.

17. The Mirror and the Mask: On Narcissism and Psychoanalytic Growth

Philip M. Bromberg

INTRODUCTION

Trying to extract some coherent view of narcissism from the ongoing controversy in the current psychoanalytic literature is somewhat like trying to chill Russian vodka by adding ice cubes; it is possible to do it, but the soul of the experience is diluted. Levenson's (1978, p. 16) suggestion that "it may not be the truth arrived at as much as the manner of arriving at the truth which is the essence of therapy", leads me to wonder if it may likewise be said that it is not the definition of narcissism arrived at as much as the struggle to arrive at one, which is the essence of recent progress in psychoanalytic thought. The struggle contains within it, an emerging shift in perspective that has begun to influence our conceptions of clinical diagnosis, the nature of human development, psychoanalytic metatheory, and the parameters of psychoanalytic treatment itself.

During the past two decades there has been a gradual but consistent movement of the mainstream of psychoanalysis in the direction of field theory, and toward the interpersonal context as the medium of both normal maturation and therapeutic change (See Bromberg, 1979a). This has brought the developmental models of psychopathology and analytic technique into closer harmony than ever before, and has focused attention on the growth of "self" as inseparable from the interrelationship of "self and other", whether in the parental environment or the therapeutic environment.

Analysts have been studying how the interpersonal field mediates the process by which self and object representations are born and internally structured; how inadequacy of interpersonal experience during various phases of maturation can lead to structural pathology of the representational world itself; how this structural pathology can lead to specific forms of character disorders traditionally considered untreatable by psychoanalysis; and how a psychoanalytic relationship with such patients might indeed be possible from a field theory orientation.

As one outcome of this paradigm shift, the subject of narcissism has become as currently fascinating and humanly real as it has formerly been wooden and artificial. The metapsychological "puppet", like Pinocchio, has come alive and gained a "self". In so doing it has become more interesting to psychoanalysts as an issue of treatment approach and as a clinical data base supplementing hysteria, than as the original construct shaped by Freud (1914) to account for certain aspects of theory.

The narcissistic personality has become accessible, as a live human being, to psychoanalytic treatment; but the term "narcissism" is now more vague and ambiguous as a hypothetical construct and as a nosological entity—"the narcissistic personality disorder". It has in fact become almost a kind of operational watershed which is used to describe those individuals whose object relations are characteristic of the developmental level of mental representation that Anna Freud (1969) calls "need satisfying", that Mahler (1972) describes as "magical omnipotence", and that Immanuel Kant might consider a systematic violation of his categorical imperative; individuals who experience other people as a means to an end rather than as an end in themselves. The defining qualities are most often described in the psychoanalytic literature as a triad of vanity, exhibitionism, and arrogant ingratitude, which for better or worse (Lasch, 1979, p.33), is what the word "narcissism" has come to mean in popular usage.

Bach (1977, p. 209) describes what it feels like from behind the analyst's couch as ". . . talking into the wind or writing on the sand, only to have one's words effaced moments later by the waves. The patient either welcomes or resents the analyst's words (and) frequently does not even register the actual content. A session which seems to have led to a certain understanding or experience of some kind may, 24 hours later, be totally forgotten."

It is a quality of unrelatedness which represents the failure in development of a spontaneous, stable, taken-for-granted self experience. The individual tends not to feel himself at the center of his own life. He is prevented from full involvement in living because he is developmentally stuck between "the mirror and the mask"—a reflected appraisal of himself, or a disguised search for one, through which the self finds or seeks affirmation of its own significance. Living becomes a process of controlling the environment and other people from behind a mask. When successful it is exhilarating; when unsuccessful there is boredom, anxiety, resentment, and emptiness. But the critical fact is that an ongoing sense of full involvement in life is missing, often without awareness. The intrinsic experience of accomplishment is transformed into one of manipulation, exploitation, and a vague feeling of fooling people. A state of well-being becomes the goal of living rather than its characteristic quality, and the moment to moment sense of being has little relevance other than as a preparation for the next moment. Existence becomes either a search or a waiting period for that moment not yet here when real life and true love will begin. The present is always imperfect in and of itself.

What keeps the person going, and often able to manage the external appearance of a relatively well-functioning life, is an internal structure referred to in the psychoanalytic literature as a "grandiose self" (Kernberg, 1975; Kohut, 1971, 1972, 1977). Its main job is to be perfect (See Rothstein, 1980); that is, to achieve approbation, to never be dependent, and to never feel lacking in any way. Although there is theoretical disagreement as to how this "grandiose self" is established, most analysts pretty much concur that it conceals beneath it a self image described by Kernberg (1975) as

a hungry, enraged, empty self, full of impotent anger at being frustrated, and fearful of a world which seems as hateful and revengeful as the patient himself (p. 233) . . . The greatest fear of these patients is to be dependent on anybody else because to depend means to hate, envy, and expose themselves to the danger of being exploited, mistreated, and frustrated (p. 235).

Consequently, any confrontation with this self image of perfection evokes an immediate need to protect it, and the other person is typically greeted with either an increased dose of disdainful aloofness or with self-righteous rage. This often poses a bit of a problem for mates, lovers, employers, friends, and analysts, should they tend to be more than a "need-satisfying object".

The picture I have been presenting is that of pathological narcissism. Whether such a thing as "normal" narcissism can be said to exist as a distinct entity is currently a controversial issue. Ernest Becker (1973) has presented a particularly compelling sociological position which examines and recasts the psychoanalytic theory of neurosis in the context of man's need to cope with existential anxiety.

"In man", Becker states (pp. 3–6),

a working level of narcissism is inseparable from self-esteem, from a basic sense of self-worth . . . it is all too absorbing and relentless to be an aberration; it expresses the heart of the creature: the desire to stand out, to be *the* one in creation. When you combine natural narcissism with the basic need for self-esteem, you create a creature who has to feel himself an object of primary value: first in the universe, representing in himself all of life.

Man, he says, is hopelessly absorbed with himself, and ". . . if everyone honestly admitted his urge to be a hero it would be a devastating release of truth". But the truth about one's need for a sense of personal heroism is not easy to admit, and thus, ". . . to become conscious of what one is doing to earn his feelings of heroism is the main self-analytic problem of life".

Becker is not taking a position that narcissism is psychiatrically healthy; rather that it is an inevitable and essential form of madness which protects us from the greater clinical madness of having to fully apprehend our own mortality in an ongoing way. As he sees it, our normal narcissism spares us from having ". . . to live a whole lifetime with the fate of death haunting one's dreams" (p. 27); a truth which if fully faced would literally drive man insane. What psychoanalysis has done, Becker asserts, is to reveal to us the complex intrapsychic and interpersonal penalties of denying the truth of man's condition. The psychological and social costs of pretending to be other than what we are is called "neurosis.".

Pathological narcissism, in this framework, is one of the particular characterological tolls that is increasingly being paid by man in contemporary society as he tries to deny his apprehension of non-being. At its core, it describes a sense of self lacking sufficient inner resources to give meaning to life simply through living it fully. Man's relentless need to validate the "self" as the goal of living may be the form of personality disorder that most fascinates psychoanalysts in our time because the experience of meaninglessness may be the context in which the feeling of non-being most typically expresses itself in our time. Peter Marin (1975) in fact believes that in current society ". . . the self replaces community, relation, neighbor, chance, or God", and sees the culturally prevailing psychological character organization as what he labels "the new narcissism".

Psychoanalytically, it can be argued that in line with Becker's perspective on the nature of the human condition, the potential for normal as well as pathological narcissism is co-existent with birth. Mahler (1972, p. 333) states that the developmental need for a separation-individuation process is based in part upon the fact that "the biological birth of the human infant and the psychological birth of the individual are not coincident in time. The former is a dramatic and readily observable, well-circumscribed event; the latter, a slowly unfolding intra-psychic process. For the more or less normal adult, the experience of being both fully 'in' and at the same time basically separate from the 'world out there' is among the givens of life that are taken for granted." But she also acknowledges (p. 338) that starting with birth and regardless of the adaptability of the outside environment, the human being is engaged in an ". . . eternal struggle against both fusion and isolation. One could regard the entire life cycle as constituting a more or less successful process of distancing from and introjection of the lost symbiotic mother, and eternal longing for the actual or fantasied 'ideal state of self', with the latter standing for a symbiotic fusion with the 'all good' symbiotic mother, who was at one time part of the self in a blissful state of well-being". In other words, simply because unlike other animals, our psychological birth takes place after our physical birth and outside of the uterus rather than inside of it, psychological maturation is inherently traumatic to some degree, and the security of the "self" is never fully stable. The potential for narcissistic pathology—difficulty in being both fully "in" and at the same time basically separate from "the world out there"—is therefore present from birth but need not develop into a characterological aggrandizement of "self" in adulthood.

Freud's (1911) example of a situation in which the pleasure principle reigns supreme and the reality of the external world is excluded, was "a bird's egg with its food supply enclosed in its shell". Ferenczi (1913) expanded on Freud's statement that the prototype of the pleasure principle was in this self-contained existence where no stimuli from the outside can impinge, and asserted that it is in fact the period of life spent in the womb which, as a stage of human development, totally represents Freud's example. It is this stage, Ferenczi argued, which truly defines omnipotence. It is not the state of having all of one's needs met, but a state in which one doesn't even need to need. It is the state of total self-sufficiency. Glatzer & Evans (1977, pp. 89–90) formulate Ferenczi's view as follows: "The clear implication of this first stage . . . this period of unconditional omnipotence . . . is that growing up is painful quite apart from the nature of the environment. The unconscious fiction of the frustrating 'outside' is ineluctable and universal. It is the inevitable consequence of being born. The cardinal importance of Ferenczi's contribution is this: The reactive rage of the child to not being fed is not due merely to the fact that he is hungry; he is more likely to be depressed. The main cause of his anger is that his illusion of self-sufficiency is constantly being shattered".

The parallel is striking between this idea of traumatic loss of omnipotence, and Becker's existential view of narcissism in man as ". . . the toll that his pretense of sanity takes as he tries to deny his true condition" (Becker, 1973, p. 30). What is called the "grandiose self" structure may be thus seen as a core patterning of self-other representation designed to protect the illusion of self-sufficiency at all costs, because in pathological narcissism it is also disguising the individual's lack of a fully individuated identity. The way in which such patients use detachment as an ego defense is illustrative. Schecter (1978, p. 82) points out that in most character structures the detachment defense attempts to convert the fear of being abondoned, an ego-passive fear, to an active movement away from relationship; the consequence is that the greater the depth of detachment, the greater will be the sense of futility; i.e., no hope for a "good relationship". In the case of pathological narcissism, however, it is my belief (Bromberg, 1979b, p. 597) that the emptiness and futility that accompany detachment do not come from the lack of hope for a "good relationship", but as a functional consequence of dimly recognizing a need for any relationship at all. The "futility" is most directly an experience of "ego depletion". It is a felt "inadequacy" of the grandiose self elicited in these individuals by evidence that they lack anything that is not contained in themselves; it is, in effect, a temporary unmasking of the illusion of self-sufficiency.

Whether we accept Becker's premise that the basis of narcissism is man's need to deny mortality by an illusion of total self-sufficiency (which he calls "heroism"), his viewpoint is paradigmatically consistent with that of Sullivan (1953, 1964a, 1964b) and Fromm (1947, 1956, 1964), and follows the direction in which interpersonal psychoanalysis and object relations theory seems to be moving; i.e., towards the concept that all narcissistic pathology is, fundamentally, mental activity designed by a grandiose interpersonal self representation to preserve its structural stability, and to maintain, protect, or restore its experience of well-being (See Schafer, 1968, pp. 191–193; Stolorow, 1975, p. 179; Sandler & Sandler, 1978, pp. 291–295; Horner, 1979, p. 32). Becker's formulation also resonates in an equally striking, although conceptually distinct way, with Kohut's (1971, 1972) position that narcissism and narcissistic rage are developmentally normal, and given the proper early environment should lead to healthy assertiveness, to a firm sense of self esteem, and to a relatively well integrated balance between feeling both in the world and separate from it. Becker (1973, p. 22) states:

The child who is well nourished and loved develops, as we said, a sense of magical omnipotence, a sense of his own indestructibility, a feeling of proven power and secure support. He can imagine himself, deep down, to be eternal. We might say that his repression of the idea of his own death is made easy for him because he is fortified against it in his very narcissistic vitality.

The clinical problem confronting contemporary psychoanalysis, however, is not metaphysical, and is no myth, even though it allegedly all started with one.

THE PROBLEM OF ANALYZABILITY

It has been written that the nymph Echo had fallen in love with a handsome youth named Narcissus, who unfortunately loved nobody but himself. Echo, however, had her own problems. She had been previously punished by a jealous goddess and had lost the gift of forming her own words, so that she could from then on only repeat the words of others. As Narcissus bent to drink one day in a quiet pool, he noticed in the mirroring surface of the water, the handsomest face he had ever seen. "I love you", said Narcissus to the handsome face. "I love *you*", repeated Echo eagerly as she stood behind him. But Narcissus neither saw nor heard her, being spellbound by the reflection in the water. He sat smiling at himself, forgetting to eat or drink, until he wasted away and died. This, by one account (D'Aulaire & D'Aulaire, 1962) may be the first recorded instance of premature termination due to an unresolved mirror transference.

The descendents of Narcissus now lie upon an analytic couch, as self-absorbed as ever, while behind them, as in the myth, sit the deter-mined but still frustrated counterparts of Echo, trying to be heard. Old narcissism or "new narcissism", it's still not easy. In some ways, though, we have progressed since that fatal day at the pool. Psychoan-alysts have begun to recognize that the solution to the problem is not located solely in the patient, and that perhaps Echo and Narcissus were less than an ideal match. One might even go as far as to suggest that Echo was working under an unnecessary handicap of her own.

Psychoanalysts, in order to practice psychoanalysis as defined by its agreed upon parameters, are bound by a particular stance which like Echo's, may have handicapped them in facilitating structural growth in narcissistic patients. Echo's burden was not just that she could only repeat what she heard, but that in so doing, she too was unable to exist as a person in her own right and thereby unable to know whether Narcissus could be reached by a different approach.

Analysts have more or less agreed that narcissistic disorders are difficult to treat and that the so-called "unmodified psychoanalytic situation" doesn't do the job. Gedo (1977, p. 792), for example, states that "In effect, no consensus has yet been reached about the appropriate analytic response to the transference manifestations of the grandiose self. Everyone is in agreement, however, about the absolute necessity of responding to these infantile claims with maximal tact and empathy . . . any failure in this regard is inevitably followed by humiliation and outrage".

In discussing the analyzability of narcissistic personality disorders, Rothstein (1982, pp. 177–178) accurately observes that certain of these patients lack the ego assets to enable them to participate in an analytic process that is relatively independent of what the analyst contributes through his own personality and approach to the patient. Because, however, these ego assets are in his view "essential prerequisities" for a genuine analytic experience, their core psychopathology is inacces-sible to interpretation and these patients are deemed unanalyzable in-asmuch as their pre-existing personality structure requires more than the unmodified psychoanalytic situation. "Interpretive attempts to fa-cilitate a working through process can evoke psychotic regressions (and) serious acting-out, sometimes including rapid disruption of the working relationship". This emphasis, Rothstein argues, is important because there are subjects who can accommodate to an analytic situation but whose analytic processes rarely develop past the regressive internalization of the analyst as a reparative narcissistically invested introject characteristic of mid-phase process. These subjects may experience significant therapeutic benefit from such a relationship. However, where reparative or 'transmuting' internalization gained in the non-verbal 'mirroring', 'holding', or 'containing' ambiance is the primary mode of therapeutic action, a therapeutic rather than analytic result had been achieved.

In other words, the prognosis for a successful analytic outcome is tied directly to a model of treatment in which the primary mode of therapeutic action is held to be that of interpretation. The patients he describes are considered unanalyzable because he feels them to be characterologically unable to utilize verbal interpretation, and able to benefit therapeutically only from "mirroring"—from "swallowing whole" the analyst's non-verbal positive attitude and unconditional acceptance.

Perhaps so. But once again, might not the problem as well as the solution be located in the nature of the relationship between Echo and Narcissus, rather than in Narcissus alone? The issue of whether interpretation or internalization of the analyst is the "genuine" agent of analytic growth may not only be irrelevant (See Strachey, 1934; Friedman, 1978), but may itself lead the analyst, like Echo, to a technique which fulfills its own prophesy of analytic failure.

The patient's sovereign need to control the object from behind a mask, often precludes an ability to "work" in the transference; i.e., to directly experience and report, as material, ongoing thoughts and feelings about the analyst and the process itself. The need to protect the stability of the grandiose self requires that he ward off any experience that leads to relinquishing his narcissistically invested representation of the analyst and the analytic situation. Right from the start, therefore, there is a frequent challenge to the conditions and formal structure of the analysis itself, in order to prevent direct experience of the transference. By the establishment of narcissistic transference configurations, the patient limits the analyst's ability to create an analytic setting which might lead to transference regression and any experience of needing more from the analyst than he is getting. The patient's only initial hope of success in treatment is that which unconsciously guides the rest of his life—to perform for the analyst and be rewarded by "cure". The analyst is therefore typically under pressure to bend his analytic structure and his approach regarding such issues as frequency of sessions, use of the couch, payment of bills, and his own characteristic level of responsiveness.

If the analyst holds a strong commitment to the concept of an "unmodified psychoanalytic situation", then any compromises he may make out of "therapeutic necessity" are simultaneously processed as "resistances" to a "genuine" analysis that has not yet begun, and which must be interpreted when the timing seems right. For certain types of patients this perspective is appropriate and most often leads to a successful outcome, but for others—narcissistic disorders in particular—it may work against its own intent and can potentially become a significant factor in either treatment impasse or a premature diagnosis of unanalyzability.

The goal of getting the patient to experience and acknowledge an ongoing transference process and to work with it analytically, is indeed the central issue. But the heart of the pathology in these patients focuses upon that being their most fundamental inability; to be both "in the world" and "separate from it" at the same time, without endangering the one internal structure they depend upon for a sense of identity— the grandiose self. The wish for the patient to enter into a "real" analysis is not in itself untherapeutic, inappropriate, or even countertransferential in the narrow use of the term; but with narcissistic disorders it is a perspective which, if too important to the analyst, may easily become the unconscious focal point which the patient holds onto in order to remain safely stuck between the mirror and the mask. As long as interpretations, no matter how tactfully administered, are directed towards the patient's transference resistance, the patient will process the experience as though the analyst were another version of a self-interested, narcissistic parental figure who is more interested in getting the patient to meet his own needs than in helping the patient. In order to ward off this perception of the analyst, the narcissistic transference configurations will become even more impenetrable or more brittle. The patient will, in other words, respond with either increased idealization of the analyst, with increased detachment, or with a marginal transference psychosis.

The clinical dilemma is genuine. There are indeed patients who, at least for long periods of time, react to interpretations only as personal feelings held by the analyst, and from the unmodified analytic stance are unanalyzable when they seem to have a serious potential for ego-disorganization or acting-out in response to this stance. If for the moment we reduce the priority of whether what we are doing conforms to the more orthodox definition of psychoanalysis, then much of the apparent disagreement becomes secondary to an approach which is potentially reconcilable with the majority of analytic viewpoints, though it most directly reflects the influence of the interpersonal position and object relations theory. It is based upon looking at the analytic situation as an open, empathic, interpersonal matrix within which the patient's representational world has maximal opportunity to become systematically repatterned and restructured at increasingly higher development levels. It is a perspective which has its deepest roots in the pioneer work of many different analysts at different points in the history of psychoanalysis, and represents a common thread linking the otherwise diverse schools of thought represented by such seminal authors as Ferenczi (1909, 1929), Strachey (1934), Sullivan (1953), Thompson (1956), Fairbairn (1952, 1954), Guntrip (1961, 1968), Winnicott (1965), Gitelson (1962), and Balint (1968).

Ernest Becker's (1964) treatise on what he views as the postscientistic "revolution in psychiatry" captures this orientation particularly vividly and without recourse to the theoretical constructs of any one school of psychoanalysis.

The patient is not struggling against himself, against forces deep within his animal nature. He is struggling rather against the loss of his world, of the whole range of action and objects that he so laboriously fashioned during his early training. He is fighting, in sum, against the subversion of himself in the only world that he knows. Each object is as much a part of him as is the built-in behavior pattern for transacting with the object. Each action is as much within his nature as the self-feeling he derives from initiating or contemplating that action. Each rule for behavior is as much a part of him as is his metabolism, the forward momentum of his life processes (p. 170). . . . The individual would have an easy time changing his early 'inauthentic' style if he could somehow disengage his own commitment to it. But rules, objects, and self-feeling are fused—taken together they constitute one's 'world'. How is one to relinquish his world unless he first gains a new one? This is the basic problem of personality change (p. 179).

He then addresses an issue which encapsulates the dilemma faced by analysts in attemping to treat narcissistic disorders; the patient's lack of an observing ego which can disembed itself sufficiently from its own world to be able to examine with the analyst the structure he is most in danger of losing should he become too clearly aware of it.

Some individuals are fortunate in their early training. . . . The result is that they have their own feeling of value pretty much in hand, so to speak. . . . Hence they can 'back off' from any *particular* object and examine it critically; they are not bound to narrow action needs. To be able to withdraw from any action-commitment long enough to appraise it critically needs the secure possession of one's own positive self-feeling. . . . The self-image does not depend hopelessly on any one object, or on any unquestionable rule. . . . Obviously this strength will be absent where . . . the rules are uncritically and inextricably fused with a particular concrete object (pp. 179–180).

Here in this final sentence is the kernel of the issue of analyzability. Individuals from whom interpersonal rules are rigidly fused with a particular concrete object representation, bring to the analytic situation a core representation of "self" which is fused equally concretely to the same interpersonal unit. Such individuals do not possess a core identity which is stable enough in its own right and flexible enough for them to 'back off' and observe themselves in the analytic process while still being immersed in it. They cannot "work" in the transference until they free themselves, at least to some degree, from the particular concrete object or part-object (Fairbairn, 1952) representation which defines their basic feeling of self-value.

For patients suffering from pathological narcissism, the "grandiose self" representation is developmentally fused to the "need-satisfying object" by a set of interpersonal operations designed to prevent the object from being little more than a mirror, and to keep the true nature of those operations "masked". The analyst and the analytic situation are primarily external versions of that concrete mental representation, and it is thus extremely difficult to help such patients mobilize their own power of critical observation to examine their narcissistic transference configurations objectively. They cannot, in Becker's terms, genuinely work on "relinquishing their old world" without a "new one" being felt as at least within their grasp. From this orientation, one aspect of the analytic process is to facilitate the patient's development of the necessary mental structure to most fully utilize it. The analytic relationship is thus the most potentially powerful and subtle instrument in the treatment process. It represents a therapeutic environment which can be flexibly adapted to the patient's developmental level and its variability, rather than a fixed set of rules to which a patient must be able to accommodate or the analyst must "modify" if the patient does not possess the "prerequisite ego assets".

The analyst is committed to an approach rather than being bound to a technique. He does not need to make a choice independent of any particular patient, between interpretation as mutative and mirroring as reparative. The therapeutic action of the analytic process is seen as containing for all patients both elements as necessary and intrinsic parts of the interpersonal field which mediates it. For any given patient, however, the relative significance of each element in the overall field will initially depend upon the developmental level of mental structure that defines his core identity. For some patients the ability to fully utilize the analytic situation will then depend upon how much growth has occurred in the establishment of a stable sense of separate identity, while for others (the traditional "good" analytic patient) it is not an issue.

Pine (1979) makes the distinction between affects which are transformed from earlier affects (such as traumatic anxiety into signal anxiety), and affects which are created when the inner psychological structure is right for it. He refers most specifically to affect states that ". . . crystallize around the child's acquisition of self-other differentiation . . ." and are ". . . first born at later stages in the developmental process when the psychological conditions for their emergence are met. These psychological conditions involve new learnings—new acquisitions of mental life . . ." (p. 93). In my view this is equally pertinent as a treatment issue where a sufficient sense of separate core identity is not present to begin with in the analysis. It implies the developmental necessity of an initial period in treatment that allows the creation of the "right inner psychological structure" upon which later acquisitions can be built. By being able to utilize the presence and emotional availability of the analyst, the patient is given a setting in which he can begin to build this "prerequisite" structure and slowly "heal" the developmentally fixated source of anxiety associated with the insufficient maturation of autonomous tension-reducing patterns of self and object representations; i.e., a core identity whose stability is relatively independent of external nourishment. In the case of pathological narcissism, before the patient can develop a genuine working alliance and the ability to value and conceptually utilize new experience of himself conveyed through another person, he must first modify the sovereignty of the grandiose self enough to permit another person to exist as a separate entity in his representational world. Without this, he is, as Rothstein (1982) argues, primarily dependent upon mirroring as a means of mediating anxiety, and will continue to ward off any experience discrepant with his self-image of needing nothing beyond what is already part of him or within his perfect ability to control in the narcissistically invested "other".

For such patients the growth of anxiety-tolerance is central to the analytic process. It moves hand-in-hand with the development of "self" and self-structuring, and is one of the key variables which determines the initial capacity of these individuals to work in the transference. It is also an ego function which should show dramatic improvement if the analytic work is accomplishing its main task. The goal of the work, as in any analysis, is for personality growth to be self-perpetuating; that is, for the patient to internalize the analyst's analytic function as an aspect of his ego autonomy (Loewald, 1960). This achievement depends upon the ability of the analysis to free the patient from the grip of the narcissistic transference as the primary source of ego-sustenance, and from the fear of ego-depletion (or "non-being") as the most powerful developmental line of anxiety.

The Question of Anxiety and the Development of "Self"

In light of the above, it is of interest to consider the possibility that the development of anxiety-tolerance and higher level "self-other" mental representation during treatment may have a parallel in normal cognitive-emotional maturation in early life that is especially relevant for these patients. Schecter (1980) presents the view that we can concieve of each form of infantile anxiety—anxiety by contagion, separation anxiety, stranger anxiety through loss of love, castration anxiety, and superego anxiety—as constituting the beginning of a developmental line which runs through childhood into adulthood. He suggests, as Pine has, that the quality of the original form of each type of anxiety is related to the developmental level of psychic structure that exists at the time, and that although each earlier line of anxiety is modified or "healed" by the subsequent development of new structure or maturation of older structure, the particular quality of the original experience continues to resonate throughout the life cycle to varying degrees for any given individual.

This orientation is particularly useful in differentiating the analytic treatment approach most suited to patients for whom an individuated core identity is taken for granted, from the approach most facilitating to patients such as narcissistic disorders, for whom it is a task to be completed through the work of the analysis itself. In this latter group of patients, the most profound source of anxiety at the onset of treatment has its origin prior to the full development of the ego and of intrapsychic conflict, and prior to the evolution of higher level ego defenses. It arises from a need to protect the fragile, poorly differentiated "self" from the threat of potential annihilation by internal and external experience that it is not yet autonomous enough to integrate, and which is thus felt as impinging, or "strange". Schecter, in fact, considers the most powerful line of anxiety that emerges in analysis to be a derivative of the early experience of stranger anxiety;

. . . it becomes clear that much of what we call resistance in psychoanalytic therapy has to do with anxiety connected with the conscious discovery of strange, new, ego-alien aspects of the self, of significant object-persons, and of their relationships (p. 551).

Stranger anxiety as a developmental line of affect has not easily fit into Freud's theory of anxiety until now; that is, until the recent new respect being paid to the structural aspects of the separation-individuation process, and to the interpersonal context which mediates the normal "healing" of more primitive sources of anxiety as later structure develops. In this sense it also helps to bridge a conceptual gap between Freud's theory of anxiety as an affect derived from motivational conflict, and Sullivan's theory of anxiety as an affect derived from structural disequilibrium of the "self".

When it does occur overtly, stranger anxiety is normally seen in infants of about seven to eight months of age, which is approximately the point in cognitive development at which there is the first evidence that an object concept has begun to develop. Fraiberg (1969) calls it the beginning of "recognition memory". Even though the infant at that point cannot be said to have a true internalized mental representation of the object since its image cannot be evoked when the object is absent, it is the beginning of the process through which the gradual loss of omnipotence becomes attached to the outside world which the infant gradually comes to accept and call "reality". It begins here because here is where the cognitive structure is first born that allows an outside and an inside to be created. The existence of this new mental structure therefore becomes in and of itself a potential source of a new line of anxiety associated with threat to "self" because "self" now begins to have a representation which organizes experience viz à viz an object. In other words, as the process of separation-individuation continues, the source of anxiety shifts slowly (or sometimes abruptly) from separation to individuation; that is, to the "self" and its own ego defenses or security operations. The greater the development of an interpersonally differentiated self and object, the more the experience of individuation and its higher level ego defenses rather than the illusion of non-separateness, mediates the integrity of the "self".

What we see as eight month stranger anxiety may be the most observable instance of failure of the interpersonal matrix to smoothly mediate the infant's rudimentary transition to a differentiated experience of "self"; it may occur in those infants for whom the birth of this new mental structure precipitates a fall from perfection which is too abrupt and thereby too discordant with previous mental organization. In this light, it would tend to be traumatic because, as Sandler (1977) suggests, the perception of "other" evokes a too discrete recognition of a non-gratifying constellation of images as "not mother"; "strangeness" and "the stranger" thus become an intolerable threat to the integrity of the newly hatching self. External reality which is too discrepant with the experience of self-contained gratification (omnipotence), reinforces the need to retain the security of omnipotent self-containment by controlling rather than internalizing reality. It is the beginning, one might say, of Narcissus and Echo at the pool; the incapacity to "take in" anything that isn't an extension of the grandiose self. It may also be the beginning of the difficulty which inhibits the normal development of more mature modes of anxiety mediation, interpersonal relatedness, and self-growth. It occurs at a time during the separation-individuation process that optimal development of self and object representation is, according to Mahler (1968, p. 20), dependent upon ". . . the child's achievement of separate functioning in the presence and emotional availability of the mother". "Even in this situation", Mahler states, "this process by its very nature continually confronts the toddler with minimal threats of object loss." Trauma during this "early practising subphase" (seven to ten months of age) interferes with what Mahler describes (1972, p. 336) as the infant's later capacity for ". . . exchanging some of his magical omnipotence for autonomy and developing self-esteem". As an adult he will thus tend to retain this early vulnerability to anxiety from a developmental source which has never "healed"; and if the developmental arrest is severe enough, his ". . . inflated, omnipotent self-object representation is the nucleus of the grandiose self which obtains in cases of pathological narcissism . . ." (Horner, 1979, p. 32).

What, then, is the most useful analytic approach in treating these individuals suffering from pathological narcissism? How does the patient ever reach the point where there is enough genuine relatedness to the analyst to form what is usually called an analyzable transference neurosis? Or to put it more operationally, how does the analysis enable the patient to assimilate anything from the analyst that he hears as less than flattering, without the grandiose self organizing the experience?

Treatment: The Integration of Mirroring and the Dissolution of the Mask

Before addressing the above question in the context of pathological narcissism, it might be useful to briefly consider my approach to the same question as it pertains to the general interpersonal model of psychoanalytic treatment (Bromberg, 1980a, pp. 243–245; 1980b, pp. 230–232). What makes the patient "trust" the analyst sufficiently to engage in a joint dismantling of his protective system with the same person who transferentially is the source of most immediate danger? Sullivan's answer (1953, pp. 152–154; 1954, pp. 217–239) was that the analyst works much like a sensitive musician; responsive to where the patient is on a gradient of anxiety, and trying to maintain it at an optimally minimal level—low enough so that the patient's defenses do not foreclose analytic inquiry, but high enough so that the defensive structure itself can be identified and explored.

In my experience, this description of keeping a finger on the pulse of the patient's level of self esteem is accurate and valuable, but incomplete; it does not address the overall quality of the patient-analyst bond, which unlike that of other relationships of minimal anxiety, allows an extraordinary degree of growth to be possible. I have suggested that the nature of this bond involves a controlled but consuming immersion by the patient in something positive, as much as it does a responsiveness to the absence of something negative. This aspect can be looked at in my view, as a shared empathic matrix between patient and analyst which, as Settlage (1977) has described, reaffirms the patient's precognitive or preverbal sense of core identity, and leads to the feeling of being "understood" as a potential cognitive bridge to being able to understand the analyst even with regard to things he does not wish to "understand". It is an ego-regulated derivative of what Sullivan (1953, pp. 37–41) depicts as the first interpersonal affirmation of core identity in the life cycle—a synchronicity between the need-tension level in the infant and the mother's responsiveness to it.

In conjunction with an appropriate working level of anxiety, it is this empathic matrix which, in my opinion, allows an analysis to take place. Tolpin (1971) puts it as follows: "By re-creating the merger and the maternal functions on which it depends, the psyche establishes an auxiliary pathway for the acquisition of tension-reducing mental structure" (p. 347). The important issue to recognize with regard to the analytic situation is that it is not a return to symbiosis, but the re-creation in the analysis of the transitional mental structure through which communication with the analyst includes the growing ability to become to himself what he experiences the analyst is to him. In a skillfully conducted analysis, the patient's "self" does not use this experience as a crutch, but is enabled by its existence to, as Tolpin puts it, ". . . perform soothing operations for itself, but now without the need for the illusory external soother" (p. 329). It is only as part of the ability to internalize the soothing function that the patient is able to utilize the analysis in its fullest sense as Rangell (1979, p. 102) describes it; ". . . a constant series of microidentifications . . . with the analyzing function of the analyst . . .". In this light I have suggested (Bromberg, 1980b, pp. 231–232) the possible advantage of viewing the interpersonal approach to analytic treatment as follows:

. . . a process of analytic inquiry mediated by maximal responsiveness to the interplay between a gradient of anxiety and a gradient of empathy. This conception has a distinct advantage over that of the 'therapeutic alliance' or the 'working alliance'. Both of these latter formulations depend on the notion of an extra-analytic bond (either global or specific) which is somehow more 'real' than the transferential bond, and has continued to remain a thorn in the side of analytic theory. Furthermore, the conception of an empathy gradient is a variable rather than a static element, and can thus deal with a much broader spectrum of psychopathology without having to modify the definition of psychoanalysis. It encompasses the fluctuating need for the analytic relationship to be more or less 'personal', for the level of empathic contact to be more or less 'deep'; and it encompasses the capacity of the patient to be more or less 'suitable' for psychoanalysis. Finally, it removes the need to introduce another 'parameter' such as an 'analytic holding environment' (Winnicott, 1955–1956; Modell, 1978) so as to conceptualize the fact that patients with more severe ego pathology require greater adaptational responsiveness from the therapist in the earlier stages of analytic treatment.

It is thus my view that regardless of who the patient is, ego growth and the ability to mature through mastering internal conflict and frustration, require an analytic setting which meets the ego's earlier and more basic need for affirmation. The need for such a setting is obviously greater in patients who begin with greater ego impairment. Ego pathology such as severe pathological narcissism does not, in this view, require a different form of treatment; it requres a greater sophistication and personal maturity on the part of the analyst in adapting to the patient's shifting need for affirmation in a way which enriches rather than contaminates the analytic field.

Affirmation, or mirroring, as ingredients in the analytic process, do not preclude interpretation as long as one accepts the idea that what needs to be interpreted can extend beyond the orthodox meaning of the term and need not focus only upon transference and resistance. When Winnicott (1971, p. 141), for example, states that ". . . psychoanalysis has been developed as a highly specialized form of playing in the service of communication with oneself and others", he is offering "playing" as a metaphor, not as a substitute for interpretation. It is a climate in which the timely and creative use of interpretation can flourish so as to maximize the patient's own creative use of the analytic experience.

There are those narcissistic disorders for whom traditional interpretation at certain stages in their analysis cannot be distinguished by them from acts of negative attribution by parental figures. The act of interpretation is indistinguishable from an attempt by the "all-knowing" parent to disqualify their reality and leave them with nothing but whatever selfishness and failure is being attributed to their behavior at that moment. These are individuals for whom the content of an interpretation directed towards a resistance will be processed as a sign of the analyst's narcissism; an instance of non-responsiveness to them, and a failure to appreciate or value them simply for who they are. The ability of these patients to eventually work in the transference is an inch by inch process, the final stage of which is the capacity to perceive a transference resistance as a transference resistance.

For certain of these individuals more than others, analytic success depends upon being able to participate in an initial period of undefinable length, in which the analysis partially protects them from stark reality which they cannot integrate, while performing its broader function of mediating their transition to a more mature and differentiated level of self and object representation (See Winnicott, 1951) capable of mediating and changing its own "reality". During this period, what Schecter (1980) calls "strangeness anxiety" stems more from the threat of failure to control the analyst and that analytic situation—failure of the grandiose self—than from having to deal with material which evokes specific areas of intrapsychic conflict. "Resistance" during this transitional period is better understood as a global defense against precipitous undermining of the "old world" rather than as an effort to ward off new insight.

It is a period in which the patient's fantasy is that there is no need for him to work; no need for him to obtain anything for himself, and that in spite of this the analyst has the power to make the analysis succeed. The proper balance between empathy and anxiety during this period is, as I see it, an analytic approach which begins to subtly challenge this fantasy without seriously threatening the patient's ability to use it to the degree he needs it transferentially. I do not share Modell's (1976) view that during this phase the patient's "cocoon" fantasy must remain unchallenged and that he will simply hatch out of it organically, nor do I agree with Kohut's (1971) similar position that narcissistic transference configurations will undergo a natural developmental evolution if the empathic "ambiance" is right. Both of these perspectives, in my view, underemphasize the fact that the patient is an adult whose ego functions are underdeveloped within a human relationship, and that he is not simply an infant in disguise. Interpretive work of a certain kind can and must be attempted right from the beginning if "empathy" is to have any meaning beyond a quasi-artificial technical maneuver designed to hopefully recapitulate infancy and repair what was orginally lacking.

The empathy-anxiety balance begins highly weighted on the side of empathy. Interpretations made during this phase are of two types which tend to overlap; neither is directed towards transference resistance or analytic resistance in general, but are not thereby valueless. Their therapeutic action is simply of a different order but to my way of thinking is every bit as "analytic" as interpretation aimed at promoting insight. At this stage, however, their analytic value has less to do with their accuracy than with the patient feeling understood. The first form of interpretation is one which Horner (1979) refers to as "structuralizing interpretation"; i.e., responding to the issue of the patient's valid need for the existing self and object structure, rather than responding to the content through which the need for that structure is being expressed at that moment. In the early phase of treatment this helps to introduce the patient to his character structure as a functional part of his personality and not simply as a piece of "illness" for which he is being blamed under the pretense of being "helped". For example, highlighting the use of detachment or self-containment as a means of avoiding the experience of inadequacy when he needs more than he can get, is a formulation that the patient can often accept and even begin to work with on a surface level without it threatening the narcissistic base of the transference itself. The general purpose of this form of interpretation is to accustom the patient to looking at himself from outside as part of an interpersonal process, but without any threat to the "mask" which he still needs in order to work at all. The second type of interpretation does address content and looks at the patient's behavior, but tries to avoid bringing the issues prematurely into the transference. Attempting to get the patient to report the minute details of specific external events and interactions, although often an ordeal for patient and analyst, is frequently a source of important movement during this phase of treatment. The goal at this stage is not to examine his transference resistance as manifested in trying to avoid the details, but to try and provide enough mirroring and understanding of his discomfort in pushing himself, that he is secure enough to take the risk. The more details he discloses, the more he becomes the agent of his own self-awareness. Through revealing details he would otherwise have omitted in order to maintain control over his self-image from behind his mask, aspects of his personality emerge which he can sometimes pick up on his own, and which can sometimes even be underscored by the analyst without the patient having to accept the analyst's reality before he is ready. Overall, the analytic approach during this early phase of treatment is one of attempting to keep the patient working at a tolerable level of frustration through maximal verbal and non-verbal responsiveness to his need to be accepted and understood on his own terms.[1] It is a stage of maximum empathy and minimum confrontation, but with sufficient anxiety to get most of the core issues out on the table.

As the patient's regressive experience deepens through the analyst's ability to protect the core fantasy of entitlement from precipitous empathic disruption in the transference, the yearnings that had been initially warded off by the illusion of self-sufficiency and idealization of the analyst gradually become more manifest in the treatment situation itself, and the balance between the gradients of empathy and anxiety begins to tilt in the opposite direction. This ushers in what might be considered the beginning of a new phase which is more confrontational but also more "real". The issue of what factors will most productively lead to this new phase is one which evokes serious differences of opinion among the various psychoanalytic schools of thought.

While for certain less seriously impaired individuals the relatively smooth evolution described by Kohut does seemingly occur, my own view is that for the larger group of more severe narcissistic disorders it is less a smooth transition than a genuinely new phase which is initiated by a certain amount of "pushing". The "pushing", which is confrontational in form, is not only needed but is developmentally facilitating in itself. It enables these patients to inch themselves out of their core fantasy of entitlement by mobilizing their newborn observing ego and focusing it not simply upon their external life, but upon the narcissistic transference itself. It is at this point that the patient's integration of mirroring is allowed to work in its own behalf. Its therapeutic value is no longer simply an aid to the acquisition of new mental structure, but is now aiding the patient's ability to use this new structure in the dissolution of the mask. It is here where I agree with Rothstein (1982,

---

[1] Lawrence Friedman (personal communication) has wryly referred to the process as "smuggling interpretations across narcissistic lines".

p. 177) that ". . . it is not the ability to establish stable narcissistic transference configurations that renders a subject analyzable. Rather it is the analysand's ability to work these through". The onset of this shift, in my experience, doesn't depend simply on how long the analyst can personally tolerate the patient's unrelatedness and self-centeredness. As the patient's narcissistic demands become more manifest in the treatment situation the analyst will become more confronting because not only is there more to confront, but also because a bridge to this new level of "reality" (See Bromberg, 1980b) has been laid by having addressed these same issues nontransferentially that now begin to be experienced and identified in the here-and-now of the patient-analyst relationship. Little by little, this permits a gradual and systematic interpretation of the underlying feelings of entitlement, and the emergence of genuine affect and a new sense of personal authenticity. The rage, emptiness, and despair that have been warded off by the grandiose self now start to be felt and mastered.

This phase marks what some schools of thought would call the *genuine* analytic work. Most prominent, especially at its onset, is intense rage in the transference. With some patients there is also concurrent movement into and out of the thin area between transference neurosis and transference psychosis, often accompanied by periods of acting-out. On the surface it may seem that at this juncture we are simply back at the pool with Echo and Narcissus. Why should one hope for an analytic outcome rather than a transference psychosis or termination? The patient is being confronted and is enraged. What makes it therapeutic simply because it is being done by an analyst? The answer, I think, is that the analyst, unlike Echo, is not out for his own self-interest, and that at this point the patient knows it at least dimly. Because of the initial phase the patient has a beginning capacity to feel another person as a separate entity and has already started to look at himself in an interpersonal context with some objectivity. They have a history together which Echo and Narcissus did not have, and if the confrontations and interpretations are being introduced gradually and empathically, the rage itself should support the individuation process, the analysis of the underlying fantasy of entitlement, and the dissolution of the mask. The rage, and often the envy, that have been attendant upon the denied yearnings, become gradually integrated as normal assertiveness and self-regard[2] as a growing sense of separateness, a therapeutic alliance, and a communicable and analyzable transference experience begins to develop. There is more and more a sense of two people being present as the patient gradually begins to accept and even enjoy the fact that he has a responsibility for the analytic work. There is less fear of losing the mask and consequently less dread of working in the transference. Interpretation and the active taking in of ideas from a perspective other than one's own becomes less a source of "strangeness anxiety". It becomes more a part of the patient's total affective thrill in his own growth rather than an impinging threat to be warded off.

This approach is independent of the analyst's personal metapsychology. It does not demand that the analyst hold the view that there are separate categories of patients: the transference neuroses, for whom unmodified psychoanalysis resolves intrapsychic conflict; and those patients with preoedipal ego impairment (narcissistic, borderline, schizoid, and character disorders) for whom modified psychoanlysis repairs damaged structure. It can accommodate, for example, Kernberg's view of narcissistic transferences as defenses against an almost inborn infantile rage, as well as Kohut's position that they are interferences or fixation points in a normal developmental process. The value of this approach is that it is exactly that . . . an approach. It does not predetermine technique. It does not require the analyst to feel he is being non-analytic if he allows a transference configuration to remain uninterpreted during a particular phase of treatment for a particular patient, nor does it require that he should allow it to do so, simply because his own analytic metatheory demands it. What it does demand is that the analyst have an ego development rationale from which he works, within which he can flexibly conceptualize the various stages of growth during the analytic process, including psychosexual growth if this is a metaphor he uses.

I am suggesting that many difficult narcissistic disorders might be analyzable if the treatment begins with a stage of analysis managed without the imposition of a classical interpretive stance or the belief

[2] See Winnicott (1950, pp. 204–218; 1971, pp. 86–94) and Kohut (1972, pp. 378–397) for a fuller theoretical elaboration of this issue.

that it is only this stance which truly defines psychoanalysis. Such patients may then gradually become more accessible and available to hearing what they do not want to hear without the narcissistic wound having to be prevented at all costs. I do not, however, believe that all individuals suffering from pathological narcissism are analyzable. In my opinion there are patients who are unanalyzable regardless of approach, and others whose particular impairment in ego development will limit how far they may be able to go in analysis. Early psychopathology is a major factor as is the potential for psychotic transference, but I prefer to use these data in determining the approach to the analytic work rather than as a diagnostic criterion of analyzability.

As to the question of how effective psychoanalysis can be at its best, in treating narcissistic disorders, I don't think we really know. I believe there is little question that we are in part fighting against cultural forces as well as intrapsychic ones, although I do not feel that culture creates pathological narcissism. I tend to agree with Kernberg (1975) that it is pretty much a developmental outcome related to parenting, but I suspect that its increased incidence culturally (Marin, 1975; Lasch, 1979) and part of the difficulty in treating it in therapy, is influenced by our socioeconomic milieu in the following way:

Talking about psychopathology is just one metaphor among other possible metaphors to describe the same phenomenon. What we call pathological narcissism someone else might not feel is an illness at all . . . that the person just needs to "grow up". In one way, of course, it is quite true. "Narcissistic psychopathology" is a way of saying that an individual is stuck at a particular level of emotional and interpersonal development, and manages to maintain his self esteem only at the expense of further growth. Growth can come about only under conditions that will allow a person to experience himself in some way that is different. It requires an environment which tends to facilitate the acceptance and integration of unpleasant but accurate experience of oneself that would otherwise be discarded because it is too discordant with one's interpersonal self representation. Psychoanalysis is an attempt to create a controlled environment which will accomplish this systematically. It is clearly not the only way that people who have been fixated at early levels of development can grow. Religion, an important friendship at a crucial moment, in fact any important relationship if it is the right one at the right time, can often get the process moving again.

Narcissistic personalities are no different than any other personality organization in this regard. A positive change in the natural environment at critical times can create influences which will foster concern, tenderness, relatedness, and appreciation. But in a social climate where the opposite characteristics tend to be almost institutionalized politically and economically, the grandiose self has a natural ally to support its already powerful claim to sovereignty. Thus, a relationship, including an analytic one, which might in a different cultural atmosphere help a person with severe narcissistic pathology see himself objectively, will tend to have less impact if in the larger scheme of things he can secretly say to himself: "We are all out for ourselves anyway". In spite of this, however, I believe that the new psychoanalytic emphasis on the whole person in an interpersonal context, is a vitalizing force which can only make psychoanalysis more open to its own continuing development, and its potential for treating serious character pathology increasingly broader.

REFERENCES

Bach, S. (1977) On the narcissistic state of consciousness. *International Journal of Psycho-Analysis*, **58**:209–233.

Balint, M. (1968) *The Basic Fault*. London: Tavistock Publications.

Becker, E. (1964) *Revolution in Psychiatry*. New York: Free Press.

Becker, E. (1973) *The Denial of Death*. New York: Free Press.

Bromberg, P. M. (1979a) Interpersonal psychoanalysis and regression. *Contemporary Psychoanalysis*, **15**:647–655.

Bromberg, P. M. (1979b) The use of detachment in narcissistic and borderline conditions. *Journal of The American Academy of Psychoanalysis*, **7**:593–600.

Bromberg, P. M. (1979c) The developmental roots of anxiety: Some observations. Paper presented at The American Academy of Psychoanalysis, November 1979.

Bromberg, P. M. (1980a) Sullivan's concept of consensual validation and the therapeutic action of psychoanalysis. *Contemporary Psychoanalysis*, **16**:237–248.

Bromberg, P. M. (1980b) Empathy, anxiety, and reality: A view from the bridge. *Contemporary Psychoanalysis*, **16**:223–236.

D'Aulaire, I. & D'Aulaire, E. P. (1962) *D'Aulaire's Book of Greek Myths*. New York: Doubleday & Company.

Fairbairn, W. R. D. (1952) *Psychoanalytic Studies of the Personality*. London: Routledge and Kegan Paul.

Fairbairn, W. R. D. (1954) *An Object-relations Theory of the Personality*. New York: Basic Books.

Ferenczi, S. (1909) Introjection and transference. *First Contributions to Psycho-Analysis*, New York: Brunner-Mazel, 1980, pp. 35–93.

Ferenczi, S. (1913) Stages in the development of the sense of reality. In: *First Contributions to Psycho-Analysis*, New York: Brunner-Mazel, 1980, pp. 213–239.

Ferenczi, S. (1929) The principle of relaxation and neocatharsis. In: *Final Contributions to the Problems and Methods of Psycho-Analysis*. New York: Brunner-Mazel, 1980, pp. 108–125.

Fraiberg, S. (1969) Libidinal object constancy and mental representation. In: *The Psychoanalytic Study of the Child*, **24:**9–47, New York, International Universities Press.

Freud, A. (1969) Discussion of John Bowlby's work. In: *The Writings of Anna Freud, Vol.* **5,** New York: International Universities Press.

Freud, S. (1911) Formulations on the two principles of mental functioning. *Standard Edition,* **12:**213–226. London: Hogarth Press, 1955.

Freud, S. (1914) On narcissism: An introduction. *Standard Edition,* **14:**67–102. London: Hogarth Press, 1957.

Friedman, L. (1978) Trends in the psychoanalytic theory of treatment. *Psychoanalytic Quarterly,* **47:**524–567.

Fromm, E. (1947) *Man For Himself.* New York: Rinehart & Company.

Fromm, E. (1956) *The Sane Society.* London: Routledge and Kegan Paul, Ch. 3.

Fromm, E. (1964) *The Heart of Man: Its Genius For Good and Evil.* New York: Harper & Row, Ch. 4.

Gedo, J. (1977) Notes on the psychoanalytic management of archaic transferences. *Journal of the American Psychoanalytic Association,* **25:**787–803.

Gitelson, M. (1962) On the curative factors in the first phase of analysis. In: *Psychoanalysis: Science and Profession.* New York: International Universities Press, 1973, pp. 311–341.

Glatzer, H. T. and Evans, W. N. (1977) On Guntrip's analysis with Fairbairn and Winnicott. *International Journal of Psychoanalytic Psychotherapy,* **6:**81–98.

Guntrip, H. J. S. (1961) *Personality Structure and Human Interaction: The Developing Synthesis of Psycho-dynamic Theory.* New York: International Universities Press.

Guntrip, H. J. S. (1968) *Schizoid Phenomena, Object-relations, and the Self.* New York: International Universities Press.

Horner, A. (1979) *Object Relations and The Developing Ego in Therapy.* New York: Jason Aronson, Inc.

Kernberg, O. (1975) *Borderline Conditions and Pathological Narcissism.* New York: Jason Aronson, Inc.

Kohut, H. (1971) *The Analysis of The Self.* New York: International Universities Press.

Kohut, H. (1972) Thoughts on narcissism and narcissistic rage. In: *The Psychoanalytic Study of The Child,* **27:**360–400, New York: Quadrangle Books.

Kohut, H. (1977) *The Restoration of The Self.* New York: International Universities Press.

Lasch, C. (1979) *The Culture of Narcissism.* New York: W. W. Norton & Company.

Levenson, E. A. (1978) Two essays in psychoanalytical psychology— **I.** Psychoanalysis: Cure or persuasion. *Contemporary Psychoanalysis,* **14:**1–30.

Loewald, H. (1960) On the therapeutic action of psychoanalysis. *International Journal of Psycho-Analysis,* **41:**16–33.

Mahler, M. S. (1968) *On Human Symbiosis and the Vicissitudes of Individuation.* New York: International Universities Press.

Mahler, M. S. (1972) On the first three subphases of the separation-individuation process. *International Journal of Psycho-Analysis,* **53:**333–338.

Marin, P. (1975) The new narcissism. *Harpers Magazine,* October 1975.

Modell, A. (1976) The 'holding environment' and the therapeutic action of psychoanalysis. *Journal of the American Psychoanalytic Association,* **24**:285–308.

Modell, A. (1978) The conceptualization of the therapeutic action of psychoanalysis: The action of the holding environment. *Bulletin of the Menninger Clinic,* **42**:493–504.

Pine, F. (1979) On the expansion of the affect array: A developmental description. *Bulletin of the Menninger Clinic,* **43**:79—95.

Rangell, L. (1979) Contemporary issues in the theory of therapy. *Journal of the American Psychoanalytic Association,* **27** (supplement):81–112.

Rothstein, A. (1980) *The Narcissistic Pursuit of Perfection.* New York: International Universities Press.

Rothstein, A. (1982) The implications of early psychopathology for the analyzability of narcissistic personality disorders. *International Journal of Psycho-Analysis,* **63**:177–188.

Sandler, A.-M. (1977) Beyond eight month anxiety. *International Journal of Psycho-Analysis,* **58**:195–208.

Sandler, J. and Sandler, A.-M. (1978) On the development of object relationships and affects. *International Journal of Psycho-Analysis,* **59**:285–296.

Schafer, R. (1968) *Aspects of Internalization.* New York: International Universities Press.

Schecter, D. E. (1978) Attachment, detachment, and psychoanalytic therapy. In: *Interpersonal Pychoanalysis: New Directions,* Ed. E. G. Witenberg. New York: Gardner Press, pp. 81–104.

Schecter, D. E. (1980) Early development roots of anxiety. *Journal of The American Academy of Psychoanalysis,* **8**:539–554.

Settlage, C. F. (1977) The psychoanalytic understanding of narcissistic and borderline personality disorders. *Journal of the American Psychoanalytic Association,* **25**:805–834.

Stolorow, R. D. (1975) Toward a functional definition of narcissism. *International Journal of Psycho-Analysis,* 56:179–186.

Strachey, J. (1934) The nature of the therapeutic action of psychoanalysis. *International Journal of Psycho-Analysis,* **15**:127–159.

Sullivan, H. S. (1953) *The Interpersonal Theory of Psychiatry.* New York: W. W. Norton & Company.

Sullivan, H. S. (1954) *The Psychiatric Interview.* New York: W. W. Norton & Company.

Sullivan, H. S. (1964a) The illusion of personal individuality. In: *The Fusion of Psychiatry and Social Science.* New York: W.W. Norton & Company, pp. 198–226.

Sullivan, H. S. (1964b) The meaning of anxiety in psychiatry and in life. In: *The Fusion of Psychiatry and Social Science.* W. W. Norton & Company, pp. 229–254.

Thompson, C. (1956) the role of the analyst's personality in therapy. In: *Interpersonal Psychoanalysis,* Ed. M. Green. New York: Basic Books, 1964.

Tolpin, M. (1971) On the beginnings of a cohesive self: An application of the concept of transmuting internalization to the study of the transitional object and signal anxiety. In: *The Psychoanalytic Study of the Child,* **26**:316–352, New York: Quadrangle Books.

Winnicott, D. W. (1950) Aggression in relation to emotional development. In: *Collected Papers: Through Paediatrics to Psycho-Analysis.* London: Tavistock Publications, 1958, pp. 204–218.

Winnicott, D. W. (1951) Transitional objects and transitional phenomena. In: *Collected*

Papers: Through Paediatrics to Psycho-Analysis. London: Tavistock Publications, 1958, pp. 229–242.

Winnicott, D. W. (1955–1956) Clinical varieties of transference. In: *Collected Papers: Through Paediatrics to Psycho-Analysis.* London: Tavistock Publications, 1958, pp. 295–299.

Winnicott, D. W. (1965) *The Maturational Processes and the Facilitating Environment.* New York: International Universities Press.

Winnicott, D. W. (1971) *Playing and Reality.* New York: Basic Books.

References

American Psychiatric Association (1980). *Diagnostic and Statistical Manual of Mental Disorders,* 3rd ed. (DSM-III). Washington, D.C.: American Psychiatric Association.

Bursten, B. (1977). The narcissistic course. In Coleman Nelson, M. *The Narcissistic Condition.* New York: Human Sciences Press.

Duruz, N. (1981). The psychoanalytic concept of narcissism, Part II: Toward a structural definition. *Psychoanal. and Contemp. Thought* 4:35–67.

Eisnitz, A. J. (1969). Narcissistic object choice, self-representation. *Int. J. Psycho-Anal.* 50:15–25.

Gedo, J. (1977). Notes on the psychoanalytic management of archaic transferences. *JAPA* 25: 787–803.

Hanley, C. and Masson, J. (1976). A critical examination of the new narcissism. *Int. J. Psycho-Anal.* 57:49–66.

Hartmann, H. (1950). Comments on the psychoanalytic theory of the ego. In *Essays on Ego Psychology.* New York: IUP, 1964, 113–141.

——and Loewenstein, R. M. (1962). Notes on the superego. In *Papers on Psychoanalytic Psychology* [Psychol. Issues, Monogr. 14]. New York: IUP, 1964, 144–181.

Jacobson, E. (1964). *The Self and the Object World.* New York: IUP.

Joffe, W. G. and Sandler, J. (1967). Some conceptual problems involved in the considerations of disorders of narcissism. *J. Child Psychother.* 2:56–66.

Kinston, W. (1982). An intrapsychic developmental schema for narcissistic disturbance. *Int. J. Psycho-Anal.* 61:383–394.

Kohut, H. (1971). *The Analysis of the Self.* New York: IUP.

Lichtenstein, H. (1964). The role of narcissism in the emergence and maintenance of a primary identity. *Int. J. Psycho-Anal.* 45:49–56.

McDougall, J. (1982). The narcissistic economy and its relation to primitive sexuality. *Contemp. Psychoanal.* 18:373–396

Moore, B. E. (1975). Toward a clarification of the concept of narcissism. *Psychoanal. Study Child.* 30:243–276.

Murray, J. M. (1964). Narcissism and the ego ideal. *JAPA* 12:482–511.

Ornstein, P. (1974). Discussion of paper by Otto. F. Kernberg, 'Further contributions to the treatment of narcissistic personalities.' *Int. J. Psycho-Anal.* 55:241–247.

Reich, A. (1953). Narcissistic object choice in women. *JAPA* 1:22–44.

Reich, W. (1949). *Character-Analysis,* 3rd ed., Wolfe, T. P. trans. New York: Orgone Institute Press, p. 158.

Rosenfeld, H. (1964). On the psychopathology of narcissism: a clinical approach. *Int. J. Psycho-Anal.* 45:332–337.

Rosenman, S. (1981). Narcissus of the myth: an essay on narcissism and victimization. In Tuttman, S.; Kaye, C.; and Zimmerman, M. *Object and Self: A Developmental Approach.* New York: IUP.

Rothstein, A. (1979). Oedipal conflicts in narcissistic personality disorders. *Int. J. Psycho-Anal.* 60:189–200.

Schwaber, E. (1979). On the self within the matrix of analytic theory—some clinical reflections and reconsiderations. *Int. J. Psycho-Anal.* 60:467–480.

Settledge, E. F. (1977). The psychoanalytic understanding of narcissistic and border-line personality disorders. *JAPA* **25**:805–834.

Teicholz, J. G. (1978). A selective review of the psychoanalytic literature on theoretical conceptualizations of narcissism. *JAPA* **26**:831–862.

Val, E. (1982). Self-esteem regulation and narcissism. *Ann. Psychoanal.* **X**:221–232.

Van der Waals, H. C. (1965). Problems of narcissism. *Bul. Menninger Clin.* **29**:293–311.

Name Index

Abraham, K., 18*n*, 91, 188–9, 227, 345, 377, 391
Adatto, C. P., 387
Adler, Alfred, 14, 34–5, 40, 117, 349
Adler, G., 420–1, 424
Alexander, F., 71
Andersen, Hans Christian, 242
Apfelbaum, B., 95, 197
Arlow, J. A., 101*n*, 197–8, 200

Bach, S., 439
Bak, R. C., 390, 393
Balint, M., 102, 203, 448
Balzac, Honoré de, 328
Becker, Ernest, 440–4, 448–9
Beckett, Samuel, 290, 333*n*
Bergler, E., 140
Bergman, Ingmar, 229
Bibring, E., 302, 365, 386, 396
Bing, J. F., 63*n*
Binswanger, L., 67
Blanck, Gertrude, 155, 157, 160, 162
Blanck, Rubin, 155, 157, 160
Blum, H. P., 421
Brenner, C., 101–2, 197–8, 200
Bromberg, Philip M., 374–5, 438–66
Buber, Martin, 304
Bursten, Ben, 4, 373–4, 377–402, 407, 410, 412, 418, 427
Busch, Wilhelm, 25

Cameron, N., 384
Cattell, J. P., 420
Chasseguet-Smirgel, J., 331*n*
Churchill, Winston, 72
Cleckley, H., 385
Cooper, Arnold M., 1, 89, 112–43, 139–40
Corwin, H. A., 421

Dahl, H., 197
D'Aulaire, E. P., 444
D'Aulaire, I., 444
Deutsch, Helene, 300, 414
Duruz, N., 8

Easser, B. R., 314
Eicke-Spengler, M., 330
Eidelberg, L., 104
Eisnitz, A., 6, 198, 200, 379
Eissler, K., 76–7
Elkisch, P., 199, 201, 396
Ellis, Havelock, 1, 17*n*, 92, 102, 112, 116
Erikson, Erik H., 89, 113, 123–4, 149, 351, 353, 377
Evans, W. N., 443

Fairbairn, W. R. D., 448–9
Federn, E., 102
Federn, P., 61*n*, 93*n*, 102
Fellini, Federico, 331
Fenichel, O., 45, 100, 216, 377
Ferenczi, S., 19*n*, 23, 45, 64*n*, 304, 442–3
Fermi, Enrico, 75
Fine, B. D., 107
Fischer, S., 342
Fliess, R, 395
Fraiberg, S., 452
Frances, A., 426
Freeman, T., 198
Freud, Anna, 108, 294, 298, 303, 387–8, 439
Freud, Sigmund, 1, 7, 13–4, 17–43, 44, 62–4, 66–9, 70, 79–80, 82–3, 85*n*, 91–5, 97–8, 100, 102–3, 105–7, 113, 115–8, 121–2, 124, 141, 145–9, 151–3, 160–1, 166, 168, 188, 199, 202–3, 223, 295, 297, 308–9, 311–3, 317–8, 345, 349–50, 352–5, 377–80, 388, 390, 439, 442, 452
Friedman, L., 358, 446, 459*n*
Fromm, Erich, 377, 443
Frosch, J., 380

Gedo, J., 10, 445
Gitelson, M., 298, 448
Glatzer, H. T., 443
Glover, E., 99, 114
Goethe, Johann Wolfgang von, 81
Gosliner, B. J., 395

Gouin Décarie, T., 99
Greenacre, P., 76–7, 397
Greene, W. A., 98
Greenson, R. R., 150, 302
Guntrip, H., 378, 448

Hanley, C., 6
Hartmann, H., 1, 14, 61n, 72, 90, 95, 104, 107, 146–7, 153–5, 160, 162, 198, 313, 350, 354–5, 378
Hazard, P., 349
Heine, Heinrich, 28
Hersey, John, 408n
Hoch, P. H., 420
Hoffer, W., 379
Holder, A., 72
Holt, R. R., 95, 197
Horner, A. J., 422–3, 444, 454, 458
Horney, Karen, 89, 113, 120–1

Ionesco, Eugene, 290

Jacobson, Edith, 1, 14, 45, 51, 71n, 72, 98, 103–4, 108, 113, 137, 158, 160–1, 198–9, 204–6, 216, 245, 252, 258, 263, 314, 346, 350, 353–4, 387, 389, 391, 393, 395, 397
Janik, A., 108n
Joffe, W. G., 7, 105, 108, 156, 205, 346
Johnson, A. M., 397
Jones, E., 64n, 91, 93n, 227
Jung, Carl Gustav, 14, 18, 23–4, 117

Kant, Immanuel, 439
Kanzer, M., 102, 203
Kaywin, L., 100
Kernberg, Otto F., 2, 10, 89–90, 95, 109n, 113, 115, 129–30, 132, 134, 137–9, 158–60, 166–70, 198, 200, 213–92, 314, 330, 375, 378, 380, 383, 403–6, 413, 419, 421–3, 426, 440, 441–2
Kernberg, P., 245
Khan, M. M. R., 296
Kinston, W., 6
Klein, Melanie, 259
Knight, Robert, 297, 390, 393
Kohut, Heinz, 2, 6–10, 14–5, 61–88, 89–90, 104, 113, 115, 123, 131–2, 134–8, 148–9, 151–60, 162, 165–70, 174–

96, 189–90, 200–2, 204, 207, 228, 245–8, 251–2, 259–60, 264–7, 269, 277–8, 286–8, 293–4, 295n, 296n, 300–1, 304–5, 310–1, 314, 323, 348–9, 356–70, 374–5, 380–2, 387, 399–400, 403–6, 407n, 408, 410, 414–22, 427, 429, 434, 440, 444, 457, 459, 461
Kramer, P., 72n
Kraus, Karl, 180n

Lasch, Christopher, 114, 125–6, 439, 462
Lazar, N., 114
Levenson, E. A., 438
Levin, S., 342, 352, 354, 369
Lewin, B. D., 51, 102, 203, 381, 386
Lewis, H. B., 348, 350–3, 365
Lewisohn, Ludwig, 81n
Lichtenstein, H., 9, 199, 201, 394
Loewald, H. W., 156, 451
Loewenstein, R. M., 1, 72, 104, 355
London, Nathaniel J., 179n, 180n
Lowenfeld, H., 352
Lynd, H. M., 348, 350–1

McDougall, J., 9
McLaughlin, F., 63n

Mahler, Margaret S., 10, 90, 113, 137, 147–53, 156, 160–2, 252, 258, 308–9, 311, 314, 323–4, 326, 394–5, 432, 439, 442, 453–4
Marburg, R., 63n
Marin, Peter, 441, 462
Masson, J., 6
Masterson, J. F., 421
Meers, D., 72
Meissner, W. W., 373–4, 403–37
Miller, Alice, 170–1, 323–47
Mitscherlich, A., 80n
Modell, Arnold H., 7, 169–70, 293–307, 356, 374, 422, 456–7
Moore, B. E., 6, 13–4, 107
Morrison, Andrew P., 7, 348–71
Mueller-Braunschweig, H., 333n
Murray, J. M., 7, 104, 200
Myerson, P. G., 300

Näcke, Paul, 17
Nadelson, T., 431
Nagera, H., 328
Nunberg, H. G., 93n, 102, 112, 120

Oremland, J., 200, 207, 379
Ornstein, P. H., 8, 168, 406, 418
Ostow, M., 102
Ovid, 336

Piers, G., 72, 349–50, 352, 354n
Pine, F., 450–1
Polatin, P., 420
Pulver, Sydney E., 89, 91–111, 115–6,
    166, 197, 201–6

Rado, Sandor, 89, 113, 121–2, 381, 386
Rangell, L., 74n, 455
Rank, Otto, 1, 17n, 64, 93–4, 103
Rapaport, D., 386
Reich, Annie, 6–7, 14–5, 44–60, 71n, 72,
    118, 137, 166, 199, 201–2, 206, 216,
    223–4, 313–4, 318–9, 355, 381, 394,
    414–5
Reich, Wilhelm, 1, 385, 396
Riesman, David, 377
Riviere, J., 227, 235
Robertson, J., 323
Rosenblatt, B., 264
Rosenfeld, H., 7, 203, 228, 235, 245, 247
Rosenman, S., 1
Ross, M., 425
Rothstein, Arnold, 9, 169–70, 308–20,
    358, 373, 440, 445, 451, 459
Rycroft, C., 296n

Sadger, J., 1, 17, 93
Sandler, A.-M., 444, 453
Sandler, J., 7, 64n, 72, 105, 108, 156,
    205, 264, 346, 355, 444
Saul, L., 71
Schafer, Roy, 113, 180n, 310n, 355, 444
Schechter, D., 354–6, 355–6, 443, 451–2
Schwaber, E., 8
Sederer, L., 351n

Seidenberg, R., 351n
Seitz, P. F. D., 72n
Settlage, C. F., 9–10, 90, 433, 455
Shakespeare, William, 144, 191
Silberer, Herbert, 39
Singer, M., 72, 349
Spitz, R. A., 99, 304, 323
Stein, M. H., 378
Sterba, R., 302
Stolorow, Robert D., 160, 166–7, 197–
    209, 444
Stone, L., 227
Strachey, J., 446, 448
Sullivan, Harry Stack, 89, 113, 118–9,
    443, 448, 452, 454–5
Szurek, S. A., 397

Tartakoff, H. H., 245, 409
Teicholz, J. G., 5, 168
Thompson, C., 448
Thrane, G., 348–9, 352
Ticho, E., 227, 245
Tolpin, Marian, 151, 156, 455
Toulmin, S., 180n
Trollope, Anthony, 69

Vaillant, G. E., 411
Val, E., 9
van der Waals, H. C., 8, 216, 245, 252,
    282
Volkan, V. D., 295n

Waelder, R., 197, 391
Webster, Noah, 44
Weiss, Edoardo, 35n
White, Marjorie Taggart, 90, 144–64,
    390
Windholz, E., 200, 207, 379
Winnicott, D, W., 89, 113, 122–3, 151,
    297, 299–301, 303–5, 323–4, 326, 338,
    340, 346, 448, 456–7, 461n
Wolf, Ernest S., 165–6, 174–96, 374
Wurmser, L., 348, 354

Zetzel, E. R., 402, 409

Subject Index

Abandonment, 273, 280, 290, 350, 352, 354, 364
Ability(ies), 330, 363, 381, 409–10
Acceptability, 394
Acceptance, 156, 277, 354, 368, 370, 375, 409, 446,, 462
  empathic, 406
Achievement(s), 145, 329–33, 339, 342 346
Action-self, 121–2
Adaptability, 442
Admiration, 130, 132, 135, 154, 159, 170, 214–5, 218, 220–1, 229, 237, 246, 253, 277, 289, 295, 329–31, 407–8, 410–2, 417, 428
Affect(s)
  false, 300
  true, 300
Affection, 341
Affirmation, 324–5, 364, 391, 440, 456
Aggrandizement, 49
Aggression, 2–3, 10, 15, 53, 138, 155, 157, 159–60, 162, 166–9, 176, 205, 220, 228, 231, 240, 247, 250–2, 261, 265–8, 276, 327, 334, 345, 349, 362, 378, 387, 393, 430–2
  classical theory of, 176
  neutralized, 157
  oral, 160, 167–8, 219, 249, 421
  pregenital, 421
Aggressive
  concern(s), 406
  dimension, 428
  drive(s), 155–7, 168
Aggressiveness, 10
Aim(s), 380
Alliance, therapeutic, 295, 301–6, 455, 461
Aloofness, 169, 224
Ambition(s), 16, 68–70, 134, 177–8, 186–7, 195–6, 215, 269–70, 357, 359–69, 400
  grandiose, 360, 368

Ambitiousness, 246
Ambivalence, 257, 343, 345, 432, 434
Anger, 128, 141, 167–8, 214, 219, 241, 249, 255–6, 272–4, 300, 327, 332, 334, 337, 344, 346, 384, 390, 433, 440
  parental, 316
Anomie, 125
Anxiety(ies), 15, 27, 48, 71n, 106, 137, 154, 169, 171, 185–6, 215, 220, 237, 239, 250, 255, 296n, 309, 327, 352, 362–3, 375, 386, 408–9, 420–1, 423, 440–1, 450–5, 457, 459
  castration, 49, 225, 296n, 317–9, 353, 362, 366, 451
  depletion, 364
  disintegration, 195
  hypochondriacal, 47, 55
  neurosis, 26, 27
  neurotic, 178
  penis, 34
  separation, 169, 255, 308, 310–1, 319, 451
  shame, 352
  stranger, 451–3
  superego, 451
  tolerance, 238
Apathy, 348, 364, 370
Approval, 130, 214, 381, 407, 415
Arrest, 435
  developmental, 406
Arrogance, 112, 373, 386, 394, 407
Aspiration(s), 356n
Assertiveness, 10, 179, 193, 444, 461
  phallic, 408
Attachment, 379, 423
  cathexes, 6
Autoerotism, 20, 98, 102, 116
Autonomy, 133, 148, 169, 193, 296, 298–9, 302, 325, 351, 353, 432–3, 451, 454
  precocious, 296
Awareness, 347, 350–1, 440

Baldwin Bählamm (W. Busch), 25*n*
Barchester Towers (A. Trollope), 69
Beauty, 2, 129, 191, 246–7, 254, 289–90,
    330
Behavior, 441
    antisocial, 237, 250, 285
Behavioral disorder(s), 165–6
Blame, 253
Body-self, 155, 186
Borderline, 366
    cases, 246
    characters, 406
    characteristics, 232, 297, 413
    condition(s), 165, 246, 404–6, 419–20,
        423, 426–7, 433–5
    disorder(s), 403, 419, 433, 435, 461
    feature(s), 424
    functioning, 429
    patient(s), 131, 215, 220, 256, 262,
        297–9, 305, 382, 419–20, 422–6,
        429–32
    state(s), 246, 296, 299, 419, 421, 431
    syndrome, 413, 422
Boredom, 131–2, 221, 229, 246, 269–71,
    278, 288, 294
Brilliance, 2, 129, 246, 333

Calmness, 177, 183, 274
Casanova (F. Fellini), 331
Castration, 350, 352, 394, 414
    complex, 34–5
    fear, 381
    threats, 1, 51
Chairs, The (E. Ionesco), 290
Character
    disorder(s), 438, 461
    differences, 379
    masochistic, 140
Clinging, 373
Cognition, 78–9, 83–4
Cognitive
    development, 452
    processes, 80
    structure, 453
Cohesion, 177–8
Cohesiveness, 201, 207, 419, 425, 430–1
    of the self, 425
Coldness, 214, 240, 261, 413
Communication, empathic, 80

Competence, 125
Competition, 129, 226
Competitiveness, 144, 394, 400, 407
Compliance, 301
Comprehension, empathic, 79
Compromises, 1, 447
Compulsion, 341
Concealment, 170
Confirmation, 289, 381, 417, 427
Conflict(s), 15, 225, 353, 354*n*, 355–6,
        366, 381, 397
    aggressive, 434
    drive theory, 365
    intrapsychic, 452, 457, 461
    oral, 225, 240
    oral-aggressive, 215, 235, 267
Confrontation(s), 166, 375, 459–60
Conscience, 37–9, 355
Consciousness, 39*n*, 67–8
Constancy, 432
Contempt, 4, 15, 255–6, 268, 277, 374,
        393, 400, 407, 411, 415
Contentment, 381, 386
Countertransference, 140, 158, 160,
        167–8, 201, 207–8, 230–1, 280,
        282, 294, 298, 300
Craving, 384
"Creative Writers and Day-Dreaming"
        (S. Freud), 34
Creativity, 15, 74–6, 85, 123, 136, 182,
        186, 290, 366
Criticism, 128–9, 159, 253, 384, 390
Cruelty, 397
Cyclothymia, 59

Danger, 381, 409
Deadness, 131, 184
Death, 423, 441, 444
Deception, 385, 393
Decompensation, 405
Dedifferentiation, 36
Defeat, 128, 140, 178, 362
Defect(s), 6, 170, 191, 352, 359, 361,
        364, 368, 370
Defense(s), 380, 422
    grandiose, 337, 339
    mechanism(s), 131, 328, 330, 381
    obsessive compulsive, 294
Defiance, 301, 317, 325

Deficit(s), 125, 426, 433
Degradations, 200
Dehumanization, 291
Dejection, 15, 178, 333, 362
Demand, 388
  exhibitionistic, 71
Demanding, 373, 388, 413
Dementia praecox, 18, 24–5, 29
Denial, 7, 49, 81, 131, 167, 295n, 296,
  305, 332, 333n, 334, 338, 352, 404,
  411
Dependency(ies), 4, 43, 113, 138, 159–
  60, 167, 198, 220, 228, 231, 235,
  255, 258–9, 263, 268, 289, 329,
  374, 383–4, 408, 423–4
  denial of, 255
  field, 351, 365
Depersonalization, 58, 236
Depletion, 165, 360–1, 367–9
Depreciation, 130, 214, 220, 231, 234,
  263, 413
Depression(s), 4, 55, 117, 140, 170–1,
  179–80, 185, 214, 222, 226, 231–3,
  239, 285, 289, 291, 317, 323, 326,
  328–9, 331–46, 350–1, 359, 361–
  2, 365–8, 370, 386, 408–9, 416,
  420, 423
  empty, 361
Depressive patients, 285, 342–3
Depressive phase, 343
Deprivation(s) 135, 140, 159
  oral, 159
Despair, 4, 178, 240, 342, 346, 361–2,
  364–5, 460
  guiltless, 370
Desperation, 383
Despondency, 363
Destruction, 218, 394
Destructiveness, 242, 268, 428–9, 431–2
Detachment, 102, 141, 275, 374, 443,
  447, 458
Devaluation, 2, 127–9, 159, 167, 218–9,
  222, 225, 230–1, 235, 246, 248,
  250, 255–6, 260–3, 267, 273, 278–
  9, 282, 393, 415, 423–4
  aggressive, 256
Differentiation, 157, 161
"Difficulty in the Path of Psycho-Analy-
  sis" (S. Freud), 19n

Diffusion, 364, 430
Disappointment(s), 90, 128, 157–8, 162,
  233, 255–6, 266–7, 273–4, 296n,
  340, 364, 387, 389, 412
Disapproval, 432
Discomfort, 388, 458
Disgust, 342, 391
Disillusionment, 104, 158, 296, 410
Disintegration, 360, 364, 381–2, 400,
  419, 426
Disorders, 434
  schizoid, 461
Disorganization, 420, 430
Dissolution, 381, 460
  of the self, 421
Distortion, 180, 424
  of the self, 180
  transferential, 418
Distress, 128, 370
Distrust, 130, 214, 413
Disturbance(s), 9, 29, 69, 134, 178, 363
  primary, 363
  secondary, 363
Doubt(s), 268, 351
Dream(s), 39, 153, 182, 417, 441
Dream-
  censor, 39
  thoughts, 39
Drive(s), 15–6, 69, 72, 74n, 77, 89, 103,
  105, 108, 155–7, 168, 205
  aggressive, 220, 252–3, 257
  control, 357
  manifestations, 2
  oral, 194
  oral-aggressive, 224
  theory, 95, 166
    psychoanalytic, 197
DSM-III, 2, 89

Echo, 1, 112, 336, 444–5, 453, 460
Echoing, 332
Ego, 3, 5, 8–9, 13–4, 19, 21, 26–9, 31–2,
  34–5, 39–42, 44–6, 48–50, 54,
  56–8, 62, 63n, 67–73, 74n, 78, 80,
  83–4, 91n, 95, 98–9, 101, 104–6,
  115–7, 120, 124, 130, 137, 146–8,
  150, 152–3, 155, 159–60, 179n,
  197–8, 217, 239, 241, 246, 247–8,
  253, 262–5, 274, 287, 293, 295,

Ego *(Continued)*
297–8, 300, 302–3, 305, 309, 311–3, 345, 348–50, 353–5, 377–82, 386–7, 390, 400, 423–4, 426, 433, 448, 450, 452, 456, 459
autonomous, 78, 82
body, 152
boundaries, 216
cathexis, 146
censor, 39*n*
classification, 378
defense, 293, 443, 452–3
deficit, 433
depletion, 443, 451
development, 45, 54, 101, 157, 199, 207, 222, 377, 461–2
differentiation, 45
disturbance, 48
function(s), 6, 9, 61*n*, 146, 155–6, 160, 199, 268, 312, 317, 425, 451, 457
growth, 456
identity, 123–4
instincts, 20–3, 30, 34, 40, 146
libido, 20–1, 27, 30, 35, 41–2, 117, 147–8
states, 44
strength, 241
structure, 298
system, 199
theory, 378–9
weakness, 232, 285, 421
Ego and the Id, The (S. Freud), 37*n*, 309, 313, 378
Ego ideal(s), 1, 3, 5–7, 11, 13–4, 16, 36–9, 42–3, 50, 54, 56–7, 59, 62, 66–8, 70–3, 95, 104, 117, 159, 216, 224–5, 261, 263–4, 311–3, 318, 333–4, 344, 348–57, 364, 396, 410, 415
disorders, 38
grandiose, 223
primitive, 216
Ego Psychology and the Psychoses (P. Federn), 61*n*
Egocentric stages, 99
Elation, 83, 386
Embarrassment, 4, 70, 348, 370, 391
Empathy, 2, 15, 77–9, 85, 90, 112, 127–30, 135–7, 158, 186, 207, 213, 258, 269, 281, 290, 296*n*, 311, 341,

369, 413, 445, 455–9
primary, 78, 81
Empathy-anxiety balance, 458
Emptiness, 2, 128, 132, 141, 159, 171, 219, 221–2, 240–1, 243, 246, 270, 274, 288–9, 291, 323, 332, 338, 360, 368–9, 412, 440, 443, 460
Endowments, 409, 411
Energies, object-related, 201
Energy, psychic, 13–4
Enfeeblement, 177, 179–80, 360
Enjoyment, 334
Enthusiasm, 131, 187, 195
Entitlement, 2, 4, 7, 10, 128–9, 140, 200, 412, 459–60
entity, 460
grandiose, 460
Envy, 7, 130, 158–9, 167, 214, 220, 222, 228, 231, 234–6, 246–7, 255–7, 261, 263, 266–8, 271, 275, 327, 330, 334, 337, 342, 346, 384, 460
oral, 198
penis, 34, 225–6
Erogenous zones, 185
Erotic cathexes, 41
Eroti(ci)sm, 41
anal, 317, 319
Erotogenic zones, 27
"Ersterwählte," 23*n*
"Ersterwähnte," 23*n*
Estrangement, 289
Exhibitionism, 2, 10, 16, 69–70, 93, 129, 134, 182–3, 187, 223, 264–5, 349, 359–60, 367, 385, 407, 416–7, 439
anal, 69
phallic, 69
urethral, 69
Exhibitionist, 385
Exhibitionistic
strivings, 71*n*
tensions, 68, 70–1
trends, 220
urge, 70
Exhilaration, 393
Exit the King (E. Ionesco), 290
Expectation(s), 141, 182, 340, 409–12
Experience, 5, 358, 363, 366–7, 374, 385, 432–3, 438–40, 444, 452–3, 462
Exploitation, 374, 410–1, 440

Exploitativeness, 129
Externalization, 391, 410

Failure(s), 7, 16, 70, 170–1, 178, 181,
    183, 206, 228, 243, 289–90, 333,
    350, 353, 354n, 359, 361–70, 382,
    435, 445–6, 456–7
Fantasy(ies) [phantasy(ies)], 2, 9, 18,
    20, 24, 29, 47–50, 52, 54–5, 67, 69,
    97, 100, 102, 117, 127, 129–30,
    132–3, 139–40, 148, 153, 159, 170,
    178, 186, 194, 202, 215, 217, 221,
    225–6, 228–9, 235, 239–41, 247,
    250, 254, 260, 272–4, 276, 279,
    281, 284, 289, 295n, 297, 301–2,
    328, 331, 333, 338, 346, 391–2,
    394, 399, 409–10, 417, 423, 457,
    459, 460
  aggressive, 274
  cocoon, 457
  grandiose, 67–70, 73, 129, 187, 194–5,
    200, 213, 246, 254, 264, 294, 297,
    368, 410, 413
  gratifying, 260
  object, 399
  omnipotent, 205, 294, 297
  passive, 410
  reunion, 390, 393
  suicidal, 239
  world, 242
Fear(s), 10, 120, 159–60, 198, 219, 225,
    229, 236, 240, 250, 255, 266, 271,
    275–6, 296n, 305, 318, 323–4,
    334, 338, 340, 394, 408, 417, 421,
    424, 440, 443
  disintegration, 196
  of rejection, 271, 288
  of retaliation, 198
Fetish, 77
Fixation(s), 6, 216, 252, 386, 390, 435
Fonction du réel, La (Janet), 24n
Forgiveness, 354, 370
Fragmentation, 165, 180n, 185, 201, 366,
    380, 382, 400, 405, 408, 418–9,
    421, 426–7
Frustration(s), 140, 150, 157, 162, 167,
    183, 203, 206, 220–1, 225, 230,
    238, 240, 250, 256, 267, 272, 274,
    278, 280, 311, 317, 332, 387, 412,
    423, 459

oral, 247
Fusion, 386, 390, 442
  regressive, 216
  symbiotic, 442
Futility, 276, 289, 323, 332, 443

Generation gap, 331n
Genetic determinants, 256
Genital(s), 27
  deficiency, 349
  visibility, 349
  vulnerability, 349
Genius(es), 215, 220
Glorification, 328
Glory, 218
Glossary (APA), 107–8
Goal(s), 178, 183, 353–6, 360–6, 368,
    385, 400, 409
  grandiose, 424
  idealized, 177, 195
  inner, 183
  self-enhancing, 178
Grandiose
  aspiration(s), 134
  inflation, 117
  isolation, 263
  person, 331, 337, 342, 346
Grandiosity, 4, 10–1, 15–6, 47, 51, 53,
    83, 112, 130, 135, 140–1, 166, 168,
    170–1, 182, 194–5, 214, 246–7,
    260, 264–6, 270, 287–8, 323, 328,
    330–3, 336–8, 341–2, 347, 358,
    362, 368, 381, 406, 408, 412–3,
    416–7, 421, 426, 428–9
  illusion of, 289
  infantile, 264–5
  phallic, 55
Gratification, 50, 133, 135, 148, 155, 217,
    234, 238, 246, 256, 260, 275, 285,
    288–90, 304, 330, 423, 453
  need, 254
  oral, 386
  sexual, 414
Gratitude, 241, 253, 255
Greatness, 177, 215, 220, 274, 318, 332,
    363
  illusions of, 318
Greed, 139, 242, 342, 389
Greediness, 277
Grievance(s), 120–1

Growth, 462
  psychoanalytic, 438
  psychosexual, 461
Guilt, 4, 7, 14, 43, 72, 141, 160, 170, 179,
    198, 225, 228, 231–6, 239–40,
    250, 255, 257–8, 261, 273, 275,
    285, 334, 348–54, 356n, 362, 366–
    7, 369–70, 381, 385, 413
Guilt-shame cycle, 350, 354n
Guilty Man, 358, 366

Hamlet (W. Shakespeare), 144
Harmony, 177–8
Hatred, 220, 222, 231, 235, 240, 257,
    267, 277
"Hedonic Control, Action-Self, and the
    Depressive Spell" (S. Rado), 121
Helplessness, 10, 15, 140, 154, 158,
    194, 278, 309, 345, 396, 428
Heroism, 441, 443
Hiding, 350, 352
"His Majesty the Baby" (S. Freud), 34
"His Majesty the Ego" (S. Freud), 34n
"History of the Psycho-Analytic Move-
    ment" (S. Freud), 35n
Hollowness, 141
Homosexual(s) 17, 30, 38
  experience, 238
  impulses, 271, 390
  urges, 390
Homosexuality, 32n, 33, 43n, 271
Hope(s) 182, 363
Hopelessness, 125, 194, 280, 328, 342,
    361–2
Hostility, 121, 350, 432
Humiliation(s), 4, 68, 128–9, 140, 170,
    255, 289, 348, 361, 370, 391, 396,
    445
Humor, 82–5
Hunger, 334, 359
Hypercathexis
  libidinous, 161
  of the object, 161
  of the self, 101
Hypersensitivity, 158, 180, 384
Hypocathexis of objects, 101–2
Hypochondria(sis), 25–7, 29, 69, 95,
    102, 117, 180
Hypochondriac, 49
Hysteria, 18, 21, 26–7, 29, 293, 439

"I," the, 115, 310n, 314–5
Id, 5, 14, 62, 146, 197, 309, 348–50, 378,
    382
Ideal(s), 36–7, 42, 68, 71–2, 83–4, 171,
    177, 182–3, 186–7, 194, 196, 217,
    311–2, 350–6, 360–3, 365–9, 400
  hungry, 191
  love, 2, 129
  parental, 355
  person, 138
  phallic, 199
  standards, 72
  state, 7, 355
  transformation of, 43
Idealization, 7, 15, 36, 66–7, 71, 76, 128,
    136, 138–9, 141, 158, 168, 215,
    217, 255, 257–9, 261–2, 266–
    7, 276–9, 296n, 302, 358–60, 363,
    368, 404, 410, 414–5, 421–2, 447,
    459
  normal, 255
  primitive, 257
Identification(s), 15, 147, 150, 156, 314,
    350, 360, 392, 396, 407–8
  empathic, 289
  positive, 350
  projective, 259
Identity, 6–7, 9, 72, 113, 123–4, 149–50,
    302, 351–2, 357, 379, 395, 427,
    430, 433, 443, 450, 452
  confusion, 9, 200
  core, 455
  crisis, 8
  formation, 9
  loss of, 9, 200
  maintenance, 9, 200
  primary, 9, 81, 200, 395, 399
Illness, 288, 423
Image, 397
  body, 54, 112, 152–3, 156
  idealized, 361
    parent, 399
  internalized ideal parental, 225
  object, 51, 137, 204, 216–7, 222, 225,
    252, 258, 262–3, 274, 280
    idealized, 262
    libidinal, 263–4
  public, 398
Imagery, 318
Imago, idealized, 418

maternal, 415
object, 4, 64, 66n, 67
parent, 63-7, 157-8, 177, 259-60, 287,
    311-2, 358, 386, 410, 414-5, 432, 434
Impairment, 128, 425, 430, 434
ego, 295
Impotence, 40, 231, 337, 424, 428
Impoverishment, 323, 345, 347, 355, 368
Impulse(s), 397, 417
aggressive, 176, 220, 354
control, 238
Impulsivity, 131
Inadequacy(ies), 6, 150, 407, 443
Incest, 390
Incompleteness, 180n
Independence, 10, 125, 170, 179, 180n,
    351, 392, 408
field, 351
Indestructibility, 444
Indifference, 2, 128-9, 220, 275
Individuality, 72, 149, 161
Individuation, 141, 149, 151, 156-7, 161,
    394-6, 400, 423, 432, 453
Infallibility, 177
Infantilism, 50, 80
ego, 48
Infatuation, 414-5, 427
Inferiority, 2, 7, 58, 69, 71n, 128-9,
    214-5, 246, 350, 407, 412, 414,
    416, 428-9
complex, 349
organ, 349
Ingratitude, 10, 439
Injury, 200
physical, 206
psychic, 206
Insecurity, 214-5, 228, 327
Insignificance, 428
Instability, 4, 415, 434
Instinct . . ., On Transformations of
    (S. Freud), 317
Instinct(s), 21, 36-7, 126, 304n
anal, 98
oral, 98
phallic, 98
sexual, 304n
theory, 96, 378-9
"Instincts and Their Vicissitudes"
    (S. Freud), 20n, 21n, 28n
Insufficiency, 228

Integration, 247, 316, 425-6, 432, 462
Intelligence, 191, 288
Interest, 308
Internalization, 147, 151, 156, 166, 181,
    259, 264, 287, 298-9, 305, 316,
    323, 360, 363, 399, 400, 427, 432,
    434, 446
Interpersonal
development, 462
relationship(s), 128, 139, 223, 237, 383
Interpretation(s), 375, 446, 456-7, 460-1
Interpretation of Dreams, The (S. Freud),
    39n
Intolerance, 228
Introject(s), 310n, 374
narcissistically invested, 446
Introjections, 432
Introspection, 369
Introversion, 18, 24, 27-8
Intrusiveness, 10, 169, 296-7
Investment
aggressive, 286
instinctual, 251, 259
in object(s), 63, 97, 106, 168, 202, 253,
    267, 286
personal, 269
Involvement, 414, 440
Invulnerability, 82, 408
Isolation, 333n, 442
social, 194-5

Jealousy, 325, 337, 342, 384
Joy, 131, 178

"Landmark Contributions," 13
Lectures, Introductory (S. Freud), 19n,
    26n, 39n
Lectures, New Introductory (S. Freud), 32n
Lethargy, 361-2
Libidinal
attraction(s), 157
availability, 433
behavior, 117
cathexis(es), 19, 25, 27, 29, 40, 44, 65,
    84, 95, 105, 146, 156, 160-1, 251-
    2, 259
of the ego, 146
of the self, 44, 61n, 89, 91n, 95, 102,
    146, 148, 155, 158, 162, 197, 199,
    203-4, 357

Libidinal *(Continued)*
 of the self-representation, 199
 conflict, 266
 development, 54, 93, 99, 108, 377–8,
  390
 drive(s), 107, 155–7, 168, 252–3
 energy, 149, 352
 excitement, 153
 fixation, 100, 201
  points, 378
 impulse(s), 176, 354
  instinctual, 25
 instinct(s), 34, 251
  primitive, 313
 investment(s), 7, 9, 77, 96, 263, 286
  in mother, 253
  in objects, 252
  of the self, 1, 61, 91–2, 94–8, 100–1,
   104–7, 109, 116–7, 205, 207, 252
 narcissistic state, 116
 object, 93–4, 116
  cathexes, 40–2
  images, 263–4
 regressions, 101
 stages, 394
 states, 44, 95
 strivings, 267
Libido, 13, 16, 18–20, 22–9, 31, 37–8,
  41–2, 46, 48, 63n, 64, 74n, 76, 95–
  6, 98–9, 101, 106, 117, 124, 148,
  151, 155, 197, 205, 349, 377, 387
 distribution(s), 61
 exhibitionistic, 71, 357
 homosexual, 38, 43, 64
 idealizing, 64, 75–6
 investment of, 5
 neutralized, 157
 self-directed, 5
 sexual object, 313
 theory, 36, 115, 120, 176
Lily in the Valley, (H. de Balzac), 328
Liveliness, 383
Loneliness, 227, 274, 280–1, 288, 290,
  323, 367
Loss, 288, 290, 317
Love-object(s), 6, 25, 30–1, 43, 149,
  153, 252, 265
Love, primary, 203–4
Lying, 128, 385

Manhood, 398
Mania, 179
Manic-depressive illness, 359n, 370
Manic-depressive states, 44
Manipulation, 384–5, 393, 410, 440
Manipulativeness, 384–5
Manliness, 373, 398
Masculine protest, 34–5
Mask, 438–40, 446–7, 454, 458–61
Masochism, 7, 68, 93, 333
Masochistic patients, 285
Masochistic tendencies, 140
Masturbation, 184
 compulsive, 185
 fantasies, 49, 97
Masturbatory activity, 201
Maturity, emotional, 194
"Me, bad," 119
"Me, good," 119
"Me, not," 119
"Me, real," 120
"Me," the, 310n, 314
Meaninglessness, 243
Mediocrity, 219
Megalomania, 18–9, 28–9, 35, 100, 106,
  117
Melancholy(ia), 59, 83
Mental Disorders, Diagnostic and Statistical Manual of (APA), 127, 384
Merger, 15, 153, 180n, 192, 200, 258,
  358–60, 363–4, 416, 423, 455
Metapsychology, 1, 91–2, 100, 108, 167,
  176, 369, 461
 conflict-drive, 167
Mirror, 9, 241, 337, 395–6, 438–9, 447,
  449
 image, 152, 200–1
Mirroring, 9, 135–6, 154, 176, 179, 180n,
  181, 188–90, 200, 331–2, 359,
  361, 363–4, 367–8, 396, 399, 414,
  446, 450–1, 454, 456, 458–9
 function, 304, 358
Mistrust, 337
"Mitty, Walter, The Secret Life of"
  (J. Thurber), 194
Mortification, 4, 10–1, 69, 104, 344, 348,
  361–2, 370, 391
Motivation, 239
 for treatment, 239

"Mourning and Melancholia"
    (S. Freud), 345
Mourning, 170, 233–4, 255, 272, 285,
    289–90, 332n, 337, 339, 342–3
My Early Life (W. Churchill), 73

"Narcismus," 17n
Narcissism, The Culture of (C. Lasch),
    125
"Narcissism, On" (S. Freud), 94, 96–7,
    100, 116, 145, 312, 352
Narcissism
    adult, 252, 288
    as a developmental stage, 97, 109,
        203, 208
    as an immature relationship to objects,
        107
    as a metapsychological problem, 216
    as a mode of relation to objects, 202
    as self-esteem, 204
    as a sexual perversion, 97, 109, 201
    as a withdrawal from objects, 107
    affective component of, 15
    body, 51–2, 199, 313
    compensatory, 59
    cosmic, 81–3
    disordered, 367
    disturbances of, 132
    drive concept of, 89, 95–6, 108, 197–
        8, 201–7
    economic definition of, 108
    functional definition of, 197, 201, 202,
        207
    "good," 106–7
    healthy, 8, 135, 149–50, 160–1, 201,
        206, 208, 324–5, 346
    infantile, 35, 42, 45, 48, 149, 248, 252–
        5, 288
    normal, 252, 254–5
    mature, 15–6, 264
    natural, 441
    normal, 18, 216, 251–4, 263, 272, 286,
        411, 440–1
    object, 6
    original, 70
    pathological, 8, 135, 139, 141, 144,
        146, 149, 155, 160, 168, 170, 191,
        213, 216–7, 222, 237, 240, 243,
        249, 251–5, 257, 259, 263–4, 269,

272, 288, 290, 440–3, 449–50, 454,
    456, 462
    pathological development of, 213
    phallic, 330, 386
    primary, 1, 3, 7, 13, 18–9, 31, 33, 41–
        2, 45, 63, 97–8, 117, 146–8, 151,
        203–4, 324, 386
    primitive, 3, 204, 263–4
    regressive, 9
    secondary, 1, 13, 45, 90, 97–8, 100,
        106, 148, 150–1, 156, 161, 203,
        312–3, 386
    self in, 7
    self-affirming nature of, 167
    theory of, 308, 319
    transformation(s) of, 61, 74, 77, 82–3,
        85
    transformed, 81
    triumph of, 82
    unhealthy, 201, 206, 208
    unmodified, 83
    untreated, 288
Narcissist(s), 15, 379, 381–2, 391–2
    phallic, 394, 396, 398–400, 412
"Narcissistic Personality, Factors in the
    Psychoanalytic Treatment" (O.
    Kernberg), 109n
"Narcissistic Personality Disorders,
    Diagnostic Criteria for," 2, 128
Narcissistic
    activity, 198–200, 205–6, 208
    anxieties, 141
    aspirations, 271, 365n
    attachments, 415
    attitudes, 207, 317
    balance, 49, 62, 273, 414
    behavior, 165, 180
        disorders, 180–1, 190, 192–3, 195
        sexually promiscuous, 268
    cathexis(es), 6, 64, 67, 79–80, 82, 85,
        200, 323, 328
        of objects, 334
    character, 114, 127, 137, 140, 192,
        216, 239, 297, 304, 361, 363, 368,
        373, 413, 426
    defense(s), 132, 222–7, 257
    disorder, 135, 293, 295–9, 301–2,
        304–5
    disturbance, 264

Narcissistic *(Continued)*
   exploitation, 412
   pathology, 165
   phallic, 408, 412
   primitive, 412
   structures, 228, 239
   traits, 404
   characteristics, 133, 405
   concerns, 381
   condition(s), 2, 15, 433, 435
   configuration(s), 200, 207, 404–6, 414–
      5, 418, 421–2, 427, 430
   conflict(s), 6, 277, 282
   consistency, 32, 380
   constellation(s), 73, 269
   defense(s), 132, 140, 223–4, 243, 255,
      267, 272–3, 277, 284, 293–7, 301–
      2, 305, 318
   deficits, 404
   delusions, 84
   demand(s), 83, 168, 193–4, 400, 412,
      460
   denial, 317
   depreciation, 289
   as a descriptive term, 213
   devaluation, 421
   development(s), 259, 316, 324–5
   dilemma, 368
   dimension, 69, 428
   disappointment(s), 415, 432
   disequilibrium, 62
   disorder(s), 3, 8, 89, 106, 115, 136,
      158, 165, 168, 171, 300, 305–6,
      367, 407, 433, 435, 445, 447–8,
      452, 456, 459, 461–2
   disturbance(s), 7, 45, 53, 170, 199–
      200, 277, 323, 326, 328–30, 333,
      336–7, 341–2, 346
   drives, 73
   dynamics, 416
   ego ideal, 38
   energy(ies), 71, 201
   entitlement(s), 1, 7, 429
   equilibrium, 411, 414–6, 420, 425
   exhibitionism, 58, 386, 407
   expectation(s), 409–10, 412
   experience(s), 4, 63, 72, 286
      primary, 311
   extremes, 423

   failure, 290
   fantasy(ies), 48–51, 59, 70, 215, 254
   feature(s), 224, 234
   feeling(s), 100, 104
   fixation(s), 100, 415–6
   formations, 434
   frustrations, 278
   function(s), 203–4, 206, 278, 326
   fusion(s), 224, 235
   grandiosity, 15, 130, 170, 215, 224,
      254, 266
   gratification(s), 135, 225, 237, 269,
      284, 288, 316, 409, 411, 414
   group, 394, 400
   humiliation, 140
   idealization, 257–9, 415
   identification, 7, 59
   imbalance, 48, 58, 71, 409, 416
   impairment, 430, 435
   individual(s), 120, 131
   injury(ies), 6, 15, 51, 62, 168, 186,
      188, 317, 353, 357, 362, 387, 405,
      422
   insult, 331*n*, 432
   interests, 34, 285
   investment, 68, 168–9, 253, 263, 308,
      310–1, 314, 405
      of the ego, 309
      secondary, 308–10, 316, 319
      in the self, 169, 253
   isolation, 422
   issues, 406, 431
   level of libidinal development, 390
   libido, 37*n*, 43, 61, 64, 68, 71, 74–7,
      81, 83, 103, 146, 154, 157, 199,
      201, 313, 353, 414
   line of development, 167
   loss, 290, 414
   love, 313
   manifestation(s) 166, 170
   mental activity, 197–8
   mortification, 69, 104
   mother(s), 170, 257, 398
      figure, 257
   need(s) 70, 176, 180, 185, 193, 195,
      238, 278, 282, 285, 323–6, 345,
      410, 417, 432, 434
      for approval, 154
   neurosis, 44

object, 314, 414, 417
  choice, 6, 33, 40, 107–8, 152–3,
    199–200, 379–81, 414, 427
  relations, 7, 9, 200–1, 204, 208, 394
  tie(s) 199, 202–3
objectives, 412
omnipotence, 9, 350
organization, 263
  pathological, 418
orientation, 48, 57, 396
parent, 66n
pathology, 6, 8–10, 44–5, 130, 136,
    139–40, 166, 368, 374, 407–9,
    412–3, 433–4, 442, 444, 463
patient(s), 7, 103, 159, 167, 169–70,
    201, 207–8, 218–9, 227–30, 232–
    3, 235, 237–8, 241, 248, 253–5,
    260, 267–8, 277, 279–80, 282,
    285–6, 290, 359, 364, 368–70, 392,
    394, 412, 431, 445
pattern(s), 160, 199–200, 386
perfection, 36, 311, 414
personality(ies), 57, 85, 129–30, 132,
    138–9, 148, 153–4, 157–60, 165,
    167, 198, 213–6, 219, 221–5, 227,
    229, 232, 234, 236, 238, 240, 243,
    245–9, 251–6, 258–9, 264–6, 268–
    70, 282, 284–91, 368, 373–4, 380–
    3, 386–7, 389–90, 395, 398–9,
    403, 405, 407, 410–2, 414, 418–27,
    430–5, 439, 463
  characteristics, 168
  disorder(s), 9, 89, 127, 129, 131–2,
    134, 137, 141, 176–7, 180, 183,
    185–6, 188, 192–4, 196, 245–
    6, 260, 265, 296n, 301, 349, 359n,
    362–3, 365–6, 403–4, 406, 418–
    9, 434, 439, 445
  disturbances, 405, 419, 422
  organization, 406–7, 418
  structure(s), 213, 226, 228, 234–5,
    243, 247–8, 250, 255, 270–1, 284–
    5, 288, 404
  treatment of, 213, 244
  types, 373, 377, 379, 383, 396–7, 408
perversion, 201–2, 208
phenomena, 166–7, 169
pleasure(s), 69, 317, 417
preoccupation with the self, 125

problems, 9, 341–2, 367, 404n
psychopathology, 462
rage, 154–5, 157–8, 168, 193, 249–50,
    255, 257, 263, 324, 357, 361, 410,
    431, 444
reaction(s), 223, 267, 350, 352
regression(s), 100, 416
relationship(s), 380, 382, 427
repair, 373, 386–7, 389, 393, 396,
    410–1
  mechanism(s), 391, 394
representational forms, 314
resistance(s), 250, 252, 254, 260–1,
    266, 268–70, 274, 280, 282, 284
response, 169
satisfaction, 37, 42, 312, 352
self, 16, 63, 67–73, 74n, 82–4, 310–2,
    357, 427
self-aggrandizement, 429
self-esteem, 353
self-inflation, 14, 47, 429
self-representation, 314
stability, 434
stage of development, 98, 216
state, 381
  primary, 373, 381
striving(s), 71n, 136, 139
structure(s), 9, 57, 73, 85, 296n, 381,
    405, 425–6
supply(ies), 129, 213, 232, 254, 326,
    331, 413
tension(s), 62, 68, 70–1, 286
threat(s), 414, 434
transference(s), 1, 8, 154, 165, 176,
    193–5, 207, 224, 226, 229, 251,
    264, 266–7, 272, 407, 418–20, 425,
    434, 446, 449, 451, 457, 459–61
trauma(ta), 51, 340, 408
triumph, 254, 288
types, 378
  of object choice, 223
victory, 317
vitality, 444
vulnerability(ies), 3–4, 67–8, 156, 410,
    412, 422–3, 429–33
withdrawal, 226, 246–7, 256, 267,
    421–2
women, 380
  phallic, 396

Narcissistic *(Continued)*
   wound(s), 387, 462
   yearning(s), 3–4, 168
Narcissus, 1, 112, 144–5, 199, 334, 336–7, 444–5, 453, 460
"Narzissismus," 17*n*
"Narzissmus," 17*n*
Need(s), 101, 148, 181, 346, 361, 367, 388–9, 406, 420, 424, 441–2, 449
   idealizing, 181
   libidinal, 343
Neediness, 384, 412
Neue Gedichte (H. Heine), 28*n*
Neurasthenia, 26–7
"Neurosis, Types of Onset of" (S. Freud), 27*n*
Neurosis(es), 18, 21–7, 29, 34–5, 37, 40–1, 120, 135, 150, 257–8, 304, 365, 367, 404–5, 408, 441
   character, 308
   classical, 131
   infantile, 296
   oedipal, 131
   transference, 125–6, 131–2, 235, 251, 258, 265, 293, 295, 301, 304–6, 454, 461
Neurotic(s), 37, 42, 162, 313, 429
   characters, 176, 406
   classical, 295, 301, 305
   conflict, 4
   disorders, 132
   illness, 41
Neutralization, 153, 313
"Nightingale, The" (H. C. Andersen), 242
"Nobel Prize complex," 410
Nonbeing, 441, 451
Noninvolvement, 167
Nonresponsiveness, 457

Object(s), 1–2, 5, 7, 10, 16, 18–19, 21, 28–9, 36, 42–3, 45, 48, 50–1, 54–5, 58, 64–7, 69–70, 74, 77, 79, 89, 95, 98–9, 101–3, 106, 112, 116–7, 135, 137–8, 147, 151, 159, 162, 169, 177, 200–1, 204–6, 222, 224–5, 227, 230, 241, 250–1, 253, 259, 261, 267, 294, 295*n*, 296*n*, 299–300, 305, 309, 310*n*, 323, 331, 344, 347, 351–2, 355, 364, 367–8, 373–4, 378–9, 381, 386, 389–90, 399, 400*4n*, 411–2, 414–7, 419, 421–9, 432, 434, 440, 446, 448–9, 452–3, 458
   attachments, 117
   cathexis(s), 19–20, 35, 42, 44–5, 48, 59, 65, 76–7, 80–1, 83, 102, 146, 148, 157, 203–4, 206
   choice, 6, 30–3, 42, 64, 94–5, 109, 116, 153, 202, 223–4, 379–80, 414
      anaclitic, 379–80
      homosexual, 116
   constancy, 161–2, 415, 431
   external, 5, 13, 151, 159, 168, 217–8, 225, 256, 262
   hunger, 294, 298–9, 305
   ideal(ized), 4, 64*n*, 137, 139, 167, 216, 218, 220, 247, 258–60, 346, 414–6, 419
   idealization of, 138
   image(s), 108, 218–9
      devaluated, 219
      external, 218
      ideal, 236
   imago, 65
   instinctual cathexes, 278
   internalized, 5, 138, 290, 310*n*
   investment(s), 63, 97, 106, 202, 253, 263, 267
   libido, 19–21, 30, 36, 41–2, 148, 202, 265, 312, 353
   loss, 59, 65, 150, 169, 296*n*, 309–10, 454
   love, 1, 6, 15, 31–2, 34, 46, 61, 63–4, 67, 74, 77, 85, 98, 116, 148–9, 216, 287, 325, 331, 337
   narcissistically cathected, 326
   narcissistically invested, 439
   need-satisfying, 449
   oedipal, 415
   omnipotent, 386, 391, 399–400, 414
   preoedipal, 415
   primary, 338, 346
   related investment, 314
   relatedness, primary, 204
   relation(s), 1, 5–7, 10, 15–6, 63, 90, 95, 98, 103, 109, 113, 116–7, 135, 144–5, 148, 150, 158, 160–2, 167–

9, 225, 252, 256, 264, 286–8, 290,
    301, 305, 308, 319, 330, 373–4,
    394, 404n, 407n, 414, 422, 424–5,
    428, 439, 444
  internalized, 248, 252–3, 255–6,
    282, 284, 286, 290, 421
  pathological, 255
  relationship(s), 55, 94–5, 98, 101, 109,
    122, 130, 154, 158, 167, 170, 198,
    202–4, 206, 213–4, 223, 225, 227,
    241, 253, 262, 272, 282, 286, 288,
    299, 301, 305, 374, 380, 406, 414,
    421
  normal, 216, 253
  pathological, 243, 252–3
  representation(s), 1–2, 5–6, 14–5,
    103, 124, 137, 141, 147–8, 156,
    159, 162, 169, 225, 247, 258, 312,
    324–6, 356, 374-5, 387, 424, 434,
    438, 449–50, 453, 457
  internalized, 218, 380
  symbiotic, 423
  transference, 267
  transitional, 298
  world, 50–1, 57, 63, 168
Obsessional types, 378
Oedipal
  conflicts, 9, 132, 263, 284
  defeat, 317
  development, 236
  fantasy, 132
  father, 318–9
  fears, 221
  formulation, 390
  involvement, 224
  period, 65
  phase, 330
  resolution, 353
  strivings, 349
  transference, 226
  wishes, 318
Oedipus complex, 14, 318, 353, 381, 400
Omnipotence, 8–9, 40, 42, 45, 64, 66,
    80, 94, 100–1, 117, 130, 132–
    3, 146, 177, 182, 200, 213, 215,
    296–7, 302, 317, 399, 404, 408,
    410, 416, 423–4, 439, 442–4, 453–
    4
Omnipotent fantasy(ies), 139, 215

Omniscience, 66, 134, 247, 410, 416, 424
Other(s), 4, 15, 356, 368, 381, 412, 438
  idealized, 4
  narcissistically invested, 451
Outbursts, aggressive, 249, 445
Overidealization, 2, 127, 129
Oversensitivity, 327, 334, 342–3
Overstimulation, 186, 367–8

Pain, 233, 328, 334, 340, 342, 346–7, 369
Panic, 289, 364, 367
Paranoia, 25, 29, 43, 390–1, 413
Paranoid
  behavior, 395
  conditions, 384
  disposition, 235
  fear, 261
  mechanism, 393
  patient(s), 391, 393, 395, 397
  rage, 235, 285
  reactions, 235, 384
Paraphrenia, 27, 29
Paraphrenic(s), 18, 25, 28–9
  disorders, 43
Passionate Pilgrim, The (W. Shake-
    speare), 191
Passive-aggressiveness, 384
Passivity, 350, 355, 365n
Pathology, 429, 431, 447
  borderline, 420, 422, 425, 429, 431,
    453
  character, 2–3, 223–5, 245, 251, 255–
    8, 313, 403, 426, 434, 463
  ego, 456
  masochistic, 139
  structure, 261, 269
    character, 269
  superego, 130, 214, 264
Perception, 67, 78–9
Perfection, 64, 70–1, 133, 157, 169–70,
    177, 225, 240, 261, 271, 312, 357,
    360, 416, 440, 453
Perfectionism, 334
Person, ideal, 217
Persona (I. Bergman), 229
Personality(ies), 70–4, 114–5, 125, 130,
    150, 165, 182, 189–93, 197, 201,
    213–5, 259, 263, 273, 288, 293,
    297, 301, 303, 305, 326, 333, 347,

Personality(ies) *(Continued)*
　　351, 373, 380, 405, 420, 422, 424,
　　430, 432–3, 435, 458–9
　alter-ego, 191
　antisocial, 214, 410
　borderline 131, 232, 246–8, 251, 373–
　　4, 380–2, 404–5, 410, 419–20,
　　427, 430–1
　　configurations, 423
　　organization, 247–8, 419
　characteristics, 262
　complementary, 380–2
　compulsive, 293
　contact-shunning, 165, 192
　craving, 373, 383, 387, 389–90, 395–6,
　　399–400
　dependent, 383
　disorder(s), 165, 180–1, 441
　　antisocial, 128, 130, 237, 384
　　borderline, 128
　　histrionic, 128
　healthy, 409
　hysterical, 223
　ideal-hungry, 165, 190–1
　manipulative, 274, 383–5, 393–5, 397–
　　400, 410
　merger-hungry, 165, 192
　mirror-hungry, 165, 190–1, 324
　neurotic, 418
　nonnarcissistic, 225
　obsessive, 223, 225, 293
　organization, 298, 404, 414, 434
　paranoid, 373, 383–4, 389–93, 397,
　　400
　passive-aggressive, 383, 398
　phallic narcissistic, 373–4, 383, 385,
　　394, 399–400, 407
　psychopathic, 410–1
　schizoid, 405, 422
　structure, 293, 445
Perversion(s), 17–8, 42, 92, 97, 146, 185,
　　331*n*, 345
　sexual, 17*n*, 89, 92, 95, 97, 116, 166,
　　201–2
Phallic narcissistic men, 331, 332
Pleasure principle, 442
Pleasure Principle, Beyond the (S. Freud),
　　22, 308
Potency, 408
Power, 2, 64, 129, 134, 177, 191, 237,

　　246–7, 254, 289–90, 385, 389–90,
　　396, 415, 444
　omnipotent, 309
Praise, 194, 221
Preoedipal
　disturbances, 314
　fears, 332
　period, 65, 254
Prestige, 191, 271, 329
Pride, 140, 329, 353, 407
Primary process, 122
　thinking, 239, 285
"Project" (S. Freud), 28*n*
Projection, 391, 411
Promiscuity, 268
Psyche, 65, 68, 78, 60, 132, 193, 200, 455
Psychic(al) energy, 13–4, 22
"Psychoanalytic Theory of the Ego,
　　Comments on" (H. Hartmann),
　　146
Psychology, Group (S. Freud), 31*n*, 36*n*,
　　37*n*, 40*n*, 43*n*
Psychology
　drive, 176, 189, 357
　ego, 1, 14, 16, 61*n*, 89–90, 110, 117–8,
　　153, 197
　group, 43
　individual, 72*n*
　of the self, 165, 174–5, 187, 196, 357,
　　362, 366
　social, 14–5, 72*n*
　structural, 357
Psychoneurosis(es), 176, 363, 406
Psychopath(s), 385, 411
Psychopathology, 72*n*, 130, 132, 135,
　　184, 195, 214, 265, 365–6, 369,
　　405–6, 419, 427, 433–4, 445, 456,
　　462
　schizoid, 422
Psychosis(es), 14, 44, 155, 165, 179, 246,
　　367, 403, 405, 419, 422
　manic-depressive, 329
　paranoid, 390
　schizophrenic, 246
　transference, 248, 421, 447
Psychotherapy, 239, 431
　supportive, 270
Psychotherapy Project of the Menninger
　　Foundation, 239
Psychotic(s), 146, 340, 392, 418

characters, 406
conditions, 384, 389
depression, 239, 290
paranoid, 390–1
regressions, 216, 445
Punishment, 352–3

Rage, 2, 7, 15, 128–30, 136, 138–40,
    154–5, 157–8, 167–9, 178, 194,
    219, 238, 240, 247, 249, 255–6,
    266–8, 274–5, 289, 298, 316, 325,
    330, 334, 342, 357, 363, 387, 421,
    440, 443, 460
  oral, 167, 214, 220, 256, 261, 266
Rapprochement, 9–10, 90, 133, 161, 374,
    432, 435
Rationalization(s), 128, 270
Reality(ies), 8, 24, 45, 47–8, 50, 53, 65,
    78, 82, 138, 147, 182, 193, 215–
    6, 247, 268, 275, 289, 295–6, 298,
    311, 317, 347, 391, 417, 453, 457,
    459–60
  testing, 50, 137, 150, 216, 258, 381
Reassurance, 359, 411
Recognition, 332, 409–10
Regression, 27, 29, 215, 227, 232, 239,
    241, 252, 258, 270, 285, 381–2,
    387, 404–5, 408, 411, 417, 419–20,
    422, 424, 426–7, 432, 434
Rejection(s), 69, 192, 206, 277, 288, 350,
    352, 354, 359, 364, 414
Relatedness, 463
Relationship, patient-analyst, 460
Remorse, 233, 348, 370
Reparation, 285, 360
Repression(s), 35–8, 41–2, 154, 293,
    295n, 379, 381, 429, 444
  pathogenic, 35
Resentment, 167, 220, 255, 392, 440
Resilience, 382, 426
Resistance(s), 410, 447, 456–7
  analytic, 458
Responsiveness, 364, 447, 456
  empathic, 406
  nonverbal, 459
  verbal, 459
Restlessness, 269, 334
Reunion, 382, 386–7, 390–1, 394, 396–7,
    400

Rupture, 382
Ruthlessness, 214, 413

Sadism, 93, 397
  oral, 198, 262
Sadistic trends, 261
Sadness, 214, 227, 234, 273–4, 337, 339
Sadomasochistic family, 397
Sadomasochistic paranoia, 390
Satisfaction(s), 140, 308, 317, 373, 379,
    388
  autoerotic, 30, 317
Schizophrenia, 18–9, 23, 95, 102, 117,
    179, 203, 366, 420
  paranoid, 5, 384
Schizophrenic(s), 366
  reaction, 239
  states, 44
Security, 182-3, 289, 309, 343
Self, Analysis of the (H. Kohut), 115
"Self and the Object World"
    (E. Jacobson), 45
Self, 1–10, 13, 15–6, 26, 44–5, 48, 51,
    53, 57–9, 62–3, 66n, 67, 69, 71–2,
    74–5, 77, 81–4, 89, 91n, 93–6,
    98–9, 103–5,107–9, 113, 115–6,
    118, 120–1, 123, 129, 131–2, 134–
    40, 146, 148, 150–2, 154–5, 159,
    161–2, 165–6, 168–70, 177–9,
    181–4, 187–90, 192, 194–5, 197–
    8, 202, 204–7, 216–9, 228, 251,
    255, 258, 260, 262, 280, 286, 296–
    7, 299–300, 302, 305, 309–12, 314,
    316, 319, 323, 325, 331, 338, 345–
    8, 351–64, 365n, 366–7, 369–70,
    380–1, 386, 392, 395–6, 398, 400,
    405, 408, 410–1, 417–8, 423–7,
    429–31, 433–4, 438–42, 449, 451–
    3, 455, 458
  as agent, 311, 314–7
    or object, 310–2, 315
  autonomous, 180n, 181, 193
  bipolar, 134, 358–9
  cohesive, 202, 418, 425
  disintegration of the, 360
  disorder(s) of the, 134, 165, 174,
    180–1, 183, 195
    primary, 179
  dissolution of the, 421
  disturbances of the

Self *(Continued)*
   primary, 178
   secondary, 178
  emptiness of, 368
  exhibitionistic, 153
  as experience, 5
  false, 122–3, 170, 300–1, 305, 326,
     332, 334, 337, 342, 346
  fragmenting, 165, 185
  functions, 9
  grandiose, 125–6, 134, 139, 153–4,
     158, 247–8, 250–1, 255–8, 260–8,
     278, 280, 282, 287–9, 354*n*, 386,
     390–1, 399–400, 406, 410, 416–8,
     422, 429, 434, 440, 443, 445–6,
     449, 451, 453–4, 457, 460, 462
   exhibitionistic, 358
  ideal, 7–8, 72, 137, 139, 145, 167, 216,
     218–20, 236, 247, 260, 348–9,
     354–6, 359*n*, 361, 364–6, 369
  idealized, 138, 158, 167
  infantile, 153, 159, 282
  integrated, 263, 453
  investment of the, 62
  loss of the, 328, 430
  nuclear, 179, 181–2, 187, 192, 359–62,
     365–8, 405
  as object, 105
  omnipotent, 153
   grandiose, 357
  overburdened, 165, 187
  overstimulated, 165, 186–7
  pathological, 260, 289
  as place, 310*n*, 315–6
  primitive, 248, 289
  real, 247, 260, 262
  sense of, 10, 431
   separate, 310
  as structure, 5, 7
  total, 185–6
  true, 122–3, 334–6, 342, 344–6
  understimulated, 184
  vulnerable, 180, 183
Self-
  absorption, 127, 203, 245
  acceptance, 171, 179, 362–3, 368, 370
  admiration, 93–4, 103, 138, 220
  aggrandizement, 48, 120, 128, 226, 410
  analysis, 280

  appreciation, 50
  assertiveness, 193–5, 392
  cathexis, 45, 102, 146, 203–4
  centeredness, 107, 112, 127, 130, 214,
     254, 273, 460
  cohesion, 2, 3, 9, 168, 200, 358,
     363–4, 374, 418, 427, 432, 434
  cohesiveness, 8, 200, 426, 430
  concept, 130, 215, 217–9, 225, 227,
     247, 257, 268, 350, 370, 391, 432
   ideal, 240
  confidence, 161, 182, 195, 334
  configurations, 251
  consciousness, 39*n*, 47, 57–8, 128
  constancy, 90, 162, 426
  containment, 453, 458
  contempt, 58
  criticism, 38–9
  deception, 340
  depletion, 202, 361, 365
  development, 136, 359
  directed libido, 5
  disorder, 178
  disturbance(s), 165, 184
  dynamism, 118–9
  enhancing goals, 178
  esteem, 1–2, 5–7, 9–11, 13–5, 44–7,
     50, 54, 56–7, 59, 68, 89–90, 94–5,
     103–8, 110, 113, 116–21, 124, 127,
     130, 132, 134, 140–1, 152–4, 156,
     158, 166, 176, 178–80, 185, 190,
     199–202, 204–6, 208, 223, 225–6,
     241, 276, 290, 325, 329, 331, 334,
     348, 351–3, 355, 358–9, 361–5,
     370, 381, 386–7, 396–7, 408, 419,
     441, 444, 454, 462
  evaluation, 50, 268
  experience, 8, 155, 241, 426
  feeling, 324–6, 448–9
  fragmentation, 188, 202
  glorification, 394, 400
  idealization, 261, 423
  identity, 162, 199
  image(s), 6, 9, 51, 54, 71*n,* 105, 108,
     137–8, 145, 159, 167, 204, 216,
     218–20, 247, 252, 258, 262–3, 274,
     280, 393–4, 408, 410–1, 426, 440,
     449, 451, 459
   actual, 218–9, 227

idealized, 225
importance, 2, 127–8, 384
inflation, 53, 120–1, 199
integration, 131, 427, 430, 433
interest(s), 61n, 103, 109–10, 460
love, 90, 94, 120–1, 144, 146, 162, 207, 216
need(s), 145, 161
organization, 122, 131, 134, 418
other differentiation, 450
other representation, 443
pathology, 181, 184, 193–4, 358, 360–1, 363–4, 367
perception(s), 105, 123
preservation, 18, 30, 146
psychology, 167, 358, 361, 365–6, 369, 374
reference, 129, 167, 213, 413
regard, 1, 8, 13, 40–1, 103, 106, 109n, 117, 129, 158, 160–1, 167, 199, 213, 413, 461
relation(s), 90, 144, 146, 150–1, 154, 156, 160–2
representation(s), 1–2, 5–8, 14, 45, 90, 103–4, 106–7, 124, 127, 137, 141, 147–8, 151–3, 156, 159–62, 166–7, 198–207, 216, 309, 314, 316–7, 319, 324–5, 346, 355–6, 424, 426, 438, 444, 450, 453, 457, 462
  grandiose, 387
reproach, 343
respect, 33, 331
stimulation, 185
structure, 258, 364, 426
sufficiency, 120, 169, 293–4, 298, 300–2, 305, 422, 443, 459
  grandiose, 294
  illusion of, 293
system, 119
Selfhood, 121
Selfishness, 125, 144, 456
Selfobject, 2–3, 9–10, 131–2, 135, 137, 148, 157, 165–6, 177, 179, 180n, 181–7, 190–2, 195, 204, 258–60, 326, 333, 346, 358–60, 362–4, 368, 370, 373–4, 386, 394, 400, 405, 408, 415, 425
  differentiation, 386

empathic, 359
ideal, 264
idealized, 181–2, 187, 192, 358–9, 361, 415
mirroring, 176, 181, 359
omnipotent, 187
parental, 187
representation, 454
understanding, 186
Separateness, 7, 149–50, 169, 296, 299, 308–10, 315, 411, 461
Separation, 141, 149–50, 156–7, 161, 169–70, 288, 309, 316, 337, 394, 400, 423, 432, 453
  anxiety, 169, 309, 316
Separation-individuation, 9, 13, 113, 149–50, 157, 161–2, 308–10, 316, 395, 432, 442, 452–3
  primary, 308
Sexual
  aims, 313
  behavior, 97
  development, 17
  deviation, 238
  excitement, 233–4
  ideal, 42–3
  impulses, 268
  instinct(s), 21–3, 30, 40, 116
  libido, 20
  love, 148
  object(s), 30–1, 95, 97, 109, 116, 153, 201, 331
  overvaluation, 31–2, 36
  satisfaction(s), 30, 36, 312
  taboo, 349
Sexuality, 14, 22, 27, 32n, 33, 36, 41, 93, 117, 136, 349, 373
  infantile, 97
Shame, 2, 4, 7, 11, 14–6, 62, 70–1, 128–9, 170–1, 193, 195, 237, 255, 329–330, 332, 334, 337, 343, 349–56, 358, 360–70, 373–4, 381, 390–1, 394, 396, 407, 410, 412, 414, 416, 420
  proneness, 351n
Shyness, 129, 194, 246
Skill(s), 178, 182
Sovereignty, 451, 463
Splits, 426

Splitting, 381, 404
Stability, 201, 207, 446
Strength, 333, 356, 397, 415
Struggle, 397, 442
Subject, 317, 351
Sublimation(s), 36–7, 48, 52, 312–3, 319
Submissiveness, 218, 223, 345
Success, 2, 129, 177–8, 228, 288, 329,
    332–3, 342, 357, 410–1
Suicidal
  attempts, 239
  fantasies, 239
  intentions, 240
  thoughts, 240, 343
Suicide(s), 155, 362
Sulking, 387–9, 413
Sunday horseman, 85n
Sunday riders, 85
Superego, 3, 5, 13–4, 37n, 46–7, 50, 56,
    58–9, 62, 65–6, 68, 71–2, 82, 84,
    130, 137–8, 146, 158–9, 197, 206,
    214, 217–8, 225, 236, 253, 258,
    262–4, 285, 287, 312, 318, 348–51,
    353, 355–6, 362, 378–9, 397, 415
  anxiety, 451
  integration, 263
  retaliation, 349
Superiority, 106, 281, 394, 423, 428
Support, 373, 411, 444
Suspicion, 195, 384, 390
Suspiciousness, 222, 231, 384, 390
Symbiosis, 147, 395, 416, 455

Talent(s), 178, 182, 288, 329–30, 363,
    409–10
Temper, 389, 397
  tantrums, 249
Tenderness, 463
Tension(s), 8, 16, 178, 186, 217, 349, 366
Termination, 460
Threat, 382, 397, 429
Three Essays (S. Freud), 20n, 30n, 93
Tolerance, 220, 232–3
Totem and Taboo (S. Freud), 19n, 43n,
    100
Tragic Man, 358, 366
"Transference, The Dynamics of"
    (C. G. Jung), 18n
Transference, 3, 10, 21–3, 25, 27, 29, 31,
    40, 79, 125, 131–2, 134–6, 146,
    153, 157–60, 165–6, 168, 176–7,
    183, 186, 195, 217, 219, 224,
    226–7, 230–3, 235, 248–50, 254–
    7, 259–61, 264–8, 273, 277, 279–
    82, 284, 293, 295, 300–1, 303–4,
    327, 343, 358, 360, 374, 380, 392,
    407n, 414–5, 417, 421, 424, 445–7,
    449, 451, 456–7, 459–61
  alter-ego, 416–7
  distortion, 180, 424
  idealizing, 134, 136, 165, 176, 259, 293
  merger, 277
  mirror, 134, 136, 153, 158, 165, 176,
    186, 254, 264–6, 277–8, 287, 293,
    416–7, 444
  negative, 229, 255, 265, 267–8, 270,
    274, 304
    dispositions, 270
  neurosis, 460
  oral-sadistic, 235
  positive, 267–8
  preoedipal, 410
  psychosis, 460
  psychotic, 462
  regression, 446
  reistance(s), 227–8, 231, 243, 374,
    447, 457–8
    negative, 270
  twinship, 417
Transformation(s), 399–400
  of ideals, 43
Transgression, 349–50
Transience, 80, 82–4
Twinship, 416

Uncertainty, 276, 334
"Unconscious, The" (S. Freud), 29n
Understanding, 311, 341, 458
  empathic, 80
Uninvolvement, 231
Uniqueness, 4, 127–8
Unpleasure, 388
Unrelatedness, 374, 439, 460
Unworthiness, 127, 129, 257, 273

Value(s), 191, 355
Vanity, 93–4, 412, 439
Victimization, 140, 431

Virtue(s), 409–10
Vigour, 177–8, 287
Vulnerability(ies), 11, 15, 176, 193, 309–10, 352, 404, 408, 410, 418, 424–5, 427–8, 431, 454
  central, 382

Weakness(es), 191, 370, 390, 397, 412, 428
Wealth, 246–7, 254, 271, 289–90
Wisdom, 15, 83–5

Wish(es), 153, 338, 362–3, 417
  aggressive, 353
  libidinal, 353
Withdrawal, 103, 202
  schizoid, 422
World, representational, 264
Worthlessness, 15, 190, 219, 359, 393, 428–9

Yearning(s), 359, 459–60
Youth, 289, 329